This Book

was presented to

The Library

by Mr B Harrison

Date March 1996.

DG 2107

A NEW APPROACH TO THE
STANDARD FORM OF BUILDING CONTRACT

A NEW APPROACH TO THE STANDARD FORM OF BUILDING CONTRACT

Glyn P. Jones MSc AIQS AIOB
Senior Lecturer, Quantity Surveying, Oxford Polytechnic

MTP
MEDICAL AND TECHNICAL PUBLISHING CO LTD OXFORD AND LANCASTER 1972

Published by

MTP
Medical and Technical Publishing Co Ltd
PO Box 51, Seacourt Tower, West Way, Oxford
PO Box 55, St Leonard's House, St Leonard's Gate, Lancaster, Lancs

SBN 852 0004 0

Text set in 11/12pt IBM Press Roman, printed by photolithography in Great Britain at The Pitman Press, Bath, and bound by Hunter and Foulis, Edinburgh

CONTENTS

FOREWORD

DAVID M. WATERHOUSE, LLB. FIArb., *Barrister of the Legal Department, NFBTE*
Formerly Legal Adviser, RIBA, and Joint Secretary, Joint Contracts Tribunal

The law and practice relating to building contracts is a highly specialized subject, and the Standard (RIBA) Form of Building Contract, around which in this country almost all building work outside the government sector is carried out, are correspondingly complicated documents; even to those who are familiar with modern building practice and management. This is inevitable in an age when construction and management techniques are becoming almost daily more specialized and sophisticated and when almost every aspect of building practice, from the drawing-board to the employment of labour on the site, is being affected by legislation in some way or another. One has therefore considerable sympathy for those who use the Standard Form (or indeed any other form of Building Contract) and admiration for the way in which most users manage to keep pace with its constant yet very necessary changes.

Nevertheless, disputes continue to arise at an alarming rate and if these are to be avoided, it is essential that the parties to the contract make themselves fully aware of their respective rights and duties as set out within the Standard Form; not only is this knowledge essential in the post-contract period whilst the job is running, but equally so at tendering stage, when a quick appreciation of the likely over-all effect of any proposed changes to the standard conditions is vital to any contractor if an intelligently estimated tender is to be submitted. Ignorance by either party of the conditions of contract can prove extremely costly: the Employer may find himself paying more for the job than he need have done; or the Contractor may find himself unable to claim moneys which he should properly have been able to recover had he been alert to the requirements of the contract. In either case vast sums of money can be spent without hope for recovery in pursuing claims through protracted arbitration proceedings or in lengthy litigation. Neither the nation nor the building industry itself can afford this wastage.

Much of this can be avoided if the users of the Standard (RIBA) Form take steps to understand thoroughly what the contract requires of them, but for this purpose there are few short cuts; a study of some at least of the available textbooks is unavoidable. The Bibliography at the end of this book lists some of these, of which only three deal specifically with the Standard (RIBA) Form, the others dealing with building contract law generally and referring to the Standard (RIBA) Form only when it is necessary to do so in order to illustrate how specific legal points are dealt with in that Form. Those textbooks which deal specifically with the Standard (RIBA) Form all adopt the well-tried and very necessary clause-by-clause approach to the subject, cross-referencing only where the text of any particular clause directly requires this; and they are basically legal textbooks.

This latest book on the subject is not such a book, and in his approach the author turns his back on tradition and he breaks entirely new ground in his treatment of the subject. By what has obviously been an impressive study, in enormous depth, of the Standard (RIBA) Form he has produced a series of 'flowcharts' which explain simply the meaning and purpose of each clause, the consequences which flow if its provisions are followed and if they are not, and the bearing which each clause has on any other clause (whether or not those other clauses are specifically mentioned in the original clause). The use of these charts ensures that every single clause in the contract, even the most apparently insignificant or unimportant, can immediately be seen in the context of all other clauses which have, expressly or by implication, any administrative, managerial, or contractual bearing on its operation. In all cases it is the practical effect, rather than the philosophy of any clause, that is covered, thus making this a practitioner's book in the fullest sense of the word.

The flowcharts may be used effectively in two ways: firstly as a prophylactic by either party as a means of anticipating the effect in operation of any clause, thus enabling the correct action to be taken in advance; and secondly (and, one hopes, more rarely) after a dispute has arisen to check whether up to that time the correct procedures have been observed, where the contractual rights or duties lie, and, if a breach is revealed, what are the remedies of the aggrieved party. Used intelligently this system can only save time and money. Looking further ahead it requires little imagination to appreciate the possibilities of such flowcharts as a basis for a computer program relating to the Standard (RIBA) Forms, and these possibilities are properly explored by the author in a chapter devoted to this topic. With the likely standardization of other contract matters (for example, National Building Specification) such programming becomes more of a probability than a mere possibility, the flowcharts providing a useful and simple starting point.

In his introductory chapters the author reveals the method he has adopted in 'paraphrasing' the wording of the various Standard (RIBA) Form Clauses; the result is undoubtedly greater clarity and the Joint Contracts Tribunal may be greatly assisted thereby when they next undertake any fundamental re-drafting of the Form.

However, even if future draftsmen do not choose to adopt this particular method of clause breakdown they should certainly study the charts because the methods used by the author, resulting in such a detailed and exhaustive cross-referencing of many of the clauses and a simplification of most (without apparent impairment of meaning), reveal several anomalies of the original drafting which clearly must be dealt with. Significant examples of this are to be found in the author's analysis of Clause 16 and the effect upon sectional completion of the required reductions in the rates of retentions and of liquidated damages: for perhaps the first time some of the real dangers of agreeing sectional completion 'ad hoc' after the contract has been let, rather than as a carefully thought-out term of the contract as tendered for, become apparent; the moral is obvious.

As one who was personally involved for a number of years in the work of the Joint Contracts Tribunal I can only express regret that a similar breakdown of the provisions of the pre-1963 Standard Forms was not available to assist the draftsmen when preparing the current 1963 editions; many of the inconsistencies and anomalies which have now been revealed might have been avoided.

This is not intended in any way as a criticism of the Joint Contracts Tribunal or of those legal draftsmen who prepared the Standard Form to their instructions; some such errors are inevitable in a task of such a size, spread over such a period of time, and more especially in the case of periodical revisions when, as must occur over a number of years, the same draftsman might not be engaged as was engaged on the preparation of the original document. The use of flowcharts of this sort, properly kept up to date (as one hopes these will be) would surely assist all who are concerned with periodic revisions of the Standard (RIBA) Form to ensure consistency of approach and to allow them to appreciate quickly the possible impact of any proposed revisions on any other relevant clauses, thus avoiding the sort of difficulty which appears to have been encountered in the past. Is it asking too much to express the hope that in the not too distant future the author might be persuaded to turn his attention to the production of similar charts showing the interrelationship of the standard forms of subcontract with the Standard (RIBA) Forms of Main Contract?

I regard this book as one of the most significant contributions made in recent years in the field of building contract management and am grateful for having been given the opportunity of contributing this Foreword. I have no hesitation in commending this book to all concerned with the use in practice of the Standard (RIBA) Form of Building Contract.

PREFACE AND ACKNOWLEDGEMENTS

Widgery L. J. (as he then was) once described the Standard Form as '. . . not just an English contract on a printed form, it is a form of contract which has a long and perhaps one may say, distinguished history, and a form of contract which is intimately known . . .'. Every practitioner in the construction industry would agree with this high-level commendation, but could every practitioner claim to have truly mastered in his mind the complexities of this important document? The Joint Contracts Tribunal's spokesman, when introducing the 'new' 1963 version to a large audience on 11 December 1962, said, '. . . once contractors and architects and quantity surveyors have got used to the new form and really mastered its provisions, they will put it away and never look at it again . . .'. With the benefit of both hindsight and these flowcharts I would now venture to suggest that these kind optimisms, regarding our ability to master the form, were really without foundation. Furthermore if we continue to accept traditional drafting techniques then practitioners will never 'know' nor 'master' the Form's complex provisions, principally because that format conceals the infinitely variable influences of 'subroutines' upon each provision. In addition, a prerequisite to any optimism concerning the Form must mean achieving unambiguous intelligibility.

If any legal statement is found to be unintelligible by a certain number of ordinary persons of a predefined intelligence, why should not that statement be rejected and a revision drawn up so that intelligibility for the majority of people is ensured, and no monopoly in understanding, for a minority, is ever created? Legislative and contractual terms affect all our lives in ever-increasing ways, and there is an urgent need to create clarity from complexity so that bureaucracy may still claim that ignorance excuses no man.

Algorithms are undoubtedly bulkier than compressed unambiguous legal statements, but, given correct binary responses to certain simple questions, the system advanced here should enable ordinary persons to solve their contract problems in the shortest possible time. More importantly, the system should result in them consistently dispensing the only correct contractual conclusion.

I realized when decomposing, or rejecting traditional legal text, without regard to syntactic policy or precedent, that the results might not satisfy legal draftsmen. However, since traditional methods and their results (according to Sachs L.J.) do not satisfy the courts, it appeared we had a mutual kind of problem. I hope they will therefore recall the compassion contained in this Indian prayer, when viewing my charts:

> Great Spirit, grant that I may
> not critize my neighbour until
> I have walked a mile in his moccasins.

Most of the work reproduced in this book was carried out at the University of Manchester Institute of Science and Technology, and was submitted there, under a thesis entitled 'Automation of the Standard Form of Building Contract by Algorithmic Methods', for a Master's degree. Professor Harper and his staff, particularly L. Gordon Bayley, W. B. Jepson, R. A. Burgess, and Dr. W. Hoff, gave invaluable aid and encouragement. F. N. Eaglestone kindly and patiently acted as a 'lighthouse' to guide me through the treacherous and troubled waters surrounding liability and indemnity.

The work which formed the background to Chapter 4, 'Computer Processing Contract Disputes', was carried out at the Oxford Polytechnic, and here I must make particular acknowledgement of the work of a colleague, Brian Clark, Principal Lecturer in Computing, who enthusiastically agreed to study the programming problems generated by this offspring of a marriage arranged between jurisprudence and cybernetics. His co-operation and programming has resulted in Chapter 4 showing the early output of what we hope may be called a jurisprudent vending machine.

I was indeed privileged to have the expert eye of David Waterhouse to scan my work, his advice on certain intricacies of the law, and his words to precede the text. For the publishers, Peter Horrobin, and Bernard Crossland (who skilfully reproduced the charts), gave me close personal attention at all times. The R.I.B.A. have kindly agreed to the Form being reproduced, so too have C.A.S.E.C., in respect of their Form of Indemnity.

The notion that algorithmic systems might remove monopolistic mystery needed time to convert into tangible results. My appreciation is expressed here for the valued privileges afforded me by the Academic Board, and Research Committee, of the Oxford Polytechnic.

Finally, and above all, I appreciate the patience and consideration of my wife and children whilst I grappled almost interminably with gobbledygook in general, and the complexities in particular of the Standard Form.

1 INTRODUCTION AND OBJECTIVES

1. M. Zander, *et al.*, *What's Wrong with the Law* (London: British Broadcasting Corporation, 1970).

2. Consumer Council Study, *Justice out of Reach* (July 1970).

INTRODUCTION

In every highly developed community which practises varied social and commercial activities, that society will formulate rules of conduct appropriate to those activities. But the twentieth-century layman, although maybe now intellectually equal to the lawyer who drafts these rules, finds himself quite unable to fully understand new and important legislation, or even day-to-day documents he may be required to agree to or use, which have been drafted for him, in the traditional way by the legal profession.

In an ideal state, the declared rules should be readily understood by every member of that community. In a welfare state, rules, regulations, obligations, rights, remedies, and every form of control proliferate, and require confirming. Commercial activities within that community and with other communities, require control documents or contracts that communicate clearly the meaning of those agreements.

Mankind has traditionally entrusted the task of confirming its rules to the legal profession, whose members have always shown an impartial concern for justice, equality, liberty, and other basic human values. Socially lawyers originated from powerful, wealthy, and sometimes charitable ancestry. With such noble and gentle backgrounds their ability to be objective and to integrate with government has always been readily accepted. But if that profession continues to produce documents which fail to communicate, inevitably laymen will decide to experiment with alternative ways of communication, probably by cybernetic means.

In questioning whether our laws or regulations need to be obscure, Sir Leslie Scarman claimed(1) that 'with fantastic skill and a high degree of precision' draftsmen do 'what they are instructed to do'. That is to say, their 'masters' are the ones who, due to insufficient consideration of the matters to be drafted, cause lack of clarity and comprehensiveness. However, within the document enclosing the above quotations, Anthony Lester states of the Rent Act of 1965:

> The legislation was drafted with grotesque and avoidable technicality. Its complex language conceals traps which only an experienced lawyer could be sure to avoid.

Members of the construction industry will no doubt confirm that the Building Regulations of 1965 appear to have suffered a fate similar to that of the Rent Act. Many experienced designers and constructors are even now, several years after, uncertain of the prohibitions or permissions of that miserable edict.

Can society accept the principle propounded by pessimistic sectors of the legal profession that you cannot simplify an inherently complex matter, therefore lay people will never understand what the law is about? On the other hand must we accept Lord Devlin's judgement(1) that 'where injustice is to be found is not so much in the cases that come to court, but in those that are never brought there'.

An independent study(2) of small claims involving goods and services declared in July 1970:

> individuals use the county courts very little for any matter at all, not consumer matters; they rarely sue and rarely defend if sued.

Of the high courts, J. F. Wilson has stated(3): 'the fact that less than six contract cases a year reach the law reports, hardly gives the impression of a field of law in urgent need of radical reform'.

This paradoxical situation has arisen despite the fact that individuals do every year raise innumerable claims. For certain reasons these claims are not pursued in the courts, nor are they settled by arbitration. This absence of formal litigation may not be a bad thing. But the underlying reasons for informal settlement, waiver, or downright despair are certainly serious.

According to the study previously mentioned, the reasons for reticence by claimants are:

(*a*) Economically the 'costs' recoverable will not cover actual legal fees and expenses involved.

(*b*) Most solicitors have little experience of litigation.

(*c*) Court procedures for dealing with technical matters are unwieldy.

Lord Justice Sachs has perhaps, by his vehement summing up of the *Bickerton* v. *North-West Regional Hospital Board* case(4), illuminated the real causes of reticence by both claimants and their advisers:

> . . . it seems to me lamentable that such a form, used to govern so many and such important activities throughout the country, should be so deviously drafted with what in parts can only be a calculated lack of forthright clarity. The time has now come for the whole to be completely redrafted so that laymen—contractors and building owners alike—can understand what are their own duties and obligations . . . At present that is not possible.

The patron saint of plain words and official English, Sir Ernest Gowers, in his epilogue to *The Complete Plain Words*(5) chastises laymen who criticize legal draftsmen for their unintelligible drafts. Piesse and Gilchrist-Smith, co-authors of one of the few texts dealing with drafting(6), accept Sir Ernest's edict completely when dealing with the intelligibility of documents. The prospective legal draftsman is warned of the dire perils involved in ignoring precedent and liberally advised in this 1965 text to 'find guidance in the discussion (on complicated statements) by Coode', who in fact wrote upon legislative expression in the Report of the Poor Law Commissioners on Local Taxation in 1843.

Sir Ernest Gowers's admonishment of laymen's criticism of draftsmen, pales under the blistering assault of Lord Justice Sachs, referred to earlier, or Lord Justice Scrutton's assailment of the draftsman responsible for the Rent Restriction Acts, 'I regret that I cannot order the costs to be paid by the draftsmen of these Acts . . .' (*Roe* v. *Russell* (1928)). More recently, R. Graham Page, as a Conservative M.P. in a letter to *The Times* (6 April 1970) wrote:

> . . . The language of the parliamentary draftsman . . . is forced on to the statute book . . . not because the Minister (or anyone else for that matter) knows what it means but because it is quicker that way.
>
> There is a fanatical belief that writing law is a monopolistic mystery of the parliamentary draftsmen's impenetrable monastery.

If by clinging to nineteenth-century methods we have reached a stage where the legal profession cannot always understand legislation as it is drafted and pumped from Parliament, or the deviousness of long-standing standard contracts, it will be an undesirable fact that society and commerce will increasingly resort to unsatisfactory settlements or waivers, through ignorance, uncertainty, high costs, or sheer despair.

Experimentation by Lewis, Horabin, and Gane(7) into an intelligent person's understanding of a small yellow leaflet accompanying twenty-million British income tax forms distributed in 1966, concluded that although the leaflet was designed to provide 'general guidance' on a newly imposed capital gains tax, 'very few' people would extract any guidance from that prose account aimed at simplifying the

3. J. F. Wilson, *Evolution or Revolution? – Prospects for Contract Law Reform* (University of Southampton, 1969).

4. I. N. Duncan Wallace, *Bickerton* v. *N.W.R.H.B.* (1969), 1 A.E.R. 977, *Hudson's Building and Engineering Contracts*, 9th and 10th editions (London: Sweet & Maxwell, 1965, 1970).

5. Sir Ernest Gowers, *The Complete Plain Words* (London: H.M.S.O., 1960).

6. E. L. Piesse and J. Gilchrist-Smith, *The Elements of Drafting* (Stevens & Sons, 1965).

7. B. N. Lewis, I. S. Horabin, and C. P. Gane, *Flow Charts, Logical Trees and Algorithms for Rules and Regulations*, CAS Occasional Paper 2 (London: H.M.S.O., 1967).

matter. The message concerned had been compressed into incomprehensible verbiage and dispensed in much the same format as are our acts and contracts.

Taxes have, of course, always troubled mankind but our sufference and payment of them has always resulted in some form of return. In our society National Insurance ranks as one such return. The National Insurance Act of 1946, however, contained this statement:

> For the purpose of this part of the schedule, a person over pensionable age, not being an insured person, shall be treated as an employed person, if he would be an insured person were he under pensionable age, and would be an employed person were he an insured person.

8. John Lyons, *Chomsky* (W. M. Collins & Co. Ltd., 1965).

This may appear to a layman to be a 'calculated' way, devised by the draftsman, of vesting in bureaucracy the right to decide a person's pension status in whatever way they consider fit, since in all probability the layman alone would not have the intellectual capacity or perseverence to decode such garble. Similarly, the layman contemplating a hire-purchase arrangement should presumably be able to satisfy himself upon Section 18, subsection 3 of the Hire-Purchase Act of 1965 dealing with the important question of warranty:

> The Condition and Warranties specified in subsection (1) of Section 17 of this Act, and, except as provided by subsection (3) of that section and by subsection (1) and (2) of this section, the condition specified in subsection (2) of that section, shall be implied notwithstanding any agreement to the contrary.

The above examples (3) are two decades apart in time but not in style. Unfortunately such examples are by no means isolated, but, of course, they are admittedly taken out of context. But even in context this method of communicating important matters can be improved upon.

Noam Chomsky believes that if an artificial language were constructed 'which violated the principles of sentence construction in a natural language then it would not be learned at all . . .'(8) and he has indicated that the linguist can scientifically account for the inability of people to analyse certain grammatically correct sentences. He compares sentence and phrase structure with bracketing in mathematics or symbolic logic. John Lyons(8) compares the statement 'old men and women' and its ambiguity, (old men) and women, or, old (men and women), with the expressions

$$(\text{where } x = 2,\ y = 3,\ z = 5) \quad (xy)+z = 11$$
$$x(y+z) = 16.$$

Determinative symbols, formulae, or equations, could preserve intelligibility and unambiguity in this way, but, even the Sumerians of Southern Mesopotamia, more than 5,000 years ago developed a system of determinatives (explanatory symbols) to use alongside their ideograms, if their simple analytical script might be ambiguous. It is however remarkable that the Oxford don who deciphers for society the contents of cuneiform contracts (Fig. 1.1), has himself to call upon a member of the legal profession to decipher any present day contract he may personally wish to enter into.

Our modern equivalent of determinatives appears to be the code of practice, or explanatory booklets. There is, however, evidence that explanatory text of even the highest order and standing in legal circles can contain subjective rather than objective statements. People may not want copious explanation, they may simply wish to know their basic obligations, rights and remedies, entrusting the legislation or agreement to be equitable in principle.

Codes of practice may be used more and more as quasi-legal documents, intended as a layman's transparent overlay to an original enactment or agreement so that he can 'see' in simple terms the real meaning of the original complex document. The Industrial Relations Act is one such original document. Parliament appears to have assimilated this morass of important social legislation and its 'ordinary' members presumably have satisfied themselves upon its detailed content and meaning. The enactment is, however, generally regarded as incomprehensible to ordinary people. As a palliative, a

Fig. 1.1. Envelope of a tablet written *c.* 1900–1700 B.C. detailing a contract regarding the extent and use of some agricultural land in Southern Iraq (note the parties' seals along the envelope edge). *Photograph: Ashmolean Museum, Oxford.*

Code of Practice has been produced to enable people to give effect to the enactment. But is it efficient to practise agreed rules one stage removed from the basic and only democratically approved version of those rules? How can society know that official explanatory text mirrors the intentions of the original Act? Could a subjective 'code-writer' with a sinister cause ever manipulate society via such a vehicle?

None of these academic questions would arise if the original enactment was intelligible. Despite the edict of Edward Heath, Prime Minister, on 4 April, 1970(9):

> I am now asking for new laws to be written in straightforward English and not in gobbledygook,

people are denied the Old English simplicity evidenced for instance in the opening 100 words of St. John's Gospel ('In the beginning was the word, and the word was with God, and the word was God . . .'). This passage was intended to be intelligible to all men, as any gospel, rule, law, or certain contracts should be and incidentally although it is 96 per cent monosyllabic, it has a Gunning Fog Index(10) of 7·4; it also compares favourably with a random *Daily Express* leading article with an index of 7·0, or a *Guardian* leading article of 10·6.

If we apply the Fog Index formula to the opening 100 words of the Standard Form of Building Contract, the subject of Lord Justice Sachs's criticism quoted earlier, we find it has an index of 16·0, and the same test applied to the next 100-word sample gives an index of 28·6, yet the two passages were 89 per cent and 86 per cent monosyllabic. Clearly the draftsman is not guilty of using words outside the reader's vocabulary. The reasons for such a high index and therefore being less readable or intelligible, are that long sentences are used. In fact the increase in index from 16·0 to 28·6 theoretically places the second word sample beyond the intelligibility of most humans if the following table of relative readability is accepted:

6–8 Children's books.

8–10 Popular papers and light fiction.

9. Conservative Trade Unionist Annual Conference (London: Sunday Times Report, 1970).

10. R. Gunning, A Formula to Establish a Measure of Readability.

10–12 Quality papers and middle-brow fiction.
12–15 Reports in general and difficult fiction.
15–20 Scientific and technical reports.
20+ Treatises, especially scientific.

It appears that shorter sentences will improve understanding. But this change alone will not produce logical solutions in cases of breach. It is also evident that much searching is involved with present format to discover relevant provisions and exceptions.

Flowcharts can break down complex sentences and separate the contents into relevant sections. With the aid of judicious binary questions calling for objective responses, and the separation of irrelevant sections by a subroutine discipline, an improvement in understanding and a reduction in the time needed to achieve that understanding is evident. Furthermore, logical solutions are capable of being automatically found by the user.

In the mechanical age an assembly line method of analytical sequence enables production to flow to a logical end-product. In this electric age we have the means to store and move information with speed and precision to make the largest problem quite as manageable as small ones.

> The breaking up of every kind of experience into uniform units in order to produce faster action and a change of form (applied knowledge) has been the secret of western power over man and nature alike(11).

The application of flowchart techniques to statutory or commercial procedures will produce a model that has all the characteristics necessary for automation in this field.

11. Marshall McLuhan, *Understanding Media: The Extensions of Man* (London: Routledge & Kegan Paul Ltd., 1964).

12. G. Sawer, *Law in Society* (Oxford: Clarendon Press, 1965).

OBJECTIVE

This work does not attempt to review the vast problems generated by man's need for an ordered, controlled and motivated compliance with rules. It is an earnest attempt to create a simple decision-reaching format at a 'low' level in a contract between man and man.

Standard Form recorded sales. N.F.B.T.E. Annual Reports, sales quoted in thousands

1963	*1964*	*1965*	*1966*	*1967*	*1968*	*1969*	*1970*
155	77	106	98	95	114	104	93

The scathing cricitism of Lord Justice Sachs quoted earlier was directed at the current *Standard Form of Building Contract*, 1963 edition, see table above. This study is directed entirely towards transforming this complex and important document into one that will:

(*a*) Enable its users to readily review and understand their obligations, rights, and remedies, and

(*b*) Provide an automatic solution technique for parties in dispute.

Theorists have long claimed 'that a mature legal system in a modern state can provide logically necessary solutions for all conceivable cases, and one only "correct" solution in each case'(12). If a contract can be regarded as 'law' between man and man then, if success in achieving the objective is at all possible, contracts are the best 'laws' to experiment with.

It is perhaps impossible to experiment to create in reality the theorist's dream of a jurisprudent vending machine without rationalizing matters to such an extent that humane reasons for nonconformity are of no concern and will not appear in the 'input' to this machine. In contracts we are concerned solely with setting out each party's obligations to the other, and the remedies available to each in the event of certain defaults. The courts will administer those remedies if one party refuses to accept the agreed remedy. Society is therefore involved in administering those 'laws' made between man and man and to that extent a rational and automatic solution-finding technique can be aimed for in the knowledge that any humane shortcoming could be resolved, as they always have been, by courts. For example, the Standard Form of Building Contract requires the Architect to objectively decide whether the work carried out is to his 'reasonable satisfaction'. Specifications are rarely comprehensive in construction projects therefore this objective test is difficult if not impossible to apply. The settlement of a dispute as to the Architect's reasonable satisfaction is no better achieved using flowcharts than it is under the present form, and until we are able to specify standards in a rational way, will remain subject to some human test which is likely to be somewhat subjective.

Flowcharting techniques simplify any plan process or procedure no matter how complex the problem. The chart arrives at correct conclusions by short simple logical steps. Flowcharts are the forerunner to computerization. Computers can store, cross-refer, retrieve, display, and provide printed out information at great speed. This technique is therefore the one adopted in this experiment to achieve the declared objective.

The use of a flowchart to project text simplifies the reasoning process, solves the question of sequence within each chart, and by subroutine methods copes with the devilish habit of cross-referencing. The simplification of complex legal sentences appears to require some considerable legal expertise. But on detailed study, it requires no more than elementary logic and the task of simplification surprisingly 'requires the use of mental operation whose validity is not determined by law'(10). Mathematical logic may in the future provide the panacea for all injustices, in the meantime our rules are not so complex when coupled to a diagrammatic method, and operated by an electric machine, that we cannot see that the mysterious and mythical legal logic is merely ordinary logic in disguise.

Work in this field is limited. Applying fundamental problems solving techniques to these forms plunges one into uninhabited territory. Any literature search proves astoundingly fruitless, leaving an impression that the arts and current techniques of drafting are known only to the practitioners. Each draftsman appears to tread in the footsteps of his forefathers. Minute changes in technique can only be detected if documents with several decades intervening are studied. All this is no real disadvantage if one wishes to return to the basic problems of communication and solution-finding.

A study of the flowcharts in Chapter 3 will indicate that a computer is not essential to this particular Contract. It can be comprehended and handled physically without the aid of the machine. However, the objectives are to investigate a system that does make use of this machine, so that it may perhaps act as a pilot for more voluminous work. Chapter 4 indicates a case dispute applied to the flowcharts using computer methods of solution-finding.

If the principles gleaned from this work are valid, it is not difficult to foresee legislation and complex standard contracts being flowcharted and securely stored on 'public' computers to which the legal profession, commerce, and even laymen can be terminally linked. We are at present content to allow E.R.N.I.E. (Electronic Random Number Indicator Equipment) to dispense favours on a few, it may not be too difficult to persuade more of us that 'he' could also dispense the only 'correct' solution in cases of dispute between man and man or even man and society.

The layman's experiments with systems to handle legal documents must advisedly stop short of territory traversed traditionally by experts in the field of law. These experiments and objectives therefore exclude any intention to produce court proof final documents, they simply use the methods and instruments of scientific technology to enable members of the construction industry to communicate correct information, and solutions to each other, and to their clients.

This flowchart format chosen for this experiment is referred to in general terms as an algorithmic method for solving problems.

2 METHOD

1. Statement box

2. Subroutine statement box

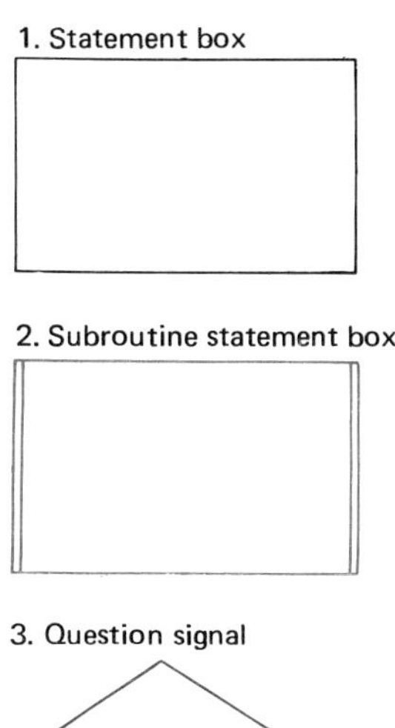

3. Question signal

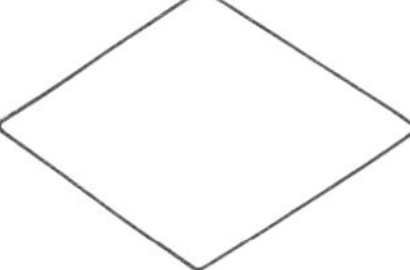

4. Connector signal

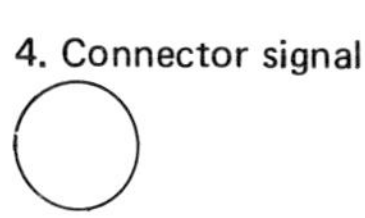

5. Stop/start signal

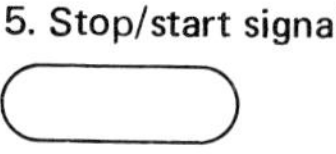

6. Annotation signal

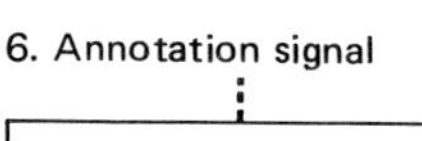

Fig. 2.1

INTRODUCTION

A legal document can be regarded as a process declaration. Flowcharts provide a pictorial representation of any process, indicating the arrangement and action of its parts by which it produces a given result. The production of flowcharts therefore involves analysing the 'system' of the legal document, to show the logical pattern of the process. This analysis will result in the process being thoroughly understood, and one objective, namely intelligibility, will thereby be achieved. From this intelligible analysis a flowchart has to be created that will be an unambiguous declaration of the legal process. The resulting flowchart will then act as an algorithm for solving disputes concerning breaches or non-compliance by either party with that declared process. Furthermore, the flowchart will enable the data and process to be handled by computer, if so desired.

A disciplined system had to be devised to create consistent and correct charts. Undisciplined total paraphrasing was completely unacceptable as a means of converting the legal phraseology into meaningful statements. This rejection was made on two grounds:

(*a*) The results would produce unfamiliar verbiage.

(*b*) Laymen's paraphrases are breeding grounds for ambiguity.

It was clear that statements would need to be constructed in a methodical way by decomposing the original text and reconstructing it by applying a set of rules to be devised which would satisfy the declared objectives (Chapter 1). Furthermore a set of symbols must be adopted to communicate the end result.

It was hoped that the rules devised would enable charts to be constructed preserving the original text as far as is possible when an existing syntactic policy is rejected. However, it will be seen later in this chapter that ordinary paraphrases or formula had to be used if unintelligible text was encountered (the test for intelligibility was subjectively applied by the author).

The requirements so far, therefore, are: (*a*) symbols (Fig. 2.1) and (*b*) method rules (p. 9). The subroutine facility contained within a flowchart could be extended to embrace mandatory amendments as they arise and non-mandatory codes which may be deemed to satisfy the intentions of an enactment or contract.

SYMBOLS

British Standards Specification 4058 defines thirty basic symbols for use in data processing, problem definition, and analysis. Six of the basic symbols available are used in this work (Fig. 2.1).

1. Statement box (Figs. 2.2 and 2.3)

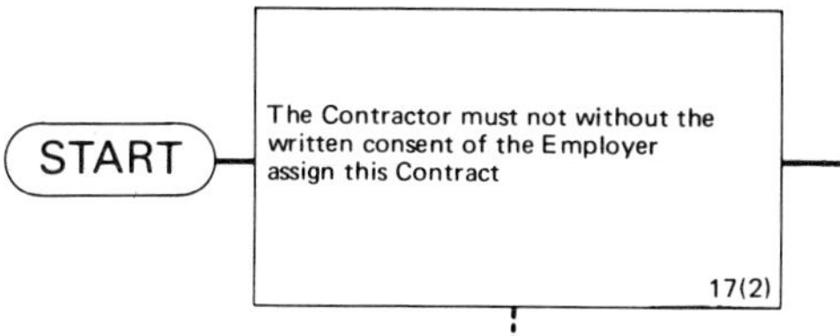
START
The Contractor must not without the written consent of the Employer assign this Contract
17(2)

Fig. 2.2

The source of the text appears in the bottom right-hand corner of each box. In certain cases for reasons of clarity and to facilitate computer processing text cannot be contained in one box. In such cases the signals :– or ; are used to denote there is overflow into succeeding boxes (Fig. 2.3).

Definition
A statement *is the description given to text originally contained in the legal document.*

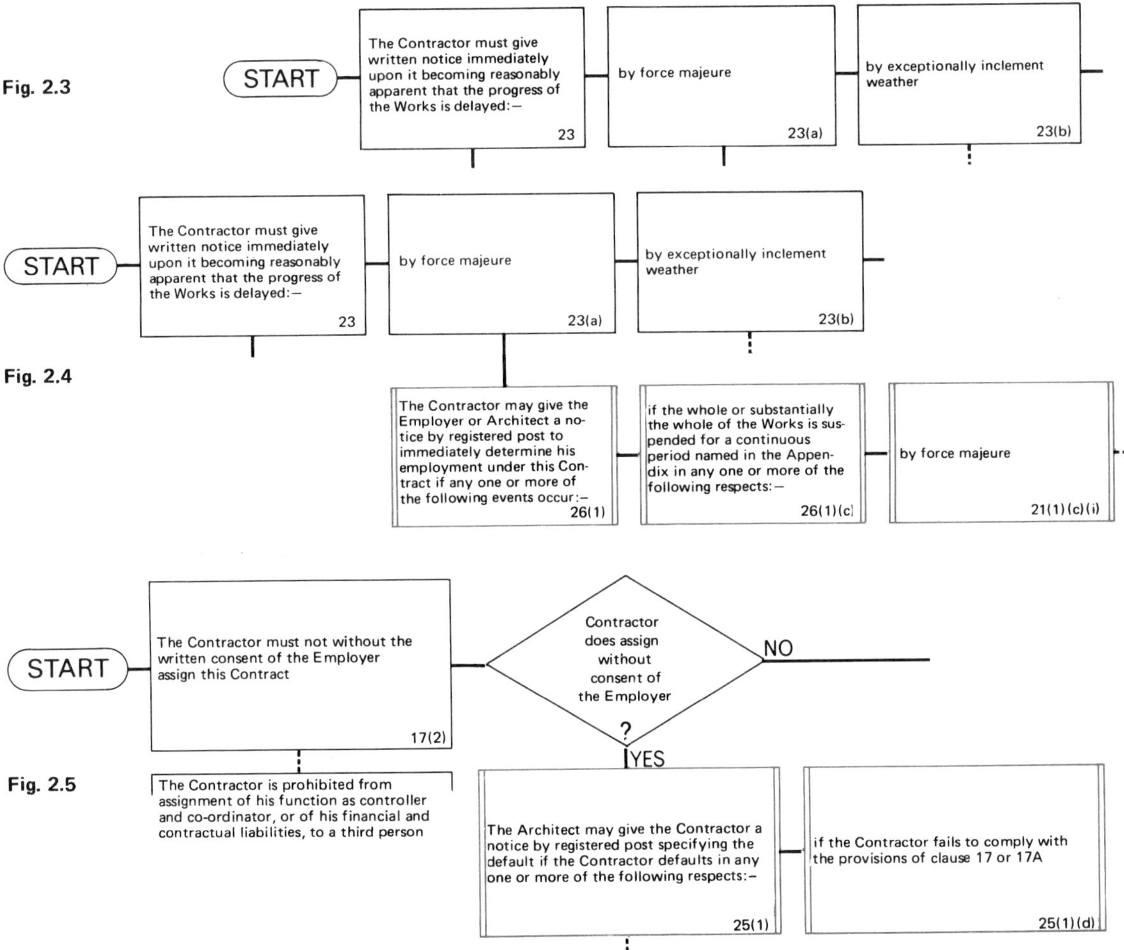
START
The Contractor must give written notice immediately upon it becoming reasonably apparent that the progress of the Works is delayed:–
23
by force majeure
23(a)
by exceptionally inclement weather
23(b)
START
The Contractor must give written notice immediately upon it becoming reasonably apparent that the progress of the Works is delayed:–
23
by force majeure
23(a)
by exceptionally inclement weather
23(b)
The Contractor may give the Employer or Architect a notice by registered post to immediately determine his employment under this Contract if any one or more of the following events occur:–
26(1)
if the whole or substantially the whole of the Works is suspended for a continuous period named in the Appendix in any one or more of the following respects:–
26(1)(c)
by force majeure
21(1)(c)(i)
START
The Contractor must not without the written consent of the Employer assign this Contract
17(2)
Contractor does assign without consent of the Employer
?
NO
YES
The Contractor is prohibited from assignment of his function as controller and co-ordinator, or of his financial and contractual liabilities, to a third person
The Architect may give the Contractor a notice by registered post specifying the default if the Contractor defaults in any one or more of the following respects:–
25(1)
if the Contractor fails to comply with the provisions of clause 17 or 17A
25(1)(d)

Fig. 2.3

Fig. 2.4

Fig. 2.5

2. **Subroutine statement box** (Fig. 2.4)

Definition
A subroutine statement *is a statement which originates from another clause in the original document and which qualifies, interacts with, or forms a logical extension to the statement, or any other subroutine statement immediately preceding.*

3. **Question signal** (Fig. 2.5)

Definition
A question *is a statement designed to challenge the text preceding to produce a binary ('yes' or 'no') response.*

4. **Connector signal** (Fig. 2.6)

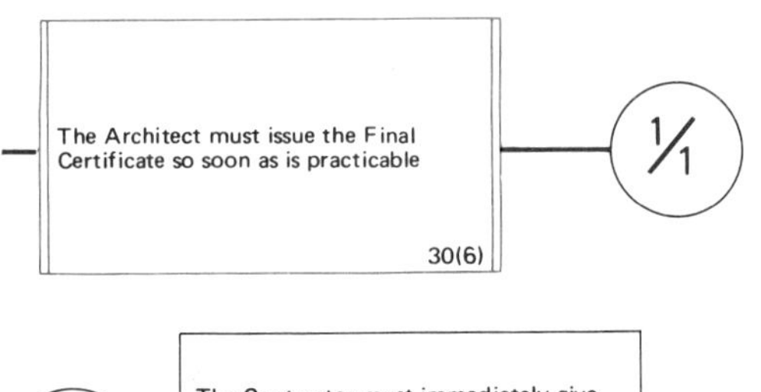
The Architect must issue the Final Certificate so soon as is practicable
30(6)
1/1
1/1
The Contractor must immediately give to the Architect a written notice specifying any discrepancy in or divergence between Contract Drawings and/or Bills if he finds any
1(2)

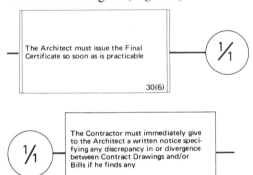

Fig. 2.6

Definition
A connector *links various sections of a chart together, enabling a chart to be divided to achieve greater clarity.*

5. **Start/stop signal** (Fig. 2.7)

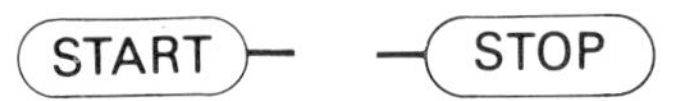
START
STOP

Fig. 2.7

Definition
Start *and* stop *signals indicate the commencement and completion point of any clause. A clause chart can be 'entered'*

into by the start signal or dependant upon any subroutine statement at the point signified by the source signal stated at the bottom right-hand corner of each box.

6. Annotation signal (Fig. 2.8)

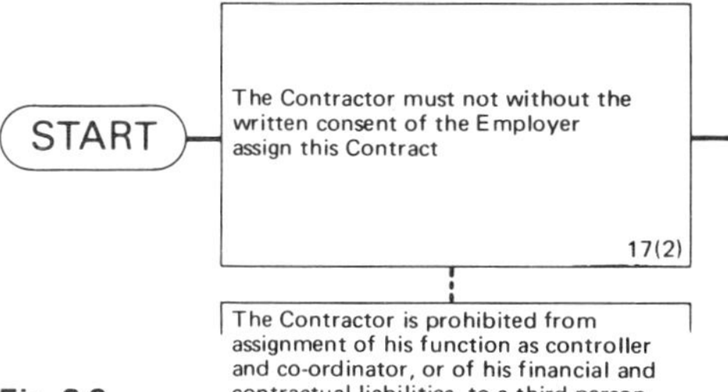
START
The Contractor must not without the written consent of the Employer assign this Contract
17(2)
The Contractor is prohibited from assignment of his function as controller and co-ordinator, or of his financial and contractual liabilities, to a third person

Fig. 2.8

Definition
The annotation *signal contains information essential to aid the user in his understanding. When a breach occurs the annotation signal is used to confirm the breach. In this Contract breaches are the responsibility of either the Employer or Contractor but the annotation identifies the person causing the breach.*

METHOD RULES
To create consistent flowcharts some informal experimentation resulted in the adoption of six rules:

1. Simplification.
2. Statement formation.
3. Sequence arrangement.
4. Questioning process.
5. Subroutine formation.
6. Annotation.

Clause 17 flowchart in Fig. 2.9 shows the above rules in application.

Rule 1. Simplification
Simplify the original text and test the results
Elementary logic is used to simplify text, and unnatural phraseology is converted into prose.

The methods used to simplify legal statements are similar to the mental deductions involved in the following example which is unrelated to law.

Statements
Jack is twice as old as he was five years ago. His mother was then six times as old as he was. She is now 35 years old.

Questions
How old is Jack?
How old was his mother when Jack was 5?
How old will Jack be when his mother is 50?
How old was Jack's mother when he was born?
What is the difference between Jack's age and his mother's?

Simplification indicates that:

(*a*) Jack is 10.

(*b*) Jack's mother was 30, five years ago.

(*c*) Jack's mother is 35.

Relevant information becomes apparent when simplification occurs, and (*b*) above can be seen to be irrelevant.

Testing of simplification is required under Rule 1 to ensure that accurate results have been obtained in relation to the task to be performed. Clearly the five questions asked must be capable of being answered from our simplified result.

The elementary logic required for this example and the testing process is the same as that required to simplify legal statements. There is no special legal or mathematical logic involved in flowcharting legal documents, although some analogous logic may be required (for example, is 'completion' in clause 1 the same as 'practical completion' in clause 15 of the Standard Form of Building Contract).

In testing simplification all possible variables must be tried, in this example; by converting each question into a binary form, i.e.

1. Is Jack 10?
2. Was Jack's mother 30 when Jack was 5?

Fig. 2.9

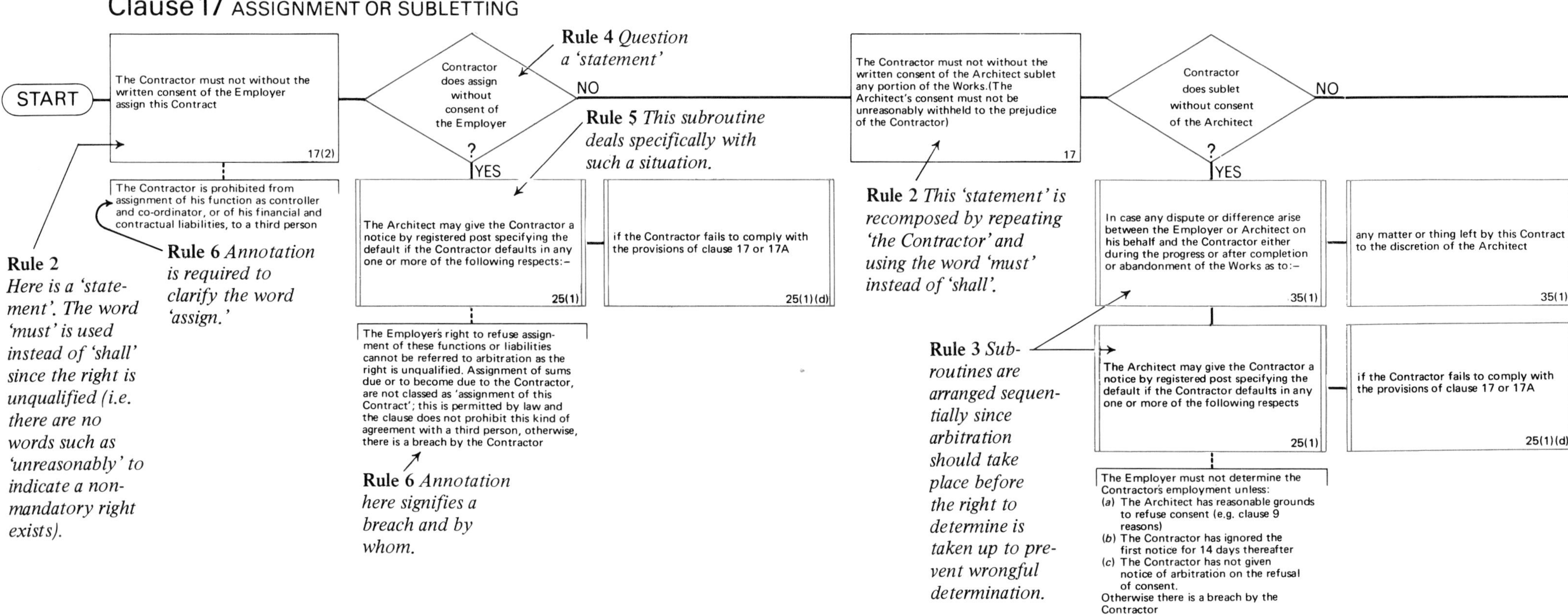

Clause 17 ASSIGNMENT OR SUBLETTING
START
The Contractor must not without the written consent of the Employer assign this Contract
17(2)
The Contractor is prohibited from assignment of his function as controller and co-ordinator, or of his financial and contractual liabilities, to a third person
Rule 2
Here is a 'statement'. The word 'must' is used instead of 'shall' since the right is unqualified (i.e. there are no words such as 'unreasonably' to indicate a non-mandatory right exists).
Rule 6 Annotation is required to clarify the word 'assign.'
Contractor does assign without consent of the Employer ?
Rule 4 Question a 'statement'
NO
YES
Rule 5 This subroutine deals specifically with such a situation.
The Architect may give the Contractor a notice by registered post specifying the default if the Contractor defaults in any one or more of the following respects:–
25(1)
if the Contractor fails to comply with the provisions of clause 17 or 17A
25(1)(d)
The Employer's right to refuse assignment of these functions or liabilities cannot be referred to arbitration as the right is unqualified. Assignment of sums due or to become due to the Contractor, are not classed as 'assignment of this Contract'; this is permitted by law and the clause does not prohibit this kind of agreement with a third person, otherwise, there is a breach by the Contractor
Rule 6 Annotation here signifies a breach and by whom.
The Contractor must not without the written consent of the Architect sublet any portion of the Works.(The Architect's consent must not be unreasonably withheld to the prejudice of the Contractor)
17
Rule 2 This 'statement' is recomposed by repeating 'the Contractor' and using the word 'must' instead of 'shall'.
Contractor does sublet without consent of the Architect ?
NO
YES
In case any dispute or difference arise between the Employer or Architect on his behalf and the Contractor either during the progress or after completion or abandonment of the Works as to:–
35(1)
any matter or thing left by this Contract to the discretion of the Architect
35(1)
Rule 3 Subroutines are arranged sequentially since arbitration should take place before the right to determine is taken up to prevent wrongful determination.
The Architect may give the Contractor a notice by registered post specifying the default if the Contractor defaults in any one or more of the following respects
25(1)
if the Contractor fails to comply with the provisions of clause 17 or 17A
25(1)(d)
The Employer must not determine the Contractor's employment unless:
(a) The Architect has reasonable grounds to refuse consent (e.g. clause 9 reasons)
(b) The Contractor has ignored the first notice for 14 days thereafter
(c) The Contractor has not given notice of arbitration on the refusal of consent.
Otherwise there is a breach by the Contractor

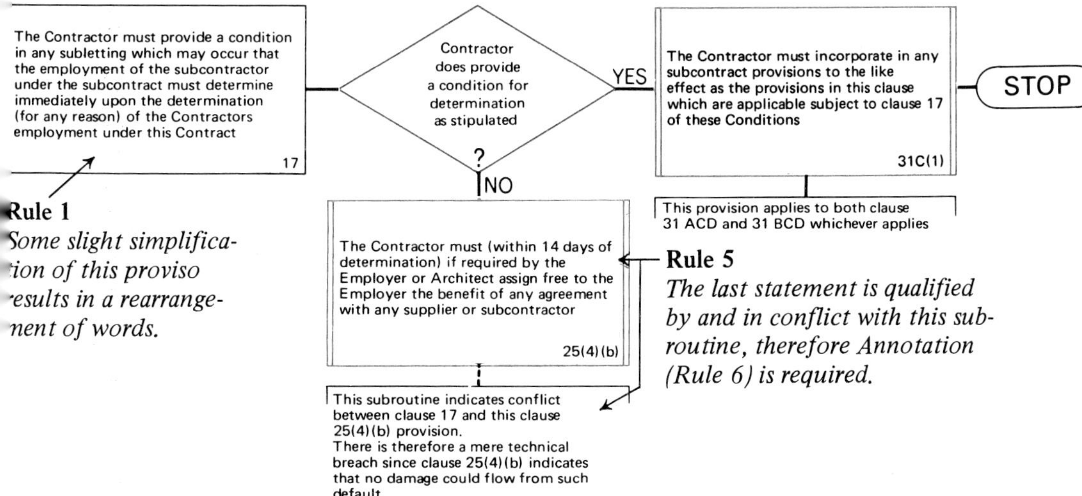
The Contractor must provide a condition in any subletting which may occur that the employment of the subcontractor under the subcontract must determine immediately upon the determination (for any reason) of the Contractors employment under this Contract
17
Contractor does provide a condition for determination as stipulated
?
YES
NO
The Contractor must incorporate in any subcontract provisions to the like effect as the provisions in this clause which are applicable subject to clause 17 of these Conditions
31C(1)
STOP
This provision applies to both clause 31 ACD and 31 BCD whichever applies
The Contractor must (within 14 days of determination) if required by the Employer or Architect assign free to the Employer the benefit of any agreement with any supplier or subcontractor
25(4)(b)
This subroutine indicates conflict between clause 17 and this clause 25(4)(b) provision.
There is therefore a mere technical breach since clause 25(4)(b) indicates that no damage could flow from such default
Rule 1
Some slight simplification of this proviso results in a rearrangement of words.
Rule 5
The last statement is qualified by and in conflict with this subroutine, therefore Annotation (Rule 6) is required.

3. Will Jack be 25 when Jack's mother is 50?
4. Was Jack's mother 25 when Jack was born?
5. Is the difference between Jack's age and his mother 25?

we can readily establish that the parameters are confined to the difference in age. From this we can deduce what our simplified statement should be (Fig. 2.10). When testing, our responses will prove the *statement* to be adequate for all its purposes.

Jack is 10 and Jack's mother is 35

Fig. 2.10

We have in the simplification kept the vital words 'Jack' and 'Jack's mother'. Similarly when analysing legal text certain words must be recognized and identified as 'irreplaceable'. This dictum is not difficult to follow in practice and just as we readily retained the words 'Jack' and 'Jack's mother' so words such as 'Contract Sum' and 'Retention', etc., from the Standard Form are logically preserved. We could replace such words by others providing they were clearly defined, for example, Prime Cost Sum or Provisional Sum. (Both would benefit from such treatment.) But this is considered an unnecessary step to take if suitable annotation can overcome the disposal of terms which are well known to most users and their purpose is equally well understood.

There must, therefore, be a consistent effort to replace the original text of legal documents into simplified statements if familiarity with such terms leads the user to a better understanding.

Ambiguities

When simplification is carried out, ambiguities may arise. The less intelligible the original statement, the more likelihood there is of ambiguity.

Example. Clause 5. The original text states:

> Unless the Architect shall otherwise instruct, in which case the contract sum shall be adjusted accordingly, the Contractor shall be responsible for and shall entirely at his own cost amend any errors arising from his own inaccurate setting out.

Taking the last part of this text first it appears to logically make the Contractor responsible for his own mistakes, and the first part of the text provides that the Architect may in suitable cases choose to accept inaccuracy with its attendant *reduction* in the contract sum. But since the word adjust is also used in clause 30 to mean both an increase or reduction, ambiguity then arises.

The objectives, however, are to simplify and not to change. The remedy in this situation lies in judicious use of annotation to ensure the user is made aware of inherent ambiguities.

More on simplification and ambiguity arising under test

Clause 16(e) of the Standard Form states:

> (e) In lieu of any sum to be paid or allowed by the Contractor under clause 22 of these Conditions in respect of any period during which the Works may remain incomplete occurring after the date on which the Employer shall have taken possession of the relevant part there shall be paid or allowed such sum as bears the same ratio to the sum which would be paid or allowed apart from the provisions of this Condition as does the Contract Sum less the total value of the said relevant part to the Contract Sum.

Simplification results must be tested under all conceivable conditions. The above statement is quite unintelligible to the user even after several surface readings. Methodical conversion into simple prose is carried out as below.

> In lieu of any sum . . . of these Conditions . . .
> (*Simplified* = instead of the Contractor paying any damages at the rate in clause 22)
>
> . . . in respect of . . . the relevant part . . .
> (*Simplified* = on the Works remaining)
>
> . . . there shall be paid . . . such sum . . .
> (*Simplified* = there must be paid a new sum equal to)
>
> . . . the same ratio . . . to the Contract Sum . . .
> (*Simplified* = new sum is to the sum in clause 22 as Contract Sum minus value of relevant part is to the Contract Sum)

In anticipation of Rule 2, Statement Formation, the above prose could be reduced by using a simple formula (Fig. 2.11).

The statement formed bears no resemblance to the original text but formulas are precise (although draftsmen make little or no use of such expression) furthermore the words:

(*a*) clause 22

(*b*) Works remaining ('remain')

(*c*) Contract Sum

(*d*) Value Relevant Part

are all preserved, and it will be seen in Test 1 that these exact words are vitally important. The intention of this original statement is to diminish the sum payable in liquidated damages on the Works remaining *pro rata* the value of the sectional part or parts of the Works handed over prior to practical completion of the whole.

Our next step, therefore, is to test the simplified statement to ensure its accuracy.

On Works remaining any damages due under clause 22 must equal x where

x : clause 22 sum

CS–VRP : CS

16(e)

Fig. 2.11

CS = Contract Sum
VRP = Value of Relevant Part

TEST 1. A Contract Sum for £100,000 has liquidated damages under clause 22 equal to £10,000 per week. The Contract is to have sectional completion in four equal parts A, B, C, and D each valued at £25,000 from the Contract Sum.

Question 1. After handing over A what damages will arise on the Works remaining?

$$x : £10,000$$
$$£100,000 - £25,000 : £100,000 \quad \therefore x = £7,500$$

Question 2. After handing over B what damages will arise on the Works remaining?

$$£100,000 - £25,000 : £100,000 \quad \therefore x = £7,500$$

Clearly the damages are not diminishing as they are intended to, in relation to the *value* handed over.

We must conclude that either (*a*) our simplification is unsound or (*b*) the original text is a misconception of the true intent.

However, the simplified statement contains the vital words 'Contract Sum' and 'relevant part' and the transposition is exact.

Let us, therefore, delve further by assuming the fault lies in the use of 'relevant part' instead of (as in our test) '*relevant parts*'.

Applying Test 1 again:

Question 1 will result in x = £7,500.
Question 2 will result in x = £5,000.
Question 3 will result in x = £2,500.
Question 4 will result in x = £0.

This is clearly the intention of the Contract.

However, elsewhere in the Contract (clause 11) provides for variations which can alter sectional values. Our simplified statement (from the original text) does not provide for such adjustments. Let us therefore test again.

TEST 2. Assume the Contract described under Test 1 contains variations which alter the values of sections A, B, C, and D as the work is in progress to:

A = £30,000
B = £30,000
C = £30,000
D = £20,000

Question 1. After handing over A what damages will arise on the Works remaining?

$$x : £10,000$$
$$£100,000 - £30,000 : £100,000 \qquad x = £7,000$$

Question 2. After handing over B what damages will arise on the Works remaining?

$$x : £10,000$$
$$£100,000 - £60,000 : £100,000 \qquad x = £4,000.$$

At this stage it is clear that this system neither relates damages to value of the new contract sums (i.e. £105,000 after A was handed over and £110,000 after B was handed over). Furthermore when C has been handed over, in constructional terms, 25 per cent of the Works remain incomplete but only £1,000 will arise in liquidated damages.

To equate damages with value, the words 'Contract Sum' have to be changed to '*Contract Sum or such other sum adjusted as necessary*'.

Applying Test 2 again and *Question 1* again:

$$\frac{x}{£105{,}000 - £30{,}000} : \frac{£10{,}000}{£105{,}000} \quad x = £7{,}140 \text{ (say)}$$

Question 2

$$\frac{x}{£110{,}000 - £60{,}000} : \frac{£10{,}000}{£110{,}000} \quad x = £4{,}550 \text{ (say)}$$

Question 3

$$\frac{x}{£115{,}000 - £90{,}000} : \frac{£10{,}000}{£115{,}000} \quad x = £2{,}170 \text{ (say)}$$

Question 4

$$\frac{x}{£110{,}000 - £110{,}000} : \frac{£10{,}000}{£110{,}000} \quad x = £0.$$

Bills of quantities would be a prerequisite in practise to enable the 'Contract Sum . . ., etc.' to be readily recognized when each section was handed over.

The policy of the original contract, when simplified, indicates an inconsistency with the policy where no sectional completion is arranged. Any delay to the Works will result in *total* application of the sum stated in clause 22. This is sensible since damage arising is not *pro rata* the *value* of the Works.

However, in the clause 16 dealing with sectional completion an attempt has been made to equate damage with value. This inconsistency and error of principle requires annotation by the chartist. It also requires careful consideration when amendment by others is contemplated since equating value with risk is practised by the insurance profession and of course the retentions held (and released) are based upon Works values.

Therefore:

(*a*) Specific sums of *damage* should be stated in *clause 22* for sectional completion effects on the total liquidated damages specified.

(*b*) The reduction of insurance risks will be calculated on *value*.

(*c*) Under present contract arrangements, retentions are held and released on *value* but specific sums based on reality rather than notional factors could be declared in this respect.

However, the principal aim of the chartist is to simplify and not to change. His findings will bring about change. In the interim his annotation will spotlight the pitfalls, and enable objective proposals to be agreed between the parties concerned.

Rule 2 Statement formation

Form statements from the results of Rule 1 which are intelligible and accurate

A legislative statement is not readily understood because it is in a form unlike 'sentence construction in a natural language' (Chomsky).

Piesse and Gilchrist discuss Coode's rule that a legislative sentence consists of four parts:

1. Case (where or when the sentence is to take effect).
2. Conditions (what is to be done to make the sentence operative).
3. Legal subject (the person to act).
4. Legal action (what that person must do).

Coode advocated sentences should consistently be arranged in the above order.

Thring's analysis of a legal sentence in its most complicated form, listed by Piesse and Gilchrist indicates five parts:

1. Case
2. Agreement or intention or declaration.
3. Conditions.
4. Exceptions.
5. Provisos.

The arrangement or order of these parts need not be in the order indicated above.

It is logical to first address the person to act and secondly inform that person what he must do. It was therefore decided to consistently arrange such statements in the following order:

1. Legal subject.
2. Legal action.
3. Case.
4. Conditions.

Furthermore, punctuation (which basically is a system of determinatives, or explanatory symbols) could be minimized by the boxing of statements in a flowchart.

The exceptions and provisos are also linked to the statements they affect by the flowchart form. When this process is applied to existing legal text the original syntax is disturbed but there seems no reason to prevent the resultant statements being repaired to court-proof standards by the draftsman and rules declared to define the legal relationship (along the lines defined in BS 4058) of statement and subroutine boxes when juxtaposed. This step would lead to the eradication of the interminable and devilishly intricate legislative sentence.

The word 'shall'

This word has proved troublesome to lawyers throughout the ages. Coode clarified the problems caused by this word being used to denote both the obligations to act and the future tense. The layman's problem, however, so far as the Standard Form of Contract is concerned is perhaps confined to understanding whether the word is denoting a mandatory or non-mandatory obligation. For example in clause 24 it states:

> . . . if the written application is made within a reasonable time of it becoming reasonably apparent that the progress of the Works or of any part thereof has been affected as aforesaid, then the Architect shall either himself ascertain or shall instruct the Quantity Surveyor to ascertain the amount of such loss and/or expense.

Such written applications frequently cite under subclauses (1), (a) and (c) dilatoriness or errors by either Architect or Quantity Surveyor as grounds for claims of loss or expense. It is not unknown or unnatural perhaps for such applications to simply be ignored, or verbally rejected by the recipient.

The Contractor in these circumstances cannot recognize readily from the surrounding verbiage whether mandatory or non-mandatory status is conferred upon this provision.

Instant identification of the status of a provision can be obtained by the use of either 'must' or 'may'. The word 'shall' has therefore been discarded in favour of either the words 'must' or 'may', dependent upon the results of the simplification process. The draftsman's use of 'deemed' can be classed as compulsory logic and furthermore requires no questioning under Rule 4.

The use of 'and/or'

Viscount Simon in *Bonitto* v. *Fuerst Bros.* (1944), A.C. 75, p. 82, crustily referred to 'the repeated use of that bastard conjunction "and/or" which has, I fear, become the commercial courts contribution to basic English'. However, in clauses 11(6) and 24(1), etc., it is used in its simplest form and is unambiguous. It has, therefore, been preserved in the simplified statements.

Once simplification has been completed and checked the next stage is the construction of new statements preserving the original text so far as is compatible with an instant and proper understanding. Simplified text is frequently longer than the original compressed text, but flowcharting requires the user only to read and understand that part which he is guided to by his binary responses to questions asked. Therefore any increase in text is not inflicted upon the reader.

By placing statements into a compartment, the reader of a chart is given pictorial aid to understand a complex situation by readily assimilated pieces of information.

Some iterative methods may be required to break down the extensive text encountered in legal documents.

Examples. See clauses 23, 24, etc.

> The use of the signals :– or ; indicates more text is to follow. The reader is therefore given a 'breathing space' or time to consider and understand fully the first part of a statement before proceeding to the next. It can be likened to providing a landing in a staircase.

These signals are used to denote that succeeding statements are to be linked to the one containing these signals.

The correct arrangement of words in new statements, derived from simplification of original text, is, of course, essential. But the use of compartments for statements enables the chartist to enjoy some considerable freedom from the nightmarish task of ensuring correct syntax occurs when long complex text is in hand. The degree of iteration used in the charting of clauses 23, 24, etc., is considered by the author to be acceptable to the reader and proves convenient when the chart is applied by computer.

Rule 3. Sequence arrangement
Once simplification has been achieved sequence and relevance becomes self-evident.

Examples. Clause 11(3).

The provisional and prime cost sum procedures when simplified indicate no relevancy with variations and provisional sum *work* or valuation. These procedures clearly belong to clauses 27 and 28. The illogical placement of these procedures leaves those clauses deficient and contributed to the disputes encountered by Bickerton and the North-West Metropolitan Hospital Board ((1969), 1 A.E.R. 977).

The charts containing connectors can break down large diagrams to manageable parts, or place relevant matter together, preserving sequence by a simple number code, i.e. Fig. 2.12.

Fig. 2.12

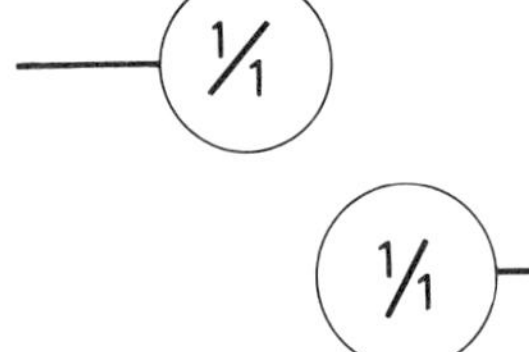
1/1
1/1

Rule 4. Questioning process
There is no simpler question than that which can be answered by a direct 'Yes' or 'No'. All questions must, therefore, be binary and consistently phrased to result in either of the above answers.

This consistency can be achieved by directing the question to the statements immediately preceding the question position, i.e. those statements which lie after the last question asked. The question position is determined by the content of the statements. Any mandatory statements will require a question and some non-mandatory statements which generate succeeding related statements will also require questioning (Fig. 2.13).

Example. Clause 2 Architect's Instructions (1)
A group of statements can be questioned by one question (see, for example, flowchart, clause 17A) simply because the statements are really one large statement placed conveniently into several compartments to enable the user to understand them more readily so that the answer in each case must be the same.

As previously stated a 'deemed' provision is classed as compulsory logic and therefore requires no questioning.

Finally, it must always be remembered that only if the question is right can the answer be right.

Rule 5. Subroutine formation
The word subroutine in computer application means that a predefined process is to be followed at a particular point, or as a result of a switch, caused by a decision resulting from a question.

The predefined process commences with the opening relevant statement elsewhere in the charts. This statement thus becomes a subroutine signal since the particular point of commencement of the subroutine is indicated in the bottom right-hand corner of each compartment.

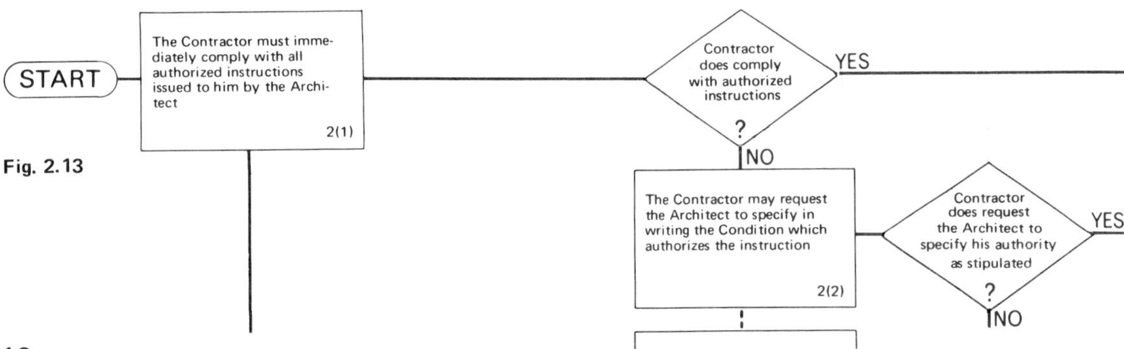
START
The Contractor must immediately comply with all authorized instructions issued to him by the Architect
2(1)
Contractor does comply with authorized instructions ?
YES
NO
The Contractor may request the Architect to specify in writing the Condition which authorizes the instruction
2(2)
Contractor does request the Architect to specify his authority as stipulated ?
YES
NO

Fig. 2.13

The opening relevant statement of the subroutine is sometimes sufficient to indicate to the reader that in his particular case the subroutine is applicable or not. If it is, he will deviate or switch into that subroutine. If it is not applicable he will take note but move logically on without switching into that subroutine.

In Chapter 4 the computer application automatically questions the reader on whether each subroutine is applicable and alternatively permits the user to choose whether to switch immediately into the subroutine or to switch after completing the viewing of statements, but before the 'stop' signal is reached.

Statements which qualify, interact or form a logical extension to a particular provision can occur, in legal documents, in any part of that document. Accuracy in recognizing such statements, so that they may be identified and positioned in the chart as subroutines, is an essential function of the chartist. Any oversight in this respect will result in an inaccurate or inconclusive result being derived.

Example. Clause 24, see flowchart.

> The provision in 24(1)(a) indicates that subroutines 23 and 26(1) are logical extensions to that particular provision. But equally or possibly more important is the interaction with clause 3(4) subroutine. This is because any shortcomings in the Contractors obligations to make a written application under clause 24(1) to claim loss and/or expense may not prevent him seeking remedies under the subroutine clause 3(4).

Rule 6. Annotation

Annotation should act as an essential aid to the reader. Anomolies and breaches are declared in annotation. Too much annotation may signify:

(*a*) Insufficient simplification has occurred, or

(*b*) The original text is tortuous, potentially ambiguous or silent.

Potential ambiguity inherent in the original text can largely be eradicated by correct charting and judicious annotation.

Anomolies must be declared as such and not changed by the chartist. This must be the function of the body responsible (or society in general) if the document is anything other than private.

A chartist who has spent long periods simplifying compressed complexity may always be inclined to voice subjective opinions in annotation. This is to be avoided if the pictorial and psychological advantages of flowcharts are to be respected.

3 FLOWCHARTS

INSTRUCTIONS ON THE USE OF FLOWCHARTS

Chapter 2 dealing with method, details the symbols used and their purpose in the flowcharts.

The reader is required to read the charts from top to bottom and left to right, in that order. The signal :– or ; appearing at the end of a statement in a box indicates the reader is required to study the variable endings or provisions to that initial statement that will be found following. An example of this signal :– in use can be seen in chart 25/3–25/4.

Arrowheads to indicate direction of 'flow' have been dispensed with except in isolated situations which require the reader to move directly to a certain position in the charts. An example of this arrow direction is evident in chart 15/16/2–STOP.

An example on the use of flowcharts

> *Brief.* An Architect instructs a Contractor by letter that he requires certain areas of facing brickwork (to cavity walls) to be removed so that a detailed visual examination of foamed cavity filling, executed and completed by nominated subcontractors, can be carried out.

The Contractor has replied to the effect that this required work will involve considerable expenditure on his part and he requires, before he will proceed, written confirmation from the Architect that these costs will be reimbursed, either by the Employer, or by the nominated subcontractor.

Procedure

Since an Architect's instruction sparked off this problem, *this will be the logical point of commencement.*

Stage 1

1. Start *Clause 2. Architect's instructions* (1).
2. Read from top to bottom and left to right, until subroutine 6(3) is reached.
3. Switch into subroutine 6(3).
4. Answer the first question: 'yes' and this informs us of the Contract provisions for payment, in addition, subroutine 23 is noted and if we switch into this subroutine we are informed of the provision for extensions in time, and the subroutine 24(1) recovery of loss and expense, *providing* the results were found to be in accordance with the Contract Standards stipulated. Finally subroutine 26(1) indicates the ultimate provision in cases where such instructions might cause substantially the whole of the Works to be suspended.

Let us, however, assume that the Contractor firmly refuses to proceed with the original instruction because the nominated subcontractor states they will not promise in writing to reimburse the Contractor because they insist they have carried out their work strictly in accordance with their quotation.

Stage 2. Clause 2. Architect's instructions (1)

1. Answer the first question: 'no'. This indicates the Contractor can request the Architect to state his authority to give such an instruction. This authority is clearly contained in

clause 6(3), therefore the Contractor is unlikely to request a statement of authority.

2. Answer the second question: 'no'. This indicates the power given to the Employer to engage others to give effect to this instruction.

Conclusion

The Contractor now realizes that under this Contract he must carry out such an instruction or be in breach. He also realizes that the Employer will have to pay his opening up costs, etc., if the work examined is found not defective. If the work examined is found defective then the Contractor must recover from the nominated subcontractor. Under the Standard Nominated Subcontract Form such costs are recoverable, and this matter is dealt with in Chapter 5 (under 'Direct and nominated subcontractors').

The chosen point of commencement on the charts is not critical, the user could choose perhaps to start at:

Clause 1. 'Contractor's obligations.'

Clause 6. 'Workmanship materials and goods.'

Clause 23. 'Extensions of time' (if the Contractor was concerned about the delay this instruction would cause).

Clause 24. 'Loss and expense by disturbance of progress.'

Clause 25. 'Determination for default by Contractor.'

Clause 26. 'Determination by the Contractor of his own employment.'

Starting at any of the above clauses will lead to the same conclusion, stated in clause 6(3), that the Architect has the authority to instruct the Contractor to open up work for inspection and the costs incurred will be reimbursed to the Contractor providing the work is in accordance with the standards called for in Contract documents.

INDEX TO FLOWCHARTS

STANDARD FORM OF BUILDING CONTRACT, 1963 (LOCAL AUTHORITIES WITH QUANTITIES) JULY 1971 REVISION

Clause 1 CONTRACTOR'S OBLIGATIONS

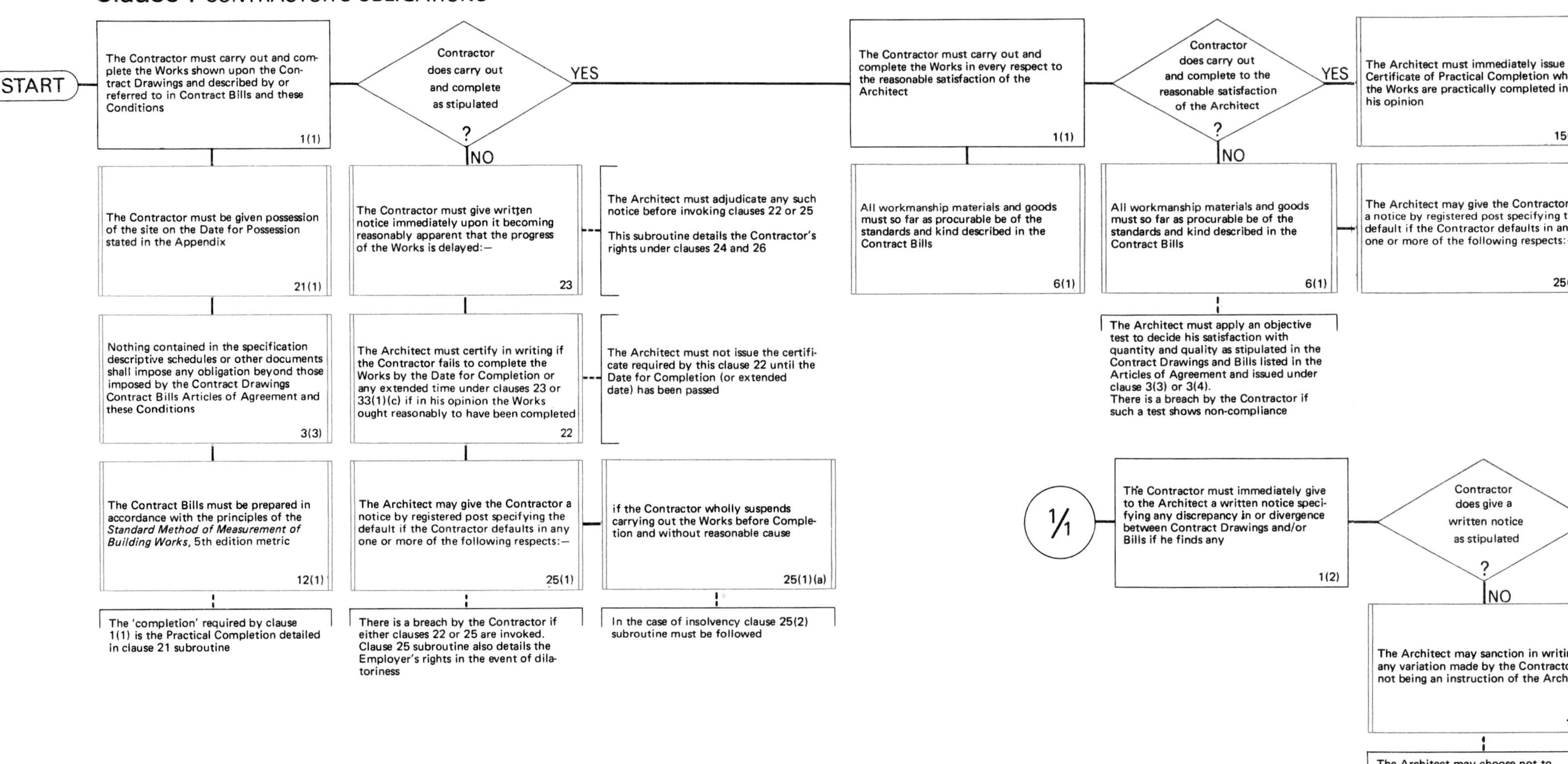
START
The Contractor must carry out and complete the Works shown upon the Contract Drawings and described by or referred to in Contract Bills and these Conditions 1(1)
Contractor does carry out and complete as stipulated ?
YES
NO
The Contractor must be given possession of the site on the Date for Possession stated in the Appendix 21(1)
The Contractor must give written notice immediately upon it becoming reasonably apparent that the progress of the Works is delayed:– 23
The Architect must adjudicate any such notice before invoking clauses 22 or 25
This subroutine details the Contractor's rights under clauses 24 and 26
Nothing contained in the specification descriptive schedules or other documents shall impose any obligation beyond those imposed by the Contract Drawings Contract Bills Articles of Agreement and these Conditions 3(3)
The Architect must certify in writing if the Contractor fails to complete the Works by the Date for Completion or any extended time under clauses 23 or 33(1)(c) if in his opinion the Works ought reasonably to have been completed 22
The Architect must not issue the certificate required by this clause 22 until the Date for Completion (or extended date) has been passed
The Contract Bills must be prepared in accordance with the principles of the *Standard Method of Measurement of Building Works*, 5th edition metric 12(1)
The Architect may give the Contractor a notice by registered post specifying the default if the Contractor defaults in any one or more of the following respects:– 25(1)
if the Contractor wholly suspends carrying out the Works before Completion and without reasonable cause 25(1)(a)
The 'completion' required by clause 1(1) is the Practical Completion detailed in clause 21 subroutine
There is a breach by the Contractor if either clauses 22 or 25 are invoked. Clause 25 subroutine also details the Employer's rights in the event of dilatoriness
In the case of insolvency clause 25(2) subroutine must be followed
The Contractor must carry out and complete the Works in every respect to the reasonable satisfaction of the Architect 1(1)
Contractor does carry out and complete to the reasonable satisfaction of the Architect ?
YES
NO
The Architect must immediately issue a Certificate of Practical Completion whe the Works are practically completed in his opinion 15(1
All workmanship materials and goods must so far as procurable be of the standards and kind described in the Contract Bills 6(1)
All workmanship materials and goods must so far as procurable be of the standards and kind described in the Contract Bills 6(1)
The Architect may give the Contractor a notice by registered post specifying th default if the Contractor defaults in any one or more of the following respects:– 25(1
The Architect must apply an objective test to decide his satisfaction with quantity and quality as stipulated in the Contract Drawings and Bills listed in the Articles of Agreement and issued under clause 3(3) or 3(4). There is a breach by the Contractor if such a test shows non-compliance
1/1
The Contractor must immediately give to the Architect a written notice specifying any discrepancy in or divergence between Contract Drawings and/or Bills if he finds any 1(2)
Contractor does give a written notice as stipulated ?
NO
The Architect may sanction in writing any variation made by the Contractor not being an instruction of the Archit 11
The Architect may choose not to invoke his powers under clause 11(1). This breach by the Contractor may have caused damage to the Employer. It may also diminish any proposed claim by the Contractor under clause 24

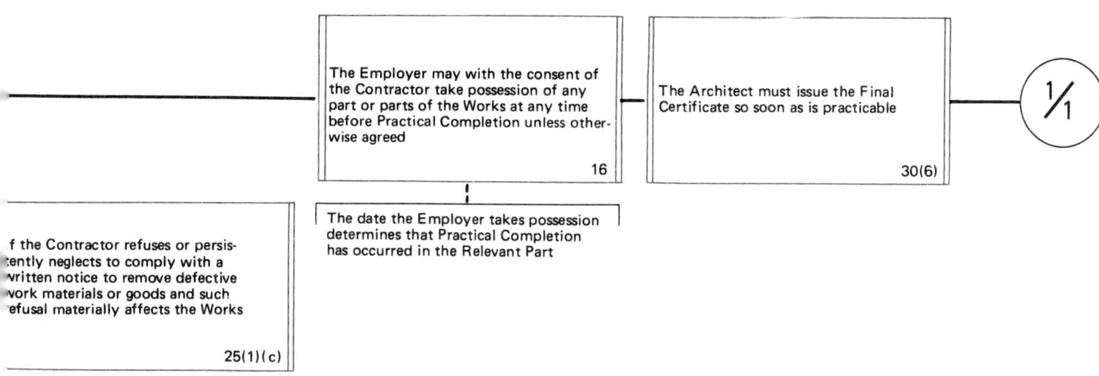
The Employer may with the consent of the Contractor take possession of any part or parts of the Works at any time before Practical Completion unless otherwise agreed
16
The Architect must issue the Final Certificate so soon as is practicable
30(6)
1/1
The date the Employer takes possession determines that Practical Completion has occurred in the Relevant Part
f the Contractor refuses or persistently neglects to comply with a written notice to remove defective work materials or goods and such refusal materially affects the Works
25(1)(c)

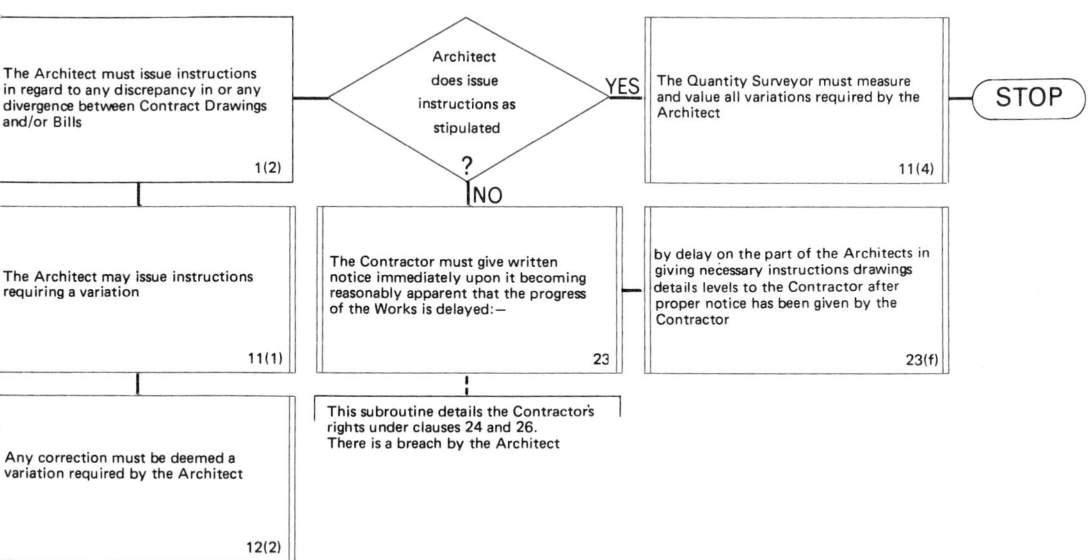
The Architect must issue instructions in regard to any discrepancy in or any divergence between Contract Drawings and/or Bills
1(2)
Architect does issue instructions as stipulated ?
YES
NO
The Quantity Surveyor must measure and value all variations required by the Architect
11(4)
STOP
The Architect may issue instructions requiring a variation
11(1)
The Contractor must give written notice immediately upon it becoming reasonably apparent that the progress of the Works is delayed:—
23
by delay on the part of the Architects in giving necessary instructions drawings details levels to the Contractor after proper notice has been given by the Contractor
23(f)
This subroutine details the Contractor's rights under clauses 24 and 26.
There is a breach by the Architect
Any correction must be deemed a variation required by the Architect
12(2)

Clause 2 ARCHITECT'S INSTRUCTIONS (1)

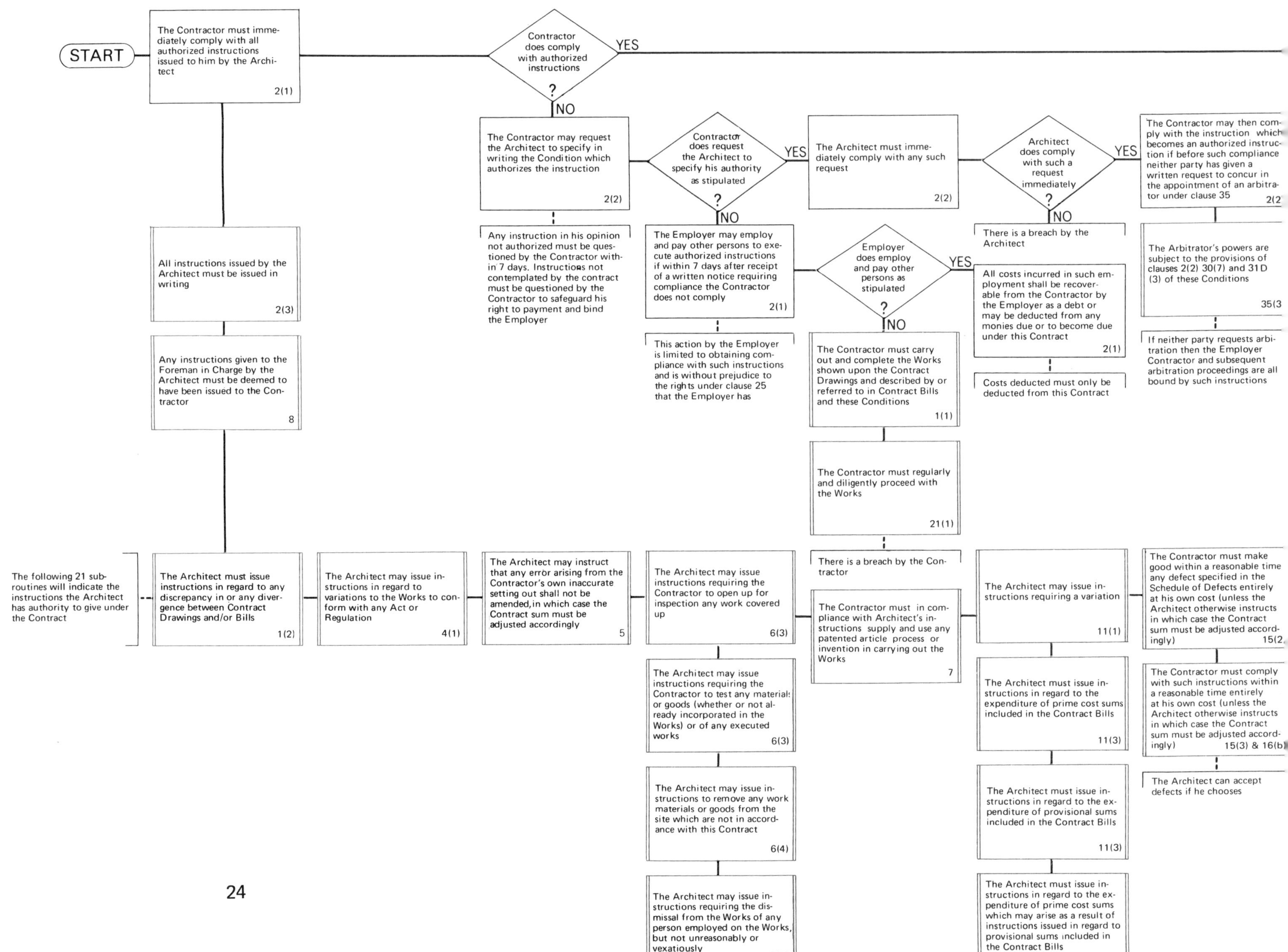
START
The Contractor must immediately comply with all authorized instructions issued to him by the Architect 2(1)
Contractor does comply with authorized instructions ?
YES
NO
The Contractor may request the Architect to specify in writing the Condition which authorizes the instruction 2(2)
Any instruction in his opinion not authorized must be questioned by the Contractor within 7 days. Instructions not contemplated by the contract must be questioned by the Contractor to safeguard his right to payment and bind the Employer
Contractor does request the Architect to specify his authority as stipulated ?
YES
NO
The Architect must immediately comply with any such request 2(2)
Architect does comply with such a request immediately ?
YES
NO
The Contractor may then comply with the instruction which becomes an authorized instruction if before such compliance neither party has given a written request to concur in the appointment of an arbitrator under clause 35 2(2
The Arbitrator's powers are subject to the provisions of clauses 2(2) 30(7) and 31D (3) of these Conditions 35(3
If neither party requests arbitration then the Employer Contractor and subsequent arbitration proceedings are all bound by such instructions
There is a breach by the Architect
The Employer may employ and pay other persons to execute authorized instructions if within 7 days after receipt of a written notice requiring compliance the Contractor does not comply 2(1)
This action by the Employer is limited to obtaining compliance with such instructions and is without prejudice to the rights under clause 25 that the Employer has
Employer does employ and pay other persons as stipulated ?
YES
NO
All costs incurred in such employment shall be recoverable from the Contractor by the Employer as a debt or may be deducted from any monies due or to become due under this Contract 2(1)
Costs deducted must only be deducted from this Contract
The Contractor must carry out and complete the Works shown upon the Contract Drawings and described by or referred to in Contract Bills and these Conditions 1(1)
The Contractor must regularly and diligently proceed with the Works 21(1)
There is a breach by the Contractor
All instructions issued by the Architect must be issued in writing 2(3)
Any instructions given to the Foreman in Charge by the Architect must be deemed to have been issued to the Contractor 8
The following 21 subroutines will indicate the instructions the Architect has authority to give under the Contract
The Architect must issue instructions in regard to any discrepancy in or any divergence between Contract Drawings and/or Bills 1(2)
The Architect may issue instructions in regard to variations to the Works to conform with any Act or Regulation 4(1)
The Architect may instruct that any error arising from the Contractor's own inaccurate setting out shall not be amended, in which case the Contract sum must be adjusted accordingly 5
The Architect may issue instructions requiring the Contractor to open up for inspection any work covered up 6(3)
The Architect may issue instructions requiring the Contractor to test any materials or goods (whether or not already incorporated in the Works) or of any executed works 6(3)
The Architect may issue instructions to remove any work materials or goods from the site which are not in accordance with this Contract 6(4)
The Architect may issue instructions requiring the dismissal from the Works of any person employed on the Works, but not unreasonably or vexatiously 6(5)
The Contractor must in compliance with Architect's instructions supply and use any patented article process or invention in carrying out the Works 7
The Architect may issue instructions requiring a variation 11(1)
The Architect must issue instructions in regard to the expenditure of prime cost sums included in the Contract Bills 11(3)
The Architect must issue instructions in regard to the expenditure of provisional sums included in the Contract Bills 11(3)
The Architect must issue instructions in regard to the expenditure of prime cost sums which may arise as a result of instructions issued in regard to provisional sums included in the Contract Bills 11(3)
The Contractor must make good within a reasonable time any defect specified in the Schedule of Defects entirely at his own cost (unless the Architect otherwise instructs in which case the Contract sum must be adjusted accordingly) 15(2
The Contractor must comply with such instructions within a reasonable time entirely at his own cost (unless the Architect otherwise instructs in which case the Contract sum must be adjusted accordingly) 15(3) & 16(b)
The Architect can accept defects if he chooses

2/1

If the Contractor disputes the basis of an instruction he should serve notice to arbitrate but nevertheless he must comply or risk being in breach if his dispute is not upheld

Any such reference on:– 35(2)

whether or not the issue of an instruction is empowered by these Conditions 35(2)

Arbitration can commence immediately but non-compliance in the meantime by the Contractor risks him being held in breach in the ensuing arbitration

The Architect may issue instructions requiring the Contractor to remove and dispose of any debris 20[C] (c)(ii)

The Architect may issue instructions to postpone any work to be executed under this Contract 21(2)

The Contractor must do all that may be reasonably required by the Architect to proceed with the Works 23

The Architect may within 14 days after such notice issue instructions to the Contractor requiring the continuation of the Works up to points of stoppage to be specified in such instructions 32(2)

The Architect may within 14 days after such notice issue instructions to the Contractor requiring the execution of such protective work as specified in such instructions 32(2)

the Architect may issue instructions requiring the Contractor to remove and/or dispose of any debris and/or damaged work and/or execute such protective work as specified in the instructions 33(1)(b)

The Architect must issue instructions in regard to what is to be done concerning such an object reported by the Contractor 34(2)

The Architect can also require the following:
clause 6(2) proof that materials etc. comply
17A (8) proof that pay and conditions comply
25(4)(b) assignment of agreements
25(4)(c) removal of Contractor's possessions
27(c) proof that payments have been made
34(2) third parties to attend antiquities
also, a Clerk of Works 'direction' can be converted into an Architect's instruction if clause 10 is complied with

Clause 2 ARCHITECT'S INSTRUCTIONS (2)

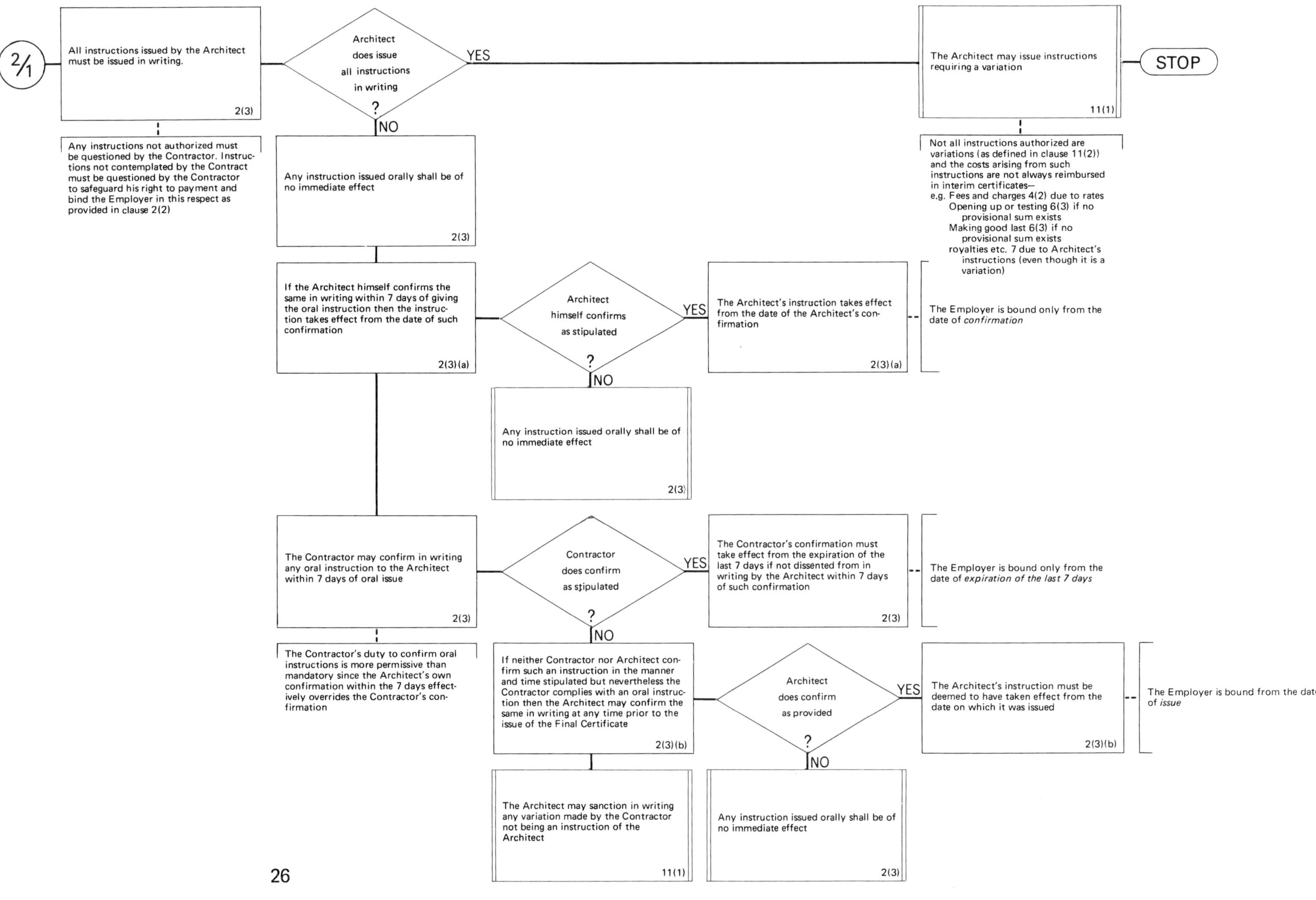

2/1
All instructions issued by the Architect must be issued in writing. 2(3)
Any instructions not authorized must be questioned by the Contractor. Instructions not contemplated by the Contract must be questioned by the Contractor to safeguard his right to payment and bind the Employer in this respect as provided in clause 2(2)
Architect does issue all instructions in writing ?
YES
The Architect may issue instructions requiring a variation 11(1)
STOP
Not all instructions authorized are variations (as defined in clause 11(2)) and the costs arising from such instructions are not always reimbursed in interim certificates—
e.g. Fees and charges 4(2) due to rates
Opening up or testing 6(3) if no provisional sum exists
Making good last 6(3) if no provisional sum exists
royalties etc. 7 due to Architect's instructions (even though it is a variation)
NO
Any instruction issued orally shall be of no immediate effect 2(3)
If the Architect himself confirms the same in writing within 7 days of giving the oral instruction then the instruction takes effect from the date of such confirmation 2(3)(a)
Architect himself confirms as stipulated ?
YES
The Architect's instruction takes effect from the date of the Architect's confirmation 2(3)(a)
The Employer is bound only from the date of confirmation
NO
Any instruction issued orally shall be of no immediate effect 2(3)
The Contractor may confirm in writing any oral instruction to the Architect within 7 days of oral issue 2(3)
The Contractor's duty to confirm oral instructions is more permissive than mandatory since the Architect's own confirmation within the 7 days effectively overrides the Contractor's confirmation
Contractor does confirm as stipulated ?
YES
The Contractor's confirmation must take effect from the expiration of the last 7 days if not dissented from in writing by the Architect within 7 days of such confirmation 2(3)
The Employer is bound only from the date of expiration of the last 7 days
NO
If neither Contractor nor Architect confirm such an instruction in the manner and time stipulated but nevertheless the Contractor complies with an oral instruction then the Architect may confirm the same in writing at any time prior to the issue of the Final Certificate 2(3)(b)
Architect does confirm as provided ?
YES
The Architect's instruction must be deemed to have taken effect from the date on which it was issued 2(3)(b)
The Employer is bound from the date of issue
NO
Any instruction issued orally shall be of no immediate effect 2(3)
The Architect may sanction in writing any variation made by the Contractor not being an instruction of the Architect 11(1)

Clause 3 CONTRACT DOCUMENTS (1)

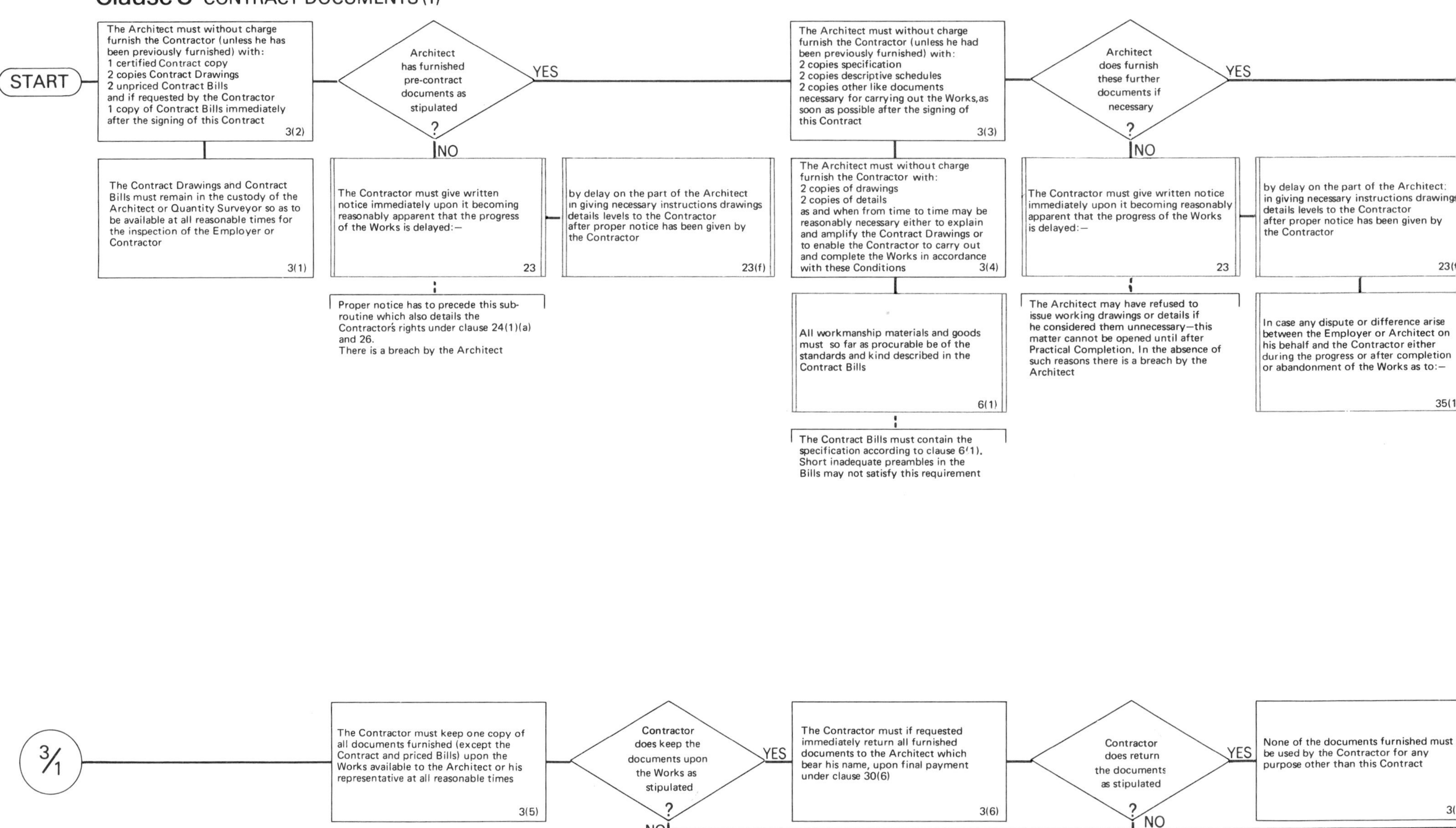

START
The Architect must without charge furnish the Contractor (unless he has been previously furnished) with:
1 certified Contract copy
2 copies Contract Drawings
2 unpriced Contract Bills
and if requested by the Contractor
1 copy of Contract Bills immediately after the signing of this Contract
3(2)
Architect has furnished pre-contract documents as stipulated ?
YES
NO
The Contract Drawings and Contract Bills must remain in the custody of the Architect or Quantity Surveyor so as to be available at all reasonable times for the inspection of the Employer or Contractor
3(1)
The Contractor must give written notice immediately upon it becoming reasonably apparent that the progress of the Works is delayed:—
23
by delay on the part of the Architect in giving necessary instructions drawings details levels to the Contractor after proper notice has been given by the Contractor
23(f)
Proper notice has to precede this sub-routine which also details the Contractor's rights under clause 24(1)(a) and 26.
There is a breach by the Architect
The Architect must without charge furnish the Contractor (unless he had been previously furnished) with:
2 copies specification
2 copies descriptive schedules
2 copies other like documents necessary for carrying out the Works, as soon as possible after the signing of this Contract
3(3)
Architect does furnish these further documents if necessary ?
YES
NO
The Architect must without charge furnish the Contractor with:
2 copies of drawings
2 copies of details
as and when from time to time may be reasonably necessary either to explain and amplify the Contract Drawings or to enable the Contractor to carry out and complete the Works in accordance with these Conditions
3(4)
All workmanship materials and goods must so far as procurable be of the standards and kind described in the Contract Bills
6(1)
The Contract Bills must contain the specification according to clause 6(1). Short inadequate preambles in the Bills may not satisfy this requirement
The Contractor must give written notice immediately upon it becoming reasonably apparent that the progress of the Works is delayed:—
23
The Architect may have refused to issue working drawings or details if he considered them unnecessary—this matter cannot be opened until after Practical Completion. In the absence of such reasons there is a breach by the Architect
by delay on the part of the Architect: in giving necessary instructions drawings details levels to the Contractor after proper notice has been given by the Contractor
23(f)
In case any dispute or difference arise between the Employer or Architect on his behalf and the Contractor either during the progress or after completion or abandonment of the Works as to:—
35(1)
3/1
The Contractor must keep one copy of all documents furnished (except the Contract and priced Bills) upon the Works available to the Architect or his representative at all reasonable times
3(5)
Contractor does keep the documents upon the Works as stipulated ?
YES
NO
There is a breach by the Contractor
The Contractor must if requested immediately return all furnished documents to the Architect which bear his name, upon final payment under clause 30(6)
3(6)
Contractor does return the documents as stipulated ?
YES
NO
None of the documents furnished must be used by the Contractor for any purpose other than this Contract
3(

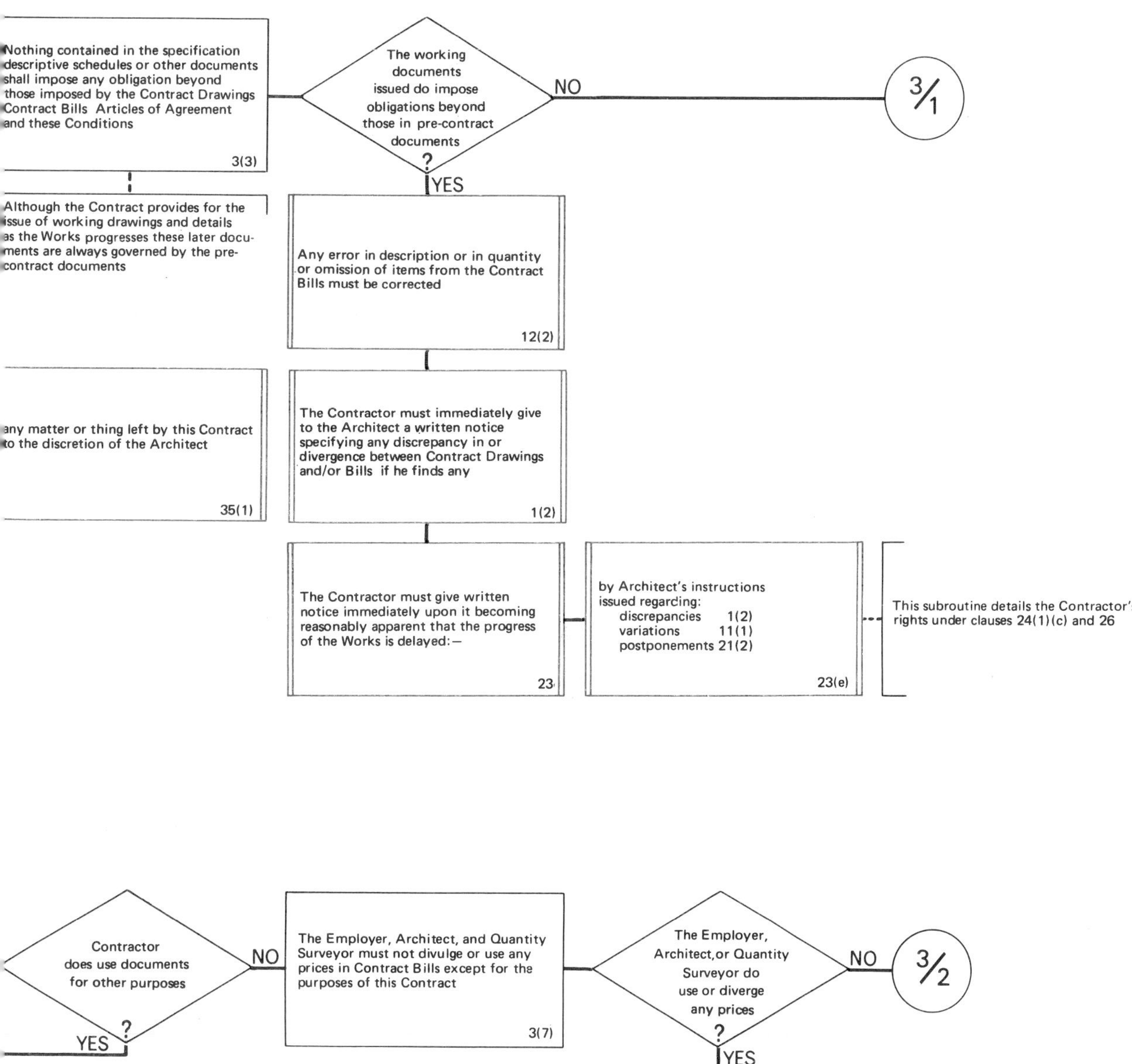
Nothing contained in the specification descriptive schedules or other documents shall impose any obligation beyond those imposed by the Contract Drawings Contract Bills Articles of Agreement and these Conditions
3(3)
The working documents issued do impose obligations beyond those in pre-contract documents ?
NO
3/1
YES
Although the Contract provides for the issue of working drawings and details as the Works progresses these later documents are always governed by the pre-contract documents
Any error in description or in quantity or omission of items from the Contract Bills must be corrected
12(2)
any matter or thing left by this Contract to the discretion of the Architect
35(1)
The Contractor must immediately give to the Architect a written notice specifying any discrepancy in or divergence between Contract Drawings and/or Bills if he finds any
1(2)
The Contractor must give written notice immediately upon it becoming reasonably apparent that the progress of the Works is delayed:—
23
by Architect's instructions issued regarding:
discrepancies 1(2)
variations 11(1)
postponements 21(2)
23(e)
This subroutine details the Contractor's rights under clauses 24(1)(c) and 26
Contractor does use documents for other purposes ?
NO
YES
The Employer, Architect, and Quantity Surveyor must not divulge or use any prices in Contract Bills except for the purposes of this Contract
3(7)
The Employer, Architect, or Quantity Surveyor do use or diverge any prices ?
NO
3/2
YES
There is a breach by the Employer, Architect, or Quantity Surveyor

Clause 3 CONTRACT DOCUMENTS (2)

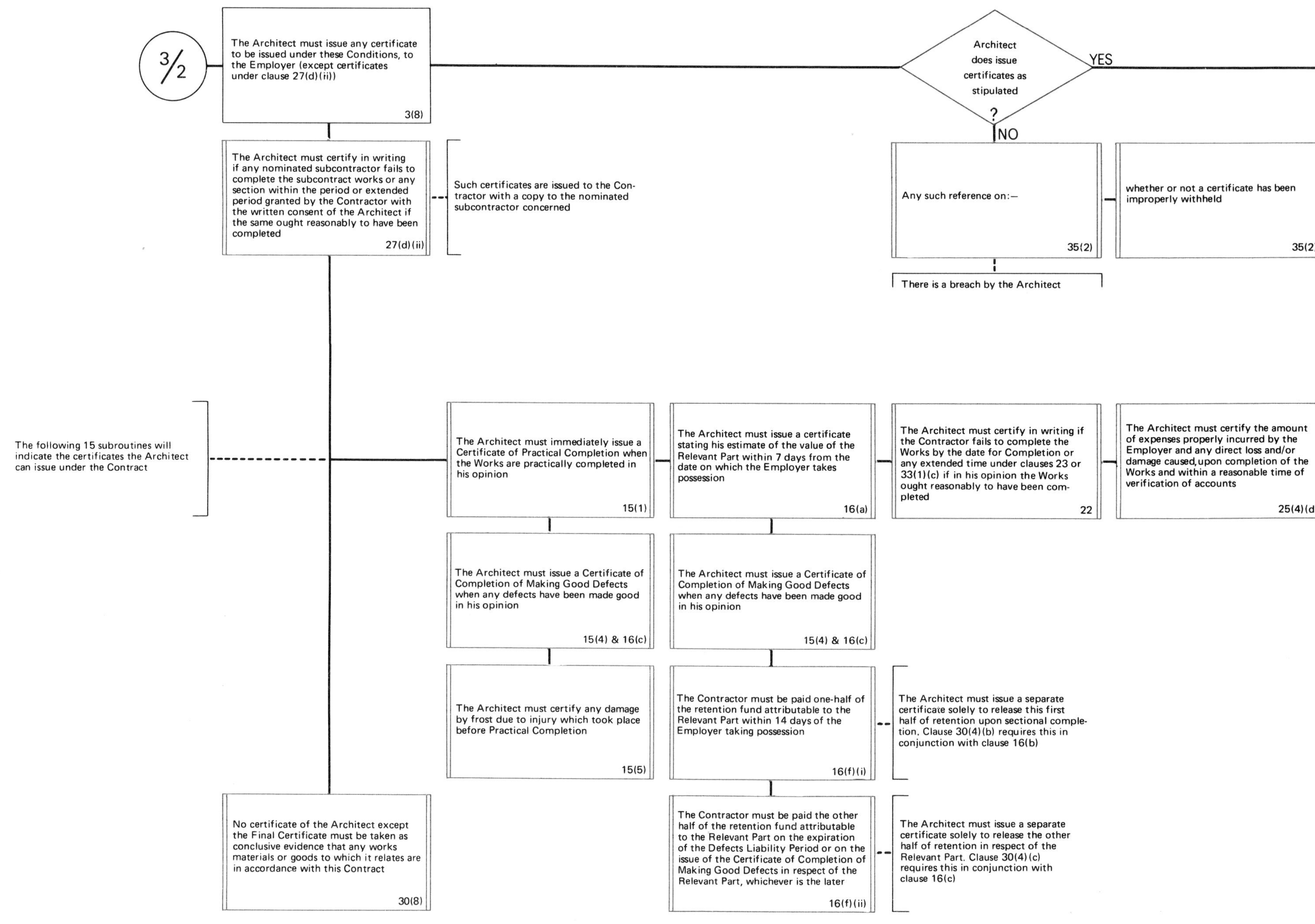

3/2
The Architect must issue any certificate to be issued under these Conditions, to the Employer (except certificates under clause 27(d)(ii))
3(8)
Architect does issue certificates as stipulated ?
YES
NO
The Architect must certify in writing if any nominated subcontractor fails to complete the subcontract works or any section within the period or extended period granted by the Contractor with the written consent of the Architect if the same ought reasonably to have been completed
27(d)(ii)
Such certificates are issued to the Contractor with a copy to the nominated subcontractor concerned
Any such reference on:—
35(2)
whether or not a certificate has been improperly withheld
35(2
There is a breach by the Architect
The following 15 subroutines will indicate the certificates the Architect can issue under the Contract
The Architect must immediately issue a Certificate of Practical Completion when the Works are practically completed in his opinion
15(1)
The Architect must issue a certificate stating his estimate of the value of the Relevant Part within 7 days from the date on which the Employer takes possession
16(a)
The Architect must certify in writing if the Contractor fails to complete the Works by the date for Completion or any extended time under clauses 23 or 33(1)(c) if in his opinion the Works ought reasonably to have been completed
22
The Architect must certify the amount of expenses properly incurred by the Employer and any direct loss and/or damage caused, upon completion of the Works and within a reasonable time of verification of accounts
25(4)(d
The Architect must issue a Certificate of Completion of Making Good Defects when any defects have been made good in his opinion
15(4) & 16(c)
The Architect must issue a Certificate of Completion of Making Good Defects when any defects have been made good in his opinion
15(4) & 16(c)
The Architect must certify any damage by frost due to injury which took place before Practical Completion
15(5)
The Contractor must be paid one-half of the retention fund attributable to the Relevant Part within 14 days of the Employer taking possession
16(f)(i)
The Architect must issue a separate certificate solely to release this first half of retention upon sectional completion. Clause 30(4)(b) requires this in conjunction with clause 16(b)
No certificate of the Architect except the Final Certificate must be taken as conclusive evidence that any works materials or goods to which it relates are in accordance with this Contract
30(8)
The Contractor must be paid the other half of the retention fund attributable to the Relevant Part on the expiration of the Defects Liability Period or on the issue of the Certificate of Completion of Making Good Defects in respect of the Relevant Part, whichever is the later
16(f)(ii)
The Architect must issue a separate certificate solely to release the other half of retention in respect of the Relevant Part. Clause 30(4)(c) requires this in conjunction with clause 16(c)

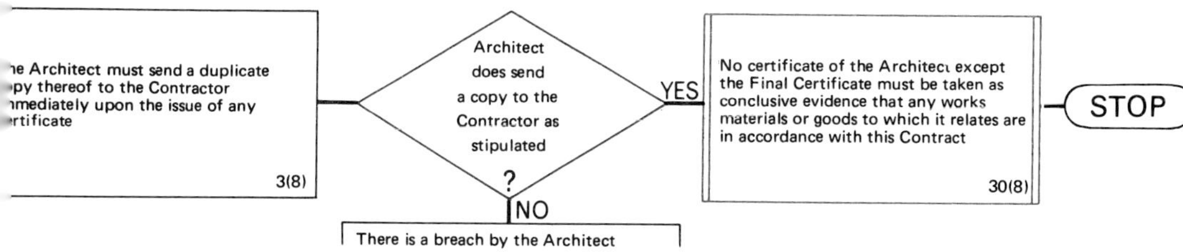

ıe Architect must send a duplicate
ɔpy thereof to the Contractor
ımediately upon the issue of any
ɛrtificate
3(8)
Architect
does send
a copy to the
Contractor as
stipulated
?
YES
NO
No certificate of the Architect except the Final Certificate must be taken as conclusive evidence that any works materials or goods to which it relates are in accordance with this Contract
30(8)
STOP
There is a breach by the Architect

ımediate arbitration is available
ıder the Contract. Clause 35(1) also
fers to the withholding of certificates
the Architect but such dispute must
vait Practical Completion before arbi-
ation commences

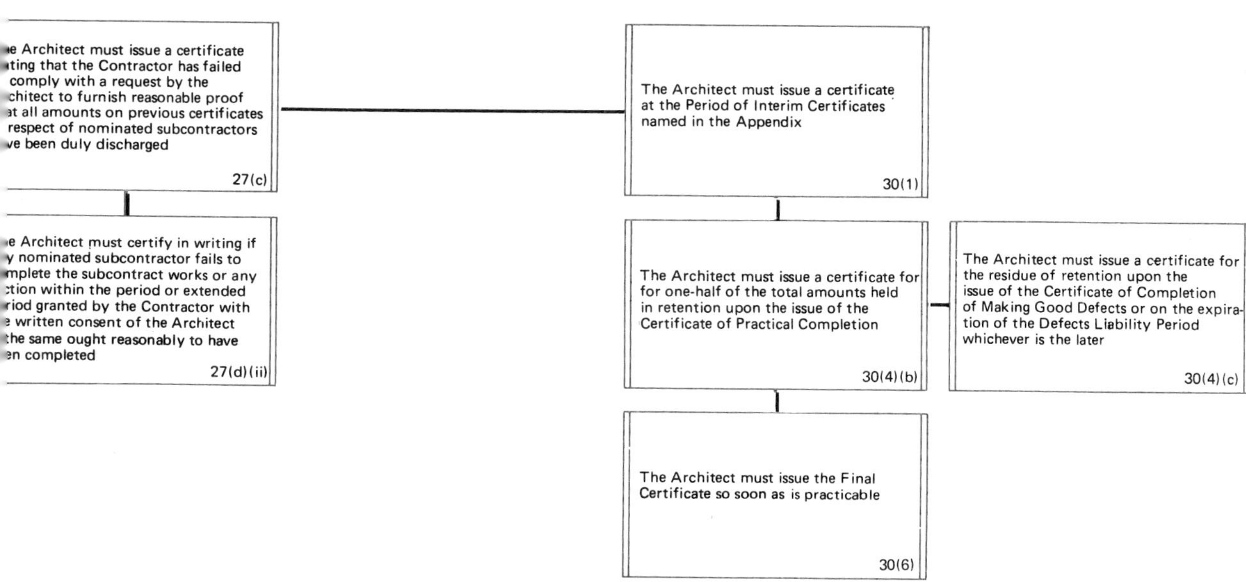

ıe Architect must issue a certificate
ating that the Contractor has failed
comply with a request by the
chitect to furnish reasonable proof
at all amounts on previous certificates
respect of nominated subcontractors
ve been duly discharged
27(c)
ıe Architect must certify in writing if
y nominated subcontractor fails to
mplete the subcontract works or any
ction within the period or extended
riod granted by the Contractor with
e written consent of the Architect
the same ought reasonably to have
en completed
27(d)(ii)
The Architect must issue a certificate at the Period of Interim Certificates named in the Appendix
30(1)
The Architect must issue a certificate for for one-half of the total amounts held in retention upon the issue of the Certificate of Practical Completion
30(4)(b)
The Architect must issue a certificate for the residue of retention upon the issue of the Certificate of Completion of Making Good Defects or on the expiration of the Defects Liability Period whichever is the later
30(4)(c)
The Architect must issue the Final Certificate so soon as is practicable
30(6)

Clause 4 STATUTORY OBLIGATIONS, NOTICES, FEES, AND CHARGES

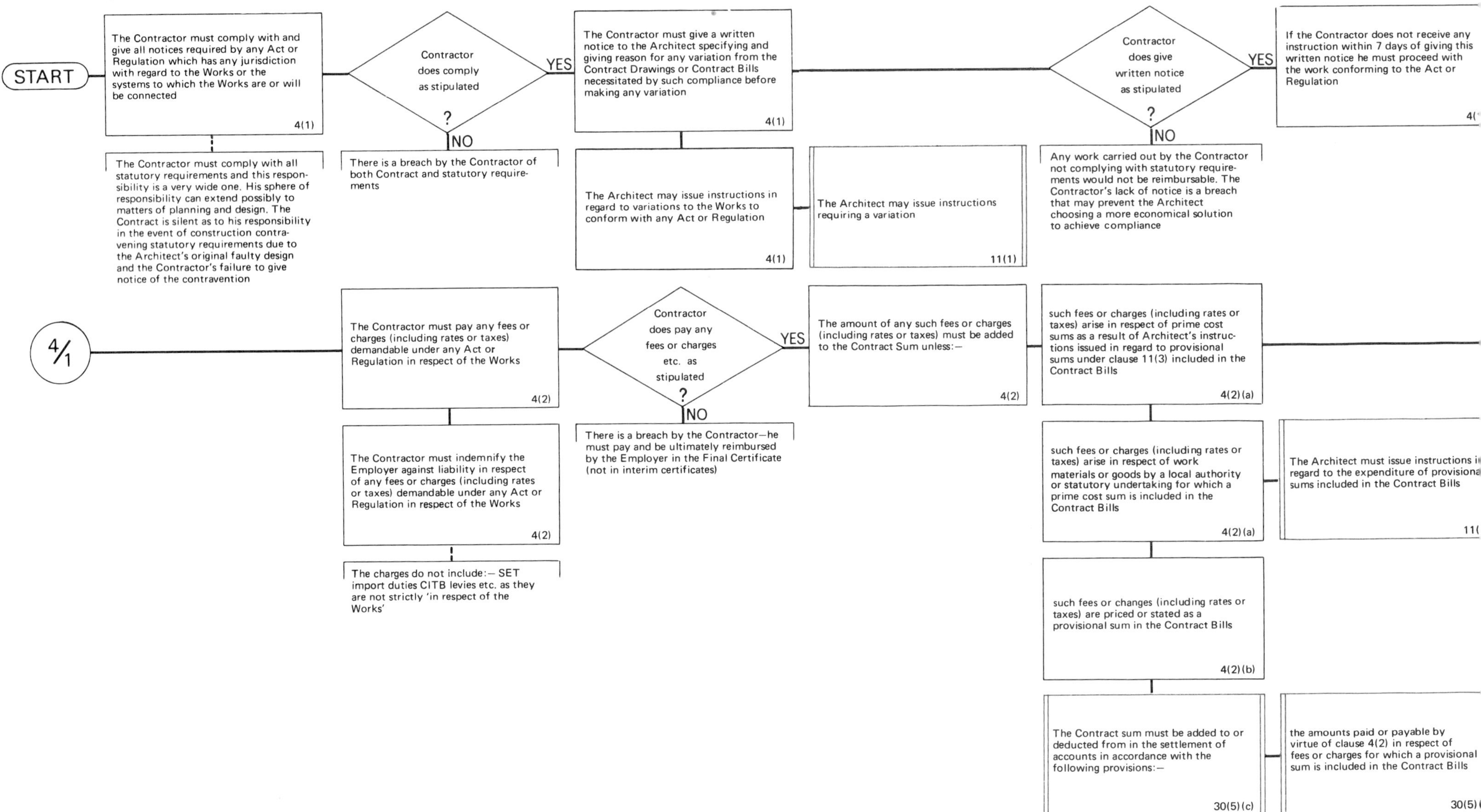

START
The Contractor must comply with and give all notices required by any Act or Regulation which has any jurisdiction with regard to the Works or the systems to which the Works are or will be connected
4(1)
The Contractor must comply with all statutory requirements and this responsibility is a very wide one. His sphere of responsibility can extend possibly to matters of planning and design. The Contract is silent as to his responsibility in the event of construction contravening statutory requirements due to the Architect's original faulty design and the Contractor's failure to give notice of the contravention
Contractor does comply as stipulated ?
YES
NO
There is a breach by the Contractor of both Contract and statutory requirements
The Contractor must give a written notice to the Architect specifying and giving reason for any variation from the Contract Drawings or Contract Bills necessitated by such compliance before making any variation
4(1)
The Architect may issue instructions in regard to variations to the Works to conform with any Act or Regulation
4(1)
The Architect may issue instructions requiring a variation
11(1)
Contractor does give written notice as stipulated ?
YES
NO
Any work carried out by the Contractor not complying with statutory requirements would not be reimbursable. The Contractor's lack of notice is a breach that may prevent the Architect choosing a more economical solution to achieve compliance
If the Contractor does not receive any instruction within 7 days of giving this written notice he must proceed with the work conforming to the Act or Regulation
4(
4/1
The Contractor must pay any fees or charges (including rates or taxes) demandable under any Act or Regulation in respect of the Works
4(2)
The Contractor must indemnify the Employer against liability in respect of any fees or charges (including rates or taxes) demandable under any Act or Regulation in respect of the Works
4(2)
The charges do not include:— SET import duties CITB levies etc. as they are not strictly 'in respect of the Works'
Contractor does pay any fees or charges etc. as stipulated ?
YES
NO
There is a breach by the Contractor—he must pay and be ultimately reimbursed by the Employer in the Final Certificate (not in interim certificates)
The amount of any such fees or charges (including rates or taxes) must be added to the Contract Sum unless:—
4(2)
such fees or charges (including rates or taxes) arise in respect of prime cost sums as a result of Architect's instructions issued in regard to provisional sums under clause 11(3) included in the Contract Bills
4(2)(a)
such fees or charges (including rates or taxes) arise in respect of work materials or goods by a local authority or statutory undertaking for which a prime cost sum is included in the Contract Bills
4(2)(a)
The Architect must issue instructions i regard to the expenditure of provisiona sums included in the Contract Bills
11(
such fees or changes (including rates or taxes) are priced or stated as a provisional sum in the Contract Bills
4(2)(b)
The Contract sum must be added to or deducted from in the settlement of accounts in accordance with the following provisions:—
30(5)(c)
the amounts paid or payable by virtue of clause 4(2) in respect of fees or charges for which a provisional sum is included in the Contract Bills
30(5)

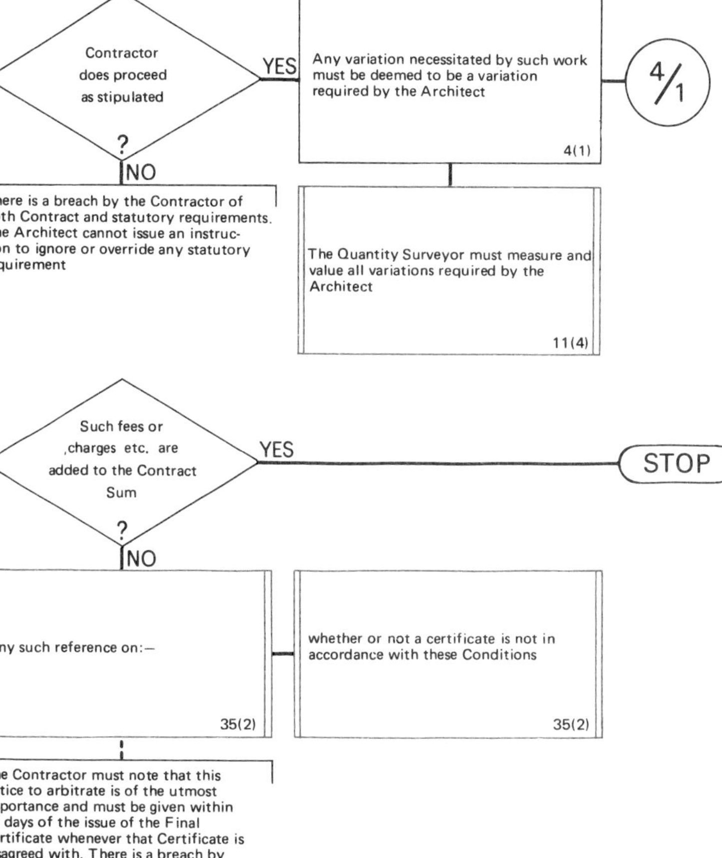
Contractor does proceed as stipulated
?
YES
NO
Any variation necessitated by such work must be deemed to be a variation required by the Architect
4(1)
4/1
The Quantity Surveyor must measure and value all variations required by the Architect
11(4)
Such fees or charges etc. are added to the Contract Sum
?
YES
NO
STOP
whether or not a certificate is not in accordance with these Conditions
35(2)
35(2)

Clause 5 SETTING OUT THE WORKS AND LEVELS

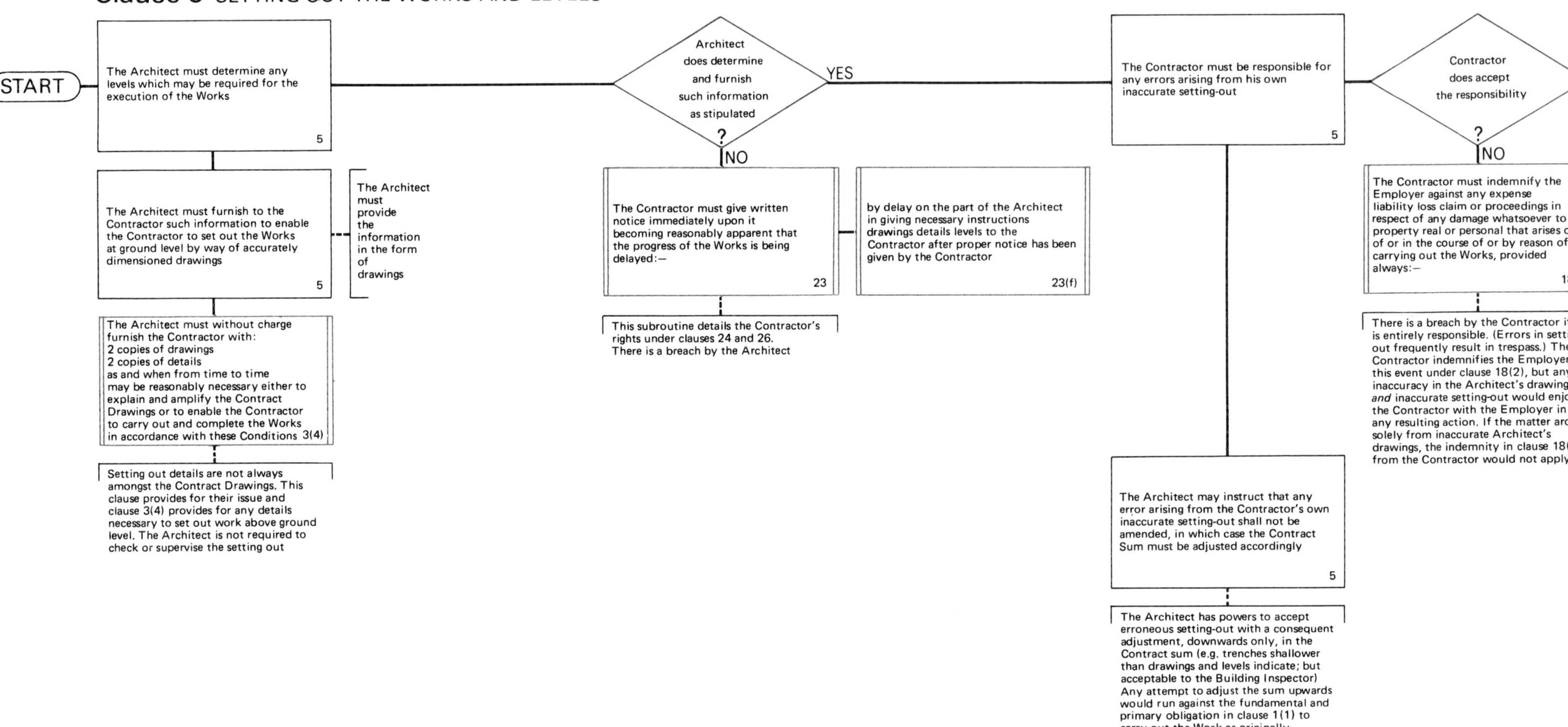

START
The Architect must determine any levels which may be required for the execution of the Works 5
The Architect must furnish to the Contractor such information to enable the Contractor to set out the Works at ground level by way of accurately dimensioned drawings 5
The Architect must provide the information in the form of drawings
The Architect must without charge furnish the Contractor with: 2 copies of drawings 2 copies of details as and when from time to time may be reasonably necessary either to explain and amplify the Contract Drawings or to enable the Contractor to carry out and complete the Works in accordance with these Conditions 3(4)
Setting out details are not always amongst the Contract Drawings. This clause provides for their issue and clause 3(4) provides for any details necessary to set out work above ground level. The Architect is not required to check or supervise the setting out
Architect does determine and furnish such information as stipulated ?
YES
NO
The Contractor must give written notice immediately upon it becoming reasonably apparent that the progress of the Works is being delayed:— 23
by delay on the part of the Architect in giving necessary instructions drawings details levels to the Contractor after proper notice has been given by the Contractor 23(f)
This subroutine details the Contractor's rights under clauses 24 and 26. There is a breach by the Architect
The Contractor must be responsible for any errors arising from his own inaccurate setting-out 5
The Architect may instruct that any error arising from the Contractor's own inaccurate setting-out shall not be amended, in which case the Contract Sum must be adjusted accordingly 5
The Architect has powers to accept erroneous setting-out with a consequent adjustment, downwards only, in the Contract sum (e.g. trenches shallower than drawings and levels indicate; but acceptable to the Building Inspector) Any attempt to adjust the sum upwards would run against the fundamental and primary obligation in clause 1(1) to carry out the Work as originally intended. Errors could be waived by Architects instruction and the Sum remain unchanged
Contractor does accept the responsibility ?
NO
The Contractor must indemnify the Employer against any expense liability loss claim or proceedings in respect of any damage whatsoever to a property real or personal that arises ou of or in the course of or by reason of carrying out the Works, provided always:— 18
There is a breach by the Contractor if h is entirely responsible. (Errors in settin out frequently result in trespass.) The Contractor indemnifies the Employer i this event under clause 18(2), but any inaccuracy in the Architect's drawings *and* inaccurate setting-out would enjoi the Contractor with the Employer in any resulting action. If the matter aros solely from inaccurate Architect's drawings, the indemnity in clause 18(2 from the Contractor would not apply

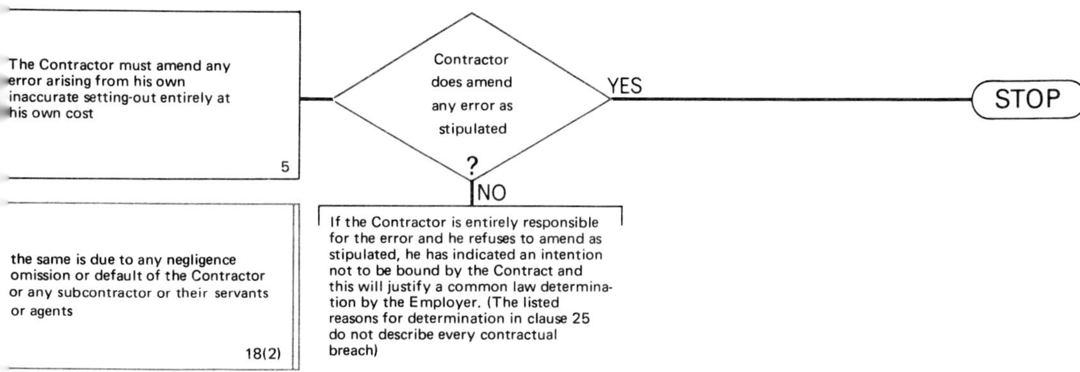

The Contractor must amend any error arising from his own inaccurate setting-out entirely at his own cost
5
Contractor does amend any error as stipulated ?
YES
STOP
NO
the same is due to any negligence omission or default of the Contractor or any subcontractor or their servants or agents
18(2)
If the Contractor is entirely responsible for the error and he refuses to amend as stipulated, he has indicated an intention not to be bound by the Contract and this will justify a common law determination by the Employer. (The listed reasons for determination in clause 25 do not describe every contractual breach)

Clause 6 WORKMANSHIP, MATERIALS, AND GOODS

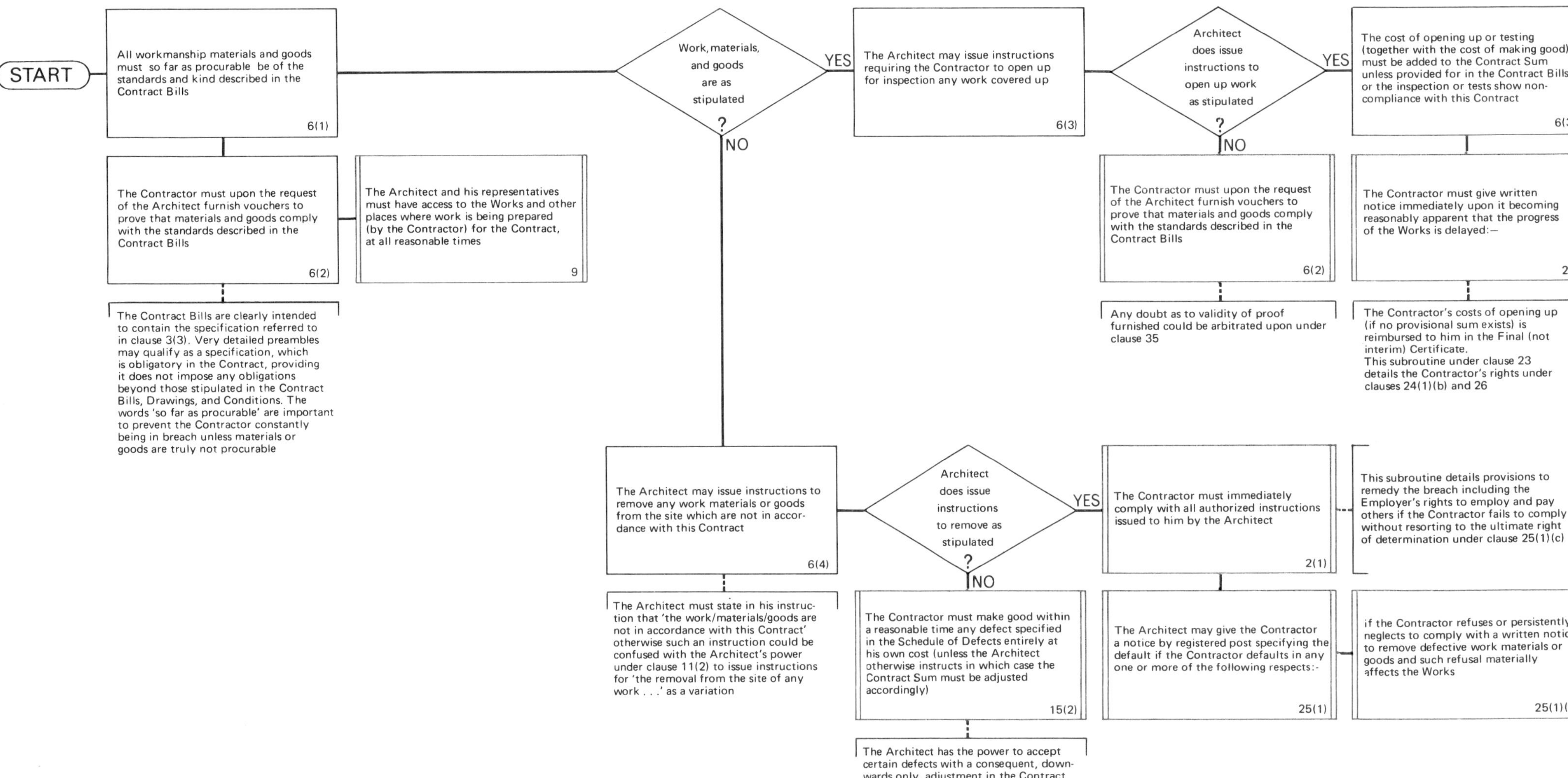

START
All workmanship materials and goods must so far as procurable be of the standards and kind described in the Contract Bills 6(1)
The Contractor must upon the request of the Architect furnish vouchers to prove that materials and goods comply with the standards described in the Contract Bills 6(2)
The Architect and his representatives must have access to the Works and other places where work is being prepared (by the Contractor) for the Contract, at all reasonable times 9
The Contract Bills are clearly intended to contain the specification referred to in clause 3(3). Very detailed preambles may qualify as a specification, which is obligatory in the Contract, providing it does not impose any obligations beyond those stipulated in the Contract Bills, Drawings, and Conditions. The words 'so far as procurable' are important to prevent the Contractor constantly being in breach unless materials or goods are truly not procurable
Work, materials, and goods are as stipulated ?
YES
NO
The Architect may issue instructions requiring the Contractor to open up for inspection any work covered up 6(3)
Architect does issue instructions to open up work as stipulated ?
YES
NO
The cost of opening up or testing (together with the cost of making good) must be added to the Contract Sum unless provided for in the Contract Bills or the inspection or tests show non-compliance with this Contract 6(3
The Contractor must upon the request of the Architect furnish vouchers to prove that materials and goods comply with the standards described in the Contract Bills 6(2)
Any doubt as to validity of proof furnished could be arbitrated upon under clause 35
The Contractor must give written notice immediately upon it becoming reasonably apparent that the progress of the Works is delayed:— 23
The Contractor's costs of opening up (if no provisional sum exists) is reimbursed to him in the Final (not interim) Certificate.
This subroutine under clause 23 details the Contractor's rights under clauses 24(1)(b) and 26
The Architect may issue instructions to remove any work materials or goods from the site which are not in accordance with this Contract 6(4)
The Architect must state in his instruction that 'the work/materials/goods are not in accordance with this Contract' otherwise such an instruction could be confused with the Architect's power under clause 11(2) to issue instructions for 'the removal from the site of any work . . .' as a variation
Architect does issue instructions to remove as stipulated ?
YES
NO
The Contractor must immediately comply with all authorized instructions issued to him by the Architect 2(1)
This subroutine details provisions to remedy the breach including the Employer's rights to employ and pay others if the Contractor fails to comply without resorting to the ultimate right of determination under clause 25(1)(c)
The Contractor must make good within a reasonable time any defect specified in the Schedule of Defects entirely at his own cost (unless the Architect otherwise instructs in which case the Contract Sum must be adjusted accordingly) 15(2)
The Architect has the power to accept certain defects with a consequent, downwards only, adjustment in the Contract Sum
The Architect may give the Contractor a notice by registered post specifying the default if the Contractor defaults in any one or more of the following respects:- 25(1)
if the Contractor refuses or persistently neglects to comply with a written notice to remove defective work materials or goods and such refusal materially affects the Works 25(1)(c

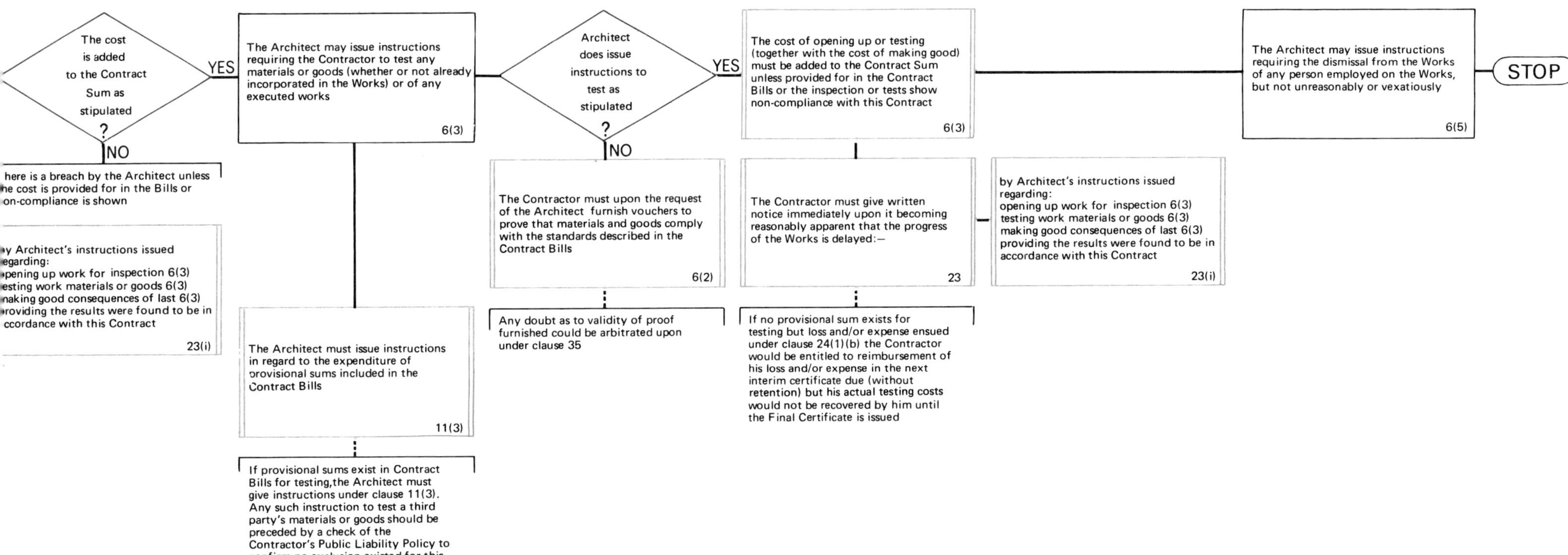

The cost is added to the Contract Sum as stipulated ?
YES
NO
here is a breach by the Architect unless he cost is provided for in the Bills or on-compliance is shown
y Architect's instructions issued egarding:
pening up work for inspection 6(3)
esting work materials or goods 6(3)
naking good consequences of last 6(3)
roviding the results were found to be in ccordance with this Contract
23(i)
The Architect may issue instructions requiring the Contractor to test any materials or goods (whether or not already incorporated in the Works) or of any executed works
6(3)
The Architect must issue instructions in regard to the expenditure of provisional sums included in the Contract Bills
11(3)
If provisional sums exist in Contract Bills for testing, the Architect must give instructions under clause 11(3). Any such instruction to test a third party's materials or goods should be preceded by a check of the Contractor's Public Liability Policy to confirm no exclusion existed for this
Architect does issue instructions to test as stipulated ?
YES
NO
The Contractor must upon the request of the Architect furnish vouchers to prove that materials and goods comply with the standards described in the Contract Bills
6(2)
Any doubt as to validity of proof furnished could be arbitrated upon under clause 35
The cost of opening up or testing (together with the cost of making good) must be added to the Contract Sum unless provided for in the Contract Bills or the inspection or tests show non-compliance with this Contract
6(3)
The Contractor must give written notice immediately upon it becoming reasonably apparent that the progress of the Works is delayed:–
23
If no provisional sum exists for testing but loss and/or expense ensued under clause 24(1)(b) the Contractor would be entitled to reimbursement of his loss and/or expense in the next interim certificate due (without retention) but his actual testing costs would not be recovered by him until the Final Certificate is issued
by Architect's instructions issued regarding:
opening up work for inspection 6(3)
testing work materials or goods 6(3)
making good consequences of last 6(3)
providing the results were found to be in accordance with this Contract
23(i)
The Architect may issue instructions requiring the dismissal from the Works of any person employed on the Works, but not unreasonably or vexatiously
6(5)
STOP

Clause 7 ROYALTIES AND PATENT RIGHTS

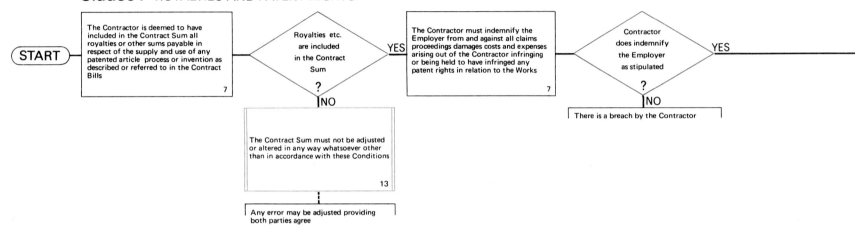

START

The Contractor is deemed to have included in the Contract Sum all royalties or other sums payable in respect of the supply and use of any patented article process or invention as described or referred to in the Contract Bills 7

Royalties etc. are included in the Contract Sum ?

NO

The Contract Sum must not be adjusted or altered in any way whatsoever other than in accordance with these Conditions 13

Any error may be adjusted providing both parties agree

YES

The Contractor must indemnify the Employer from and against all claims proceedings damages costs and expenses arising out of the Contractor infringing or being held to have infringed any patent rights in relation to the Works 7

Contractor does indemnify the Employer as stipulated ?

NO

There is a breach by the Contractor

YES

ROYALTIES AND PATENT RIGHTS ARISING FROM ARCHITECT'S INSTRUCTIONS

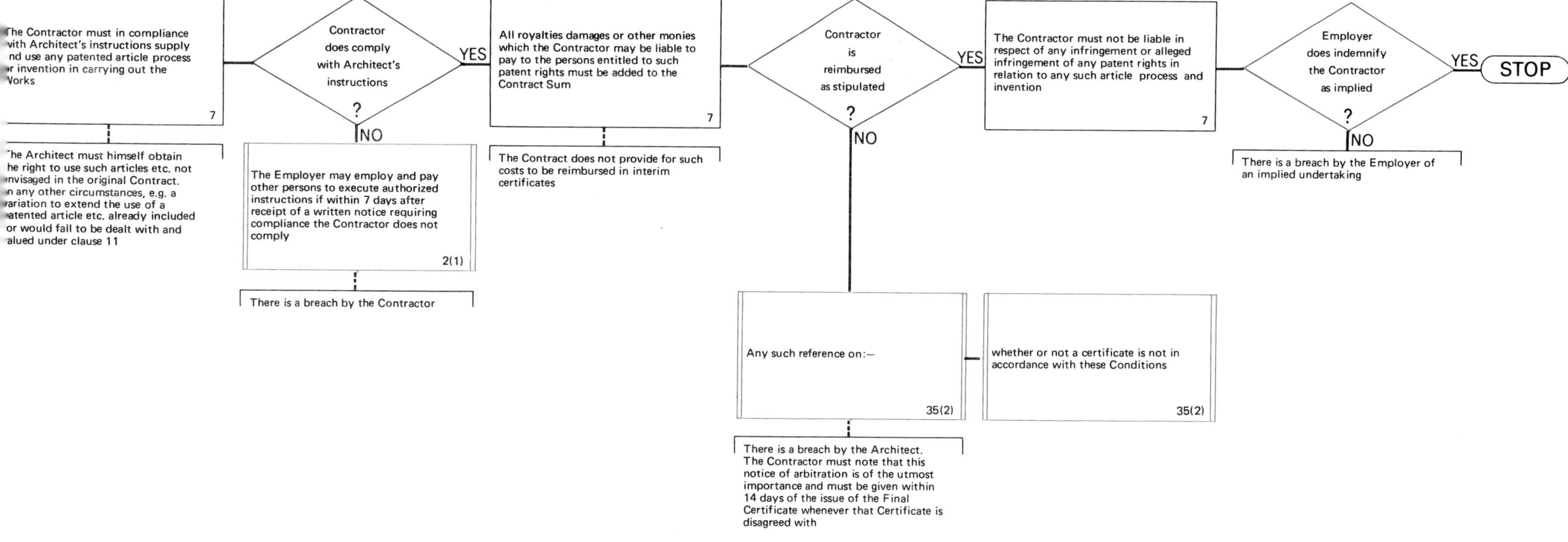

The Contractor must in compliance with Architect's instructions supply and use any patented article process or invention in carrying out the Works
7
The Architect must himself obtain the right to use such articles etc. not envisaged in the original Contract. In any other circumstances, e.g. a variation to extend the use of a patented article etc. already included or would fall to be dealt with and valued under clause 11
Contractor does comply with Architect's instructions ?
YES
NO
The Employer may employ and pay other persons to execute authorized instructions if within 7 days after receipt of a written notice requiring compliance the Contractor does not comply
2(1)
There is a breach by the Contractor
All royalties damages or other monies which the Contractor may be liable to pay to the persons entitled to such patent rights must be added to the Contract Sum
7
The Contract does not provide for such costs to be reimbursed in interim certificates
Contractor is reimbursed as stipulated ?
YES
NO
Any such reference on:–
35(2)
whether or not a certificate is not in accordance with these Conditions
35(2)
There is a breach by the Architect. The Contractor must note that this notice of arbitration is of the utmost importance and must be given within 14 days of the issue of the Final Certificate whenever that Certificate is disagreed with
The Contractor must not be liable in respect of any infringement or alleged infringement of any patent rights in relation to any such article process and invention
7
Employer does indemnify the Contractor as implied ?
YES
STOP
NO
There is a breach by the Employer of an implied undertaking

Clause 8 FOREMAN IN CHARGE

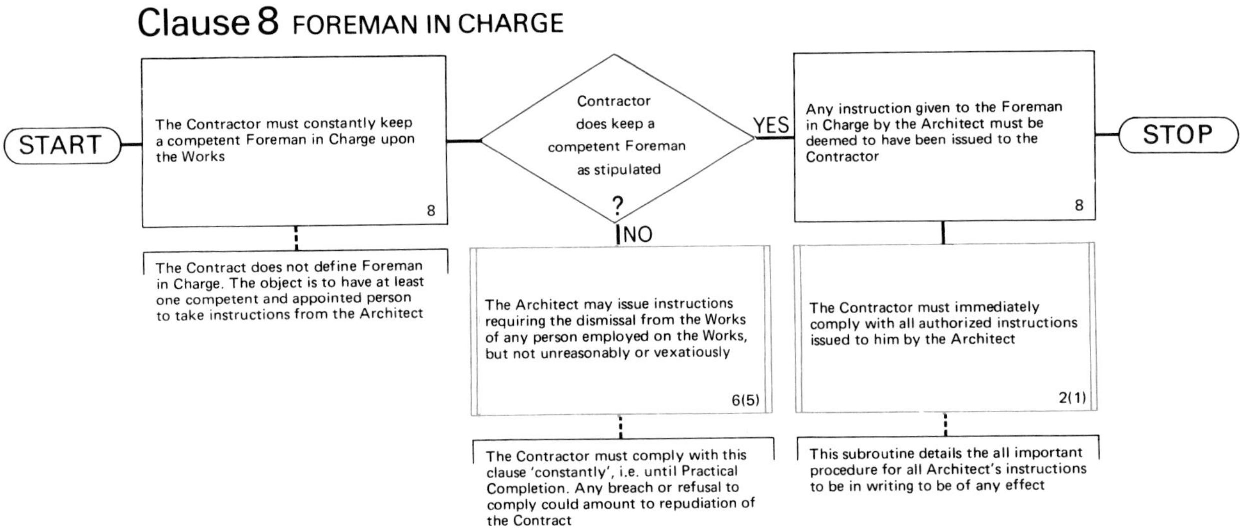
START
The Contractor must constantly keep a competent Foreman in Charge upon the Works
8
The Contract does not define Foreman in Charge. The object is to have at least one competent and appointed person to take instructions from the Architect
Contractor does keep a competent Foreman as stipulated
?
YES
NO
The Architect may issue instructions requiring the dismissal from the Works of any person employed on the Works, but not unreasonably or vexatiously
6(5)
The Contractor must comply with this clause 'constantly', i.e. until Practical Completion. Any breach or refusal to comply could amount to repudiation of the Contract
Any instruction given to the Foreman in Charge by the Architect must be deemed to have been issued to the Contractor
8
STOP
The Contractor must immediately comply with all authorized instructions issued to him by the Architect
2(1)
This subroutine details the all important procedure for all Architect's instructions to be in writing to be of any effect

Clause 9 ACCESS FOR ARCHITECT

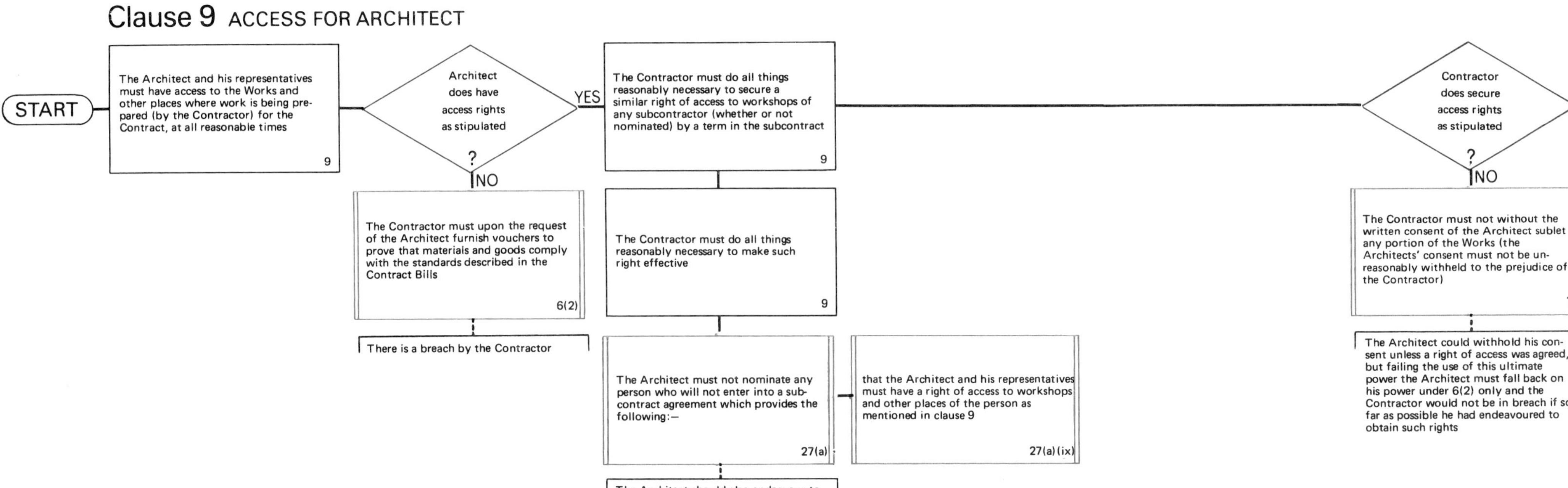

START
The Architect and his representatives must have access to the Works and other places where work is being prepared (by the Contractor) for the Contract, at all reasonable times
9
Architect does have access rights as stipulated ?
YES
NO
The Contractor must upon the request of the Architect furnish vouchers to prove that materials and goods comply with the standards described in the Contract Bills
6(2)
There is a breach by the Contractor
The Contractor must do all things reasonably necessary to secure a similar right of access to workshops of any subcontractor (whether or not nominated) by a term in the subcontract
9
The Contractor must do all things reasonably necessary to make such right effective
9
The Architect must not nominate any person who will not enter into a subcontract agreement which provides the following:—
27(a)
that the Architect and his representatives must have a right of access to workshops and other places of the person as mentioned in clause 9
27(a)(ix)
The Architect should also endeavour to secure this access right when inviting tenders from nominated suppliers to satisfy clause 28(b)(i)
Contractor does secure access rights as stipulated ?
NO
The Contractor must not without the written consent of the Architect sublet any portion of the Works (the Architects' consent must not be unreasonably withheld to the prejudice of the Contractor)
17
The Architect could withhold his consent unless a right of access was agreed, but failing the use of this ultimate power the Architect must fall back on his power under 6(2) only and the Contractor would not be in breach if so far as possible he had endeavoured to obtain such rights

STOP

Clause 10 CLERK OF WORKS

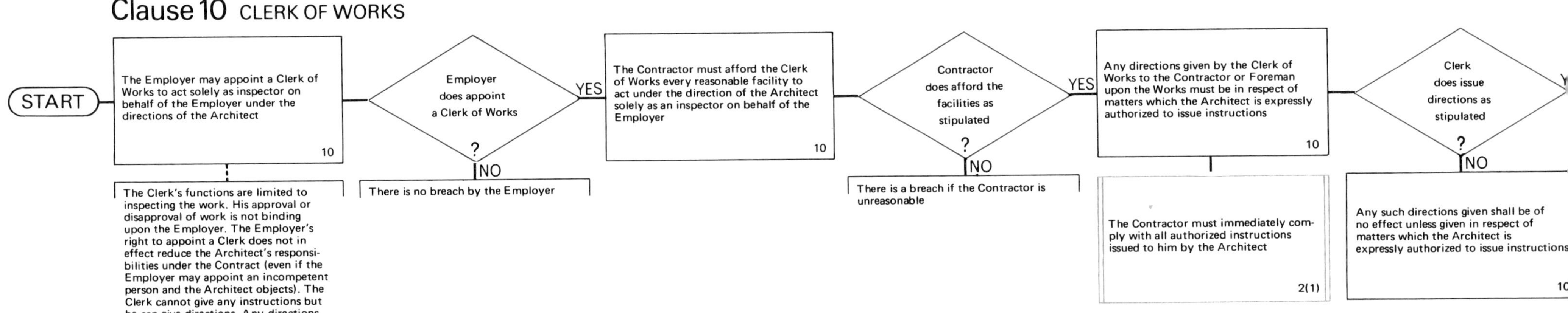
START
The Employer may appoint a Clerk of Works to act solely as inspector on behalf of the Employer under the directions of the Architect
10
The Clerk's functions are limited to inspecting the work. His approval or disapproval of work is not binding upon the Employer. The Employer's right to appoint a Clerk does not in effect reduce the Architect's responsibilities under the Contract (even if the Employer may appoint an incompetent person and the Architect objects). The Clerk cannot give any instructions but he can give directions. Any directions given are subject to approval or veto by the Architect
Employer does appoint a Clerk of Works ?
YES
NO
There is no breach by the Employer
The Contractor must afford the Clerk of Works every reasonable facility to act under the direction of the Architect solely as an inspector on behalf of the Employer
10
Contractor does afford the facilities as stipulated ?
YES
NO
There is a breach if the Contractor is unreasonable
Any directions given by the Clerk of Works to the Contractor or Foreman upon the Works must be in respect of matters which the Architect is expressly authorized to issue instructions
10
The Contractor must immediately comply with all authorized instructions issued to him by the Architect
2(1)
Clerk does issue directions as stipulated ?
NO
Any such directions given shall be of no effect unless given in respect of matters which the Architect is expressly authorized to issue instructions

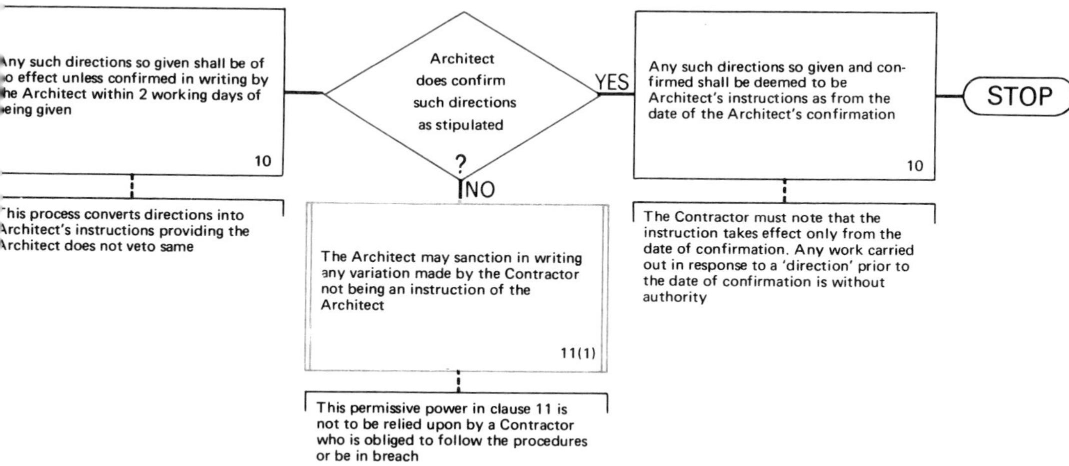

ny such directions so given shall be of
o effect unless confirmed in writing by
he Architect within 2 working days of
eing given
10
his process converts directions into
rchitect's instructions providing the
rchitect does not veto same
Architect does confirm such directions as stipulated ?
YES
NO
The Architect may sanction in writing any variation made by the Contractor not being an instruction of the Architect
11(1)
This permissive power in clause 11 is not to be relied upon by a Contractor who is obliged to follow the procedures or be in breach
Any such directions so given and confirmed shall be deemed to be Architect's instructions as from the date of the Architect's confirmation
10
The Contractor must note that the instruction takes effect only from the date of confirmation. Any work carried out in response to a 'direction' prior to the date of confirmation is without authority
STOP

Clause 11 VARIATIONS AND PROVISIONAL SUM WORK

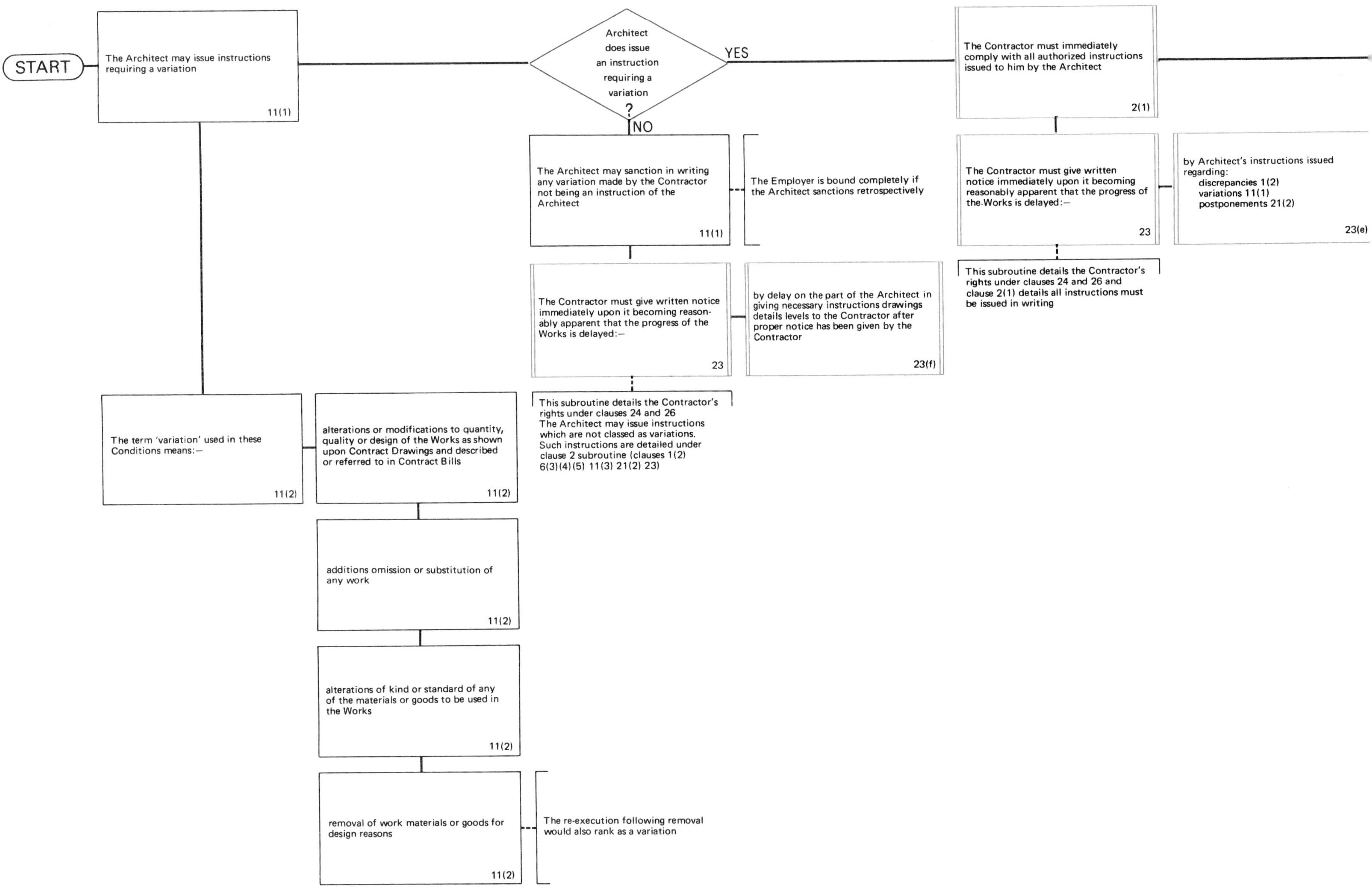

START
The Architect may issue instructions requiring a variation 11(1)
Architect does issue an instruction requiring a variation ?
YES
NO
The Contractor must immediately comply with all authorized instructions issued to him by the Architect 2(1)
The Architect may sanction in writing any variation made by the Contractor not being an instruction of the Architect 11(1)
The Employer is bound completely if the Architect sanctions retrospectively
The Contractor must give written notice immediately upon it becoming reasonably apparent that the progress of the Works is delayed:– 23
by Architect's instructions issued regarding:
discrepancies 1(2)
variations 11(1)
postponements 21(2)
23(e)
This subroutine details the Contractor's rights under clauses 24 and 26 and clause 2(1) details all instructions must be issued in writing
The Contractor must give written notice immediately upon it becoming reasonably apparent that the progress of the Works is delayed:– 23
by delay on the part of the Architect in giving necessary instructions drawings details levels to the Contractor after proper notice has been given by the Contractor 23(f)
This subroutine details the Contractor's rights under clauses 24 and 26
The Architect may issue instructions which are not classed as variations. Such instructions are detailed under clause 2 subroutine (clauses 1(2) 6(3)(4)(5) 11(3) 21(2) 23)
The term 'variation' used in these Conditions means:– 11(2)
alterations or modifications to quantity, quality or design of the Works as shown upon Contract Drawings and described or referred to in Contract Bills 11(2)
additions omission or substitution of any work 11(2)
alterations of kind or standard of any of the materials or goods to be used in the Works 11(2)
removal of work materials or goods for design reasons 11(2)
The re-execution following removal would also rank as a variation

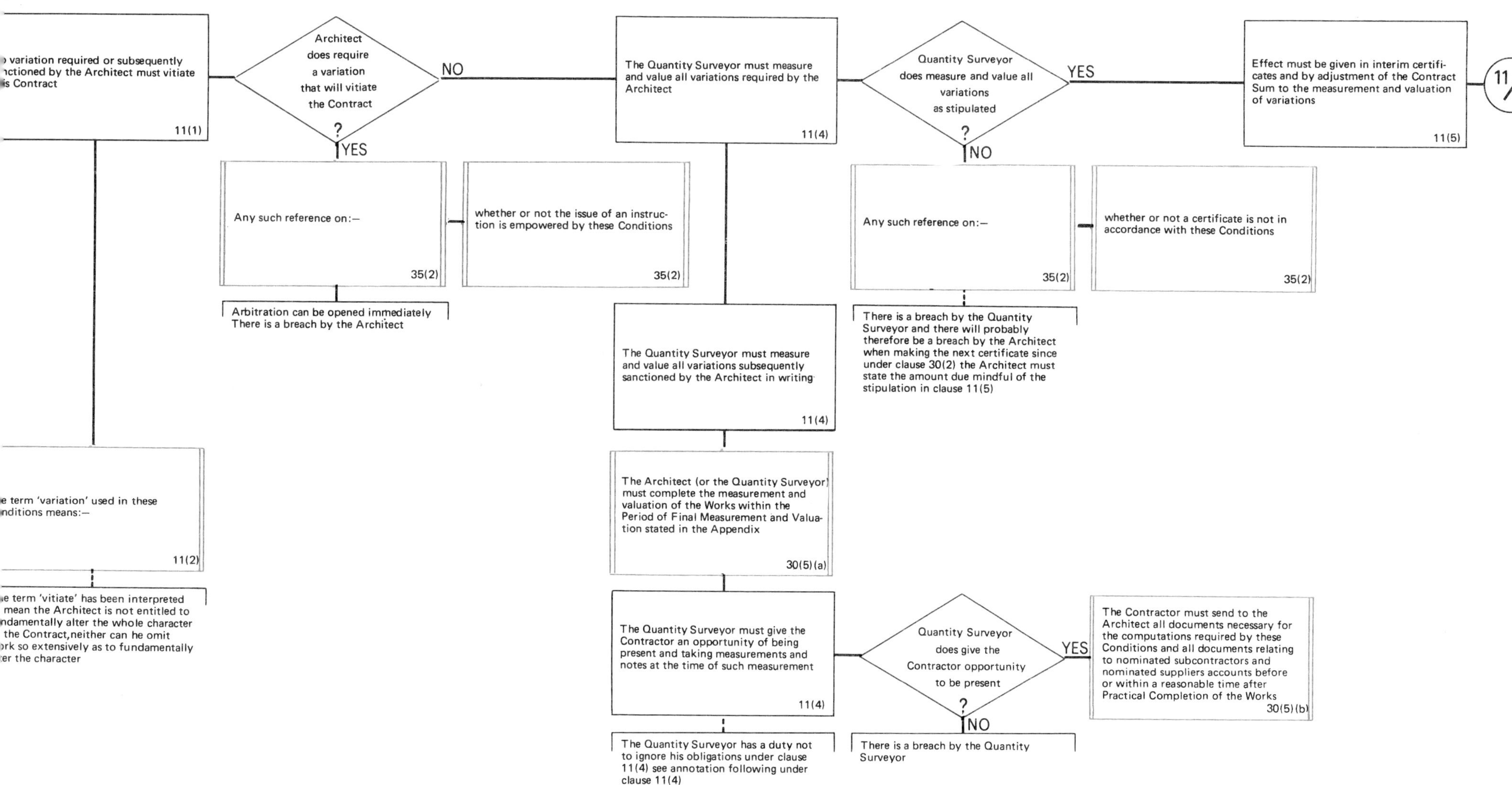
variation required or subsequently
ctioned by the Architect must vitiate
s Contract
11(1)
Architect
does require
a variation
that will vitiate
the Contract
?
NO
YES
The Quantity Surveyor must measure and value all variations required by the Architect
11(4)
Quantity Surveyor
does measure and value all
variations
as stipulated
?
YES
NO
Effect must be given in interim certificates and by adjustment of the Contract Sum to the measurement and valuation of variations
11(5)
11/1
Any such reference on:–
35(2)
whether or not the issue of an instruction is empowered by these Conditions
35(2)
Arbitration can be opened immediately
There is a breach by the Architect
Any such reference on:–
35(2)
whether or not a certificate is not in accordance with these Conditions
35(2)
There is a breach by the Quantity Surveyor and there will probably therefore be a breach by the Architect when making the next certificate since under clause 30(2) the Architect must state the amount due mindful of the stipulation in clause 11(5)
The Quantity Surveyor must measure and value all variations subsequently sanctioned by the Architect in writing
11(4)
e term 'variation' used in these
nditions means:–
11(2)
e term 'vitiate' has been interpreted
mean the Architect is not entitled to
ndamentally alter the whole character
the Contract, neither can he omit
rk so extensively as to fundamentally
er the character
The Architect (or the Quantity Surveyor) must complete the measurement and valuation of the Works within the Period of Final Measurement and Valuation stated in the Appendix
30(5)(a)
The Quantity Surveyor must give the Contractor an opportunity of being present and taking measurements and notes at the time of such measurement
11(4)
Quantity Surveyor
does give the
Contractor opportunity
to be present
?
YES
NO
The Contractor must send to the Architect all documents necessary for the computations required by these Conditions and all documents relating to nominated subcontractors and nominated suppliers accounts before or within a reasonable time after Practical Completion of the Works
30(5)(b)
The Quantity Surveyor has a duty not to ignore his obligations under clause 11(4) see annotation following under clause 11(4)
There is a breach by the Quantity Surveyor

Clause 11 VARIATIONS AND PROVISIONAL SUM WORK

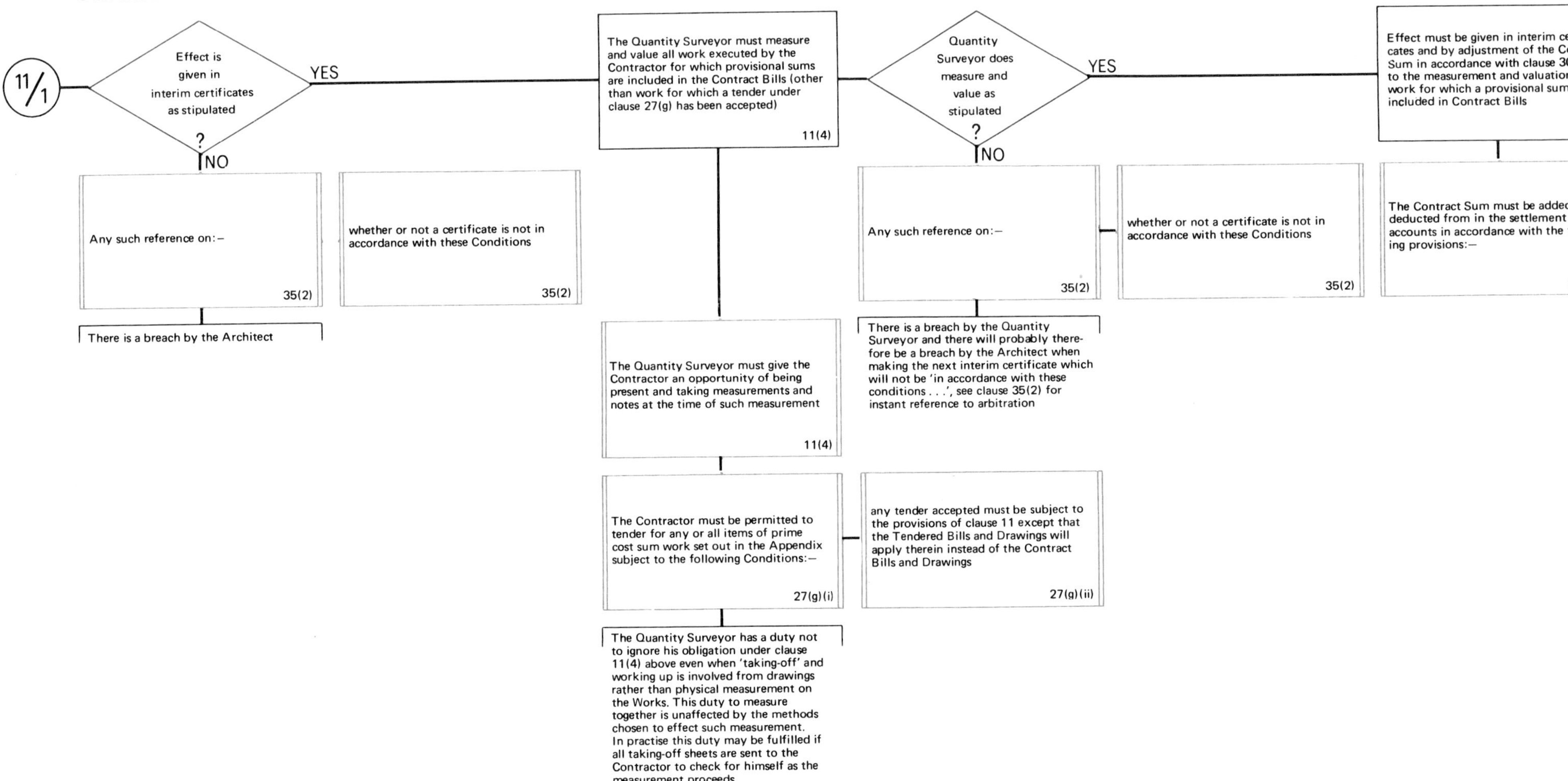

11/1
Effect is given in interim certificates as stipulated ?
YES
NO
Any such reference on:– 35(2)
whether or not a certificate is not in accordance with these Conditions 35(2)
There is a breach by the Architect
The Quantity Surveyor must measure and value all work executed by the Contractor for which provisional sums are included in the Contract Bills (other than work for which a tender under clause 27(g) has been accepted) 11(4)
The Quantity Surveyor must give the Contractor an opportunity of being present and taking measurements and notes at the time of such measurement 11(4)
The Contractor must be permitted to tender for any or all items of prime cost sum work set out in the Appendix subject to the following Conditions:– 27(g)(i)
any tender accepted must be subject to the provisions of clause 11 except that the Tendered Bills and Drawings will apply therein instead of the Contract Bills and Drawings 27(g)(ii)
The Quantity Surveyor has a duty not to ignore his obligation under clause 11(4) above even when 'taking-off' and working up is involved from drawings rather than physical measurement on the Works. This duty to measure together is unaffected by the methods chosen to effect such measurement. In practise this duty may be fulfilled if all taking-off sheets are sent to the Contractor to check for himself as the measurement proceeds
Quantity Surveyor does measure and value as stipulated ?
YES
NO
Any such reference on:– 35(2)
whether or not a certificate is not in accordance with these Conditions 35(2)
There is a breach by the Quantity Surveyor and there will probably therefore be a breach by the Architect when making the next interim certificate which will not be 'in accordance with these conditions . . .', see clause 35(2) for instant reference to arbitration
Effect must be given in interim certificates and by adjustment of the Contra Sum in accordance with clause 30(5)(to the measurement and valuation of work for which a provisional sum is included in Contract Bills 11
The Contract Sum must be added to o deducted from in the settlement of accounts in accordance with the follov ing provisions:– 30(5)

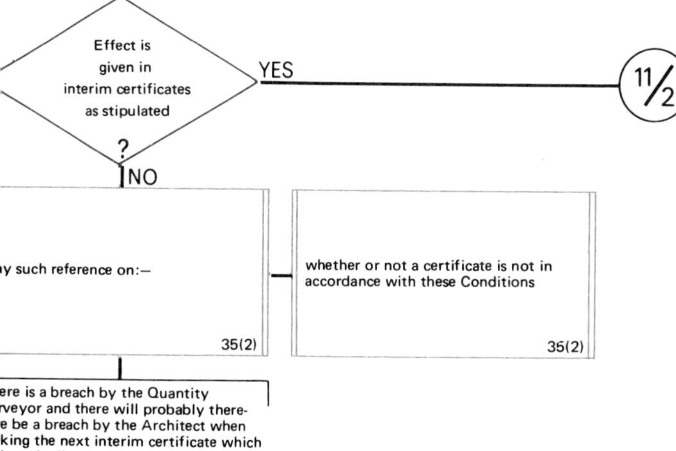
Effect is given in interim certificates as stipulated ?
YES
11/2
NO
-y such reference on:—
35(2)
whether or not a certificate is not in accordance with these Conditions
35(2)
-ere is a breach by the Quantity
-rveyor and there will probably there-
-e be a breach by the Architect when
-king the next interim certificate which
-l not be 'in accordance with these
-nditions . . . , see clause 35(2) for
-tant reference to arbitration

Clause 11 VALUATION OF VARIATIONS AND PROVISIONAL SUM WORK

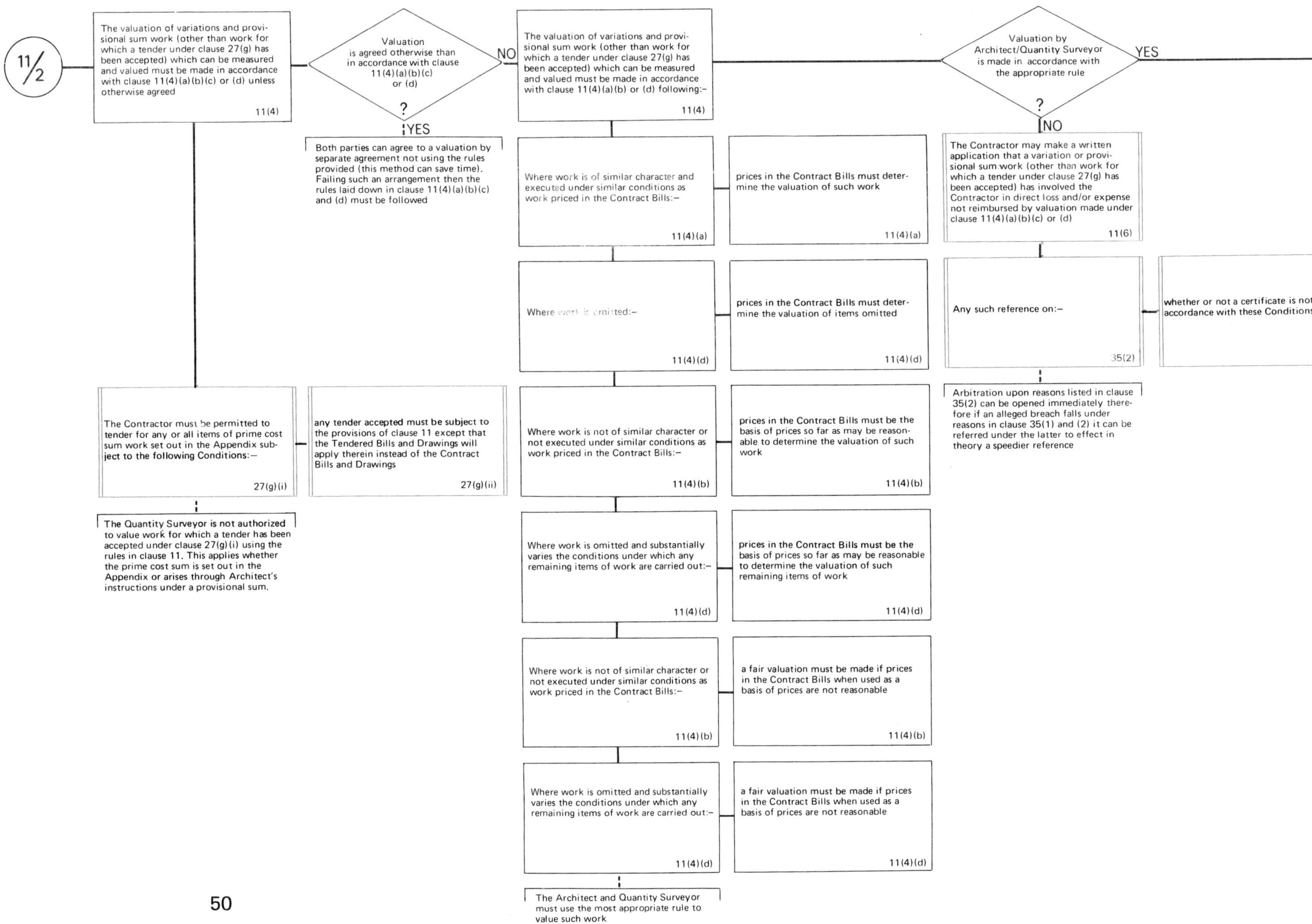

11/2
The valuation of variations and provisional sum work (other than work for which a tender under clause 27(g) has been accepted) which can be measured and valued must be made in accordance with clause 11(4)(a)(b)(c) or (d) unless otherwise agreed
11(4)
Valuation is agreed otherwise than in accordance with clause 11(4)(a)(b)(c) or (d)
?
NO
YES
Both parties can agree to a valuation by separate agreement not using the rules provided (this method can save time). Failing such an arrangement then the rules laid down in clause 11(4)(a)(b)(c) and (d) must be followed
The valuation of variations and provisional sum work (other than work for which a tender under clause 27(g) has been accepted) which can be measured and valued must be made in accordance with clause 11(4)(a)(b) or (d) following:–
11(4)
Valuation by Architect/Quantity Surveyor is made in accordance with the appropriate rule
?
YES
NO
Where work is of similar character and executed under similar conditions as work priced in the Contract Bills:–
11(4)(a)
prices in the Contract Bills must determine the valuation of such work
11(4)(a)
The Contractor may make a written application that a variation or provisional sum work (other than work for which a tender under clause 27(g) has been accepted) has involved the Contractor in direct loss and/or expense not reimbursed by valuation made under clause 11(4)(a)(b)(c) or (d)
11(6)
Where work is omitted:–
11(4)(d)
prices in the Contract Bills must determine the valuation of items omitted
11(4)(d)
Any such reference on:–
35(2)
whether or not a certificate is not in accordance with these Conditions
Arbitration upon reasons listed in clause 35(2) can be opened immediately therefore if an alleged breach falls under reasons in clause 35(1) and (2) it can be referred under the latter to effect in theory a speedier reference
The Contractor must be permitted to tender for any or all items of prime cost sum work set out in the Appendix subject to the following Conditions:–
27(g)(i)
any tender accepted must be subject to the provisions of clause 11 except that the Tendered Bills and Drawings will apply therein instead of the Contract Bills and Drawings
27(g)(ii)
The Quantity Surveyor is not authorized to value work for which a tender has been accepted under clause 27(g)(i) using the rules in clause 11. This applies whether the prime cost sum is set out in the Appendix or arises through Architect's instructions under a provisional sum.
Where work is not of similar character or not executed under similar conditions as work priced in the Contract Bills:–
11(4)(b)
prices in the Contract Bills must be the basis of prices so far as may be reasonable to determine the valuation of such work
11(4)(b)
Where work is omitted and substantially varies the conditions under which any remaining items of work are carried out:–
11(4)(d)
prices in the Contract Bills must be the basis of prices so far as may be reasonable to determine the valuation of such remaining items of work
11(4)(d)
Where work is not of similar character or not executed under similar conditions as work priced in the Contract Bills:–
11(4)(b)
a fair valuation must be made if prices in the Contract Bills when used as a basis of prices are not reasonable
11(4)(b)
Where work is omitted and substantially varies the conditions under which any remaining items of work are carried out:–
11(4)(d)
a fair valuation must be made if prices in the Contract Bills when used as a basis of prices are not reasonable
11(4)(d)
The Architect and Quantity Surveyor must use the most appropriate rule to value such work

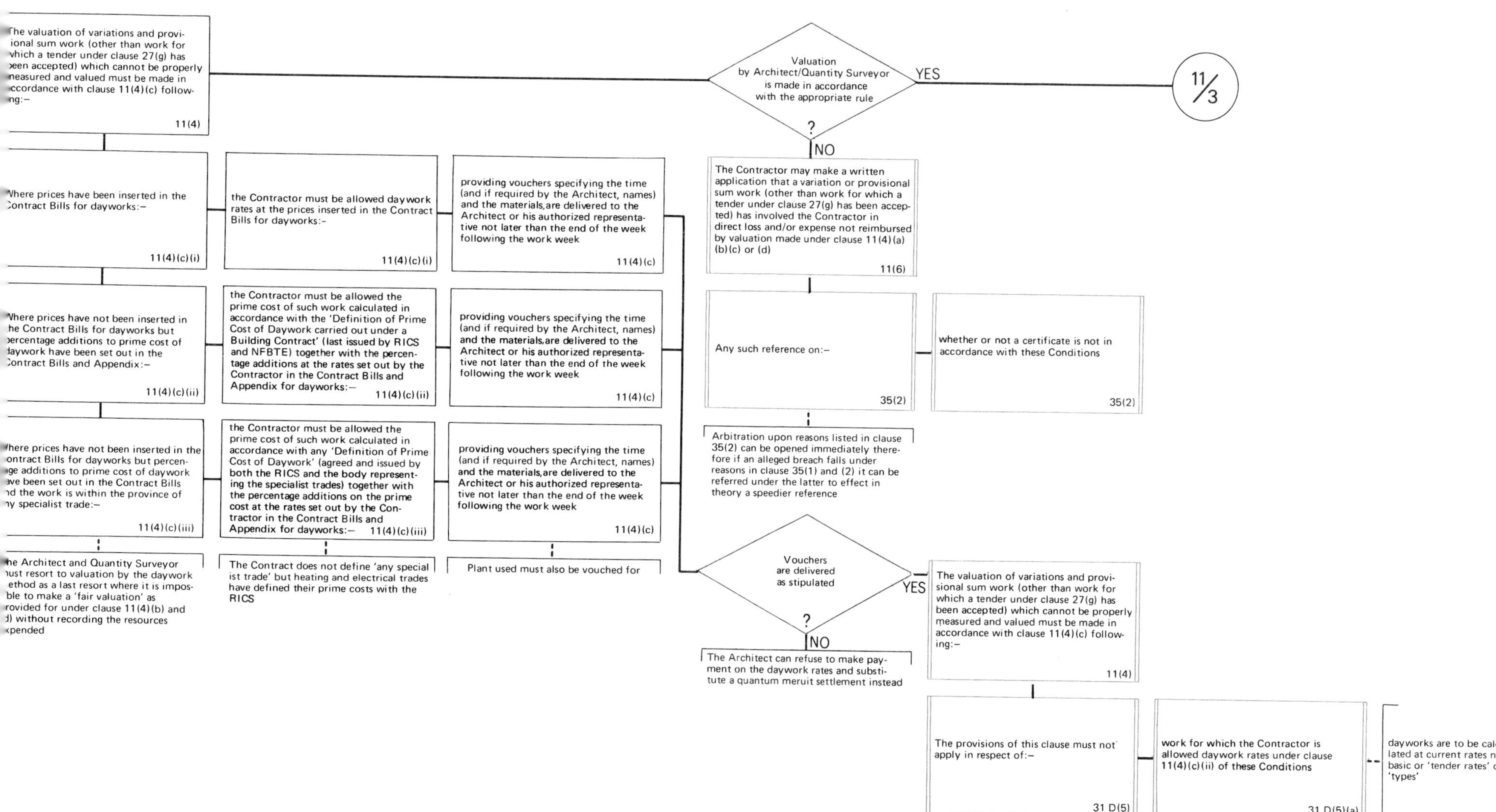

The valuation of variations and provisional sum work (other than work for which a tender under clause 27(g) has been accepted) which cannot be properly measured and valued must be made in accordance with clause 11(4)(c) following:– 11(4)
Valuation by Architect/Quantity Surveyor is made in accordance with the appropriate rule ?
YES
11/3
NO
Where prices have been inserted in the Contract Bills for dayworks:– 11(4)(c)(i)
the Contractor must be allowed daywork rates at the prices inserted in the Contract Bills for dayworks:– 11(4)(c)(i)
providing vouchers specifying the time (and if required by the Architect, names) and the materials, are delivered to the Architect or his authorized representative not later than the end of the week following the work week 11(4)(c)
The Contractor may make a written application that a variation or provisional sum work (other than work for which a tender under clause 27(g) has been accepted) has involved the Contractor in direct loss and/or expense not reimbursed by valuation made under clause 11(4)(a)(b)(c) or (d) 11(6)
Where prices have not been inserted in the Contract Bills for dayworks but percentage additions to prime cost of daywork have been set out in the Contract Bills and Appendix:– 11(4)(c)(ii)
the Contractor must be allowed the prime cost of such work calculated in accordance with the 'Definition of Prime Cost of Daywork carried out under a Building Contract' (last issued by RICS and NFBTE) together with the percentage additions at the rates set out by the Contractor in the Contract Bills and Appendix for dayworks:– 11(4)(c)(ii)
providing vouchers specifying the time (and if required by the Architect, names) and the materials, are delivered to the Architect or his authorized representative not later than the end of the week following the work week 11(4)(c)
Any such reference on:– 35(2)
whether or not a certificate is not in accordance with these Conditions 35(2)
Arbitration upon reasons listed in clause 35(2) can be opened immediately therefore if an alleged breach falls under reasons in clause 35(1) and (2) it can be referred under the latter to effect in theory a speedier reference
Where prices have not been inserted in the Contract Bills for dayworks but percentage additions to prime cost of daywork have been set out in the Contract Bills and the work is within the province of any specialist trade:– 11(4)(c)(iii)
the Contractor must be allowed the prime cost of such work calculated in accordance with any 'Definition of Prime Cost of Daywork' (agreed and issued by both the RICS and the body representing the specialist trades) together with the percentage additions on the prime cost at the rates set out by the Contractor in the Contract Bills and Appendix for dayworks:– 11(4)(c)(iii)
providing vouchers specifying the time (and if required by the Architect, names) and the materials, are delivered to the Architect or his authorized representative not later than the end of the week following the work week 11(4)(c)
The Architect and Quantity Surveyor must resort to valuation by the daywork method as a last resort where it is impossible to make a 'fair valuation' as provided for under clause 11(4)(b) and (d) without recording the resources expended
The Contract does not define 'any special ist trade' but heating and electrical trades have defined their prime costs with the RICS
Plant used must also be vouched for
Vouchers are delivered as stipulated ?
YES
NO
The Architect can refuse to make payment on the daywork rates and substitute a quantum meruit settlement instead
The valuation of variations and provisional sum work (other than work for which a tender under clause 27(g) has been accepted) which cannot be properly measured and valued must be made in accordance with clause 11(4)(c) following:– 11(4)
The provisions of this clause must not apply in respect of:– 31 D(5)
work for which the Contractor is allowed daywork rates under clause 11(4)(c)(ii) of these Conditions 31 D(5)(a)
dayworks are to be calculated at current rates not basic or 'tender rates' or 'types'

Clause 11 DIRECT LOSS, ETC., ARISING FROM VARIATIONS OR PROVISIONAL SUM WORK

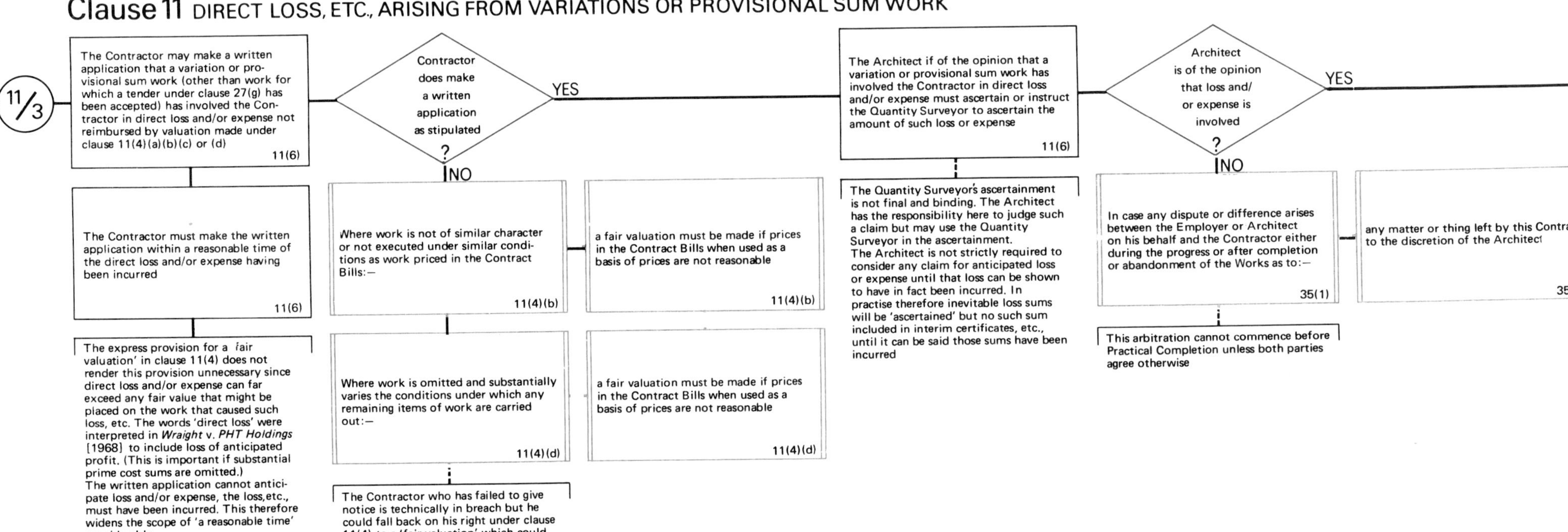

11/3
The Contractor may make a written application that a variation or provisional sum work (other than work for which a tender under clause 27(g) has been accepted) has involved the Contractor in direct loss and/or expense not reimbursed by valuation made under clause 11(4)(a)(b)(c) or (d) 11(6)
Contractor does make a written application as stipulated ?
YES
NO
The Architect if of the opinion that a variation or provisional sum work has involved the Contractor in direct loss and/or expense must ascertain or instruct the Quantity Surveyor to ascertain the amount of such loss or expense 11(6)
Architect is of the opinion that loss and/ or expense is involved ?
YES
NO
The Contractor must make the written application within a reasonable time of the direct loss and/or expense having been incurred 11(6)
Where work is not of similar character or not executed under similar conditions as work priced in the Contract Bills:— 11(4)(b)
a fair valuation must be made if prices in the Contract Bills when used as a basis of prices are not reasonable 11(4)(b)
The Quantity Surveyor's ascertainment is not final and binding. The Architect has the responsibility here to judge such a claim but may use the Quantity Surveyor in the ascertainment. The Architect is not strictly required to consider any claim for anticipated loss or expense until that loss can be shown to have in fact been incurred. In practise therefore inevitable loss sums will be 'ascertained' but no such sum included in interim certificates, etc., until it can be said those sums have been incurred
In case any dispute or difference arises between the Employer or Architect on his behalf and the Contractor either during the progress or after completion or abandonment of the Works as to:— 35(1)
any matter or thing left by this Contrac to the discretion of the Architect 35(
This arbitration cannot commence before Practical Completion unless both parties agree otherwise
The express provision for a 'fair valuation' in clause 11(4) does not render this provision unnecessary since direct loss and/or expense can far exceed any fair value that might be placed on the work that caused such loss, etc. The words 'direct loss' were interpreted in *Wraight* v. *PHT Holdings* [1968] to include loss of anticipated profit. (This is important if substantial prime cost sums are omitted.) The written application cannot anticipate loss and/or expense, the loss,etc., must have been incurred. This therefore widens the scope of 'a reasonable time' considerably
Where work is omitted and substantially varies the conditions under which any remaining items of work are carried out:— 11(4)(d)
a fair valuation must be made if prices in the Contract Bills when used as a basis of prices are not reasonable 11(4)(d)
The Contractor who has failed to give notice is technically in breach but he could fall back on his right under clause 11(4) to a 'fair valuation' which could include a certain amount of direct loss and/or expense providing it produced a fair value on the work involved.
'A reasonable time' was interpreted in *Tersons Ltd.* v. *Stevenage Development Corp.* [1965] in a liberal way. The Contract does not call for evidence of loss or expense by the Contractor but there is an implied duty to show such evidence

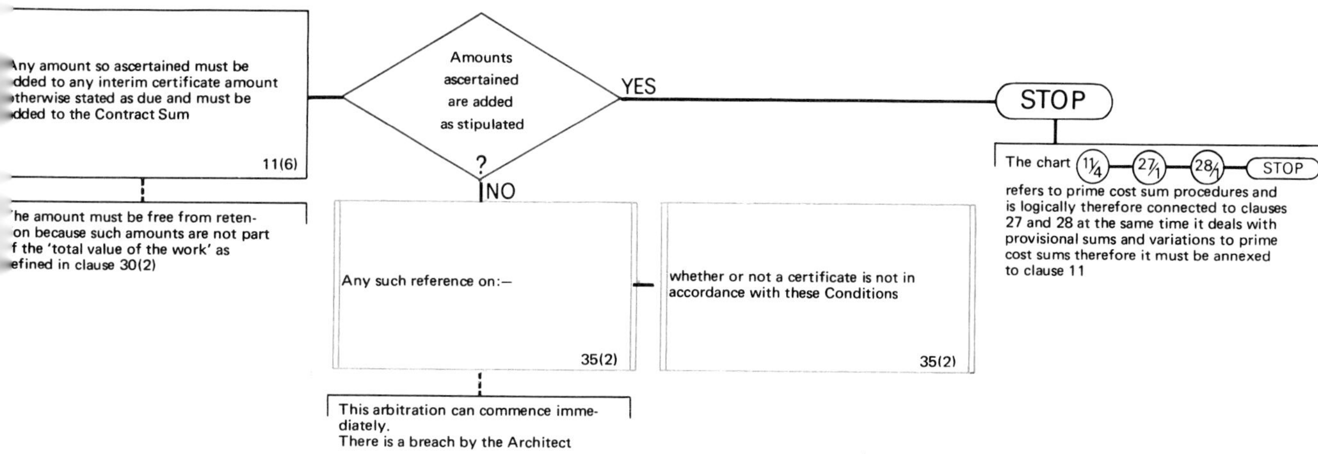

Any amount so ascertained must be added to any interim certificate amount otherwise stated as due and must be added to the Contract Sum
11(6)
The amount must be free from retention because such amounts are not part of the 'total value of the work' as defined in clause 30(2)
Amounts ascertained are added as stipulated
?
YES
NO
STOP
The chart 11/4 — 27/1 — 28/1 — STOP
refers to prime cost sum procedures and is logically therefore connected to clauses 27 and 28 at the same time it deals with provisional sums and variations to prime cost sums therefore it must be annexed to clause 11
Any such reference on:—
35(2)
whether or not a certificate is not in accordance with these Conditions
35(2)
This arbitration can commence immediately.
There is a breach by the Architect

Clause 11 PROVISIONAL AND PRIME COST SUM PROCEDURES

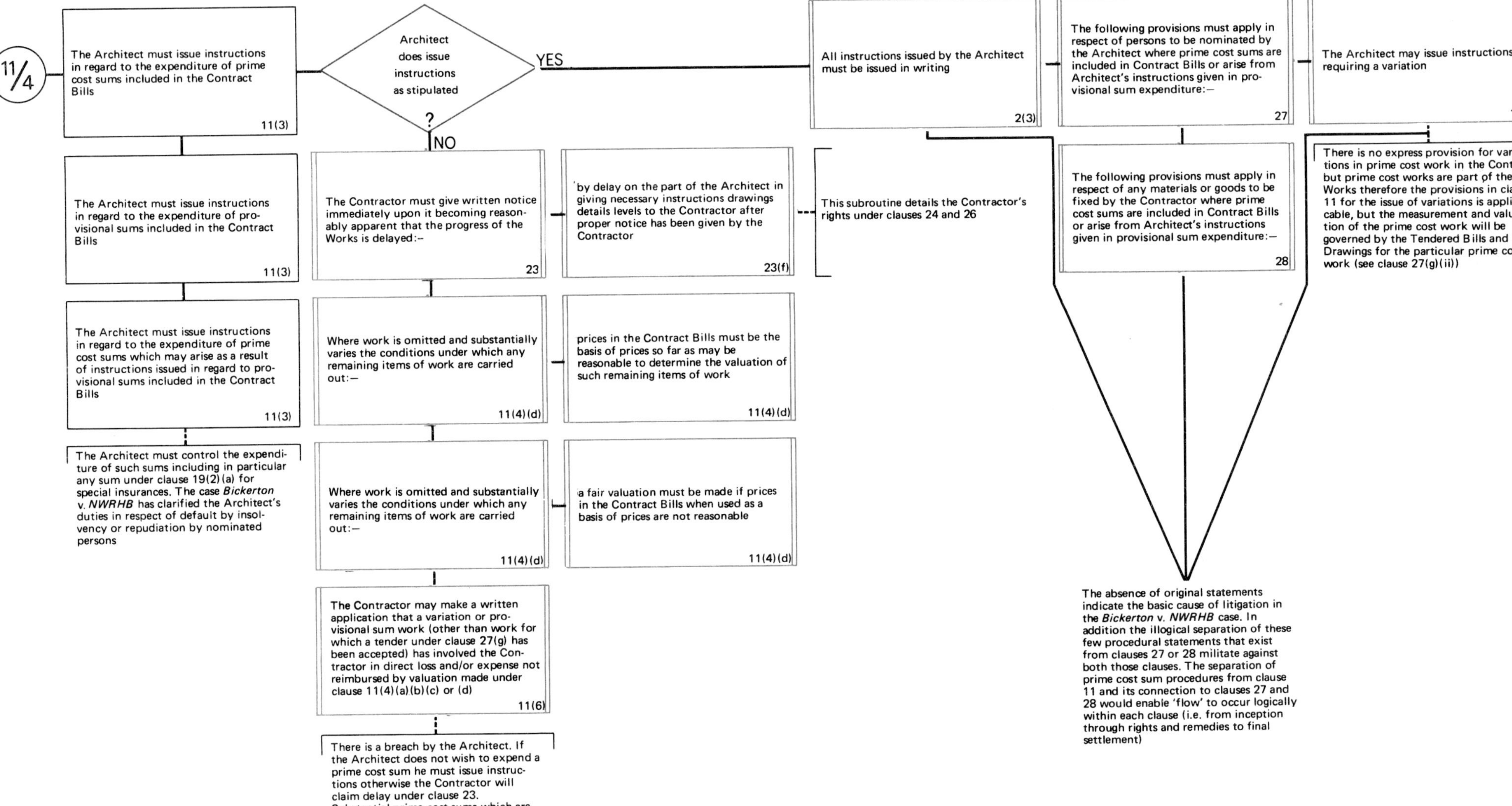

11/4
The Architect must issue instructions in regard to the expenditure of prime cost sums included in the Contract Bills
11(3)
Architect does issue instructions as stipulated ?
YES
NO
All instructions issued by the Architect must be issued in writing
2(3)
The following provisions must apply in respect of persons to be nominated by the Architect where prime cost sums are included in Contract Bills or arise from Architect's instructions given in provisional sum expenditure:–
27
The Architect may issue instructions requiring a variation
11(1
The Architect must issue instructions in regard to the expenditure of provisional sums included in the Contract Bills
11(3)
The Contractor must give written notice immediately upon it becoming reasonably apparent that the progress of the Works is delayed:–
23
by delay on the part of the Architect in giving necessary instructions drawings details levels to the Contractor after proper notice has been given by the Contractor
23(f)
This subroutine details the Contractor's rights under clauses 24 and 26
The following provisions must apply in respect of any materials or goods to be fixed by the Contractor where prime cost sums are included in Contract Bills or arise from Architect's instructions given in provisional sum expenditure:–
28
There is no express provision for variations in prime cost work in the Contract but prime cost works are part of the Works therefore the provisions in clause 11 for the issue of variations is applicable, but the measurement and valuation of the prime cost work will be governed by the Tendered Bills and Drawings for the particular prime cost work (see clause 27(g)(ii))
The Architect must issue instructions in regard to the expenditure of prime cost sums which may arise as a result of instructions issued in regard to provisional sums included in the Contract Bills
11(3)
Where work is omitted and substantially varies the conditions under which any remaining items of work are carried out:–
11(4)(d)
prices in the Contract Bills must be the basis of prices so far as may be reasonable to determine the valuation of such remaining items of work
11(4)(d)
The Architect must control the expenditure of such sums including in particular any sum under clause 19(2)(a) for special insurances. The case Bickerton v. NWRHB has clarified the Architect's duties in respect of default by insolvency or repudiation by nominated persons
Where work is omitted and substantially varies the conditions under which any remaining items of work are carried out:–
11(4)(d)
a fair valuation must be made if prices in the Contract Bills when used as a basis of prices are not reasonable
11(4)(d)
The Contractor may make a written application that a variation or provisional sum work (other than work for which a tender under clause 27(g) has been accepted) has involved the Contractor in direct loss and/or expense not reimbursed by valuation made under clause 11(4)(a)(b)(c) or (d)
11(6)
The absence of original statements indicate the basic cause of litigation in the Bickerton v. NWRHB case. In addition the illogical separation of these few procedural statements that exist from clauses 27 or 28 militate against both those clauses. The separation of prime cost sum procedures from clause 11 and its connection to clauses 27 and 28 would enable 'flow' to occur logically within each clause (i.e. from inception through rights and remedies to final settlement)
There is a breach by the Architect. If the Architect does not wish to expend a prime cost sum he must issue instructions otherwise the Contractor will claim delay under clause 23. Substantial prime cost sums which are omitted can raise claims under clause 11(4)(d), due to the varying conditions of remaining work, and a claim under clause 11(6) due to direct loss and/or expense

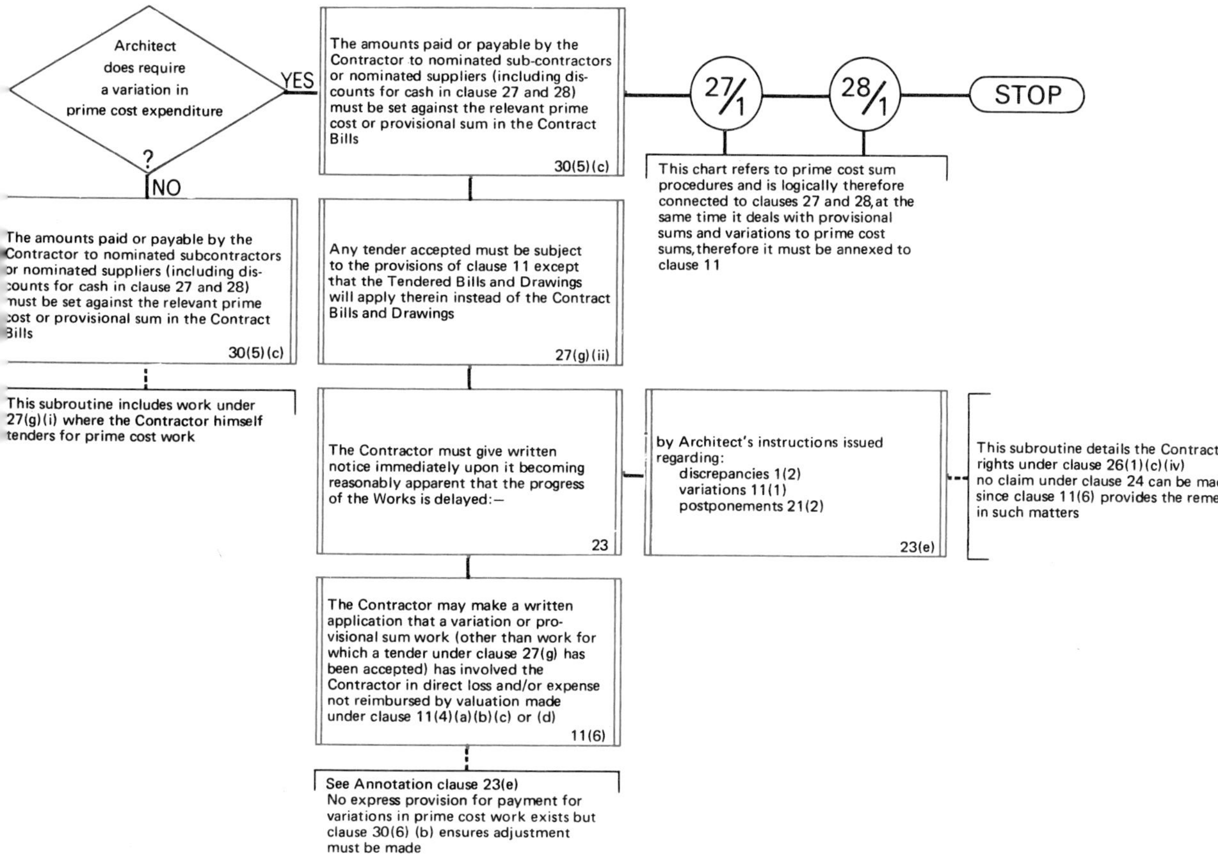

Architect
does require
a variation in
prime cost expenditure
?
YES
NO
The amounts paid or payable by the Contractor to nominated sub-contractors or nominated suppliers (including discounts for cash in clause 27 and 28) must be set against the relevant prime cost or provisional sum in the Contract Bills
30(5)(c)
27/1
28/1
STOP
This chart refers to prime cost sum procedures and is logically therefore connected to clauses 27 and 28, at the same time it deals with provisional sums and variations to prime cost sums, therefore it must be annexed to clause 11
The amounts paid or payable by the Contractor to nominated subcontractors or nominated suppliers (including discounts for cash in clause 27 and 28) must be set against the relevant prime cost or provisional sum in the Contract Bills
30(5)(c)
This subroutine includes work under 27(g)(i) where the Contractor himself tenders for prime cost work
Any tender accepted must be subject to the provisions of clause 11 except that the Tendered Bills and Drawings will apply therein instead of the Contract Bills and Drawings
27(g)(ii)
The Contractor must give written notice immediately upon it becoming reasonably apparent that the progress of the Works is delayed:—
23
by Architect's instructions issued regarding:
discrepancies 1(2)
variations 11(1)
postponements 21(2)
23(e)
This subroutine details the Contractor's rights under clause 26(1)(c)(iv) no claim under clause 24 can be made since clause 11(6) provides the remedy in such matters
The Contractor may make a written application that a variation or provisional sum work (other than work for which a tender under clause 27(g) has been accepted) has involved the Contractor in direct loss and/or expense not reimbursed by valuation made under clause 11(4)(a)(b)(c) or (d)
11(6)
See Annotation clause 23(e)
No express provision for payment for variations in prime cost work exists but clause 30(6) (b) ensures adjustment must be made

Clause 12 CONTRACT BILLS

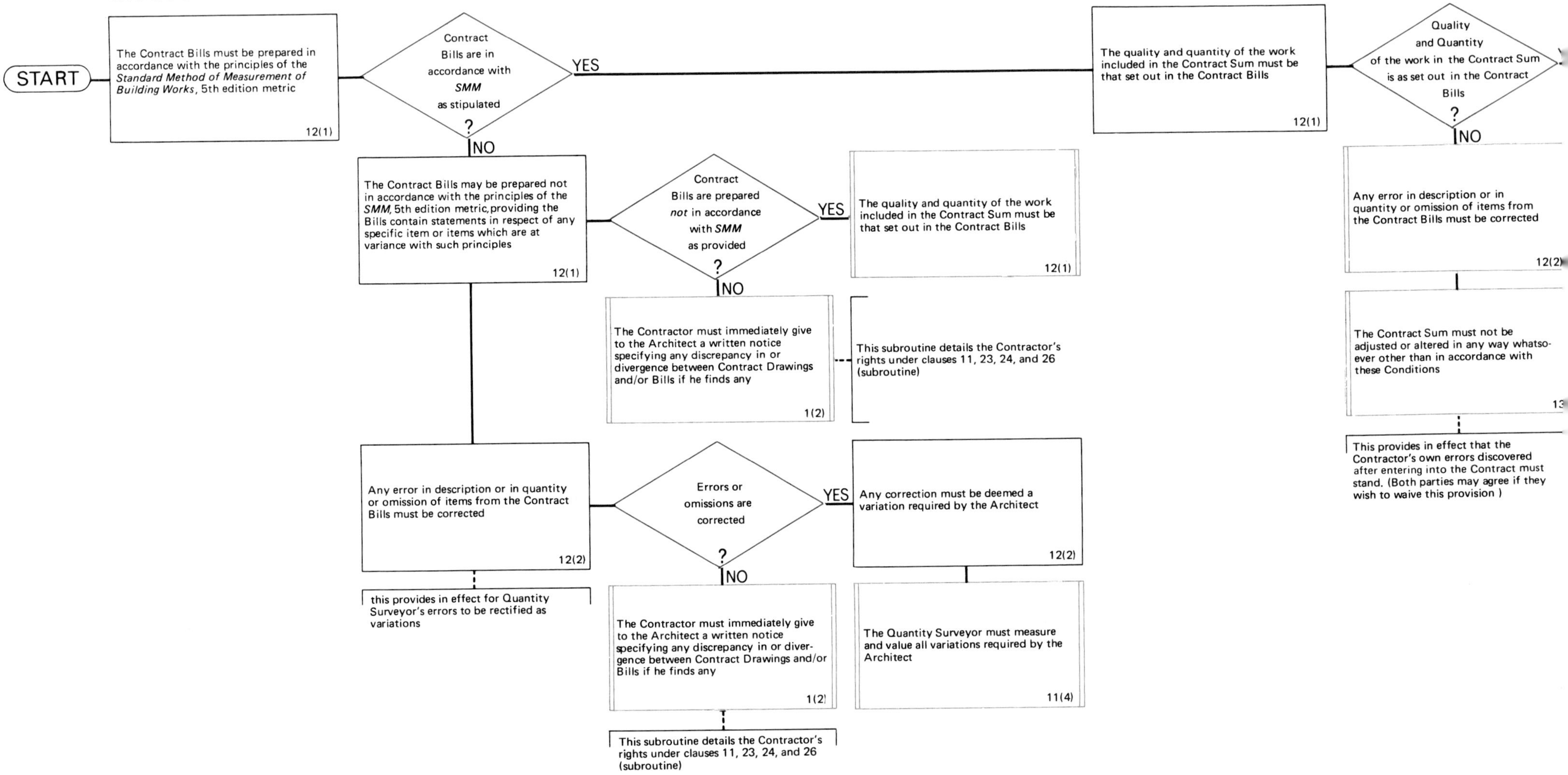

START

The Contract Bills must be prepared in accordance with the principles of the *Standard Method of Measurement of Building Works*, 5th edition metric
12(1)

Contract Bills are in accordance with *SMM* as stipulated ?

YES

The quality and quantity of the work included in the Contract Sum must be that set out in the Contract Bills
12(1)

Quality and Quantity of the work in the Contract Sum is as set out in the Contract Bills ?

NO

Any error in description or in quantity or omission of items from the Contract Bills must be corrected
12(2)

The Contract Sum must not be adjusted or altered in any way whatsoever other than in accordance with these Conditions
13

This provides in effect that the Contractor's own errors discovered after entering into the Contract must stand. (Both parties may agree if they wish to waive this provision)

NO

The Contract Bills may be prepared not in accordance with the principles of the *SMM*, 5th edition metric, providing the Bills contain statements in respect of any specific item or items which are at variance with such principles
12(1)

Contract Bills are prepared *not* in accordance with *SMM* as provided ?

YES

The quality and quantity of the work included in the Contract Sum must be that set out in the Contract Bills
12(1)

NO

The Contractor must immediately give to the Architect a written notice specifying any discrepancy in or divergence between Contract Drawings and/or Bills if he finds any
1(2)

This subroutine details the Contractor's rights under clauses 11, 23, 24, and 26 (subroutine)

Any error in description or in quantity or omission of items from the Contract Bills must be corrected
12(2)

this provides in effect for Quantity Surveyor's errors to be rectified as variations

Errors or omissions are corrected ?

YES

Any correction must be deemed a variation required by the Architect
12(2)

The Quantity Surveyor must measure and value all variations required by the Architect
11(4)

NO

The Contractor must immediately give to the Architect a written notice specifying any discrepancy in or divergence between Contract Drawings and/or Bills if he finds any
1(2)

This subroutine details the Contractor's rights under clauses 11, 23, 24, and 26 (subroutine)

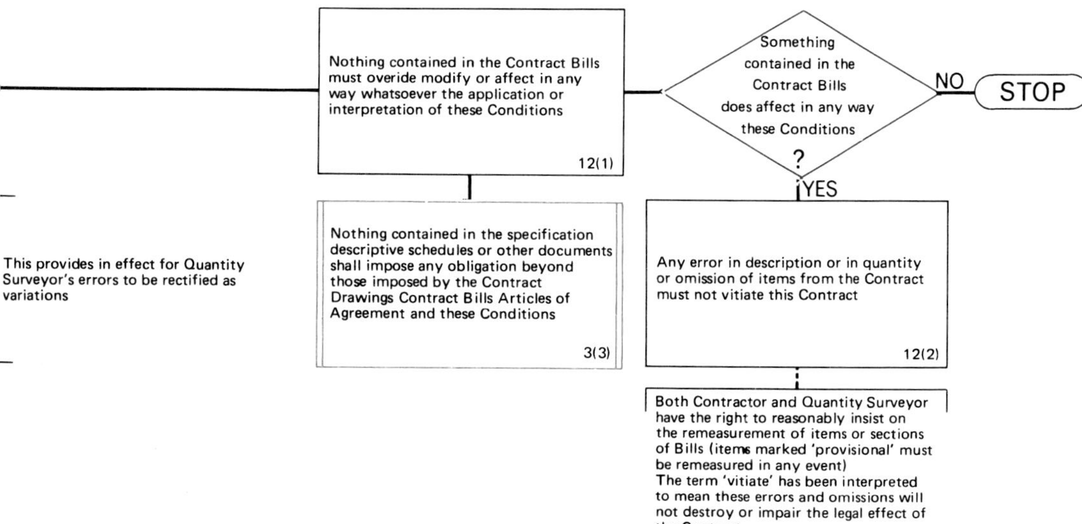
Nothing contained in the Contract Bills must overide modify or affect in any way whatsoever the application or interpretation of these Conditions
12(1)
Something contained in the Contract Bills does affect in any way these Conditions ?
NO
STOP
YES
This provides in effect for Quantity Surveyor's errors to be rectified as variations
Nothing contained in the specification descriptive schedules or other documents shall impose any obligation beyond those imposed by the Contract Drawings Contract Bills Articles of Agreement and these Conditions
3(3)
Any error in description or in quantity or omission of items from the Contract must not vitiate this Contract
12(2)
Both Contractor and Quantity Surveyor have the right to reasonably insist on the remeasurement of items or sections of Bills (items marked 'provisional' must be remeasured in any event)
The term 'vitiate' has been interpreted to mean these errors and omissions will not destroy or impair the legal effect of the Contract

Clause 13 CONTRACT SUM

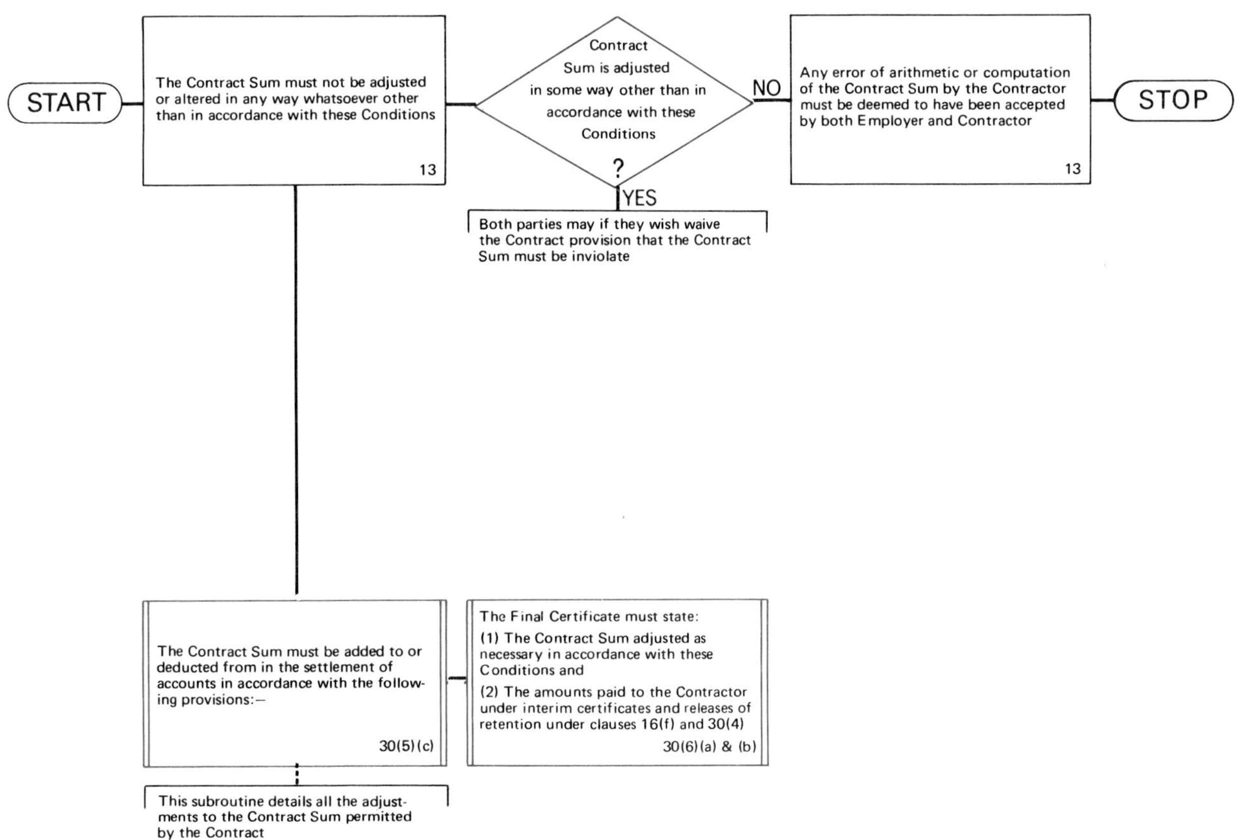

START
The Contract Sum must not be adjusted or altered in any way whatsoever other than in accordance with these Conditions
13
Contract Sum is adjusted in some way other than in accordance with these Conditions
?
NO
YES
Any error of arithmetic or computation of the Contract Sum by the Contractor must be deemed to have been accepted by both Employer and Contractor
13
STOP
Both parties may if they wish waive the Contract provision that the Contract Sum must be inviolate
The Contract Sum must be added to or deducted from in the settlement of accounts in accordance with the following provisions:—
30(5)(c)
The Final Certificate must state:
(1) The Contract Sum adjusted as necessary in accordance with these Conditions and
(2) The amounts paid to the Contractor under interim certificates and releases of retention under clauses 16(f) and 30(4)
30(6)(a) & (b)
This subroutine details all the adjustments to the Contract Sum permitted by the Contract

Clause 14 UNFIXED MATERIALS AND GOODS ON-SITE

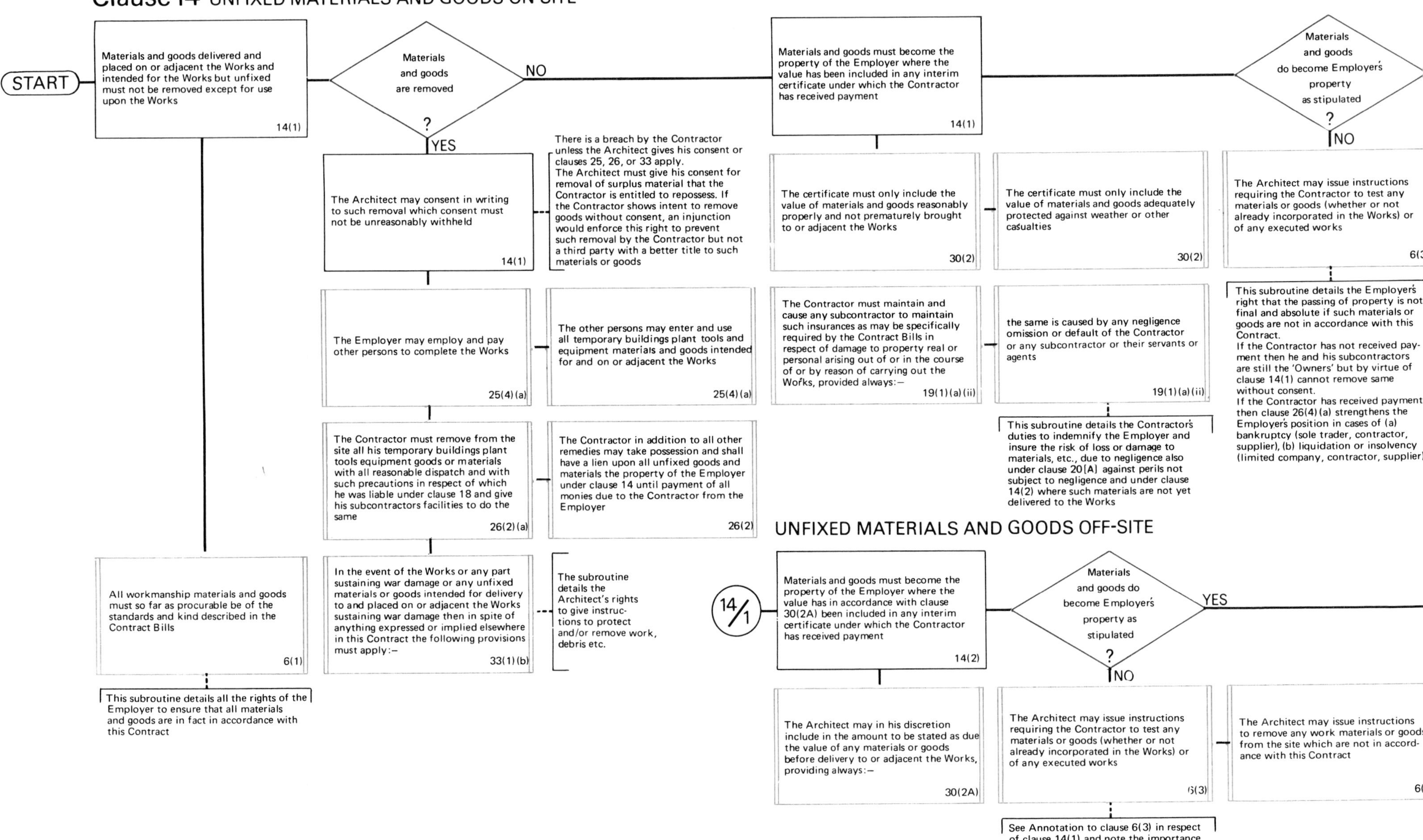

START
Materials and goods delivered and placed on or adjacent the Works and intended for the Works but unfixed must not be removed except for use upon the Works 14(1)
Materials and goods are removed ?
NO
YES
The Architect may consent in writing to such removal which consent must not be unreasonably withheld 14(1)
There is a breach by the Contractor unless the Architect gives his consent or clauses 25, 26, or 33 apply. The Architect must give his consent for removal of surplus material that the Contractor is entitled to repossess. If the Contractor shows intent to remove goods without consent, an injunction would enforce this right to prevent such removal by the Contractor but not a third party with a better title to such materials or goods
The Employer may employ and pay other persons to complete the Works 25(4)(a)
The other persons may enter and use all temporary buildings plant tools and equipment materials and goods intended for and on or adjacent the Works 25(4)(a)
The Contractor must remove from the site all his temporary buildings plant tools equipment goods or materials with all reasonable dispatch and with such precautions in respect of which he was liable under clause 18 and give his subcontractors facilities to do the same 26(2)(a)
The Contractor in addition to all other remedies may take possession and shall have a lien upon all unfixed goods and materials the property of the Employer under clause 14 until payment of all monies due to the Contractor from the Employer 26(2)
All workmanship materials and goods must so far as procurable be of the standards and kind described in the Contract Bills 6(1)
This subroutine details all the rights of the Employer to ensure that all materials and goods are in fact in accordance with this Contract
In the event of the Works or any part sustaining war damage or any unfixed materials or goods intended for delivery to and placed on or adjacent the Works sustaining war damage then in spite of anything expressed or implied elsewhere in this Contract the following provisions must apply:– 33(1)(b)
The subroutine details the Architect's rights to give instructions to protect and/or remove work, debris etc.
Materials and goods must become the property of the Employer where the value has been included in any interim certificate under which the Contractor has received payment 14(1)
Materials and goods do become Employer's property as stipulated ?
NO
The certificate must only include the value of materials and goods reasonably properly and not prematurely brought to or adjacent the Works 30(2)
The certificate must only include the value of materials and goods adequately protected against weather or other casualties 30(2)
The Architect may issue instructions requiring the Contractor to test any materials or goods (whether or not already incorporated in the Works) or of any executed works 6(3
The Contractor must maintain and cause any subcontractor to maintain such insurances as may be specifically required by the Contract Bills in respect of damage to property real or personal arising out of or in the course of or by reason of carrying out the Works, provided always:– 19(1)(a)(ii)
the same is caused by any negligence omission or default of the Contractor or any subcontractor or their servants or agents 19(1)(a)(ii)
This subroutine details the Contractor's duties to indemnify the Employer and insure the risk of loss or damage to materials, etc., due to negligence also under clause 20[A] against perils not subject to negligence and under clause 14(2) where such materials are not yet delivered to the Works
This subroutine details the Employer's right that the passing of property is not final and absolute if such materials or goods are not in accordance with this Contract. If the Contractor has not received payment then he and his subcontractors are still the 'Owners' but by virtue of clause 14(1) cannot remove same without consent. If the Contractor has received payment then clause 26(4)(a) strengthens the Employer's position in cases of (a) bankruptcy (sole trader, contractor, supplier), (b) liquidation or insolvency (limited company, contractor, supplier)
UNFIXED MATERIALS AND GOODS OFF-SITE
14/1
Materials and goods must become the property of the Employer where the value has in accordance with clause 30(2A) been included in any interim certificate under which the Contractor has received payment 14(2)
Materials and goods do become Employer's property as stipulated ?
YES
NO
The Architect may in his discretion include in the amount to be stated as due the value of any materials or goods before delivery to or adjacent the Works, providing always:– 30(2A)
The Architect may issue instructions requiring the Contractor to test any materials or goods (whether or not already incorporated in the Works) or of any executed works 6(3)
The Architect may issue instructions to remove any work materials or goods from the site which are not in accordance with this Contract 6(
See Annotation to clause 6(3) in respect of clause 14(1) and note the importance under clause 30(2A) of proof of ownership

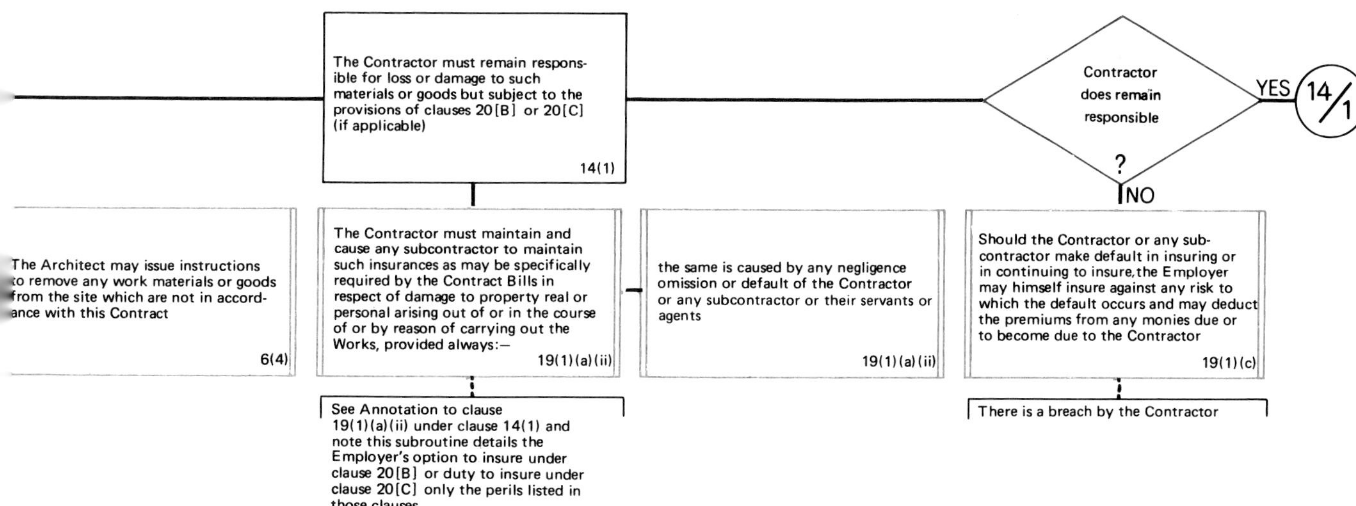

The Contractor must remain responsible for loss or damage to such materials or goods but subject to the provisions of clauses 20[B] or 20[C] (if applicable)
14(1)
Contractor does remain responsible
?
YES
NO
14/1
The Architect may issue instructions to remove any work materials or goods from the site which are not in accordance with this Contract
6(4)
The Contractor must maintain and cause any subcontractor to maintain such insurances as may be specifically required by the Contract Bills in respect of damage to property real or personal arising out of or in the course of or by reason of carrying out the Works, provided always:—
19(1)(a)(ii)
the same is caused by any negligence omission or default of the Contractor or any subcontractor or their servants or agents
19(1)(a)(ii)
Should the Contractor or any subcontractor make default in insuring or in continuing to insure, the Employer may himself insure against any risk to which the default occurs and may deduct the premiums from any monies due or to become due to the Contractor
19(1)(c)
See Annotation to clause 19(1)(a)(ii) under clause 14(1) and note this subroutine details the Employer's option to insure under clause 20[B] or duty to insure under clause 20[C] only the perils listed in those clauses
There is a breach by the Contractor

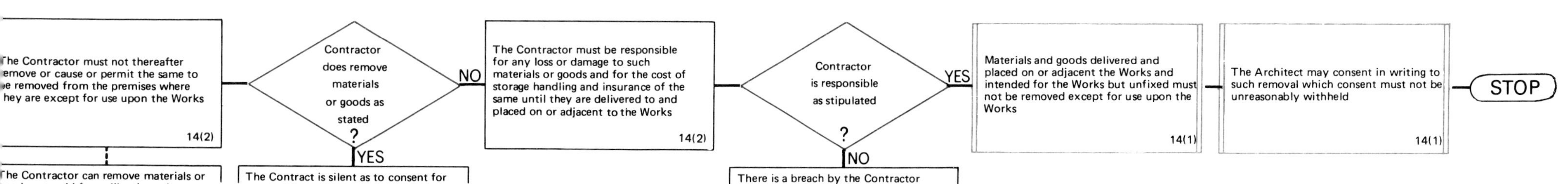

The Contractor must not thereafter remove or cause or permit the same to be removed from the premises where they are except for use upon the Works
14(2)
Contractor does remove materials or goods as stated
?
NO
YES
The Contractor must be responsible for any loss or damage to such materials or goods and for the cost of storage handling and insurance of the same until they are delivered to and placed on or adjacent to the Works
14(2)
Contractor is responsible as stipulated
?
YES
NO
Materials and goods delivered and placed on or adjacent the Works and intended for the Works but unfixed must not be removed except for use upon the Works
14(1)
The Architect may consent in writing to such removal which consent must not be unreasonably withheld
14(1)
STOP
The Contractor can remove materials or goods not paid for unlike the strict provision under clause 14(1) which prohibits any removal whether paid for or not
The Contract is silent as to consent for removal from off-site stores (for e.g. surplus). (It is also silent in respect of clause 25 procedure for 'other persons' to recover.) However, clause 26(2) permits the Contractor to have a lien on such materials or goods in the event of his own determination.
There is a breach by the Contractor if he removes for reasons other than stated above
There is a breach by the Contractor

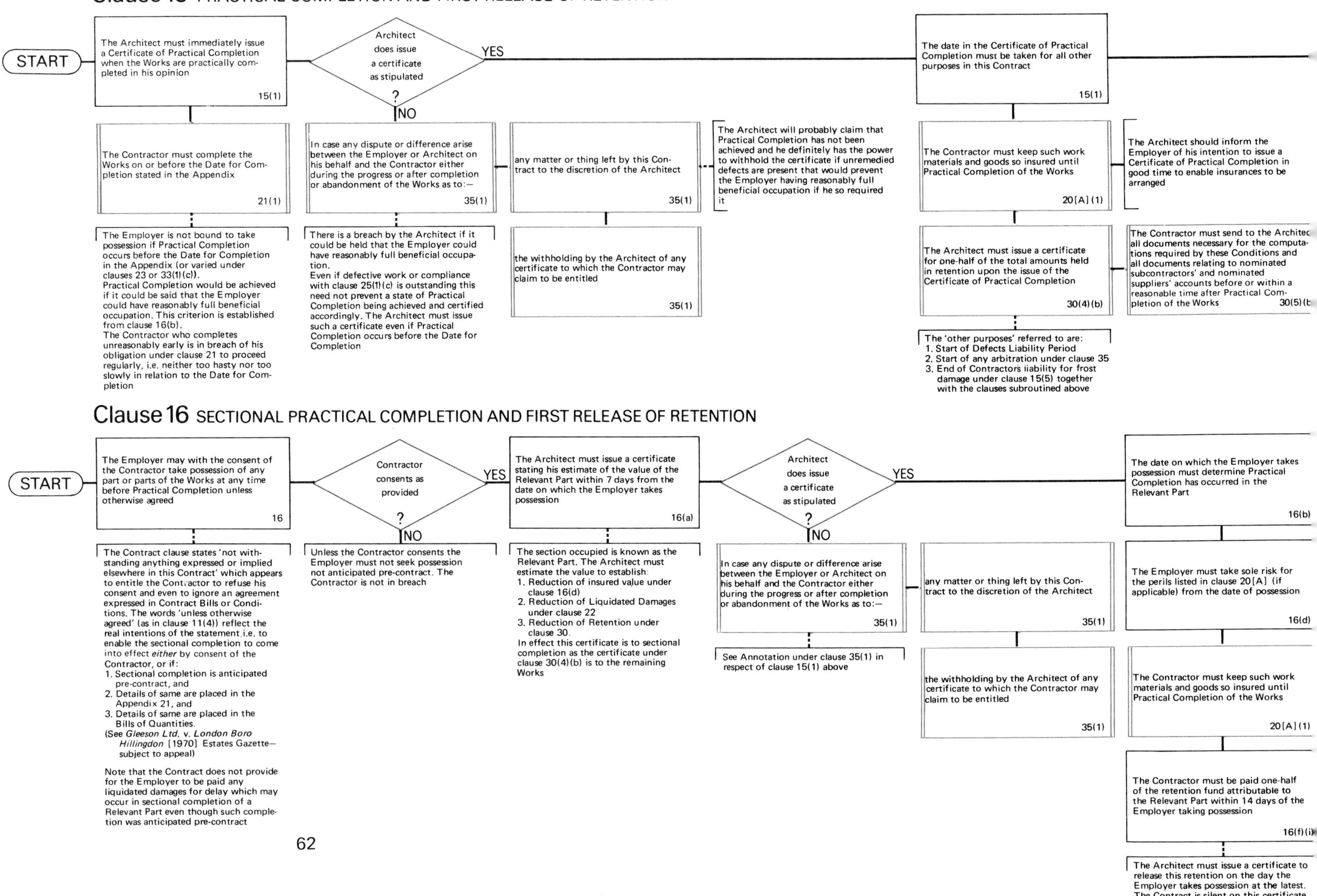

Clause 15 PRACTICAL COMPLETION AND FIRST RELEASE OF RETENTION
START
The Architect must immediately issue a Certificate of Practical Completion when the Works are practically completed in his opinion 15(1)
Architect does issue a certificate as stipulated ?
YES
NO
The date in the Certificate of Practical Completion must be taken for all other purposes in this Contract 15(1)
The Contractor must complete the Works on or before the Date for Completion stated in the Appendix 21(1)
In case any dispute or difference arise between the Employer or Architect on his behalf and the Contractor either during the progress or after completion or abandonment of the Works as to:— 35(1)
any matter or thing left by this Contract to the discretion of the Architect 35(1)
The Architect will probably claim that Practical Completion has not been achieved and he definitely has the power to withhold the certificate if unremedied defects are present that would prevent the Employer having reasonably full beneficial occupation if he so required it
The Contractor must keep such work materials and goods so insured until Practical Completion of the Works 20[A](1)
The Architect should inform the Employer of his intention to issue a Certificate of Practical Completion in good time to enable insurances to be arranged
The Employer is not bound to take possession if Practical Completion occurs before the Date for Completion in the Appendix (or varied under clauses 23 or 33(1)(c)). Practical Completion would be achieved if it could be said that the Employer could have reasonably full beneficial occupation. This criterion is established from clause 16(b). The Contractor who completes unreasonably early is in breach of his obligation under clause 21 to proceed regularly, i.e. neither too hasty nor too slowly in relation to the Date for Completion
There is a breach by the Architect if it could be held that the Employer could have reasonably full beneficial occupation. Even if defective work or compliance with clause 25(1)(c) is outstanding this need not prevent a state of Practical Completion being achieved and certified accordingly. The Architect must issue such a certificate even if Practical Completion occurs before the Date for Completion
the withholding by the Architect of any certificate to which the Contractor may claim to be entitled 35(1)
The Architect must issue a certificate for one-half of the total amounts held in retention upon the issue of the Certificate of Practical Completion 30(4)(b)
The Contractor must send to the Architect all documents necessary for the computations required by these Conditions and all documents relating to nominated subcontractors' and nominated suppliers' accounts before or within a reasonable time after Practical Completion of the Works 30(5)(b)
The 'other purposes' referred to are:
1. Start of Defects Liability Period
2. Start of any arbitration under clause 35
3. End of Contractors liability for frost damage under clause 15(5) together with the clauses subroutined above
Clause 16 SECTIONAL PRACTICAL COMPLETION AND FIRST RELEASE OF RETENTION
START
The Employer may with the consent of the Contractor take possession of any part or parts of the Works at any time before Practical Completion unless otherwise agreed 16
Contractor consents as provided ?
YES
NO
The Architect must issue a certificate stating his estimate of the value of the Relevant Part within 7 days from the date on which the Employer takes possession 16(a)
Architect does issue a certificate as stipulated ?
YES
NO
The date on which the Employer takes possession must determine Practical Completion has occurred in the Relevant Part 16(b)
The Contract clause states 'not withstanding anything expressed or implied elsewhere in this Contract' which appears to entitle the Contractor to refuse his consent and even to ignore an agreement expressed in Contract Bills or Conditions. The words 'unless otherwise agreed' (as in clause 11(4)) reflect the real intentions of the statement i.e. to enable the sectional completion to come into effect *either* by consent of the Contractor, or if:
1. Sectional completion is anticipated pre-contract, and
2. Details of same are placed in the Appendix 21, and
3. Details of same are placed in the Bills of Quantities.
(See *Gleeson Ltd.* v. *London Boro Hillingdon* [1970] Estates Gazette—subject to appeal)
Note that the Contract does not provide for the Employer to be paid any liquidated damages for delay which may occur in sectional completion of a Relevant Part even though such completion was anticipated pre-contract
Unless the Contractor consents the Employer must not seek possession not anticipated pre-contract. The Contractor is not in breach
The section occupied is known as the Relevant Part. The Architect must estimate the value to establish:
1. Reduction of insured value under clause 16(d)
2. Reduction of Liquidated Damages under clause 22
3. Reduction of Retention under clause 30.
In effect this certificate is to sectional completion as the certificate under clause 30(4)(b) is to the remaining Works
In case any dispute or difference arise between the Employer or Architect on his behalf and the Contractor either during the progress or after completion or abandonment of the Works as to:— 35(1)
See Annotation under clause 35(1) in respect of clause 15(1) above
any matter or thing left by this Contract to the discretion of the Architect 35(1)
the withholding by the Architect of any certificate to which the Contractor may claim to be entitled 35(1)
The Employer must take sole risk for the perils listed in clause 20[A] (if applicable) from the date of possession 16(d)
The Contractor must keep such work materials and goods so insured until Practical Completion of the Works 20[A](1)
The Contractor must be paid one-half of the retention fund attributable to the Relevant Part within 14 days of the Employer taking possession 16(f)(i)
The Architect must issue a certificate to release this retention on the day the Employer takes possession at the latest. The Contract is silent on this certificate

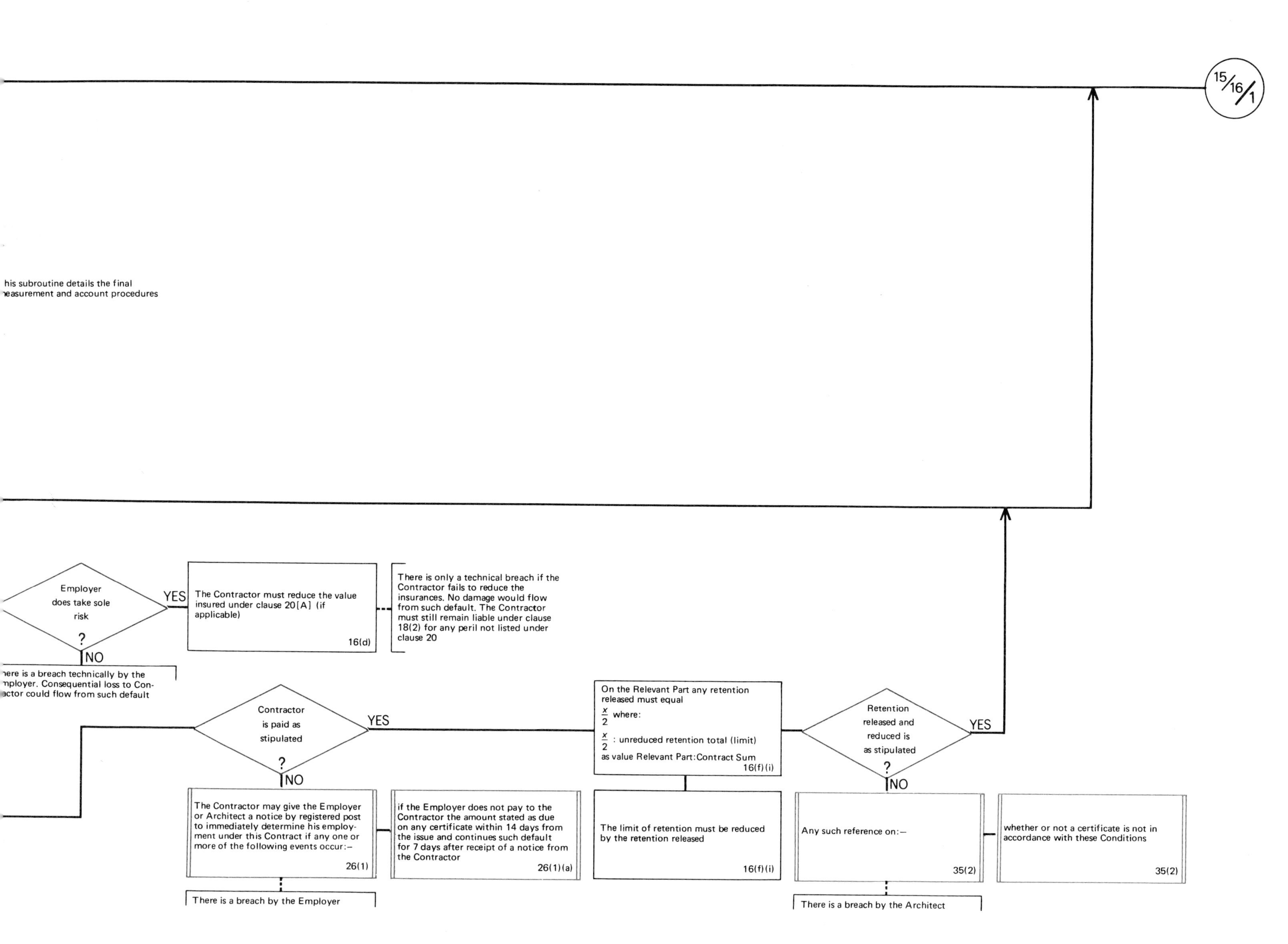
15/16/1
his subroutine details the final
neasurement and account procedures
Employer does take sole risk ?
YES
NO
The Contractor must reduce the value insured under clause 20[A] (if applicable)
16(d)
There is only a technical breach if the Contractor fails to reduce the insurances. No damage would flow from such default. The Contractor must still remain liable under clause 18(2) for any peril not listed under clause 20
nere is a breach technically by the
nployer. Consequential loss to Con-
actor could flow from such default
Contractor is paid as stipulated ?
YES
NO
On the Relevant Part any retention released must equal $\frac{x}{2}$ where:
$\frac{x}{2}$: unreduced retention total (limit)
as value Relevant Part:Contract Sum
16(f)(i)
Retention released and reduced is as stipulated ?
YES
NO
The Contractor may give the Employer or Architect a notice by registered post to immediately determine his employment under this Contract if any one or more of the following events occur:–
26(1)
if the Employer does not pay to the Contractor the amount stated as due on any certificate within 14 days from the issue and continues such default for 7 days after receipt of a notice from the Contractor
26(1)(a)
The limit of retention must be reduced by the retention released
16(f)(i)
Any such reference on:–
35(2)
whether or not a certificate is not in accordance with these Conditions
35(2)
There is a breach by the Employer
There is a breach by the Architect

Clauses 15 and 16 DEFECTS LIABILITIES, FINAL RELEASE OF RETENTIONS, AND REDUCTION OF DAMAGES ON SECTIONAL COMPLETION (1)

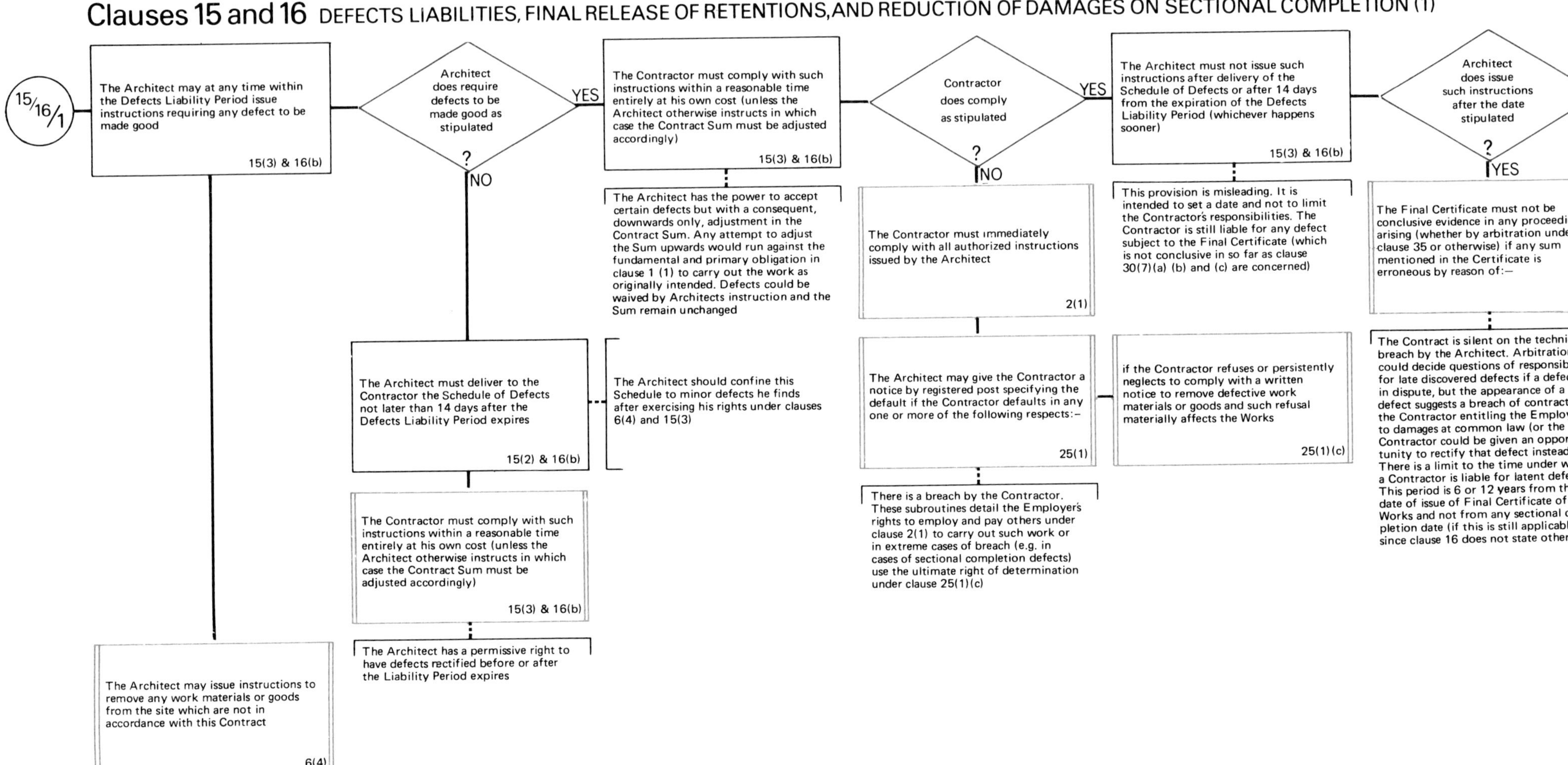

15/16/1
The Architect may at any time within the Defects Liability Period issue instructions requiring any defect to be made good
15(3) & 16(b)
Architect does require defects to be made good as stipulated ?
YES
NO
The Contractor must comply with such instructions within a reasonable time entirely at his own cost (unless the Architect otherwise instructs in which case the Contract Sum must be adjusted accordingly)
15(3) & 16(b)
The Architect has the power to accept certain defects but with a consequent, downwards only, adjustment in the Contract Sum. Any attempt to adjust the Sum upwards would run against the fundamental and primary obligation in clause 1 (1) to carry out the work as originally intended. Defects could be waived by Architects instruction and the Sum remain unchanged
Contractor does comply as stipulated ?
YES
NO
The Contractor must immediately comply with all authorized instructions issued by the Architect
2(1)
The Architect may give the Contractor a notice by registered post specifying the default if the Contractor defaults in any one or more of the following respects:–
25(1)
There is a breach by the Contractor. These subroutines detail the Employer's rights to employ and pay others under clause 2(1) to carry out such work or in extreme cases of breach (e.g. in cases of sectional completion defects) use the ultimate right of determination under clause 25(1)(c)
The Architect must not issue such instructions after delivery of the Schedule of Defects or after 14 days from the expiration of the Defects Liability Period (whichever happens sooner)
15(3) & 16(b)
This provision is misleading. It is intended to set a date and not to limit the Contractor's responsibilities. The Contractor is still liable for any defect subject to the Final Certificate (which is not conclusive in so far as clause 30(7)(a) (b) and (c) are concerned)
if the Contractor refuses or persistently neglects to comply with a written notice to remove defective work materials or goods and such refusal materially affects the Works
25(1)(c)
Architect does issue such instructions after the date stipulated ?
YES
The Final Certificate must not be conclusive evidence in any proceeding arising (whether by arbitration under clause 35 or otherwise) if any sum mentioned in the Certificate is erroneous by reason of:–
30
The Contract is silent on the technica breach by the Architect. Arbitration could decide questions of responsibili for late discovered defects if a defect in dispute, but the appearance of a defect suggests a breach of contract b the Contractor entitling the Employer to damages at common law (or the Contractor could be given an opportunity to rectify that defect instead). There is a limit to the time under whi a Contractor is liable for latent defect This period is 6 or 12 years from the date of issue of Final Certificate of th Works and not from any sectional co pletion date (if this is still applicable) since clause 16 does not state otherwi
The Architect must deliver to the Contractor the Schedule of Defects not later than 14 days after the Defects Liability Period expires
15(2) & 16(b)
The Architect should confine this Schedule to minor defects he finds after exercising his rights under clauses 6(4) and 15(3)
The Contractor must comply with such instructions within a reasonable time entirely at his own cost (unless the Architect otherwise instructs in which case the Contract Sum must be adjusted accordingly)
15(3) & 16(b)
The Architect has a permissive right to have defects rectified before or after the Liability Period expires
The Architect may issue instructions to remove any work materials or goods from the site which are not in accordance with this Contract
6(4)
The Architect should instruct that all defects, other than minor ones, be rectified under either clause 6(4) or 15(3) as early as possible. This is sensible policy in view of the possibility that defects rectified just prior to the date of issue of the Final Certificate under clause 30(6) may manifest themselves again, after the Final Certificate has been issued. Thus raising problems under clause 30(7)(b)

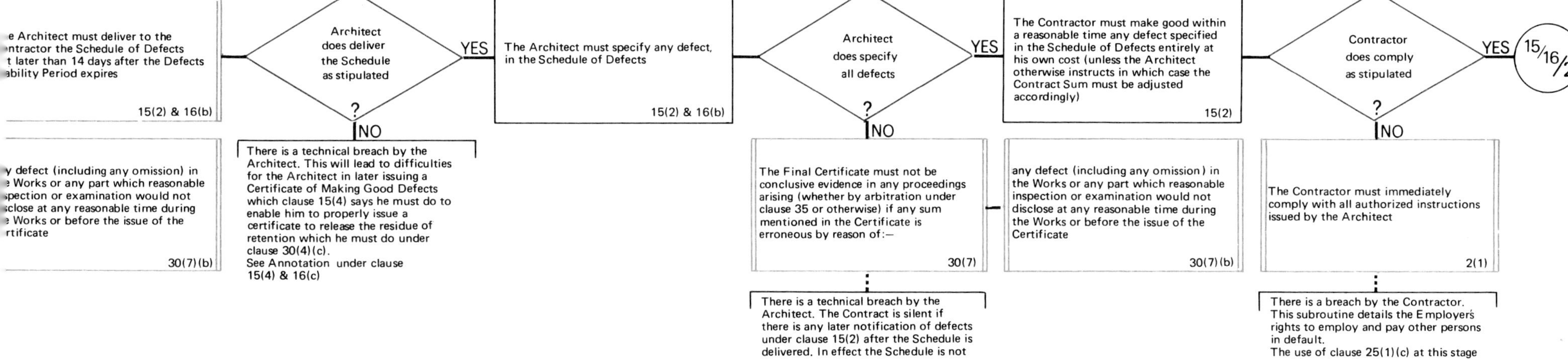

e Architect must deliver to the
ntractor the Schedule of Defects
t later than 14 days after the Defects
ability Period expires
15(2) & 16(b)
Architect
does deliver
the Schedule
as stipulated
?
YES
NO
The Architect must specify any defect, in the Schedule of Defects
15(2) & 16(b)
Architect
does specify
all defects
?
YES
NO
The Contractor must make good within a reasonable time any defect specified in the Schedule of Defects entirely at his own cost (unless the Architect otherwise instructs in which case the Contract Sum must be adjusted accordingly)
15(2)
Contractor
does comply
as stipulated
?
YES
NO
15/16/2
y defect (including any omission) in
e Works or any part which reasonable
spection or examination would not
sclose at any reasonable time during
e Works or before the issue of the
rtificate
30(7)(b)
There is a technical breach by the Architect. This will lead to difficulties for the Architect in later issuing a Certificate of Making Good Defects which clause 15(4) says he must do to enable him to properly issue a certificate to release the residue of retention which he must do under clause 30(4)(c).
See Annotation under clause 15(4) & 16(c)
The Final Certificate must not be conclusive evidence in any proceedings arising (whether by arbitration under clause 35 or otherwise) if any sum mentioned in the Certificate is erroneous by reason of:—
30(7)
any defect (including any omission) in the Works or any part which reasonable inspection or examination would not disclose at any reasonable time during the Works or before the issue of the Certificate
30(7)(b)
The Contractor must immediately comply with all authorized instructions issued by the Architect
2(1)
There is a technical breach by the Architect. The Contract is silent if there is any later notification of defects under clause 15(2) after the Schedule is delivered. In effect the Schedule is not final and absolute, it simply sets out formally the Contractor's task and not his liabilities. It also sets in motion procedures leading to clause 15(4) and the release of retention under clause 30(4)(c) and issue of Final Certificate. Even a Certificate of Completion of Making Good Defects is not conclusive since clause 30(8) states this. The Final Certificate is almost final and absolute except for latent defects, etc., under clause 30(7)(a) (b) and (c)
There is a breach by the Contractor. This subroutine details the Employer's rights to employ and pay other persons in default.
The use of clause 25(1)(c) at this stage would not be effective

Clauses 15 and 16 DEFECTS LIABILITIES, FINAL RELEASE OF RETENTIONS, AND REDUCTION OF DAMAGES ON SECTIONAL COMPLETION (2)

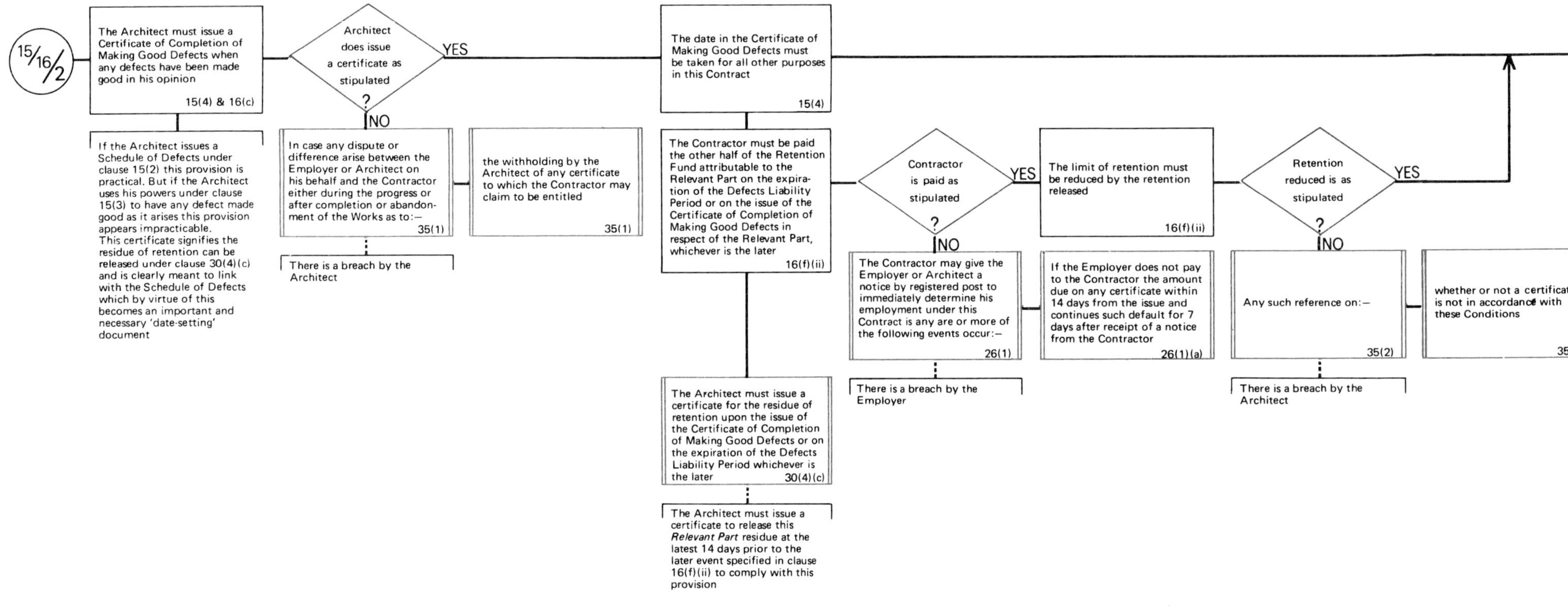

15/16/2
The Architect must issue a Certificate of Completion of Making Good Defects when any defects have been made good in his opinion 15(4) & 16(c)
If the Architect issues a Schedule of Defects under clause 15(2) this provision is practical. But if the Architect uses his powers under clause 15(3) to have any defect made good as it arises this provision appears impracticable. This certificate signifies the residue of retention can be released under clause 30(4)(c) and is clearly meant to link with the Schedule of Defects which by virtue of this becomes an important and necessary 'date-setting' document
Architect does issue a certificate as stipulated ?
YES
NO
In case any dispute or difference arise between the Employer or Architect on his behalf and the Contractor either during the progress or after completion or abandonment of the Works as to:– 35(1)
the withholding by the Architect of any certificate to which the Contractor may claim to be entitled 35(1)
There is a breach by the Architect
The date in the Certificate of Making Good Defects must be taken for all other purposes in this Contract 15(4)
The Contractor must be paid the other half of the Retention Fund attributable to the Relevant Part on the expiration of the Defects Liability Period or on the issue of the Certificate of Completion of Making Good Defects in respect of the Relevant Part, whichever is the later 16(f)(ii)
The Architect must issue a certificate for the residue of retention upon the issue of the Certificate of Completion of Making Good Defects or on the expiration of the Defects Liability Period whichever is the later 30(4)(c)
The Architect must issue a certificate to release this *Relevant Part* residue at the latest 14 days prior to the later event specified in clause 16(f)(ii) to comply with this provision
Contractor is paid as stipulated ?
YES
NO
The Contractor may give the Employer or Architect a notice by registered post to immediately determine his employment under this Contract is any are or more of the following events occur:– 26(1)
There is a breach by the Employer
The limit of retention must be reduced by the retention released 16(f)(ii)
If the Employer does not pay to the Contractor the amount due on any certificate within 14 days from the issue and continues such default for 7 days after receipt of a notice from the Contractor 26(1)(a)
Retention reduced is as stipulated ?
YES
NO
Any such reference on:– 35(2)
There is a breach by the Architect
whether or not a certificate is not in accordance with these Conditions 35(

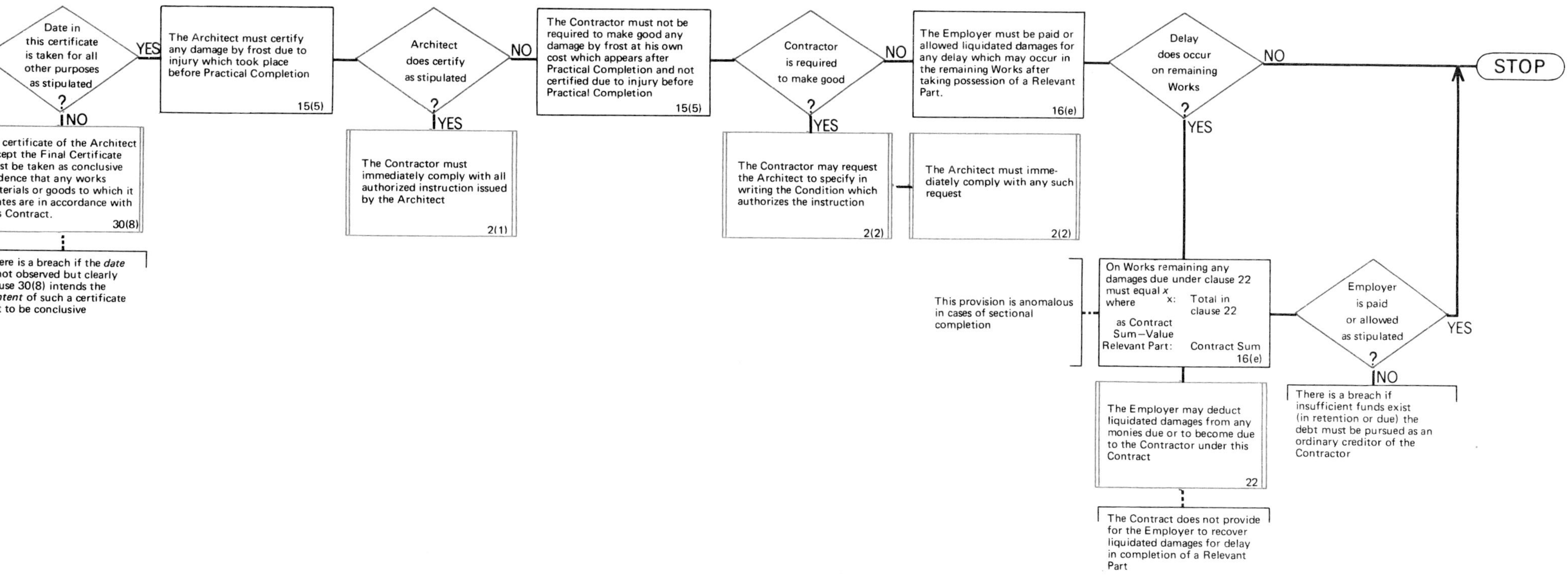

Date in this certificate is taken for all other purposes as stipulated ?
YES
NO
certificate of the Architect ept the Final Certificate st be taken as conclusive dence that any works terials or goods to which it ates are in accordance with Contract. 30(8)
ere is a breach if the *date* not observed but clearly use 30(8) intends the *ntent* of such a certificate to be conclusive
The Architect must certify any damage by frost due to injury which took place before Practical Completion 15(5)
Architect does certify as stipulated ?
NO
YES
The Contractor must immediately comply with all authorized instruction issued by the Architect 2(1)
The Contractor must not be required to make good any damage by frost at his own cost which appears after Practical Completion and not certified due to injury before Practical Completion 15(5)
Contractor is required to make good ?
NO
YES
The Contractor may request the Architect to specify in writing the Condition which authorizes the instruction 2(2)
The Architect must immediately comply with any such request 2(2)
The Employer must be paid or allowed liquidated damages for any delay which may occur in the remaining Works after taking possession of a Relevant Part. 16(e)
Delay does occur on remaining Works ?
NO
YES
STOP
This provision is anomalous in cases of sectional completion
On Works remaining any damages due under clause 22 must equal *x* where x: Total in clause 22 as Contract Sum–Value Relevant Part: Contract Sum 16(e)
The Employer may deduct liquidated damages from any monies due or to become due to the Contractor under this Contract 22
The Contract does not provide for the Employer to recover liquidated damages for delay in completion of a Relevant Part
Employer is paid or allowed as stipulated ?
YES
NO
There is a breach if insufficient funds exist (in retention or due) the debt must be pursued as an ordinary creditor of the Contractor

Clause 17 ASSIGNMENT OR SUBLETTING

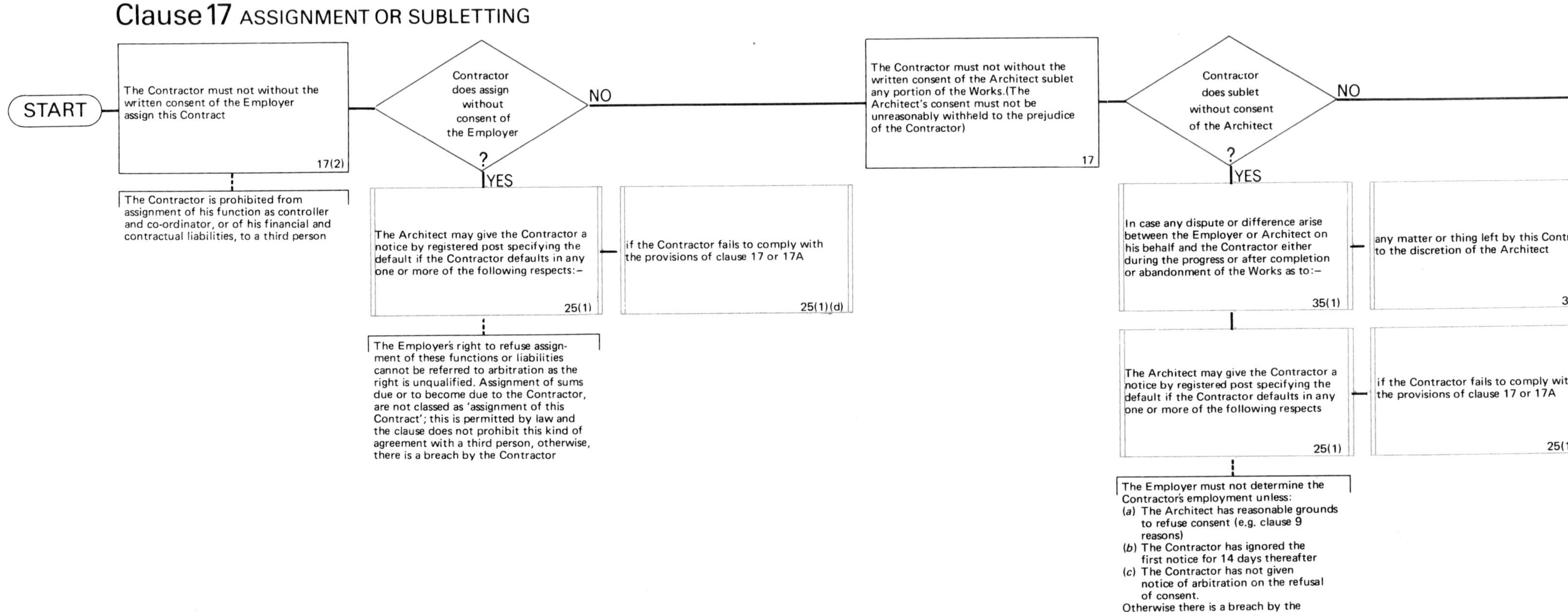
START
The Contractor must not without the written consent of the Employer assign this Contract
17(2)
The Contractor is prohibited from assignment of his function as controller and co-ordinator, or of his financial and contractual liabilities, to a third person
Contractor does assign without consent of the Employer ?
NO
YES
The Architect may give the Contractor a notice by registered post specifying the default if the Contractor defaults in any one or more of the following respects:–
25(1)
if the Contractor fails to comply with the provisions of clause 17 or 17A
25(1)(d)
The Employer's right to refuse assignment of these functions or liabilities cannot be referred to arbitration as the right is unqualified. Assignment of sums due or to become due to the Contractor, are not classed as 'assignment of this Contract'; this is permitted by law and the clause does not prohibit this kind of agreement with a third person, otherwise, there is a breach by the Contractor
The Contractor must not without the written consent of the Architect sublet any portion of the Works.(The Architect's consent must not be unreasonably withheld to the prejudice of the Contractor)
17
Contractor does sublet without consent of the Architect ?
NO
YES
In case any dispute or difference arise between the Employer or Architect on his behalf and the Contractor either during the progress or after completion or abandonment of the Works as to:–
35(1)
any matter or thing left by this Contra
to the discretion of the Architect
35
The Architect may give the Contractor a notice by registered post specifying the default if the Contractor defaults in any one or more of the following respects
25(1)
if the Contractor fails to comply with the provisions of clause 17 or 17A
25(1)
The Employer must not determine the Contractor's employment unless:
(a) The Architect has reasonable grounds to refuse consent (e.g. clause 9 reasons)
(b) The Contractor has ignored the first notice for 14 days thereafter
(c) The Contractor has not given notice of arbitration on the refusal of consent.
Otherwise there is a breach by the Contractor

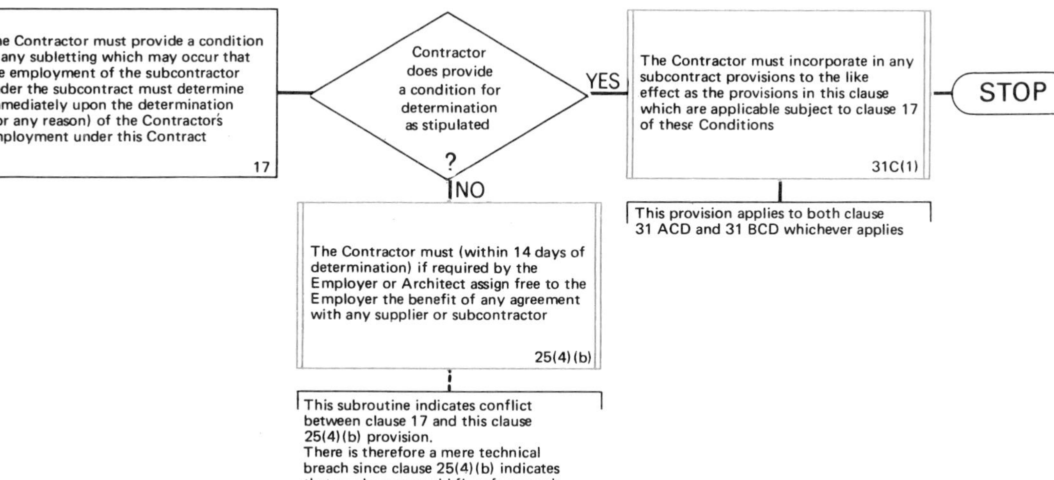
he Contractor must provide a condition
any subletting which may occur that
e employment of the subcontractor
der the subcontract must determine
mediately upon the determination
or any reason) of the Contractor's
nployment under this Contract
17
Contractor
does provide
a condition for
determination
as stipulated
?
YES
NO
The Contractor must incorporate in any
subcontract provisions to the like
effect as the provisions in this clause
which are applicable subject to clause 17
of these Conditions
31C(1)
STOP
This provision applies to both clause
31 ACD and 31 BCD whichever applies
The Contractor must (within 14 days of
determination) if required by the
Employer or Architect assign free to the
Employer the benefit of any agreement
with any supplier or subcontractor
25(4)(b)
This subroutine indicates conflict
between clause 17 and this clause
25(4)(b) provision.
There is therefore a mere technical
breach since clause 25(4)(b) indicates
that no damage could flow from such
default

Clause 17A FAIR WAGES AND CONDITIONS

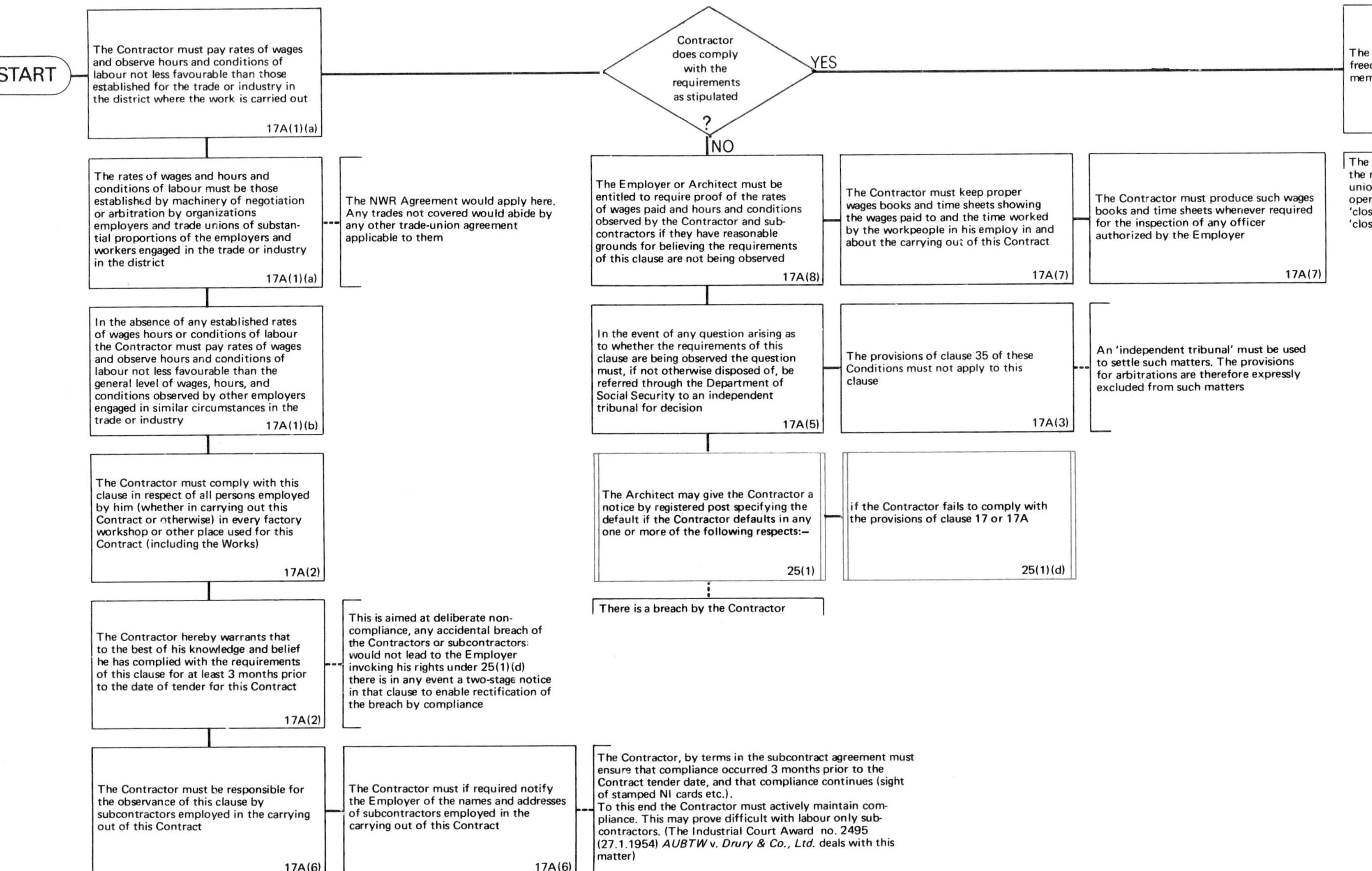
START
The Contractor must pay rates of wages and observe hours and conditions of labour not less favourable than those established for the trade or industry in the district where the work is carried out 17A(1)(a)
Contractor does comply with the requirements as stipulated ?
YES
NO
The Contractor must recognize the freedom of his workpeople to be members of trade unions 17
The Industrial Relations Act now exte the rights not to be a member of a trad union or for an 'Agency Shop' to be operated but not the imposition of a 'closed shop'. In certain circumstances 'closed shop' can be operated
The rates of wages and hours and conditions of labour must be those established by machinery of negotiation or arbitration by organizations employers and trade unions of substantial proportions of the employers and workers engaged in the trade or industry in the district 17A(1)(a)
The NWR Agreement would apply here. Any trades not covered would abide by any other trade-union agreement applicable to them
The Employer or Architect must be entitled to require proof of the rates of wages paid and hours and conditions observed by the Contractor and subcontractors if they have reasonable grounds for believing the requirements of this clause are not being observed 17A(8)
The Contractor must keep proper wages books and time sheets showing the wages paid to and the time worked by the workpeople in his employ in and about the carrying out of this Contract 17A(7)
The Contractor must produce such wages books and time sheets whenever required for the inspection of any officer authorized by the Employer 17A(7)
In the absence of any established rates of wages hours or conditions of labour the Contractor must pay rates of wages and observe hours and conditions of labour not less favourable than the general level of wages, hours, and conditions observed by other employers engaged in similar circumstances in the trade or industry 17A(1)(b)
In the event of any question arising as to whether the requirements of this clause are being observed the question must, if not otherwise disposed of, be referred through the Department of Social Security to an independent tribunal for decision 17A(5)
The provisions of clause 35 of these Conditions must not apply to this clause 17A(3)
An 'independent tribunal' must be used to settle such matters. The provisions for arbitrations are therefore expressly excluded from such matters
The Contractor must comply with this clause in respect of all persons employed by him (whether in carrying out this Contract or otherwise) in every factory workshop or other place used for this Contract (including the Works) 17A(2)
The Architect may give the Contractor a notice by registered post specifying the default if the Contractor defaults in any one or more of the following respects:– 25(1)
if the Contractor fails to comply with the provisions of clause 17 or 17A 25(1)(d)
There is a breach by the Contractor
The Contractor hereby warrants that to the best of his knowledge and belief he has complied with the requirements of this clause for at least 3 months prior to the date of tender for this Contract 17A(2)
This is aimed at deliberate non-compliance, any accidental breach of the Contractors or subcontractors would not lead to the Employer invoking his rights under 25(1)(d) there is in any event a two-stage notice in that clause to enable rectification of the breach by compliance
The Contractor must be responsible for the observance of this clause by subcontractors employed in the carrying out of this Contract 17A(6)
The Contractor must if required notify the Employer of the names and addresses of subcontractors employed in the carrying out of this Contract 17A(6)
The Contractor, by terms in the subcontract agreement must ensure that compliance occurred 3 months prior to the Contract tender date, and that compliance continues (sight of stamped NI cards etc.).
To this end the Contractor must actively maintain compliance. This may prove difficult with labour only subcontractors. (The Industrial Court Award no. 2495 (27.1.1954) AUBTW v. Drury & Co., Ltd. deals with this matter)

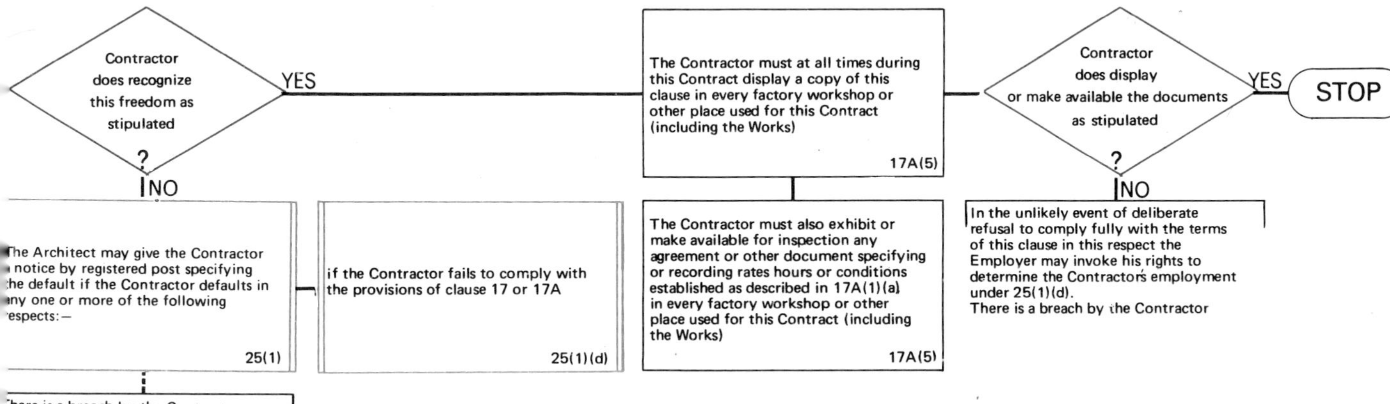

Contractor
does recognize
this freedom as
stipulated
?
YES
NO
The Contractor must at all times during this Contract display a copy of this clause in every factory workshop or other place used for this Contract (including the Works)
17A(5)
Contractor
does display
or make available the documents
as stipulated
?
YES
STOP
NO
The Architect may give the Contractor a notice by registered post specifying the default if the Contractor defaults in any one or more of the following respects:—
25(1)
if the Contractor fails to comply with the provisions of clause 17 or 17A
25(1)(d)
The Contractor must also exhibit or make available for inspection any agreement or other document specifying or recording rates hours or conditions established as described in 17A(1)(a) in every factory workshop or other place used for this Contract (including the Works)
17A(5)
In the unlikely event of deliberate refusal to comply fully with the terms of this clause in this respect the Employer may invoke his rights to determine the Contractor's employment under 25(1)(d).
There is a breach by the Contractor
There is a breach by the Contractor

Clause 18 LIABILITIES AND INDEMNITIES

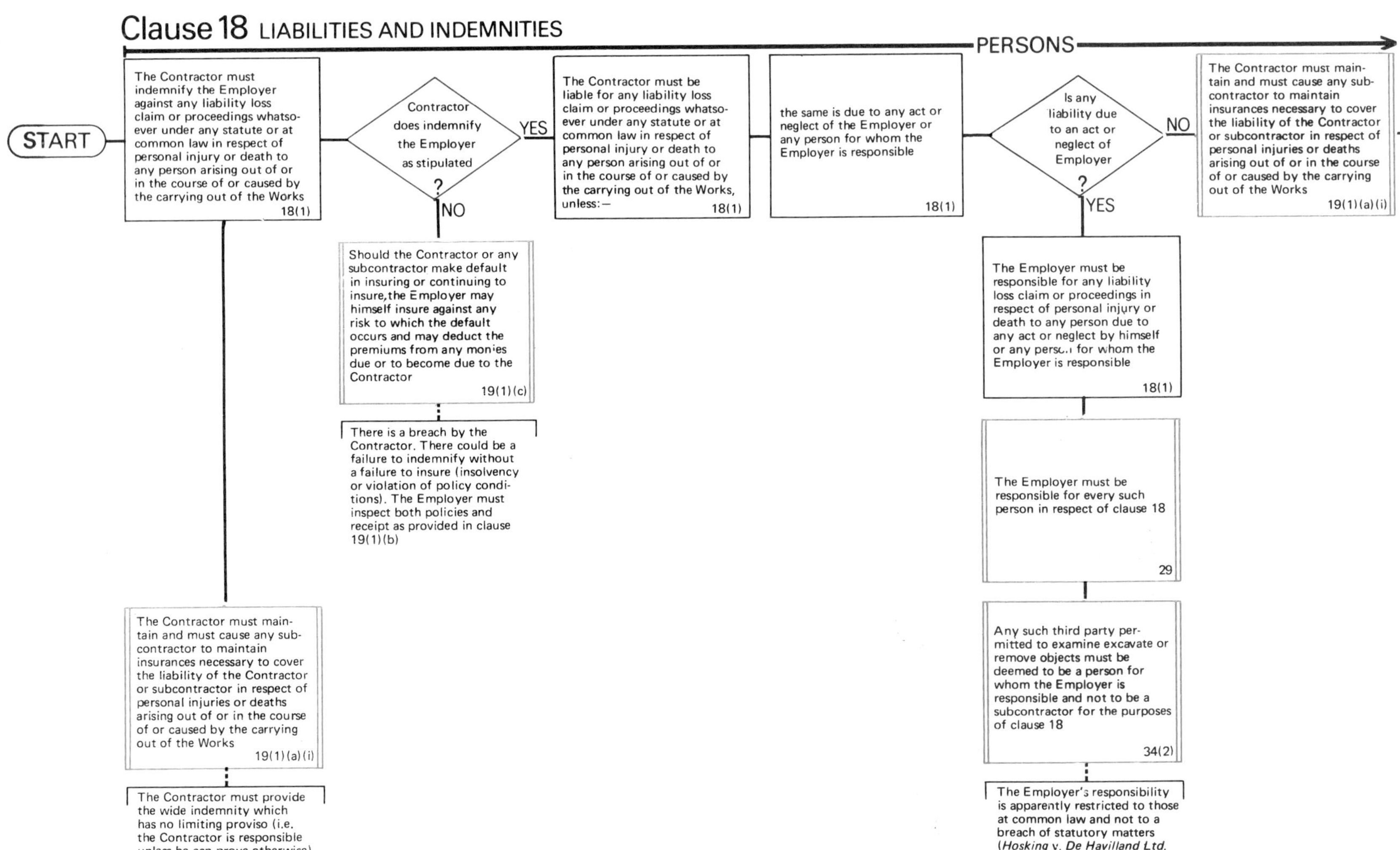
PERSONS
START
The Contractor must indemnify the Employer against any liability loss claim or proceedings whatsoever under any statute or at common law in respect of personal injury or death to any person arising out of or in the course of or caused by the carrying out of the Works 18(1)
Contractor does indemnify the Employer as stipulated ?
YES
NO
The Contractor must be liable for any liability loss claim or proceedings whatsoever under any statute or at common law in respect of personal injury or death to any person arising out of or in the course of or caused by the carrying out of the Works, unless:— 18(1)
the same is due to any act or neglect of the Employer or any person for whom the Employer is responsible 18(1)
Is any liability due to an act or neglect of Employer ?
NO
YES
The Contractor must maintain and must cause any subcontractor to maintain insurances necessary to cover the liability of the Contractor or subcontractor in respect of personal injuries or deaths arising out of or in the course of or caused by the carrying out of the Works 19(1)(a)(i)
The Contractor must indemni the Employer against any expense liability loss claim or proceedings in respect of any damage whatsoever to any property real or personal that arises out of or in the course or by reason of carrying out the Works, provided always:– 18(
Should the Contractor or any subcontractor make default in insuring or continuing to insure, the Employer may himself insure against any risk to which the default occurs and may deduct the premiums from any monies due or to become due to the Contractor 19(1)(c)
There is a breach by the Contractor. There could be a failure to indemnify without a failure to insure (insolvency or violation of policy conditions). The Employer must inspect both policies and receipt as provided in clause 19(1)(b)
The Employer must be responsible for any liability loss claim or proceedings in respect of personal injury or death to any person due to any act or neglect by himself or any person for whom the Employer is responsible 18(1)
The Employer must be responsible for every such person in respect of clause 18 29
Any such third party permitted to examine excavate or remove objects must be deemed to be a person for whom the Employer is responsible and not to be a subcontractor for the purposes of clause 18 34(2)
The Employer's responsibility is apparently restricted to those at common law and not to a breach of statutory matters (*Hosking* v. *De Havilland Ltd.* [1949] 1 AER 540)
The Contractor must maintain and must cause any subcontractor to maintain insurances necessary to cover the liability of the Contractor or subcontractor in respect of personal injuries or deaths arising out of or in the course of or caused by the carrying out of the Works 19(1)(a)(i)
The Contractor must provide the wide indemnity which has no limiting proviso (i.e. the Contractor is responsible unless he can prove otherwise)
The Contractor must maintain and cause any subcontractor to maintain such insurances as may be specifically required by the Contract Bills in respect of damage to property real or personal arising out of or in the course of or by reason of carrying out the Works, provided always:— 19(1)(a)
The Contractor's indemnity here is less wide than under clause 18(1) by virtue of the proviso and the optional clause 20[B] or [C] (i.e. the Contractor will assume responsibility providing that responsibility is clearly his)

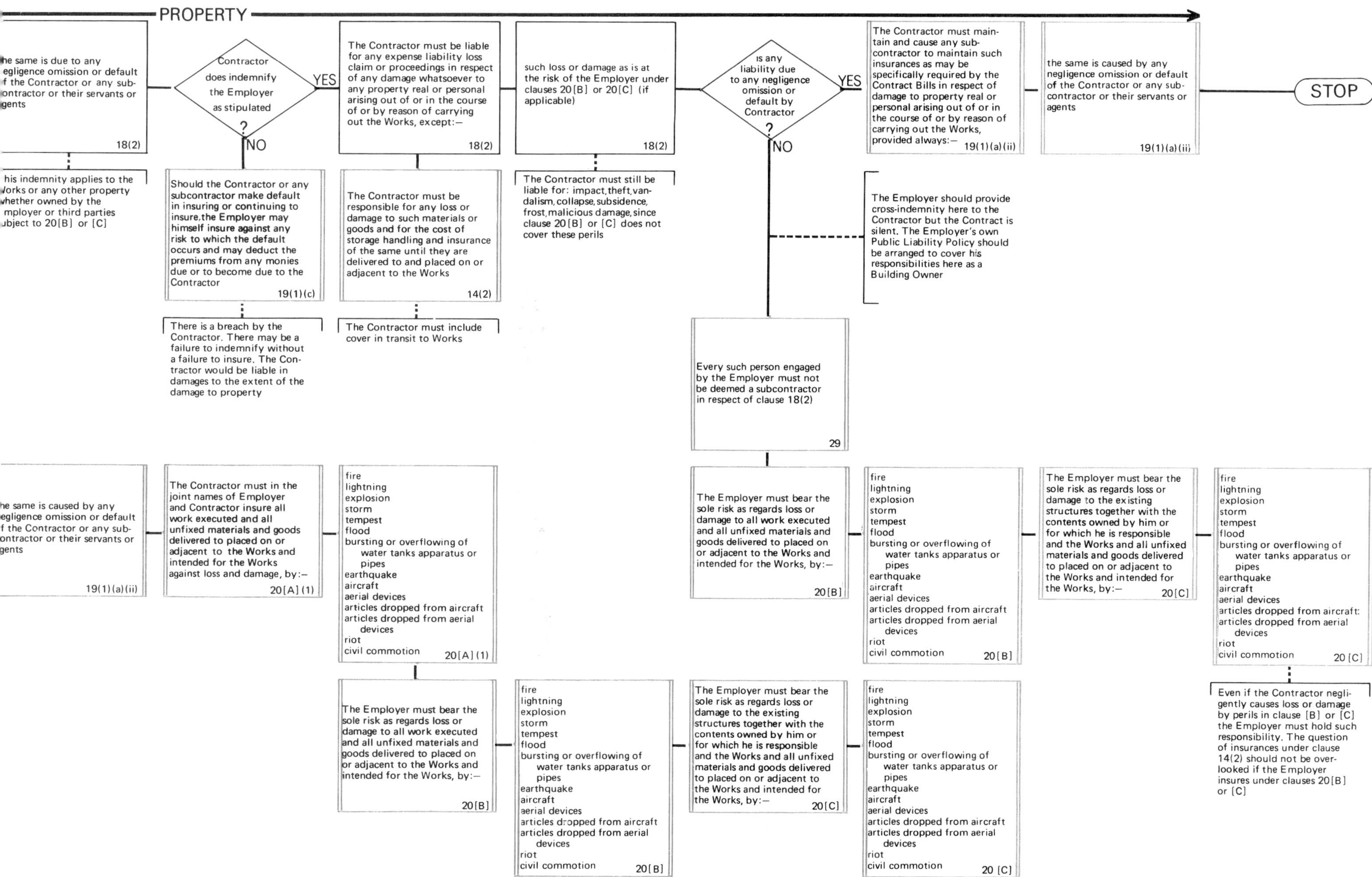
PROPERTY
he same is due to any egligence omission or default f the Contractor or any sub-ontractor or their servants or gents 18(2)
his indemnity applies to the Vorks or any other property whether owned by the mployer or third parties ubject to 20[B] or [C]
Contractor does indemnify the Employer as stipulated ?
YES
NO
Should the Contractor or any subcontractor make default in insuring or continuing to insure, the Employer may himself insure against any risk to which the default occurs and may deduct the premiums from any monies due or to become due to the Contractor 19(1)(c)
There is a breach by the Contractor. There may be a failure to indemnify without a failure to insure. The Contractor would be liable in damages to the extent of the damage to property
The Contractor must be liable for any expense liability loss claim or proceedings in respect of any damage whatsoever to any property real or personal arising out of or in the course of or by reason of carrying out the Works, except:— 18(2)
The Contractor must be responsible for any loss or damage to such materials or goods and for the cost of storage handling and insurance of the same until they are delivered to and placed on or adjacent to the Works 14(2)
The Contractor must include cover in transit to Works
such loss or damage as is at the risk of the Employer under clauses 20[B] or 20[C] (if applicable) 18(2)
The Contractor must still be liable for: impact, theft, vandalism, collapse, subsidence, frost, malicious damage, since clause 20[B] or [C] does not cover these perils
Is any liability due to any negligence omission or default by Contractor ?
YES
NO
The Employer should provide cross-indemnity here to the Contractor but the Contract is silent. The Employer's own Public Liability Policy should be arranged to cover his responsibilities here as a Building Owner
Every such person engaged by the Employer must not be deemed a subcontractor in respect of clause 18(2) 29
The Contractor must maintain and cause any subcontractor to maintain such insurances as may be specifically required by the Contract Bills in respect of damage to property real or personal arising out of or in the course of or by reason of carrying out the Works, provided always:— 19(1)(a)(ii)
the same is caused by any negligence omission or default of the Contractor or any sub-contractor or their servants or agents 19(1)(a)(ii)
STOP
he same is caused by any egligence omission or default f the Contractor or any sub-ontractor or their servants or gents 19(1)(a)(ii)
The Contractor must in the joint names of Employer and Contractor insure all work executed and all unfixed materials and goods delivered to placed on or adjacent to the Works and intended for the Works against loss and damage, by:— 20[A](1)
fire lightning explosion storm tempest flood bursting or overflowing of water tanks apparatus or pipes earthquake aircraft aerial devices articles dropped from aircraft articles dropped from aerial devices riot civil commotion 20[A](1)
The Employer must bear the sole risk as regards loss or damage to all work executed and all unfixed materials and goods delivered to placed on or adjacent to the Works and intended for the Works, by:— 20[B]
fire lightning explosion storm tempest flood bursting or overflowing of water tanks apparatus or pipes earthquake aircraft aerial devices articles dropped from aircraft articles dropped from aerial devices riot civil commotion 20[B]
The Employer must bear the sole risk as regards loss or damage to the existing structures together with the contents owned by him or for which he is responsible and the Works and all unfixed materials and goods delivered to placed on or adjacent to the Works and intended for the Works, by:— 20[C]
fire lightning explosion storm tempest flood bursting or overflowing of water tanks apparatus or pipes earthquake aircraft aerial devices articles dropped from aircraft articles dropped from aerial devices riot civil commotion 20 [C]
The Employer must bear the sole risk as regards loss or damage to all work executed and all unfixed materials and goods delivered to placed on or adjacent to the Works and intended for the Works, by:— 20[B]
fire lightning explosion storm tempest flood bursting or overflowing of water tanks apparatus or pipes earthquake aircraft aerial devices articles dropped from aircraft articles dropped from aerial devices riot civil commotion 20[B]
The Employer must bear the sole risk as regards loss or damage to the existing structures together with the contents owned by him or for which he is responsible and the Works and all unfixed materials and goods delivered to placed on or adjacent to the Works and intended for the Works, by:— 20[C]
fire lightning explosion storm tempest flood bursting or overflowing of water tanks apparatus or pipes earthquake aircraft aerial devices articles dropped from aircraft articles dropped from aerial devices riot civil commotion 20 [C]
Even if the Contractor negligently causes loss or damage by perils in clause [B] or [C] the Employer must hold such responsibility. The question of insurances under clause 14(2) should not be overlooked if the Employer insures under clauses 20[B] or [C]

Clause 19 INSURANCES

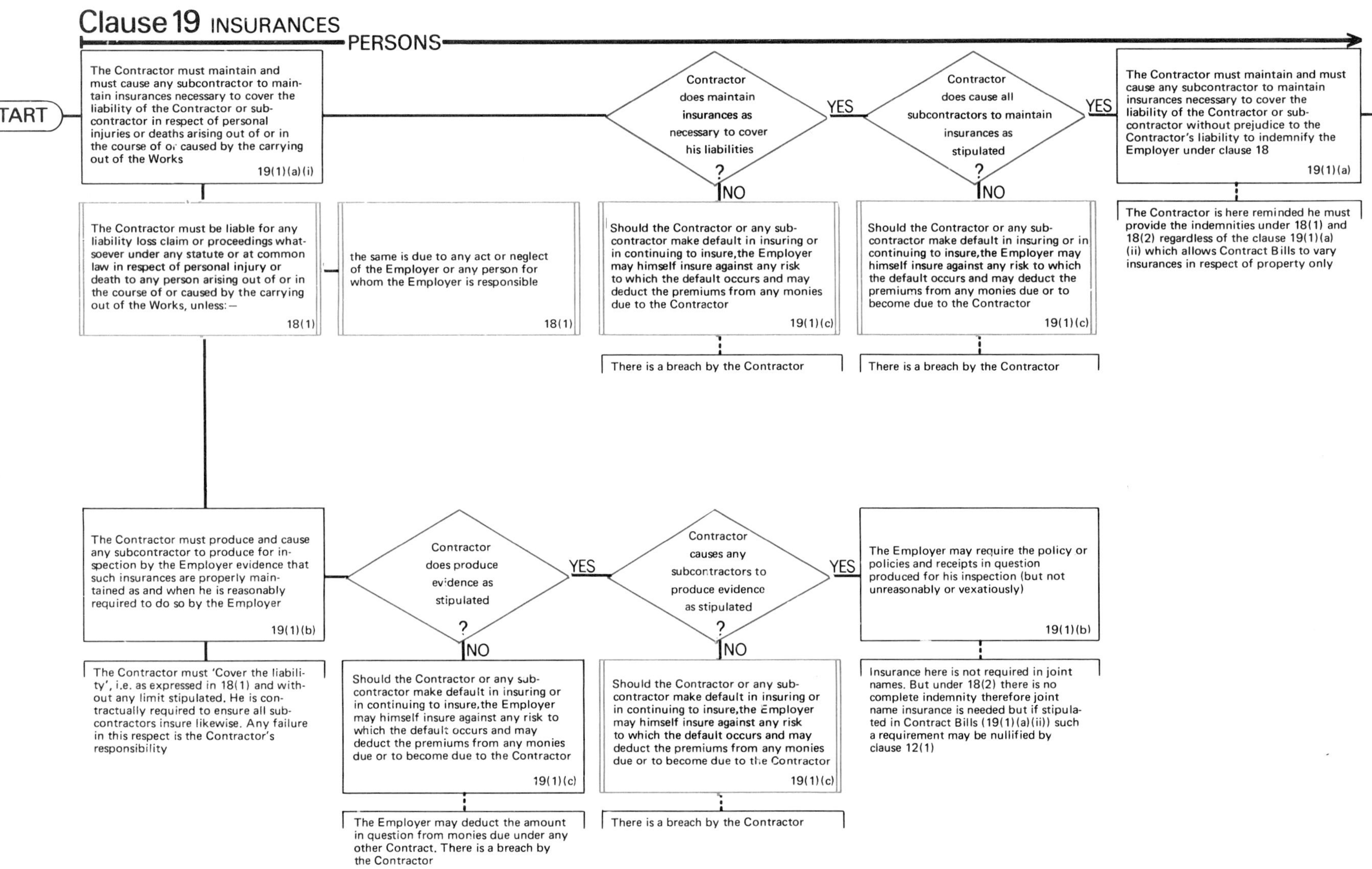
PERSONS
START
The Contractor must maintain and must cause any subcontractor to maintain insurances necessary to cover the liability of the Contractor or subcontractor in respect of personal injuries or deaths arising out of or in the course of or caused by the carrying out of the Works 19(1)(a)(i)
Contractor does maintain insurances as necessary to cover his liabilities ?
YES
Contractor does cause all subcontractors to maintain insurances as stipulated ?
YES
The Contractor must maintain and must cause any subcontractor to maintain insurances necessary to cover the liability of the Contractor or subcontractor without prejudice to the Contractor's liability to indemnify the Employer under clause 18 19(1)(a)
The Contractor is here reminded he must provide the indemnities under 18(1) and 18(2) regardless of the clause 19(1)(a)(ii) which allows Contract Bills to vary insurances in respect of property only
The Contractor must be liable for any liability loss claim or proceedings whatsoever under any statute or at common law in respect of personal injury or death to any person arising out of or in the course of or caused by the carrying out of the Works, unless:— 18(1)
the same is due to any act or neglect of the Employer or any person for whom the Employer is responsible 18(1)
NO
Should the Contractor or any subcontractor make default in insuring or in continuing to insure, the Employer may himself insure against any risk to which the default occurs and may deduct the premiums from any monies due to the Contractor 19(1)(c)
There is a breach by the Contractor
NO
Should the Contractor or any subcontractor make default in insuring or in continuing to insure, the Employer may himself insure against any risk to which the default occurs and may deduct the premiums from any monies due or to become due to the Contractor 19(1)(c)
There is a breach by the Contractor
The Contractor must produce and cause any subcontractor to produce for inspection by the Employer evidence that such insurances are properly maintained as and when he is reasonably required to do so by the Employer 19(1)(b)
Contractor does produce evidence as stipulated ?
YES
Contractor causes any subcontractors to produce evidence as stipulated ?
YES
The Employer may require the policy or policies and receipts in question produced for his inspection (but not unreasonably or vexatiously) 19(1)(b)
Insurance here is not required in joint names. But under 18(2) there is no complete indemnity therefore joint name insurance is needed but if stipulated in Contract Bills (19(1)(a)(ii)) such a requirement may be nullified by clause 12(1)
The Contractor must 'Cover the liability', i.e. as expressed in 18(1) and without any limit stipulated. He is contractually required to ensure all subcontractors insure likewise. Any failure in this respect is the Contractor's responsibility
NO
Should the Contractor or any subcontractor make default in insuring or in continuing to insure, the Employer may himself insure against any risk to which the default occurs and may deduct the premiums from any monies due or to become due to the Contractor 19(1)(c)
The Employer may deduct the amount in question from monies due under any other Contract. There is a breach by the Contractor
NO
Should the Contractor or any subcontractor make default in insuring or in continuing to insure, the Employer may himself insure against any risk to which the default occurs and may deduct the premiums from any monies due or to become due to the Contractor 19(1)(c)
There is a breach by the Contractor

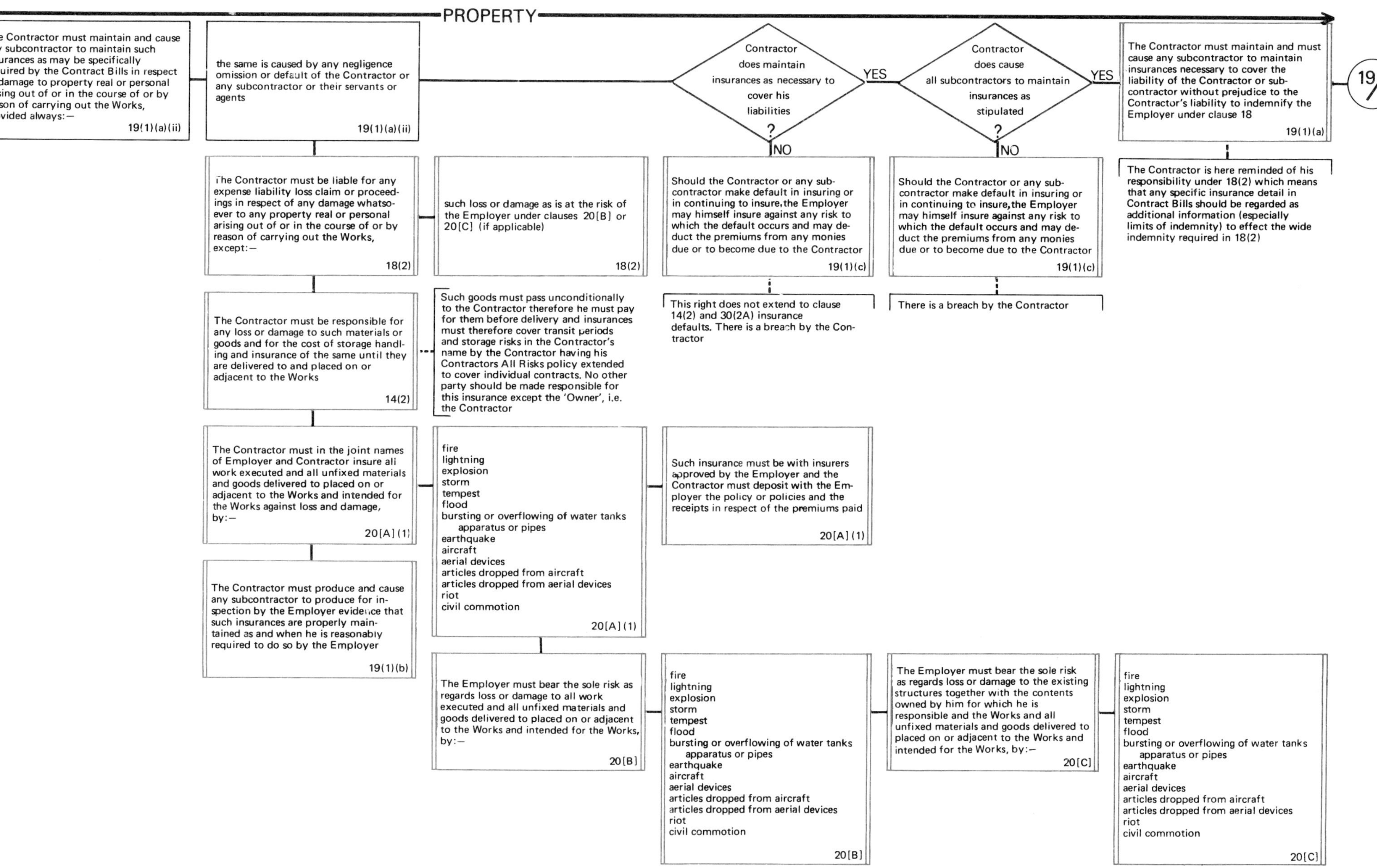

PROPERTY
’he Contractor must maintain and cause ny subcontractor to maintain such nsurances as may be specifically equired by the Contract Bills in respect f damage to property real or personal rising out of or in the course of or by eason of carrying out the Works, rovided always:— 19(1)(a)(ii)
the same is caused by any negligence omission or default of the Contractor or any subcontractor or their servants or agents 19(1)(a)(ii)
Contractor does maintain insurances as necessary to cover his liabilities ?
YES
NO
Contractor does cause all subcontractors to maintain insurances as stipulated ?
YES
NO
The Contractor must maintain and must cause any subcontractor to maintain insurances necessary to cover the liability of the Contractor or sub-contractor without prejudice to the Contractor's liability to indemnify the Employer under clause 18 19(1)(a)
19/1
The Contractor must be liable for any expense liability loss claim or proceedings in respect of any damage whatsoever to any property real or personal arising out of or in the course of or by reason of carrying out the Works, except:— 18(2)
such loss or damage as is at the risk of the Employer under clauses 20[B] or 20[C] (if applicable) 18(2)
Should the Contractor or any sub-contractor make default in insuring or in continuing to insure, the Employer may himself insure against any risk to which the default occurs and may deduct the premiums from any monies due or to become due to the Contractor 19(1)(c)
Should the Contractor or any sub-contractor make default in insuring or in continuing to insure, the Employer may himself insure against any risk to which the default occurs and may deduct the premiums from any monies due or to become due to the Contractor 19(1)(c)
The Contractor is here reminded of his responsibility under 18(2) which means that any specific insurance detail in Contract Bills should be regarded as additional information (especially limits of indemnity) to effect the wide indemnity required in 18(2)
This right does not extend to clause 14(2) and 30(2A) insurance defaults. There is a breach by the Contractor
There is a breach by the Contractor
The Contractor must be responsible for any loss or damage to such materials or goods and for the cost of storage handling and insurance of the same until they are delivered to and placed on or adjacent to the Works 14(2)
Such goods must pass unconditionally to the Contractor therefore he must pay for them before delivery and insurances must therefore cover transit periods and storage risks in the Contractor's name by the Contractor having his Contractors All Risks policy extended to cover individual contracts. No other party should be made responsible for this insurance except the 'Owner', i.e. the Contractor
The Contractor must in the joint names of Employer and Contractor insure all work executed and all unfixed materials and goods delivered to placed on or adjacent to the Works and intended for the Works against loss and damage, by:— 20[A](1)
fire
lightning
explosion
storm
tempest
flood
bursting or overflowing of water tanks apparatus or pipes
earthquake
aircraft
aerial devices
articles dropped from aircraft
articles dropped from aerial devices
riot
civil commotion
20[A](1)
Such insurance must be with insurers approved by the Employer and the Contractor must deposit with the Employer the policy or policies and the receipts in respect of the premiums paid 20[A](1)
The Contractor must produce and cause any subcontractor to produce for inspection by the Employer evidence that such insurances are properly maintained as and when he is reasonably required to do so by the Employer 19(1)(b)
The Employer must bear the sole risk as regards loss or damage to all work executed and all unfixed materials and goods delivered to placed on or adjacent to the Works and intended for the Works, by:— 20[B]
fire
lightning
explosion
storm
tempest
flood
bursting or overflowing of water tanks apparatus or pipes
earthquake
aircraft
aerial devices
articles dropped from aircraft
articles dropped from aerial devices
riot
civil commotion
20[B]
The Employer must bear the sole risk as regards loss or damage to the existing structures together with the contents owned by him for which he is responsible and the Works and all unfixed materials and goods delivered to placed on or adjacent to the Works and intended for the Works, by:— 20[C]
fire
lightning
explosion
storm
tempest
flood
bursting or overflowing of water tanks apparatus or pipes
earthquake
aircraft
aerial devices
articles dropped from aircraft
articles dropped from aerial devices
riot
civil commotion
20[C]

Clause 19 SPECIAL INSURANCE FOR THE EMPLOYER

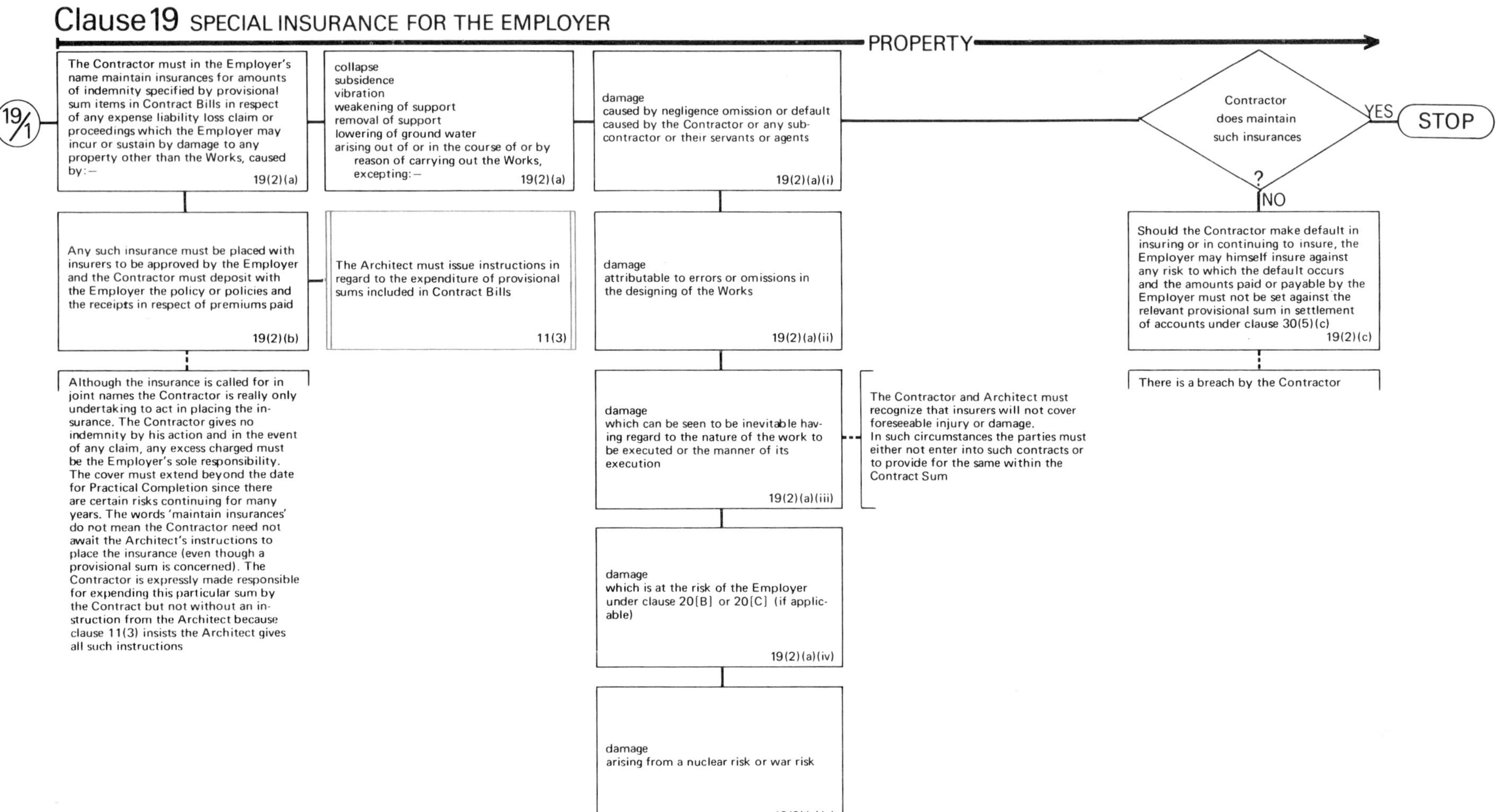

PROPERTY
19/1
The Contractor must in the Employer's name maintain insurances for amounts of indemnity specified by provisional sum items in Contract Bills in respect of any expense liability loss claim or proceedings which the Employer may incur or sustain by damage to any property other than the Works, caused by:— 19(2)(a)
collapse
subsidence
vibration
weakening of support
removal of support
lowering of ground water
arising out of or in the course of or by reason of carrying out the Works, excepting:— 19(2)(a)
damage caused by negligence omission or default caused by the Contractor or any sub-contractor or their servants or agents 19(2)(a)(i)
Contractor does maintain such insurances ?
YES
STOP
NO
Any such insurance must be placed with insurers to be approved by the Employer and the Contractor must deposit with the Employer the policy or policies and the receipts in respect of premiums paid 19(2)(b)
The Architect must issue instructions in regard to the expenditure of provisional sums included in Contract Bills 11(3)
damage attributable to errors or omissions in the designing of the Works 19(2)(a)(ii)
Should the Contractor make default in insuring or in continuing to insure, the Employer may himself insure against any risk to which the default occurs and the amounts paid or payable by the Employer must not be set against the relevant provisional sum in settlement of accounts under clause 30(5)(c) 19(2)(c)
Although the insurance is called for in joint names the Contractor is really only undertaking to act in placing the insurance. The Contractor gives no indemnity by his action and in the event of any claim, any excess charged must be the Employer's sole responsibility. The cover must extend beyond the date for Practical Completion since there are certain risks continuing for many years. The words 'maintain insurances' do not mean the Contractor need not await the Architect's instructions to place the insurance (even though a provisional sum is concerned). The Contractor is expressly made responsible for expending this particular sum by the Contract but not without an instruction from the Architect because clause 11(3) insists the Architect gives all such instructions
damage which can be seen to be inevitable having regard to the nature of the work to be executed or the manner of its execution 19(2)(a)(iii)
The Contractor and Architect must recognize that insurers will not cover foreseeable injury or damage. In such circumstances the parties must either not enter into such contracts or to provide for the same within the Contract Sum
There is a breach by the Contractor
damage which is at the risk of the Employer under clause 20[B] or 20[C] (if applicable) 19(2)(a)(iv)
damage arising from a nuclear risk or war risk 19(2)(a)(v)

Clause 20 [A] INSURANCES BY CONTRACTOR (OPTIONAL)

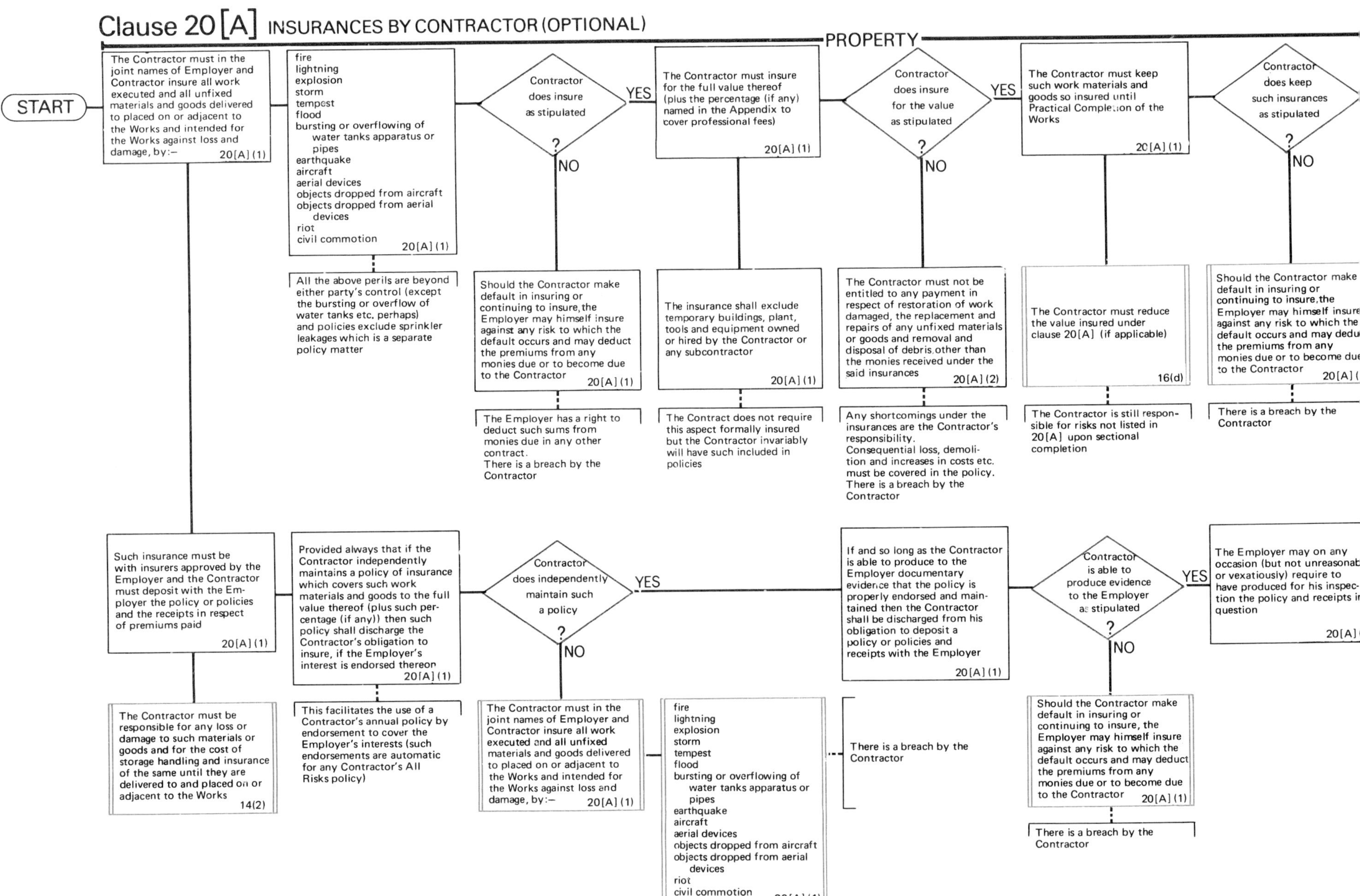

PROPERTY
START
The Contractor must in the joint names of Employer and Contractor insure all work executed and all unfixed materials and goods delivered to placed on or adjacent to the Works and intended for the Works against loss and damage, by:– 20[A](1)
fire
lightning
explosion
storm
tempest
flood
bursting or overflowing of water tanks apparatus or pipes
earthquake
aircraft
aerial devices
objects dropped from aircraft
objects dropped from aerial devices
riot
civil commotion 20[A](1)
All the above perils are beyond either party's control (except the bursting or overflow of water tanks etc. perhaps) and policies exclude sprinkler leakages which is a separate policy matter
Contractor does insure as stipulated ?
YES
NO
Should the Contractor make default in insuring or continuing to insure, the Employer may himself insure against any risk to which the default occurs and may deduct the premiums from any monies due or to become due to the Contractor 20[A](1)
The Employer has a right to deduct such sums from monies due in any other contract. There is a breach by the Contractor
The Contractor must insure for the full value thereof (plus the percentage (if any) named in the Appendix to cover professional fees) 20[A](1)
The insurance shall exclude temporary buildings, plant, tools and equipment owned or hired by the Contractor or any subcontractor 20[A](1)
The Contract does not require this aspect formally insured but the Contractor invariably will have such included in policies
Contractor does insure for the value as stipulated ?
YES
NO
The Contractor must not be entitled to any payment in respect of restoration of work damaged, the replacement and repairs of any unfixed materials or goods and removal and disposal of debris other than the monies received under the said insurances 20[A](2)
Any shortcomings under the insurances are the Contractor's responsibility. Consequential loss, demolition and increases in costs etc. must be covered in the policy. There is a breach by the Contractor
The Contractor must keep such work materials and goods so insured until Practical Completion of the Works 20[A](1)
The Contractor must reduce the value insured under clause 20[A] (if applicable) 16(d)
The Contractor is still responsible for risks not listed in 20[A] upon sectional completion
Contractor does keep such insurances as stipulated ?
NO
Should the Contractor make default in insuring or continuing to insure, the Employer may himself insure against any risk to which the default occurs and may dedu… the premiums from any monies due or to become due to the Contractor 20[A](
There is a breach by the Contractor
Such insurance must be with insurers approved by the Employer and the Contractor must deposit with the Employer the policy or policies and the receipts in respect of premiums paid 20[A](1)
The Contractor must be responsible for any loss or damage to such materials or goods and for the cost of storage handling and insurance of the same until they are delivered to and placed on or adjacent to the Works 14(2)
Provided always that if the Contractor independently maintains a policy of insurance which covers such work materials and goods to the full value thereof (plus such percentage (if any)) then such policy shall discharge the Contractor's obligation to insure, if the Employer's interest is endorsed thereon 20[A](1)
This facilitates the use of a Contractor's annual policy by endorsement to cover the Employer's interests (such endorsements are automatic for any Contractor's All Risks policy)
Contractor does independently maintain such a policy ?
YES
NO
The Contractor must in the joint names of Employer and Contractor insure all work executed and all unfixed materials and goods delivered to placed on or adjacent to the Works and intended for the Works against loss and damage, by:– 20[A](1)
fire
lightning
explosion
storm
tempest
flood
bursting or overflowing of water tanks apparatus or pipes
earthquake
aircraft
aerial devices
objects dropped from aircraft
objects dropped from aerial devices
riot
civil commotion 20[A](1)
There is a breach by the Contractor
If and so long as the Contractor is able to produce to the Employer documentary evidence that the policy is properly endorsed and maintained then the Contractor shall be discharged from his obligation to deposit a policy or policies and receipts with the Employer 20[A](1)
Contractor is able to produce evidence to the Employer as stipulated ?
YES
NO
Should the Contractor make default in insuring or continuing to insure, the Employer may himself insure against any risk to which the default occurs and may deduct the premiums from any monies due or to become due to the Contractor 20[A](1)
There is a breach by the Contractor
The Employer may on any occasion (but not unreasonab… or vexatiously) require to have produced for his inspection the policy and receipts in question 20[A]

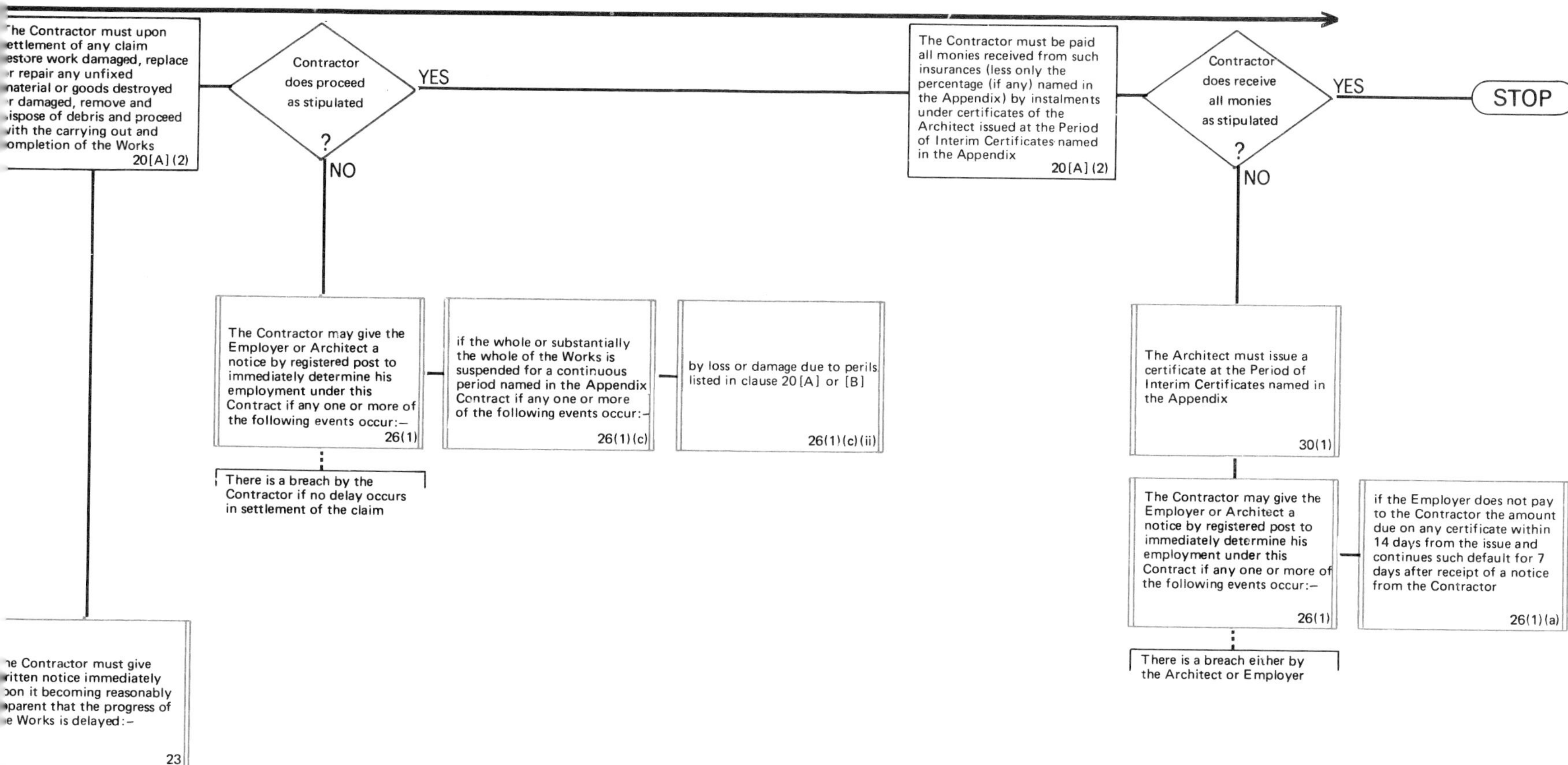

'he Contractor must upon settlement of any claim estore work damaged, replace r repair any unfixed material or goods destroyed r damaged, remove and dispose of debris and proceed with the carrying out and completion of the Works 20[A](2)
Contractor does proceed as stipulated ?
YES
NO
The Contractor must be paid all monies received from such insurances (less only the percentage (if any) named in the Appendix) by instalments under certificates of the Architect issued at the Period of Interim Certificates named in the Appendix 20[A](2)
Contractor does receive all monies as stipulated ?
YES
NO
STOP
The Contractor may give the Employer or Architect a notice by registered post to immediately determine his employment under this Contract if any one or more of the following events occur:– 26(1)
if the whole or substantially the whole of the Works is suspended for a continuous period named in the Appendix Contract if any one or more of the following events occur:– 26(1)(c)
by loss or damage due to perils listed in clause 20[A] or [B] 26(1)(c)(ii)
There is a breach by the Contractor if no delay occurs in settlement of the claim
The Architect must issue a certificate at the Period of Interim Certificates named in the Appendix 30(1)
The Contractor may give the Employer or Architect a notice by registered post to immediately determine his employment under this Contract if any one or more of the following events occur:– 26(1)
if the Employer does not pay to the Contractor the amount due on any certificate within 14 days from the issue and continues such default for 7 days after receipt of a notice from the Contractor 26(1)(a)
There is a breach either by the Architect or Employer
ne Contractor must give written notice immediately pon it becoming reasonably pparent that the progress of e Works is delayed:– 23
e Contractor must always e this notice even if gligence on his part caused contributed to the loss or mage since clause 23 calls on the Contractor to nstantly endeavour to prevent ay also to do all that the chitect may require to ercome the delay

Clause 20[B] INSURANCES BY EMPLOYER (OPTIONAL) PROPERTY

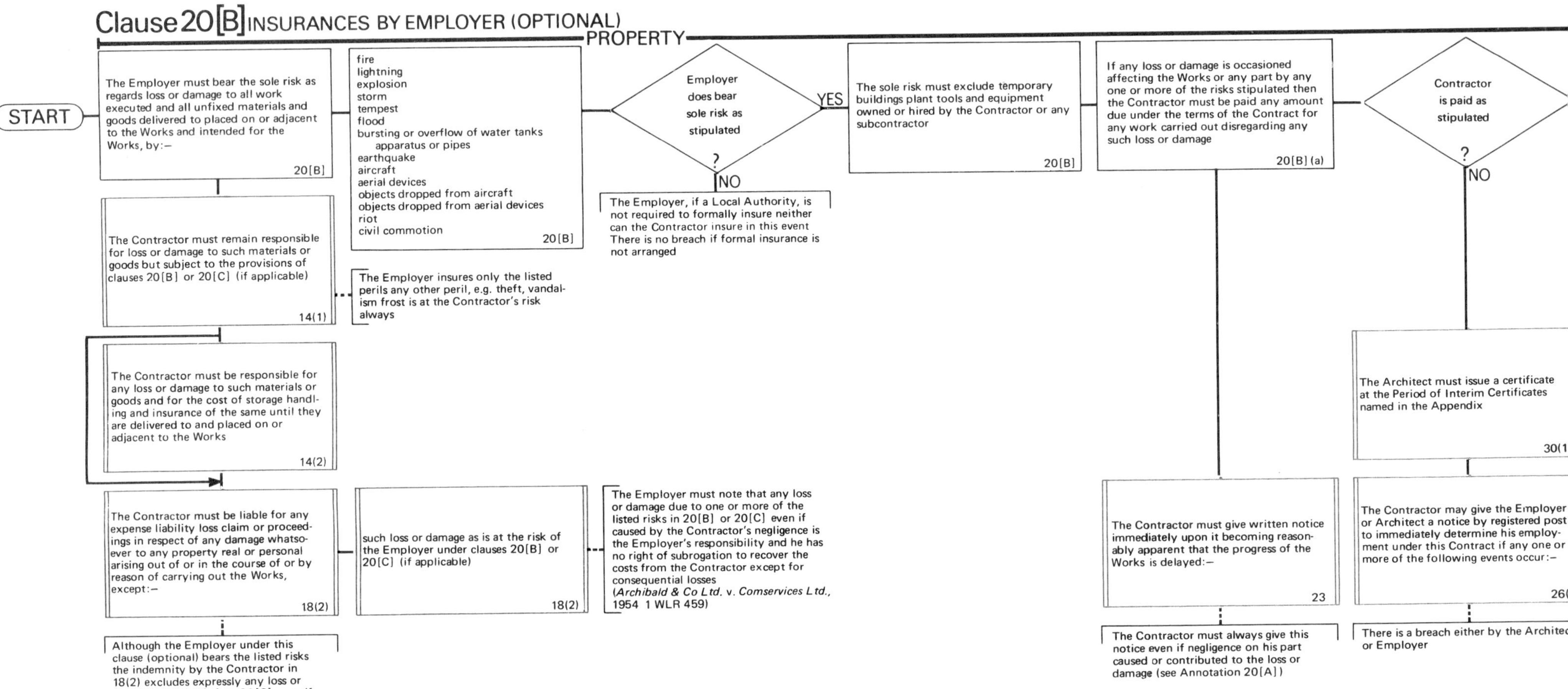

START
The Employer must bear the sole risk as regards loss or damage to all work executed and all unfixed materials and goods delivered to placed on or adjacent to the Works and intended for the Works, by:– 20[B]
fire
lightning
explosion
storm
tempest
flood
bursting or overflow of water tanks apparatus or pipes
earthquake
aircraft
aerial devices
objects dropped from aircraft
objects dropped from aerial devices
riot
civil commotion 20[B]
Employer does bear sole risk as stipulated ?
YES
NO
The sole risk must exclude temporary buildings plant tools and equipment owned or hired by the Contractor or any subcontractor 20[B]
If any loss or damage is occasioned affecting the Works or any part by any one or more of the risks stipulated then the Contractor must be paid any amount due under the terms of the Contract for any work carried out disregarding any such loss or damage 20[B] (a)
Contractor is paid as stipulated ?
NO
The Employer, if a Local Authority, is not required to formally insure neither can the Contractor insure in this event There is no breach if formal insurance is not arranged
The Contractor must remain responsible for loss or damage to such materials or goods but subject to the provisions of clauses 20[B] or 20[C] (if applicable) 14(1)
The Employer insures only the listed perils any other peril, e.g. theft, vandalism frost is at the Contractor's risk always
The Contractor must be responsible for any loss or damage to such materials or goods and for the cost of storage handling and insurance of the same until they are delivered to and placed on or adjacent to the Works 14(2)
The Architect must issue a certificate at the Period of Interim Certificates named in the Appendix 30(1
The Contractor must be liable for any expense liability loss claim or proceedings in respect of any damage whatsoever to any property real or personal arising out of or in the course of or by reason of carrying out the Works, except:– 18(2)
such loss or damage as is at the risk of the Employer under clauses 20[B] or 20[C] (if applicable) 18(2)
The Employer must note that any loss or damage due to one or more of the listed risks in 20[B] or 20[C] even if caused by the Contractor's negligence is the Employer's responsibility and he has no right of subrogation to recover the costs from the Contractor except for consequential losses (*Archibald & Co Ltd. v. Comservices Ltd.*, 1954 1 WLR 459)
The Contractor must give written notice immediately upon it becoming reasonably apparent that the progress of the Works is delayed:– 23
The Contractor may give the Employer or Architect a notice by registered post to immediately determine his employment under this Contract if any one or more of the following events occur:– 26(
The Contractor must always give this notice even if negligence on his part caused or contributed to the loss or damage (see Annotation 20[A])
There is a breach either by the Architec or Employer
Although the Employer under this clause (optional) bears the listed risks the indemnity by the Contractor in 18(2) excludes expressly any loss or damage under 20[B] or 20[C] even if Contractor's negligence caused the loss or damage (e.g. failure to properly protect against storms). This optional clause therefore has little if any advantage in practise since Insurers would require higher premiums because of the loss of subrogation rights except for consequential losses

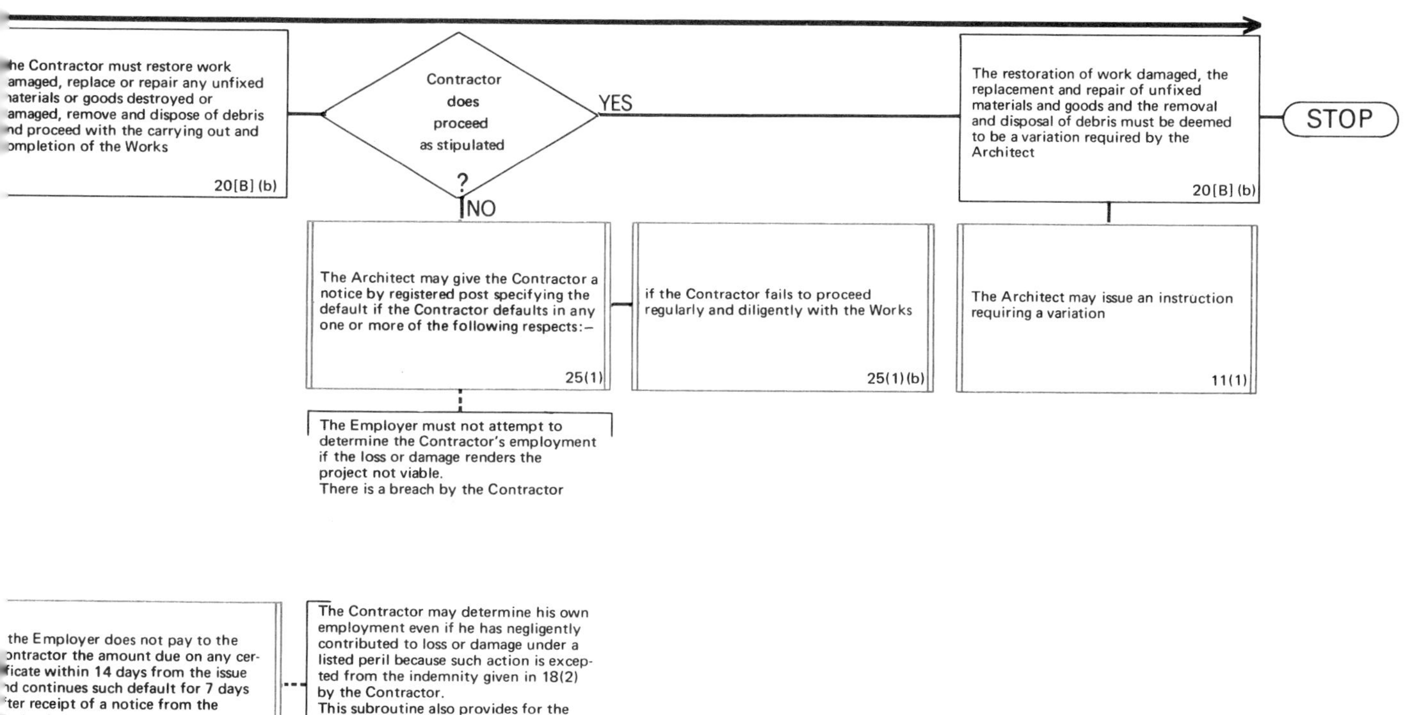

he Contractor must restore work amaged, replace or repair any unfixed naterials or goods destroyed or amaged, remove and dispose of debris nd proceed with the carrying out and ompletion of the Works
20[B] (b)
Contractor does proceed as stipulated
?
YES
NO
The restoration of work damaged, the replacement and repair of unfixed materials and goods and the removal and disposal of debris must be deemed to be a variation required by the Architect
20[B] (b)
STOP
The Architect may give the Contractor a notice by registered post specifying the default if the Contractor defaults in any one or more of the following respects:–
25(1)
if the Contractor fails to proceed regularly and diligently with the Works
25(1)(b)
The Architect may issue an instruction requiring a variation
11(1)
The Employer must not attempt to determine the Contractor's employment if the loss or damage renders the project not viable.
There is a breach by the Contractor
the Employer does not pay to the ontractor the amount due on any cer- ficate within 14 days from the issue nd continues such default for 7 days ter receipt of a notice from the ontractor
26(1)(a)
The Contractor may determine his own employment even if he has negligently contributed to loss or damage under a listed peril because such action is excep- ted from the indemnity given in 18(2) by the Contractor.
This subroutine also provides for the Contractor to determine his own em- ployment for other reasons connected with loss or damage

Clause 20[C] INSURANCES BY EMPLOYER (NO OPTION)

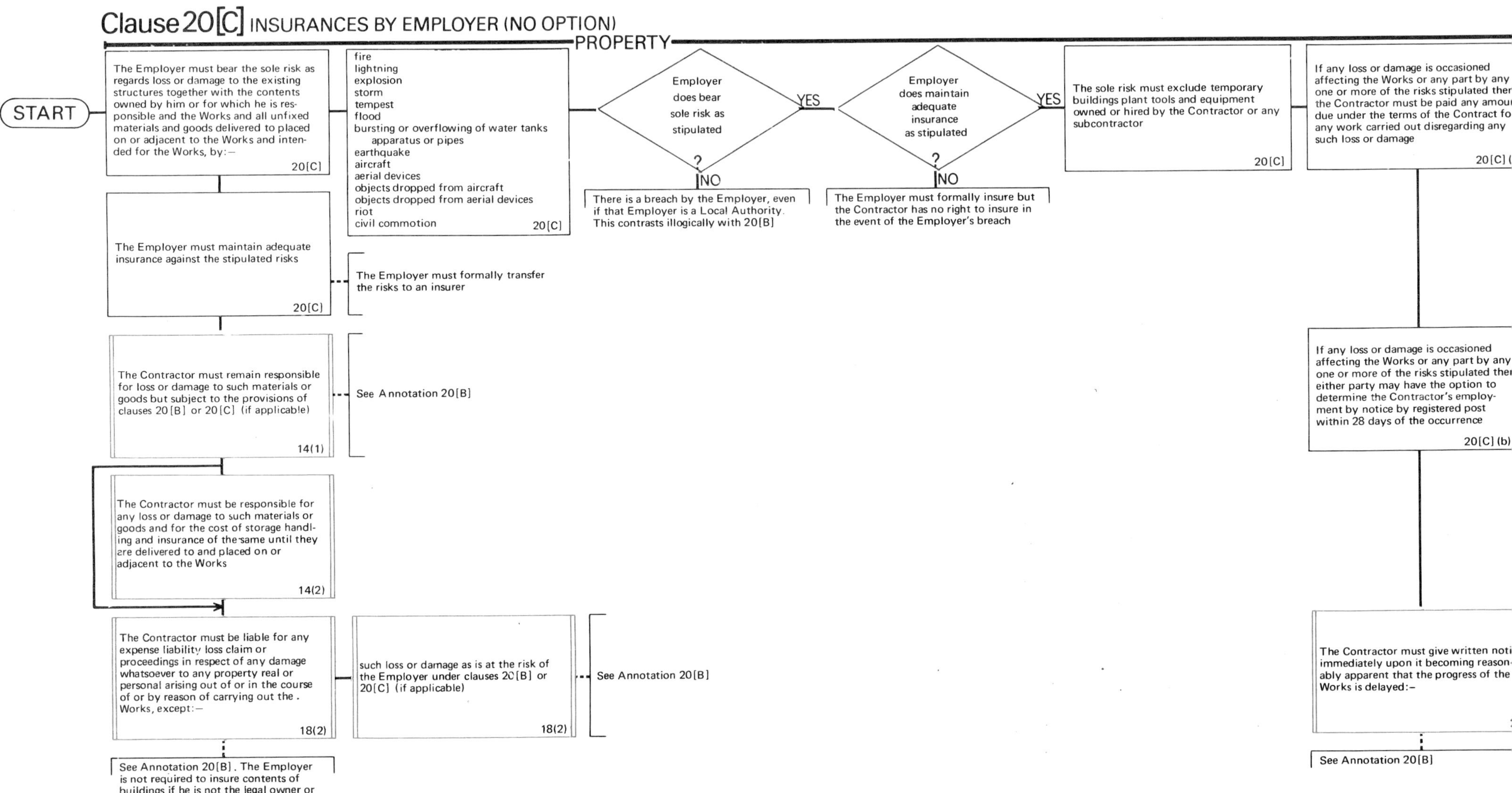

PROPERTY
START
The Employer must bear the sole risk as regards loss or damage to the existing structures together with the contents owned by him or for which he is responsible and the Works and all unfixed materials and goods delivered to placed on or adjacent to the Works and intended for the Works, by:– 20[C]
fire
lightning
explosion
storm
tempest
flood
bursting or overflowing of water tanks apparatus or pipes
earthquake
aircraft
aerial devices
objects dropped from aircraft
objects dropped from aerial devices
riot
civil commotion 20[C]
Employer does bear sole risk as stipulated ?
YES
NO
There is a breach by the Employer, even if that Employer is a Local Authority. This contrasts illogically with 20[B]
Employer does maintain adequate insurance as stipulated ?
YES
NO
The Employer must formally insure but the Contractor has no right to insure in the event of the Employer's breach
The sole risk must exclude temporary buildings plant tools and equipment owned or hired by the Contractor or any subcontractor 20[C]
If any loss or damage is occasioned affecting the Works or any part by any one or more of the risks stipulated ther the Contractor must be paid any amou due under the terms of the Contract fo any work carried out disregarding any such loss or damage 20[C] (
The Employer must maintain adequate insurance against the stipulated risks 20[C]
The Employer must formally transfer the risks to an insurer
The Contractor must remain responsible for loss or damage to such materials or goods but subject to the provisions of clauses 20[B] or 20[C] (if applicable) 14(1)
See Annotation 20[B]
If any loss or damage is occasioned affecting the Works or any part by any one or more of the risks stipulated the either party may have the option to determine the Contractor's employment by notice by registered post within 28 days of the occurrence 20[C] (b)
The Contractor must be responsible for any loss or damage to such materials or goods and for the cost of storage handling and insurance of the same until they are delivered to and placed on or adjacent to the Works 14(2)
The Contractor must be liable for any expense liability loss claim or proceedings in respect of any damage whatsoever to any property real or personal arising out of or in the course of or by reason of carrying out the Works, except:– 18(2)
such loss or damage as is at the risk of the Employer under clauses 20[B] or 20[C] (if applicable) 18(2)
See Annotation 20[B]
The Contractor must give written noti immediately upon it becoming reason ably apparent that the progress of the Works is delayed:–
See Annotation 20[B]. The Employer is not required to insure contents of buildings if he is not the legal owner or legally responsible for same. Ecclesiastical property owners cannot always obtain the cover stipulated particularly in respect of storm damage. This matter must be agreed between the parties
See Annotation 20[B]

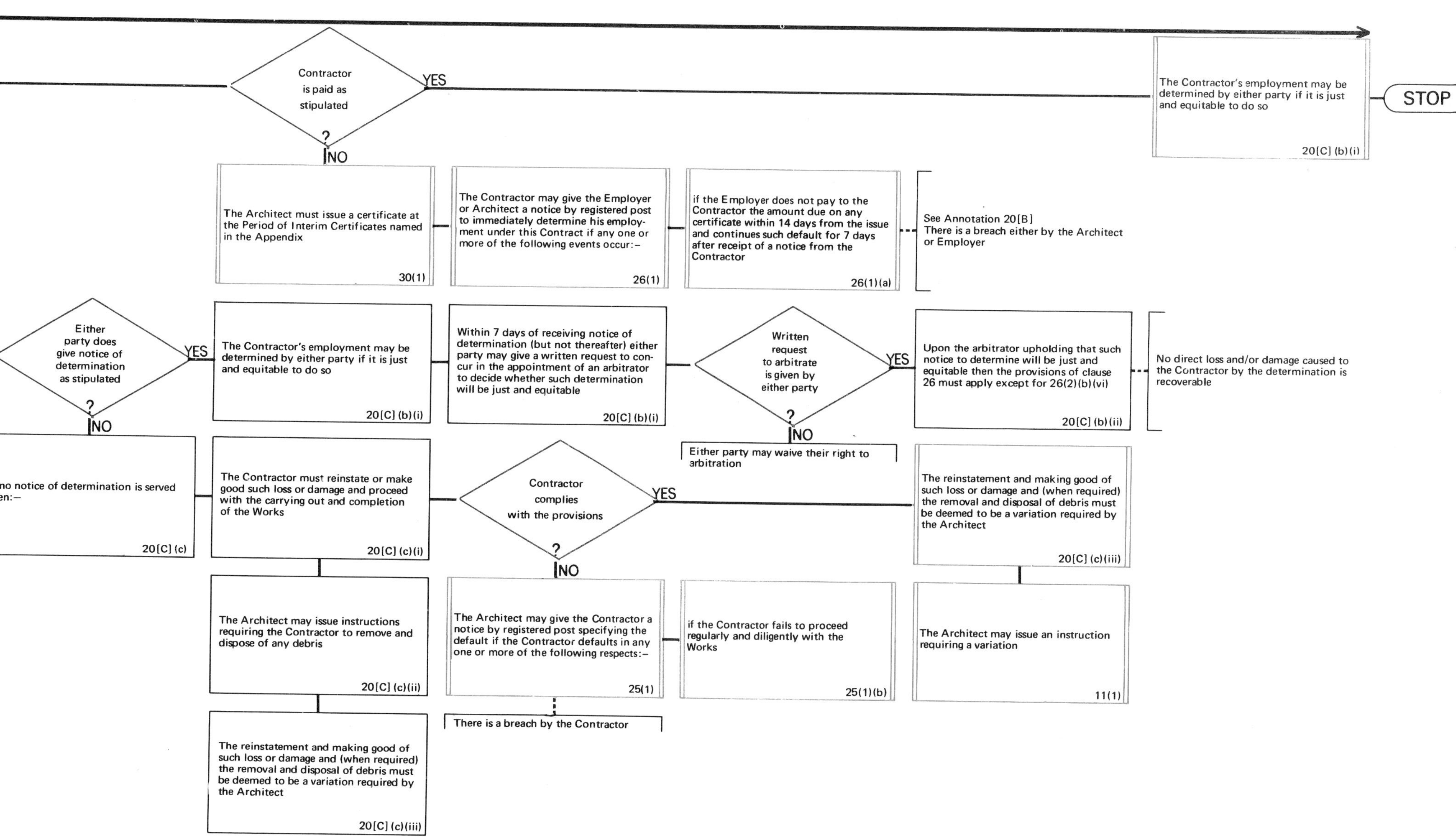

Contractor is paid as stipulated
?
YES
NO
The Contractor's employment may be determined by either party if it is just and equitable to do so
20[C] (b)(i)
STOP
The Architect must issue a certificate at the Period of Interim Certificates named in the Appendix
30(1)
The Contractor may give the Employer or Architect a notice by registered post to immediately determine his employment under this Contract if any one or more of the following events occur:–
26(1)
if the Employer does not pay to the Contractor the amount due on any certificate within 14 days from the issue and continues such default for 7 days after receipt of a notice from the Contractor
26(1)(a)
See Annotation 20[B]
There is a breach either by the Architect or Employer
Either party does give notice of determination as stipulated
The Contractor's employment may be determined by either party if it is just and equitable to do so
20[C] (b)(i)
Within 7 days of receiving notice of determination (but not thereafter) either party may give a written request to concur in the appointment of an arbitrator to decide whether such determination will be just and equitable
20[C] (b)(i)
Written request to arbitrate is given by either party
Either party may waive their right to arbitration
Upon the arbitrator upholding that such notice to determine will be just and equitable then the provisions of clause 26 must apply except for 26(2)(b)(vi)
20[C] (b)(ii)
No direct loss and/or damage caused to the Contractor by the determination is recoverable
no notice of determination is served
en:–
20[C] (c)
The Contractor must reinstate or make good such loss or damage and proceed with the carrying out and completion of the Works
20[C] (c)(i)
Contractor complies with the provisions
The reinstatement and making good of such loss or damage and (when required) the removal and disposal of debris must be deemed to be a variation required by the Architect
20[C] (c)(iii)
The Architect may issue instructions requiring the Contractor to remove and dispose of any debris
20[C] (c)(ii)
The Architect may give the Contractor a notice by registered post specifying the default if the Contractor defaults in any one or more of the following respects:–
25(1)
if the Contractor fails to proceed regularly and diligently with the Works
25(1)(b)
The Architect may issue an instruction requiring a variation
11(1)
There is a breach by the Contractor
The reinstatement and making good of such loss or damage and (when required) the removal and disposal of debris must be deemed to be a variation required by the Architect
20[C] (c)(iii)

Clause 21 POSSESSION COMPLETION AND POSTPONEMENT

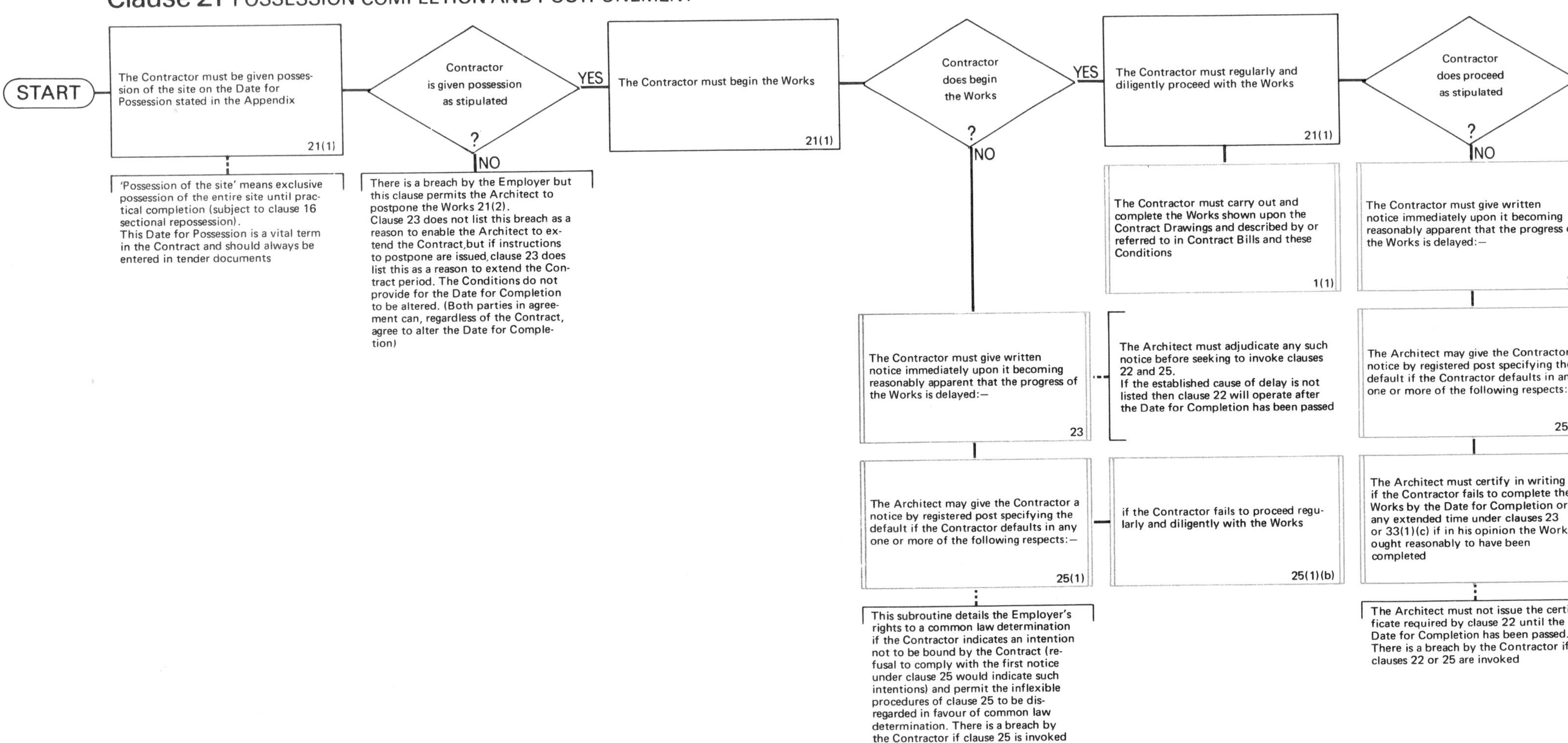

START
The Contractor must be given possession of the site on the Date for Possession stated in the Appendix
21(1)
'Possession of the site' means exclusive possession of the entire site until practical completion (subject to clause 16 sectional repossession).
This Date for Possession is a vital term in the Contract and should always be entered in tender documents
Contractor is given possession as stipulated
?
YES
NO
There is a breach by the Employer but this clause permits the Architect to postpone the Works 21(2).
Clause 23 does not list this breach as a reason to enable the Architect to extend the Contract,but if instructions to postpone are issued, clause 23 does list this as a reason to extend the Contract period. The Conditions do not provide for the Date for Completion to be altered. (Both parties in agreement can, regardless of the Contract, agree to alter the Date for Completion)
The Contractor must begin the Works
21(1)
Contractor does begin the Works
?
YES
NO
The Contractor must give written notice immediately upon it becoming reasonably apparent that the progress of the Works is delayed:—
23
The Architect may give the Contractor a notice by registered post specifying the default if the Contractor defaults in any one or more of the following respects:—
25(1)
This subroutine details the Employer's rights to a common law determination if the Contractor indicates an intention not to be bound by the Contract (refusal to comply with the first notice under clause 25 would indicate such intentions) and permit the inflexible procedures of clause 25 to be disregarded in favour of common law determination. There is a breach by the Contractor if clause 25 is invoked
The Contractor must regularly and diligently proceed with the Works
21(1)
The Contractor must carry out and complete the Works shown upon the Contract Drawings and described by or referred to in Contract Bills and these Conditions
1(1)
The Architect must adjudicate any such notice before seeking to invoke clauses 22 and 25.
If the established cause of delay is not listed then clause 22 will operate after the Date for Completion has been passed
if the Contractor fails to proceed regularly and diligently with the Works
25(1)(b)
Contractor does proceed as stipulated
?
NO
The Contractor must give written notice immediately upon it becoming reasonably apparent that the progress of the Works is delayed:—
2
The Architect may give the Contractor notice by registered post specifying the default if the Contractor defaults in any one or more of the following respects:—
25(
The Architect must certify in writing if the Contractor fails to complete the Works by the Date for Completion or any extended time under clauses 23 or 33(1)(c) if in his opinion the Works ought reasonably to have been completed
The Architect must not issue the certificate required by clause 22 until the Date for Completion has been passed.
There is a breach by the Contractor if clauses 22 or 25 are invoked

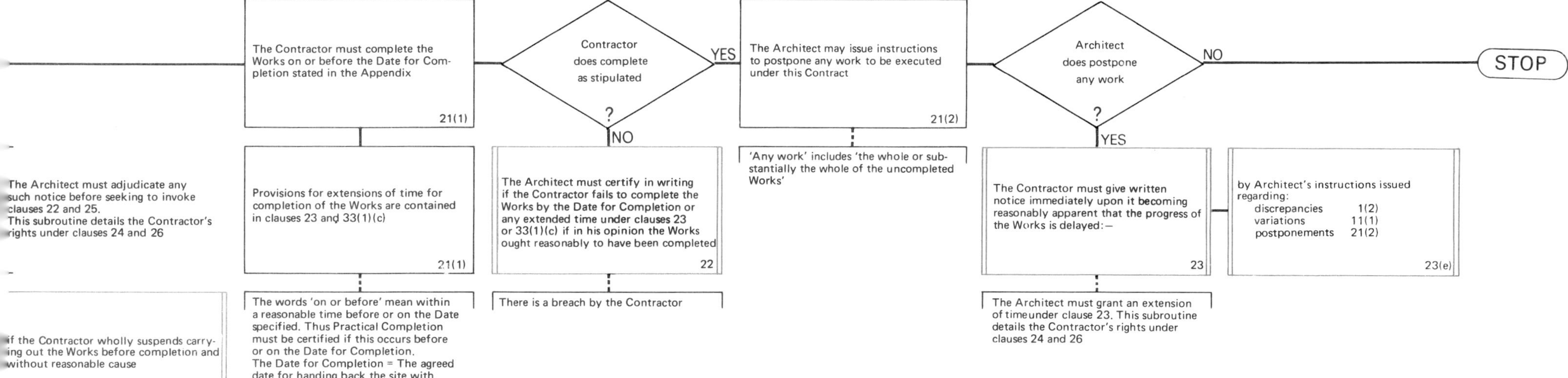
The Contractor must complete the Works on or before the Date for Completion stated in the Appendix
21(1)
Contractor does complete as stipulated ?
YES
NO
The Architect may issue instructions to postpone any work to be executed under this Contract
21(2)
Architect does postpone any work ?
NO
YES
STOP
The Architect must adjudicate any such notice before seeking to invoke clauses 22 and 25.
This subroutine details the Contractor's rights under clauses 24 and 26
Provisions for extensions of time for completion of the Works are contained in clauses 23 and 33(1)(c)
21(1)
The Architect must certify in writing if the Contractor fails to complete the Works by the Date for Completion or any extended time under clauses 23 or 33(1)(c) if in his opinion the Works ought reasonably to have been completed
22
'Any work' includes 'the whole or substantially the whole of the uncompleted Works'
The Contractor must give written notice immediately upon it becoming reasonably apparent that the progress of the Works is delayed:—
23
by Architect's instructions issued regarding:
discrepancies 1(2)
variations 11(1)
postponements 21(2)
23(e)
if the Contractor wholly suspends carrying out the Works before completion and without reasonable cause
25(1)(a)
This subroutine details all the Employer's rights of determination, in addition clause 25(1)(d) details his common law rights
The words 'on or before' mean within a reasonable time before or on the Date specified. Thus Practical Completion must be certified if this occurs before or on the Date for Completion.
The Date for Completion = The agreed date for handing back the site with completed Works
The Date of 'Practical Completion' = The actual date when the Works are practically complete
The Date of Completion of Making Good Defects = The actual date when all known defects are made good
There is a breach by the Contractor
The Architect must grant an extension of time under clause 23. This subroutine details the Contractor's rights under clauses 24 and 26

Clause 22 DAMAGES FOR NON-COMPLETION

START

The Architect must certify in writing if the Contractor fails to complete the Works by the Date for Completion or any extended time under clauses 23 or 33(1)(c) if in his opinion the Works ought reasonably to have been completed 22

Architect does certify as stipulated ? YES / NO

The Contractor must give written notice immediately upon it becoming reasonably apparent that the progress of the Works is delayed:– 23

In the event of the Works or any part sustaining war damage or any unfixed materials or goods intended for delivered to and placed on or adjacent the Works sustaining war damage then in spite of anything expressed or implied in this Contract the following provisions must apply:– 33(1)

The Architect's certificate issued under clause 22 is a condition precedent to the Employer being entitled to deduct or be paid damages

In case any dispute or difference arise between the Employer or Architect on his behalf and the Contractor either during the progress or after completion or abandonment of the Works as to:– 35(1)

any matter or thing left by this Contract to the discretion of the Architect 35(1)

There is a breach by the Architect preventing the Employer from recovering damages.
The Architect must not issue this certificate until the Date for Completion has been passed. If a claim has been entered under clause 23 the Architect must adjudicate on this 'as soon as he is able' as possibly it influences the Date for Completion

The Contractor must pay or allow the Employer liquidated damages for the period the Works remain incomplete at the rate stated in the Appendix 22

Contractor does pay or allow damages as stipulated ? YES / NO

The Employer may deduct liquidated damages from any monies due or to become due to the Contractor under this Contract 22

Any balance expressed in the Final Certificate must be subject to any deductions authorized by these Conditions 30(6)

The balance to be expressed must not be altered by any sum due to the Employer for damages. But the balance is subject to *deductions* for any such sum

Any such reference on:– 35(2)

whether or not a certificate is not in accordance with these Conditions 35(2

The Employer must be paid or allowed liquidated damages for any delay which may occur in the remaining Works after taking possession of a Relevant Part 16(e)

The Architect must not himself deduct damages from the total to be stated as due although he can set out the calculated sum involved, but this is not one of his duties under the Contract.
Any interim certificate issued after the Date for Completion (or extended date) can be subjected to such a deduction under clause 22 from sums due to the Contractor.
If there are no sums due to the Contractor he must 'pay' such sums.
The Contract does not provide for liquidated damages to be paid if delay occurs in sectional completion.
The provisions for fluctuations in cost (clause 31) must continue to run in periods of delay since liquidated damages are deemed to cover such eventualities

STOP

ere is a breach by the Contractor
less notice to arbitrate is given. (Arbi-
tion may conclude otherwise.) The
tificate referred to here is that of
n-completion.
e debt cannot be set against other
ntracts if insufficient funds exist

Clause 23 EXTENSIONS OF TIME (1)

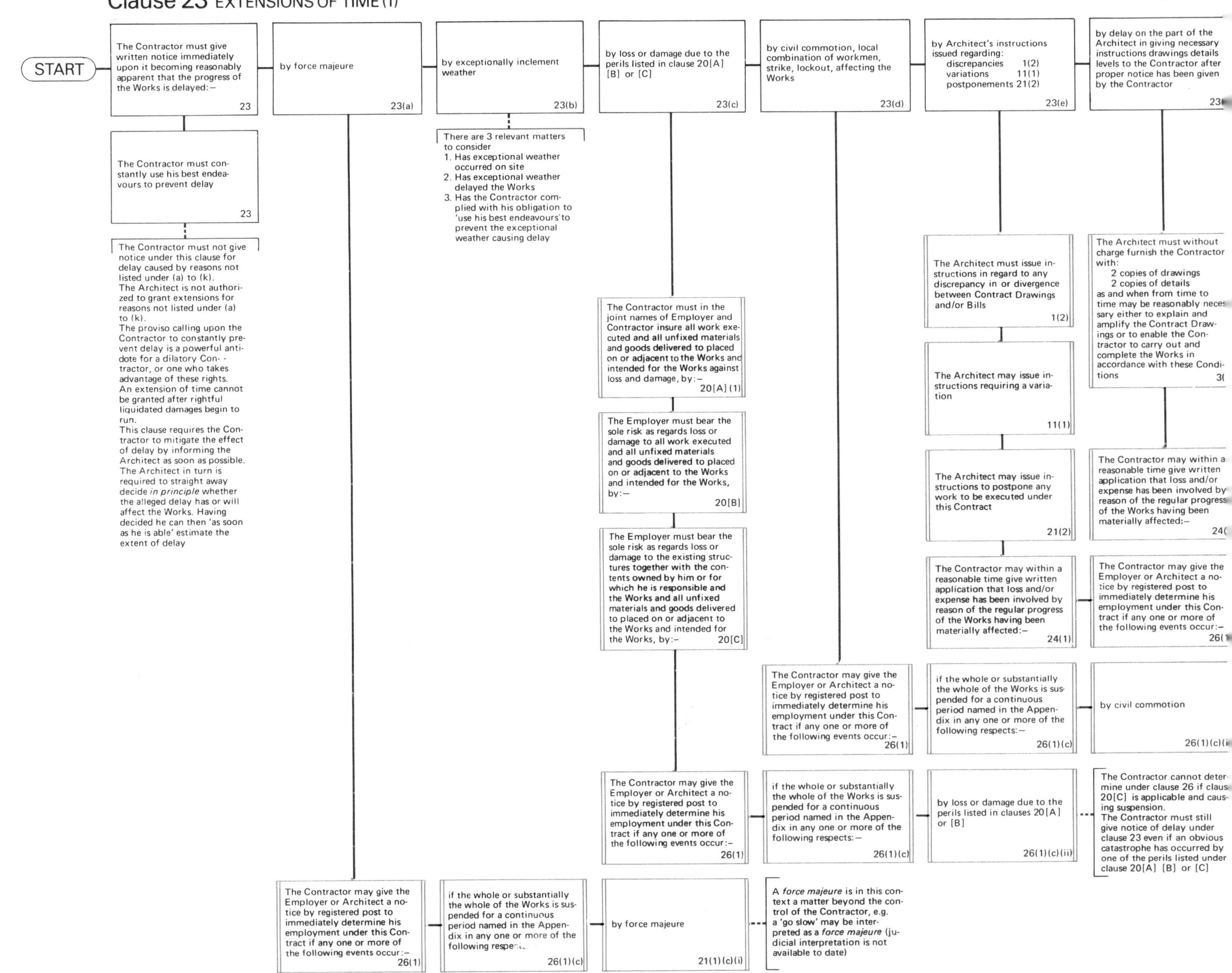

START
The Contractor must give written notice immediately upon it becoming reasonably apparent that the progress of the Works is delayed:– 23
The Contractor must constantly use his best endeavours to prevent delay 23
The Contractor must not give notice under this clause for delay caused by reasons not listed under (a) to (k). The Architect is not authorized to grant extensions for reasons not listed under (a) to (k). The proviso calling upon the Contractor to constantly prevent delay is a powerful antidote for a dilatory Contractor, or one who takes advantage of these rights. An extension of time cannot be granted after rightful liquidated damages begin to run. This clause requires the Contractor to mitigate the effect of delay by informing the Architect as soon as possible. The Architect in turn is required to straight away decide in principle whether the alleged delay has or will affect the Works. Having decided he can then 'as soon as he is able' estimate the extent of delay
by force majeure 23(a)
by exceptionally inclement weather 23(b)
There are 3 relevant matters to consider 1. Has exceptional weather occurred on site 2. Has exceptional weather delayed the Works 3. Has the Contractor complied with his obligation to 'use his best endeavours' to prevent the exceptional weather causing delay
by loss or damage due to the perils listed in clause 20[A] [B] or [C] 23(c)
by civil commotion, local combination of workmen, strike, lockout, affecting the Works 23(d)
by Architect's instructions issued regarding: discrepancies 1(2) variations 11(1) postponements 21(2) 23(e)
by delay on the part of the Architect in giving necessary instructions drawings details levels to the Contractor after proper notice has been given by the Contractor 23
The Contractor must in the joint names of Employer and Contractor insure all work executed and all unfixed materials and goods delivered to placed on or adjacent to the Works and intended for the Works against loss and damage, by:– 20[A] (1)
The Employer must bear the sole risk as regards loss or damage to all work executed and all unfixed materials and goods delivered to placed on or adjacent to the Works and intended for the Works, by:– 20[B]
The Employer must bear the sole risk as regards loss or damage to the existing structures together with the contents owned by him or for which he is responsible and the Works and all unfixed materials and goods delivered to placed on or adjacent to the Works and intended for the Works, by:– 20[C]
The Contractor may give the Employer or Architect a notice by registered post to immediately determine his employment under this Contract if any one or more of the following events occur:– 26(1)
if the whole or substantially the whole of the Works is suspended for a continuous period named in the Appendix in any one or more of the following respects:– 26(1)(c)
by loss or damage due to the perils listed in clauses 20[A] or [B] 26(1)(c)(ii)
The Contractor cannot determine under clause 26 if clause 20[C] is applicable and causing suspension. The Contractor must still give notice of delay under clause 23 even if an obvious catastrophe has occurred by one of the perils listed under clause 20[A] [B] or [C]
The Architect must issue instructions in regard to any discrepancy in or divergence between Contract Drawings and/or Bills 1(2)
The Architect may issue instructions requiring a variation 11(1)
The Architect may issue instructions to postpone any work to be executed under this Contract 21(2)
The Contractor may within a reasonable time give written application that loss and/or expense has been involved by reason of the regular progress of the Works having been materially affected:– 24(1)
The Architect must without charge furnish the Contractor with: 2 copies of drawings 2 copies of details as and when from time to time may be reasonably nece sary either to explain and amplify the Contract Drawings or to enable the Contractor to carry out and complete the Works in accordance with these Conditions 3(
The Contractor may within a reasonable time give written application that loss and/or expense has been involved by reason of the regular progress of the Works having been materially affected:– 24(
The Contractor may give the Employer or Architect a notice by registered post to immediately determine his employment under this Contract if any one or more of the following events occur:– 26(1
The Contractor may give the Employer or Architect a notice by registered post to immediately determine his employment under this Contract if any one or more of the following events occur:– 26(1)
if the whole or substantially the whole of the Works is suspended for a continuous period named in the Appendix in any one or more of the following respects:– 26(1)(c)
by civil commotion 26(1)(c)(i
The Contractor may give the Employer or Architect a notice by registered post to immediately determine his employment under this Contract if any one or more of the following events occur:– 26(1)
if the whole or substantially the whole of the Works is suspended for a continuous period named in the Appendix in any one or more of the following respects 26(1)(c)
by force majeure 21(1)(c)(i)
A force majeure is in this context a matter beyond the control of the Contractor, e.g. a 'go slow' may be interpreted as a force majeure (judicial interpretation is not available to date)

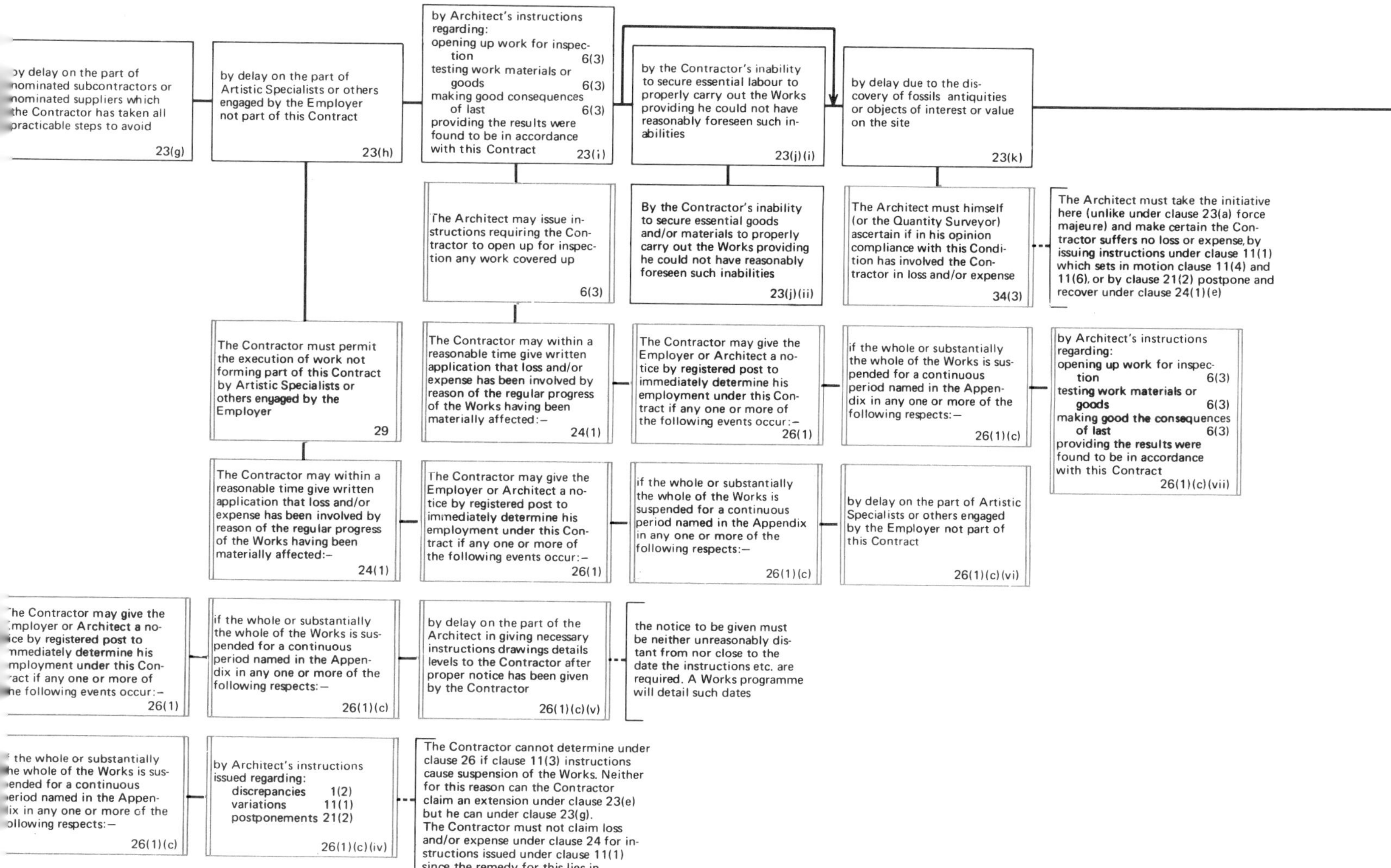

by delay on the part of nominated subcontractors or nominated suppliers which the Contractor has taken all practicable steps to avoid 23(g)
by delay on the part of Artistic Specialists or others engaged by the Employer not part of this Contract 23(h)
by Architect's instructions regarding: opening up work for inspection 6(3) testing work materials or goods 6(3) making good consequences of last 6(3) providing the results were found to be in accordance with this Contract 23(i)
by the Contractor's inability to secure essential labour to properly carry out the Works providing he could not have reasonably foreseen such inabilities 23(j)(i)
by delay due to the discovery of fossils antiquities or objects of interest or value on the site 23(k)
23/1
The Architect may issue instructions requiring the Contractor to open up for inspection any work covered up 6(3)
By the Contractor's inability to secure essential goods and/or materials to properly carry out the Works providing he could not have reasonably foreseen such inabilities 23(j)(ii)
The Architect must himself (or the Quantity Surveyor) ascertain if in his opinion compliance with this Condition has involved the Contractor in loss and/or expense 34(3)
The Architect must take the initiative here (unlike under clause 23(a) force majeure) and make certain the Contractor suffers no loss or expense, by issuing instructions under clause 11(1) which sets in motion clause 11(4) and 11(6), or by clause 21(2) postpone and recover under clause 24(1)(e)
The Contractor must permit the execution of work not forming part of this Contract by Artistic Specialists or others engaged by the Employer 29
The Contractor may within a reasonable time give written application that loss and/or expense has been involved by reason of the regular progress of the Works having been materially affected:– 24(1)
The Contractor may give the Employer or Architect a notice by registered post to immediately determine his employment under this Contract if any one or more of the following events occur:– 26(1)
if the whole or substantially the whole of the Works is suspended for a continuous period named in the Appendix in any one or more of the following respects:– 26(1)(c)
by Architect's instructions regarding: opening up work for inspection 6(3) testing work materials or goods 6(3) making good the consequences of last 6(3) providing the results were found to be in accordance with this Contract 26(1)(c)(vii)
The Contractor may within a reasonable time give written application that loss and/or expense has been involved by reason of the regular progress of the Works having been materially affected:– 24(1)
The Contractor may give the Employer or Architect a notice by registered post to immediately determine his employment under this Contract if any one or more of the following events occur:– 26(1)
if the whole or substantially the whole of the Works is suspended for a continuous period named in the Appendix in any one or more of the following respects:– 26(1)(c)
by delay on the part of Artistic Specialists or others engaged by the Employer not part of this Contract 26(1)(c)(vi)
The Contractor may give the Employer or Architect a notice by registered post to immediately determine his employment under this Contract if any one or more of the following events occur:– 26(1)
if the whole or substantially the whole of the Works is suspended for a continuous period named in the Appendix in any one or more of the following respects:– 26(1)(c)
by delay on the part of the Architect in giving necessary instructions drawings details levels to the Contractor after proper notice has been given by the Contractor 26(1)(c)(v)
the notice to be given must be neither unreasonably distant from nor close to the date the instructions etc. are required. A Works programme will detail such dates
if the whole or substantially the whole of the Works is suspended for a continuous period named in the Appendix in any one or more of the following respects:– 26(1)(c)
by Architect's instructions issued regarding: discrepancies 1(2) variations 11(1) postponements 21(2) 26(1)(c)(iv)
The Contractor cannot determine under clause 26 if clause 11(3) instructions cause suspension of the Works. Neither for this reason can the Contractor claim an extension under clause 23(e) but he can under clause 23(g). The Contractor must not claim loss and/or expense under clause 24 for instructions issued under clause 11(1) since the remedy for this lies in clause 11(6)
The word strike is unqualified therefore an unofficial strike would be included

Clause 23 EXTENSIONS OF TIME (2)

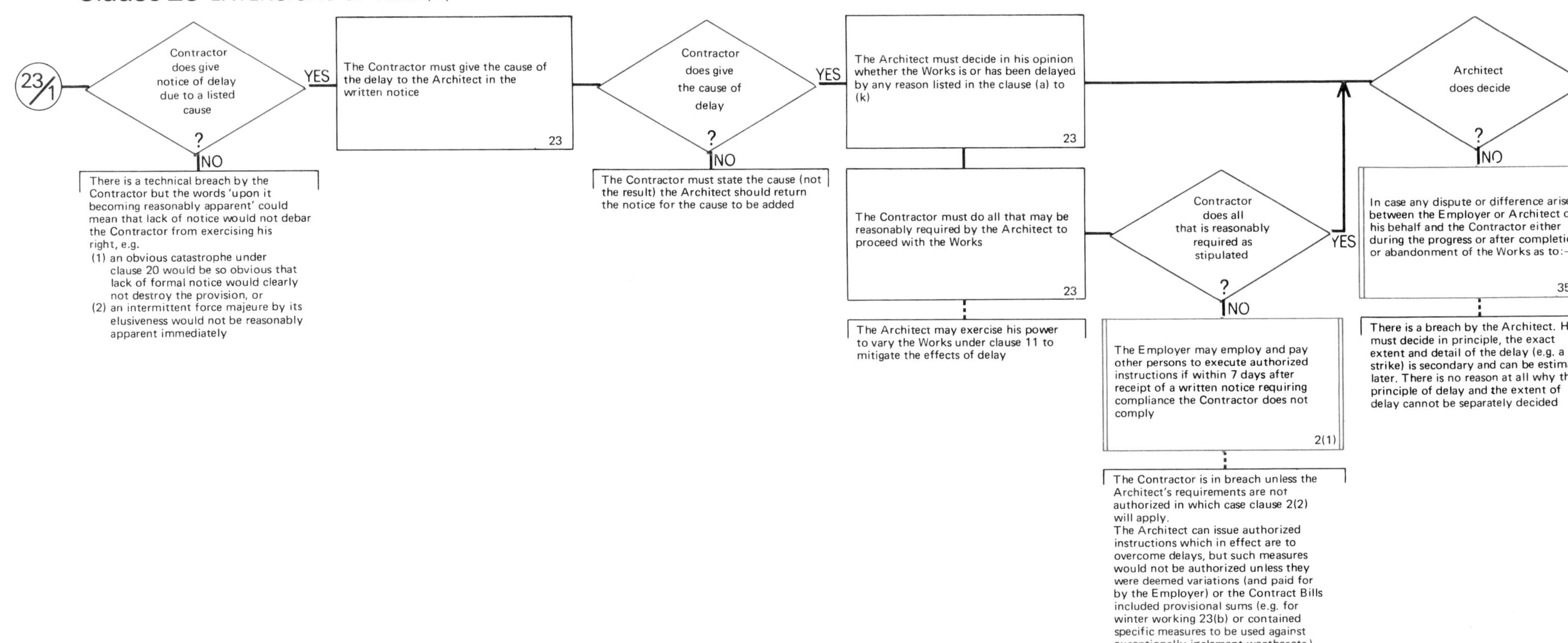

23/1
Contractor does give notice of delay due to a listed cause ?
YES
NO
There is a technical breach by the Contractor but the words 'upon it becoming reasonably apparent' could mean that lack of notice would not debar the Contractor from exercising his right, e.g.
(1) an obvious catastrophe under clause 20 would be so obvious that lack of formal notice would clearly not destroy the provision, or
(2) an intermittent force majeure by its elusiveness would not be reasonably apparent immediately
The Contractor must give the cause of the delay to the Architect in the written notice
23
Contractor does give the cause of delay ?
YES
NO
The Contractor must state the cause (not the result) the Architect should return the notice for the cause to be added
The Architect must decide in his opinion whether the Works is or has been delayed by any reason listed in the clause (a) to (k)
23
The Contractor must do all that may be reasonably required by the Architect to proceed with the Works
23
The Architect may exercise his power to vary the Works under clause 11 to mitigate the effects of delay
Contractor does all that is reasonably required as stipulated ?
YES
NO
The Employer may employ and pay other persons to execute authorized instructions if within 7 days after receipt of a written notice requiring compliance the Contractor does not comply
2(1)
The Contractor is in breach unless the Architect's requirements are not authorized in which case clause 2(2) will apply.
The Architect can issue authorized instructions which in effect are to overcome delays, but such measures would not be authorized unless they were deemed variations (and paid for by the Employer) or the Contract Bills included provisional sums (e.g. for winter working 23(b) or contained specific measures to be used against exceptionally inclement weather etc.)
Architect does decide ?
NO
In case any dispute or difference arise between the Employer or Architect on his behalf and the Contractor either during the progress or after completion or abandonment of the Works as to:—
35(1
There is a breach by the Architect. He must decide in principle, the exact extent and detail of the delay (e.g. a strike) is secondary and can be estimated later. There is no reason at all why the principle of delay and the extent of delay cannot be separately decided

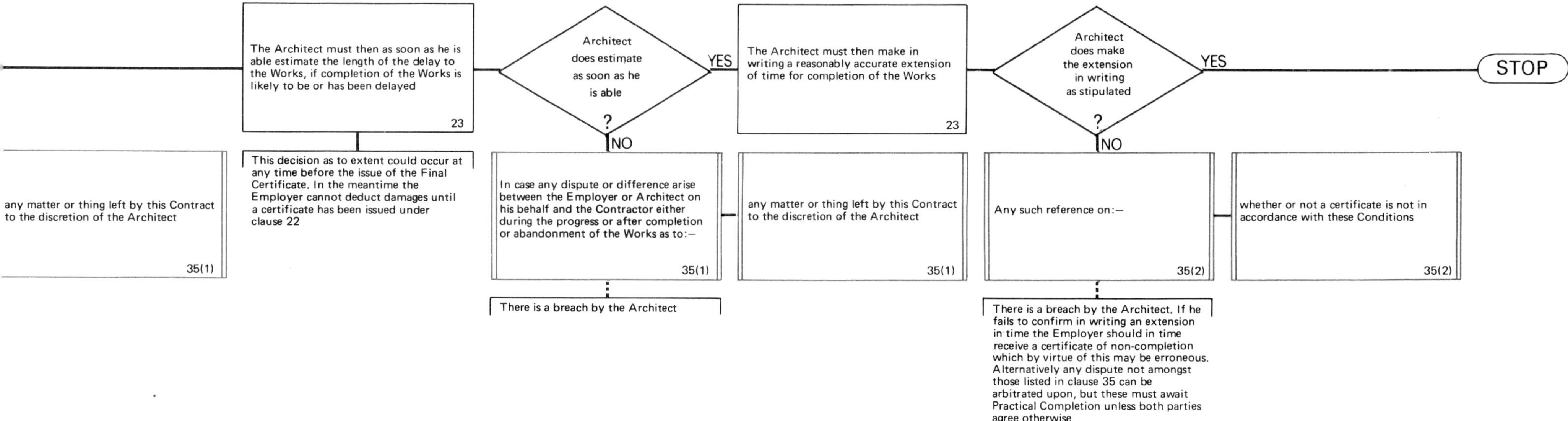
The Architect must then as soon as he is able estimate the length of the delay to the Works, if completion of the Works is likely to be or has been delayed
23
Architect does estimate as soon as he is able ?
YES
NO
The Architect must then make in writing a reasonably accurate extension of time for completion of the Works
23
Architect does make the extension in writing as stipulated ?
YES
NO
STOP
any matter or thing left by this Contract to the discretion of the Architect
35(1)
This decision as to extent could occur at any time before the issue of the Final Certificate. In the meantime the Employer cannot deduct damages until a certificate has been issued under clause 22
In case any dispute or difference arise between the Employer or Architect on his behalf and the Contractor either during the progress or after completion or abandonment of the Works as to:—
35(1)
any matter or thing left by this Contract to the discretion of the Architect
35(1)
Any such reference on:—
35(2)
whether or not a certificate is not in accordance with these Conditions
35(2)
There is a breach by the Architect
There is a breach by the Architect. If he fails to confirm in writing an extension in time the Employer should in time receive a certificate of non-completion which by virtue of this may be erroneous. Alternatively any dispute not amongst those listed in clause 35 can be arbitrated upon, but these must await Practical Completion unless both parties agree otherwise

Clause 24 LOSS AND EXPENSE BY DISTURBANCE OF PROGRESS (1)

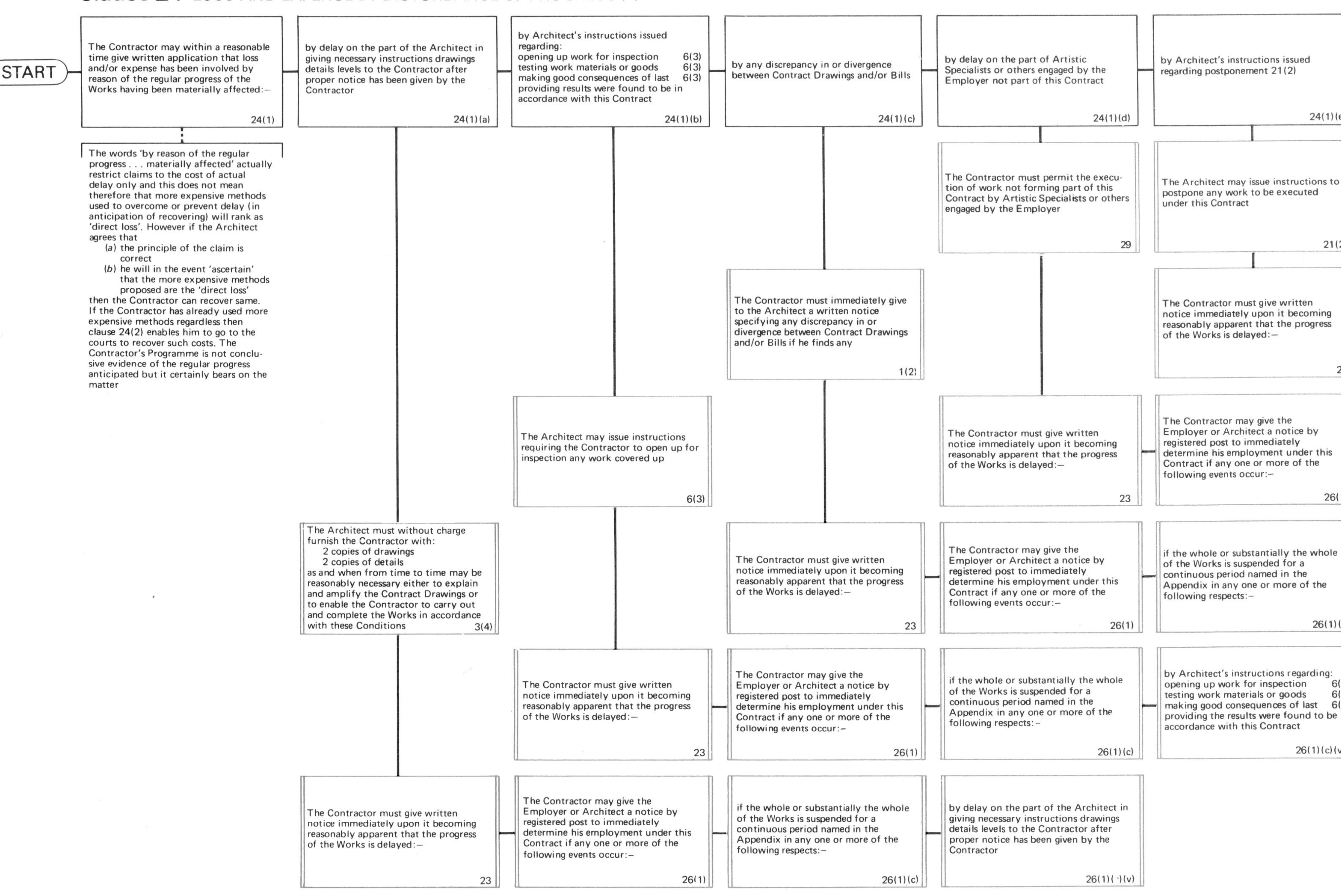

START
The Contractor may within a reasonable time give written application that loss and/or expense has been involved by reason of the regular progress of the Works having been materially affected:– 24(1)
The words 'by reason of the regular progress . . . materially affected' actually restrict claims to the cost of actual delay only and this does not mean therefore that more expensive methods used to overcome or prevent delay (in anticipation of recovering) will rank as 'direct loss'. However if the Architect agrees that
(a) the principle of the claim is correct
(b) he will in the event 'ascertain' that the more expensive methods proposed are the 'direct loss'
then the Contractor can recover same. If the Contractor has already used more expensive methods regardless then clause 24(2) enables him to go to the courts to recover such costs. The Contractor's Programme is not conclusive evidence of the regular progress anticipated but it certainly bears on the matter
by delay on the part of the Architect in giving necessary instructions drawings details levels to the Contractor after proper notice has been given by the Contractor 24(1)(a)
The Architect must without charge furnish the Contractor with: 2 copies of drawings 2 copies of details as and when from time to time may be reasonably necessary either to explain and amplify the Contract Drawings or to enable the Contractor to carry out and complete the Works in accordance with these Conditions 3(4)
The Contractor must give written notice immediately upon it becoming reasonably apparent that the progress of the Works is delayed:– 23
by Architect's instructions issued regarding: opening up work for inspection 6(3) testing work materials or goods 6(3) making good consequences of last 6(3) providing results were found to be in accordance with this Contract 24(1)(b)
The Architect may issue instructions requiring the Contractor to open up for inspection any work covered up 6(3)
The Contractor must give written notice immediately upon it becoming reasonably apparent that the progress of the Works is delayed:– 23
The Contractor may give the Employer or Architect a notice by registered post to immediately determine his employment under this Contract if any one or more of the following events occur:– 26(1)
by any discrepancy in or divergence between Contract Drawings and/or Bills 24(1)(c)
The Contractor must immediately give to the Architect a written notice specifying any discrepancy in or divergence between Contract Drawings and/or Bills if he finds any 1(2)
The Contractor must give written notice immediately upon it becoming reasonably apparent that the progress of the Works is delayed:– 23
The Contractor may give the Employer or Architect a notice by registered post to immediately determine his employment under this Contract if any one or more of the following events occur:– 26(1)
if the whole or substantially the whole of the Works is suspended for a continuous period named in the Appendix in any one or more of the following respects:– 26(1)(c)
by delay on the part of Artistic Specialists or others engaged by the Employer not part of this Contract 24(1)(d)
The Contractor must permit the execution of work not forming part of this Contract by Artistic Specialists or others engaged by the Employer 29
The Contractor must give written notice immediately upon it becoming reasonably apparent that the progress of the Works is delayed:– 23
The Contractor may give the Employer or Architect a notice by registered post to immediately determine his employment under this Contract if any one or more of the following events occur:– 26(1)
if the whole or substantially the whole of the Works is suspended for a continuous period named in the Appendix in any one or more of the following respects:– 26(1)(c)
by delay on the part of the Architect in giving necessary instructions drawings details levels to the Contractor after proper notice has been given by the Contractor 26(1)(c)(v)
by Architect's instructions issued regarding postponement 21(2) 24(1)(e
The Architect may issue instructions to postpone any work to be executed under this Contract 21(2
The Contractor must give written notice immediately upon it becoming reasonably apparent that the progress of the Works is delayed:– 2
The Contractor may give the Employer or Architect a notice by registered post to immediately determine his employment under this Contract if any one or more of the following events occur:– 26(1
if the whole or substantially the whole of the Works is suspended for a continuous period named in the Appendix in any one or more of the following respects:– 26(1)(
by Architect's instructions regarding: opening up work for inspection 6(testing work materials or goods 6(making good consequences of last 6(providing the results were found to be i accordance with this Contract 26(1)(c)(v

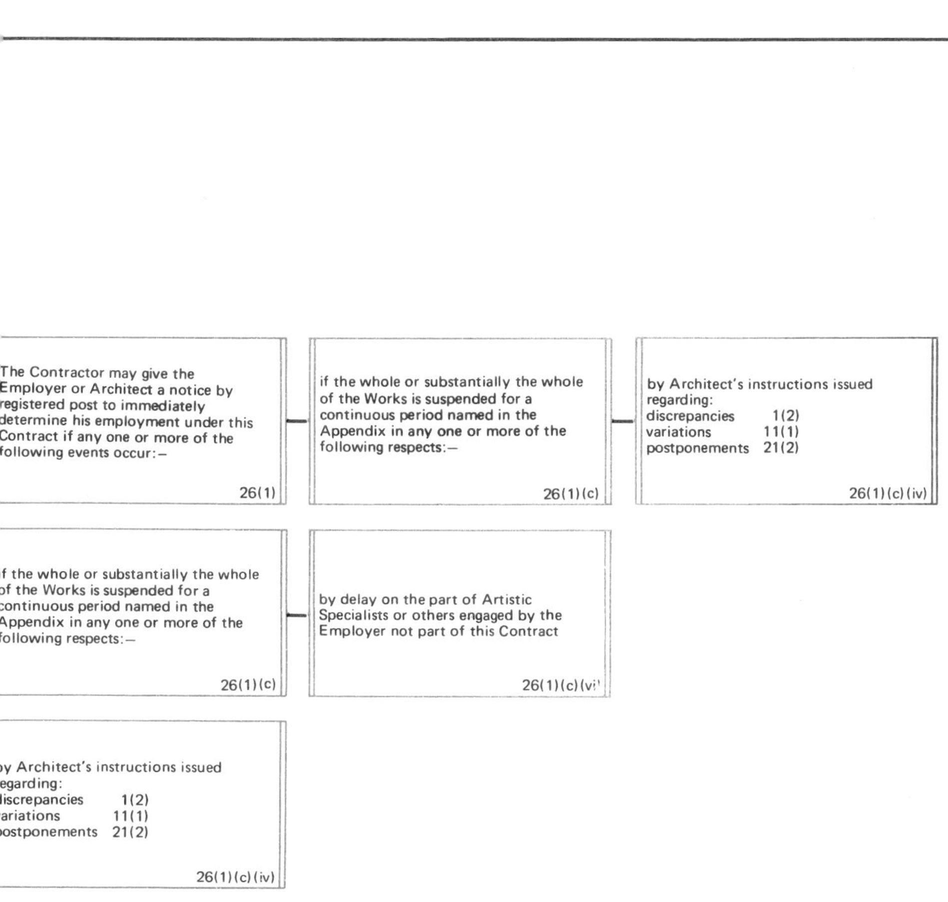
The Contractor may give the
Employer or Architect a notice by
registered post to immediately
determine his employment under this
Contract if any one or more of the
following events occur:—
26(1)
if the whole or substantially the whole
of the Works is suspended for a
continuous period named in the
Appendix in any one or more of the
following respects:—
26(1)(c)
by Architect's instructions issued
regarding:
discrepancies 1(2)
variations 11(1)
postponements 21(2)
26(1)(c)(iv)
if the whole or substantially the whole
of the Works is suspended for a
continuous period named in the
Appendix in any one or more of the
following respects:—
26(1)(c)
by delay on the part of Artistic
Specialists or others engaged by the
Employer not part of this Contract
26(1)(c)(vi)
by Architect's instructions issued
regarding:
discrepancies 1(2)
variations 11(1)
postponements 21(2)
26(1)(c)(iv)

Contractor does give the application as stipulated ?

YES → 24/1

NO

The Contractor may possess other rights and remedies

24(2)

Although written notice is a condition precedent to action by the Architect lack of formal notice may not prevent the Contractor from recovering at Common Law with wider scope than the reasons listed in this clause.
If notice had already been given by the Contractor under clause 23 this breach would be a technical one only and would not prevent recovery even under this Contract provision

Clause 24 LOSS AND EXPENSE BY DISTURBANCE OF PROGRESS (2)

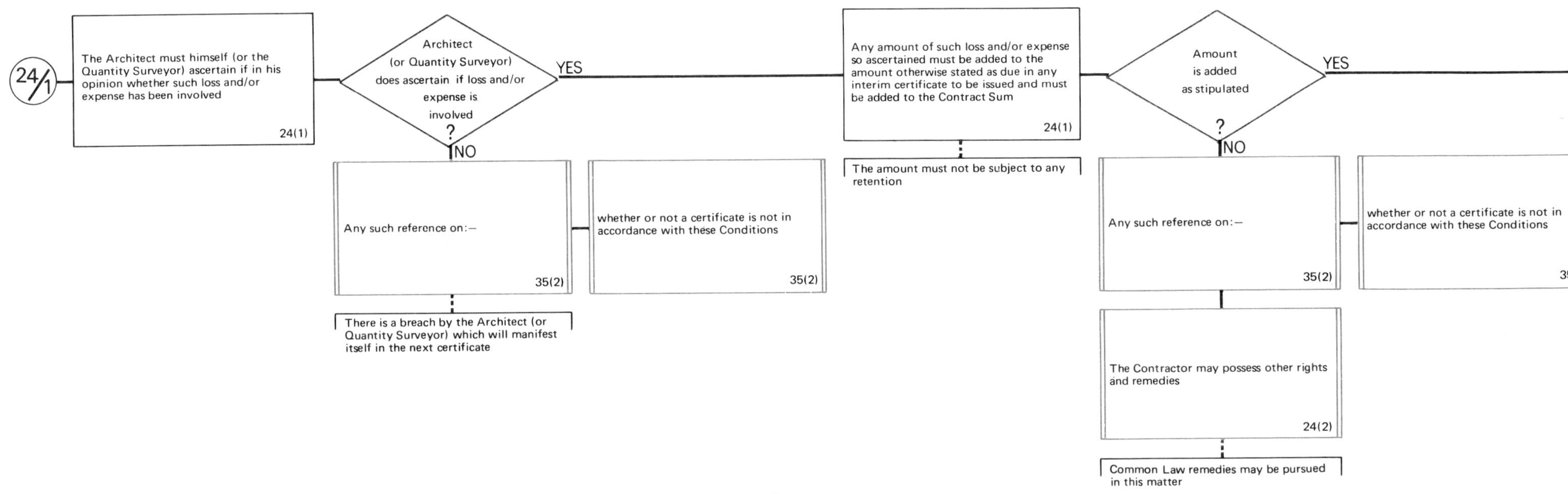

24/1
The Architect must himself (or the Quantity Surveyor) ascertain if in his opinion whether such loss and/or expense has been involved
24(1)
Architect (or Quantity Surveyor) does ascertain if loss and/or expense is involved ?
YES
NO
Any such reference on:—
35(2)
whether or not a certificate is not in accordance with these Conditions
35(2)
There is a breach by the Architect (or Quantity Surveyor) which will manifest itself in the next certificate
Any amount of such loss and/or expense so ascertained must be added to the amount otherwise stated as due in any interim certificate to be issued and must be added to the Contract Sum
24(1)
The amount must not be subject to any retention
Amount is added as stipulated ?
YES
NO
Any such reference on:—
35(2)
whether or not a certificate is not in accordance with these Conditions
The Contractor may possess other rights and remedies
24(2)
Common Law remedies may be pursued in this matter

STOP

here is a breach by the Architect

Clause 25 DETERMINATION FOR DEFAULT BY CONTRACTOR

START

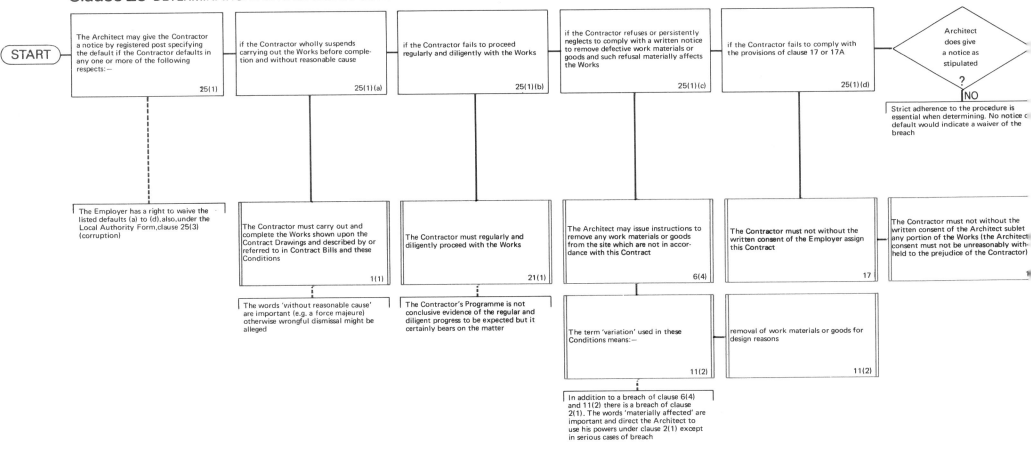

The Architect may give the Contractor a notice by registered post specifying the default if the Contractor defaults in any one or more of the following respects:— 25(1)

The Employer has a right to waive the listed defaults (a) to (d), also, under the Local Authority Form, clause 25(3) (corruption)

if the Contractor wholly suspends carrying out the Works before completion and without reasonable cause 25(1)(a)

The Contractor must carry out and complete the Works shown upon the Contract Drawings and described by or referred to in Contract Bills and these Conditions 1(1)

The words 'without reasonable cause' are important (e.g. a force majeure) otherwise wrongful dismissal might be alleged

if the Contractor fails to proceed regularly and diligently with the Works 25(1)(b)

The Contractor must regularly and diligently proceed with the Works 21(1)

The Contractor's Programme is not conclusive evidence of the regular and diligent progress to be expected but it certainly bears on the matter

if the Contractor refuses or persistently neglects to comply with a written notice to remove defective work materials or goods and such refusal materially affects the Works 25(1)(c)

The Architect may issue instructions to remove any work materials or goods from the site which are not in accordance with this Contract 6(4)

The term 'variation' used in these Conditions means:— 11(2)

removal of work materials or goods for design reasons 11(2)

In addition to a breach of clause 6(4) and 11(2) there is a breach of clause 2(1). The words 'materially affected' are important and direct the Architect to use his powers under clause 2(1) except in serious cases of breach

if the Contractor fails to comply with the provisions of clause 17 or 17A 25(1)(d)

The Contractor must not without the written consent of the Employer assign this Contract 17

The Contractor must not without the written consent of the Architect sublet any portion of the Works (the Architect consent must not be unreasonably withheld to the prejudice of the Contractor)

Architect does give a notice as stipulated ?

NO

Strict adherence to the procedure is essential when determining. No notice of default would indicate a waiver of the breach

25

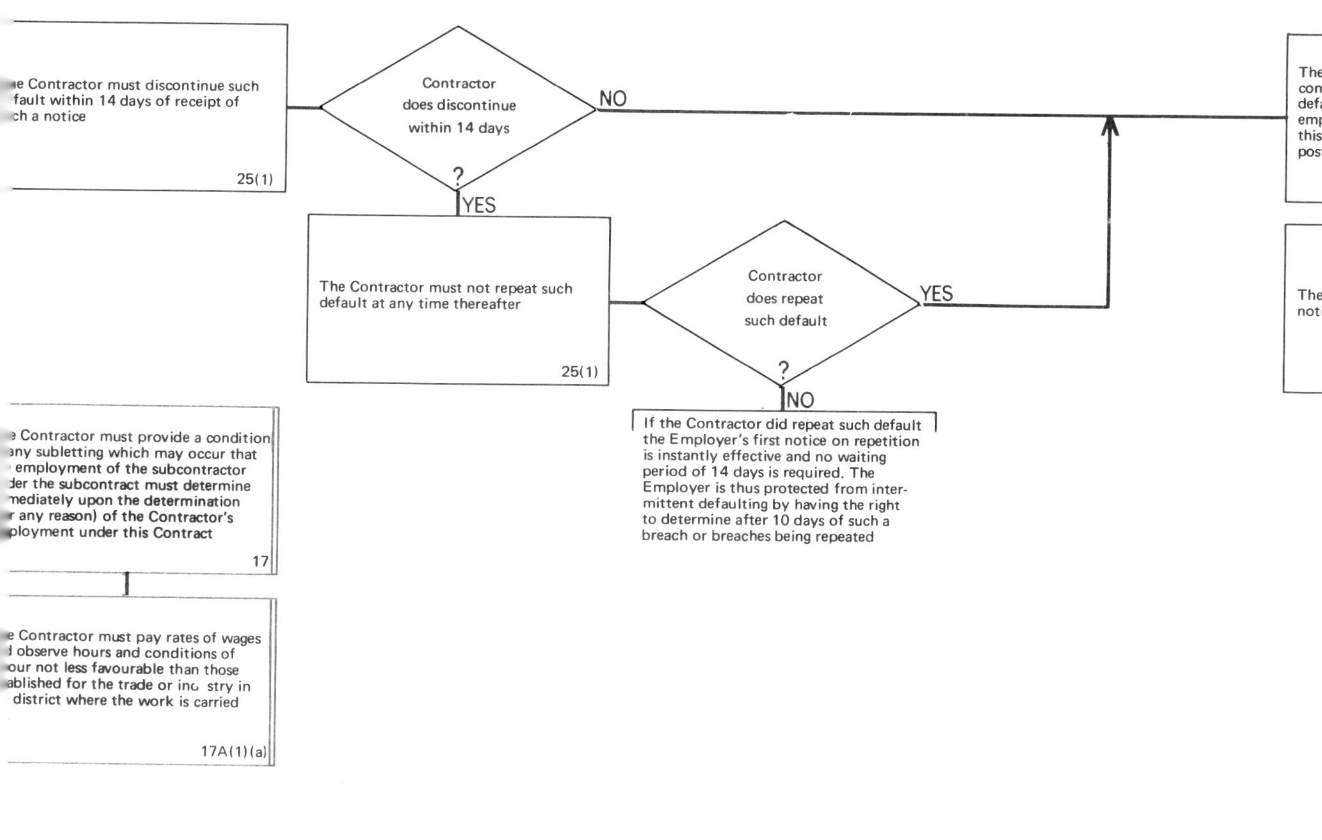

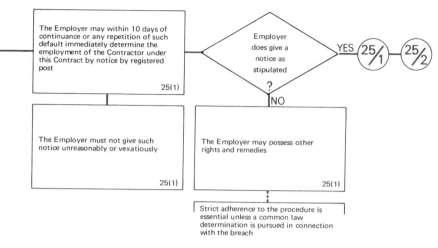

ıe Contractor must discontinue such
fault within 14 days of receipt of
ch a notice
25(1)
Contractor does discontinue within 14 days ?
NO
YES
The Contractor must not repeat such default at any time thereafter
25(1)
Contractor does repeat such default ?
YES
NO
If the Contractor did repeat such default the Employer's first notice on repetition is instantly effective and no waiting period of 14 days is required. The Employer is thus protected from intermittent defaulting by having the right to determine after 10 days of such a breach or breaches being repeated
ɘ Contractor must provide a condition
ıny subletting which may occur that
employment of the subcontractor
der the subcontract must determine
mediately upon the determination
r any reason) of the Contractor's
ployment under this Contract
17
e Contractor must pay rates of wages
l observe hours and conditions of
our not less favourable than those
ablished for the trade or industry in
district where the work is carried
17A(1)(a)

The Employer may within 10 days of continuance or any repetition of such default immediately determine the employment of the Contractor under this Contract by notice by registered post

25(1)

Employer does give a notice as stipulated ?

YES 25/1 — 25/2

NO

The Employer must not give such notice unreasonably or vexatiously

25(1)

The Employer may possess other rights and remedies

25(1)

Strict adherence to the procedure is essential unless a common law determination is pursued in connection with the breach

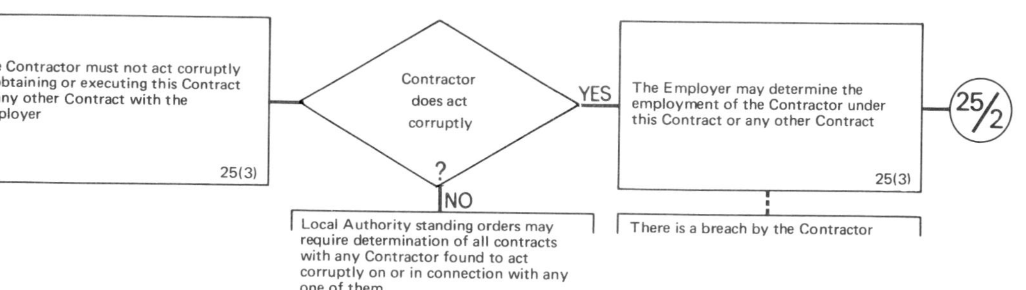

ɘ Contractor must not act corruptly
btaining or executing this Contract
ıny other Contract with the
ployer
25(3)
Contractor does act corruptly ?
YES
NO
The Employer may determine the employment of the Contractor under this Contract or any other Contract
25(3)
25/2
There is a breach by the Contractor
Local Authority standing orders may require determination of all contracts with any Contractor found to act corruptly on or in connection with any one of them

Clause 25 PROCEDURE AFTER SERVING NOTICE FOR DEFAULTS BY CONTRACTOR

25/2

The Employer may employ and pay other persons to complete the Works 25(4)(a)

Employer does employ and pay others to complete?

YES

The other persons may enter and use all temporary buildings plant tools and equipment materials and goods intended for and on or adjacent the Works 25(4)(a)

Materials and goods delivered and placed on or adjacent the Works and intended for the Works but unfixed must not be removed except for use upon the Works 14(1)

The Employer must ensure any surplus materials are reserved for the Contractor

Materials and goods must become the property of the Employer where the value has in accordance with clause 30(2A) been included in any interim certificate under which the Contractor has received payment 14(2)

The Contract is silent as to procedure for the Employer to recover such materials or goods

NO

The Employer may decide to revoke his determination and instruct the Contractor to proceed with his employment in spite of the breach

Other persons do enter and use as stipulated?

NO

The Contractor must if required in writing by the Architect (but not before) remove within a reasonable time any temporary buildings plant tools equipment materials and goods belonging to or hired by him 25(4)(c)

YES

The Contractor must (within 14 days of determination) if required by the Employer or Architect assign free to the Employer the benefit of any agreement with any supplier or subcontractor 25(4)(b)

The Contractor must provide a condition in any subletting which may occur that the employment of the sub-contractor under the sub-contract must determine immediately upon the determination (for any reason) of the Contractor's employment under this Contract 17

Employer does require assignment as stipulated?

NO

The Employer need not since clauses 17 and 27 and clause 28 provide for the next appointed Contractor to start up fresh agreements in effect

The Architect must not nominate any person who wi[ll] not enter into a subcontract agreement which provides the following:— 27(a)

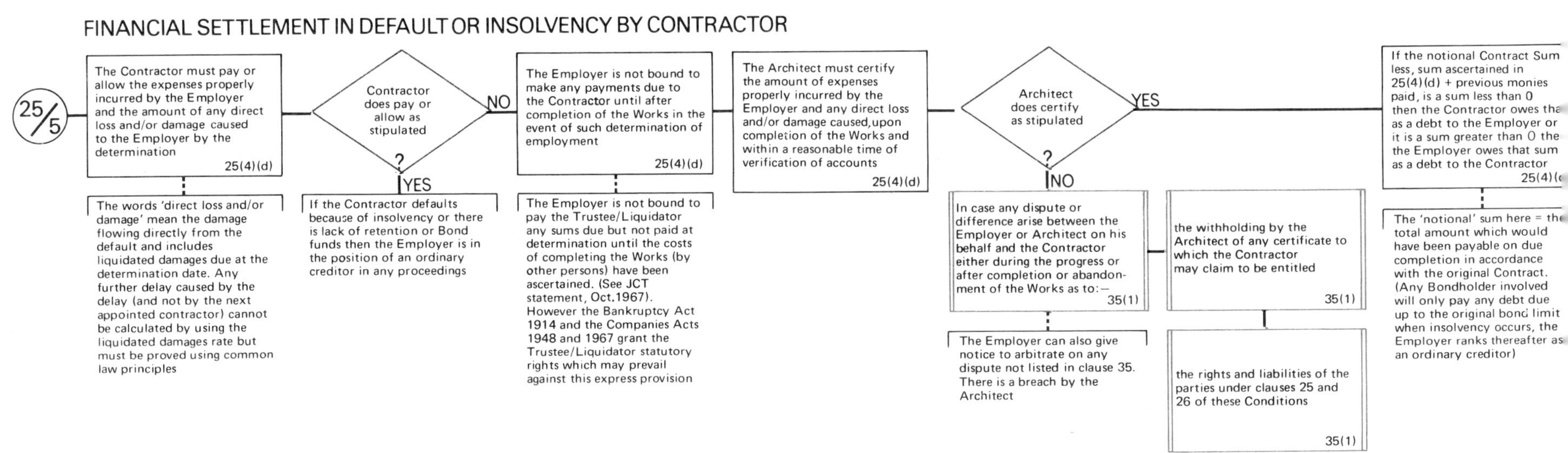

FINANCIAL SETTLEMENT IN DEFAULT OR INSOLVENCY BY CONTRACTOR
25/5
The Contractor must pay or allow the expenses properly incurred by the Employer and the amount of any direct loss and/or damage caused to the Employer by the determination 25(4)(d)
The words 'direct loss and/or damage' mean the damage flowing directly from the default and includes liquidated damages due at the determination date. Any further delay caused by the delay (and not by the next appointed contractor) cannot be calculated by using the liquidated damages rate but must be proved using common law principles
Contractor does pay or allow as stipulated?
NO
The Employer is not bound to make any payments due to the Contractor until after completion of the Works in the event of such determination of employment 25(4)(d)
The Employer is not bound to pay the Trustee/Liquidator any sums due but not paid at determination until the costs of completing the Works (by other persons) have been ascertained. (See JCT statement, Oct.1967). However the Bankruptcy Act 1914 and the Companies Acts 1948 and 1967 grant the Trustee/Liquidator statutory rights which may prevail against this express provision
YES
If the Contractor defaults because of insolvency or there is lack of retention or Bond funds then the Employer is in the position of an ordinary creditor in any proceedings
The Architect must certify the amount of expenses properly incurred by the Employer and any direct loss and/or damage caused, upon completion of the Works and within a reasonable time of verification of accounts 25(4)(d)
Architect does certify as stipulated?
YES
If the notional Contract Sum less, sum ascertained in 25(4)(d) + previous monies paid, is a sum less than 0 then the Contractor owes that as a debt to the Employer or it is a sum greater than 0 the the Employer owes that sum as a debt to the Contractor 25(4)(
The 'notional' sum here = the total amount which would have been payable on due completion in accordance with the original Contract. (Any Bondholder involved will only pay any debt due up to the original bond limit when insolvency occurs, the Employer ranks thereafter as an ordinary creditor)
NO
In case any dispute or difference arise between the Employer or Architect on his behalf and the Contractor either during the progress or after completion or abandonment of the Works as to:— 35(1)
The Employer can also give notice to arbitrate on any dispute not listed in clause 35. There is a breach by the Architect
the withholding by the Architect of any certificate to which the Contractor may claim to be entitled 35(1)
the rights and liabilities of the parties under clauses 25 and 26 of these Conditions 35(1)

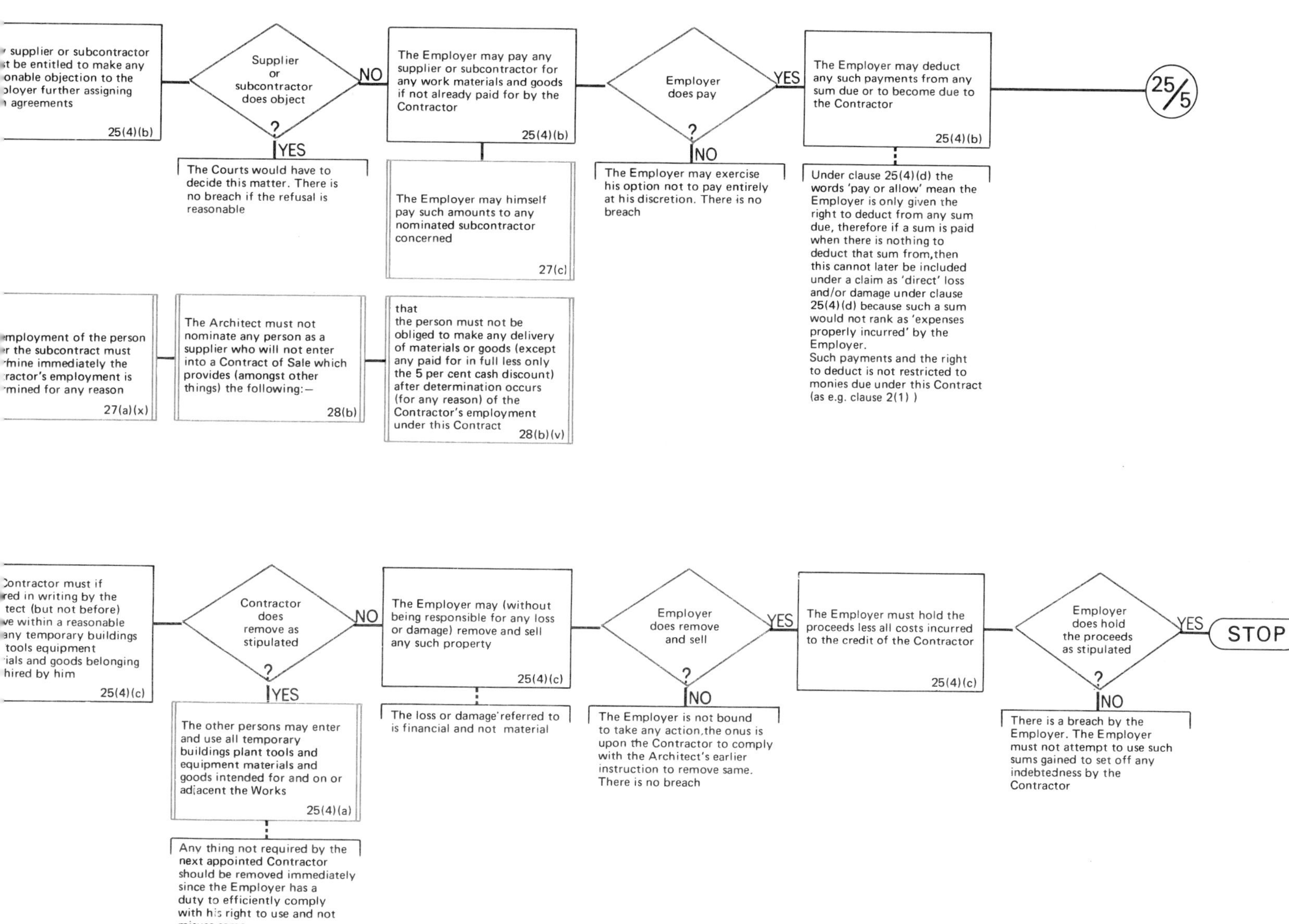

supplier or subcontractor
t be entitled to make any
onable objection to the
ployer further assigning
agreements
25(4)(b)
Supplier or subcontractor does object ?
NO
YES
The Courts would have to decide this matter. There is no breach if the refusal is reasonable
The Employer may pay any supplier or subcontractor for any work materials and goods if not already paid for by the Contractor
25(4)(b)
The Employer may himself pay such amounts to any nominated subcontractor concerned
27(c)
Employer does pay ?
YES
NO
The Employer may exercise his option not to pay entirely at his discretion. There is no breach
The Employer may deduct any such payments from any sum due or to become due to the Contractor
25(4)(b)
Under clause 25(4)(d) the words 'pay or allow' mean the Employer is only given the right to deduct from any sum due, therefore if a sum is paid when there is nothing to deduct that sum from, then this cannot later be included under a claim as 'direct' loss and/or damage under clause 25(4)(d) because such a sum would not rank as 'expenses properly incurred' by the Employer.
Such payments and the right to deduct is not restricted to monies due under this Contract (as e.g. clause 2(1))
25/5
mployment of the person
r the subcontract must
mine immediately the
ractor's employment is
mined for any reason
27(a)(x)
The Architect must not nominate any person as a supplier who will not enter into a Contract of Sale which provides (amongst other things) the following:—
28(b)
that the person must not be obliged to make any delivery of materials or goods (except any paid for in full less only the 5 per cent cash discount) after determination occurs (for any reason) of the Contractor's employment under this Contract
28(b)(v)
ontractor must if
red in writing by the
tect (but not before)
ve within a reasonable
ny temporary buildings
tools equipment
ials and goods belonging
hired by him
25(4)(c)
Contractor does remove as stipulated ?
NO
YES
The other persons may enter and use all temporary buildings plant tools and equipment materials and goods intended for and on or adjacent the Works
25(4)(a)
Any thing not required by the next appointed Contractor should be removed immediately since the Employer has a duty to efficiently comply with his right to use and not misuse same
The Employer may (without being responsible for any loss or damage) remove and sell any such property
25(4)(c)
The loss or damage referred to is financial and not material
Employer does remove and sell ?
YES
NO
The Employer is not bound to take any action, the onus is upon the Contractor to comply with the Architect's earlier instruction to remove same. There is no breach
The Employer must hold the proceeds less all costs incurred to the credit of the Contractor
25(4)(c)
Employer does hold the proceeds as stipulated ?
YES
STOP
NO
There is a breach by the Employer. The Employer must not attempt to use such sums gained to set off any indebtedness by the Contractor

Clause 25 DETERMINATION IN THE EVENT OF CONTRACTOR'S INSOLVENCY

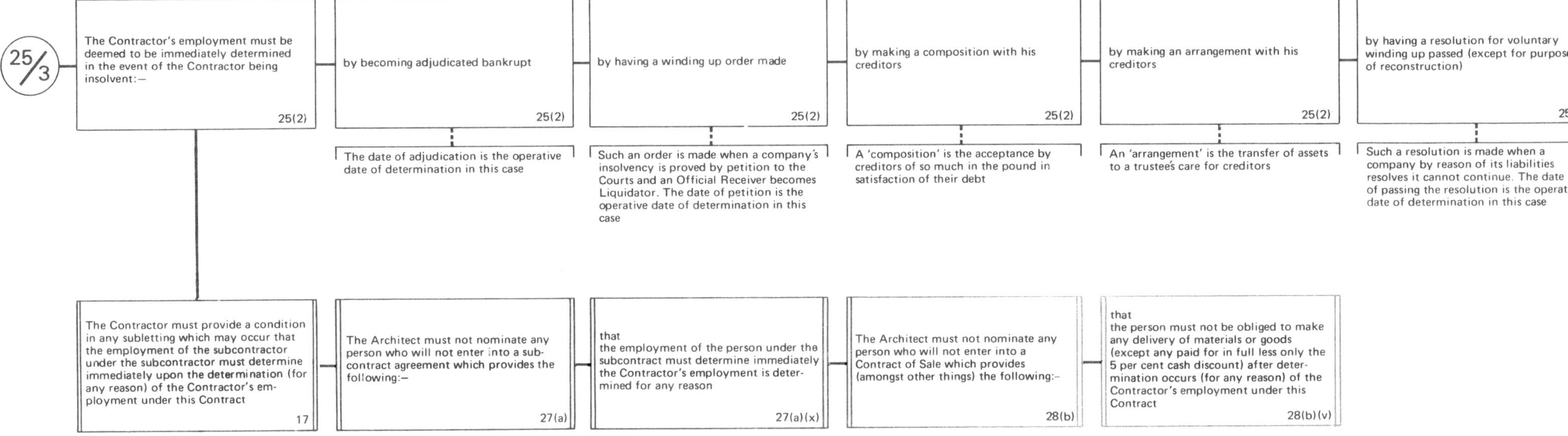

25/3
The Contractor's employment must be deemed to be immediately determined in the event of the Contractor being insolvent:–
25(2)
by becoming adjudicated bankrupt
25(2)
The date of adjudication is the operative date of determination in this case
by having a winding up order made
25(2)
Such an order is made when a company's insolvency is proved by petition to the Courts and an Official Receiver becomes Liquidator. The date of petition is the operative date of determination in this case
by making a composition with his creditors
25(2)
A 'composition' is the acceptance by creditors of so much in the pound in satisfaction of their debt
by making an arrangement with his creditors
25(2)
An 'arrangement' is the transfer of assets to a trustee's care for creditors
by having a resolution for voluntary winding up passed (except for purposes of reconstruction)
25(2
Such a resolution is made when a company by reason of its liabilities resolves it cannot continue. The date of passing the resolution is the operative date of determination in this case
The Contractor must provide a condition in any subletting which may occur that the employment of the subcontractor under the subcontractor must determine immediately upon the determination (for any reason) of the Contractor's employment under this Contract
17
The Architect must not nominate any person who will not enter into a sub-contract agreement which provides the following:–
27(a)
that the employment of the person under the subcontract must determine immediately the Contractor's employment is determined for any reason
27(a)(x)
The Architect must not nominate any person who will not enter into a Contract of Sale which provides (amongst other things) the following:–
28(b)
that the person must not be obliged to make any delivery of materials or goods (except any paid for in full less only the 5 per cent cash discount) after determination occurs (for any reason) of the Contractor's employment under this Contract
28(b)(v)

PROCEDURE AFTER AUTOMATIC DETERMINATION FOLLOWED BY AN ADOPTION IN INSOLVENCY

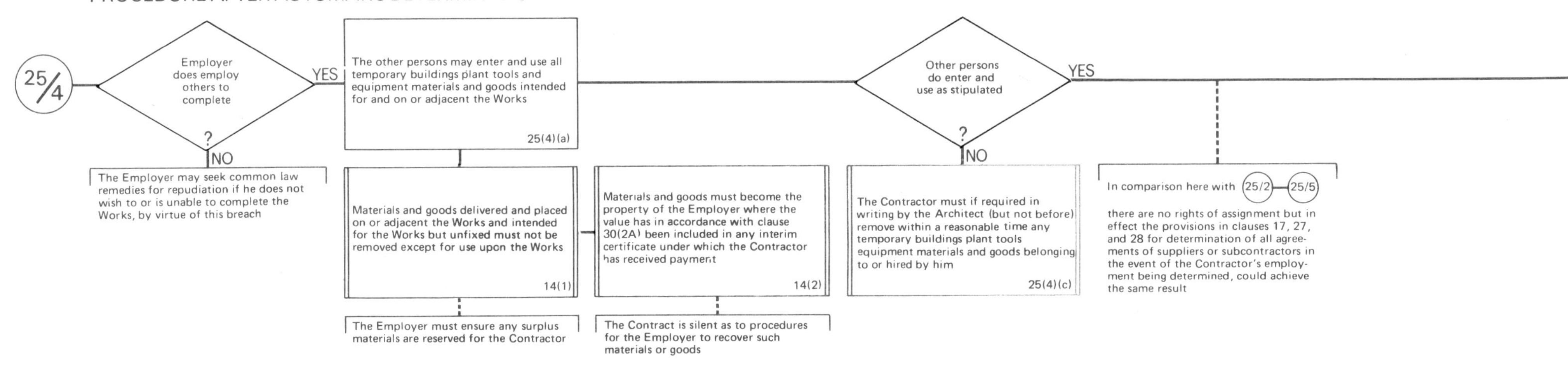

25/4
Employer does employ others to complete ?
YES
NO
The Employer may seek common law remedies for repudiation if he does not wish to or is unable to complete the Works, by virtue of this breach
The other persons may enter and use all temporary buildings plant tools and equipment materials and goods intended for and on or adjacent the Works
25(4)(a)
Materials and goods delivered and placed on or adjacent the Works and intended for the Works but unfixed must not be removed except for use upon the Works
14(1)
The Employer must ensure any surplus materials are reserved for the Contractor
Materials and goods must become the property of the Employer where the value has in accordance with clause 30(2A) been included in any interim certificate under which the Contractor has received payment
14(2)
The Contract is silent as to procedures for the Employer to recover such materials or goods
Other persons do enter and use as stipulated ?
YES
NO
The Contractor must if required in writing by the Architect (but not before) remove within a reasonable time any temporary buildings plant tools equipment materials and goods belonging to or hired by him
25(4)(c)
In comparison here with 25/2 – 25/5
there are no rights of assignment but in effect the provisions in clauses 17, 27, and 28 for determination of all agreements of suppliers or subcontractors in the event of the Contractor's employment being determined, could achieve the same result

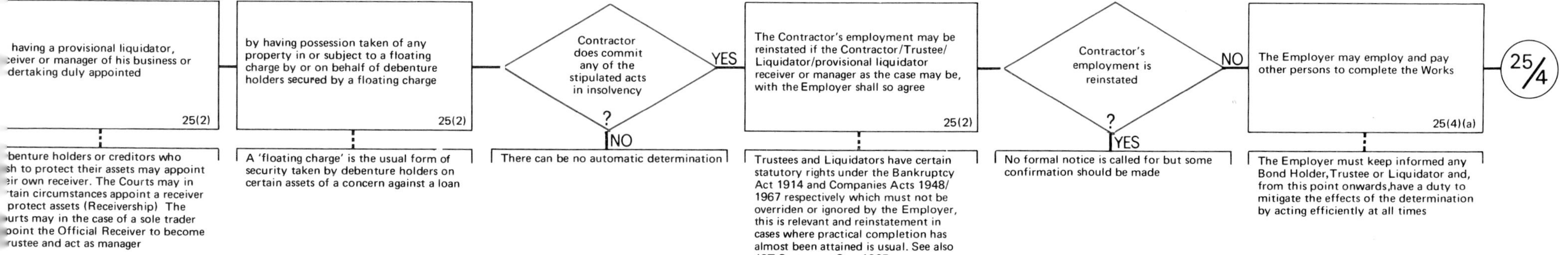
having a provisional liquidator,
ceiver or manager of his business or
dertaking duly appointed
25(2)
by having possession taken of any property in or subject to a floating charge by or on behalf of debenture holders secured by a floating charge
25(2)
Contractor does commit any of the stipulated acts in insolvency ?
YES
NO
The Contractor's employment may be reinstated if the Contractor/Trustee/ Liquidator/provisional liquidator receiver or manager as the case may be, with the Employer shall so agree
25(2)
Contractor's employment is reinstated ?
NO
YES
The Employer may employ and pay other persons to complete the Works
25(4)(a)
25/4
benture holders or creditors who
sh to protect their assets may appoint
eir own receiver. The Courts may in
tain circumstances appoint a receiver
protect assets (Receivership) The
urts may in the case of a sole trader
point the Official Receiver to become
rustee and act as manager
A 'floating charge' is the usual form of security taken by debenture holders on certain assets of a concern against a loan
There can be no automatic determination
Trustees and Liquidators have certain statutory rights under the Bankruptcy Act 1914 and Companies Acts 1948/ 1967 respectively which must not be overriden or ignored by the Employer, this is relevant and reinstatement in cases where practical completion has almost been attained is usual. See also JCT Statement Oct. 1967
No formal notice is called for but some confirmation should be made
The Employer must keep informed any Bond Holder, Trustee or Liquidator and, from this point onwards, have a duty to mitigate the effects of the determination by acting efficiently at all times

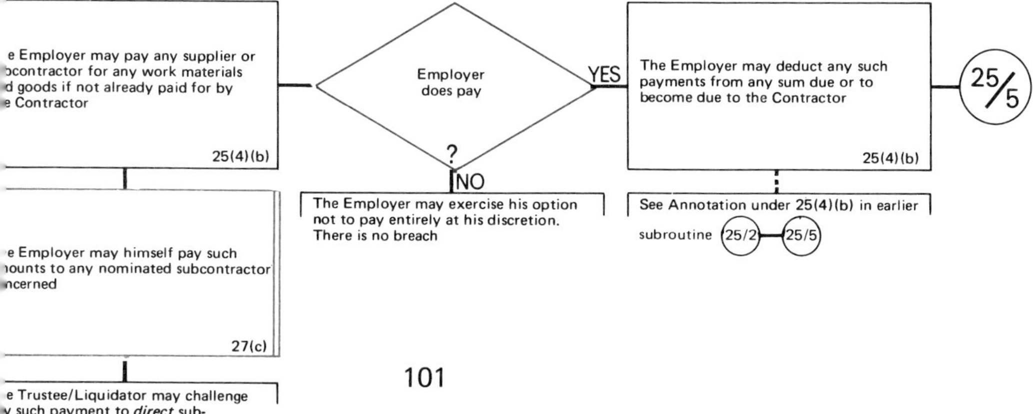
e Employer may pay any supplier or
bcontractor for any work materials
d goods if not already paid for by
e Contractor
25(4)(b)
Employer does pay ?
YES
NO
The Employer may deduct any such payments from any sum due or to become due to the Contractor
25(4)(b)
25/5
e Employer may himself pay such
nounts to any nominated subcontractor
ncerned
27(c)
The Employer may exercise his option not to pay entirely at his discretion. There is no breach
See Annotation under 25(4)(b) in earlier subroutine 25/2—25/5
e Trustee/Liquidator may challenge
y such payment to *direct* sub-
ntractors or suppliers (see JCT
atement, Oct.1967)

Clause 26 DETERMINATION BY THE CONTRACTOR OF HIS OWN EMPLOYMENT

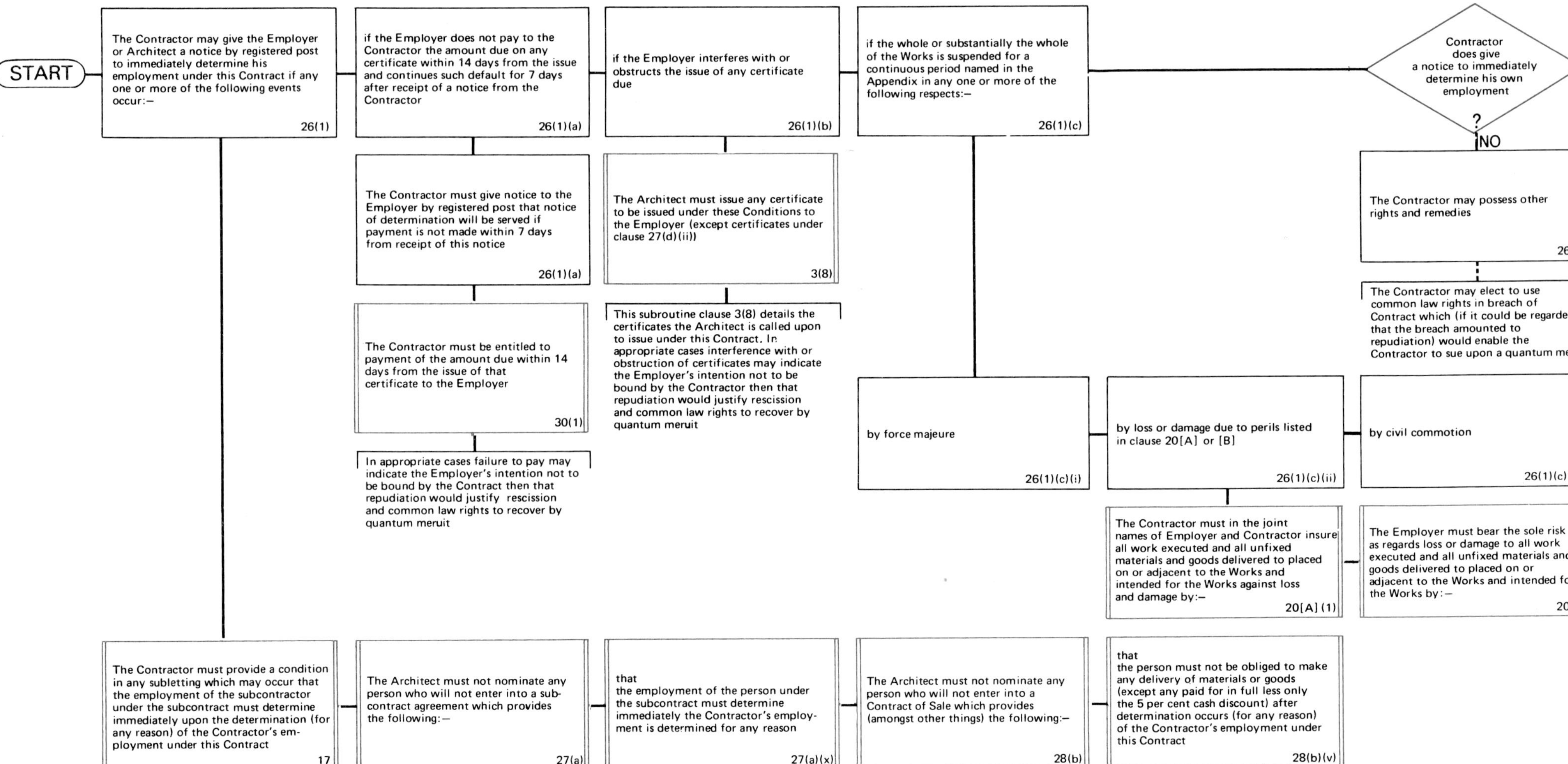

START
The Contractor may give the Employer or Architect a notice by registered post to immediately determine his employment under this Contract if any one or more of the following events occur:– 26(1)
if the Employer does not pay to the Contractor the amount due on any certificate within 14 days from the issue and continues such default for 7 days after receipt of a notice from the Contractor 26(1)(a)
if the Employer interferes with or obstructs the issue of any certificate due 26(1)(b)
if the whole or substantially the whole of the Works is suspended for a continuous period named in the Appendix in any one or more of the following respects:– 26(1)(c)
Contractor does give a notice to immediately determine his own employment ?
NO
The Contractor must give notice to the Employer by registered post that notice of determination will be served if payment is not made within 7 days from receipt of this notice 26(1)(a)
The Architect must issue any certificate to be issued under these Conditions to the Employer (except certificates under clause 27(d)(ii)) 3(8)
The Contractor may possess other rights and remedies 26(
The Contractor must be entitled to payment of the amount due within 14 days from the issue of that certificate to the Employer 30(1)
This subroutine clause 3(8) details the certificates the Architect is called upon to issue under this Contract. In appropriate cases interference with or obstruction of certificates may indicate the Employer's intention not to be bound by the Contractor then that repudiation would justify rescission and common law rights to recover by quantum meruit
The Contractor may elect to use common law rights in breach of Contract which (if it could be regarded that the breach amounted to repudiation) would enable the Contractor to sue upon a quantum mer
In appropriate cases failure to pay may indicate the Employer's intention not to be bound by the Contract then that repudiation would justify rescission and common law rights to recover by quantum meruit
by force majeure 26(1)(c)(i)
by loss or damage due to perils listed in clause 20[A] or [B] 26(1)(c)(ii)
by civil commotion 26(1)(c)(i
The Contractor must in the joint names of Employer and Contractor insure all work executed and all unfixed materials and goods delivered to placed on or adjacent to the Works and intended for the Works against loss and damage by:– 20[A](1)
The Employer must bear the sole risk as regards loss or damage to all work executed and all unfixed materials and goods delivered to placed on or adjacent to the Works and intended for the Works by:– 20[
The Contractor must provide a condition in any subletting which may occur that the employment of the subcontractor under the subcontract must determine immediately upon the determination (for any reason) of the Contractor's employment under this Contract 17
The Architect must not nominate any person who will not enter into a sub-contract agreement which provides the following:– 27(a)
that the employment of the person under the subcontract must determine immediately the Contractor's employment is determined for any reason 27(a)(x)
The Architect must not nominate any person who will not enter into a Contract of Sale which provides (amongst other things) the following:– 28(b)
that the person must not be obliged to make any delivery of materials or goods (except any paid for in full less only the 5 per cent cash discount) after determination occurs (for any reason) of the Contractor's employment under this Contract 28(b)(v)

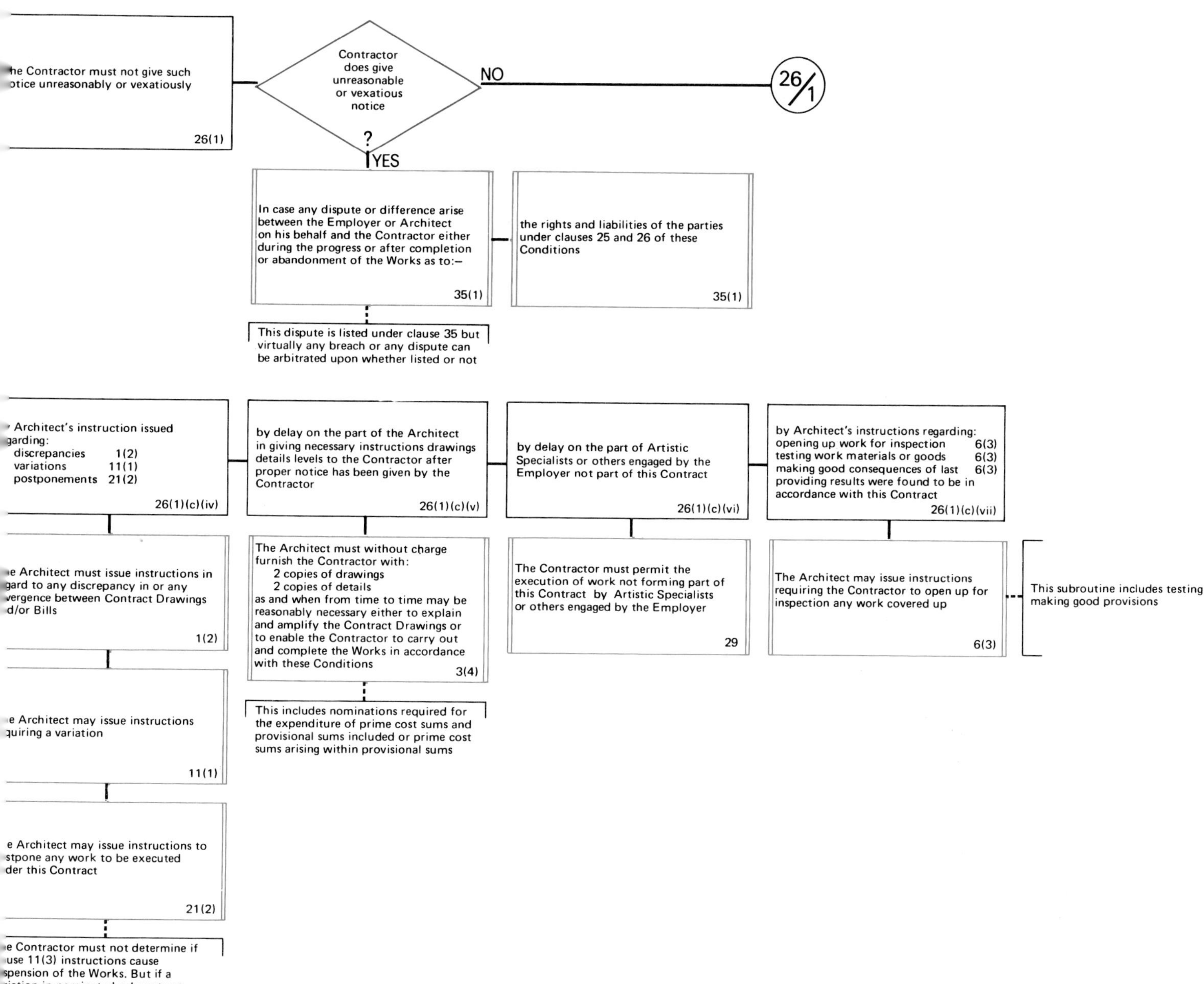

he Contractor must not give such
otice unreasonably or vexatiously
26(1)
Contractor does give unreasonable or vexatious notice ?
NO
26/1
YES
In case any dispute or difference arise between the Employer or Architect on his behalf and the Contractor either during the progress or after completion or abandonment of the Works as to:–
35(1)
the rights and liabilities of the parties under clauses 25 and 26 of these Conditions
35(1)
This dispute is listed under clause 35 but virtually any breach or any dispute can be arbitrated upon whether listed or not
Architect's instruction issued
garding:
discrepancies 1(2)
variations 11(1)
postponements 21(2)
26(1)(c)(iv)
by delay on the part of the Architect in giving necessary instructions drawings details levels to the Contractor after proper notice has been given by the Contractor
26(1)(c)(v)
by delay on the part of Artistic Specialists or others engaged by the Employer not part of this Contract
26(1)(c)(vi)
by Architect's instructions regarding:
opening up work for inspection 6(3)
testing work materials or goods 6(3)
making good consequences of last 6(3)
providing results were found to be in accordance with this Contract
26(1)(c)(vii)
e Architect must issue instructions in
gard to any discrepancy in or any
vergence between Contract Drawings
d/or Bills
1(2)
The Architect must without charge furnish the Contractor with:
2 copies of drawings
2 copies of details
as and when from time to time may be reasonably necessary either to explain and amplify the Contract Drawings or to enable the Contractor to carry out and complete the Works in accordance with these Conditions
3(4)
The Contractor must permit the execution of work not forming part of this Contract by Artistic Specialists or others engaged by the Employer
29
The Architect may issue instructions requiring the Contractor to open up for inspection any work covered up
6(3)
This subroutine includes testing and making good provisions
This includes nominations required for the expenditure of prime cost sums and provisional sums included or prime cost sums arising within provisional sums
e Architect may issue instructions
quiring a variation
11(1)
e Architect may issue instructions to
stpone any work to be executed
der this Contract
21(2)
e Contractor must not determine if
use 11(3) instructions cause
spension of the Works. But if a
iation in nominated subcontract
rk requiring an instruction under
use 11(1) causes such suspension then
e Contractor can determine

Clause 26 AGREED AND ACCRUED RIGHTS OF THE PARTIES UPON SUCH DETERMINATION

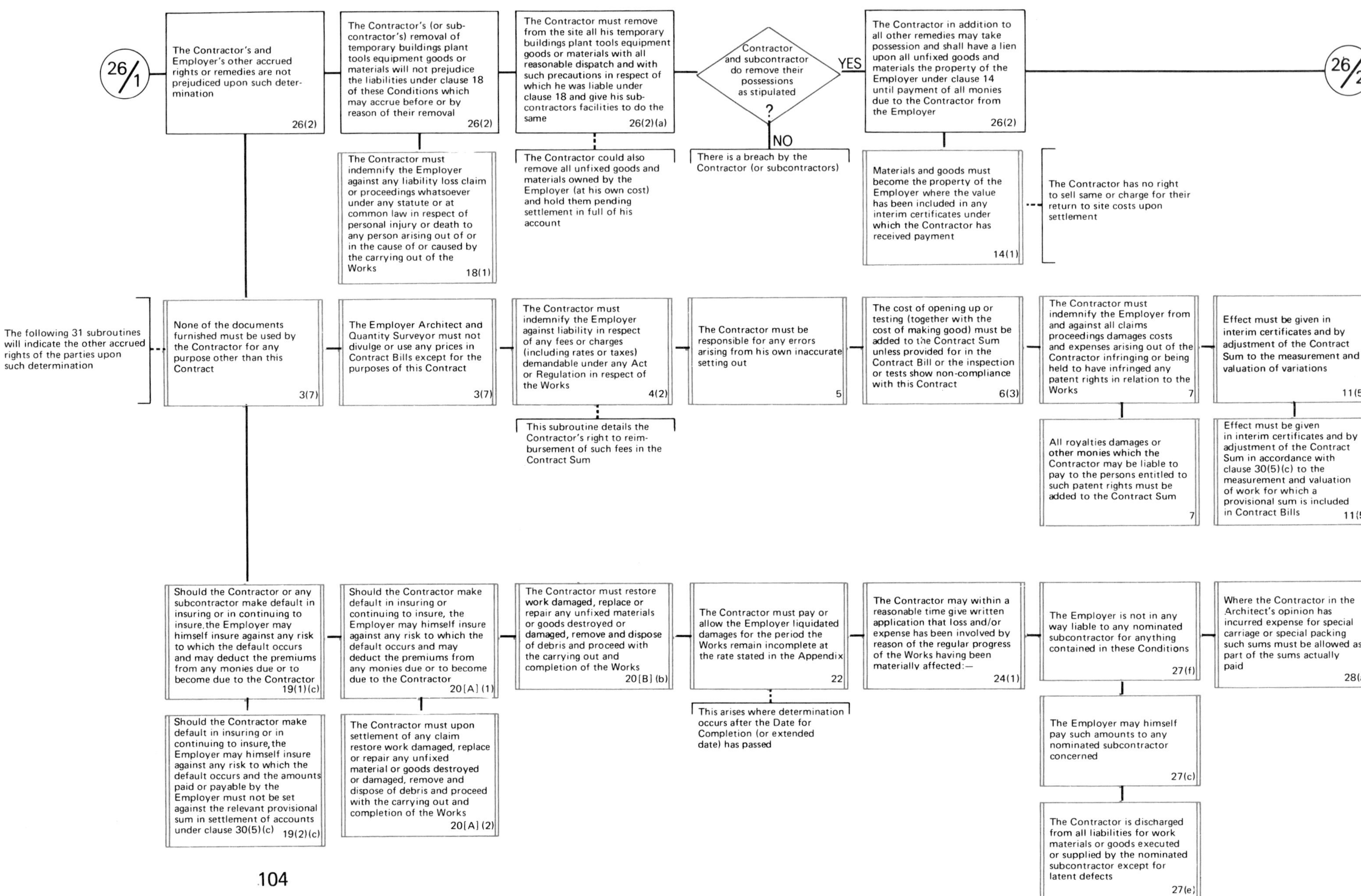

26/1
The Contractor's and Employer's other accrued rights or remedies are not prejudiced upon such determination 26(2)
The Contractor's (or subcontractor's) removal of temporary buildings plant tools equipment goods or materials will not prejudice the liabilities under clause 18 of these Conditions which may accrue before or by reason of their removal 26(2)
The Contractor must indemnify the Employer against any liability loss claim or proceedings whatsoever under any statute or at common law in respect of personal injury or death to any person arising out of or in the cause of or caused by the carrying out of the Works 18(1)
The Contractor must remove from the site all his temporary buildings plant tools equipment goods or materials with all reasonable dispatch and with such precautions in respect of which he was liable under clause 18 and give his subcontractors facilities to do the same 26(2)(a)
The Contractor could also remove all unfixed goods and materials owned by the Employer (at his own cost) and hold them pending settlement in full of his account
Contractor and subcontractor do remove their possessions as stipulated ?
YES
NO
There is a breach by the Contractor (or subcontractors)
The Contractor in addition to all other remedies may take possession and shall have a lien upon all unfixed goods and materials the property of the Employer under clause 14 until payment of all monies due to the Contractor from the Employer 26(2)
26/2
Materials and goods must become the property of the Employer where the value has been included in any interim certificates under which the Contractor has received payment 14(1)
The Contractor has no right to sell same or charge for their return to site costs upon settlement
The following 31 subroutines will indicate the other accrued rights of the parties upon such determination
None of the documents furnished must be used by the Contractor for any purpose other than this Contract 3(7)
The Employer Architect and Quantity Surveyor must not divulge or use any prices in Contract Bills except for the purposes of this Contract 3(7)
The Contractor must indemnify the Employer against liability in respect of any fees or charges (including rates or taxes) demandable under any Act or Regulation in respect of the Works 4(2)
This subroutine details the Contractor's right to reimbursement of such fees in the Contract Sum
The Contractor must be responsible for any errors arising from his own inaccurate setting out 5
The cost of opening up or testing (together with the cost of making good) must be added to the Contract Sum unless provided for in the Contract Bill or the inspection or tests show non-compliance with this Contract 6(3)
The Contractor must indemnify the Employer from and against all claims proceedings damages costs and expenses arising out of the Contractor infringing or being held to have infringed any patent rights in relation to the Works 7
All royalties damages or other monies which the Contractor may be liable to pay to the persons entitled to such patent rights must be added to the Contract Sum 7
Effect must be given in interim certificates and by adjustment of the Contract Sum to the measurement and valuation of variations 11(5)
Effect must be given in interim certificates and by adjustment of the Contract Sum in accordance with clause 30(5)(c) to the measurement and valuation of work for which a provisional sum is included in Contract Bills 11(5)
Should the Contractor or any subcontractor make default in insuring or in continuing to insure, the Employer may himself insure against any risk to which the default occurs and may deduct the premiums from any monies due or to become due to the Contractor 19(1)(c)
Should the Contractor make default in insuring or in continuing to insure, the Employer may himself insure against any risk to which the default occurs and the amounts paid or payable by the Employer must not be set against the relevant provisional sum in settlement of accounts under clause 30(5)(c) 19(2)(c)
Should the Contractor make default in insuring or continuing to insure, the Employer may himself insure against any risk to which the default occurs and may deduct the premiums from any monies due or to become due to the Contractor 20[A](1)
The Contractor must upon settlement of any claim restore work damaged, replace or repair any unfixed material or goods destroyed or damaged, remove and dispose of debris and proceed with the carrying out and completion of the Works 20[A](2)
The Contractor must restore work damaged, replace or repair any unfixed materials or goods destroyed or damaged, remove and dispose of debris and proceed with the carrying out and completion of the Works 20[B](b)
The Contractor must pay or allow the Employer liquidated damages for the period the Works remain incomplete at the rate stated in the Appendix 22
This arises where determination occurs after the Date for Completion (or extended date) has passed
The Contractor may within a reasonable time give written application that loss and/or expense has been involved by reason of the regular progress of the Works having been materially affected:— 24(1)
The Employer is not in any way liable to any nominated subcontractor for anything contained in these Conditions 27(f)
The Employer may himself pay such amounts to any nominated subcontractor concerned 27(c)
The Contractor is discharged from all liabilities for work materials or goods executed or supplied by the nominated subcontractor except for latent defects 27(e)
Where the Contractor in the Architect's opinion has incurred expense for special carriage or special packing such sums must be allowed as part of the sums actually paid 28(a)

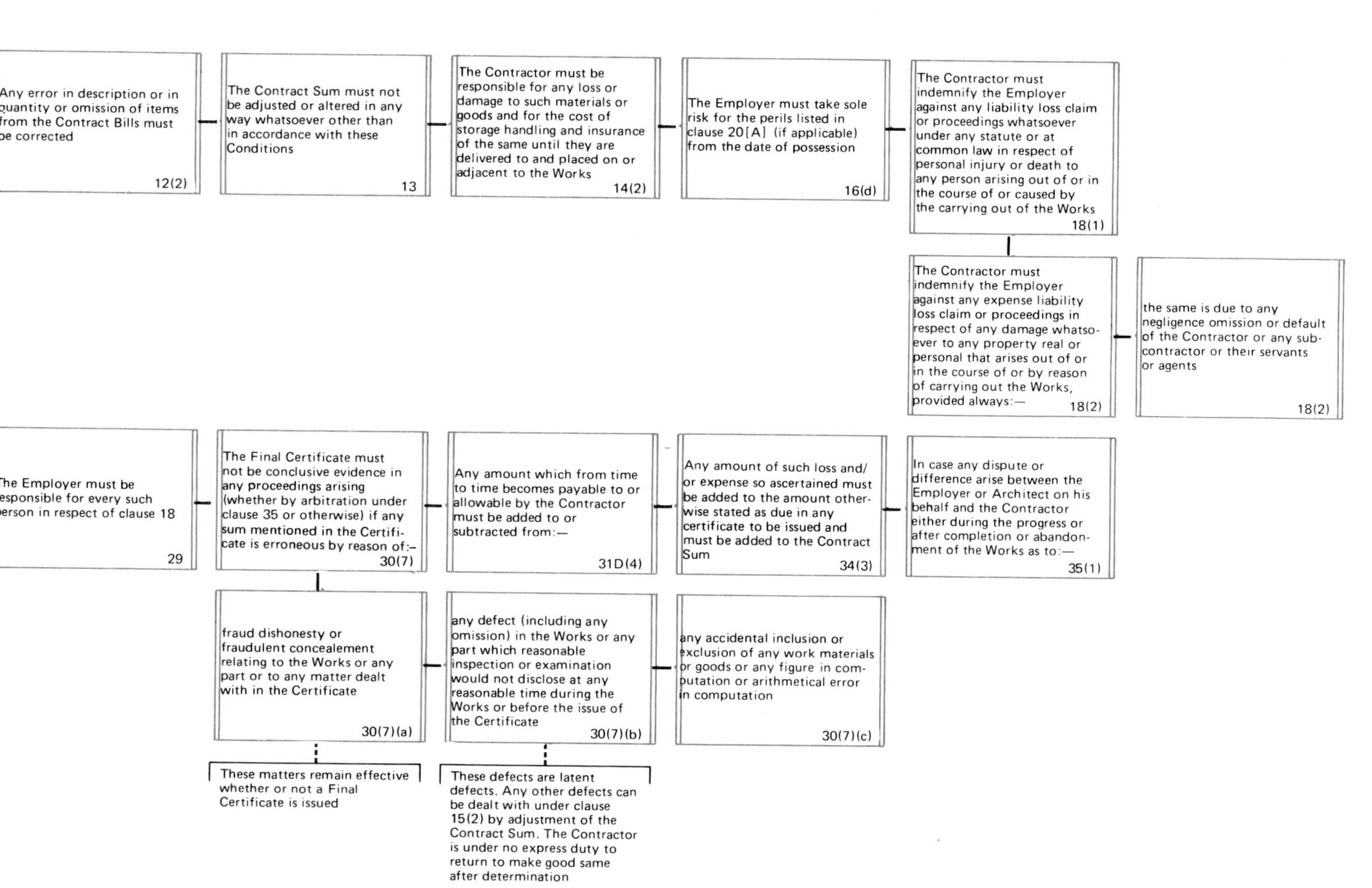
Any error in description or in quantity or omission of items from the Contract Bills must be corrected
12(2)
The Contract Sum must not be adjusted or altered in any way whatsoever other than in accordance with these Conditions
13
The Contractor must be responsible for any loss or damage to such materials or goods and for the cost of storage handling and insurance of the same until they are delivered to and placed on or adjacent to the Works
14(2)
The Employer must take sole risk for the perils listed in clause 20[A] (if applicable) from the date of possession
16(d)
The Contractor must indemnify the Employer against any liability loss claim or proceedings whatsoever under any statute or at common law in respect of personal injury or death to any person arising out of or in the course of or caused by the carrying out of the Works
18(1)
The Contractor must indemnify the Employer against any expense liability loss claim or proceedings in respect of any damage whatsoever to any property real or personal that arises out of or in the course of or by reason of carrying out the Works, provided always:—
18(2)
the same is due to any negligence omission or default of the Contractor or any sub-contractor or their servants or agents
18(2)
The Employer must be responsible for every such person in respect of clause 18
29
The Final Certificate must not be conclusive evidence in any proceedings arising (whether by arbitration under clause 35 or otherwise) if any sum mentioned in the Certificate is erroneous by reason of:–
30(7)
Any amount which from time to time becomes payable to or allowable by the Contractor must be added to or subtracted from:—
31D(4)
Any amount of such loss and/or expense so ascertained must be added to the amount otherwise stated as due in any certificate to be issued and must be added to the Contract Sum
34(3)
In case any dispute or difference arise between the Employer or Architect on his behalf and the Contractor either during the progress or after completion or abandonment of the Works as to:—
35(1)
fraud dishonesty or fraudulent concealement relating to the Works or any part or to any matter dealt with in the Certificate
30(7)(a)
any defect (including any omission) in the Works or any part which reasonable inspection or examination would not disclose at any reasonable time during the Works or before the issue of the Certificate
30(7)(b)
any accidental inclusion or exclusion of any work materials or goods or any figure in computation or arithmetical error in computation
30(7)(c)
These matters remain effective whether or not a Final Certificate is issued
These defects are latent defects. Any other defects can be dealt with under clause 15(2) by adjustment of the Contract Sum. The Contractor is under no express duty to return to make good same after determination

Clause 26 FINANCIAL SETTLEMENT UPON SUCH DETERMINATION

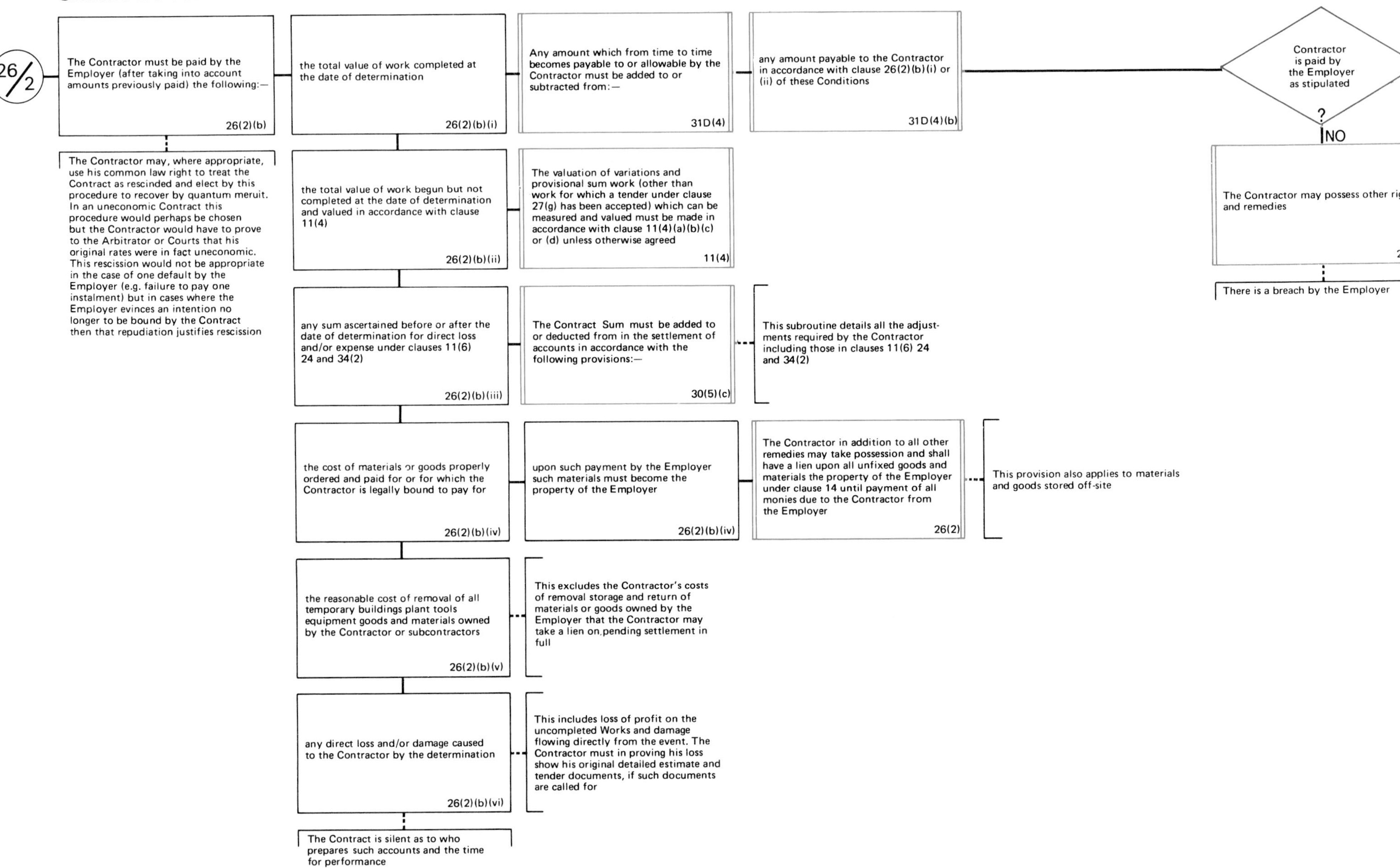

26/2
The Contractor must be paid by the Employer (after taking into account amounts previously paid) the following:— 26(2)(b)
The Contractor may, where appropriate, use his common law right to treat the Contract as rescinded and elect by this procedure to recover by quantum meruit. In an uneconomic Contract this procedure would perhaps be chosen but the Contractor would have to prove to the Arbitrator or Courts that his original rates were in fact uneconomic. This rescission would not be appropriate in the case of one default by the Employer (e.g. failure to pay one instalment) but in cases where the Employer evinces an intention no longer to be bound by the Contract then that repudiation justifies rescission
the total value of work completed at the date of determination 26(2)(b)(i)
Any amount which from time to time becomes payable to or allowable by the Contractor must be added to or subtracted from:— 31D(4)
any amount payable to the Contractor in accordance with clause 26(2)(b)(i) or (ii) of these Conditions 31D(4)(b)
Contractor is paid by the Employer as stipulated ?
NO
The Contractor may possess other rights and remedies 26(1)
There is a breach by the Employer
the total value of work begun but not completed at the date of determination and valued in accordance with clause 11(4) 26(2)(b)(ii)
The valuation of variations and provisional sum work (other than work for which a tender under clause 27(g) has been accepted) which can be measured and valued must be made in accordance with clause 11(4)(a)(b)(c) or (d) unless otherwise agreed 11(4)
any sum ascertained before or after the date of determination for direct loss and/or expense under clauses 11(6) 24 and 34(2) 26(2)(b)(iii)
The Contract Sum must be added to or deducted from in the settlement of accounts in accordance with the following provisions:— 30(5)(c)
This subroutine details all the adjustments required by the Contractor including those in clauses 11(6) 24 and 34(2)
the cost of materials or goods properly ordered and paid for or for which the Contractor is legally bound to pay for 26(2)(b)(iv)
upon such payment by the Employer such materials must become the property of the Employer 26(2)(b)(iv)
The Contractor in addition to all other remedies may take possession and shall have a lien upon all unfixed goods and materials the property of the Employer under clause 14 until payment of all monies due to the Contractor from the Employer 26(2)
This provision also applies to materials and goods stored off-site
the reasonable cost of removal of all temporary buildings plant tools equipment goods and materials owned by the Contractor or subcontractors 26(2)(b)(v)
This excludes the Contractor's costs of removal storage and return of materials or goods owned by the Employer that the Contractor may take a lien on pending settlement in full
any direct loss and/or damage caused to the Contractor by the determination 26(2)(b)(vi)
This includes loss of profit on the uncompleted Works and damage flowing directly from the event. The Contractor must in proving his loss show his original detailed estimate and tender documents, if such documents are called for
The Contract is silent as to who prepares such accounts and the time for performance

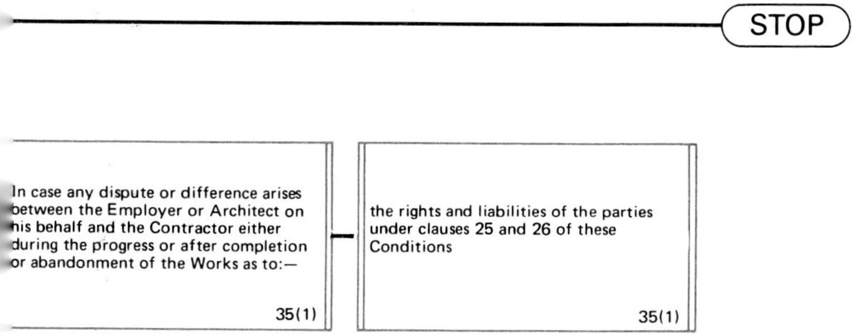

STOP

In case any dispute or difference arises between the Employer or Architect on his behalf and the Contractor either during the progress or after completion or abandonment of the Works as to:— 35(1)

the rights and liabilities of the parties under clauses 25 and 26 of these Conditions 35(1)

Clause 27 NOMINATED SUBCONTRACTORS

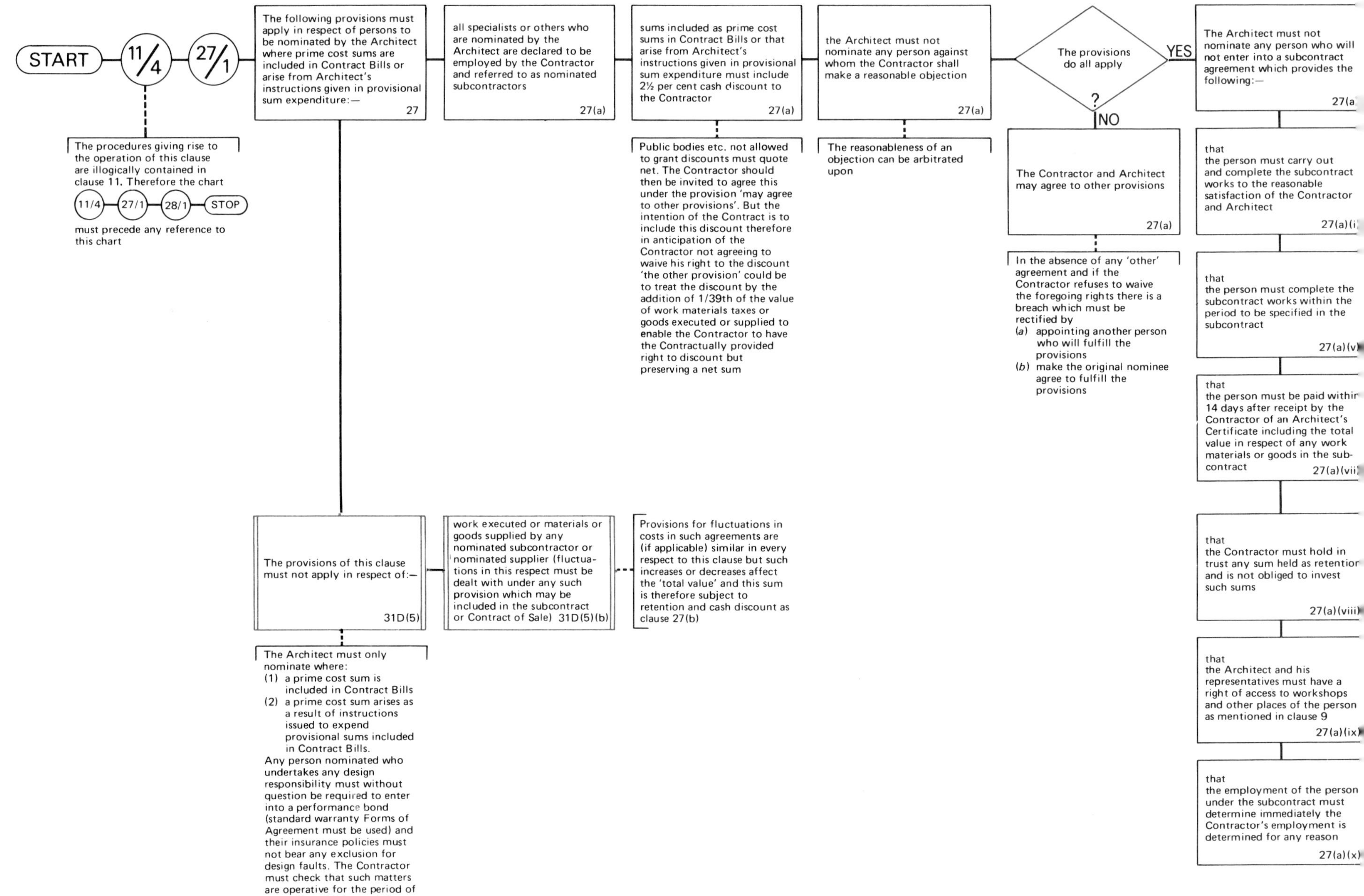

START
11/4
27/1
The following provisions must apply in respect of persons to be nominated by the Architect where prime cost sums are included in Contract Bills or arise from Architect's instructions given in provisional sum expenditure:— 27
all specialists or others who are nominated by the Architect are declared to be employed by the Contractor and referred to as nominated subcontractors 27(a)
sums included as prime cost sums in Contract Bills or that arise from Architect's instructions given in provisional sum expenditure must include 2½ per cent cash discount to the Contractor 27(a)
the Architect must not nominate any person against whom the Contractor shall make a reasonable objection 27(a)
The provisions do all apply ?
YES
NO
The Architect must not nominate any person who will not enter into a subcontract agreement which provides the following:— 27(a
that the person must carry out and complete the subcontract works to the reasonable satisfaction of the Contractor and Architect 27(a)(i
that the person must complete the subcontract works within the period to be specified in the subcontract 27(a)(v
that the person must be paid within 14 days after receipt by the Contractor of an Architect's Certificate including the total value in respect of any work materials or goods in the sub-contract 27(a)(vii
that the Contractor must hold in trust any sum held as retention and is not obliged to invest such sums 27(a)(viii
that the Architect and his representatives must have a right of access to workshops and other places of the person as mentioned in clause 9 27(a)(ix
that the employment of the person under the subcontract must determine immediately the Contractor's employment is determined for any reason 27(a)(x)
The procedures giving rise to the operation of this clause are illogically contained in clause 11. Therefore the chart
11/4
27/1
28/1
STOP
must precede any reference to this chart
Public bodies etc. not allowed to grant discounts must quote net. The Contractor should then be invited to agree this under the provision 'may agree to other provisions'. But the intention of the Contract is to include this discount therefore in anticipation of the Contractor not agreeing to waive his right to the discount 'the other provision' could be to treat the discount by the addition of 1/39th of the value of work materials taxes or goods executed or supplied to enable the Contractor to have the Contractually provided right to discount but preserving a net sum
The reasonableness of an objection can be arbitrated upon
The Contractor and Architect may agree to other provisions 27(a)
In the absence of any 'other' agreement and if the Contractor refuses to waive the foregoing rights there is a breach which must be rectified by
(a) appointing another person who will fulfill the provisions
(b) make the original nominee agree to fulfill the provisions
The provisions of this clause must not apply in respect of:— 31D(5)
work executed or materials or goods supplied by any nominated subcontractor or nominated supplier (fluctuations in this respect must be dealt with under any such provision which may be included in the subcontract or Contract of Sale) 31D(5)(b)
Provisions for fluctuations in costs in such agreements are (if applicable) similar in every respect to this clause but such increases or decreases affect the 'total value' and this sum is therefore subject to retention and cash discount as clause 27(b)
The Architect must only nominate where:
(1) a prime cost sum is included in Contract Bills
(2) a prime cost sum arises as a result of instructions issued to expend provisional sums included in Contract Bills.
Any person nominated who undertakes any design responsibility must without question be required to enter into a performance bond (standard warranty Forms of Agreement must be used) and their insurance policies must not bear any exclusion for design faults. The Contractor must check that such matters are operative for the period of years (6 or 12) beyond the anticipated date of Final Certificate.

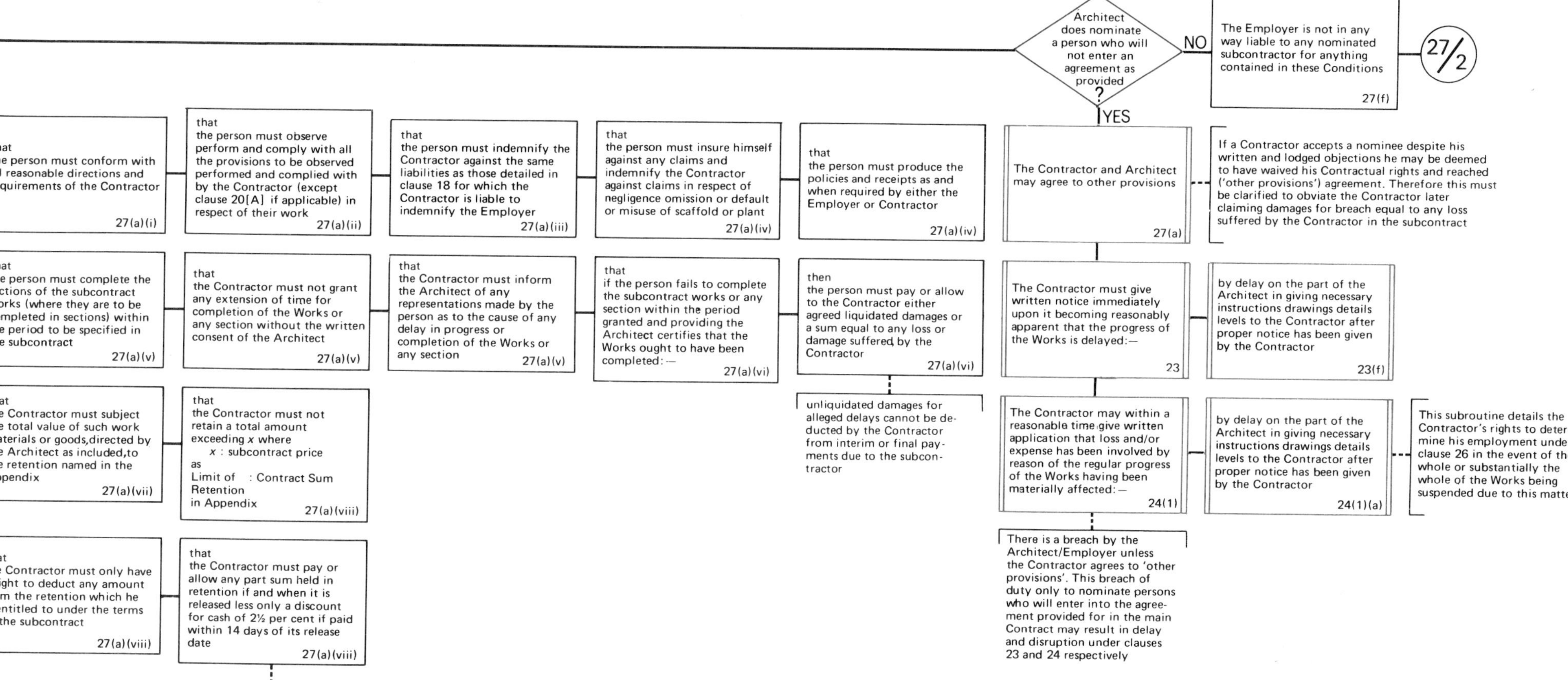

Architect does nominate a person who will not enter an agreement as provided ?
NO
The Employer is not in any way liable to any nominated subcontractor for anything contained in these Conditions 27(f)
27/2
YES
hat
he person must conform with
ll reasonable directions and
equirements of the Contractor
27(a)(i)
that the person must observe perform and comply with all the provisions to be observed performed and complied with by the Contractor (except clause 20[A] if applicable) in respect of their work 27(a)(ii)
that the person must indemnify the Contractor against the same liabilities as those detailed in clause 18 for which the Contractor is liable to indemnify the Employer 27(a)(iii)
that the person must insure himself against any claims and indemnify the Contractor against claims in respect of negligence omission or default or misuse of scaffold or plant 27(a)(iv)
that the person must produce the policies and receipts as and when required by either the Employer or Contractor 27(a)(iv)
The Contractor and Architect may agree to other provisions 27(a)
If a Contractor accepts a nominee despite his written and lodged objections he may be deemed to have waived his Contractual rights and reached ('other provisions') agreement. Therefore this must be clarified to obviate the Contractor later claiming damages for breach equal to any loss suffered by the Contractor in the subcontract
hat
he person must complete the
ections of the subcontract
orks (where they are to be
ompleted in sections) within
he period to be specified in
he subcontract
27(a)(v)
that the Contractor must not grant any extension of time for completion of the Works or any section without the written consent of the Architect 27(a)(v)
that the Contractor must inform the Architect of any representations made by the person as to the cause of any delay in progress or completion of the Works or any section 27(a)(v)
that if the person fails to complete the subcontract works or any section within the period granted and providing the Architect certifies that the Works ought to have been completed: — 27(a)(vi)
then the person must pay or allow to the Contractor either agreed liquidated damages or a sum equal to any loss or damage suffered by the Contractor 27(a)(vi)
unliquidated damages for alleged delays cannot be deducted by the Contractor from interim or final payments due to the subcontractor
The Contractor must give written notice immediately upon it becoming reasonably apparent that the progress of the Works is delayed: — 23
by delay on the part of the Architect in giving necessary instructions drawings details levels to the Contractor after proper notice has been given by the Contractor 23(f)
hat
he Contractor must subject
he total value of such work
aterials or goods,directed by
he Architect as included,to
he retention named in the
ppendix
27(a)(vii)
that the Contractor must not retain a total amount exceeding x where
x : subcontract price
as
Limit of : Contract Sum Retention in Appendix 27(a)(viii)
The Contractor may within a reasonable time give written application that loss and/or expense has been involved by reason of the regular progress of the Works having been materially affected: — 24(1)
by delay on the part of the Architect in giving necessary instructions drawings details levels to the Contractor after proper notice has been given by the Contractor 24(1)(a)
This subroutine details the Contractor's rights to determine his employment under clause 26 in the event of the whole or substantially the whole of the Works being suspended due to this matter
hat
e Contractor must only have
right to deduct any amount
om the retention which he
entitled to under the terms
the subcontract
27(a)(viii)
that the Contractor must pay or allow any part sum held in retention if and when it is released less only a discount for cash of 2½ per cent if paid within 14 days of its release date 27(a)(viii)
The words 'by whomsoever held' in this clause mean that the Contractor himself can hold retention
There is a breach by the Architect/Employer unless the Contractor agrees to 'other provisions'. This breach of duty only to nominate persons who will enter into the agreement provided for in the main Contract may result in delay and disruption under clauses 23 and 24 respectively

Clause 27 PAYMENTS TO NOMINATED SUBCONTRACTORS

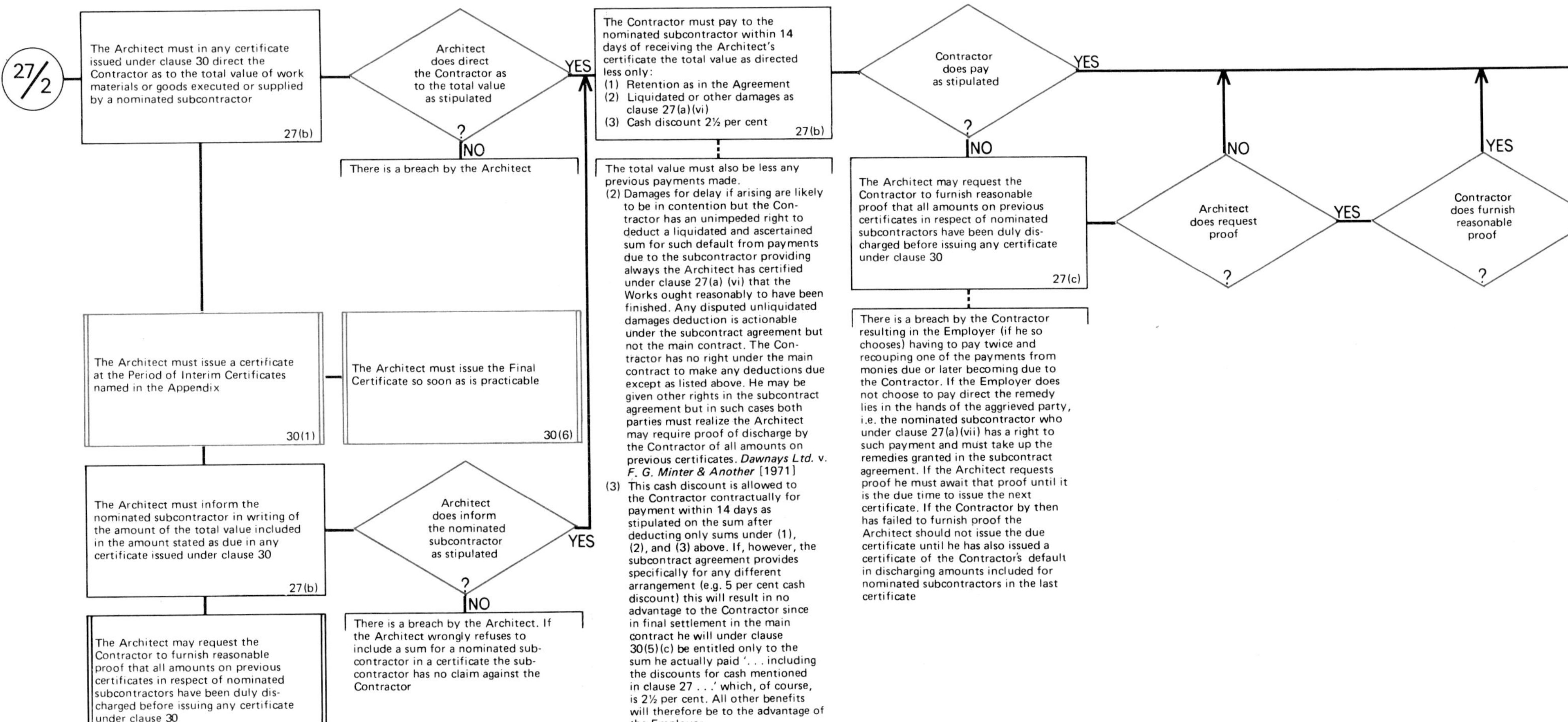
27/2
The Architect must in any certificate issued under clause 30 direct the Contractor as to the total value of work materials or goods executed or supplied by a nominated subcontractor 27(b)
Architect does direct the Contractor as to the total value as stipulated ?
YES
NO
There is a breach by the Architect
The Contractor must pay to the nominated subcontractor within 14 days of receiving the Architect's certificate the total value as directed less only:
(1) Retention as in the Agreement
(2) Liquidated or other damages as clause 27(a)(vi)
(3) Cash discount 2½ per cent 27(b)
The total value must also be less any previous payments made.
(2) Damages for delay if arising are likely to be in contention but the Contractor has an unimpeded right to deduct a liquidated and ascertained sum for such default from payments due to the subcontractor providing always the Architect has certified under clause 27(a) (vi) that the Works ought reasonably to have been finished. Any disputed unliquidated damages deduction is actionable under the subcontract agreement but not the main contract. The Contractor has no right under the main contract to make any deductions due except as listed above. He may be given other rights in the subcontract agreement but in such cases both parties must realize the Architect may require proof of discharge by the Contractor of all amounts on previous certificates. Dawnays Ltd. v. F. G. Minter & Another [1971]
(3) This cash discount is allowed to the Contractor contractually for payment within 14 days as stipulated on the sum after deducting only sums under (1), (2), and (3) above. If, however, the subcontract agreement provides specifically for any different arrangement (e.g. 5 per cent cash discount) this will result in no advantage to the Contractor since in final settlement in the main contract he will under clause 30(5)(c) be entitled only to the sum he actually paid '. . . including the discounts for cash mentioned in clause 27 . . .' which, of course, is 2½ per cent. All other benefits will therefore be to the advantage of the Employer
Contractor does pay as stipulated ?
YES
NO
The Architect may request the Contractor to furnish reasonable proof that all amounts on previous certificates in respect of nominated subcontractors have been duly discharged before issuing any certificate under clause 30 27(c)
There is a breach by the Contractor resulting in the Employer (if he so chooses) having to pay twice and recouping one of the payments from monies due or later becoming due to the Contractor. If the Employer does not choose to pay direct the remedy lies in the hands of the aggrieved party, i.e. the nominated subcontractor who under clause 27(a)(vii) has a right to such payment and must take up the remedies granted in the subcontract agreement. If the Architect requests proof he must await that proof until it is the due time to issue the next certificate. If the Contractor by then has failed to furnish proof the Architect should not issue the due certificate until he has also issued a certificate of the Contractor's default in discharging amounts included for nominated subcontractors in the last certificate
NO
Architect does request proof ?
YES
YES
Contractor does furnish reasonable proof ?
The Architect must issue a certificate at the Period of Interim Certificates named in the Appendix 30(1)
The Architect must issue the Final Certificate so soon as is practicable 30(6)
The Architect must inform the nominated subcontractor in writing of the amount of the total value included in the amount stated as due in any certificate issued under clause 30 27(b)
Architect does inform the nominated subcontractor as stipulated ?
YES
NO
There is a breach by the Architect. If the Architect wrongly refuses to include a sum for a nominated subcontractor in a certificate the subcontractor has no claim against the Contractor
The Architect may request the Contractor to furnish reasonable proof that all amounts on previous certificates in respect of nominated subcontractors have been duly discharged before issuing any certificate under clause 30 27(c)

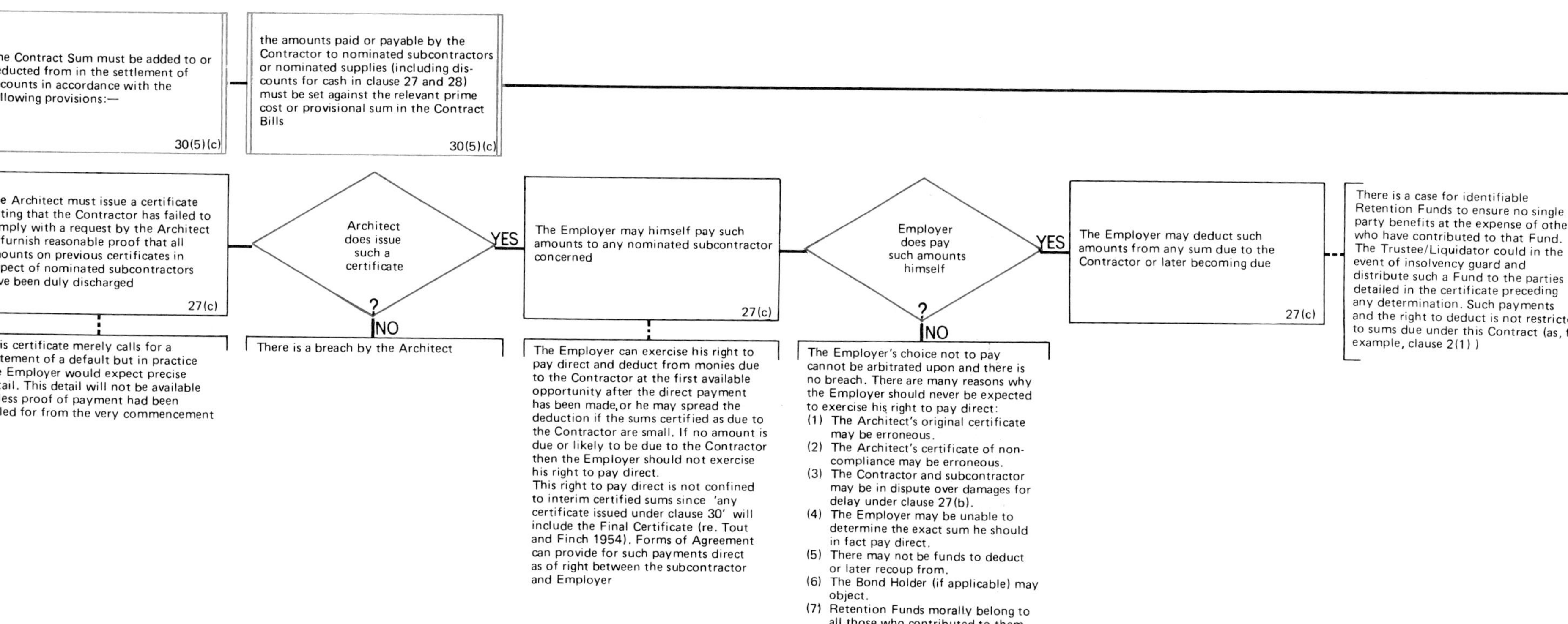

he Contract Sum must be added to or
educted from in the settlement of
counts in accordance with the
ollowing provisions:—
30(5)(c)
the amounts paid or payable by the
Contractor to nominated subcontractors
or nominated supplies (including discounts for cash in clause 27 and 28)
must be set against the relevant prime
cost or provisional sum in the Contract
Bills
30(5)(c)
27/3
he Architect must issue a certificate
ating that the Contractor has failed to
mply with a request by the Architect
furnish reasonable proof that all
nounts on previous certificates in
spect of nominated subcontractors
ve been duly discharged
27(c)
Architect
does issue
such a
certificate
?
YES
NO
The Employer may himself pay such
amounts to any nominated subcontractor
concerned
27(c)
Employer
does pay
such amounts
himself
?
YES
NO
The Employer may deduct such
amounts from any sum due to the
Contractor or later becoming due
27(c)
There is a case for identifiable
Retention Funds to ensure no single
party benefits at the expense of others
who have contributed to that Fund.
The Trustee/Liquidator could in the
event of insolvency guard and
distribute such a Fund to the parties
detailed in the certificate preceding
any determination. Such payments
and the right to deduct is not restricted
to sums due under this Contract (as, for
example, clause 2(1))
is certificate merely calls for a
atement of a default but in practice
e Employer would expect precise
tail. This detail will not be available
less proof of payment had been
lled for from the very commencement
There is a breach by the Architect
The Employer can exercise his right to
pay direct and deduct from monies due
to the Contractor at the first available
opportunity after the direct payment
has been made,or he may spread the
deduction if the sums certified as due to
the Contractor are small. If no amount is
due or likely to be due to the Contractor
then the Employer should not exercise
his right to pay direct.
This right to pay direct is not confined
to interim certified sums since 'any
certificate issued under clause 30' will
include the Final Certificate (re. Tout
and Finch 1954). Forms of Agreement
can provide for such payments direct
as of right between the subcontractor
and Employer
The Employer's choice not to pay
cannot be arbitrated upon and there is
no breach. There are many reasons why
the Employer should never be expected
to exercise his right to pay direct:
(1) The Architect's original certificate
may be erroneous.
(2) The Architect's certificate of non-
compliance may be erroneous.
(3) The Contractor and subcontractor
may be in dispute over damages for
delay under clause 27(b).
(4) The Employer may be unable to
determine the exact sum he should
in fact pay direct.
(5) There may not be funds to deduct
or later recoup from.
(6) The Bond Holder (if applicable) may
object.
(7) Retention Funds morally belong to
all those who contributed to them.

Clause 27 PAYMENTS TO NOMINATED SUBCONTRACTORS (continued)

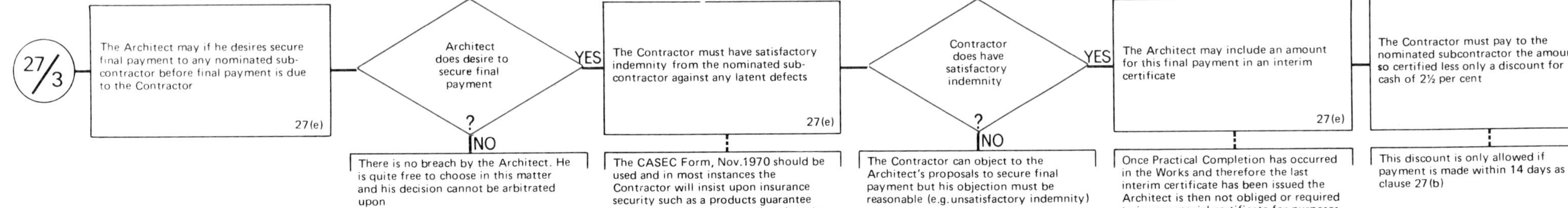

27/3
The Architect may if he desires secure final payment to any nominated sub-contractor before final payment is due to the Contractor
27(e)
Architect does desire to secure final payment ?
YES
NO
The Contractor must have satisfactory indemnity from the nominated sub-contractor against any latent defects
27(e)
Contractor does have satisfactory indemnity ?
YES
NO
The Architect may include an amount for this final payment in an interim certificate
27(e)
The Contractor must pay to the nominated subcontractor the amount so certified less only a discount for cash of 2½ per cent
There is no breach by the Architect. He is quite free to choose in this matter and his decision cannot be arbitrated upon
The CASEC Form, Nov.1970 should be used and in most instances the Contractor will insist upon insurance security such as a products guarantee policy or at least evidence that the sub-contractor's current policies are in fact extended and endorsed for the Contractor to cover the risk and must remain to cover claims up to 6 or 12 years (if applicable) from the date of the issue of the Final Certificate under the main contract. (At this stage the anticipated date will suffice but subject to adjustment later)
The Contractor can object to the Architect's proposals to secure final payment but his objection must be reasonable (e.g. unsatisfactory indemnity)
Once Practical Completion has occurred in the Works and therefore the last interim certificate has been issued the Architect is then not obliged or required to issue a special certificate for purposes of securing such payment
This discount is only allowed if payment is made within 14 days as clause 27(b)

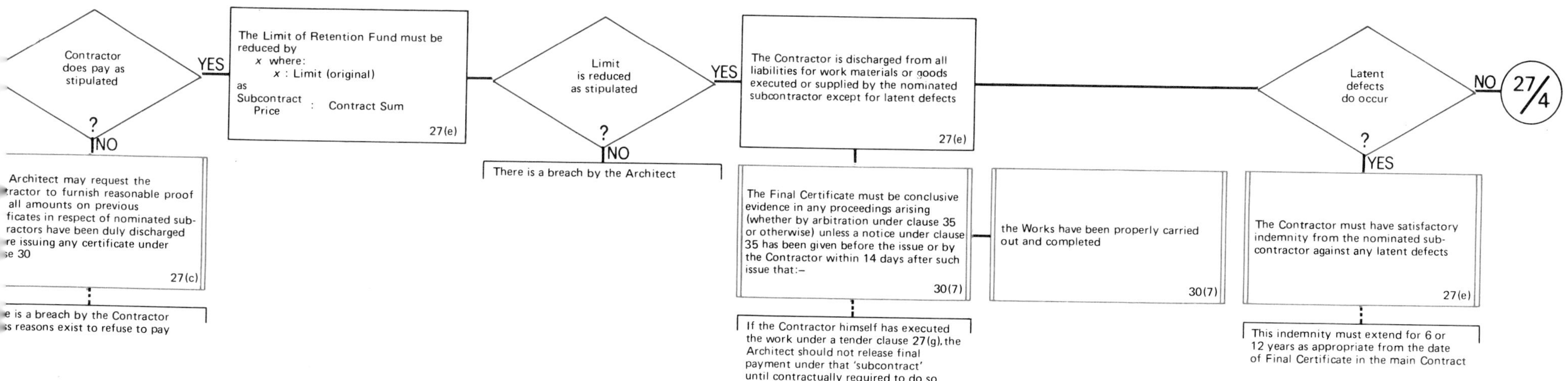

Contractor does pay as stipulated
?
YES
NO
Architect may request the [cut off]tractor to furnish reasonable proof [cut off] all amounts on previous [cut off]ficates in respect of nominated sub-[cut off]ractors have been duly discharged [cut off]re issuing any certificate under [cut off]se 30
27(c)
[cut off]e is a breach by the Contractor [cut off]s reasons exist to refuse to pay
The Limit of Retention Fund must be reduced by
x where:
x : Limit (original)
as
Subcontract Price : Contract Sum
27(e)
Limit is reduced as stipulated
?
NO
There is a breach by the Architect
YES
The Contractor is discharged from all liabilities for work materials or goods executed or supplied by the nominated subcontractor except for latent defects
27(e)
The Final Certificate must be conclusive evidence in any proceedings arising (whether by arbitration under clause 35 or otherwise) unless a notice under clause 35 has been given before the issue or by the Contractor within 14 days after such issue that:–
30(7)
the Works have been properly carried out and completed
30(7)
If the Contractor himself has executed the work under a tender clause 27(g), the Architect should not release final payment under that 'subcontract' until contractually required to do so
Latent defects do occur
?
NO
27/4
YES
The Contractor must have satisfactory indemnity from the nominated sub-contractor against any latent defects
27(e)
This indemnity must extend for 6 or 12 years as appropriate from the date of Final Certificate in the main Contract

Clause 27 DELAY BY NOMINATED SUBCONTRACTOR

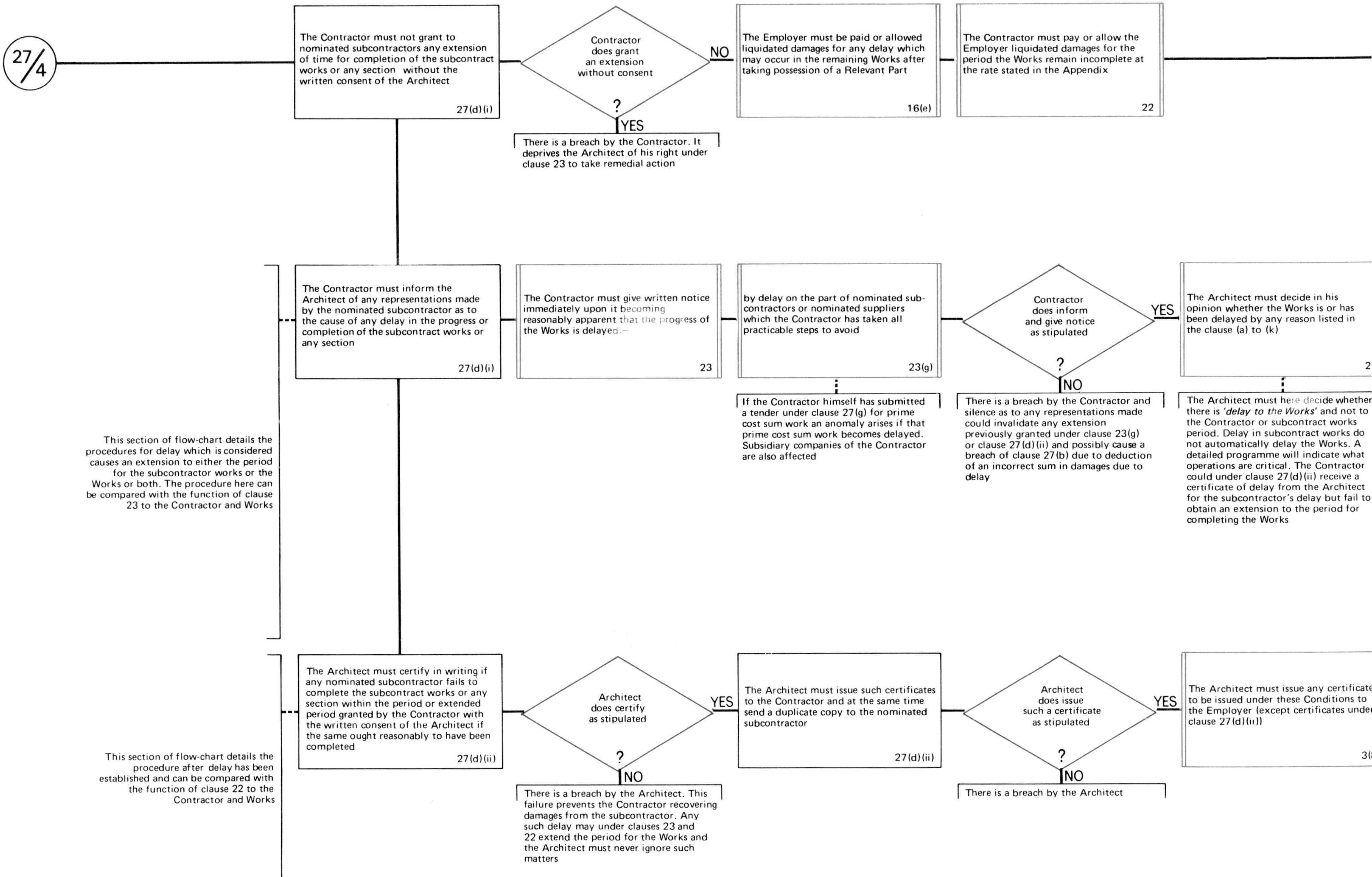

27/4
The Contractor must not grant to nominated subcontractors any extension of time for completion of the subcontract works or any section without the written consent of the Architect
27(d)(i)
Contractor does grant an extension without consent
?
NO
YES
There is a breach by the Contractor. It deprives the Architect of his right under clause 23 to take remedial action
The Employer must be paid or allowed liquidated damages for any delay which may occur in the remaining Works after taking possession of a Relevant Part
16(e)
The Contractor must pay or allow the Employer liquidated damages for the period the Works remain incomplete at the rate stated in the Appendix
22
This section of flow-chart details the procedures for delay which is considered causes an extension to either the period for the subcontractor works or the Works or both. The procedure here can be compared with the function of clause 23 to the Contractor and Works
The Contractor must inform the Architect of any representations made by the nominated subcontractor as to the cause of any delay in the progress or completion of the subcontract works or any section
27(d)(i)
The Contractor must give written notice immediately upon it becoming reasonably apparent that the progress of the Works is delayed
23
by delay on the part of nominated sub-contractors or nominated suppliers which the Contractor has taken all practicable steps to avoid
23(g)
If the Contractor himself has submitted a tender under clause 27(g) for prime cost sum work an anomaly arises if that prime cost sum work becomes delayed. Subsidiary companies of the Contractor are also affected
Contractor does inform and give notice as stipulated
?
YES
NO
There is a breach by the Contractor and silence as to any representations made could invalidate any extension previously granted under clause 23(g) or clause 27(d)(ii) and possibly cause a breach of clause 27(b) due to deduction of an incorrect sum in damages due to delay
The Architect must decide in his opinion whether the Works is or has been delayed by any reason listed in the clause (a) to (k)
The Architect must here decide whether there is *'delay to the Works'* and not to the Contractor or subcontract works period. Delay in subcontract works do not automatically delay the Works. A detailed programme will indicate what operations are critical. The Contractor could under clause 27(d)(ii) receive a certificate of delay from the Architect for the subcontractor's delay but fail to obtain an extension to the period for completing the Works
This section of flow-chart details the procedure after delay has been established and can be compared with the function of clause 22 to the Contractor and Works
The Architect must certify in writing if any nominated subcontractor fails to complete the subcontract works or any section within the period or extended period granted by the Contractor with the written consent of the Architect if the same ought reasonably to have been completed
27(d)(ii)
Architect does certify as stipulated
?
YES
NO
There is a breach by the Architect. This failure prevents the Contractor recovering damages from the subcontractor. Any such delay may under clauses 23 and 22 extend the period for the Works and the Architect must never ignore such matters
The Architect must issue such certificates to the Contractor and at the same time send a duplicate copy to the nominated subcontractor
27(d)(ii)
Architect does issue such a certificate as stipulated
?
YES
NO
There is a breach by the Architect
The Architect must issue any certificate to be issued under these Conditions to the Employer (except certificates under clause 27(d)(ii))

27/5

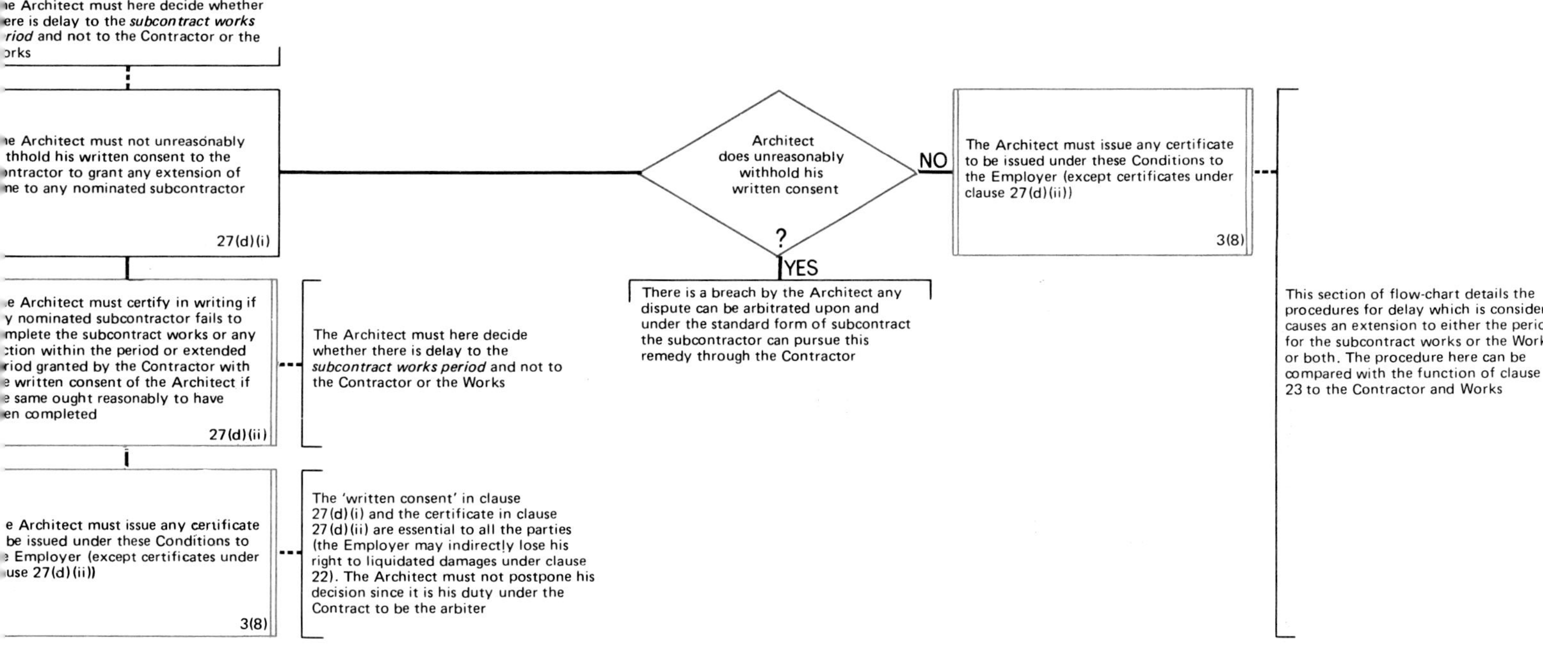

ne Architect must here decide whether ere is delay to the *subcontract works riod* and not to the Contractor or the orks
ne Architect must not unreasonably thhold his written consent to the ntractor to grant any extension of ne to any nominated subcontractor
27(d)(i)
Architect does unreasonably withhold his written consent
?
NO
YES
The Architect must issue any certificate to be issued under these Conditions to the Employer (except certificates under clause 27(d)(ii))
3(8)
There is a breach by the Architect any dispute can be arbitrated upon and under the standard form of subcontract the subcontractor can pursue this remedy through the Contractor
e Architect must certify in writing if y nominated subcontractor fails to mplete the subcontract works or any ction within the period or extended riod granted by the Contractor with e written consent of the Architect if e same ought reasonably to have en completed
27(d)(ii)
The Architect must here decide whether there is delay to the *subcontract works period* and not to the Contractor or the Works
e Architect must issue any certificate be issued under these Conditions to e Employer (except certificates under use 27(d)(ii))
3(8)
The 'written consent' in clause 27(d)(i) and the certificate in clause 27(d)(ii) are essential to all the parties (the Employer may indirectly lose his right to liquidated damages under clause 22). The Architect must not postpone his decision since it is his duty under the Contract to be the arbiter
This section of flow-chart details the procedures for delay which is considered causes an extension to either the period for the subcontract works or the Works or both. The procedure here can be compared with the function of clause 23 to the Contractor and Works

s section of flow-chart details the cedure after delay has been ablished and can be compared with function of clause 22 to the ntractor and Works

Clause 27 PRIME COST SUMS WORK FOR WHICH CONTRACTOR TENDERS

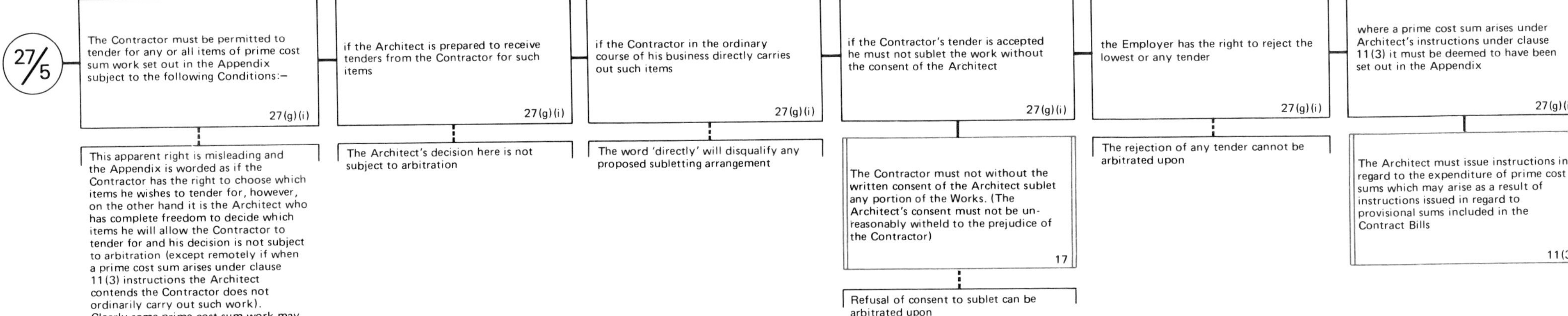
27/5
The Contractor must be permitted to tender for any or all items of prime cost sum work set out in the Appendix subject to the following Conditions:–
27(g)(i)
if the Architect is prepared to receive tenders from the Contractor for such items
27(g)(i)
if the Contractor in the ordinary course of his business directly carries out such items
27(g)(i)
if the Contractor's tender is accepted he must not sublet the work without the consent of the Architect
27(g)(i)
the Employer has the right to reject the lowest or any tender
27(g)(i)
where a prime cost sum arises under Architect's instructions under clause 11(3) it must be deemed to have been set out in the Appendix
27(g)(
The Architect's decision here is not subject to arbitration
The word 'directly' will disqualify any proposed subletting arrangement
The Contractor must not without the written consent of the Architect sublet any portion of the Works. (The Architect's consent must not be unreasonably witheld to the prejudice of the Contractor)
17
Refusal of consent to sublet can be arbitrated upon
The rejection of any tender cannot be arbitrated upon
The Architect must issue instructions in regard to the expenditure of prime cost sums which may arise as a result of instructions issued in regard to provisional sums included in the Contract Bills
11(

This apparent right is misleading and the Appendix is worded as if the Contractor has the right to choose which items he wishes to tender for, however, on the other hand it is the Architect who has complete freedom to decide which items he will allow the Contractor to tender for and his decision is not subject to arbitration (except remotely if when a prime cost sum arises under clause 11(3) instructions the Architect contends the Contractor does not ordinarily carry out such work).
Clearly some prime cost sum work may already be promised to certain specialists and these must be indicated in the tender documents.
The Employer has the ultimate veto in that he can reject any tender in any case without being subject to arbitration.
Contractors should declare any interests they may have in subsidiary companies and the like if any risk of collusion might arise in connection with such tenders (Local Authority provisions under clause 25(3) exist in this respect).
Contractor's tenders must be explicit on questions of: (1) discounts for cash, (2) profit, (3) attendances, (4) fluctuations
which provisions should be adhered to for clarity and Contractual reasons.
Architects and Employers must not overlook the problems that might arise in the event of any delay occurring in the prime cost sum work by subsidiary companies of, and the Contractor, and the anomalous position then arising under clause 23(g)

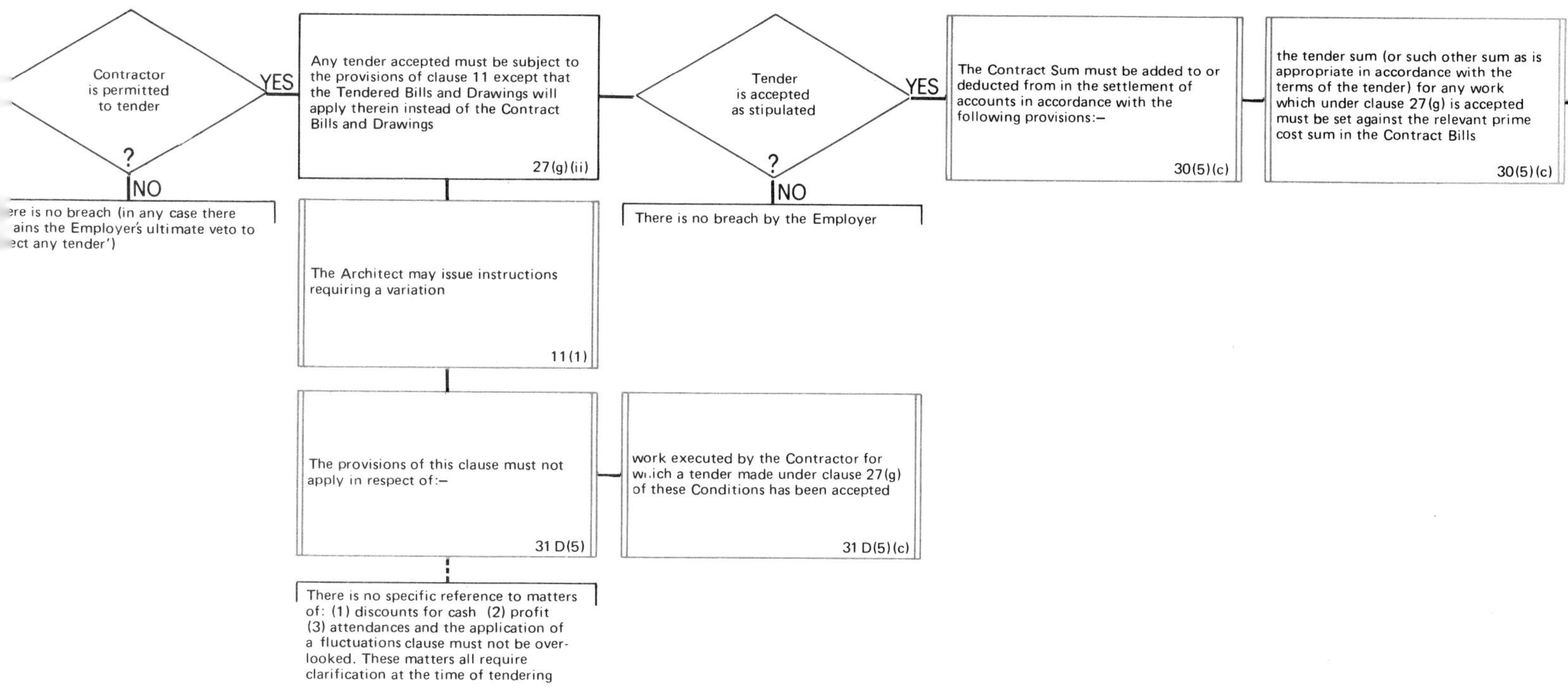
Contractor is permitted to tender
?
YES
NO
…ere is no breach (in any case there …ains the Employer's ultimate veto to …ect any tender')
Any tender accepted must be subject to the provisions of clause 11 except that the Tendered Bills and Drawings will apply therein instead of the Contract Bills and Drawings
27(g)(ii)
The Architect may issue instructions requiring a variation
11(1)
The provisions of this clause must not apply in respect of:–
31 D(5)
There is no specific reference to matters of: (1) discounts for cash (2) profit (3) attendances and the application of a fluctuations clause must not be overlooked. These matters all require clarification at the time of tendering
Tender is accepted as stipulated
?
YES
NO
There is no breach by the Employer
work executed by the Contractor for which a tender made under clause 27(g) of these Conditions has been accepted
31 D(5)(c)
The Contract Sum must be added to or deducted from in the settlement of accounts in accordance with the following provisions:–
30(5)(c)
the tender sum (or such other sum as is appropriate in accordance with the terms of the tender) for any work which under clause 27(g) is accepted must be set against the relevant prime cost sum in the Contract Bills
30(5)(c)
STOP

Clause 28 NOMINATED SUPPLIERS

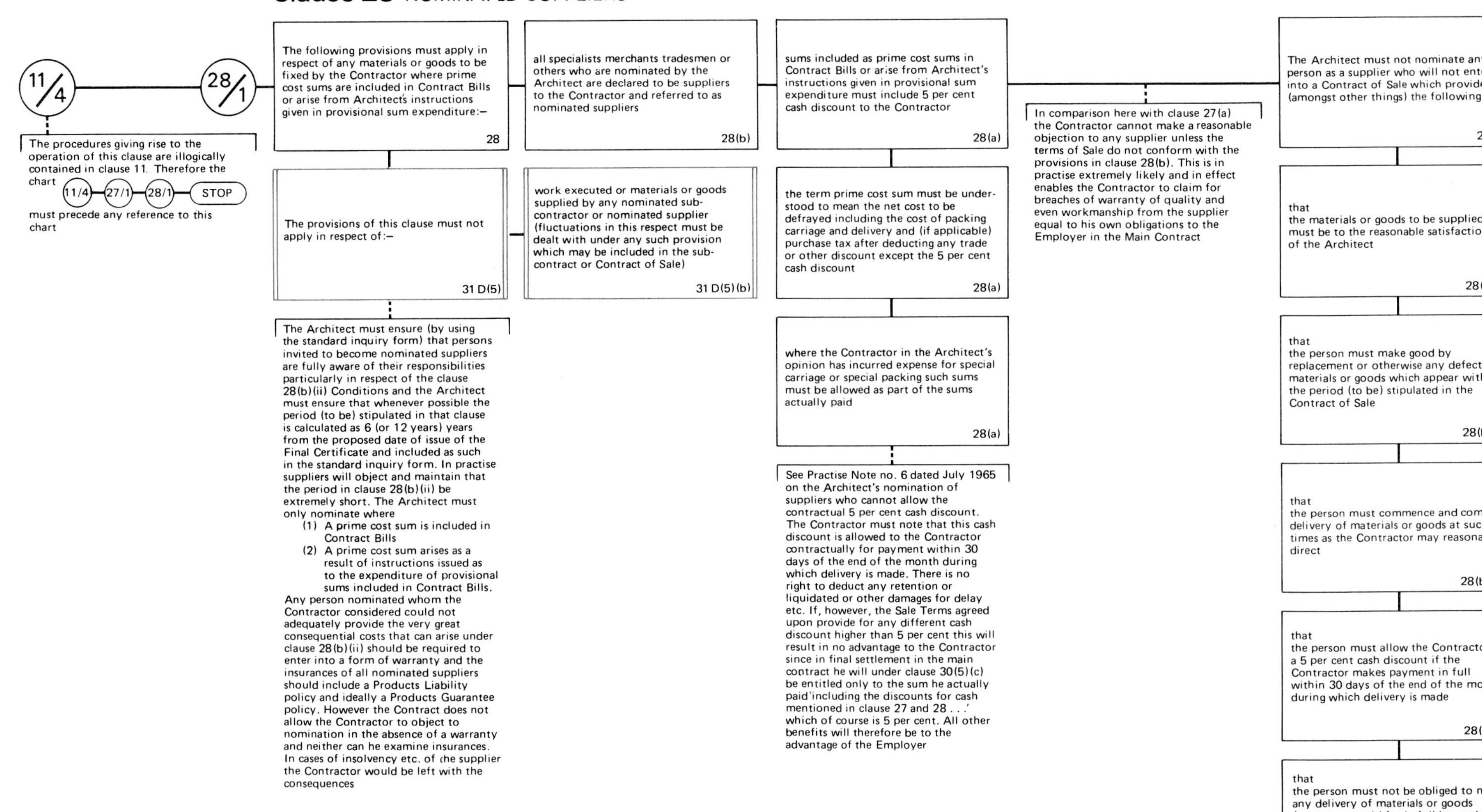

11/4
28/1
The procedures giving rise to the operation of this clause are illogically contained in clause 11. Therefore the chart
11/4 27/1 28/1 STOP
must precede any reference to this chart
The following provisions must apply in respect of any materials or goods to be fixed by the Contractor where prime cost sums are included in Contract Bills or arise from Architect's instructions given in provisional sum expenditure:–
28
The provisions of this clause must not apply in respect of:–
31 D(5)
The Architect must ensure (by using the standard inquiry form) that persons invited to become nominated suppliers are fully aware of their responsibilities particularly in respect of the clause 28(b)(ii) Conditions and the Architect must ensure that whenever possible the period (to be) stipulated in that clause is calculated as 6 (or 12 years) years from the proposed date of issue of the Final Certificate and included as such in the standard inquiry form. In practise suppliers will object and maintain that the period in clause 28(b)(ii) be extremely short. The Architect must only nominate where
(1) A prime cost sum is included in Contract Bills
(2) A prime cost sum arises as a result of instructions issued as to the expenditure of provisional sums included in Contract Bills.
Any person nominated whom the Contractor considered could not adequately provide the very great consequential costs that can arise under clause 28(b)(ii) should be required to enter into a form of warranty and the insurances of all nominated suppliers should include a Products Liability policy and ideally a Products Guarantee policy. However the Contract does not allow the Contractor to object to nomination in the absence of a warranty and neither can he examine insurances. In cases of insolvency etc. of the supplier the Contractor would be left with the consequences
all specialists merchants tradesmen or others who are nominated by the Architect are declared to be suppliers to the Contractor and referred to as nominated suppliers
28(b)
work executed or materials or goods supplied by any nominated sub-contractor or nominated supplier (fluctuations in this respect must be dealt with under any such provision which may be included in the sub-contract or Contract of Sale)
31 D(5)(b)
sums included as prime cost sums in Contract Bills or arise from Architect's instructions given in provisional sum expenditure must include 5 per cent cash discount to the Contractor
28(a)
the term prime cost sum must be understood to mean the net cost to be defrayed including the cost of packing carriage and delivery and (if applicable) purchase tax after deducting any trade or other discount except the 5 per cent cash discount
28(a)
where the Contractor in the Architect's opinion has incurred expense for special carriage or special packing such sums must be allowed as part of the sums actually paid
28(a)
See Practise Note no. 6 dated July 1965 on the Architect's nomination of suppliers who cannot allow the contractual 5 per cent cash discount. The Contractor must note that this cash discount is allowed to the Contractor contractually for payment within 30 days of the end of the month during which delivery is made. There is no right to deduct any retention or liquidated or other damages for delay etc. If, however, the Sale Terms agreed upon provide for any different cash discount higher than 5 per cent this will result in no advantage to the Contractor since in final settlement in the main contract he will under clause 30(5)(c) be entitled only to the sum he actually paid 'including the discounts for cash mentioned in clause 27 and 28 . . .' which of course is 5 per cent. All other benefits will therefore be to the advantage of the Employer
In comparison here with clause 27(a) the Contractor cannot make a reasonable objection to any supplier unless the terms of Sale do not conform with the provisions in clause 28(b). This is in practise extremely likely and in effect enables the Contractor to claim for breaches of warranty of quality and even workmanship from the supplier equal to his own obligations to the Employer in the Main Contract
The Architect must not nominate any person as a supplier who will not enter into a Contract of Sale which provides (amongst other things) the following:–
28(b
that the materials or goods to be supplied must be to the reasonable satisfaction of the Architect
28(b)
that the person must make good by replacement or otherwise any defects in materials or goods which appear within the period (to be) stipulated in the Contract of Sale
28(b)(
that the person must commence and comple delivery of materials or goods at such times as the Contractor may reasonably direct
28(b)(i
that the person must allow the Contractor a 5 per cent cash discount if the Contractor makes payment in full within 30 days of the end of the month during which delivery is made
28(b)(
that the person must not be obliged to mak any delivery of materials or goods (except any paid for in full less only the 5 per cent cash discount) after determination occurs (for any reason) the Contractor's employment under th Contract
28(b)

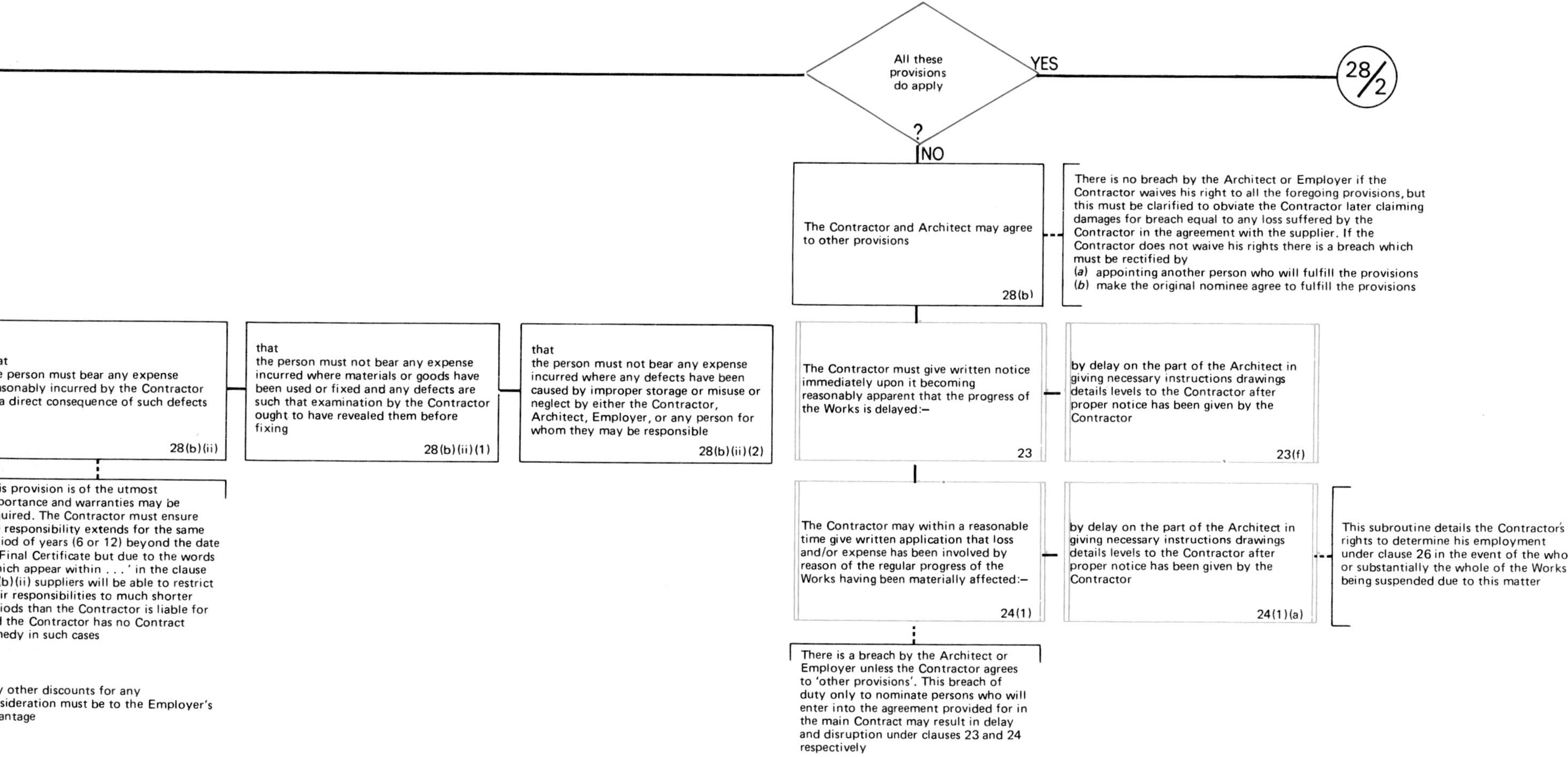

All these provisions do apply
?
YES
NO
28/2
The Contractor and Architect may agree to other provisions
28(b)
There is no breach by the Architect or Employer if the Contractor waives his right to all the foregoing provisions, but this must be clarified to obviate the Contractor later claiming damages for breach equal to any loss suffered by the Contractor in the agreement with the supplier. If the Contractor does not waive his rights there is a breach which must be rectified by
(a) appointing another person who will fulfill the provisions
(b) make the original nominee agree to fulfill the provisions
hat
he person must bear any expense
easonably incurred by the Contractor
s a direct consequence of such defects
28(b)(ii)
that
the person must not bear any expense incurred where materials or goods have been used or fixed and any defects are such that examination by the Contractor ought to have revealed them before fixing
28(b)(ii)(1)
that
the person must not bear any expense incurred where any defects have been caused by improper storage or misuse or neglect by either the Contractor, Architect, Employer, or any person for whom they may be responsible
28(b)(ii)(2)
The Contractor must give written notice immediately upon it becoming reasonably apparent that the progress of the Works is delayed:–
23
by delay on the part of the Architect in giving necessary instructions drawings details levels to the Contractor after proper notice has been given by the Contractor
23(f)
his provision is of the utmost
nportance and warranties may be
quired. The Contractor must ensure
e responsibility extends for the same
eriod of years (6 or 12) beyond the date
Final Certificate but due to the words
which appear within . . . ' in the clause
8(b)(ii) suppliers will be able to restrict
eir responsibilities to much shorter
eriods than the Contractor is liable for
d the Contractor has no Contract
medy in such cases
The Contractor may within a reasonable time give written application that loss and/or expense has been involved by reason of the regular progress of the Works having been materially affected:–
24(1)
by delay on the part of the Architect in giving necessary instructions drawings details levels to the Contractor after proper notice has been given by the Contractor
24(1)(a)
This subroutine details the Contractor's rights to determine his employment under clause 26 in the event of the whole or substantially the whole of the Works being suspended due to this matter
There is a breach by the Architect or Employer unless the Contractor agrees to 'other provisions'. This breach of duty only to nominate persons who will enter into the agreement provided for in the main Contract may result in delay and disruption under clauses 23 and 24 respectively
ny other discounts for any
nsideration must be to the Employer's
vantage

Clause 28 PAYMENT TO NOMINATED SUPPLIERS

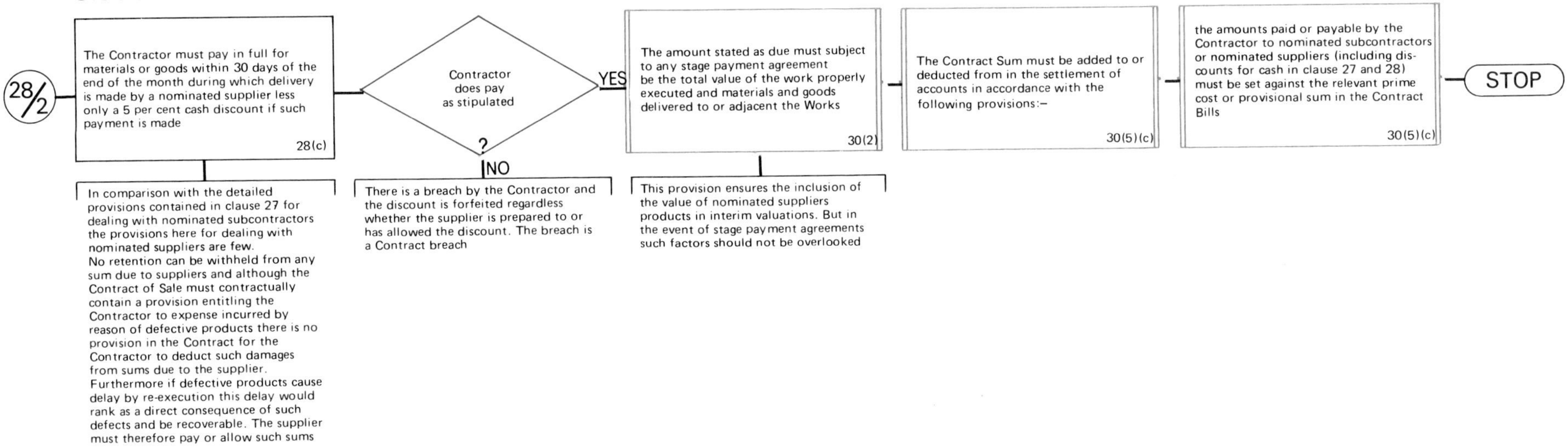

28/2

The Contractor must pay in full for materials or goods within 30 days of the end of the month during which delivery is made by a nominated supplier less only a 5 per cent cash discount if such payment is made 28(c)

In comparison with the detailed provisions contained in clause 27 for dealing with nominated subcontractors the provisions here for dealing with nominated suppliers are few.
No retention can be withheld from any sum due to suppliers and although the Contract of Sale must contractually contain a provision entitling the Contractor to expense incurred by reason of defective products there is no provision in the Contract for the Contractor to deduct such damages from sums due to the supplier.
Furthermore if defective products cause delay by re-execution this delay would rank as a direct consequence of such defects and be recoverable. The supplier must therefore pay or allow such sums

Contractor does pay as stipulated ?

NO

There is a breach by the Contractor and the discount is forfeited regardless whether the supplier is prepared to or has allowed the discount. The breach is a Contract breach

YES

The amount stated as due must subject to any stage payment agreement be the total value of the work properly executed and materials and goods delivered to or adjacent the Works 30(2)

This provision ensures the inclusion of the value of nominated suppliers products in interim valuations. But in the event of stage payment agreements such factors should not be overlooked

The Contract Sum must be added to or deducted from in the settlement of accounts in accordance with the following provisions:– 30(5)(c)

the amounts paid or payable by the Contractor to nominated subcontractors or nominated suppliers (including discounts for cash in clause 27 and 28) must be set against the relevant prime cost or provisional sum in the Contract Bills 30(5)(c)

STOP

Clause 29 ARTISTIC SPECIALISTS ENGAGED BY THE EMPLOYER

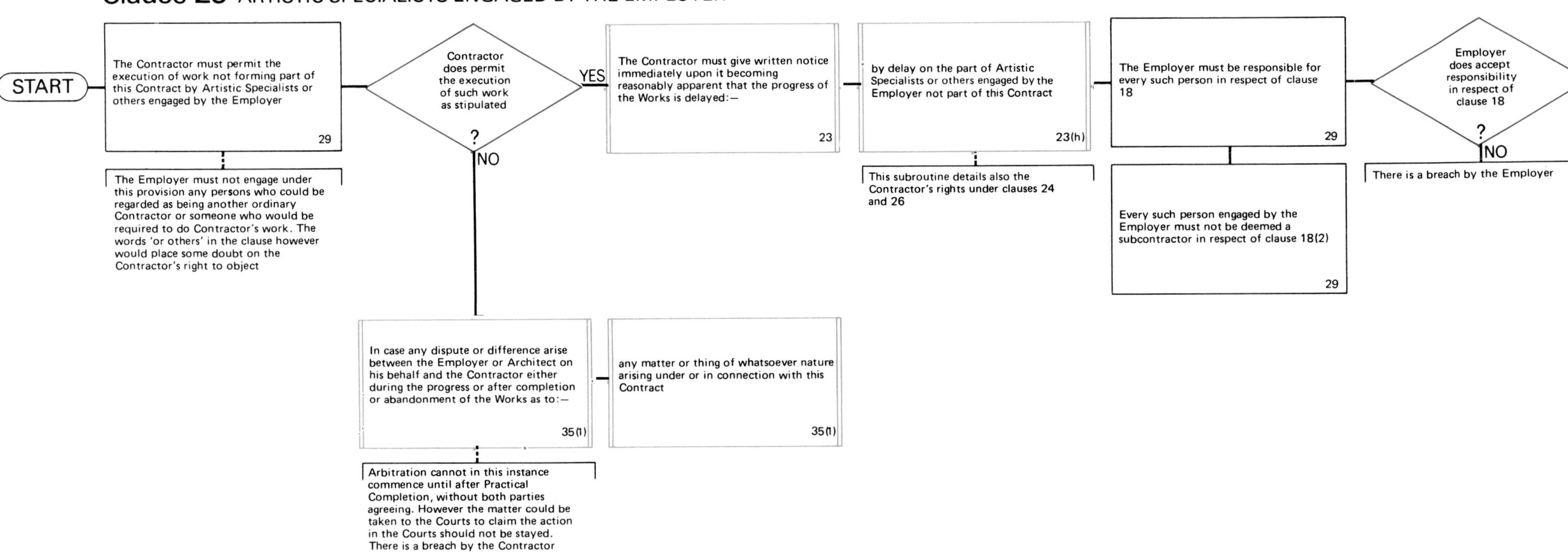

START
The Contractor must permit the execution of work not forming part of this Contract by Artistic Specialists or others engaged by the Employer
29
The Employer must not engage under this provision any persons who could be regarded as being another ordinary Contractor or someone who would be required to do Contractor's work. The words 'or others' in the clause however would place some doubt on the Contractor's right to object
Contractor does permit the execution of such work as stipulated
?
YES
NO
The Contractor must give written notice immediately upon it becoming reasonably apparent that the progress of the Works is delayed:—
23
by delay on the part of Artistic Specialists or others engaged by the Employer not part of this Contract
23(h)
This subroutine details also the Contractor's rights under clauses 24 and 26
The Employer must be responsible for every such person in respect of clause 18
29
Every such person engaged by the Employer must not be deemed a subcontractor in respect of clause 18(2)
29
Employer does accept responsibility in respect of clause 18
?
NO
There is a breach by the Employer
In case any dispute or difference arise between the Employer or Architect on his behalf and the Contractor either during the progress or after completion or abandonment of the Works as to:—
35(1)
any matter or thing of whatsoever nature arising under or in connection with this Contract
35(1)
Arbitration cannot in this instance commence until after Practical Completion, without both parties agreeing. However the matter could be taken to the Courts to claim the action in the Courts should not be stayed.
There is a breach by the Contractor

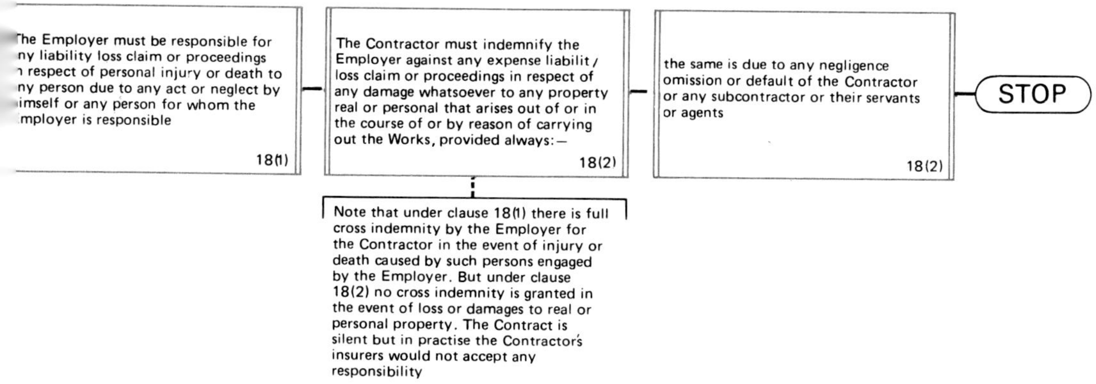

The Employer must be responsible for any liability loss claim or proceedings in respect of personal injury or death to any person due to any act or neglect by himself or any person for whom the Employer is responsible

18(1)

The Contractor must indemnify the Employer against any expense liability loss claim or proceedings in respect of any damage whatsoever to any property real or personal that arises out of or in the course of or by reason of carrying out the Works, provided always:—

18(2)

Note that under clause 18(1) there is full cross indemnity by the Employer for the Contractor in the event of injury or death caused by such persons engaged by the Employer. But under clause 18(2) no cross indemnity is granted in the event of loss or damages to real or personal property. The Contract is silent but in practise the Contractor's insurers would not accept any responsibility

the same is due to any negligence omission or default of the Contractor or any subcontractor or their servants or agents

18(2)

STOP

Clause 30 INTERIM PAYMENT CERTIFICATES (1)

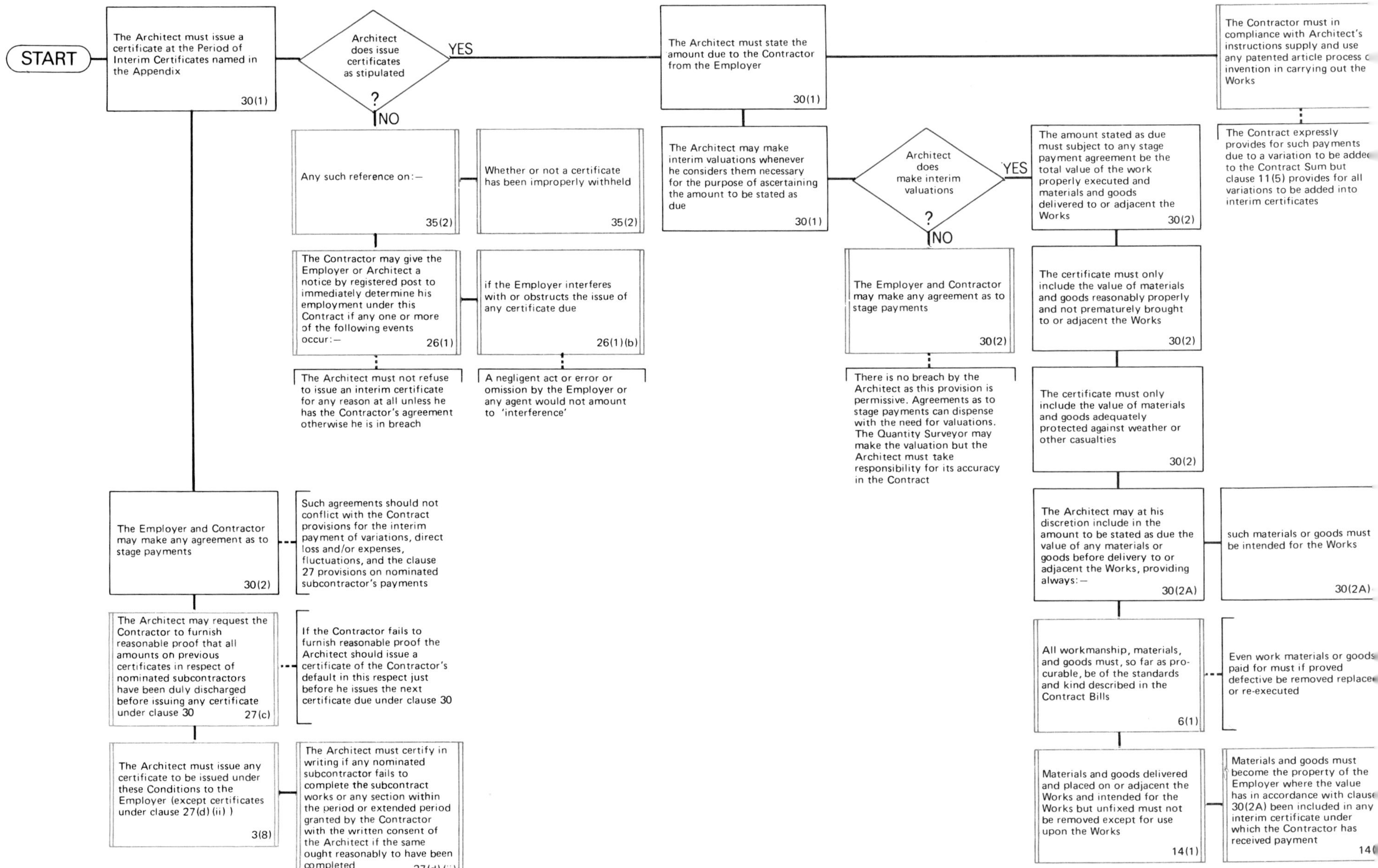

START
The Architect must issue a certificate at the Period of Interim Certificates named in the Appendix 30(1)
Architect does issue certificates as stipulated ?
YES
NO
The Architect must state the amount due to the Contractor from the Employer 30(1)
The Contractor must in compliance with Architect's instructions supply and use any patented article process or invention in carrying out the Works
The Contract expressly provides for such payments due to a variation to be added to the Contract Sum but clause 11(5) provides for all variations to be added into interim certificates
Any such reference on:– 35(2)
Whether or not a certificate has been improperly withheld 35(2)
The Contractor may give the Employer or Architect a notice by registered post to immediately determine his employment under this Contract if any one or more of the following events occur:– 26(1)
if the Employer interferes with or obstructs the issue of any certificate due 26(1)(b)
The Architect must not refuse to issue an interim certificate for any reason at all unless he has the Contractor's agreement otherwise he is in breach
A negligent act or error or omission by the Employer or any agent would not amount to 'interference'
The Architect may make interim valuations whenever he considers them necessary for the purpose of ascertaining the amount to be stated as due 30(1)
Architect does make interim valuations ?
YES
NO
The amount stated as due must subject to any stage payment agreement be the total value of the work properly executed and materials and goods delivered to or adjacent the Works 30(2)
The Employer and Contractor may make any agreement as to stage payments 30(2)
There is no breach by the Architect as this provision is permissive. Agreements as to stage payments can dispense with the need for valuations. The Quantity Surveyor may make the valuation but the Architect must take responsibility for its accuracy in the Contract
The certificate must only include the value of materials and goods reasonably properly and not prematurely brought to or adjacent the Works 30(2)
The certificate must only include the value of materials and goods adequately protected against weather or other casualties 30(2)
The Employer and Contractor may make any agreement as to stage payments 30(2)
Such agreements should not conflict with the Contract provisions for the interim payment of variations, direct loss and/or expenses, fluctuations, and the clause 27 provisions on nominated subcontractor's payments
The Architect may at his discretion include in the amount to be stated as due the value of any materials or goods before delivery to or adjacent the Works, providing always:– 30(2A)
such materials or goods must be intended for the Works 30(2A)
The Architect may request the Contractor to furnish reasonable proof that all amounts on previous certificates in respect of nominated subcontractors have been duly discharged before issuing any certificate under clause 30 27(c)
If the Contractor fails to furnish reasonable proof the Architect should issue a certificate of the Contractor's default in this respect just before he issues the next certificate due under clause 30
All workmanship, materials, and goods must, so far as procurable, be of the standards and kind described in the Contract Bills 6(1)
Even work materials or goods paid for must if proved defective be removed replaced or re-executed
The Architect must issue any certificate to be issued under these Conditions to the Employer (except certificates under clause 27(d)(ii)) 3(8)
The Architect must certify in writing if any nominated subcontractor fails to complete the subcontract works or any section within the period or extended period granted by the Contractor with the written consent of the Architect if the same ought reasonably to have been completed 27(d)(ii)
Materials and goods delivered and placed on or adjacent the Works and intended for the Works but unfixed must not be removed except for use upon the Works 14(1)
Materials and goods must become the property of the Employer where the value has in accordance with clause 30(2A) been included in any interim certificate under which the Contractor has received payment

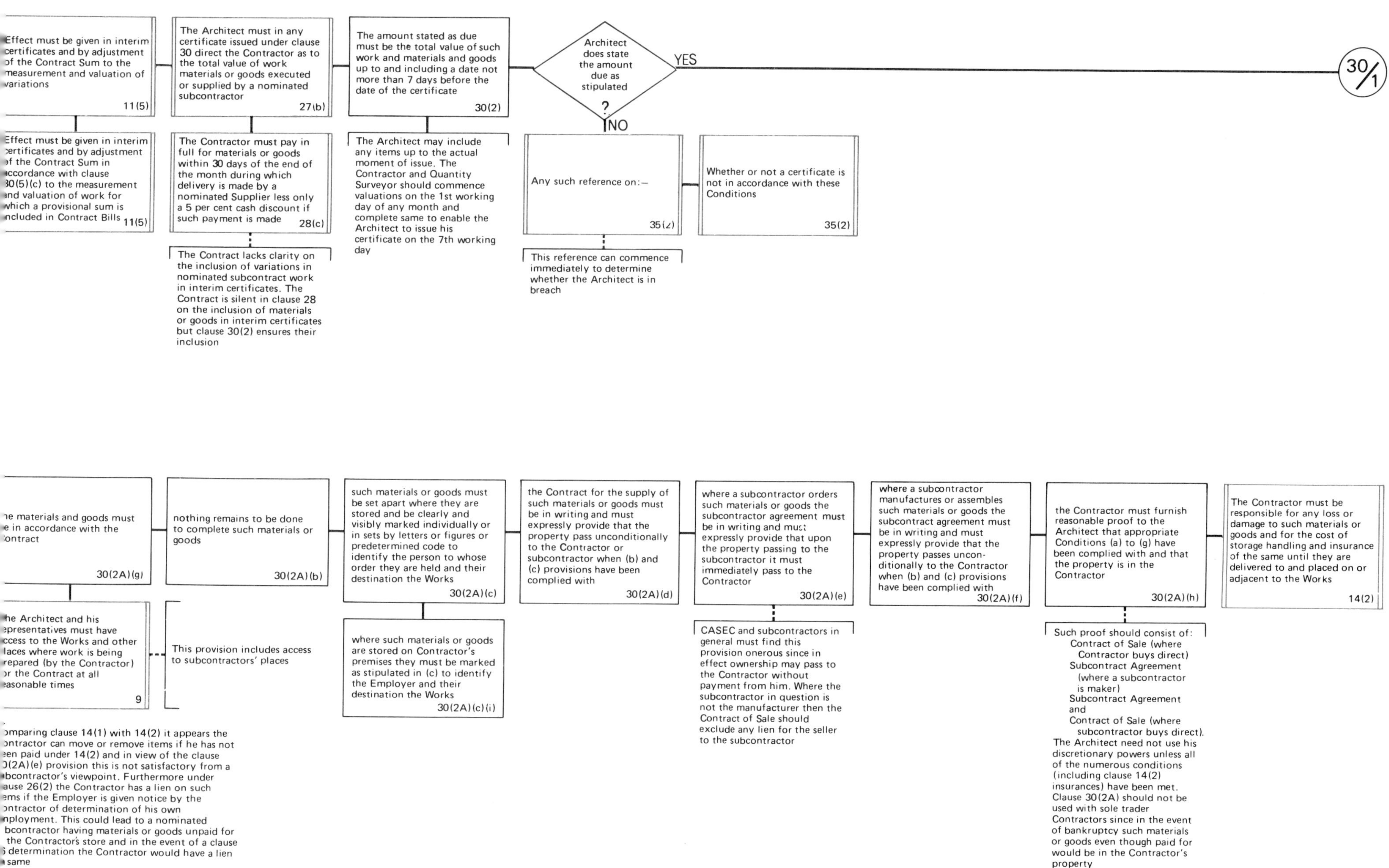

Effect must be given in interim certificates and by adjustment of the Contract Sum to the measurement and valuation of variations 11(5)
The Architect must in any certificate issued under clause 30 direct the Contractor as to the total value of work materials or goods executed or supplied by a nominated subcontractor 27(b)
The amount stated as due must be the total value of such work and materials and goods up to and including a date not more than 7 days before the date of the certificate 30(2)
Architect does state the amount due as stipulated ?
YES
NO
30/1
Effect must be given in interim certificates and by adjustment of the Contract Sum in accordance with clause 30(5)(c) to the measurement and valuation of work for which a provisional sum is included in Contract Bills 11(5)
The Contractor must pay in full for materials or goods within 30 days of the end of the month during which delivery is made by a nominated Supplier less only a 5 per cent cash discount if such payment is made 28(c)
The Contract lacks clarity on the inclusion of variations in nominated subcontract work in interim certificates. The Contract is silent in clause 28 on the inclusion of materials or goods in interim certificates but clause 30(2) ensures their inclusion
The Architect may include any items up to the actual moment of issue. The Contractor and Quantity Surveyor should commence valuations on the 1st working day of any month and complete same to enable the Architect to issue his certificate on the 7th working day
Any such reference on:– 35(2)
Whether or not a certificate is not in accordance with these Conditions 35(2)
This reference can commence immediately to determine whether the Architect is in breach
The materials and goods must be in accordance with the Contract 30(2A)(g)
nothing remains to be done to complete such materials or goods 30(2A)(b)
such materials or goods must be set apart where they are stored and be clearly and visibly marked individually or in sets by letters or figures or predetermined code to identify the person to whose order they are held and their destination the Works 30(2A)(c)
the Contract for the supply of such materials or goods must be in writing and must expressly provide that the property pass unconditionally to the Contractor or subcontractor when (b) and (c) provisions have been complied with 30(2A)(d)
where a subcontractor orders such materials or goods the subcontractor agreement must be in writing and must expressly provide that upon the property passing to the subcontractor it must immediately pass to the Contractor 30(2A)(e)
where a subcontractor manufactures or assembles such materials or goods the subcontract agreement must be in writing and must expressly provide that the property passes unconditionally to the Contractor when (b) and (c) provisions have been complied with 30(2A)(f)
the Contractor must furnish reasonable proof to the Architect that appropriate Conditions (a) to (g) have been complied with and that the property is in the Contractor 30(2A)(h)
The Contractor must be responsible for any loss or damage to such materials or goods and for the cost of storage handling and insurance of the same until they are delivered to and placed on or adjacent to the Works 14(2)
The Architect and his representatives must have access to the Works and other places where work is being prepared (by the Contractor) for the Contract at all reasonable times 9
This provision includes access to subcontractors' places
where such materials or goods are stored on Contractor's premises they must be marked as stipulated in (c) to identify the Employer and their destination the Works 30(2A)(c)(i)
CASEC and subcontractors in general must find this provision onerous since in effect ownership may pass to the Contractor without payment from him. Where the subcontractor in question is not the manufacturer then the Contract of Sale should exclude any lien for the seller to the subcontractor
Such proof should consist of: Contract of Sale (where Contractor buys direct) Subcontract Agreement (where a subcontractor is maker) Subcontract Agreement and Contract of Sale (where subcontractor buys direct). The Architect need not use his discretionary powers unless all of the numerous conditions (including clause 14(2) insurances) have been met. Clause 30(2A) should not be used with sole trader Contractors since in the event of bankruptcy such materials or goods even though paid for would be in the Contractor's property
Comparing clause 14(1) with 14(2) it appears the Contractor can move or remove items if he has not been paid under 14(2) and in view of the clause 30(2A)(e) provision this is not satisfactory from a subcontractor's viewpoint. Furthermore under clause 26(2) the Contractor has a lien on such items if the Employer is given notice by the Contractor of determination of his own employment. This could lead to a nominated subcontractor having materials or goods unpaid for in the Contractor's store and in the event of a clause 26 determination the Contractor would have a lien on same

Clause 30 INTERIM PAYMENT CERTIFICATES (2)

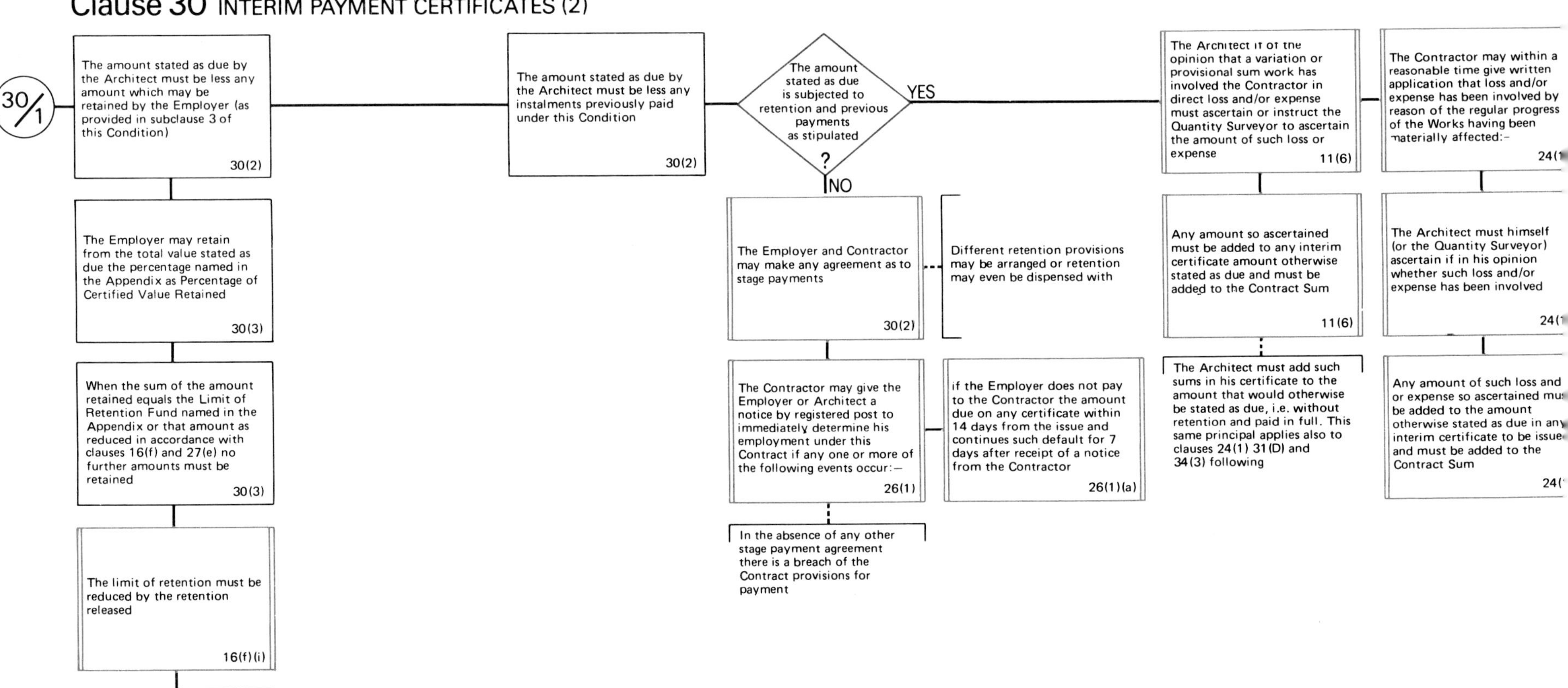

30/1
The amount stated as due by the Architect must be less any amount which may be retained by the Employer (as provided in subclause 3 of this Condition) 30(2)
The Employer may retain from the total value stated as due the percentage named in the Appendix as Percentage of Certified Value Retained 30(3)
When the sum of the amount retained equals the Limit of Retention Fund named in the Appendix or that amount as reduced in accordance with clauses 16(f) and 27(e) no further amounts must be retained 30(3)
The limit of retention must be reduced by the retention released 16(f)(i)
The Limit of Retention Fund must be reduced by x where x : Limit (original) as Subcontract Price : ContractSum 27(e)
The amount stated as due by the Architect must be less any instalments previously paid under this Condition 30(2)
The amount stated as due is subjected to retention and previous payments as stipulated ?
YES
NO
The Employer and Contractor may make any agreement as to stage payments 30(2)
Different retention provisions may be arranged or retention may even be dispensed with
The Contractor may give the Employer or Architect a notice by registered post to immediately determine his employment under this Contract if any one or more of the following events occur:– 26(1)
if the Employer does not pay to the Contractor the amount due on any certificate within 14 days from the issue and continues such default for 7 days after receipt of a notice from the Contractor 26(1)(a)
In the absence of any other stage payment agreement there is a breach of the Contract provisions for payment
The Architect if of the opinion that a variation or provisional sum work has involved the Contractor in direct loss and/or expense must ascertain or instruct the Quantity Surveyor to ascertain the amount of such loss or expense 11(6)
Any amount so ascertained must be added to any interim certificate amount otherwise stated as due and must be added to the Contract Sum 11(6)
The Architect must add such sums in his certificate to the amount that would otherwise be stated as due, i.e. without retention and paid in full. This same principal applies also to clauses 24(1) 31(D) and 34(3) following
The Contractor may within a reasonable time give written application that loss and/or expense has been involved by reason of the regular progress of the Works having been materially affected:– 24(1
The Architect must himself (or the Quantity Surveyor) ascertain if in his opinion whether such loss and/or expense has been involved 24(1
Any amount of such loss and or expense so ascertained mus be added to the amount otherwise stated as due in any interim certificate to be issue and must be added to the Contract Sum 24(

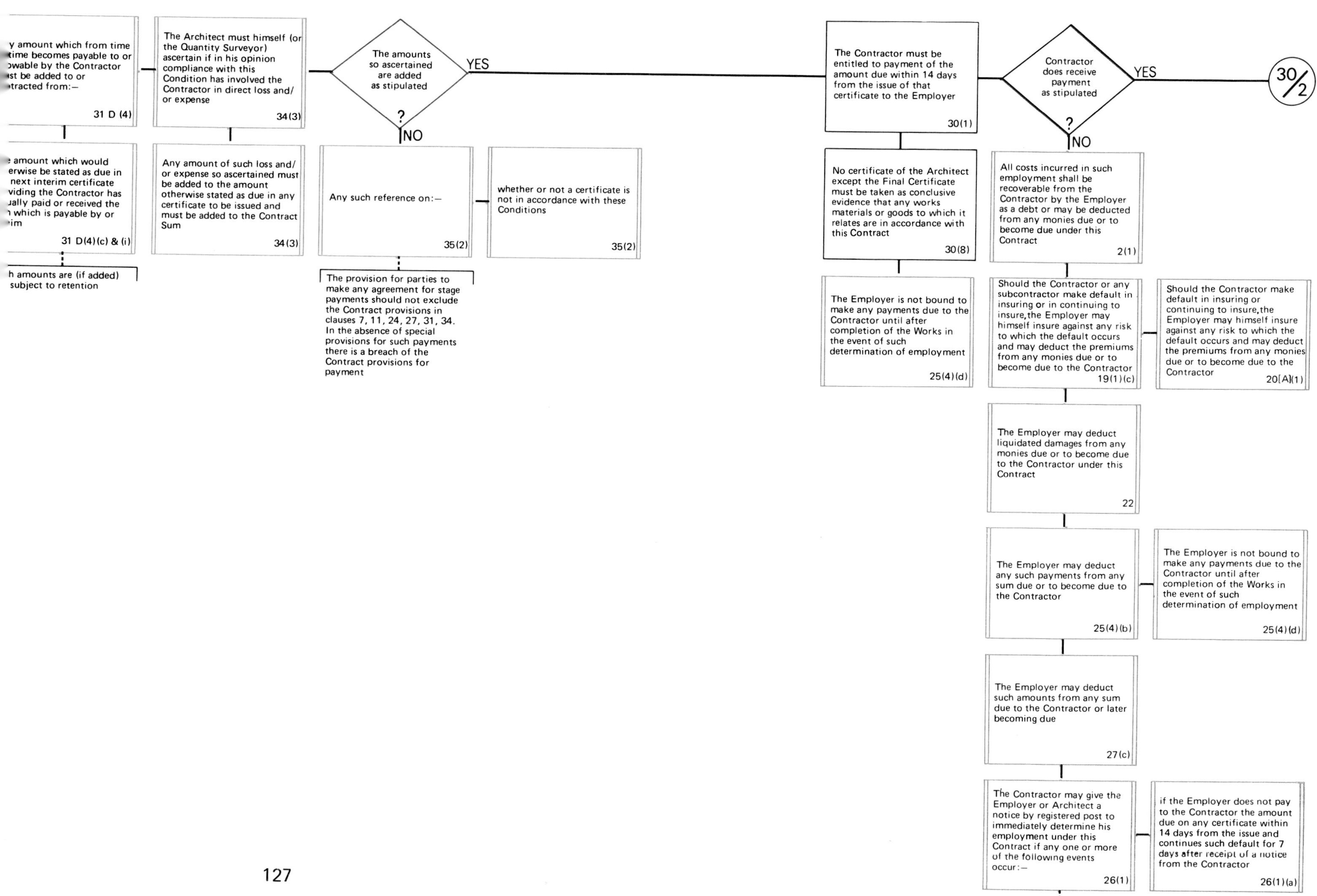
y amount which from time
time becomes payable to or
owable by the Contractor
st be added to or
tracted from:–
31 D (4)
The Architect must himself (or the Quantity Surveyor) ascertain if in his opinion compliance with this Condition has involved the Contractor in direct loss and/or expense
34(3)
The amounts so ascertained are added as stipulated
?
YES
NO
The Contractor must be entitled to payment of the amount due within 14 days from the issue of that certificate to the Employer
30(1)
Contractor does receive payment as stipulated
?
YES
NO
30/2
e amount which would
erwise be stated as due in
next interim certificate
viding the Contractor has
ually paid or received the
which is payable by or
im
31 D(4)(c) & (i)
h amounts are (if added)
subject to retention
Any amount of such loss and/or expense so ascertained must be added to the amount otherwise stated as due in any certificate to be issued and must be added to the Contract Sum
34(3)
Any such reference on:–
35(2)
whether or not a certificate is not in accordance with these Conditions
35(2)
The provision for parties to make any agreement for stage payments should not exclude the Contract provisions in clauses 7, 11, 24, 27, 31, 34. In the absence of special provisions for such payments there is a breach of the Contract provisions for payment
No certificate of the Architect except the Final Certificate must be taken as conclusive evidence that any works materials or goods to which it relates are in accordance with this Contract
30(8)
All costs incurred in such employment shall be recoverable from the Contractor by the Employer as a debt or may be deducted from any monies due or to become due under this Contract
2(1)
The Employer is not bound to make any payments due to the Contractor until after completion of the Works in the event of such determination of employment
25(4)(d)
Should the Contractor or any subcontractor make default in insuring or in continuing to insure, the Employer may himself insure against any risk to which the default occurs and may deduct the premiums from any monies due or to become due to the Contractor
19(1)(c)
Should the Contractor make default in insuring or continuing to insure, the Employer may himself insure against any risk to which the default occurs and may deduct the premiums from any monies due or to become due to the Contractor
20[A](1)
The Employer may deduct liquidated damages from any monies due or to become due to the Contractor under this Contract
22
The Employer may deduct any such payments from any sum due or to become due to the Contractor
25(4)(b)
The Employer is not bound to make any payments due to the Contractor until after completion of the Works in the event of such determination of employment
25(4)(d)
The Employer may deduct such amounts from any sum due to the Contractor or later becoming due
27(c)
The Contractor may give the Employer or Architect a notice by registered post to immediately determine his employment under this Contract if any one or more of the following events occur:–
26(1)
if the Employer does not pay to the Contractor the amount due on any certificate within 14 days from the issue and continues such default for 7 days after receipt of a notice from the Contractor
26(1)(a)
Subject to the permitted deductions there is a breach by the Employer

Clause 30 RETENTION CERTIFICATES

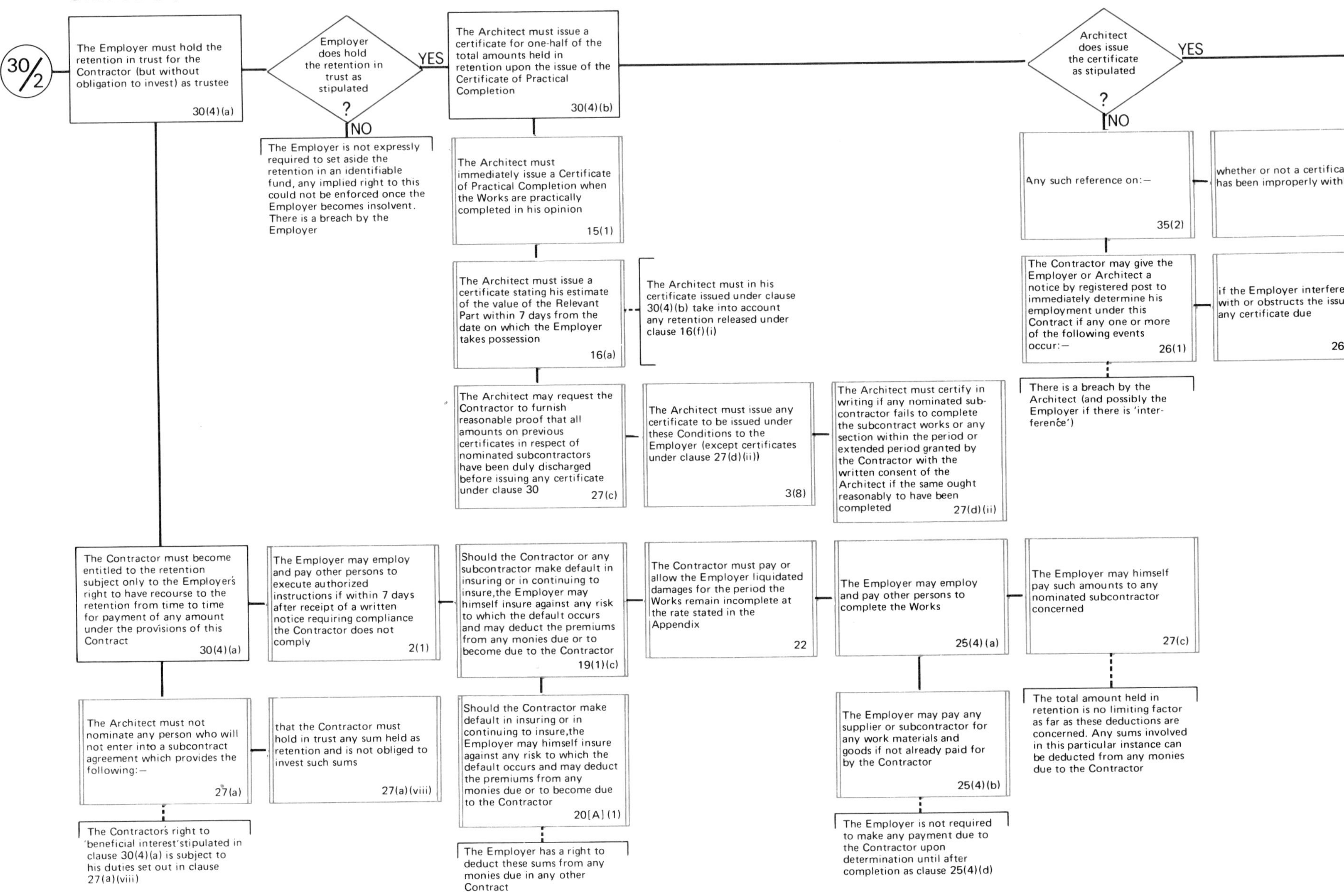

30/2
The Employer must hold the retention in trust for the Contractor (but without obligation to invest) as trustee 30(4)(a)
Employer does hold the retention in trust as stipulated ?
YES
NO
The Employer is not expressly required to set aside the retention in an identifiable fund, any implied right to this could not be enforced once the Employer becomes insolvent. There is a breach by the Employer
The Architect must issue a certificate for one-half of the total amounts held in retention upon the issue of the Certificate of Practical Completion 30(4)(b)
The Architect must immediately issue a Certificate of Practical Completion when the Works are practically completed in his opinion 15(1)
The Architect must issue a certificate stating his estimate of the value of the Relevant Part within 7 days from the date on which the Employer takes possession 16(a)
The Architect must in his certificate issued under clause 30(4)(b) take into account any retention released under clause 16(f)(i)
The Architect may request the Contractor to furnish reasonable proof that all amounts on previous certificates in respect of nominated subcontractors have been duly discharged before issuing any certificate under clause 30 27(c)
The Architect must issue any certificate to be issued under these Conditions to the Employer (except certificates under clause 27(d)(ii)) 3(8)
The Architect must certify in writing if any nominated subcontractor fails to complete the subcontract works or any section within the period or extended period granted by the Contractor with the written consent of the Architect if the same ought reasonably to have been completed 27(d)(ii)
Architect does issue the certificate as stipulated ?
YES
NO
Any such reference on:– 35(2)
whether or not a certificate has been improperly withhe
3
The Contractor may give the Employer or Architect a notice by registered post to immediately determine his employment under this Contract if any one or more of the following events occur:– 26(1)
if the Employer interferes with or obstructs the issue any certificate due
26(1
There is a breach by the Architect (and possibly the Employer if there is 'interference')
The Contractor must become entitled to the retention subject only to the Employer's right to have recourse to the retention from time to time for payment of any amount under the provisions of this Contract 30(4)(a)
The Employer may employ and pay other persons to execute authorized instructions if within 7 days after receipt of a written notice requiring compliance the Contractor does not comply 2(1)
Should the Contractor or any subcontractor make default in insuring or in continuing to insure, the Employer may himself insure against any risk to which the default occurs and may deduct the premiums from any monies due or to become due to the Contractor 19(1)(c)
The Contractor must pay or allow the Employer liquidated damages for the period the Works remain incomplete at the rate stated in the Appendix 22
The Employer may employ and pay other persons to complete the Works 25(4)(a)
The Employer may himself pay such amounts to any nominated subcontractor concerned 27(c)
The Architect must not nominate any person who will not enter into a subcontract agreement which provides the following:– 27(a)
that the Contractor must hold in trust any sum held as retention and is not obliged to invest such sums 27(a)(viii)
Should the Contractor make default in insuring or in continuing to insure, the Employer may himself insure against any risk to which the default occurs and may deduct the premiums from any monies due or to become due to the Contractor 20[A](1)
The Employer may pay any supplier or subcontractor for any work materials and goods if not already paid for by the Contractor 25(4)(b)
The total amount held in retention is no limiting factor as far as these deductions are concerned. Any sums involved in this particular instance can be deducted from any monies due to the Contractor
The Contractor's right to 'beneficial interest' stipulated in clause 30(4)(a) is subject to his duties set out in clause 27(a)(viii)
The Employer has a right to deduct these sums from any monies due in any other Contract
The Employer is not required to make any payment due to the Contractor upon determination until after completion as clause 25(4)(d)

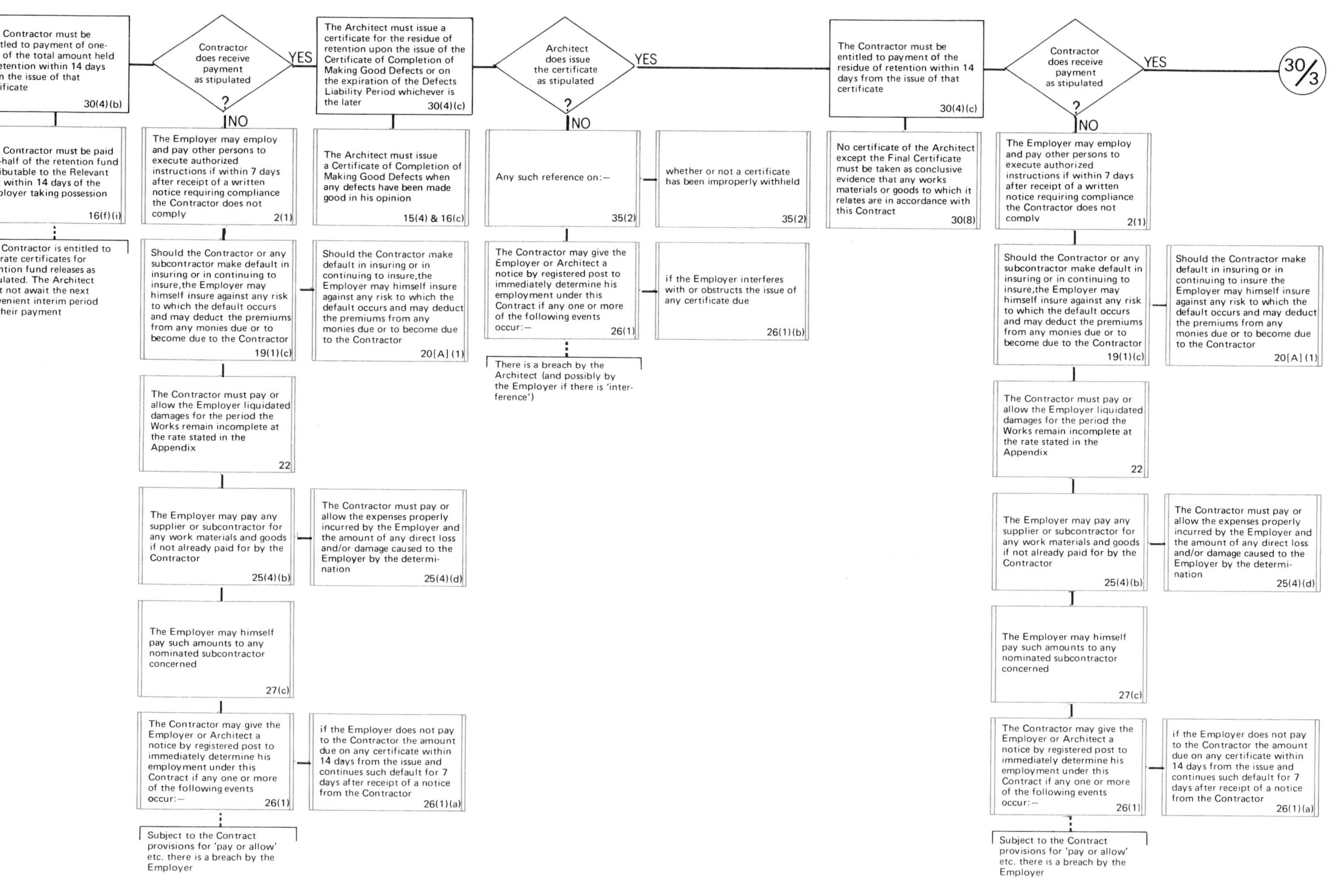

Contractor must be
itled to payment of one-
of the total amount held
etention within 14 days
n the issue of that
tificate
30(4)(b)
Contractor does receive payment as stipulated ?
YES
NO
The Architect must issue a certificate for the residue of retention upon the issue of the Certificate of Completion of Making Good Defects or on the expiration of the Defects Liability Period whichever is the later
30(4)(c)
Architect does issue the certificate as stipulated ?
YES
NO
The Contractor must be entitled to payment of the residue of retention within 14 days from the issue of that certificate
30(4)(c)
Contractor does receive payment as stipulated ?
YES
NO
30/3
Contractor must be paid
-half of the retention fund
ributable to the Relevant
t within 14 days of the
ployer taking possession
16(f)(i)
Contractor is entitled to
arate certificates for
ntion fund releases as
ulated. The Architect
st not await the next
venient interim period
their payment
The Employer may employ and pay other persons to execute authorized instructions if within 7 days after receipt of a written notice requiring compliance the Contractor does not comply
2(1)
Should the Contractor or any subcontractor make default in insuring or in continuing to insure, the Employer may himself insure against any risk to which the default occurs and may deduct the premiums from any monies due or to become due to the Contractor
19(1)(c)
Should the Contractor make default in insuring or in continuing to insure, the Employer may himself insure against any risk to which the default occurs and may deduct the premiums from any monies due or to become due to the Contractor
20[A](1)
The Contractor must pay or allow the Employer liquidated damages for the period the Works remain incomplete at the rate stated in the Appendix
22
The Employer may pay any supplier or subcontractor for any work materials and goods if not already paid for by the Contractor
25(4)(b)
The Contractor must pay or allow the expenses properly incurred by the Employer and the amount of any direct loss and/or damage caused to the Employer by the determination
25(4)(d)
The Employer may himself pay such amounts to any nominated subcontractor concerned
27(c)
The Contractor may give the Employer or Architect a notice by registered post to immediately determine his employment under this Contract if any one or more of the following events occur:—
26(1)
if the Employer does not pay to the Contractor the amount due on any certificate within 14 days from the issue and continues such default for 7 days after receipt of a notice from the Contractor
26(1)(a)
Subject to the Contract provisions for 'pay or allow' etc. there is a breach by the Employer
The Architect must issue a Certificate of Completion of Making Good Defects when any defects have been made good in his opinion
15(4) & 16(c)
Any such reference on:—
35(2)
whether or not a certificate has been improperly withheld
35(2)
The Contractor may give the Employer or Architect a notice by registered post to immediately determine his employment under this Contract if any one or more of the following events occur:—
26(1)
if the Employer interferes with or obstructs the issue of any certificate due
26(1)(b)
There is a breach by the Architect (and possibly by the Employer if there is 'interference')
No certificate of the Architect except the Final Certificate must be taken as conclusive evidence that any works materials or goods to which it relates are in accordance with this Contract
30(8)
The Employer may employ and pay other persons to execute authorized instructions if within 7 days after receipt of a written notice requiring compliance the Contractor does not comply
2(1)
Should the Contractor or any subcontractor make default in insuring or in continuing to insure, the Employer may himself insure against any risk to which the default occurs and may deduct the premiums from any monies due or to become due to the Contractor
19(1)(c)
Should the Contractor make default in insuring or in continuing to insure the Employer may himself insure against any risk to which the default occurs and may deduct the premiums from any monies due or to become due to the Contractor
20[A](1)
The Contractor must pay or allow the Employer liquidated damages for the period the Works remain incomplete at the rate stated in the Appendix
22
The Employer may pay any supplier or subcontractor for any work materials and goods if not already paid for by the Contractor
25(4)(b)
The Contractor must pay or allow the expenses properly incurred by the Employer and the amount of any direct loss and/or damage caused to the Employer by the determination
25(4)(d)
The Employer may himself pay such amounts to any nominated subcontractor concerned
27(c)
The Contractor may give the Employer or Architect a notice by registered post to immediately determine his employment under this Contract if any one or more of the following events occur:—
26(1)
if the Employer does not pay to the Contractor the amount due on any certificate within 14 days from the issue and continues such default for 7 days after receipt of a notice from the Contractor
26(1)(a)
Subject to the Contract provisions for 'pay or allow' etc. there is a breach by the Employer

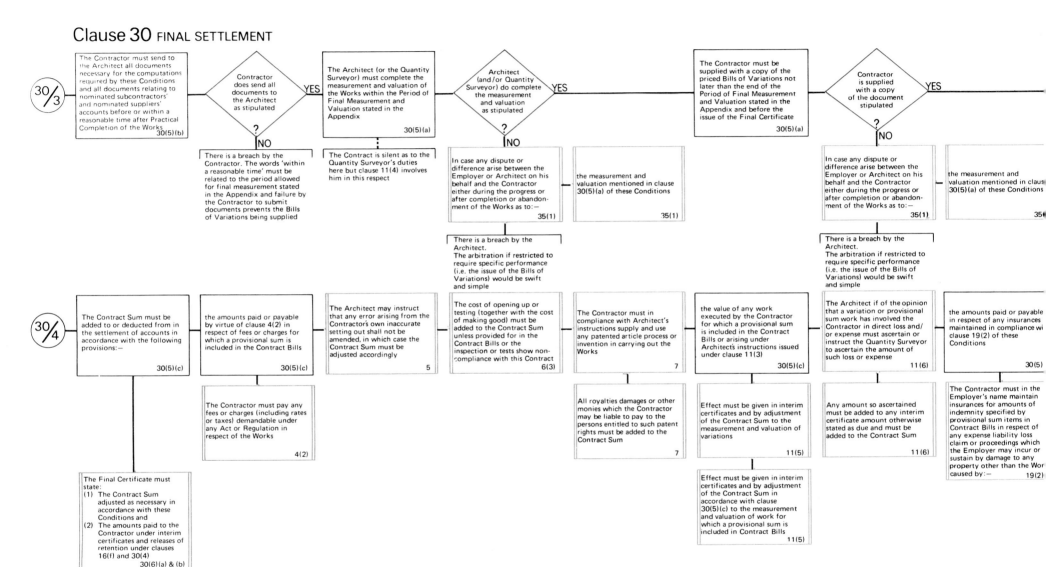

Clause 30 FINAL SETTLEMENT

30/3

The Contractor must send to the Architect all documents necessary for the computations required by these Conditions and all documents relating to nominated subcontractors' and nominated suppliers' accounts before or within a reasonable time after Practical Completion of the Works 30(5)(b)

Contractor does send all documents to the Architect as stipulated ?

NO: There is a breach by the Contractor. The words 'within a reasonable time' must be related to the period allowed for final measurement stated in the Appendix and failure by the Contractor to submit documents prevents the Bills of Variations being supplied

YES: The Architect (or the Quantity Surveyor) must complete the measurement and valuation of the Works within the Period of Final Measurement and Valuation stated in the Appendix 30(5)(a)

The Contract is silent as to the Quantity Surveyor's duties here but clause 11(4) involves him in this respect

Architect (and/or Quantity Surveyor) do complete the measurement and valuation as stipulated ?

NO: In case any dispute or difference arise between the Employer or Architect on his behalf and the Contractor either during the progress or after completion or abandonment of the Works as to:— 35(1)

the measurement and valuation mentioned in clause 30(5)(a) of these Conditions 35(1)

There is a breach by the Architect. The arbitration if restricted to require specific performance (i.e. the issue of the Bills of Variations) would be swift and simple

YES: The Contractor must be supplied with a copy of the priced Bills of Variations not later than the end of the Period of Final Measurement and Valuation stated in the Appendix and before the issue of the Final Certificate 30(5)(a)

Contractor is supplied with a copy of the document stipulated ?

NO: In case any dispute or difference arise between the Employer or Architect on his behalf and the Contractor either during the progress or after completion or abandonment of the Works as to:— 35(1)

the measurement and valuation mentioned in claus[e] 30(5)(a) of these Conditions 35[(1)]

There is a breach by the Architect. The arbitration if restricted to require specific performance (i.e. the issue of the Bills of Variations) would be swift and simple

YES

30/4

The Contract Sum must be added to or deducted from in the settlement of accounts in accordance with the following provisions:— 30(5)(c)

The Final Certificate must state:
(1) The Contract Sum adjusted as necessary in accordance with these Conditions and
(2) The amounts paid to the Contractor under interim certificates and releases of retention under clauses 16(f) and 30(4)
30(6)(a) & (b)

the amounts paid or payable by virtue of clause 4(2) in respect of fees or charges for which a provisional sum is included in the Contract Bills 30(5)(c)

The Contractor must pay any fees or charges (including rates or taxes) demandable under any Act or Regulation in respect of the Works 4(2)

The Architect may instruct that any error arising from the Contractor's own inaccurate setting out shall not be amended, in which case the Contract Sum must be adjusted accordingly 5

The cost of opening up or testing (together with the cost of making good) must be added to the Contract Sum unless provided for in the Contract Bills or the inspection or tests show non-compliance with this Contract 6(3)

The Contractor must in compliance with Architect's instructions supply and use any patented article process or invention in carrying out the Works 7

All royalties damages or other monies which the Contractor may be liable to pay to the persons entitled to such patent rights must be added to the Contract Sum 7

the value of any work executed by the Contractor for which a provisional sum is included in the Contract Bills or arising under Architect's instructions issued under clause 11(3) 30(5)(c)

Effect must be given in interim certificates and by adjustment of the Contract Sum to the measurement and valuation of variations 11(5)

Effect must be given in interim certificates and by adjustment of the Contract Sum in accordance with clause 30(5)(c) to the measurement and valuation of work for which a provisional sum is included in Contract Bills 11(5)

The Architect if of the opinion that a variation or provisional sum work has involved the Contractor in direct loss and/or expense must ascertain or instruct the Quantity Surveyor to ascertain the amount of such loss or expense 11(6)

Any amount so ascertained must be added to any interim certificate amount otherwise stated as due and must be added to the Contract Sum 11(6)

the amounts paid or payable in respect of any insurances maintained in compliance wi[th] clause 19(2) of these Conditions 30(5)

The Contractor must in the Employer's name maintain insurances for amounts of indemnity specified by provisional sum items in Contract Bills in respect of any expense liability loss claim or proceedings which the Employer may incur or sustain by damage to any property other than the Wor[ks] caused by:— 19(2)

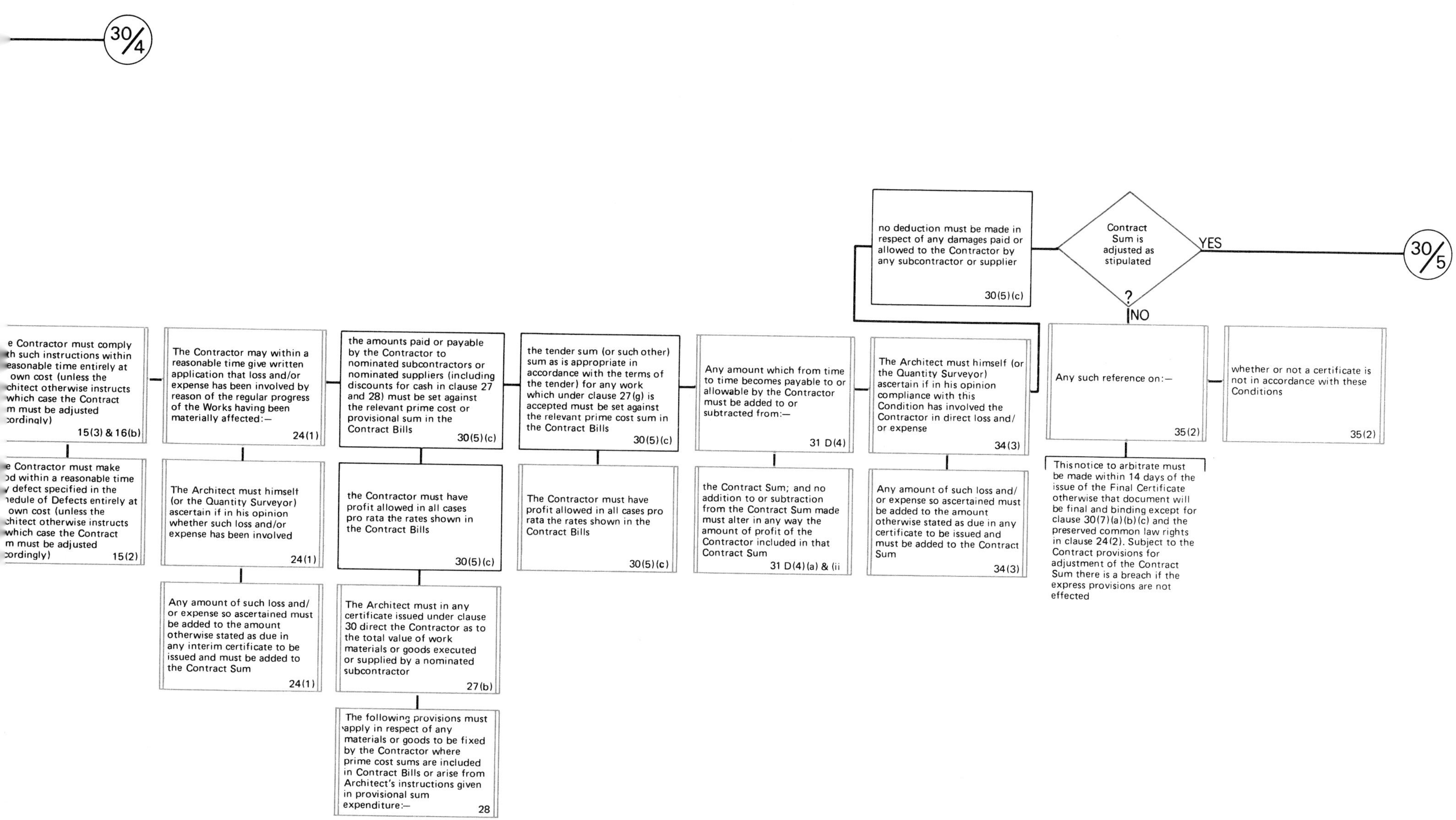

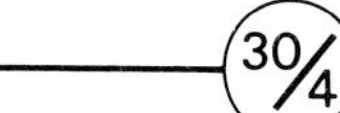

30/4

e Contractor must comply
th such instructions within
easonable time entirely at
own cost (unless the
chitect otherwise instructs
which case the Contract
m must be adjusted
cordingly)
15(3) & 16(b)

e Contractor must make
od within a reasonable time
y defect specified in the
hedule of Defects entirely at
own cost (unless the
chitect otherwise instructs
which case the Contract
m must be adjusted
cordingly) 15(2)

The Contractor may within a reasonable time give written application that loss and/or expense has been involved by reason of the regular progress of the Works having been materially affected:— 24(1)

The Architect must himself (or the Quantity Surveyor) ascertain if in his opinion whether such loss and/or expense has been involved 24(1)

Any amount of such loss and/or expense so ascertained must be added to the amount otherwise stated as due in any interim certificate to be issued and must be added to the Contract Sum 24(1)

the amounts paid or payable by the Contractor to nominated subcontractors or nominated suppliers (including discounts for cash in clause 27 and 28) must be set against the relevant prime cost or provisional sum in the Contract Bills 30(5)(c)

the Contractor must have profit allowed in all cases pro rata the rates shown in the Contract Bills 30(5)(c)

The Architect must in any certificate issued under clause 30 direct the Contractor as to the total value of work materials or goods executed or supplied by a nominated subcontractor 27(b)

The following provisions must apply in respect of any materials or goods to be fixed by the Contractor where prime cost sums are included in Contract Bills or arise from Architect's instructions given in provisional sum expenditure:— 28

the tender sum (or such other) sum as is appropriate in accordance with the terms of the tender) for any work which under clause 27(g) is accepted must be set against the relevant prime cost sum in the Contract Bills 30(5)(c)

The Contractor must have profit allowed in all cases pro rata the rates shown in the Contract Bills 30(5)(c)

Any amount which from time to time becomes payable to or allowable by the Contractor must be added to or subtracted from:— 31 D(4)

the Contract Sum; and no addition to or subtraction from the Contract Sum made must alter in any way the amount of profit of the Contractor included in that Contract Sum 31 D(4)(a) & (ii

The Architect must himself (or the Quantity Surveyor) ascertain if in his opinion compliance with this Condition has involved the Contractor in direct loss and/or expense 34(3)

Any amount of such loss and/or expense so ascertained must be added to the amount otherwise stated as due in any certificate to be issued and must be added to the Contract Sum 34(3)

no deduction must be made in respect of any damages paid or allowed to the Contractor by any subcontractor or supplier 30(5)(c)

Contract Sum is adjusted as stipulated ?

YES

30/5

NO

Any such reference on:— 35(2)

whether or not a certificate is not in accordance with these Conditions 35(2)

This notice to arbitrate must be made within 14 days of the issue of the Final Certificate otherwise that document will be final and binding except for clause 30(7)(a)(b)(c) and the preserved common law rights in clause 24(2). Subject to the Contract provisions for adjustment of the Contract Sum there is a breach if the express provisions are not effected

Clause 30 FINAL CERTIFICATE

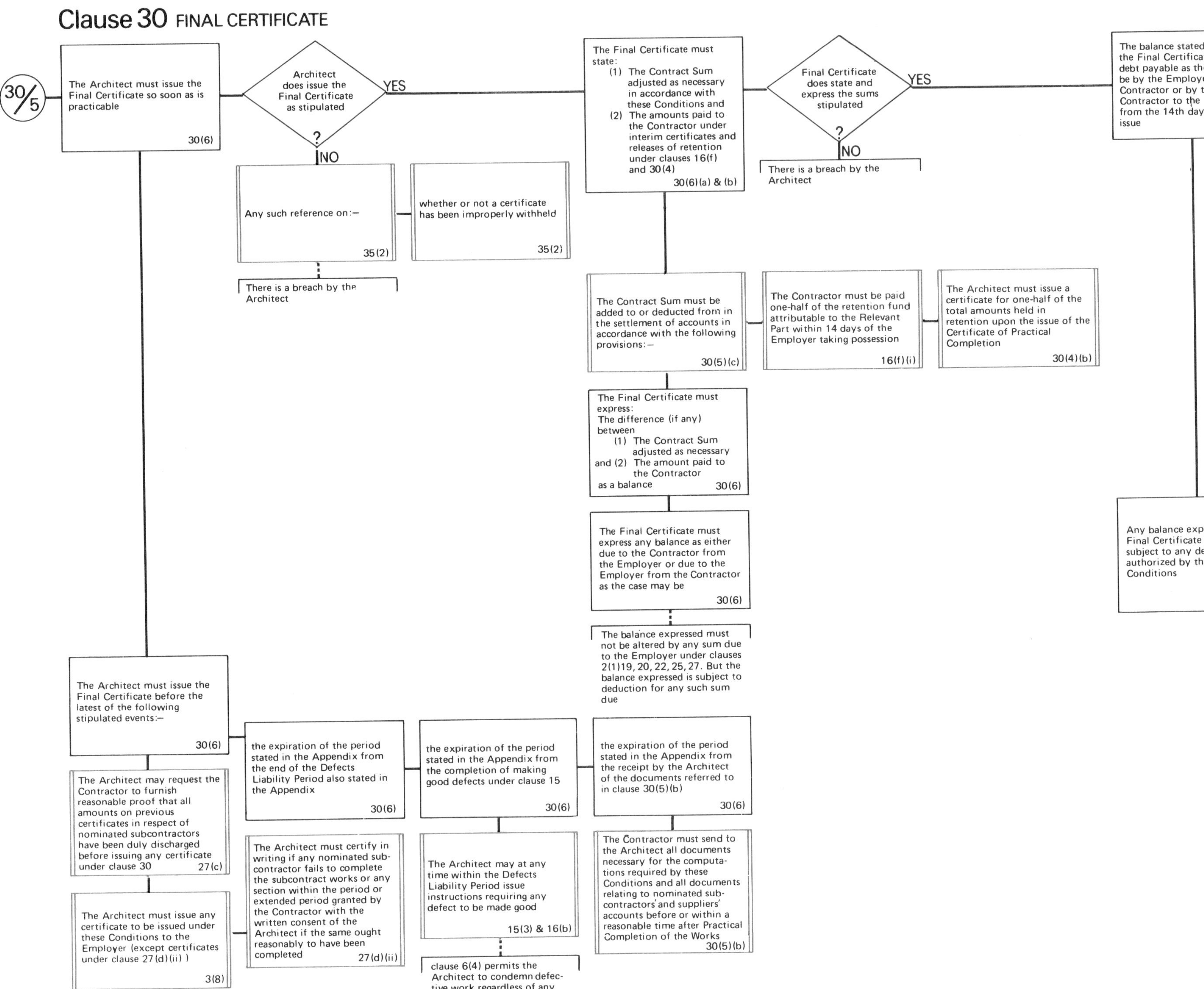

30/5
The Architect must issue the Final Certificate so soon as is practicable 30(6)
Architect does issue the Final Certificate as stipulated ?
YES
NO
Any such reference on:– 35(2)
whether or not a certificate has been improperly withheld 35(2)
There is a breach by the Architect
The Final Certificate must state: (1) The Contract Sum adjusted as necessary in accordance with these Conditions and (2) The amounts paid to the Contractor under interim certificates and releases of retention under clauses 16(f) and 30(4) 30(6)(a) & (b)
Final Certificate does state and express the sums stipulated ?
YES
NO
There is a breach by the Architect
The balance stated as due in the Final Certificate must be a debt payable as the case may be by the Employer to the Contractor or by the Contractor to the Employer as from the 14th day after the issue 30(6)
The Contract Sum must be added to or deducted from in the settlement of accounts in accordance with the following provisions:– 30(5)(c)
The Contractor must be paid one-half of the retention fund attributable to the Relevant Part within 14 days of the Employer taking possession 16(f)(i)
The Architect must issue a certificate for one-half of the total amounts held in retention upon the issue of the Certificate of Practical Completion 30(4)(b)
The Final Certificate must express: The difference (if any) between (1) The Contract Sum adjusted as necessary and (2) The amount paid to the Contractor as a balance 30(6)
The Final Certificate must express any balance as either due to the Contractor from the Employer or due to the Employer from the Contractor as the case may be 30(6)
The balance expressed must not be altered by any sum due to the Employer under clauses 2(1)19, 20, 22, 25, 27. But the balance expressed is subject to deduction for any such sum due
Any balance expressed in the Final Certificate must be subject to any deductions authorized by these Conditions 30(6)
The Architect must issue the Final Certificate before the latest of the following stipulated events:– 30(6)
the expiration of the period stated in the Appendix from the end of the Defects Liability Period also stated in the Appendix 30(6)
the expiration of the period stated in the Appendix from the completion of making good defects under clause 15 30(6)
the expiration of the period stated in the Appendix from the receipt by the Architect of the documents referred to in clause 30(5)(b) 30(6)
The Architect may request the Contractor to furnish reasonable proof that all amounts on previous certificates in respect of nominated subcontractors have been duly discharged before issuing any certificate under clause 30 27(c)
The Architect must issue any certificate to be issued under these Conditions to the Employer (except certificates under clause 27(d)(ii)) 3(8)
The Architect must certify in writing if any nominated subcontractor fails to complete the subcontract works or any section within the period or extended period granted by the Contractor with the written consent of the Architect if the same ought reasonably to have been completed 27(d)(ii)
The Architect may at any time within the Defects Liability Period issue instructions requiring any defect to be made good 15(3) & 16(b)
clause 6(4) permits the Architect to condemn defective work regardless of any prearranged defects liability period
The Contractor must send to the Architect all documents necessary for the computations required by these Conditions and all documents relating to nominated subcontractors' and suppliers' accounts before or within a reasonable time after Practical Completion of the Works 30(5)(b)

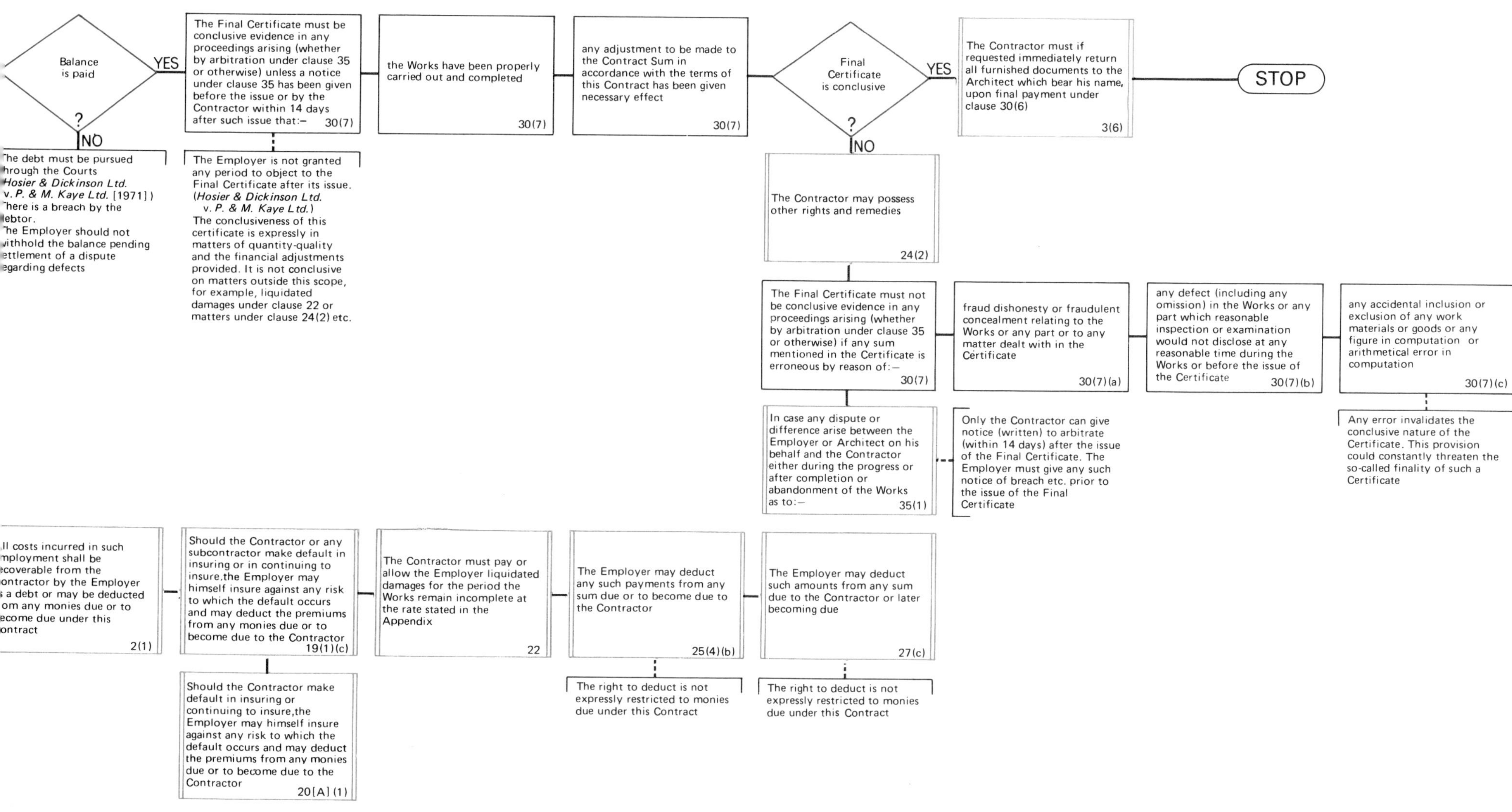

Balance is paid
YES
?
NO
The Final Certificate must be conclusive evidence in any proceedings arising (whether by arbitration under clause 35 or otherwise) unless a notice under clause 35 has been given before the issue or by the Contractor within 14 days after such issue that:– 30(7)
the Works have been properly carried out and completed 30(7)
any adjustment to be made to the Contract Sum in accordance with the terms of this Contract has been given necessary effect 30(7)
Final Certificate is conclusive
YES
?
NO
The Contractor must if requested immediately return all furnished documents to the Architect which bear his name, upon final payment under clause 30(6) 3(6)
STOP
he debt must be pursued hrough the Courts Hosier & Dickinson Ltd. v. P. & M. Kaye Ltd. [1971]) here is a breach by the ebtor. he Employer should not vithhold the balance pending ettlement of a dispute egarding defects
The Employer is not granted any period to object to the Final Certificate after its issue. (Hosier & Dickinson Ltd. v. P. & M. Kaye Ltd.) The conclusiveness of this certificate is expressly in matters of quantity-quality and the financial adjustments provided. It is not conclusive on matters outside this scope, for example, liquidated damages under clause 22 or matters under clause 24(2) etc.
The Contractor may possess other rights and remedies 24(2)
The Final Certificate must not be conclusive evidence in any proceedings arising (whether by arbitration under clause 35 or otherwise) if any sum mentioned in the Certificate is erroneous by reason of:– 30(7)
fraud dishonesty or fraudulent concealment relating to the Works or any part or to any matter dealt with in the Certificate 30(7)(a)
any defect (including any omission) in the Works or any part which reasonable inspection or examination would not disclose at any reasonable time during the Works or before the issue of the Certificate 30(7)(b)
any accidental inclusion or exclusion of any work materials or goods or any figure in computation or arithmetical error in computation 30(7)(c)
In case any dispute or difference arise between the Employer or Architect on his behalf and the Contractor either during the progress or after completion or abandonment of the Works as to:– 35(1)
Only the Contractor can give notice (written) to arbitrate (within 14 days) after the issue of the Final Certificate. The Employer must give any such notice of breach etc. prior to the issue of the Final Certificate
Any error invalidates the conclusive nature of the Certificate. This provision could constantly threaten the so-called finality of such a Certificate
ll costs incurred in such mployment shall be ecoverable from the ontractor by the Employer a debt or may be deducted om any monies due or to ecome due under this ontract 2(1)
Should the Contractor or any subcontractor make default in insuring or in continuing to insure,the Employer may himself insure against any risk to which the default occurs and may deduct the premiums from any monies due or to become due to the Contractor 19(1)(c)
The Contractor must pay or allow the Employer liquidated damages for the period the Works remain incomplete at the rate stated in the Appendix 22
The Employer may deduct any such payments from any sum due or to become due to the Contractor 25(4)(b)
The Employer may deduct such amounts from any sum due to the Contractor or later becoming due 27(c)
Should the Contractor make default in insuring or continuing to insure,the Employer may himself insure against any risk to which the default occurs and may deduct the premiums from any monies due or to become due to the Contractor 20[A](1)
The right to deduct is not expressly restricted to monies due under this Contract
The right to deduct is not expressly restricted to monies due under this Contract

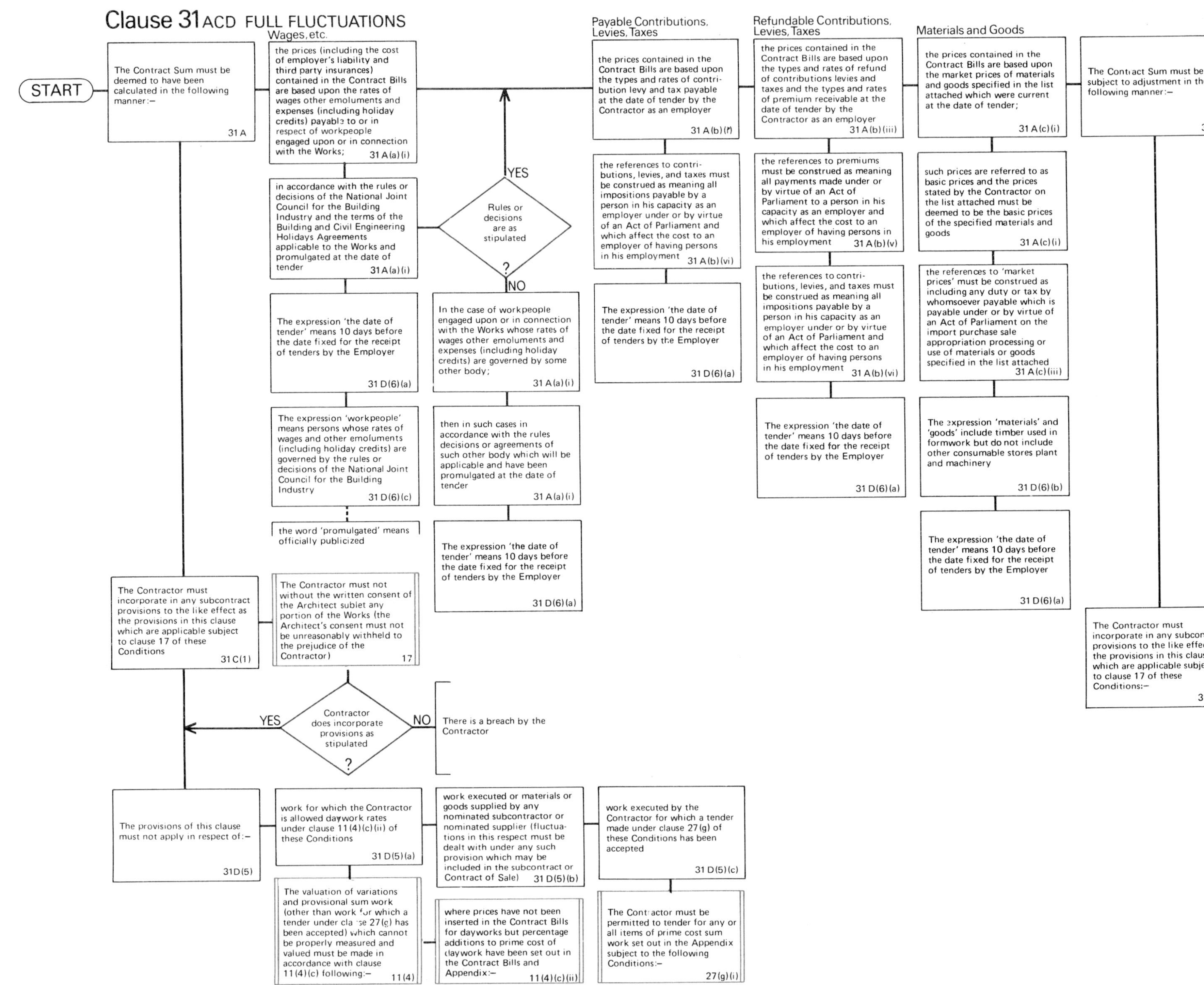
Clause 31ACD FULL FLUCTUATIONS
START
The Contract Sum must be deemed to have been calculated in the following manner:– 31 A
Wages, etc.
the prices (including the cost of employer's liability and third party insurances) contained in the Contract Bills are based upon the rates of wages other emoluments and expenses (including holiday credits) payable to or in respect of workpeople engaged upon or in connection with the Works; 31 A(a)(i)
in accordance with the rules or decisions of the National Joint Council for the Building Industry and the terms of the Building and Civil Engineering Holidays Agreements applicable to the Works and promulgated at the date of tender 31 A(a)(i)
Rules or decisions are as stipulated ?
YES
NO
The expression 'the date of tender' means 10 days before the date fixed for the receipt of tenders by the Employer 31 D(6)(a)
In the case of workpeople engaged upon or in connection with the Works whose rates of wages other emoluments and expenses (including holiday credits) are governed by some other body; 31 A(a)(i)
The expression 'workpeople' means persons whose rates of wages and other emoluments (including holiday credits) are governed by the rules or decisions of the National Joint Council for the Building Industry 31 D(6)(c)
then in such cases in accordance with the rules decisions or agreements of such other body which will be applicable and have been promulgated at the date of tender 31 A(a)(i)
the word 'promulgated' means officially publicized
The expression 'the date of tender' means 10 days before the date fixed for the receipt of tenders by the Employer 31 D(6)(a)
Payable Contributions, Levies, Taxes
the prices contained in the Contract Bills are based upon the types and rates of contribution levy and tax payable at the date of tender by the Contractor as an employer 31 A(b)(i)
the references to contributions, levies, and taxes must be construed as meaning all impositions payable by a person in his capacity as an employer under or by virtue of an Act of Parliament and which affect the cost to an employer of having persons in his employment 31 A(b)(vi)
The expression 'the date of tender' means 10 days before the date fixed for the receipt of tenders by the Employer 31 D(6)(a)
Refundable Contributions, Levies, Taxes
the prices contained in the Contract Bills are based upon the types and rates of refund of contributions levies and taxes and the types and rates of premium receivable at the date of tender by the Contractor as an employer 31 A(b)(iii)
the references to premiums must be construed as meaning all payments made under or by virtue of an Act of Parliament to a person in his capacity as an employer and which affect the cost to an employer of having persons in his employment 31 A(b)(v)
the references to contributions, levies, and taxes must be construed as meaning all impositions payable by a person in his capacity as an employer under or by virtue of an Act of Parliament and which affect the cost to an employer of having persons in his employment 31 A(b)(vi)
The expression 'the date of tender' means 10 days before the date fixed for the receipt of tenders by the Employer 31 D(6)(a)
Materials and Goods
the prices contained in the Contract Bills are based upon the market prices of materials and goods specified in the list attached which were current at the date of tender; 31 A(c)(i)
such prices are referred to as basic prices and the prices stated by the Contractor on the list attached must be deemed to be the basic prices of the specified materials and goods 31 A(c)(i)
the references to 'market prices' must be construed as including any duty or tax by whomsoever payable which is payable under or by virtue of an Act of Parliament on the import purchase sale appropriation processing or use of materials or goods specified in the list attached 31 A(c)(iii)
The expression 'materials' and 'goods' include timber used in formwork but do not include other consumable stores plant and machinery 31 D(6)(b)
The expression 'the date of tender' means 10 days before the date fixed for the receipt of tenders by the Employer 31 D(6)(a)
The Contract Sum must be subject to adjustment in the following manner:– 31
The Contractor must incorporate in any subcontract provisions to the like effect as the provisions in this clause which are applicable subject to clause 17 of these Conditions:– 31C
The Contractor must incorporate in any subcontract provisions to the like effect as the provisions in this clause which are applicable subject to clause 17 of these Conditions 31 C(1)
The Contractor must not without the written consent of the Architect sublet any portion of the Works (the Architect's consent must not be unreasonably withheld to the prejudice of the Contractor) 17
Contractor does incorporate provisions as stipulated ?
YES
NO
There is a breach by the Contractor
The provisions of this clause must not apply in respect of:– 31D(5)
work for which the Contractor is allowed daywork rates under clause 11(4)(c)(ii) of these Conditions 31 D(5)(a)
work executed or materials or goods supplied by any nominated subcontractor or nominated supplier (fluctuations in this respect must be dealt with under any such provision which may be included in the subcontract or Contract of Sale) 31 D(5)(b)
work executed by the Contractor for which a tender made under clause 27(g) of these Conditions has been accepted 31 D(5)(c)
The valuation of variations and provisional sum work (other than work for which a tender under clause 27(g) has been accepted) which cannot be properly measured and valued must be made in accordance with clause 11(4)(c) following:– 11(4)
where prices have not been inserted in the Contract Bills for dayworks but percentage additions to prime cost of daywork have been set out in the Contract Bills and Appendix:– 11(4)(c)(ii)
The Contractor must be permitted to tender for any or all items of prime cost sum work set out in the Appendix subject to the following Conditions:– 27(g)(i)

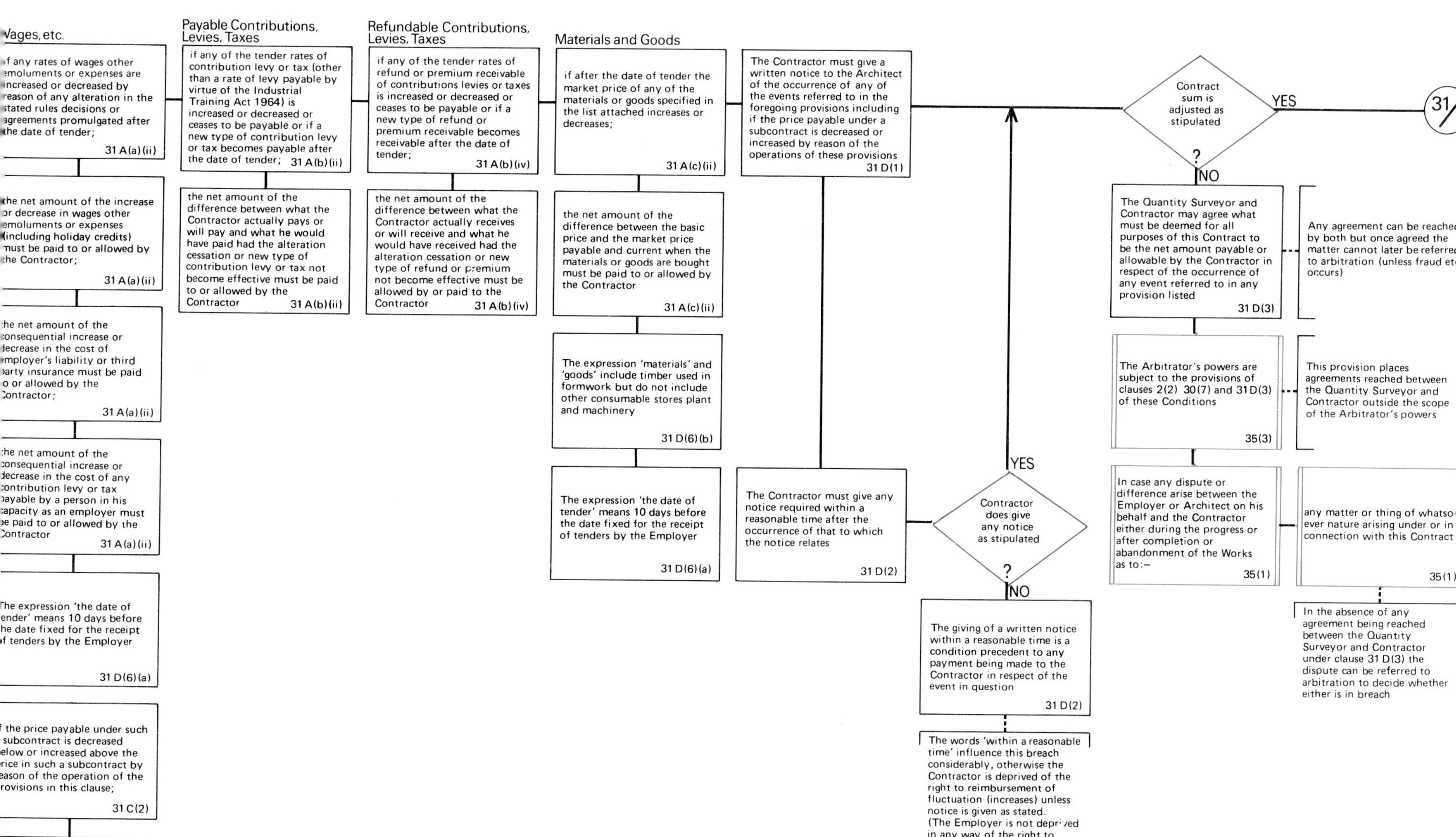
Wages, etc.
if any rates of wages other emoluments or expenses are increased or decreased by reason of any alteration in the stated rules decisions or agreements promulgated after the date of tender; 31 A(a)(ii)
the net amount of the increase or decrease in wages other emoluments or expenses (including holiday credits) must be paid to or allowed by the Contractor; 31 A(a)(ii)
the net amount of the consequential increase or decrease in the cost of employer's liability or third party insurance must be paid to or allowed by the Contractor; 31 A(a)(ii)
the net amount of the consequential increase or decrease in the cost of any contribution levy or tax payable by a person in his capacity as an employer must be paid to or allowed by the Contractor 31 A(a)(ii)
The expression 'the date of tender' means 10 days before the date fixed for the receipt of tenders by the Employer 31 D(6)(a)
if the price payable under such subcontract is decreased below or increased above the price in such a subcontract by reason of the operation of the provisions in this clause; 31 C(2)
the net amount of the decrease or increase must be allowed by or paid to the Contractor under this Contract 31 C(2)
Payable Contributions, Levies, Taxes
if any of the tender rates of contribution levy or tax (other than a rate of levy payable by virtue of the Industrial Training Act 1964) is increased or decreased or ceases to be payable or if a new type of contribution levy or tax becomes payable after the date of tender; 31 A(b)(ii)
the net amount of the difference between what the Contractor actually pays or will pay and what he would have paid had the alteration cessation or new type of contribution levy or tax not become effective must be paid to or allowed by the Contractor 31 A(b)(ii)
Refundable Contributions, Levies, Taxes
if any of the tender rates of refund or premium receivable of contributions levies or taxes is increased or decreased or ceases to be payable or if a new type of refund or premium receivable becomes receivable after the date of tender; 31 A(b)(iv)
the net amount of the difference between what the Contractor actually receives or will receive and what he would have received had the alteration cessation or new type of refund or premium not become effective must be allowed by or paid to the Contractor 31 A(b)(iv)
Materials and Goods
if after the date of tender the market price of any of the materials or goods specified in the list attached increases or decreases; 31 A(c)(ii)
the net amount of the difference between the basic price and the market price payable and current when the materials or goods are bought must be paid to or allowed by the Contractor 31 A(c)(ii)
The expression 'materials' and 'goods' include timber used in formwork but do not include other consumable stores plant and machinery 31 D(6)(b)
The expression 'the date of tender' means 10 days before the date fixed for the receipt of tenders by the Employer 31 D(6)(a)
The Contractor must give a written notice to the Architect of the occurrence of any of the events referred to in the foregoing provisions including if the price payable under a subcontract is decreased or increased by reason of the operations of these provisions 31 D(1)
The Contractor must give any notice required within a reasonable time after the occurrence of that to which the notice relates 31 D(2)
Contractor does give any notice as stipulated ?
YES
NO
The giving of a written notice within a reasonable time is a condition precedent to any payment being made to the Contractor in respect of the event in question 31 D(2)
The words 'within a reasonable time' influence this breach considerably, otherwise the Contractor is deprived of the right to reimbursement of fluctuation (increases) unless notice is given as stated. (The Employer is not deprived in any way of the right to decreases in costs)
Contract sum is adjusted as stipulated ?
YES
31/1
NO
The Quantity Surveyor and Contractor may agree what must be deemed for all purposes of this Contract to be the net amount payable or allowable by the Contractor in respect of the occurrence of any event referred to in any provision listed 31 D(3)
Any agreement can be reached by both but once agreed the matter cannot later be referred to arbitration (unless fraud etc. occurs)
The Arbitrator's powers are subject to the provisions of clauses 2(2) 30(7) and 31 D(3) of these Conditions 35(3)
This provision places agreements reached between the Quantity Surveyor and Contractor outside the scope of the Arbitrator's powers
In case any dispute or difference arise between the Employer or Architect on his behalf and the Contractor either during the progress or after completion or abandonment of the Works as to:– 35(1)
any matter or thing of whatsoever nature arising under or in connection with this Contract 35(1)
In the absence of any agreement being reached between the Quantity Surveyor and Contractor under clause 31 D(3) the dispute can be referred to arbitration to decide whether either is in breach

Clause 31BCD LIMITED FLUCTUATIONS

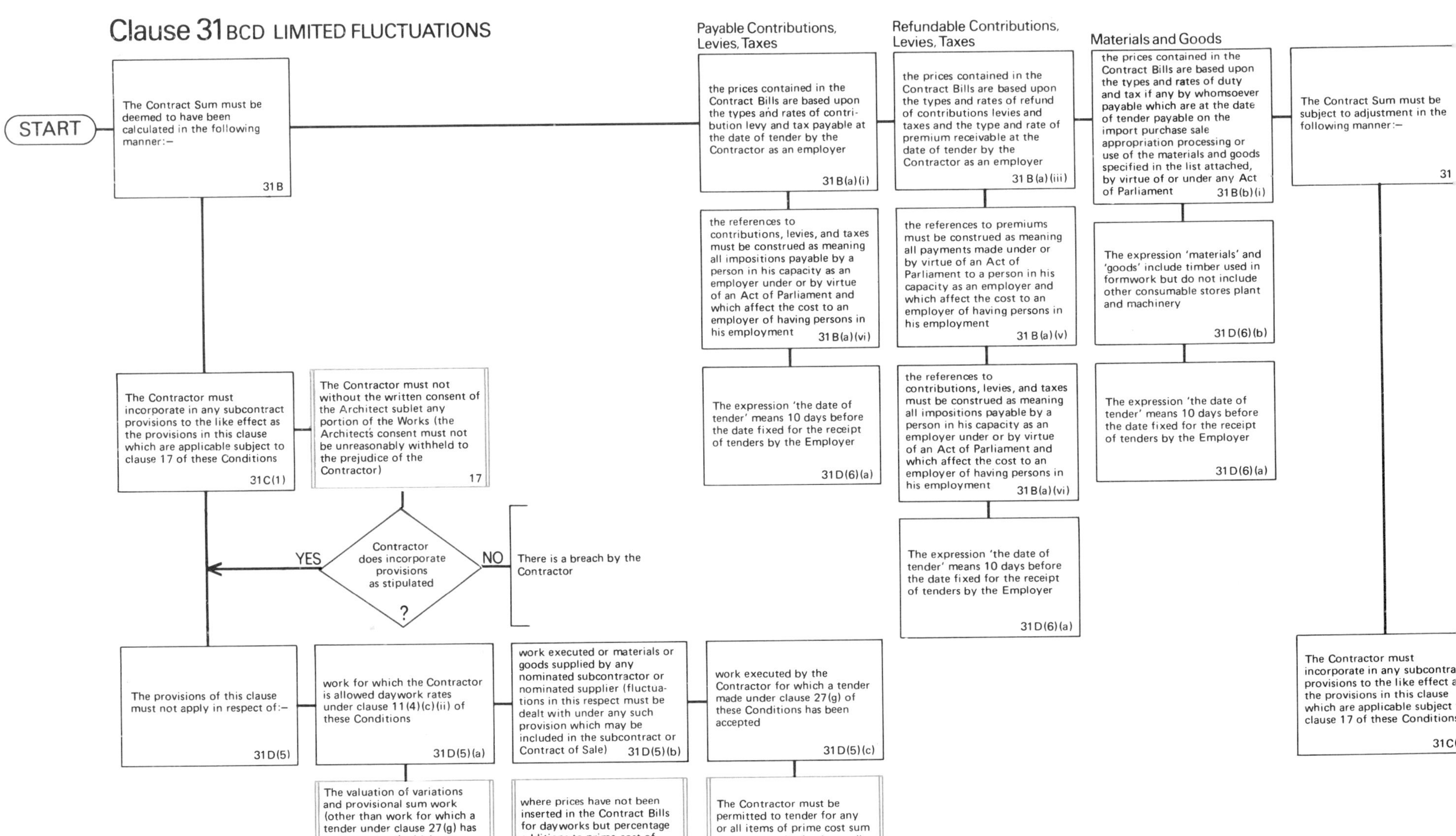
START
The Contract Sum must be deemed to have been calculated in the following manner:– 31B
Payable Contributions, Levies, Taxes
the prices contained in the Contract Bills are based upon the types and rates of contribution levy and tax payable at the date of tender by the Contractor as an employer 31B(a)(i)
the references to contributions, levies, and taxes must be construed as meaning all impositions payable by a person in his capacity as an employer under or by virtue of an Act of Parliament and which affect the cost to an employer of having persons in his employment 31B(a)(vi)
The expression 'the date of tender' means 10 days before the date fixed for the receipt of tenders by the Employer 31D(6)(a)
Refundable Contributions, Levies, Taxes
the prices contained in the Contract Bills are based upon the types and rates of refund of contributions levies and taxes and the type and rate of premium receivable at the date of tender by the Contractor as an employer 31B(a)(iii)
the references to premiums must be construed as meaning all payments made under or by virtue of an Act of Parliament to a person in his capacity as an employer and which affect the cost to an employer of having persons in his employment 31B(a)(v)
the references to contributions, levies, and taxes must be construed as meaning all impositions payable by a person in his capacity as an employer under or by virtue of an Act of Parliament and which affect the cost to an employer of having persons in his employment 31B(a)(vi)
The expression 'the date of tender' means 10 days before the date fixed for the receipt of tenders by the Employer 31D(6)(a)
Materials and Goods
the prices contained in the Contract Bills are based upon the types and rates of duty and tax if any by whomsoever payable which are at the date of tender payable on the import purchase sale appropriation processing or use of the materials and goods specified in the list attached, by virtue of or under any Act of Parliament 31B(b)(i)
The expression 'materials' and 'goods' include timber used in formwork but do not include other consumable stores plant and machinery 31D(6)(b)
The expression 'the date of tender' means 10 days before the date fixed for the receipt of tenders by the Employer 31D(6)(a)
The Contract Sum must be subject to adjustment in the following manner:– 31
The Contractor must incorporate in any subcontract provisions to the like effect as the provisions in this clause which are applicable subject to clause 17 of these Conditions 31C(1)
The Contractor must not without the written consent of the Architect sublet any portion of the Works (the Architect's consent must not be unreasonably withheld to the prejudice of the Contractor) 17
Contractor does incorporate provisions as stipulated ?
YES
NO
There is a breach by the Contractor
The provisions of this clause must not apply in respect of:– 31D(5)
work for which the Contractor is allowed daywork rates under clause 11(4)(c)(ii) of these Conditions 31D(5)(a)
work executed or materials or goods supplied by any nominated subcontractor or nominated supplier (fluctuations in this respect must be dealt with under any such provision which may be included in the subcontract or Contract of Sale) 31D(5)(b)
work executed by the Contractor for which a tender made under clause 27(g) of these Conditions has been accepted 31D(5)(c)
The valuation of variations and provisional sum work (other than work for which a tender under clause 27(g) has been accepted) which cannot be properly measured and valued must be made in accordance with clause 11(4)(c) following:– 11(4)
where prices have not been inserted in the Contract Bills for dayworks but percentage additions to prime cost of daywork have been set out in the Contract Bills and Appendix:– 11(4)(c)(ii)
The Contractor must be permitted to tender for any or all items of prime cost sum work set out in the Appendix subject to the following Conditions:– 27(g)(i)
The Contractor must incorporate in any subcontra[ct] provisions to the like effect a[s] the provisions in this clause which are applicable subject [to] clause 17 of these Conditions 31C

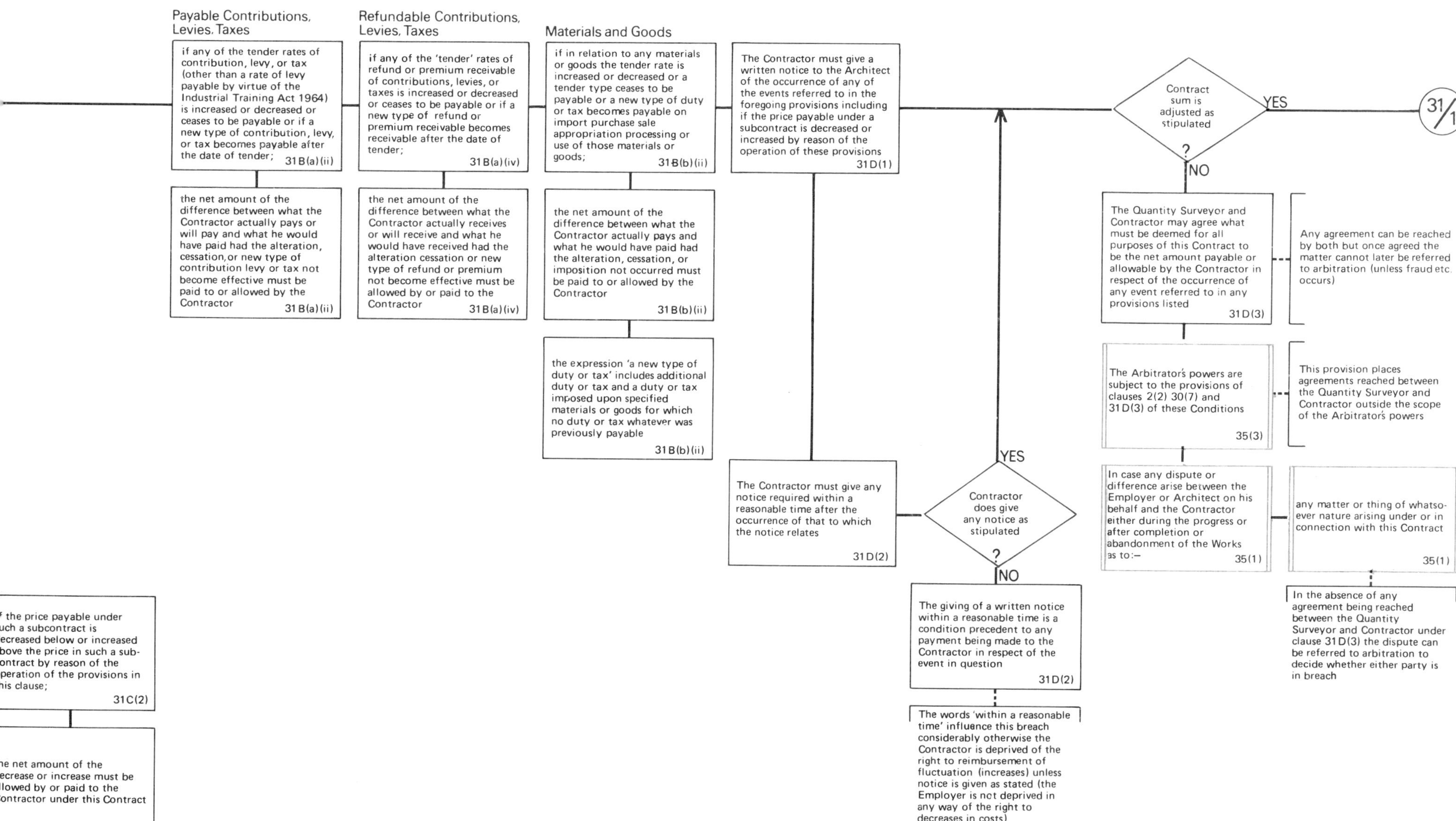
Payable Contributions, Levies, Taxes
if any of the tender rates of contribution, levy, or tax (other than a rate of levy payable by virtue of the Industrial Training Act 1964) is increased or decreased or ceases to be payable or if a new type of contribution, levy, or tax becomes payable after the date of tender; 31B(a)(ii)
the net amount of the difference between what the Contractor actually pays or will pay and what he would have paid had the alteration, cessation, or new type of contribution levy or tax not become effective must be paid to or allowed by the Contractor 31B(a)(ii)
Refundable Contributions, Levies, Taxes
if any of the 'tender' rates of refund or premium receivable of contributions, levies, or taxes is increased or decreased or ceases to be payable or if a new type of refund or premium receivable becomes receivable after the date of tender; 31B(a)(iv)
the net amount of the difference between what the Contractor actually receives or will receive and what he would have received had the alteration cessation or new type of refund or premium not become effective must be allowed by or paid to the Contractor 31B(a)(iv)
Materials and Goods
if in relation to any materials or goods the tender rate is increased or decreased or a tender type ceases to be payable or a new type of duty or tax becomes payable on import purchase sale appropriation processing or use of those materials or goods; 31B(b)(ii)
the net amount of the difference between what the Contractor actually pays and what he would have paid had the alteration, cessation, or imposition not occurred must be paid to or allowed by the Contractor 31B(b)(ii)
the expression 'a new type of duty or tax' includes additional duty or tax and a duty or tax imposed upon specified materials or goods for which no duty or tax whatever was previously payable 31B(b)(ii)
The Contractor must give a written notice to the Architect of the occurrence of any of the events referred to in the foregoing provisions including if the price payable under a subcontract is decreased or increased by reason of the operation of these provisions 31D(1)
Contract sum is adjusted as stipulated ?
YES
31/1
NO
The Quantity Surveyor and Contractor may agree what must be deemed for all purposes of this Contract to be the net amount payable or allowable by the Contractor in respect of the occurrence of any event referred to in any provisions listed 31D(3)
Any agreement can be reached by both but once agreed the matter cannot later be referred to arbitration (unless fraud etc. occurs)
The Arbitrator's powers are subject to the provisions of clauses 2(2) 30(7) and 31D(3) of these Conditions 35(3)
This provision places agreements reached between the Quantity Surveyor and Contractor outside the scope of the Arbitrator's powers
In case any dispute or difference arise between the Employer or Architect on his behalf and the Contractor either during the progress or after completion or abandonment of the Works as to:— 35(1)
any matter or thing of whatsoever nature arising under or in connection with this Contract 35(1)
In the absence of any agreement being reached between the Quantity Surveyor and Contractor under clause 31D(3) the dispute can be referred to arbitration to decide whether either party is in breach
The Contractor must give any notice required within a reasonable time after the occurrence of that to which the notice relates 31D(2)
Contractor does give any notice as stipulated ?
YES
NO
The giving of a written notice within a reasonable time is a condition precedent to any payment being made to the Contractor in respect of the event in question 31D(2)
The words 'within a reasonable time' influence this breach considerably otherwise the Contractor is deprived of the right to reimbursement of fluctuation (increases) unless notice is given as stated (the Employer is not deprived in any way of the right to decreases in costs)
the price payable under uch a subcontract is ecreased below or increased bove the price in such a sub- ontract by reason of the peration of the provisions in his clause; 31C(2)
he net amount of the ecrease or increase must be llowed by or paid to the Contractor under this Contract 31C(2)

Clause 31 SETTLEMENT OF FLUCTUATIONS

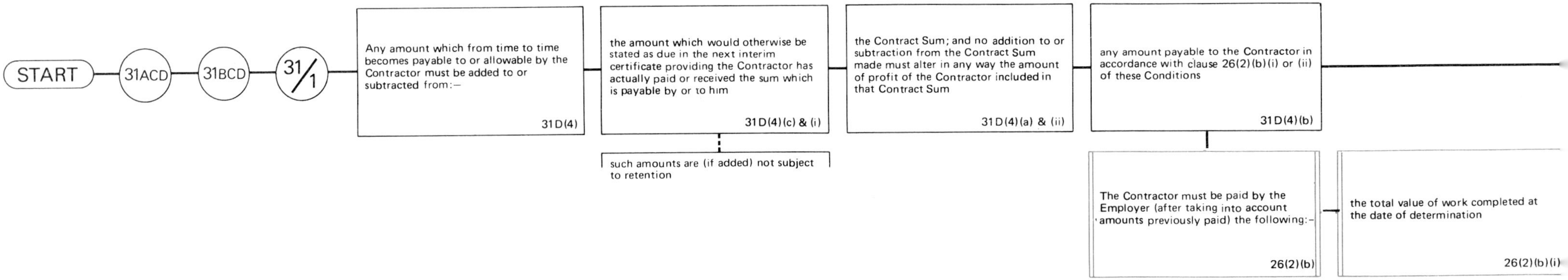

START — 31ACD — 31BCD — 31/1

Any amount which from time to time becomes payable to or allowable by the Contractor must be added to or subtracted from:–

31D(4)

the amount which would otherwise be stated as due in the next interim certificate providing the Contractor has actually paid or received the sum which is payable by or to him

31D(4)(c) & (i)

such amounts are (if added) not subject to retention

the Contract Sum; and no addition to or subtraction from the Contract Sum made must alter in any way the amount of profit of the Contractor included in that Contract Sum

31D(4)(a) & (ii)

any amount payable to the Contractor in accordance with clause 26(2)(b)(i) or (ii) of these Conditions

31D(4)(b)

The Contractor must be paid by the Employer (after taking into account amounts previously paid) the following:–

26(2)(b)

the total value of work completed at the date of determination

26(2)(b)(i)

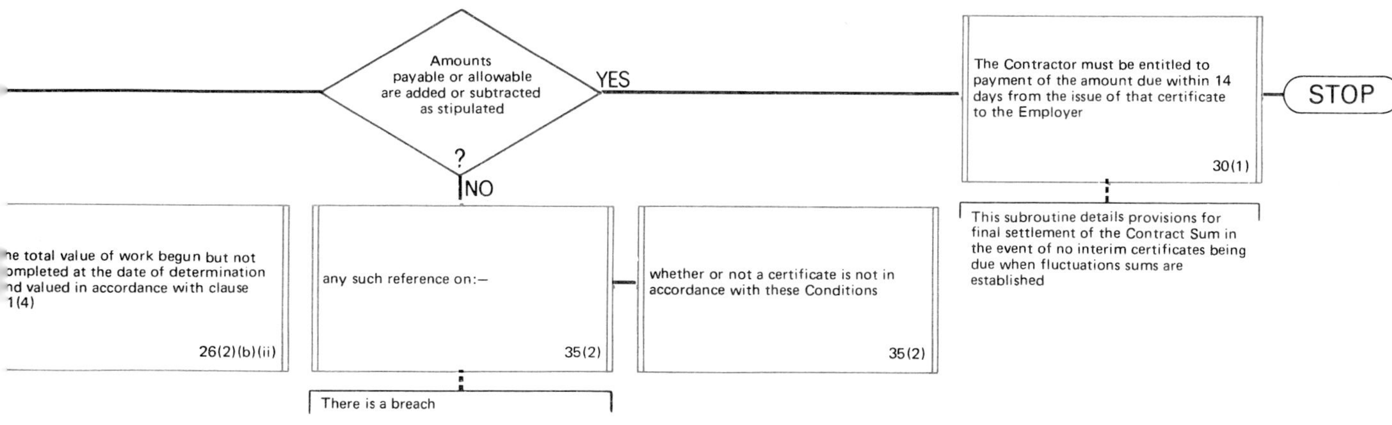
Amounts payable or allowable are added or subtracted as stipulated
?
YES
NO
The Contractor must be entitled to payment of the amount due within 14 days from the issue of that certificate to the Employer
30(1)
STOP
This subroutine details provisions for final settlement of the Contract Sum in the event of no interim certificates being due when fluctuations sums are established
he total value of work begun but not ompleted at the date of determination nd valued in accordance with clause 1(4)
26(2)(b)(ii)
any such reference on:–
35(2)
whether or not a certificate is not in accordance with these Conditions
35(2)
There is a breach

Clause 32 OUTBREAK OF HOSTILITIES

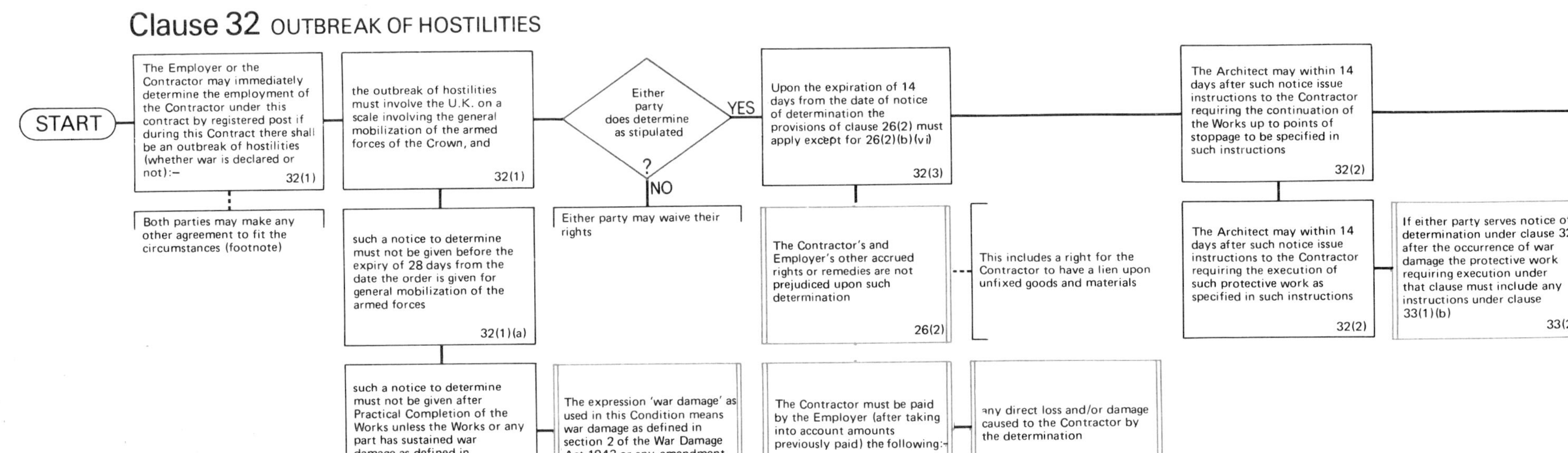

START
The Employer or the Contractor may immediately determine the employment of the Contractor under this contract by registered post if during this Contract there shall be an outbreak of hostilities (whether war is declared or not):– 32(1)
Both parties may make any other agreement to fit the circumstances (footnote)
the outbreak of hostilities must involve the U.K. on a scale involving the general mobilization of the armed forces of the Crown, and 32(1)
such a notice to determine must not be given before the expiry of 28 days from the date the order is given for general mobilization of the armed forces 32(1)(a)
such a notice to determine must not be given after Practical Completion of the Works unless the Works or any part has sustained war damage as defined in clause 33(4) 32(1)(b)
Either party does determine as stipulated ?
YES
NO
Either party may waive their rights
The expression 'war damage' as used in this Condition means war damage as defined in section 2 of the War Damage Act 1943 or any amendment 33(4)
Upon the expiration of 14 days from the date of notice of determination the provisions of clause 26(2) must apply except for 26(2)(b)(vi) 32(3)
The Contractor's and Employer's other accrued rights or remedies are not prejudiced upon such determination 26(2)
This includes a right for the Contractor to have a lien upon unfixed goods and materials
The Contractor must be paid by the Employer (after taking into account amounts previously paid) the following:- 26(2)(b)
any direct loss and/or damage caused to the Contractor by the determination 26(2)(b)(vi)
The Architect may within 14 days after such notice issue instructions to the Contractor requiring the continuation of the Works up to points of stoppage to be specified in such instructions 32(2)
The Architect may within 14 days after such notice issue instructions to the Contractor requiring the execution of such protective work as specified in such instructions 32(2)
If either party serves notice of determination under clause 32 after the occurrence of war damage the protective work requiring execution under that clause must include any instructions under clause 33(1)(b) 33(2)

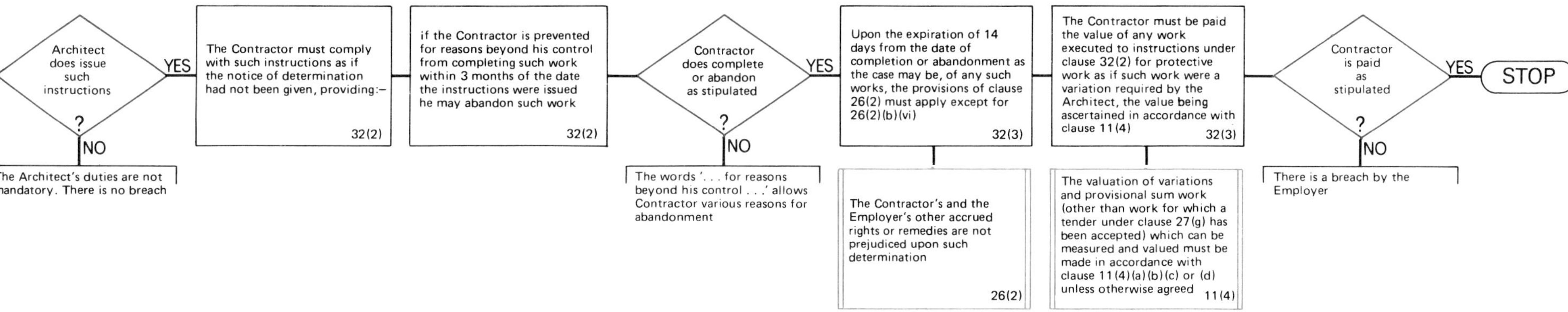
Architect does issue such instructions ?
YES
NO
The Architect's duties are not mandatory. There is no breach
The Contractor must comply with such instructions as if the notice of determination had not been given, providing:–
32(2)
if the Contractor is prevented for reasons beyond his control from completing such work within 3 months of the date the instructions were issued he may abandon such work
32(2)
Contractor does complete or abandon as stipulated ?
YES
NO
The words '. . . for reasons beyond his control . . .' allows Contractor various reasons for abandonment
Upon the expiration of 14 days from the date of completion or abandonment as the case may be, of any such works, the provisions of clause 26(2) must apply except for 26(2)(b)(vi)
32(3)
The Contractor's and the Employer's other accrued rights or remedies are not prejudiced upon such determination
26(2)
The Contractor must be paid the value of any work executed to instructions under clause 32(2) for protective work as if such work were a variation required by the Architect, the value being ascertained in accordance with clause 11(4)
32(3)
The valuation of variations and provisional sum work (other than work for which a tender under clause 27(g) has been accepted) which can be measured and valued must be made in accordance with clause 11(4)(a)(b)(c) or (d) unless otherwise agreed
11(4)
Contractor is paid as stipulated ?
YES
NO
There is a breach by the Employer
STOP

Clause 33 WAR DAMAGE

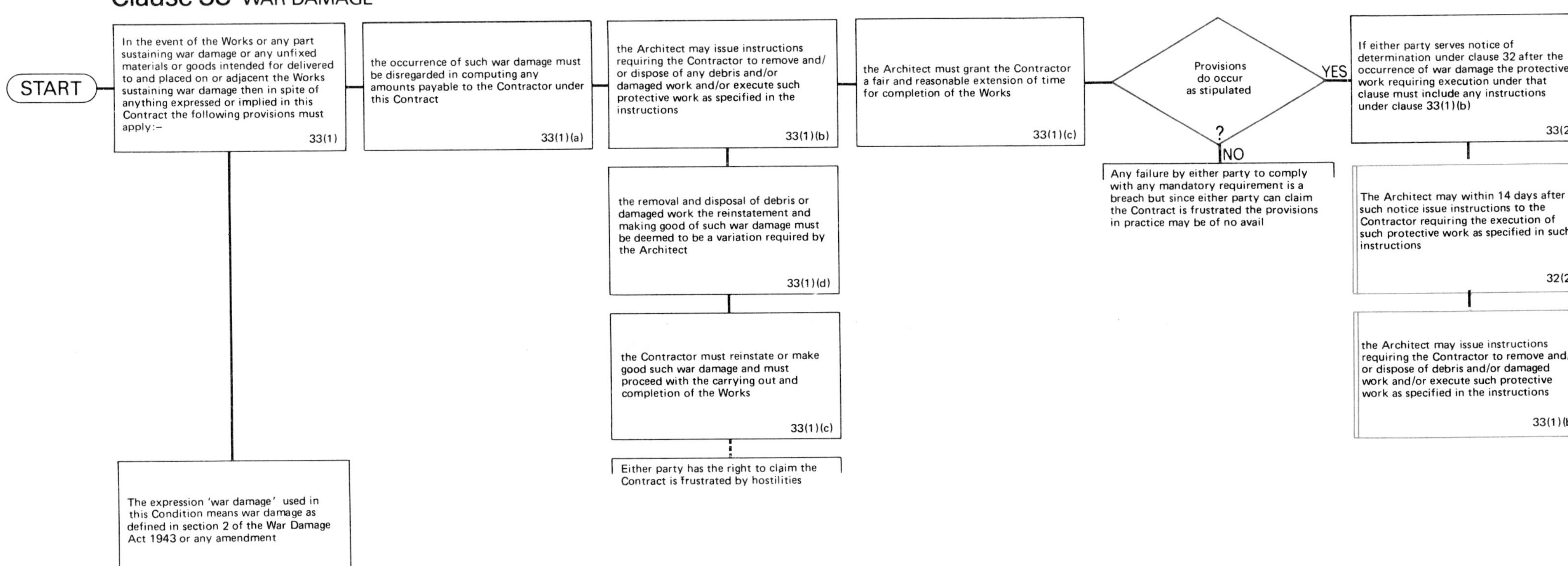
START
In the event of the Works or any part sustaining war damage or any unfixed materials or goods intended for delivered to and placed on or adjacent the Works sustaining war damage then in spite of anything expressed or implied in this Contract the following provisions must apply:– 33(1)
the occurrence of such war damage must be disregarded in computing any amounts payable to the Contractor under this Contract 33(1)(a)
the Architect may issue instructions requiring the Contractor to remove and/or dispose of any debris and/or damaged work and/or execute such protective work as specified in the instructions 33(1)(b)
the Architect must grant the Contractor a fair and reasonable extension of time for completion of the Works 33(1)(c)
Provisions do occur as stipulated ?
YES
NO
If either party serves notice of determination under clause 32 after the occurrence of war damage the protective work requiring execution under that clause must include any instructions under clause 33(1)(b) 33(2
Any failure by either party to comply with any mandatory requirement is a breach but since either party can claim the Contract is frustrated the provisions in practice may be of no avail
the removal and disposal of debris or damaged work the reinstatement and making good of such war damage must be deemed to be a variation required by the Architect 33(1)(d)
The Architect may within 14 days after such notice issue instructions to the Contractor requiring the execution of such protective work as specified in such instructions 32(2
the Contractor must reinstate or make good such war damage and must proceed with the carrying out and completion of the Works 33(1)(c)
the Architect may issue instructions requiring the Contractor to remove and/or dispose of debris and/or damaged work and/or execute such protective work as specified in the instructions 33(1)(b
Either party has the right to claim the Contract is frustrated by hostilities
The expression 'war damage' used in this Condition means war damage as defined in section 2 of the War Damage Act 1943 or any amendment 33(4)

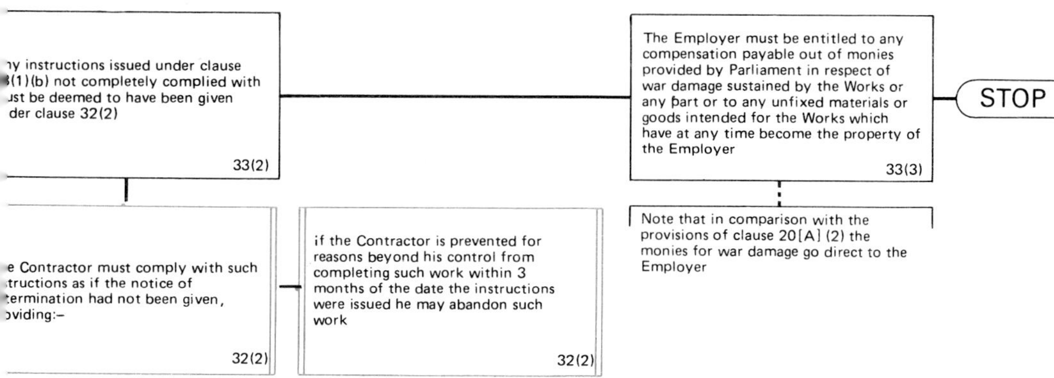

ny instructions issued under clause
(1)(b) not completely complied with
ust be deemed to have been given
der clause 32(2)
33(2)
The Employer must be entitled to any compensation payable out of monies provided by Parliament in respect of war damage sustained by the Works or any part or to any unfixed materials or goods intended for the Works which have at any time become the property of the Employer
33(3)
STOP
e Contractor must comply with such
tructions as if the notice of
termination had not been given,
oviding:–
32(2)
if the Contractor is prevented for reasons beyond his control from completing such work within 3 months of the date the instructions were issued he may abandon such work
32(2)
Note that in comparison with the provisions of clause 20[A] (2) the monies for war damage go direct to the Employer

Clause 34 DISCOVERIES ON THE SITE

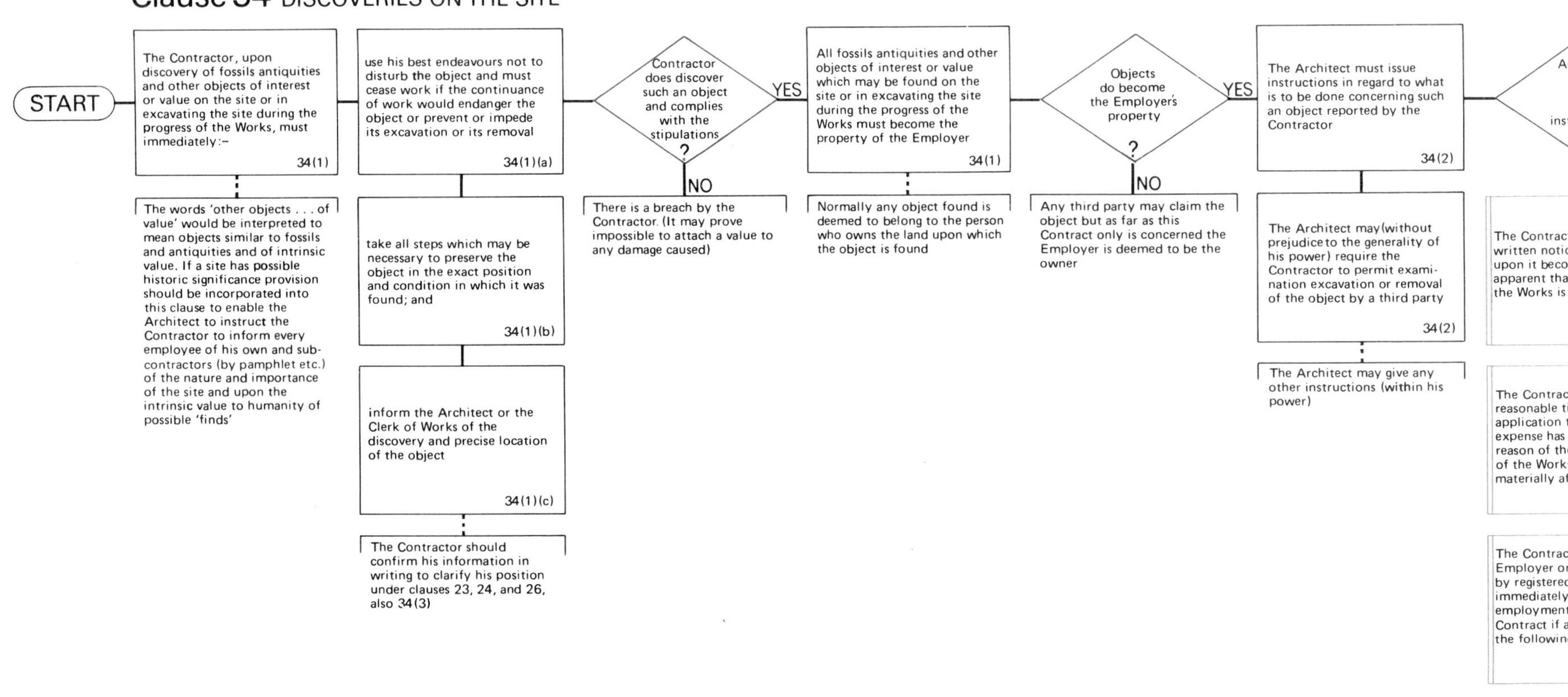
START
The Contractor, upon discovery of fossils antiquities and other objects of interest or value on the site or in excavating the site during the progress of the Works, must immediately:– 34(1)
The words 'other objects . . . of value' would be interpreted to mean objects similar to fossils and antiquities and of intrinsic value. If a site has possible historic significance provision should be incorporated into this clause to enable the Architect to instruct the Contractor to inform every employee of his own and sub-contractors (by pamphlet etc.) of the nature and importance of the site and upon the intrinsic value to humanity of possible 'finds'
use his best endeavours not to disturb the object and must cease work if the continuance of work would endanger the object or prevent or impede its excavation or its removal 34(1)(a)
take all steps which may be necessary to preserve the object in the exact position and condition in which it was found; and 34(1)(b)
inform the Architect or the Clerk of Works of the discovery and precise location of the object 34(1)(c)
The Contractor should confirm his information in writing to clarify his position under clauses 23, 24, and 26, also 34(3)
Contractor does discover such an object and complies with the stipulations ?
YES
NO
There is a breach by the Contractor. (It may prove impossible to attach a value to any damage caused)
All fossils antiquities and other objects of interest or value which may be found on the site or in excavating the site during the progress of the Works must become the property of the Employer 34(1)
Normally any object found is deemed to belong to the person who owns the land upon which the object is found
Objects do become the Employer's property ?
YES
NO
Any third party may claim the object but as far as this Contract only is concerned the Employer is deemed to be the owner
The Architect must issue instructions in regard to what is to be done concerning such an object reported by the Contractor 34(2)
The Architect may (without prejudice to the generality of his power) require the Contractor to permit examination excavation or removal of the object by a third party 34(2)
The Architect may give any other instructions (within his power)
Architect does issue such instructions ?
NO
The Contractor must give written notice immediately upon it becoming reasonably apparent that the progress of the Works is delayed:–
The Contractor may within reasonable time give written application that loss and/or expense has been involved by reason of the regular progress of the Works having been materially affected:– 24
The Contractor may give the Employer or Architect a notice by registered post to immediately determine his employment under this Contract if any one or more the following events occur:– 26
There is a breach by the Architect

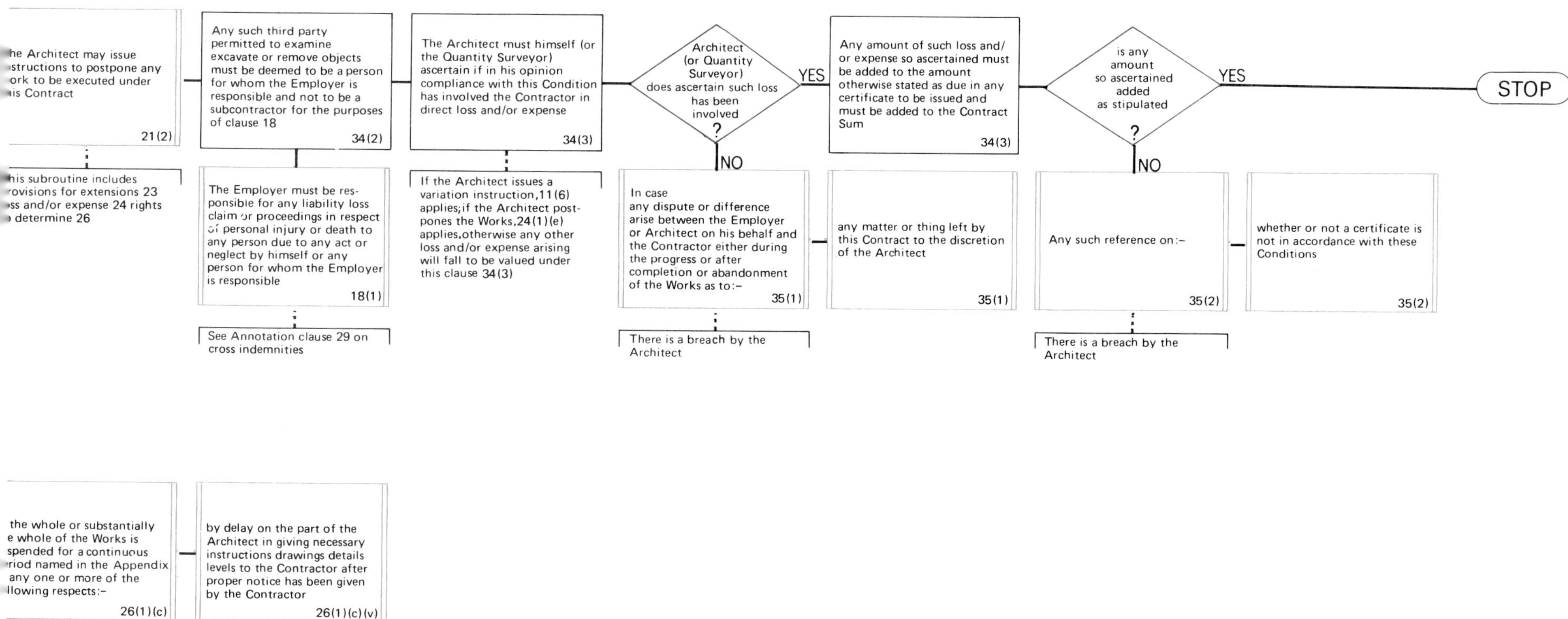

he Architect may issue
structions to postpone any
ork to be executed under
is Contract
21(2)
his subroutine includes
rovisions for extensions 23
ss and/or expense 24 rights
determine 26
Any such third party
permitted to examine
excavate or remove objects
must be deemed to be a person
for whom the Employer is
responsible and not to be a
subcontractor for the purposes
of clause 18
34(2)
The Employer must be res-
ponsible for any liability loss
claim or proceedings in respect
of personal injury or death to
any person due to any act or
neglect by himself or any
person for whom the Employer
is responsible
18(1)
See Annotation clause 29 on
cross indemnities
The Architect must himself (or
the Quantity Surveyor)
ascertain if in his opinion
compliance with this Condition
has involved the Contractor in
direct loss and/or expense
34(3)
If the Architect issues a
variation instruction,11(6)
applies;if the Architect post-
pones the Works,24(1)(e)
applies,otherwise any other
loss and/or expense arising
will fall to be valued under
this clause 34(3)
Architect
(or Quantity
Surveyor)
does ascertain such loss
has been
involved
?
YES
NO
In case
any dispute or difference
arise between the Employer
or Architect on his behalf and
the Contractor either during
the progress or after
completion or abandonment
of the Works as to:–
35(1)
There is a breach by the
Architect
Any amount of such loss and/
or expense so ascertained must
be added to the amount
otherwise stated as due in any
certificate to be issued and
must be added to the Contract
Sum
34(3)
any matter or thing left by
this Contract to the discretion
of the Architect
35(1)
is any
amount
so ascertained
added
as stipulated
?
YES
NO
STOP
Any such reference on:–
35(2)
There is a breach by the
Architect
whether or not a certificate is
not in accordance with these
Conditions
35(2)
the whole or substantially
e whole of the Works is
spended for a continuous
riod named in the Appendix
any one or more of the
llowing respects:–
26(1)(c)
by delay on the part of the
Architect in giving necessary
instructions drawings details
levels to the Contractor after
proper notice has been given
by the Contractor
26(1)(c)(v)

Clause 35 ARBITRATION

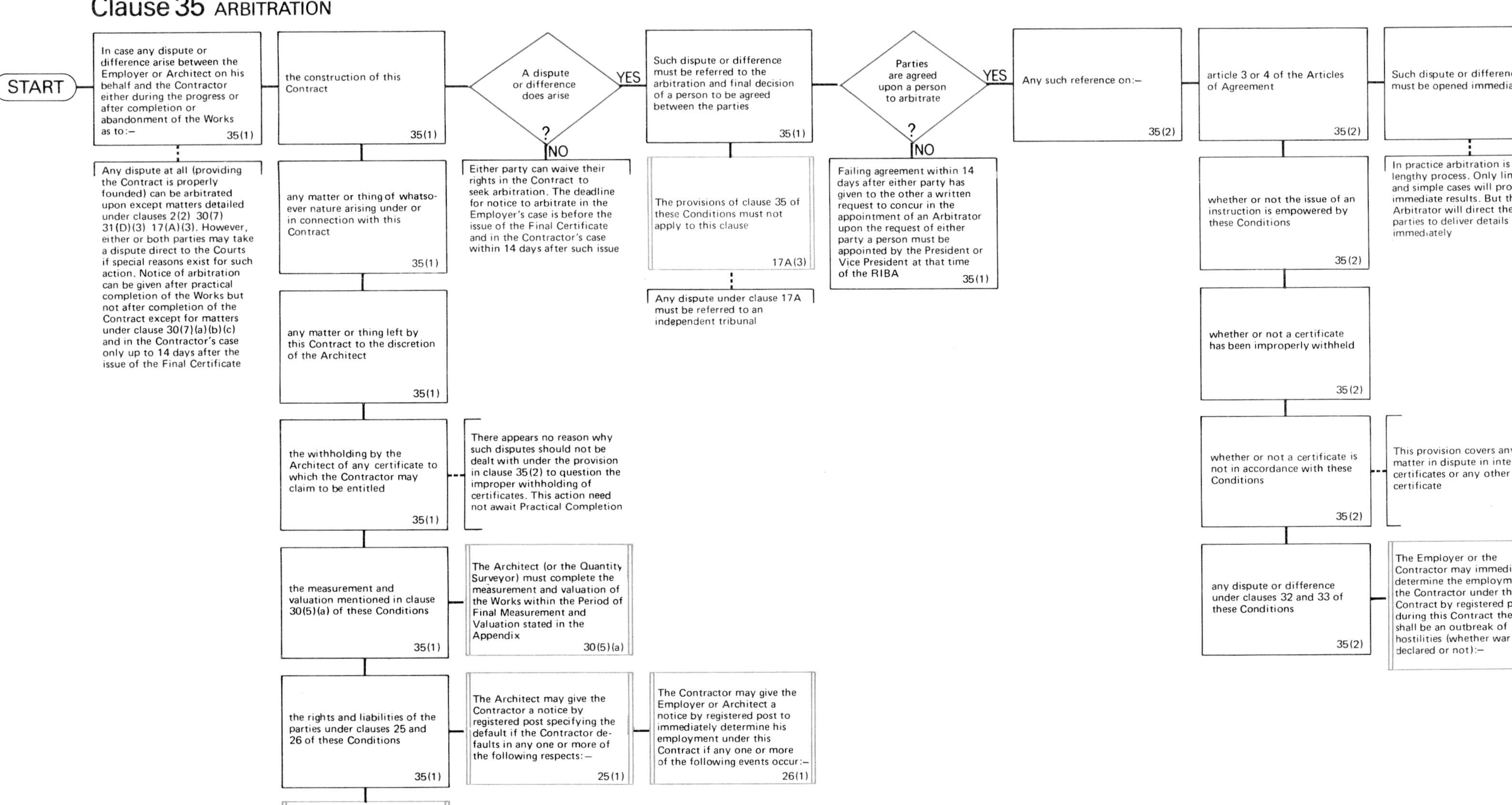
START
In case any dispute or difference arise between the Employer or Architect on his behalf and the Contractor either during the progress or after completion or abandonment of the Works as to:– 35(1)
Any dispute at all (providing the Contract is properly founded) can be arbitrated upon except matters detailed under clauses 2(2) 30(7) 31(D)(3) 17(A)(3). However, either or both parties may take a dispute direct to the Courts if special reasons exist for such action. Notice of arbitration can be given after practical completion of the Works but not after completion of the Contract except for matters under clause 30(7)(a)(b)(c) and in the Contractor's case only up to 14 days after the issue of the Final Certificate
the construction of this Contract 35(1)
any matter or thing of whatsoever nature arising under or in connection with this Contract 35(1)
any matter or thing left by this Contract to the discretion of the Architect 35(1)
the withholding by the Architect of any certificate to which the Contractor may claim to be entitled 35(1)
There appears no reason why such disputes should not be dealt with under the provision in clause 35(2) to question the improper withholding of certificates. This action need not await Practical Completion
the measurement and valuation mentioned in clause 30(5)(a) of these Conditions 35(1)
The Architect (or the Quantity Surveyor) must complete the measurement and valuation of the Works within the Period of Final Measurement and Valuation stated in the Appendix 30(5)(a)
the rights and liabilities of the parties under clauses 25 and 26 of these Conditions 35(1)
The Architect may give the Contractor a notice by registered post specifying the default if the Contractor defaults in any one or more of the following respects:– 25(1)
The Contractor may give the Employer or Architect a notice by registered post to immediately determine his employment under this Contract if any one or more of the following events occur:– 26(1)
Within 7 days of receiving notice of determination (but not thereafter) either party may give a written request to concur in the appointment of an arbitrator to decide whether such determination will be just and equitable 20[C] (b)(i)
A dispute or difference does arise ?
YES
NO
Either party can waive their rights in the Contract to seek arbitration. The deadline for notice to arbitrate in the Employer's case is before the issue of the Final Certificate and in the Contractor's case within 14 days after such issue
Such dispute or difference must be referred to the arbitration and final decision of a person to be agreed between the parties 35(1)
The provisions of clause 35 of these Conditions must not apply to this clause 17A(3)
Any dispute under clause 17A must be referred to an independent tribunal
Parties are agreed upon a person to arbitrate ?
YES
NO
Failing agreement within 14 days after either party has given to the other a written request to concur in the appointment of an Arbitrator upon the request of either party a person must be appointed by the President or Vice President at that time of the RIBA 35(1)
Any such reference on:– 35(2)
article 3 or 4 of the Articles of Agreement 35(2)
whether or not the issue of an instruction is empowered by these Conditions 35(2)
whether or not a certificate has been improperly withheld 35(2)
whether or not a certificate is not in accordance with these Conditions 35(2)
any dispute or difference under clauses 32 and 33 of these Conditions 35(2)
Such dispute or difference must be opened immediat
In practice arbitration is a lengthy process. Only limi and simple cases will prod immediate results. But the Arbitrator will direct the parties to deliver details immediately
This provision covers any matter in dispute in interir certificates or any other certificate
The Employer or the Contractor may immediat determine the employmen the Contractor under this Contract by registered pos during this Contract there shall be an outbreak of hostilities (whether war is declared or not):–

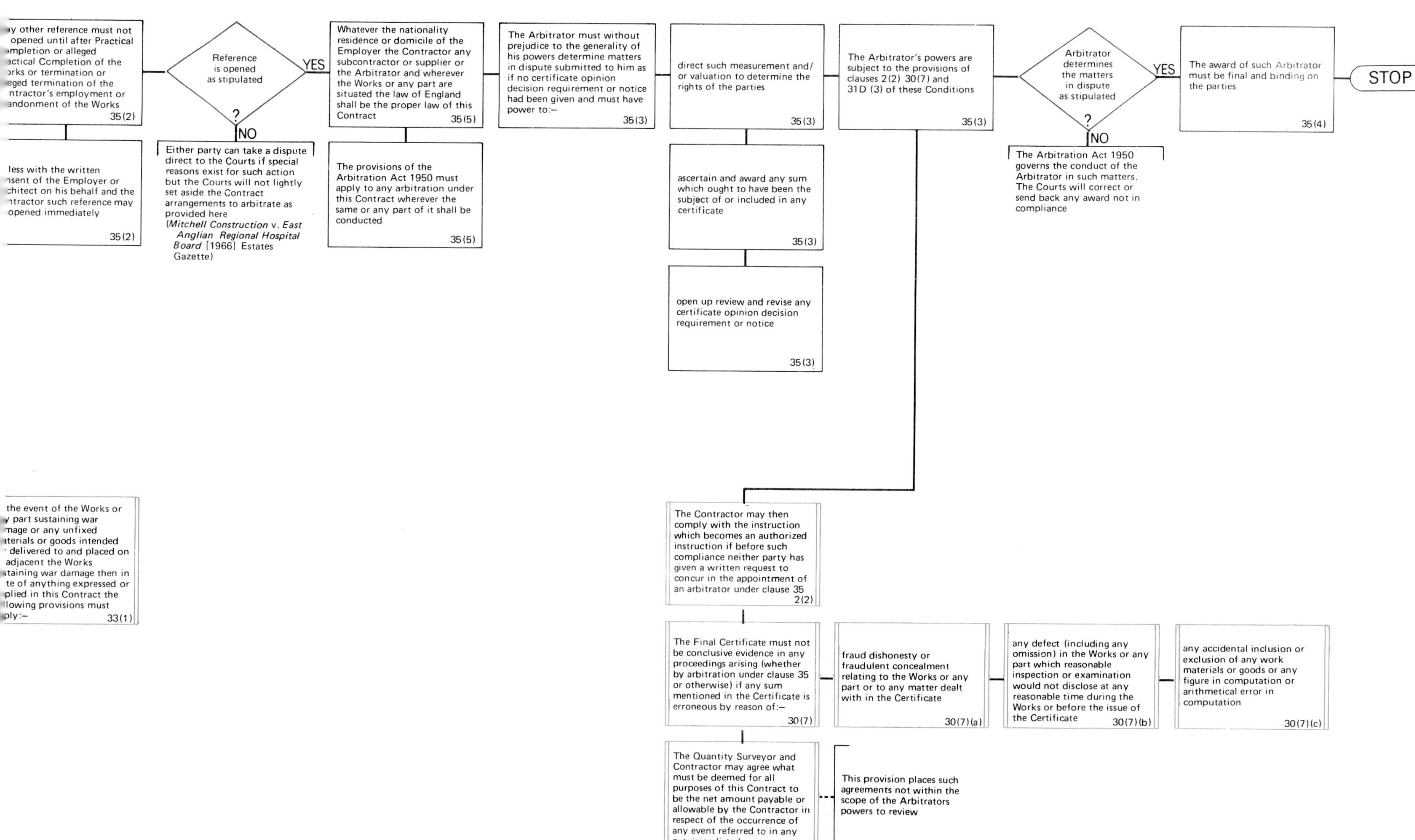

…y other reference must not … opened until after Practical …mpletion or alleged …actical Completion of the …orks or termination or …eged termination of the …ntractor's employment or …andonment of the Works 35(2)
…less with the written …nsent of the Employer or …chitect on his behalf and the …ntractor such reference may … opened immediately 35(2)
Reference is opened as stipulated ?
YES
NO
Either party can take a dispute direct to the Courts if special reasons exist for such action but the Courts will not lightly set aside the Contract arrangements to arbitrate as provided here (Mitchell Construction v. East Anglian Regional Hospital Board [1966] Estates Gazette)
Whatever the nationality residence or domicile of the Employer the Contractor any subcontractor or supplier or the Arbitrator and wherever the Works or any part are situated the law of England shall be the proper law of this Contract 35(5)
The provisions of the Arbitration Act 1950 must apply to any arbitration under this Contract wherever the same or any part of it shall be conducted 35(5)
The Arbitrator must without prejudice to the generality of his powers determine matters in dispute submitted to him as if no certificate opinion decision requirement or notice had been given and must have power to:– 35(3)
direct such measurement and/or valuation to determine the rights of the parties 35(3)
ascertain and award any sum which ought to have been the subject of or included in any certificate 35(3)
open up review and revise any certificate opinion decision requirement or notice 35(3)
The Arbitrator's powers are subject to the provisions of clauses 2(2) 30(7) and 31D (3) of these Conditions 35(3)
Arbitrator determines the matters in dispute as stipulated ?
YES
NO
The Arbitration Act 1950 governs the conduct of the Arbitrator in such matters. The Courts will correct or send back any award not in compliance
The award of such Arbitrator must be final and binding on the parties 35(4)
STOP
…the event of the Works or …y part sustaining war …mage or any unfixed …aterials or goods intended … delivered to and placed on … adjacent the Works …staining war damage then in …te of anything expressed or …plied in this Contract the …llowing provisions must …ply:– 33(1)
The Contractor may then comply with the instruction which becomes an authorized instruction if before such compliance neither party has given a written request to concur in the appointment of an arbitrator under clause 35 2(2)
The Final Certificate must not be conclusive evidence in any proceedings arising (whether by arbitration under clause 35 or otherwise) if any sum mentioned in the Certificate is erroneous by reason of:– 30(7)
fraud dishonesty or fraudulent concealment relating to the Works or any part or to any matter dealt with in the Certificate 30(7)(a)
any defect (including any omission) in the Works or any part which reasonable inspection or examination would not disclose at any reasonable time during the Works or before the issue of the Certificate 30(7)(b)
any accidental inclusion or exclusion of any work materials or goods or any figure in computation or arithmetical error in computation 30(7)(c)
The Quantity Surveyor and Contractor may agree what must be deemed for all purposes of this Contract to be the net amount payable or allowable by the Contractor in respect of the occurrence of any event referred to in any provision listed 31D(3)
This provision places such agreements not within the scope of the Arbitrators powers to review

4 COMPUTER PROCESSING CONTRACT DISPUTES

> The instruments of scientific technology have no will of their own, no inborn inclination either to good or to evil. They are servants of man, and everything depends on the use man makes of them(1).

1. Harry W. Jones (ed.), *Law and the Social Role of Science* (New York: Rockefeller University Press, 1966).

INTRODUCTION

A flowchart is normally the forerunner to program writing. In most cases of computer application, the machine is used for numerical manipulation. But in this work the flowcharts in Chapter 3 are not the series of machine orders normally associated with such charts. They are simply concerned with an analytical display of text in a predefined manner determined by either set order or responses to binary questions.

If the Standard Form of Contract is regarded as a 'system' then that system has been analysed and presented for transposition to a computer in flowchart form. There has in effect been created a large-scale town map of the Standard Form. The boxes of text are stored at an address which can be called up by the user or will be automatically called up by the system if that address is a subroutine. If the user requires certain information on an obligation or remedy he will call up a certain address evident from an index, that address will in turn take him methodically to further relevant addresses to complete the search. At various crossroads *en route* binary questions will objectively, and then automatically, lead to the correct destination, thus solving the problem in the shortest possible time by the elimination of journeys along routes which cannot lead the searcher to his correct destination.

The system can provide reviews, case lists, and word lists on request and also completely monitors the analysis of the dispute as it develops interactively at the computer terminal.

In order to examine the feasibility of using an interactive system, certain clauses were set up and tested for disputes and reviews, and a particular kind of dispute was run on this partial system.

The user, seated at a typewriter keyboard, is required only to type the particular clause numbers he requires. If he chooses to use the dispute program he will in addition use a simple 'yes' or 'no' key to answer the binary questions. Great care was taken to ensure that the user is communicated with in sensible English rather than computer code. 'Decisions' from the system are printed in red to draw attention to such matters.

The case study that follows was considered suitably involved, to test the computer monitored system, on the following counts:

1. Complex design responsibilities are involved.

2. Explicit and implied obligations are involved.

3. It illustrates contract procedures and the benefit of both 'review' and 'dispute' programs.

4. It investigates contract provisions for the recovery of direct loss, etc., arising from breaches.

5. It gauges and illustrates the ability required, in a complex dispute, by the user so that correct responses are input to the all-important binary questions.

CASE STUDY

Details

Brief Description of Building. Multistorey steel-framed building about 150 m long × 30 m wide × 25 m high.

Form of Contract. Standard Form of Building Contract, private edition *with* quantities, 1963.

Documents. Contract Drawings (general details to small scale: no steelwork drawings). Contract Bill (*S.M.M.*, 5th edition (Imperial) used). No specification but Bill contained detailed preambles.

Dispute. The Contractor had preplanned to encase in concrete the structural steelwork in 5 sections working 2 sections at a time, each section encased vertically to roof level using 2 lots of scaffold. The scaffold from section 1 on its encasing completion being reused on section 3 and 5. The scaffold from section 2 being reused on section 4. The encasement was planned to commence once the frame was completely in its final form. The steelwork and precast concrete floor beams were the subject of separate prime cost sums. The subcontractor for the steelwork had also been responsible for the structural design of the steelwork frame. The quotation submitted by this subcontractor to the Architect prior to the tender stage stated they had designed the steelwork 'as structurally cased' in accordance with BSS 449/1959. The Bill of Quantities in turn called upon the Contractor to encase steel 'in accordance with BSS 449'.

The British Standards document (dated 1959) contains over a hundred pages and refers to twenty other British standards or codes but in no case does it refer to the method order or detail of encasement of steelwork.

A separate clause in the Bill of Quantities requires the Contractor not to 'permit anything to be done to cause forces or applied loads to be applied to the Works greater than those for which the Works had been designed'.

A steel erection drawing issued by the Architect after site work commenced made no reference to methods or restrictions on encasement. The Bill of Quantities contained no express reference to methods to be imposed upon the Contractor.

Immediately after commencement of encasement the Architect has written a letter to the Contractor and insisted that 'to ensure stability no precast flooring could be fixed until the steelwork had been encased up to 4th Floor level (out of 6 Floors) throughout the complete length of the structure'.

The Contractor considers this instruction interferes with his planned methods and will therefore impose a restriction not stated at the outset. This will cause some financial loss, also some delay.

At this stage he does not intend to change his proposed method unless the Architect agrees to reimburse his loss and also extends the date for completion.

The Architect maintains that according to clause 1(1) the Contractor must carry out the Works in every respect to the reasonable satisfaction of the Architect and therefore must follow his instruction in this matter.

Stage 1

The initial problem is deciding just where to begin, however it will be seen later that the precise point of commencement is not critical. So long as one starts in the right field, the charts and programs will bring the searcher home to roost onto the correct conclusion.

From the brief details of the Case Study and with reference to the index (Fig. 4.1, pp. 152–62), the following decisions can be made:

1. *Clause 2. Architect's instructions*

It is clear that the Architect has by virtue of his letter to the Contractor issued an 'instruction' albeit unorthodox and uncertain in authority, we must therefore test this clause.

2. *Clause 1. Contractor's obligations*

Since the Architect considers he has a right to have the work *carried out* to his satisfaction, and he quotes this clause as his authority in this respect then we must test this clause.

The index also lists certain clauses which may bear on the matter:

Clause 3. Contract Documents.
Clause 12. Contract Bills.
Clause 6. Workmanship, materials, and goods.
Clause 11(6). Direct loss, etc.
Clause 24. Loss and expense by disturbance of progress.

The above are noted for probable review or test under program B (dispute). We might also regard the nominated subcontractor, as designer, is involved in this, but since the Architect is apparently taking responsibility in this particular matter the above list will be examined before clause 27 is reviewed.

We are now ready to apply the problem to the computer stored analysis, program B.

Stage 2

Commentary and details of this stage are shown upon Fig. 4.1 (pp. 152–62).

Fig. 4.1

STAGE 2

STANDARD FORM OF BUILDING CONTRACT 1963 (LA WITH QUANTITIES) JULY 1971 REVISION

THIS PROGRAM ENABLES CONTRACTING PARTIES

(A) TO REVIEW THEIR OBLIGATIONS RIGHTS AND REMEDIES, OR

(B) IN THE EVENT OF EITHER PARTY NOT COMPLYING WITH ANY OF THOSE OBLIGATIONS THE PROGRAM WILL, BY QUESTIONING THE PARTIES, LOGICALLY PRODUCE THE CORRECT CONTRACTUAL DECISION

THE FOLLOWING PROVISIONS ARE INCORPORATED IN THIS CONTRACT.

1	CONTRACTOR'S OBLIGATIONS.	2	ARCHITECT'S INSTRUCTIONS.	3	CONTRACT DOCUMENTS.
4	STATUTORY OBLIGATIONS,NOTICES, FEES AND CHARGES.	5	SETTING OUT THE WORKS AND LEVELS.	6	WORKMANSHIP, MATERIALS AND GOODS.
7	ROYALTIES AND PATENT RIGHTS.	8	FOREMAN IN CHARGE.	9	ACCESS FOR ARCHITECT.
10	CLERK OF WORKS.	11	VARIATIONS AND PROVISIONAL SUM WORK.	11	VALUATION OF VARIATIONS AND PROVISIONAL SUM WORK.
11	DIRECT LOSS ETC. ARISING FROM VARIATIONS OR PROVISIONAL SUM WORK.	11	PROVISIONAL AND PRIME COST SUM PROCEDURES.	12	CONTRACT BILLS.
13	CONTRACT SUM.	14	UNFIXED MATERIALS AND GOODS ON SITE.	14	UNFIXED MATERIALS AND GOODS OFF SITE.
15	PRACTICAL COMPLETION AND FIRST RELEASE OF RETENTION.	16	SECTIONAL PRACTICAL COMPLETION AND FIRST RELEASE OF RETENTION.	15&16	DEFECTS LIABILITIES, FINAL RELEASE OF RETENTIONS AND REDUCTION OF DAMAGES ON SECTIONAL COMPLETION.
17	ASSIGNMENT OF SUBLETTING.	17A	FAIR WAGES AND CONDITIONS.	18	LIABILITIES AND INDEMNITIES.
19	INSURANCES.	19	SPECIAL INSURANCES FOR THE EMPLOYER.	20(A)	INSURANCES BY CONTRACTOR (NEW WORK OPTIONAL).
20(B)	INSURANCES BY EMPLOYER(NEW WORK OPTIONAL).	20(C)	INSURANCES BY EMPLOYER (ALTERATIONS NO OPTION).	21	POSSESSION, COMPLETION AND POSTPONEMENT.
22	DAMAGES FOR NON COMPLETION.	23	EXTENSIONS OF TIME.	24	LOSS AND EXPENSE BY DISTURBANCE OF PROGRESS.
25	DETERMINATION FOR DEFAULTS BY CONTRACTOR. PROCEDURE AFTER SERVING NOTICE FOR DEFAULTS BY CONTRACTOR. DETERMINATION IN THE EVENT OF CONTRACTOR'S INSOLVENCY. PROCEDURE AFTER AUTOMATIC DETERMINATION FOLLOWED BY ADOPTION IN INSOLVENCY. FINANCIAL SETTLEMENT IN DEFAULT OR INSOLVENCY BY CONTRACTOR.	26	DETERMINATION BY THE CONTRACTOR OF HIS OWN EMPLOYMENT. AGREED AND ACCRUED RIGHTS OF THE PARTIES UPON SUCH DETERMINATION. FINANCIAL SETTLEMENT UPON SUCH DETERMINATION.	27	NOMINATED SUBCONTRACTORS. PAYMENTS TO NOMINATED SUBCONTRACTORS. DELAY BY NOMINATED SUBCONTRACTORS. P.C. SUMS WORK FOR WHICH CONTRACTOR TENDERS.
28	NOMINATED SUPPLIERS. PAYMENT TO NOMINATED SUPPLIERS.	29	ARTISTIC SPECIALISTS ENGAGED BY THE EMPLOYER.	30	INTERIM PAYMENT CERTIFICATES. RETENTION CERTIFICATES. FINAL SETTLEMENT. FINAL CERTIFICATE.
31ACD	FULL FLUCTUATIONS.	31BCD	LIMITED FLUCTUATIONS.	31	SETTLEMENT OF FLUCTUATIONS.
32	OUTBREAK OF HOSTILITIES.	33	WAR DAMAGE.	34	DISCOVERIES ON THE SITE.
35	ARBITRATION.				

```
WHICH PROVISION DO YOU WISH TO EXAMINE ?
TYPE THE NUMBER

2

YOU HAVE ASKED TO EXAMINE PROVISION  2 IS THIS CORRECT ?
TYPE YES OR NO

YES

ARE YOU CONCERNED WITH

   (A) A REVIEW OF THE PROVISIONS, OR
   (B) A DISPUTE

TYPE A OR B

B

YOU ARE CONCERNED WITH A DISPUTE ?

IS THIS CORRECT?
TYPE YES OR NO

YES
```

CLAUSE 2 ARCHITECTS INSTRUCTIONS

STATEMENT

THE CONTRACTOR MUST IMMEDIATELY COMPLY WITH ALL AUTHORISED INSTRUCTIONS ISSUED TO HIM BY THE ARCHITECT. 2(1)

SUBROUTINES

ALL INSTRUCTIONS ISSUED BY THE ARCHITECT MUST BE ISSUED IN WRITING. 2(3)

ANY INSTRUCTIONS GIVEN TO THE FOREMAN-IN-CHARGE BY THE ARCHITECT SHALL BE DEEMED TO HAVE BEEN ISSUED TO THE CONTRACTOR. 8

DO YOU WISH TO EXAMINE ANY SUBROUTINE NOW? ANSWER GIVEN - NO

NOTICE

THE FOLLOWING 21 SUB-ROUTINES WILL INDICATE THE INSTRUCTIONS THE ARCHITECT HAS AUTHORITY TO GIVE UNDER THE CONTRACT.

DO YOU WISH TO EXAMINE THESE SUBROUTINES NOW? ANSWER GIVEN - YES

THE ARCHITECT MUST ISSUE INSTRUCTIONS IN REGARD TO ANY DISCREPANCIES IN OR DIVERGENCE BETWEEN CONTRACT DRAWINGS AND/OR BILLS. 1(2)

THE ARCHITECT MAY ISSUE INSTRUCTIONS IN REGARD TO SUCH VARIATIONS. 4(1)

THE ARCHITECT MAY INSTRUCT THAT ANY ERROR ARISING FROM THE CONTRACTORS OWN INNACCURATE SETTING OUT SHALL NOT BE AMENDED IN WHICH CASE THE CONTRACT SUMS MUST BE ADJUSTED ACCORDINGLY. 5

THE ARCHITECT MAY ISSUE INSTRUCTIONS REQUIRING THE CONTRACTOR TO OPEN UP FOR INSPECTION ANY WORK COVERED UP. 6(2)

THE ARCHITECT MAY ISSUE INSTRUCTIONS REQUIRING THE CONTRACTOR TO TEST ANY MATERIALS OR GOODS (WHETHER OR NOT ALREADY INCORPORATED IN THE WORKS)OR OF ANY EXECUTED WORK. 6(3)

THE ARCHITECT MAY ISSUE INSTRUCTIONS TO REMOVE ANY WORK MATERIALS OR GOODS FROM THE SITE WHICH ARE NOT IN ACCORDANCE WITH THIS CONTRACT. 6 (4)

THE ARCHITECT MAY ISSUE INSTRUCTIONS REQUIRING THE DISMISSAL FROM THE WORKS OF ANY PERSON EMPLOYED ON THE WORKS, BUT NOT UNREASONABLY OR VEXATIOUSLY. 6(5).

THE CONTRACTOR MUST,IN COMPLIANCE WITH ARCHITECTS INSTRUCTIONS,SUPPLY AND USE ANY PATENTED ARTICLE,PROCESS OR INVENTION IN CARRYING OUT THE WORKS. 7

THE ARCHITECT MAY ISSUE INSTRUCTIONS REQUIRING A VARIATION. 11(1).

THE ARCHITECT MUST ISSUE INSTRUCTIONS IN REGARD TO THE EXPENDITURE OF PRIME COST SUMS INCLUDED IN THE CONTRACT BILLS. 11(3)

THE ARCHITECT MUST ISSUE INSTRUCTIONS IN REGARD TO THE EXPENDITURE OF PROVISIONAL SUMS INCLUDED IN THE CONTRACT BILLS. 11(3)

THE ARCHITECT MUST ISSUE INSTRUCTIONS IN REGARD TO THE EXPENDITURE OF PRIME COST SUMS WHICH MAY ARISE AS A RESULT OF INSTRUCTIONS ISSUED IN REGARD TO PROVISIONAL SUMS INCLUDED IN THE CONTRACT BILLS. 11(3)

From the 21 subroutines listed the only relevant grounds for such an instruction would appear to the Contractor to be either under clause 1(2) or clause 11 – both would in effect admit there was an error in the Contract Bills!

THE CONTRACTOR MUST MAKE GOOD WITHIN A REASONABLE TIME ANY DEFECT SPECIFIED IN THE SCHEDULE OF DEFECTS ENTIRELY AT HIS OWN COST (UNLESS THE ARCHITECT OTHERWISE INSTRUCTS IN WHICH CASE THE CONTRACT SUM MUST BE ADJUSTED ACCORDINGLY). 15(2)

THE CONTRACTOR MUST COMPLY WITH SUCH INSTRUCTIONS WITHIN A REASONABLE TIME ENTIRELY AT HIS OWN COST(UNLESS THE ARCHITECT OTHERWISE INSTRUCTS IN WHICH CASE THE CONTRACT SUM MUST BE ADJUSTED ACCORDINGLY). 15(3)&16(B)

THE ARCHITECT CAN ACCEPT DEFECTS IF HE CHOOSES.

THE ARCHITECT MAY ISSUE INSTRUCTIONS REQUIRING THE CONTRACTOR TO REMOVE AND DISPOSE OF ANY DEBRIS. 20(C)(C)(II)

THE ARCHITECT MAY ISSUE INSTRUCTIONS TO POSTPONE ANY WORK TO BE EXECUTED IN THIS CONTRACT. 21(2)

THE CONTRACTOR MUST DO ALL THAT MAY BE REASONABLY REQUIRED BY THE ARCHITECT TO PROCEED WITH THE WORKS. 23

THE ARCHITECT MAY WITHIN 14 DAYS AFTER SUCH NOTICE ISSUE INSTRUCTIONS TO THE CONTRACTOR REQUIRING THE CONTINUATION OF THE WORKS UP TO THE POINTS OF STOPPAGE TO BE SPECIFIED IN SUCH INSTRUCTIONS. 32(2)

THE ARCHITECT MAY WITHIN 14 DAYS AFTER SUCH NOTICE ISSUE INSTRUCTIONS TO THE CONTRACTOR REQUIRING THE EXECUTION OF SUCH PROTECTIVE WORK AS SPECIFIED IN SUCH INSTRUCTIONS. 32(2)

THE ARCHITECT MAY ISSUE INSTRUCTIONS REQUIRING THE CONTRACTOR TO REMOVE AND/OR DISPOSE OF ANY DEBRIS AND/OR DAMAGED WORK AND/OR EXECUTE SUCH PROTECTIVE WORK AS SPECIFIED IN THE INSTRUCTIONS. 33(1)(B)

THE ARCHITECT MUST ISSUE INSTRUCTIONS IN REGARD TO WHAT IS TO BE DONE CONCERNING SUCH AN OBJECT REPORTED BY THE CONTRACTOR. 34(2)

THE ARCHITECT MUST ISSUE INSTRUCTIONS IN REGARD TO WHAT IS TO BE DONE CONCERNING SUCH AN OBJECT REPORTED BY THE CONTRACTOR. 34(2)

CONTRACTOR DOES COMPLY WITH AUTHORIZED INSTRUCTIONS? ANSWER GIVEN - NO

DECISION

STATEMENT

THE CONTRACTOR MAY REQUEST THE ARCHITECT TO SPECIFY IN WRITING THE CONDITION WHICH AUTHORISES THE INSTRUCTION. 2(2)

ANY INSTRUCTION IN HIS OPINION NOT AUTHORISED MUST BE QUESTIONED BY THE CONTRACTOR WITHIN 7 DAYS. INSTRUCTIONS NOT CONTEMPLATED BY THE CONTRACT MUST BE QUESTIONED BY THE CONTRACTOR TO SAFEGUARD HIS RIGHT TO PAYMENT AND BIND THE EMPLOYER.

The Contractor must at this stage request the Architect to specify the condition. In the meantime the Contractor can review clause 2 to see what should happen next.

REVIEW OF CLAUSE 2

THE CONTRACTOR MUST IMMEDIATELY COMPLY WITH ALL AUTHORISED INSTRUCTIONS ISSUED TO HIM BY THE ARCHITECT. 2(1)

THE CONTRACTOR MAY REQUEST THE ARCHITECT TO

MUST BE QUESTIONED BY THE CONTRACTOR WITHIN 7 DAYS. INSTRUCTIONS NOT CONTEMPLATED BY THE CONTRACT MUST BE QUESTIONED BY THE CONTRACTOR TO SAFEGUARD HIS RIGHT TO PAYMENT AND BIND THE EMPLOYER.

THE ARCHITECT MUST IMMEDIATELY COMPLY WITH ANY SUCH REQUEST. 2(2)

THE CONTRACTOR MAY THEN COMPLY WITH THE INSTRUCTION WHICH BECOMES AN AUTHORISED INSTRUCTION IF BEFORE SUCH COMPLIANCE NEITHER PARTY HAS GIVEN A WRITTEN REQUEST TO CONCUR IN THE APPOINTMENT OF AN ARBITRATOR UNDER CLAUSE 35 2(2)

IF THE CONTRACTOR DISPUTES THE BASIS OF AN INSTRUCTION HE SHOULD SERVE NOTICE TO ARBITRATE BUT NEVERTHELESS HE MUST COMPLY OR RISK BEING IN BREACH IF HIS DISPUTE IS NOT UPHELD .

THE EMPLOYER MAY EMPLOY AND PAY OTHER PERSONS TO EXECUTE AUTHORISED INSTRUCTIONS IF WITHIN 7 DAYS AFTER RECEIPT OF A WRITTEN NOTICE REQUIRING COMPLIANCE THE CONTRACTOR DOES NOT COMPLY. 2(1)

THIS ACTION BY THE EMPLOYER IS LIMITED TO OBTAINING COMPLIANCE WITH SUCH INSTRUCTIONS AND IS WITHOUT PREJUDICE TO THE RIGHTS UNDER CLAUSE 25 THAT THE EMPLOYER HAS.

ALL COSTS INCURRED IN SUCH EMPLOYMENT SHALL BE DEDUCTABLE FROM THE CONTRACTOR BY THE EMPLOYER AS A DEBT OR MAY BE DEDUCTED FROM ANY MONIES DUE OR TO BECOME DUE UNDER THIS CONTRACT. 2(1)

COSTS DEDUCTED MUST ONLY BE DEDUCTED FROM THIS CONTRACT.

ALL INSTRUCTIONS ISSUED BY THE ARCHITECT MUST BE ISSUED IN WRITING. 2(3)

ANY INSTRUCTIONS NOT AUTHORISED MUST BE QUESTIONED BY THE CONTRACTOR.INSTRUCTIONS NOT CONTEMPLATED BY THE CONTRACT MUST BE QUESTIONED BY THE CONTRACTOR TO SAFEGUARD HIS RIGHT TO PAYMENT AND BIND THE EMPLOYER IN THIS RESPECT AS PROVIDED IN CLAUSE 2(2).

ANY INSTRUCTION ISSUED ORALLY SHALL BE OF NO IMMEDIATE EFFECT. 2(3)

IF THE ARCHITECT HIMSELF CONFIRMS THE SAME IN WRITING WITHIN 7 DAYS OF GIVING THE ORAL INSTRUCTION THEN THE INSTRUCTION TAKES EFFECT FROM THE DATE OF SUCH CONFIRMATION. 2(3)(A)

THE ARCHITECTS INSTRUCTION TAKES EFFECT FROM THE DATE OF THE ARCHITECTS CONFIRMATION. 2(3)(A)

THE EMPLOYER IS BOUND ONLY FROM THE DATE OF CONFIRMATION.

THE CONTRACTOR MAY CONFIRM IN WRITING ANY ORAL INSTRUCTION TO THE ARCHITECT WITHIN 7 DAYS OF ORAL ISSUE. 2(3)

THE CONTRACTORS DUTY TO CONFIRM ORAL INSTRUCTIONS IS MORE PERMISSIVE THAN MANDATORY SINCE THE ARCHITECTS OWN CONFIRMATION WITHIN 7 DAYS EFFECTIVELY OVERRIDES THE CONTRACTORS CONFIRMATION

THE CONTRACTORS CONFIRMATION MUST TAKE EFFECT FROM THE EXPIRATION OF THE LAST 7 DAYS IF NOT DISSENTED FROM IN WRITING BY THE ARCHITECT WITHIN 7 DAYS OF SUCH CONFIRMATION. 2(3)

```
                                        THE EMPLOYER IS BOUND
                                        ONLY FROM THE DATE OF
                                        EXPIRATION OF THE LAST
                                        7 DAYS.

IF NEITHER CONTRACTOR NOR ARCHITECT CONFIRM SUCH
 AN INSTRUCTION IN THE MANNER AND TIME
STIPULATED BUT NEVERTHELESS THE CONTRACTOR
COMPLIES WITH AN ORAL INSTRUCTION THEN THE
ARCHITECT MAY CONFIRM THE SAME IN WRITING AT ANY
TIME PRIOR TO THE ISSUE OF THE FINAL
CERTIFICATE.   2(3)(B)

THE ARCHITECTS INSTRUCTION MUST BE DEEMED TO
HAVE TAKEN EFFECT FROM THE DATE ON WHICH IT WAS
ISSUED.   2(3)(B)

                                        THE EMPLOYER IS BOUND
                                        FROM THE DATE OF ISSUE.

                                                        DO YOU REQUIRE
                                                        A WORD LIST?        ANSWER GIVEN
                                                                                    - NO

                                                        DO YOU REQUIRE
                                                        A CASE LIST?        ANSWER GIVEN
                                                                                    - YES

 ARCHITECTS INSTRUCTIONS
 -----------------------

    (1) NEODOX LTD V SWINTON + PENDLEBURY B.C.(1958) Q.B.D(SPECIAL PAPER).
    (2) CLAYTON V WOODMAN (1962) Q.B.533 - (1962) 1 W.L.R.585.
    (3) EAST HAM B.C V BERNARD SUNLEY (1966) A.C.406
    (4) AMF(INTERNATIONAL) V MAGNET BOWLING LTD (1968) W.L.R 1028

 WHICH PROVISION DO YOU WISH TO EXAMINE?
 TYPE THE NUMBER

 1

 YOU HAVE ASKED TO EXAMINE PROVISION  1 IS THIS CORRECT?
 TYPE YES OR NO

YES

 ARE YOU CONCERNED WITH

    (A) A REVIEW OF THE PROVISIONS, OR
    (B) A DISPUTE

 TYPE A OR B

B

 YOU ARE CONCERNED WITH A DISPUTE?

 IS THIS CORRECT?
 TYPE YES OR NO

YES

 CLAUSE  1          CONTRACTOR'S  OBLIGATIONS
 ---------          -------------------------

 STATEMENT
 ---------

THE CONTRACTOR MUST CARRY OUT AND COMPLETE THE
WORKS SHOWN UPON THE CONTRACT DRAWINGS AND
DESCRIBED BY OR REFERRED TO IN CONTRACT BILLS
AND THESE CONDITIONS.   1(1).

 SUBROUTINES
 -----------

THE CONTRACTOR MUST BE GIVEN POSSESSION OF THE
SITE ON THE DATE FOR POSSESSION STATED IN THE
APPENDIX.   21(1).
```

Upon receipt of the Contractors request, the Architect must specify the condition number which permits him to issue such instructions. The Architect considers the Contractor is obliged under clause 1 to comply with his instruction. Prior to confirming this however he decides to call up clause 1 program B to check this.

NOTHING CONTAINED IN THE SPECIFICATION DESCRIPTIVE SCHEDULES OR OTHER DOCUMENTS SHALL IMPOSE ANY OBLIGATION BEYOND THOSE IMPOSED BY THE CONTRACT DRAWINGS BILLS ARTICLES OF AGREEMENT AND THESE CONDITIONS. 3(3).

THE CONTRACT BILLS MUST BE PREPARED IN ACCORDANCE WITH THE PRINCIPLES OF THE STANDARD METHOD OF MEASUREMENT OF BUILDING WORKS 5TH EDITION METRIC. 12(1).

This subroutine 3(3) is relevant and is bound up with subroutine 12(1). The Architect will therefore decide to examine both.

THE 'COMPLETION' REQUIRED BY CLAUSE 1 (1) IS THE PRACTICAL COMPLETION DETAILED IN CLAUSE 21 SUBROUTINE.

DO YOU WISH TO EXAMINE ANY SUBROUTINE NOW? ANSWER GIVEN - YES

TYPE THE SUBROUTINE NUMBER(S) YOU WISH TO EXAMINE SEPARATED WITH COMMAS

3(3),12(1)

EXAMINATION OF SUBROUTINE 3(3)

STATEMENT

NOTHING CONTAINED IN THE SPECIFICATION DESCRIPTIVE SCHEDULES OR OTHER DOCUMENTS SHALL IMPOSE ANY OBLIGATION BEYOND THOSE IMPOSED BY THE CONTRACT DRAWINGS BILLS ARTICLES OF AGREEMENT AND THESE CONDITIONS. 3(3).

ALTHOUGH THE CONTRACT PROVIDES FOR THE ISSUE OF WORKING DRAWINGS AND DETAILS AS THE WORKS PROGRESSES THESE LATER DOCUMENTS ARE ALWAYS GOVERNED BY THE PRE-CONTRACT DOCUMENTS.

A correct response to this question in these circumstances must be "Yes" since the Architect has in fact issued a letter (a "working document") which imposes an obligation beyond those imposed by the pre-contract documents which are silent as to any express method of erection required.

THE WORKING DOCUMENTS ISSUED DO IMPOSE OBLIGATIONS BEYOND THOSE IN PRE-CONTRACT DOCUMENTS? ANSWER GIVEN - YES

DECISION

SUBROUTINES

ANY ERROR IN DESCRIPTION OR IN QUANTITY OR OMISSION OF ITEMS FROM THE CONTRACT BILLS MUST BE CORRECTED. 12(2)

This decision indicates the procedures to be followed by both parties in the circumstances.

THE CONTRACTOR MUST IMMEDIATELY GIVE TO THE ARCHITECT A WRITTEN NOTICE SPECIFYING ANY DISCREPANCY IN OR DIVERGENCE BETWEEN CONTRACT DRAWINGS AND/OR BILLS IF HE FINDS ANY. 1(2).

THE CONTRACTOR MUST GIVE WRITTEN NOTICE IMMEDIATELY UPON IT BECOMING REASONABLY APPARENT THAT THE PROGRESS OF THE WORKS IS DELAYED- 23.

BY, ARCHITECTS INSTRUCTIONS ISSUED REGARDING- DISCREPANCIES 1(2) VARIATIONS 11(1) POSTPONEMENTS 21(2) 23(E)

THIS SUBROUTINE DETAILS THE CONTRACTORS RIGHTS UNDER CLAUSES 24(1)(C) AND 26.

END OF EXAMINATION OF SUBROUTINE 3(3)

EXAMINATION OF SUBROUTINE 12(1)

STATEMENT

THE CONTRACT BILLS MUST BE PREPARED IN ACCORDANCE WITH THE PRINCIPLES OF THE STANDARD METHOD OF MEASUREMENT OF BUILDING WORKS 5TH EDITION METRIC. 12(1).

CONTRACT BILLS ARE IN ACCORDANCE WITH SMM AS STIPULATED? ANSWER GIVEN - NO

A correct response to this question in these circumstances must be – "No" since the SMM clause B 6 requires any imposed restrictions on methods of working must be stated as an item in Contract Bills.

DECISION

STATEMENT

THE CONTRACT BILLS MAY BE PREPARED NOT IN ACCORDANCE WITH THE PRINCIPLES OF THE SMM 5TH EDITION METRIC PROVIDING THE BILLS CONTAIN STATEMENTS IN RESPECT OF ANY SPECIFIC ITEM OR ITEMS WHICH ARE AT VARIANCE WITH SUCH PRINCIPLES. 12(1)

DECISION

SUBROUTINE

THE CONTRACTOR MUST IMMEDIATELY GIVE TO THE ARCHITECT A WRITTEN NOTICE SPECIFYING ANY DISCREPANCY IN OR DIVERGENCE BETWEEN CONTRACT DRAWINGS AND/OR BILLS IF HE FINDS ANY. 1(2).

This decision brings us back to clause 1 and indicates the Contractors procedures and rights in the circumstances.

THIS SUBROUTINE DETAILS THE CONTRACTORS RIGHTS UNDER CLAUSES 11,23,24 AND 26 (SUBROUTINES).

END OF EXAMINATION OF SUBROUTINE 12(1)

STATEMENT

THE CONTRACTOR MUST CARRY OUT AND COMPLETE THE WORKS SHOWN UPON THE CONTRACT DRAWINGS AND DESCRIBED BY OR REFERRED TO IN CONTRACT BILLS AND THESE CONDITIONS. 1(1).

CONTRACTOR DOES CARRY OUT AND COMPLETE AS STIPULATED? ANSWER GIVEN - NO

DECISION

SUBROUTINES

THE CONTRACTOR MUST GIVE WRITTEN NOTICE IMMEDIATELY UPON IT BECOMING REASONABLY APPARENT THAT THE PROGRESS OF THE WORKS IS DELAYED- 23.

THE ARCHITECT MUST ADJUDICATE ANY SUCH NOTICE BEFORE INVOKING CLAUSES 22 OR 25 THIS SUBROUTINE DETAILS THE CONTRACTORS RIGHTS UNDER CLAUSES 24 AND 26.

THE ARCHITECT MUST CERTIFY IN WRITING IF THE CONTRACTOR FAILS TO COMPLETE THE WORKS BY THE DATE FOR COMPLETION OR ANY EXTENDED TIME UNDER CLAUSES 23 OR 33(1)(C). 22.

THE ARCHITECT MUST NOT ISSUE THE CERTIFICATE REQUIRED BY THIS CLAUSE 22 UNTIL THE DATE FOR COMPLETION (OR EXTENDED DATE) HAS BEEN PASSED.

This decision warns of the Contractors duty under clause 23 to give notice of delay if in fact this dispute does cause delay and the Architect is warned not to attempt to determine the Contractors employment if a 'reasonable' cause exists.

THE ARCHITECT MAY GIVE THE CONTRACTOR A NOTICE BY REGISTERED POST IF THE CONTRACTOR DEFAULTS IN ANY ONE OR MORE OF THE FOLLOWING RESPECTS.- 25(1)

IF THE CONTRACTOR WHOLLY SUSPENDS CARRYING OUT THE WORKS BEFORE COMPLETION AND WITHOUT REASONABLE CAUSE. 25(1)(A).

IN THE CASE OF INSOLVENCY CLAUSE 25(2) SUBROUTINE MUST BE FOLLOWED.

THERE IS A BREACH BY THE CONTRACTOR IF EITHER CLAUSES 22 OR 25 ARE INVOKED CLAUSE 25 SUBROUTINE ALSO DETAILS THE EMPLOYERS RIGHTS IN THE EVENT OF DILATORINESS.

THE MACHINE WILL PAUSE WHILE YOU CONSIDER THE DECISION.PRESS THE 'PROGRAM START' BUTTON WHEN YOU WISH TO CONTINUE

STATEMENT

THE CONTRACTOR MUST CARRY OUT AND COMPLETE THE WORKS IN EVERY RESPECT TO THE REASONABLE SATISFACTION OF THE A9CHITECT. 1(1).

SUBROUTINE

ALL WORKMANSHIP MATERIALS AND GOODS MUST SO FAR AS PROCURABLE BE OF THE STANDARDS AND KIND DESCRIBED IN THE CONTRACT BILLS. 6(1)

DO YOU WISH TO EXAMINE THE SUBROUTINE NOW? ANSWER GIVEN - YES

This subroutine which qualifies the Contractors obligation stated in clause 1(1) must be examined by the Architect to discover exactly what the obligation extends to.

EXAMINATION OF SUBROUTINE 6(1)

STATEMENTS

ALL WORKMANSHIP MATERIALS AND GOODS MUST SO FAR AS PROCURABLE BE OF THE STANDARDS AND KIND DESCRIBED IN THE CONTRACT BILLS. 6(1)

THE CONTRACTOR MUST UPON THE REQUEST OF THE ARCHITECT FURNISH VOUCHE9S TO PROVE THAT MATERIALS AND GOODS COMPLY WITH THE STANDARDS DESCRIBED IN THE CONTRACT BILLS. 6(2)

THE CONTRACT BILLS ARE CLEARLY INTENDED TO CONTAIN THE SPECIFICATION REFERRED TO IN CLAUSE 3(3). VERY DETAILED PREAMBLES MAY QUALIFY AS A SPECIFICATION WHICH IS OBLIGATORY IN THE CONTRACT, PROVIDING IT DOES NOT IMPOSE ANY OBLIGATIONS BEYOND THOSE STIPULATED IN THE CONTRACT BILLS, DRAWINGS AND CONDITIONS. THE WORDS 'SO FAR AS PROCURABLE' ARE IMPORTANT TO PREVENT THE CONTRACTOR CONSTANTLY BEING IN BREACH UNLESS MATERIALS OR GOODS ARE TRULY NOT PROCURABLE.

```
SUBROUTINE
----------

THE ARCHITECT AND HIS REPRESENTATIVES MUST HAVE
ACCESS TO THE WORKS AND OTHER PLACES WHERE WORK
IS BEING PREPARED (BY THE CONTRACTOR) FOR THE
CONTRACT AT ALL REASONABLE TIMES.   9

                                        DO YOU WISH TO EXAMINE
                                        THE SUBROUTINE NOW?   ANSWER GIVEN
                                                                    - NO

                                        WORK, MATERIALS AND
                                        GOODS ARE AS STIPULATED?ANSWER GIVEN
                                                                    - NO

DECISION
--------

THE ARCHITECT MAY ISSUE INSTRUCTIONS TO REMOVE
ANY WORK MATERIALS OR GOODS FROM THE SITE WHICH
ARE NOT IN ACCORDANCE WITH THIS CONTRACT.   6
(4)

                             THE ARCHITECT MUST STATE
                             IN HIS INSTRUCTIONS
                             THAT 'THE WORK/
                             MATERIA S/GOODS ARE NOT
                             IN ACCORDANCE WITH THIS
                             CONTRACT' OTHERWISE
                             SUCH AN INSTRUCTION
                             COULD BE CONFUSED WITH
                             THE ARCHITECTS POWER
                             UNDER CLAUSE 11(2) TO
                             ISSUE INSTRUCTIONS FOR
                             'THE REMOVAL FROM THE
                             SITE OF ANY WORK...' AS
                             A VARIATION.

THE MACHINE WILL PAUSE WHILE YOU CONSIDER THE
DECISION.PRESS THE 'PROGRAM START' BUTTON WHEN
YOU WISH TO CONTINUE.

                                        ARCHITECT DOES ISSUE
                                        INSTRUCTIONS TO REMOVE
                                        AS STIPULATED?        ANSWER GIVEN
                                                                    - NO

DECISION
--------

SUBROUTINE
----------

THE CONTRACTOR MUST MAKE GOOD WITHIN A
REASONABLE TIME ANY DEFECT SPECIFIED IN THE
SCHEDULE OF DEFECTS ENTIRELY AT HIS OWN COST
(UNLESS THE ARCHITECT OTHERWISE INSTRUCTS IN
WHICH CASE THE CONTRACT SUM MUST BE ADJUSTED
ACCORDINGLY).   15(2)

                             THE ARCHITECT HAS THE
                             POWER TO ACCEPT CERTAIN
                             DEFECTS WITH A
                             CONSEQUENT, DOWNWARDS
                             ONLY, ADJUSTMENT IN THE
                             CONTRACT SUM.

THE MACHINE WILL PAUSE WHILE YOU CONSIDER THE
DECISION.PRESS THE 'PROGRAM START' BUTTON WHEN
YOU WISH TO CONTINUE.

STATEMENT
---------

THE CONTRACTOR MUST CARRY OUT AND COMPLETE THE
WORKS IN EVERY RESPECT TO THE REASONABLE
SATISFACTION OF THE ARCHITECT.   1(1).

                                        CONTRACTOR DOES CARRY
                                        OUT AND COMPLETE TO THE
                                        REASONABLE SATISFACTION
                                        OF THE ARCHITECT?     ANSWER GIVEN
                                                                    - NO
```

Although the subroutine 6(1) clearly indicates that the Contractors obligations extend only so far as the standards described in Contract Bills – the Architect may still consider there is some implied obligation to follow his instruction and therefore may respond "No" to this question.

If a statement is followed by subroutines which are examined, then that statement is repeated to the user upon completion of subroutine examinations prior to a question being asked.

DECISION

SUBROUTINES

ALL WORKMANSHIP MATERIALS AND GOODS MUST SO FAR AS PROCURABLE BE OF THE STANDARDS AND KIND DESCRIBED IN THE CONTRACT BILLS. 6(1)

This decision refers us back to clause 6(1) which has already been examined and the annotation reminds the Architect that all work must be as described in Contract Bills.

THE ARCHITECT MAY GIVE THE CONTRACTOR A NOTICE BY REGISTERED POST IF THE CONTRACTOR DEFAULTS IN ANY ONE OR MORE OF THE FOLLOWING RESPECTS.- 25(1)

IF THE CONTRACTOR REFUSES OR PERSISTENTLY NEGLECTS TO COMPLY WITH A WRITTEN NOTICE TO REMOVE DEFECTIVE WORK MATERIALS OR GOODS AND SUCH REFUSAL MATERIALLY AFFECTS THE WORKS. 25(1)(C).

THE ARCHITECT MUST APPLY AN OBJECTIVE TEST TO DECIDE HIS SATISFACTION WITH QUANTITY AND QUALITY AS STIPULATED IN THE CONTRACT DRAWINGS AND BILLS LISTED IN THE ARTICLES OF AGREEMENT AND ISSUED UNDER CLAUSE 3(3) OR 3(4) THERE IS A BREACH BY THE CONTRACTOR IF SUCH A TEST SHOWS NON-COMPLIANCE.

THE MACHINE WILL PAUSE WHILE YOU CONSIDER THE DECISION.PRESS THE 'PROGRAM START' BUTTON WHEN YOU WISH TO CONTINUE

SUBROUTINES

THE ARCHITECT MUST IMMEDIATELY ISSUE A CERTIFICATE OF PRACTICAL COMPLETION WHEN THE WORKS ARE PRACTICALLY COMPLETED IN HIS OPINION. 15(1).

THE EMPLOYER MAY WITH THE CONSENT OF THE CONTRACTOR TAKE POSSESSION OF ANY PART OR PARTS OF THE WORKS AT ANY TIME BEFORE PRACTICAL COMPLETION. 16

THE DATE THE EMPLOYER TAKES POSSESSION DETERMINES THAT PRACTICAL COMPLETION HAS OCCURRED IN THE RELEVANT PART.

THE ARCHITECT MUST ISSUE THE FINAL CERTIFICATE SO SOON AS IS PRACTICABLE. 30(6).

DO YOU WISH TO EXAMINE ANY SUBROUTINE NOW? ANSWER GIVEN - NO

STATEMENT

THE CONTRACTOR MUST IMMEDIATELY GIVE TO THE ARCHITECT A WRITTEN NOTICE SPECIFYING ANY DISCREPANCY IN OR DIVERGENCE BETWEEN CONTRACT DRAWINGS AND/OR BILLS IF HE FINDS ANY. 1(2).

CONTRACTOR DOES GIVE A WRITTEN NOTICE AS STIPULATED? ANSWER GIVEN - YES

STATEMENT

THE ARCHITECT MUST ISSUE INSTRUCTIONS IN REGARD TO ANY DISCREPANCIES IN OR DIVERGENCE BETWEEN CONTRACT DRAWINGS AND/OR BILLS. 1(2)

```
SUBROUTINES
-----------

THE ARCHITECT MAY ISSUE INSTRUCTIONS REQUIRING
A VARIATION.   11(1).

ANY CORRECTION MUST BE DEEMED A VARIATION
REQUIRED BY THE ARCHITECT.   12(2).
                                                  DO YOU WISH TO EXAMINE
                                                  ANY SUBROUTINE NOW?        ANSWER GIVEN
                                                                                        - NO
                                                  ARCHITECT DOES ISSUE
                                                  INSTRUCTIONS AS
                                                  STIPULATED?                ANSWER GIVEN
                                                                                        - NO

DECISION
--------

SUBROUTINE
----------

THE CONTRACTOR MUST GIVE WRITTEN NOTICE
IMMEDIATELY UPON IT BECOMING REASONABLY APPARENT
THAT THE PROGRESS OF THE WORKS IS DELAYED-    23.

BY DELAY ON THE PART OF THE ARCHITECT IN GIVING
NECESSARY INSTRUCTIONS,DRAWINGS,DETAILS,LEVELS
TO THE CONTRACTOR AFTER PROPER NOTICE HAS BEEN
GIVEN BY THE CONTRACTOR.   23(F).

                                    THIS SUBROUTINE DETAILS
                                    THE CONTRACTORS RIGHTS
                                    UNDER CLAUSES 24 AND 26
                                    THERE IS A BREACH BY
                                    THE ARCHITECT.

SUBROUTINE
----------

THE QUANTITY SURVEYOR MUST MEASURE AND VALUE
ALL VARIATIONS REQUIRED BY THE ARCHITECT.   11
(4)
                                                  DO YOU WISH TO EXAMINE
                                                  THE SUBROUTINE NOW?        ANSWER GIVEN
                                                                                        - NO

                                    THIS IS THE END OF
                                          CLAUSE 1
                                    DEALING WITH THE
                                        CONTRACTOR'S
                                         OBLIGATIONS

                                                  DO YOU REQUIRE
                                                  A WORD LIST?               ANSWER GIVEN
                                                                                        - NO

                                                  DO YOU REQUIRE
                                                  A CASE LIST?               ANSWER GIVEN
                                                                                        - NO
```

This decision indicates the position when the Contractor notifies the Architect of a discrepancy (in his own opinion) and the Architect does not then issue instructions in response to such a notice.

END OF STAGE 2

At this point it is clear that if an Architect wishes to impose any special methods upon a Contractor then the SMM (B.6) requires this to be stated and if it is not then there is a discrepancy in the Bill concerned.
The Contractor must now be given an instruction under clause 2 (either under I (2) or II(1) conditions) to bind the Employer to pay the costs involved.

Stage 3
The Contractor considers he *will* incur direct loss and expense due to this instruction given.

He will, therefore, review clauses 11(6) and 24 since he is uncertain whether to claim reimbursement of the damages under the provisions of clause 11(6) or clause 24 or both.

This stage is detailed in Fig. 4.2 (pp. 164–7).

Fig. 4.2

STAGE 3

```
WHICH PROVISION DO YOU WISH TO EXAMINE?
TYPE THE NUMBER

11

YOU HAVE ASKED TO EXAMINE PROVISION 11 IS THIS CORRECT?
TYPE YES OR NO

YES

ARE YOU CONCERNED WITH

   (A) A REVIEW OF THE PROVISIONS, OR
   (B) A DISPUTE

TYPE A OR B

A

YOU ARE CONCERNED WITH A REVIEW?

IS THIS CORRECT?
TYPE YES OR NO

YES

CLAUSE 11          DIRECT LOSS ETC. ARISING FROM VARIATIONS OR PROVISIONAL SUM WORK.
---------          -----------------------------------------------------------------


REVIEW OF CLAUSE 11
-------------------

THE CONTRACTOR MAY MAKE A WRITTEN APPLICATION
THAT A VARIATION OR PROVISIONAL SUM WORK (OTHER
THAN WORK FOR WHICH A TENDER UDER CLAUSE 27(G)
HAS BEEN ACCEPTED) HAS INVOLVED THE CONTRACTOR
IN DIRECT LOSS AND/OR EXPENSE NOT REIMBURSED BY
VALUATION MADE UNDER CLAUSE 11(4)(A)(B)(C) OR
(D).  11(6)

THE CONTRACTOR MUST MAKE THE WRITTEN
APPLICATION WITHIN A REASONABLE TIME OF THE
DIRECT LOSS AND/OR EXPENSE HAVING BEEN INCURRED.
   11(6)
```

The actual loss caused by the instruction will be claimed under clause 11(6) unless a fair valuation is agreed under clause 11(4).

```
THE EXPRESS PROVISION
FOR A 'FAIR VALUATION'
IN CLAUSE 11(4) DOES
NOT RENDER THIS
PROVISION UNNECESSARY
SINCE DIRECT LOSS AND/
OR EXPENSE CAN FAR
EXCEED ANY FAIR VALUE
THAT MIGHT BE PLACED ON
THE WORK THAT CAUSED
SUCH LOSS ETC. THE
WORDS DIRECT LOSS WERE
INTERPRETED IN WRAIGHT
V PHT HOLDINGS (1968)
TO INCLUDE LOSS OF
PROFIT. (THIS IS
IMPORTANT IF SUB
STANTIAL PRIME COST
SUMS ARE OMITTED) THE
WRITTEN APPLICATION
CANNOT ANTICIPATE LOSS
AND/OR EXPENSE, THE
LOSS ETC MUST HAVE BEEN
INCURRED.THIS THEREFORE
WIDENS THE SCOPE OF
'A REASONABLE TIME'
CONSIDERABLY.  E   <

THE ARCHITECT IF OF THE OPINION THAT A
VARIATION OR PROVISIONAL SUM WORK HAS INVOLVED
THE CONTRACTOR IN DIRECT LOSS AND/OR EXPENSE
MUST ASCERTAIN OR INSTRUCT THE QUANTITY SURVEYOR
 TO ASCERTAIN THE AMOUNT OF SUCH LOSS OR EXPENSE
    11(6)
```

```
THE QUANTITY SURVEYORS
ASCERTAINMENT IS NOT
FINAL AND BINDING. THE
ARCHITECT HAS THE
RESPONSIBILITY HERE TO
JUDGE SUCH A CLAIM BUT
MAY USE THE QUANTITY
SURVEYOR IN THE
ASCERTAINMENT. THE
ARCHITECT IS NOT
STRICTLY REQUIRED TO
CONSIDER ANY CLAIM FOR
ANTICIPATED LOSS OR
EXPENSE BUT IN THE CASE
OF EXTENDED
'PRELIMINARIES' SUMS HE
WILL ARRANGE FOR SUCH
AMOUNTS TO BE BROUGHT
INTO THE ASCERTAINMENT
WHEN THEY HAVE BEEN
INCURRED BUT NOT BEFORE.

ANY AMOUNT SO ASCERTAINED MUST BE ADDED TO ANY
INTERIM CERTIFICATE AMOUNT OTHERWISE STATED AS
DUE AND MUST BE ADDED TO THE CONTRACT SUM.
11(6)

THE AMOUNT MUST BE FREE
FROM RETENTION BECAUSE
SUCH AMOUNTS ARE NOT
PART OF THE 'TOTAL
VALUE OF THE WORK' AS
DEFINED IN CLAUSE 30
(2)

DO YOU REQUIRE
A WORD LIST?                ANSWER GIVEN
                                         - NO

DO YOU REQUIRE
A CASE LIST?                ANSWER GIVEN
                                         - NO

WHICH PROVISION DO YOU WISH TO EXAMINE?
TYPE THE NUMBER

24

YOU HAVE ASKED TO EXAMINE PROVISION 24 IS THIS CORRECT?
TYPE YES OR NO

YES

ARE YOU CONCERNED WITH

   (A) A REVIEW OF THE PROVISIONS, OR
   (B) A DISPUTE

TYPE A OR B

A

YOU ARE CONCERNED WITH A REVIEW?

IS THIS CORRECT?
TYPE YES OR NO

YES
```

CLAUSE 24 LOSS AND EXPENSE BY DISTURBANCE OF PROGRESS

REVIEW OF CLAUSE 24

The actual loss caused by the delay only will be recovered under this clause. Furthermore this review indicates that any amounts so ascertained are to be added to the next interim valuation due and not subjected to retention.

THE CONTRACTOR MAY WITHIN A REASONABLE TIME GIVE WRITTEN APPLICATION THAT LOSS AND/OR EXPENSE HAS BEEN INVOLVED BY REASON OF THE REGULAR PROGRESS OF THE WORKS HAVING BEEN MATERIALLY AFFECTED- 24(1)

THE WORDS 'BY REASON OF THE REGULAR PROGRESS... MATERIALLY AFFECTED' ACTUALLYRESTRICT CLAIMS TO THE COST OF ACTUAL DELAY ONLY AND THIS DOES NOT MEAN THEREFORE THAT MORE EXPENSIVE METHODS USED TO OVERCOME OR PREVENT DELAY (IN ANTICIPATION OF RECOVERING) WILL RANK AS 'DIRECT LOSS'. HOWEVER IF THE ARCHITECT AGREES THAT-(A) THE PRINCIPAL OF THE CLAIM IS CORRECT (B) HE WILL IN THE EVENT 'ASCERTAIN' THAT THE MORE EXPENSIVE METHODS PROPOSED ARE THE 'DIRECT LOSS'-THEN THE CONTRACTOR CAN RECOVER SAME. IF THE CONTRACTOR HAS ALREADY USED MORE EXPENSIVE METHODS REGARDLESS THEN CLAUSE 24(2) ENABLES HIM TO GO TO THE COURTS TO RECOVER SUCH COSTS. THE CONTRACTORS PROGRAMME IS NOT CONCLUSIVE EVIDENCE OF THE REGULAR PROGRESS ANTICIPATED BUT IT CERTAINLY BEARS ON THE MATTER.

BY DELAY ON THE PART OF THE ARCHITECT IN GIVING NECESSARY INSTRUCTIONS,DRAWINGS,DETAILS, LEVELS TO THE CONTRACTOR AFTER PROPER NOTICE HAS BEEN GIVEN BY THE CONTRACTOR. 24(1)(A)

BY ARCHITECTS INSTRUCTIONS ISSUED REGARDING-OPENING UP WORK FOR INSPECTION 6(3)-TESTING WORK MATERIALS OR GOODS 6(3)-MAKING GOOD CONSEQUENCES OF LAST 6(3)-PROVIDING RESULTS WERE FOUND TO BE IN ACCORDANCE WITH THIS CONTRACT. 24(1)(B)

BY ANY DISCREPANCY IN OR DIVERGENCE BETWEEN CONTRACT DRAWINGS AND/OR BILLS. 24(1)(C)

BY DELAY ON THE PART OF ARTISTIC SPECIALISTS ENGAGED BY THE EMPLOYER NOT PART OF THIS CONTRACT. 24(1)(D)

BY ARCHITECTS INSTRUCTIONS ISSUED REGARDING POSTPONEMENT. 21(2)

THE CONTRACTOR MAY POSSESS OTHER RIGHTS AND REMEDIES. 24(2)

ALTHOUGH WRITTEN NOTICE IS A CONDITION PRECEDENT TO ACTION BY THE ARCHITECT LACK OF FORMAL NOTICE MAY NOT PREVENT THE CONTRACTOR FROM RECOVERING AT COMMON LAW WITH WIDER SCOPE THAN THE REASONS LISTED IN THIS CLAUSE. IF NOTICE HAS ALREADY BEEN GIVEN BY THE CONTRACTOR UNDER CLAUSE 23 THIS DEFAULT WOULD BE A TECHNICAL ONE ONLY AND WOULD NOT PREVENT RECOVERY EVEN UNDER THIS CONTRACT PROVISION.

THE ARCHITECT MUST HIMSELF (OR THE QUANTITY SURVEYOR) ASCERTAIN IF IN HIS OPINION WHETHER SUCH LOSS AND/OR EXPENSE HAS BEEN INVOLVED. 24(1)

ANY AMOUNT OF SUCH LOSS AND/OR EXPENSE SO ASCERTAINED MUST BE ADDED TO THE AMOUNT OTHERWISE STATED AS DUE IN ANY INTERIM CERTIFICATE TO BE ISSUED AND MUST BE ADDED TO THE CONTRACT SUM. 24(1)

THE AMOUNT MUST NOT BE SUBJECT TO ANY RETENTION.

DO YOU REQUIRE A WORD LIST? ANSWER GIVEN - NO

DO YOU REQUIRE A CASE LIST? ANSWER GIVEN - NO

END OF STAGE 3

SUMMARY

If the test cases referred to in connection with clause 2 are examined it will be seen from the judgements in those cases that, unless a contract expressly specifies certain methods of working, any intervention by the Architect to impose his own preferred method will expose the Employer to a claim for a variation.

Providing the Architect ensures that at the end, when the structural frame and flooring are complete, the Employer has a sound building, then he will have performed his function in the contract. If the designer of the frame relied particularly upon a certain method or order of encasement to stabilize the structure during its erection then BS 449 calls upon that designer to consider safety in such matters as part and parcel of the *design*. This would mean a prohibition on any method of encasement other than that required by the designer.

In the absence of instructions regarding methods and standards the Contractor must carry out any work in accordance with the standards implied by law, i.e.

> he must exercise skill and care, using materials of good quality suitable for their intended purpose.

The Architect in this dispute would probably consider that his preferred methods are an implied obligation if safety or stability are concerned, however, BS 449 is silent upon such matters except to say the designer must consider such matters in his design. In this case, however, the design was the responsibility of a nominated person who became a subcontractor to the main contractor. The flowcharts indicate under clauses 17, 18, 19, 20, and 27 the importance of ensuring that design responsibilities rest with those who carry out the design and that the responsibility is adequately backed by indemnification. Both the Architect and the Contractor require this protection from the nominated subcontractor. Thus if the Contractor had carried out these works unfettered by this imposition but in the event the frame had in fact collapsed, then the design fault responsibility would clearly rest eventually with the nominated subcontractor who would be (or should be) adequately insured in this respect. In fact a review of clause 27 would indicate that the Contractor could even object to the nomination of the proposed subcontractor unless such safeguards were available. For the Contractor to be aware of any collapse risk during encasement he would in effect be required to himself 'design' the structural frame concerned. Design responsibilities should never be blurred between the parties concerned and clause 4 requires some clarification in this respect so far as design compliance with Regulations are concerned, and the local authorities responsibilities to ensure compliance is uncertain.

In the pre-1963 form of contract it was possible for an Architect to give such an instruction regarding contract work by an express provision in clause 1 of that form. However, that express provision has since been removed. The Architect can only instruct and direct the Contractor as to the final result he requires, how the Contractor achieves these results is his own business *unless* specific provisions on *method or order* exist in Contract bills, drawings or a specification. The contract does provide in clause 6(3) for the Architect to test any work executed at any stage, this facility would enable an Architect to prevent unacceptable final results arising, furthermore the Contractor would have to pay the costs of such tests if they indicated the work did not or would not comply with the required final result.

CONCLUSIONS

The machine discipline causes the user to proceed logically step by step through the problem, and in particular the user is constantly cross-referred to another area of the contract that will influence the result. No matter at which clause the user starts the search, providing he enters any one of the clauses 1, 2, 3, 6, 11, 12, 24 (and any person studying the brief would be reasonably bound to enter at least one of these clauses), he will be directed eventually to the same logical conclusion and be directed to give all the correct contract notices at the correct time.

This can be evidenced if we assumed for instance the search was commenced at clause 1 instead of clause 2. Clause 1 refers to 3(3) which in turn asked the user whether working documents issued imposed any obligation beyond those in pre-contract documents. From here we are referred to 1(2) and asked if we think there is a divergence, if so, have we informed the Architect? This then takes us in turn to clause 11 and 12. If we turn to clause 11 this tells us that if the Architect has not issued an instruction requiring a variation, but nevertheless we consider delay has been caused, then clause 11 contains provision for him to later sanction his instruction, if he so decides, also that clause 23 should be referred to in the case of delay. If we are in doubt as to the basis of the instruction given then we are referred to clauses 1, 6, 11, 21, and 23.

And so the method ensures the user explores every relevant avenue signposted by the machine, almost regardless of the starting-point decided upon, working like an accurate road-map in conjunction with correct signposting.

Furthermore, from the review of clause 24 (24(1) Annotation) it can be seen how important it is to settle such matters in principle before commencing to use more expensive methods of construction to overcome such problems, although clause 24(2) enables the Contractor to go 'outside' the Contract to recover such costs in certain circumstances. The subroutine 24(1)(a) also states if delay had occurred then a written notice under clause 23 should be given and in extreme cases of delay clause 26 could be invoked to determine the Contractor's employment in the Contract. These final measures would have all been founded on correct contract provisions and procedures.

All of the foregoing can be gleaned from flowcharts without resort to machined monitoring. But thousands of small contractors, and owners, may prefer a 'machined' settlement obtained through a 'dispute centre' or trade bureaux in this way, rather than risk harming a relationship through subjective argument.

5 PROBLEMS IN PRACTICE

INTRODUCTION

There is in existence a great deal of expert legal commentary already available to the industry upon all aspects of this contract. Certain problems, however, seem to arise, or cause doubts, in practice in spite of this fountain of advice. This chapter examines some of these areas of potential dispute which fall partly outside the scope of the systems flowcharts, but nevertheless may be put to the system for a solution.

Judging from the areas of complexity evidenced in flowcharts (clauses 11 and 30), foremost amongst these problems has been the settlement of variations, claims, and the delay in issue of final certificates. These difficulties have combined to cause many cash flow crises within the industry. Commentators have suggested ways of reducing the difficulties ranging from the complete prohibition of change orders to advice on giving notice to arbitrate in the matter. The detailed analysis of contract provisions in respect of variations, clause 11(6) claims, and the settlement of final accounts will indicate that if the industry continues to accept variations then it must make some radical change in methods of managing variations.

Variable insurance policy practice, when coupled up to the very complex Standard Contract provisions, combines to create an almost incomprehensible mixture of meaningless verbiage, racked by exclusions and exceptions to such an extent that it is feared that many construction companies may be unaware of the exact cover required by the Contract, or afforded by their insurers. An attempt has been made therefore to clear some of the ground surrounding this particular problem.

All subcontractors are part and parcel of the construction process, but direct subcontractors are barely recognized in the Standard Conditions. They frequently labour along in an informal alliance with a contractor whilst collectively contributing the major share of a project. This attracts onerous risks and responsibilities without any recourse to the Employer, even for prompt payment, nor are there any effective remedies against dilatory Contractors. Nominated subcontractors on the other hand are provided for in detail. The section following on direct and nominated subcontractors indicates that standard forms of subcontract in use, are numerically less than contractors in existence. Some attention is therefore given to these relationships which are essential to the main contract.

The flowcharts in Chapter 3 should guide the user through problems of practice specifically concerned with the Conditions, but those described in the following pages require more than compliance with the flowchart discipline to ensure effective control.

It is also important to realize that many problems arise in practice which appear to be concerned with the Contract but when analysed are in fact not pure contract difficulties. An example follows to illustrate this point.

HOSPITAL PROJECT

Standard Form of Building Contract, 1963 edition with quantities

Tender date: June 1963

The hospital occupies the whole area of the site and involves excavating to reduce levels. Below the reduced levels, bases are excavated, concreted, and nominated subcontractors erect a steel structural frame.

Owing to the limited amount of original ground retained between each base it would be impossible for the steel erection crane to move around the site. It was also impossible for a crane to operate from outside the site boundary.

The Contractor therefore reduced the whole site area to the level of base tops to allow movement of the crane. Upon completion of crane activities the site was brought up to formation level with hardcore.

A dispute arose because the Contractor claimed:

(*a*) Additional excavation (between bases),

(*b*) Hardcore filling to make up levels,

but the Employers, Architect, and Quantity Surveyor maintained the Contractor should ascertain for himself the site conditions governing the work and make suitable financial allowances. The Contractor claimed that the Standard Method of Measurement required contract bills to deal with the matters claimed under (*a*) and (*b*) above.

A study of the dispute details will indicate:

1. The S.M.M. clause B20 calls for special attendance (*i.e.*, *provision of temporary access and hardstandings*) upon nominated subcontractors to be detailed in the contract bills.

2. The S.M.M. clause B13 calls for particulars to be given of temporary roads and access to be given in the contract bills, this is particularly necessary in this situation since at the pre-tender stage no contractor can be aware or have knowledge of nominated subcontractors' requirements other than those detailed under the 'general' and 'special' attendance terms.

3. The response of the Employers, Architect, and Quantity Surveyor could result in the tendering contractors realizing that contiguous excavations would cause access problems thus causing them to plan on phased work which would naturally cause extra costs to the nominated steel erectors and other sectors which would eventually rest with the client.

4. The named Quantity Surveyor must consider such problems when taking-off (R. D. Wood states in *Principles of Quantity Surveying*: 'contiguous excavation needs some careful thought . . .' by the taker-off). This is *not* to say he must consider *how* will the Contractor carry out the work but he must consider (and measure accordingly) factors emanating from the works design or location that generate work items measurable in accord with the S.M.M., as detailed under 1 above, otherwise the Contractor, unfettered by any stipulated restriction, *could* plan to carry out the work as detailed in 3 above.

Thus it can be seen that this dispute is not so directly concerned with the contract as with the so-called principles of the S.M.M. If this aspect can be agreed, that there is an error in the Contract Bills, then of course the flowcharts (clause 12) will indicate clearly how the matter should be dealt with. If this point is not predetermined, then inevitably the flowchart dispute program will ask:

> Contract Bills are in accordance with S.M.M. as stipulated?
> Answer 'Yes' or 'No'.

If both parties cannot agree whether or not there is an error, then the program will instruct the aggrieved party what to do in the circumstances, and later (clause 1(2)) states there is a breach.

This may appear to the other party to be a failure by the system to dispense 'the only correct solution'. But in fact it is a failure on the part of the S.M.M. to indicate unambiguously what duties the Quantity Surveyor has in this respect, which in turn must cause one of the users to input an incorrect response to the question put to him.

This raises a valid question whether the system can cope with incorrect responses to the binary questions. There is no reason to prevent checks being built into the system to obviate incorrect responses, particularly to certain questions which can be anticipated may result in genuinely objective but nevertheless incorrect responses. However, such checks would extend the program time involved for both correct and incorrect respondents. Suitable annotation could be used to warn users of the need to consider certain questions in depth prior to proceeding. However for the main part the binary questions and system have all been designed to eradicate possibly difficult questions.

VARIATIONS AND PROVISIONAL SUM WORK

> Building Research Station studies show that variations are usually too cheap. The present system in my view makes variations far too easy; they should be made more difficult, perhaps punitively . . . (1).

1. E. R. Skoyles, *Architect's Journal*, 28 January 1970.

The 'Action on Banwell' report maintained that variations 'are endemic to the building process' and the system, i.e. the *Standard Form of Building Contract* certainly makes variations easy. Without immediately adopting a punitive attitude to variations, some attention should be paid to current procedures, in an effort to identify reasons for the inadequate valuation of variations.

The Conditions of Contract provide a set of comprehensive rules for the valuation of variations in clause 11(4)(a)(b)(c) and (d). Alternatively, providing both parties agree, a 'separate agreement' may be reached without resort to the set of rules provided. Furthermore, if a Contractor considers loss and/or expense has arisen due to variations, then clause 11(6) entitles him to reimbursement of such sums. Clearly in view of these comprehensive provisions, any reasons there may be for inadequate valuations will not be found within the *Standard Form of Building Contract.*

The consequences of not reaching a 'separate agreement' may well be that insufficient time is available to enable the Quantity Surveyor to meticulously take-off, work-up, and produce draft Bills of Variation (valued in accordance with the rules), in time for inclusion into the Architect's interim certificate following the carrying out of the work involved. This is one major cause of cash flow problems in industry. Interim certificates are 'not in accordance with these Conditions . . .' (clause 35(2)) and this failure is commulative, resulting in widespread delay in final account settlement. But delays in valuing are not to be confused with improper or inadequate valuations, although delays will certainly contribute to the real costs of variations.

The valuation of variations is a clear-cut process particularly providing variations are for work of similar character and executed under similar conditions and do not change the character or conditions of other work to be carried out. The contract documents detail the contract character and physical conditions, but clause 11 permits reasonable changes in the work listed or shown in the documents. It is obvious, therefore, bearing clause 11 in mind, that most variations if issued in good time will not be unexpected and will not in themselves automatically change the character or conditions anticipated.

However, H. T. Burke in his paper 'Contractor's Claims and Other Problems' maintains:

> You have, in submitting your tender, offered to execute the works for the contract sum, these works being of certain character to be executed under certain conditions in a given time . . . and your obligation does not extend beyond that point.

But this alleged certainty of character and physical conditions is qualified by this all-important clause 11 condition which permits sums to be expended upon work which cannot entirely be foreseen and, more importantly, permits unpredictable variations in the work stipulated.

The original rates inserted by a Contractor, therefore, into a Bill must be for the listed work, but mindful of the strong possibility that provisional or variation work will have some influence upon his general continuity, productivity, and final work quantity.

However, Burke maintains:

> There is, indeed, hardly any variation which can be made to the contract work without altering the character or conditions under which the work has to be performed.

But since it is acknowledged that variations are in fact endemic to the building process, the Contractor must expect to assimilate a reasonable degree of variation before he could maintain his bill rates did not provide a suitable basis for the valuation of any variation, and this fact should be reflected by Contractors in the contract sum, via the rates therein. It follows that most variations must be valued using the bill rates, either as they stand or as a basis for valuations. If work is required which has absolutely no comparison with work already listed in the original bill, then a fair value or separate agreement can be arranged as provided for in clause 11(4).

The statement that almost any variation alters the character or physical conditions of the work to be performed, if correct, would in effect place a premium upon almost any variation by automatically causing that work to be valued at new rates above the level of the bill rates or, failing this, bringing clause 11(6) into play. This punitive theory appears to be out of line with the real purport of the present contract provisions which recognize that variations are in fact endemic. The Contractor cannot in effect therefore claim variation work is a nuisance and must be valued accordingly, or that his work is automatically hindered simply because variations are being issued. It is only when change, hindrance or omission can be claimed to be of an unreasonable degree that the Contractor's original bill rates will logically not suffice, and a new basis for valuation or clause 11(6) may be brought into play to cover his deficit. It would be true to say that any one variation is *capable* of altering the character or physical conditions under which the work has to be performed, but it is not correct to assume that any one or series of variations does in fact alter the character or conditions(2).

2. Swedish priced bills of quantity are used to value variations, but only up to a 25 per cent increase or decrease in the work varied, but always up to a contract value of 0·5 per cent of the contract sum (Bjorn Bindslev, 'Contract Procedures and Techniques in Europe and Scandinavia', *Chartered Surveyor*, September 1971).

Variations certainly militate against Contractors who wish to preplan work at the pre-contract stage. In practice, however, conventional estimating techniques often pay scant regard anyway to any detailed plan of work, method or required resources at the stage when rates are actually inserted into bills of quantity. Even formal programs put forward to satisfy contract conditions are not always necessarily followed in detail by site managers.

Thus the present-day Contract Bill is in effect a document largely containing national notional rates which have been formulated without detailed regard to interwoven activities or particular resources and methods. The consistency of these notional rates appears to confirm that contractors do recognize the uncertainty of the work programme as presented to them during the pre-contract stage. There is, however, a possibility that contractors may reduce their notional rates, when work is difficult to obtain, to such a level that their rates prove quite inadequate if the clause 11 provisions are vigorously employed. Claims are then wrongly put forward under the clause 11(6) heading to recover none the less genuine losses to the Contractor.

The Building Research Station has developed operational format bills of quantity which facilitate all site control and management functions. Paradoxically, the construction industry has not indicated yet that it is ready for a fundamental change in its source document format. The operational bill format, when developed into an acceptable form, would minimize both notional estimating and the use of variations. In the meantime, Contractors, in the face of reduced profits, relentlessly pare down their notional rates inserted into Contract Bills regardless of the undoubted affect that a reasonable degree of variation has upon productivity.

Any Contractor forwarding claims under clause 11(6) has an implied obligation to show evidence that detailed and skilled valuation took place originally, when establishing the Contract Bill rates. It is however, not uncommon to find standard rates being used by Contractors for the majority of operations in many Bills for works of widely differing character and physical conditions. Bureaux pricing is sometimes used whereby works are rapidly rated without proper regard for a Contractor's real capabilities, resources, or even a site visit.

It would not be difficult in such circumstances for Architects and Quantity Surveyors to resist clause 11(6) claims on the grounds that loss and/or expense arose more by virtue of unskilled estimating than by the anticipative tribulations inflicted by variations.

Operational estimating techniques must replace our less skilfull pre-contract methods if the identification of cost and loss, etc., under clause 11(6) is to be founded upon skilled valuation rather than notional convictions. This would then lead to variations being valued so that they would not be described as 'too cheap'.

CLAIMS BY CONTRACTORS TO RECOVER DIRECT LOSS AND/OR EXPENSE

The Contract contains the words direct loss and/or expense (or damage) to describe the damages recoverable by the Contractor in the event of certain acts being committed by the Employer. The words 'loss' and 'expense' on the face of it give no guidance upon the question of overhead costs or profit. Furthermore the word 'direct' is, to a layman, quite misleading.

Legal understanding, and interpretation, of these words indicate that the Contractor is entitled to recover direct costs caused by additional or more expensive methods or losses by reduced productivity. In addition, indirect costs such as project and general overheads, interest upon working capital, and, above all perhaps, anticipated profits are all recoverable when such words are used to define the extent of reimbursement.

Categories of admissable claims

There are four categories of claim admissable under the Contract. Two of these categories have express procedures laid down in detail under clauses 11(6), 24, 26, and 34(3).

The four categories are:

1. (*a*) To recover direct loss or expense caused by variations or provisional sum work *(clause 11(6))*.
   (*b*) To recover direct loss or expense caused by disturbance of regular progress *(clauses 24 and 34(3))*.

2. To recover loss or damaged caused by determination *(clause 26)*.

3. To recover damages caused by a breach of Conditions where no express procedures for making claims are laid down.

4. To recover damages upon rescinding the Contract due to frustration.

Categories 1 and 2 are to be judged by the Architect according to the Contract.

Categories 3 and 4 are outside the Architect's jurisdiction.

Claims under category 1 and 2, are intended by the Contract to be settled with a minimum of delay and a maximum of efficiency because the Contract envisaged such events occurring and saw fit to formalize and streamline the procedures accordingly.

Category 1(a). Direct loss or expense caused by variations or provisional sum work (clause 11(6)).
If a 'fair valuation' is not made under the rules laid down in clause 11(4) and if a 'separate agreement' cannot be reached to value variations or provisional sum work which the Contractor claims have unreasonably affected the character or physical conditions, then such matters can be rectified by the use of the clause 11(6) facilities. The direct loss and/or expense suffered may far exceed any 'fair valuation' that might be placed upon the activity or activities concerned.

Category 1(b). Direct loss or expense caused by disturbance of regular progress (clause 24 and 34(3))
If the progress of the Works is affected by any of the detailed causes listed in clause 24(1)(a)(b)(c)(d) or (e) or in clause 34(3), then the Contractor may have such breaches rectified by the use of the detailed procedures within those clauses.

Category 2. Direct loss or damaged caused by determination (clause 26)
If the Employer commits breaches as detailed in clause 26(1)(a)(b)(c) or (d) and the Contractor properly determines his own employment in the Contract, apart from recovering the costs listed in subclause (2)(a) and (b)(i)(ii)(iii)(iv) and (v), the Contractor is entitled to recover any direct loss and/or damage caused by the determination.

The Contract inconsistently in this clause (1)(c)(i) and (iii) regards suspension of the Works by reason of 'force majeure' or 'civil commotion' in the same light as breaches caused by matters within the Employer's control. The Contract right to damages and a lien upon all unfixed goods and materials in such circumstances conflicts with more equitable principles that damages in such situations should not be recoverable.

Category 3. Claims for a breach of any condition where no express procedures are laid down within the Contract
The Employer may for example commit breaches which prevent a Contractor from starting the Works by (*a*) failing to give any possession, or (*b*) prevent the Contractor from proceeding as planned by failing to give full or prompt possession on the date stated in the Appendix. Such breaches would give rise to damage in the case of (*a*) equal to the anticipated profit on the Works, and in the case of (*b*) equal to the direct loss and/or expense caused. Any claim made under this heading cannot be settled by the Architect although the Employer could make an express arrangement with the Architect to ascertain what damages had arisen, and to settle such a dispute for the Employer.

Category 4. Claims to rescind the Contract due to frustration
This category of claim rarely occurs but could arise in connection with hostilities as detailed in clause 32(3). The Law Reform (Frustrated Contracts) Act 1943 would apply in such events. Frustration is not readily defined in contractual terms. The recovery of damage in such claims may well be nominal, although confusingly clause 26(1)(c)(i) and (iii) as previously stated do include 'force majeure' and 'civil commotion' (which are both possible grounds for claiming frustration) as contractual grounds for the recover of damage under that clause.

The admissibility of sums claimed
The words direct loss and/or expense (or damage). really mean all the financial damages not too remote that they could not be directly attributable to the event.

Damages can be divided into two categories:
(*a*) Direct damages (*b*) Consequential damages
Direct damage can occur in operations carried out, and consequential damage can arise directly from those events to cause loss and/or expense.

(*a*) *Direct damage headings*

1. Main Contractor's labour utilization and productivity, material costs and waste factors, plant (including scaffold and other like equipment) utilization, and expenses.
2. Direct subcontractors' work.
3. Direct suppliers' charges (increases due to variations reducing quantity, etc.)
4. Nominated subcontractors' work (claimed from the Contractor).
5. Nominated suppliers' charges (claimed from the Contractor).

(*b*) *Consequential damage headings*

1. Preliminaries:
    - Project overheads
    - Firm price allowances
    - Bonds
    - Insurances
    - Water/electricity
    - Other risk or item allowances.
2. General overheads costs.
3. Working capital costs.
4. Profit capable of being earned.

Claims procedures
The Contract lays down implicit procedures to be followed when claims under categories 1 and 2 are being made. Clause 30(5)(c), chart 4–5 (pp. 130–31) illustrate this point. However, there are circumstances when a claim which might fail through non-compliance with the stated procedures could still succeed by submission of the claim under category 3. Clause 24(1)(a) chart (p. 92) illustrates this particular point.

Example. If a claim is made under clause 24(1)(a) without a written application being made 'within a reasonable time', the chart indicates that there has in effect been a breach of clause 3(4) and such breaches are rectifiable alternatively under category 3 claims. But any damages agreed ought to be considerably adjusted since the Contractor, by not giving notice, has not done everything he reasonably could be expected to do to mitigate the loss, etc., caused.

There is an implied obligation under clause 11(6) and 24 upon the Contractor to give evidence to the Architect of any loss and/or expense he may claim to have suffered as a result of variations or the disruptive causes listed. The Contractor must assist the Architect or Quantity Surveyor in their duties by ensuring claims made are:

1. Based soundly upon contractual rights.
2. Accurate in every detail.
3. Backed up with factual information.
4. Preceded by the correct contractual notices and procedures.

Furthermore, this duty extends to mitigating the claimed loss or expense in any reasonable way.

So long as conventional bills only require rates to be representative of a Contractor's notional resources all lumped together, the establishing of the effect of variation or disruption in monetary terms will continue to be based upon arbitrary percentage factors added to or taken from those bill rates. In the circumstances this method of settlement appears to be the only reasonable and practical way, in the absence of more sophisticated estimating and site control techniques. Such techniques cannot be developed if industry and the Contract continues to permit partially designed buildings to be commenced and the inevitable variations to be declared endemic.

Prime cost sums

Subclause (3) should be separated from clause 11 and placed with clauses 27 and 28. There is no Contract provision for dealing with variations in prime cost work. Original prime cost sums should be required by the Contract to be accurately assessed and described. This is at present implied but not explicit.

The Contractor must not use his power under clause 26 to determine if instructions given to him under clause 11(3) cause suspension of the Works. But if a variation in nominated subcontract work is required this would require an instruction to be issued under clause 11(1) then if this caused suspension in the Works the Contractor would be entitled to determine using his powers under clause 26. The original completion date for a contract is set inclusive of prime cost and provisional sum work, the absence from clause 23(e) of any reference to instructions issued under 11(3) confirms therefore that:

(*a*) The Architect cannot create new prime cost or provisional sums.

(*b*) Clauses 27 and 28 ensure that nominated persons must comply within the Contractor's programme.

(*c*) Provisional sums must be confined to works which cannot entirely be foreseen (as defined in S.M.M. A7) which implies a small part of the whole Works.

There would appear to be a case for the inclusion of delay in provisional sum instruction under clause 11(3) into clause 23(e) because of the element of unknown in such work.

INSURANCE MATTERS

Introduction

The clauses 18, 19, and 20 deal with the parties liabilities, indemnities, and insurance responsibilities.

The complexity of these clauses when coupled up to the bewildering methods of varying policies to provide flexibility in cover, can in itself create a substantial risk, and problems or disputes.

In effect, the Contract is calling for insurances which on the face of it are not available from the British insurance profession. Furthermore, insurance companies do not have a standard form of insurance policy which would enable the parties concerned to readily see how close the available policies come to satisfying the Contract requirements.

This fact was recognized as far as clause 19(2)(a) was concerned when in 1968 a revision to accord with the current insurance practise resulted. The British Insurance Association advised on the redrafting of that Contract clause resulting in insurance being readily available for the perils listed therein at reasonable premiums.

Table A (p. 179) indicates the policies available to the construction industry and their relevance in the Standard Form.

Table B (p. 180) indicates some of the exclusions or endorsements to be found in the relevant available policies and whether such exclusions, etc., are acceptable under the Standard Form.

Exclusions and endorsements are used by insurers to prevent certain loss or to motivate the insured to take care, or to reduce premiums. These variations are a result of claims experience or varying assessment by the underwriter of the risks.

Exclusions may exclude certain risks, endorsements may delete exclusions. Some endorsements may delete an exclusion but impose an unrealistic limit of indemnity within the endorsement.

The limit of indemnity can be varied in the case of a Public Liability Policy. A basic limit may be £250,000 but the 'collapse' perils therein may be only £10,000.

Any attempt to increase such a limit may involve substantial excess provisions coupled with an increase in premium of substantial sums particularly if the insurer is not a specialist in construction insurance matters.

By reference to the charts 18, 19, and 20 (pp. 72–83) together with Tables A and B it can be deduced that the Architect cannot be expected to have expert knowledge of insurance matters under the Contract, or in his terms of engagement with the Employer (unless an express agreement to this effect is entered into). However, the Contract expects the Architect to consider certain insurance matters at the pre-contract stage and prior to commencement of the Works.

The Contract bills must specify the limit of indemnity required in respect of clause 19(1)(b) and do likewise in the case of clause 19(2)(a) insurance provisions which must be the subject of a provisional sum if this insurance is specifically required. The bills should also instruct the Contractor to insure as required by clauses 19(1)(a) and (b) and this should then be adequate discharge of the Architect's duties at this pre-contract stage.

The Contractor must then immediately post-contract, produce and cause any subcontractor to produce for inspection by the Employer evidence that proper insurances are in existence and are being maintained. It is at this stage that any Employer (or Architect if he has expressly agreed to do so) or Contractor (in respect of subcontractors) will run into a myriad of matters to consider, as detailed in Tables A and B.

Apart from the exclusions to be considered there are certain matters to check to avoid accidental default by:

1. The nature and extent of a Contractor's (or subcontractor's) business as actually entered in a policy should not conflict with the nature and extent of the proposed Works (or subcontract works). Certain policy conditions in this respect may also be violated by mistake or otherwise.

2. The Employer's Liability Policy should be extended to cover 'labour only' subcontractors by endorsement and a check made that the payroll costs are being added to the Contractor's own payroll total to ensure that cover (which is based upon such totals) is provided.

3. The Public Liability Policy should also be extended to cover 'labour only' subcontractors.

4. *The Public Liability Policy* should have a limit of indemnity never less than £250,000 for any one occurrence of personal injury, etc., and the limit for property claims should be set to reflect the value, size, nature, and extent of the Works and adjacent property, particularly mindful of the collapse type peril which may be subjected to much lower indemnity levels.

5. *The Contractor's All Risks Policy* if issued for a specific contract must be for the Works period (i.e. to Practical Completion) and any extension in the Works period must have a similar insurance extension. When an extension does

occur an insurer may vary the terms especially if a claim has arisen during the earlier Works period. An annual type policy obviates the latter problem but the policy usually has a higher excess and has a maximum liability and/or duration for any one Works period imposed.

6. *The Fire and Special Perils Policy* risks are also covered under a Contractor's All Risks Policy at a fractionally higher premium. Any Employer insuring under clause 20 should take out a Contractor's All Risks Policy. If a building is to house equipment which is extremely valuable (for example, computers) and such equipment is to be delivered under a separate contract say just before Practical Completion it could under clause 20 suffer damage from one of the perils listed in that clause. The Contractor's own Public Liability Policy would cover such risks, but the limit of indemnity in his Public Liability Policy may be only a fraction of the sum total damage.

7. Contractors seeking insurances are required to complete proposal forms describing and classifying their activities, under headings of 'hazardous' undertakings.

From this proposal the insurer assesses the premium.

If, however, in practice the Contractor becomes involved largely in 'hazardous' undertakings which on his proposal form were marked 'nil' or 'minimal' there may well be problems arising in the event of a claim.

Typical 'hazardous' undertakings are:

(1) The construction, alteration or repair of sewers, involving open excavation work exceeding 5 m in depth.

(2) Any work of demolition except demolition:
  (i) of buildings or part of a building, when such work forms part of a contract for reconstruction, alteration or repair by the insured,
  (ii) of other structures not exceeding 4 m in height and not forming part of any building.

(3) Tree-felling, pile-driving, blasting, diving, tunnelling, water diversion, work within or behind dams; quarrying or sand or gravel-getting.

(4) Erecting steel or iron frame structures.

(5) The construction, alteration, or repair of towers, steeples, blast furnaces, or chimney shafts, railroads, docks, or harbours.

(6) The digging or boring of wells; the repair of wells exceeding 6 m in depth from surface.

(7) The plastering of churches, chapels, cinemas, exhibitions, music halls, public halls, or theatres.

(8) Painting or glazing work on roofs, hangars, bridges, viaducts, gasometers, blast furnaces, or other lofty structures.

(9) The construction, alteration, or repair of viaducts or bridges.

(10) Operations of a special hazard not specified above (particulars to be given).

It is clearly a tall order to expect any of the parties involved in the Contract to check insurance matters in such depth, however, the fact remains that there is lurking in that verbiage possible ruination on both sides. Some simple system of checking must in the near future be found.

The Employer's Liability (Defective Equipment) Act 1969 now requires an employer to be liable for defects in equipment even if he was not negligent. The Employer's Liability (Compulsory Insurance) Act 1969 which came into force on 1 January 1972 will bring about revisions and review of such insurance policies.

A standard set of basic policies for construction work consisting of:

Employer's Liability Policy

Public Liability Policy

Contractor's All Risks Policy

Fire and Special Perils Policy

19(2)(a) Liability Policy

using standard phraseology for the policies and exclusions would enable the parties to check whether exclusions were acceptable still leaving the insurer with the veto provided by the exclusion.

Table A. Indicating policies available and their relevance in the Standard Form

Policy name	*Details of cover provided*	*19(1)(a)*	*19(1)(b)*	*19(2)(a)*	*20[A]*	*20[B]*	*20[C]*	*14(2)*
Employer's Liability	Liabilities of the Employer (i.e. in this case the Contractor) to his own employees for personal injuries or death and the consequential loss arising.	○						
Public Liability	Liabilities of the Contractor for claims by the public (other than from his own employees) for personal injury or death and the consequential loss arising. Liabilities of the Contractor for claims by the public for loss or damage to property real or personal (other than the Contractor's own property) and the consequential loss arising. (This policy could be extended to encompass the Employer's responsibilities under clause 19(2)(a) but a special '19(2)(a) Liability Policy' or an extended 'Contractor's All Risks' Policy would be advisable.)	○	○	●				
19(2)(a) Liability	Liabilities of the Client for claims by third parties for adjacent properties and the consequential loss arising.			○				
Contractor's All Risks	Loss or damage to the Works and certain materials or goods by any perils but *not* the consequential loss arising. (This Policy assists the Public Liability Policy cover for clause 19(1)(b) by covering Works property in the insureds control which is excluded from the Public Liability Policy. This Policy can be extended to cover clause 19(2)(a) risks for the Employer (Client). This Policy can be extended to cover materials and goods stored off-site.)		●	●	○	○	○	●
Fire and Special Perils	Loss or damage to the Works and certain materials or goods caused by only the perils listed in the Policy but *not* the consequential loss arising.				○	○	○	
Contractor's Combined	Liabilities and loss or damage as detailed under: Employer's Liability Public Liability Contractor's All Risks } This Policy can be on an annual or single contract basis.	○	○		○			
'Liability' Policy	Liabilities only (*not* loss or damage) as detailed under: Employer's Liability Public Liability	○	○					

Table B. Indicating some exclusions or endorsements and their acceptibility under the Standard Form

Policy name	*Exclusions or endorsements*	*Probable*	*Possible*	*Acceptable*		
				Yes	*No*	*?*
Employer's Liability	(1) Activities outside the U.K.	O		O		
	(2) Hazardous activities.	O				O
Public Liability	(1) Activities outside the U.K.	O		O		
	(2) Hazardous activities. (The perils listed under clause 19(2)(a) are normally excluded from this policy hence the need for a special policy or the removal of these exclusions to provide for the special insurances for the client under that 19(2)(a) clause if this policy is extended.)	O				O
	(3) Contractual Liabilities express or implied. (The Contractor's Plant Association Hire Documents make their operator an 'employee' of the Contractor hiring, thus making the Contractor responsible for him and his acts. An adjoining owner may grant rights for cranes or persons to pass over his land subject to no liabilities upon that owner.)		O		O	
	(4) Liabilities for acts of subcontractors.		O		O	
	(5) Injuries, etc., to employees.	O		O		
	(6) War and kindred risks, radioactive contamination, explosive nuclear assemblies, sonic boom damage.	O		O		
	(7) Property belonging to or held in trust by or in the care or control of the insured. (Property belonging to the insured is always excluded but the rest of the exclusion is unacceptable if under clause 6(3) tests of other persons property is called for.)	O			O	

Table B *continued*

Policy name	*Exclusions or endorsements*	*Probable*	*Possible*	*Acceptable*		
				Yes	*No*	*?*
Public Liability *continued*	(8) Property on which the insured is or has been working upon. (This is to exclude defective workmanship, but it is not acceptable when a peril listed in clause 20 occurs.)	O				O
	(9) Vibration, removal, or weakening of support.		O		O	
	(10) Fire and/or explosion. (This exclusion is acceptable if other policies carry the risks.)	O				O
	(11) Use of passenger lifts, locomotives, aircraft and watercraft. (This exclusion is acceptable if other policies carry the risks or if the risks cannot arise.)	O				O
	(12) Use of cranes or hoists.		O		O	
	(13) Use of hoists or lifts for work-people on site. (This exclusion is acceptable if other policies carry the risks or if the risks cannot arise.)		O			O
	(14) Defective drains, sewers, pollution.		O		O	
	(15) Licensed motor vehicles and mechanical plant.	O		O		
	(16) Unlicensed motor vehicles and mechanical plant.		O		O	
	(17) Products liability. (Any Contractor who supplies goods or materials (for example, joinery) requires this cover for 6 or 12 years from Final Certificate.)	O				O
	(18) Inevitable or deliberate injuries or damage. (For example, if in 500 dwellings faults develop in say 10 which the insurer accepts under the Product Liability which is not excluded, the insurer may then claim the faults in the first 10 units are inherent and that it is inevitable that the faults will manifest themselves in the remaining 490 dwellings. This in effect excludes defective workmanship.)	O		O		

Table B *continued*

Policy name	*Exclusions or endorsements*	*Probable*	*Possible*	*Acceptable*		
				Yes	*No*	*?*
Contractor's All Risks	(1) War and kindred risks, radioactive contamination, explosive nuclear assemblies, sonic boom damage.	O		O		
	(2) Defective workmanship, material, or design plans or specifications.	O		O		
	(3) Loss or damage to plant and equipment, own or hired.	O				O
	(4) Loss solely due to use or occupation by the client of any portion for which Practical Completion has occurred.	O		O		
	(5) Wear and tear and gradual deterioration.	O		O		
Fire and Special Perils	(1) War and kindred risks, radioactive contamination and explosive nuclear assemblies, sonic boom damage.	O		O		
	(2) Consequential loss (including loss of profits). (The consequential loss referred to here refers to a business interruption which is possible to cover under a separate policy for 'Business Interruption' or 'Advance Profits'.)	O		O		
	(3) Fire through the property's own spontaneous combustion or heating.	O		O		
	(4) Frost subsidence or landslip. (A 'frost' is not a 'storm' and is covered under the Contractor's All Risks Policy.)	O		O		
	(5) Damage to fences, gates, and boardings.	O			O	
	(6) Damage to movable property in the open.	O			O	
	(7) Riot and civil commotion loss or damage where: (*a*) caused by requisition by the authorities, (*b*) caused by cessation of work.	O		O		

Table B *continued*

Policy name	*Exclusions and endorsements*
19(2)(a) Liability Contractor's Combined 'Liability' Policy	These three policies consist of combinations of the three basic policies: Employer's Liability Public Liability Contractor's All Risks except the 'Liability' Policy does not include the Contractor's All Risks Policy. Any exclusions and endorsements to be found in the basic policies listed above will therefore appear in any combination of such policies.

Clause 18. Liabilities and indemnities
This clause details the liabilities and indemnities the Contractor is to be responsible for under the Contract. Clauses 19 and 20 follow to detail the formal insurances required by the Contract.

Clause 18 (1) (Persons)
This provides clear-cut procedures in the event of any injury or death to any persons. Any claim whatever is deemed by the Contract to be the Contractor's liability and he must indemnify the Employer in any proceedings whatsoever *unless* the claim was due to any act or neglect of the Employer or any person for whom the Employer is responsible. (The Contract is silent as to whether the Architect or Quantity Surveyor or Clerk of Works are regarded as persons for whom the Employer is responsible but clause 29 and 34 does specify two classes of such person, i.e. artists, etc., and third parties permitted to examine antiquities found.)

This is a sensible arrangement, most claims rest with the Contractor, in any event thereby removing, for the moment, the question whether any of the multitude of subcontractors or even the Employer himself or person he is responsible for are to answer such claims. In cases of personal injuries or deaths, arrangements that clearly pinpoint the person responsible are socially (and contractually) desirable. The Contractor has a contract right under clause 19(1)(a) to cause any subcontractor to insure the same liabilities as the Contractor holds in respect of personal injuries and death, but the Contract makes the Contractor responsible if any subcontractor defaults in respect of insurance provisions.

Clause 19(1)(a) calls for insurance (with no limit of indemnity) from the Contractor to cover his liabilities and such insurance carries a right of subrogation for the insurer to recover any damages that may be apportioned to other persons in an action thereby enabling the responsibility to finally rest with the right person.

However the indemnity given by the Contractor (and by the subcontractor to the Contractor) could not be relied upon in the case *Richardson* v. *Bucks, C. C. and Others* (1971), Times Law Reports, where Richardson sued Bucks, C. C., Sydney Green (Civil Engineering) Ltd., and Roads Reconstruction (Contracting) Ltd. (Employer, Contractor, Subcontractor respectively), for injuries sustained by falling from a scooter. The Courts held that Bucks, C. C. and Others were not responsible, but their costs of defending the action to which they were entitled could not be recovered from Richardson who was impecunious. The Court of Appeal decided on the question of such costs, that all three defendants should pay their own, on the basis that the indemnity was intended to apply to matters arising from the construction work that the Contractor (or subcontractors) could have prevented by taking proper care, and was not intended to indemnify the Employer against fanciful or malicious (and therefore unsuccessful) claims.

The Employer must clearly have a Public Liability Policy and Employer's Liability Policy in existence to cover his activities as a building 'Owner' as from the date of possession given in the Appendix. The Employer's Liability (Compulsory Insurance) Act 1965 requires an Employer to be insured for at least £2 million from any one claim for bodily injury or disease sustained by employees. Certain bodies are exempt from the Acts requirements to insure and local authorities are one such body.

Clause 18(2) (Property)
The wide indemnity provided by the Contractor under clause 18(1) is not required of him under clause 18(2) which deals with property (real or personal). This indemnity given by the Contractor is conditional upon him having been negligent or has omitted to do something or has defaulted in his obligations in some way, or his servants, subcontractors, or agents.

This change in method from clause 18(1) is perhaps sensible since claims under this head could sometimes result from faults in design rather than construction. The Contractor indemnifies the Employer therefore *providing* he has been negligent, etc., or his servants, subcontractors, or agents.

However, the indemnity given by the Contractor could not be relied upon by the Employer in the case *A.M.F. (International) Ltd.* v. *Magnet Bowling Ltd and G. P. Trentham Ltd.* (1968), 1 W.L.R. 1028, where the Employer was held to have been negligent towards a third party, bringing the claim, by the Contractor, that caused the loss and damage in question. The Employer did, however, recover his contribution in fact from the Contractor due to the breaches in the Contract.

Because of this case some Bills may call for joint insurance under clause 19(1)(b) to protect the Employer but since the Contract does not call for joint insurance and clause 12(1) expressly states the Bills must not alter or modify the Conditions this procedure is not effective, the Contract can be altered but tampering with the form is not recommended, therefore separate insurance arrangements dealing with such matters should be made by the Employer. (There is no reason at all why both parties should not agree to joint insurance without altering the Contract or calling for this in the Contract Bills.)

The Contractor has a Contract right under clause 19(1)(b) to cause any subcontractor to insure the same liabilities as the Contractor holds under this clause in respect of damage to any property (real or personal), both the Works themselves and adjacent property owned by the Employer or third persons.

Conclusions

Clause 18

1. The differences in the indemnities in clause 18(1) for personal injury and in clause 18(2) for damage to property are confusing to the user. Uniform indemnities would prove simpler and ought not affect the premiums required.

2. The word 'injury' is used to denote both personal injury and damage to property. This should be avoided to ensure clarity.

3. The separation of indemnity, liability, and insurance provisions under clauses 18, 19, and 20 (not forgetting clause 14(2)) does not simplify the understanding. These matters would best be dealt with under one heading.

4. The exception in the indemnity required of the Contractor, if the Employer is negligent, appears to extend to the Employers breach of statutory duties but in fact *Hosking* v. *De Havilland Ltd.* (1949), 1 A.E.R. 540, indicates that this is not so, the Contract should therefore clarify this point.

5. The question of the Employer's responsibility for the Architect, Quantity Surveyor, and Clerk of Works requires confirmation, to be consistent with the express statements to that effect in clauses 29 and 34.

Insurances

Clauses 19 and 20 (optional 30(2A) and 14(2))
These two clauses stipulate the risks which are to be formally transferred to insurance companies (except where Local Authorities are the Employers and choose to carry the risk under the 20(B) option).

Clause 19(1)(a) calls for insurance to match the requirements of clause 18(1).

Clause 19(1)(b) calls for insurance to match the requirements of clause 18(2).

Clause 19(2)(a) calls for insurance to cover the Employer against special risks inherent in the Works, but in respect of damage to property outside the Works.

Clause 20(A)(B)(C) calls for insurance to cover the Works against perils outside the control of either the Contractor or Employer.

However, 'No insurance policy covers every risk although a number of policy holders expect it to do so, especially when a claim occurs . . .'(3).

3. F. N. Eaglestone, *The RIBA Contract and the Insurance Market.* (PH Press Ltd, 1964).

Clauses 19(1)(a) and (b)

Contract Bills frequently call upon the Contractor to provide unattainable insurances or on the other hand some give no details at all. Since Public Liability policies are always subject to a limit of indemnity it is clear that the Architect must give details of the limit in this respect in the Contract Bills, this detail coupled with instructions to insure as required in clauses 19(1)(a) and (b) will be sufficient minimum detail to satisfy both the Contract and the Contract Bills requirement. Any attempt to impose more onerous liabilities or obtain wider indemnities will run against clause 12 which prohibits the alteration or modification of the Contract by anything stated in Contract Bills.

The limits of indemnity are therefore to be considered in the pre-contract stage and will be governed by the size, nature, value, and eventual contents of the Works together with its adjacent properties and environment. But the degree of risk is not *pro rata* to the size or value of the project, hence insurers will grant high levels of indemnity with low increases in premium for such policies as they have available. These policies are subject to exclusions some of which the insurer will remove upon an increase of premium but some exclusion must remain inviolable. The Contract Bills should therefore indicate in addition to limits of indemnity, the exclusions and endorsement which will not be acceptable. This information will enable the Contractor's estimator and insurer to evaluate the particular project requirements (see Table B for details of exclusions, etc., acceptable or otherwise).

Clause 19(2)(a)

The Contract requires the Architect to consider at the design stage whether the proposed Works might at any period in time be likely to cause damage to adjacent property by:

collapse
subsidence
vibration
weakening or removal of support
lowering ground water

caused by risks inherent in the Works and not by negligence on the part of the Contractor.

If the answer to this question is in any way in the affirmative the Architect should approach suitable insurers, who specialize in such matters, to conduct a survey of the risks and to advise the Architect on the limits of indemnity to be provided. The quotation of the insurer will include the survey fee and this sum will become the provisional sum required under clause 19(2)(a) to be stated in Bills. There will be an excess to bear in the event of any claim which will be the Employer's responsibility to pay in the event of a claim arising, this excess sum might be added into the provisional sum or alternatively made a Contingency Item.

Although the insurance is said to be in joint names in the Contract this insurance policy will not indemnify the Contractor and any claim exceeding the insurance limit will rest solely with the Employer.

It must be realized that such insurance does not cover the Works themselves, nor personal injury to third parties caused by the perils listed. But since any collapse, etc., would indicate a probable fault in design, this would be a matter for the Architect's own Professional Indemnity.

However, there are certain aspects in this matter worthy of consideration:

1. What is the limit of the Architect's indemnity and how does this compare with the likely financial costs arising from a claim or claims?

2. What is the Contractor's responsibility under clause 1(1) wherein he is required to carry out and complete the Works regardless of the fact that clause 19(2)(a) does not cover the Works?

3. What is the Contractor's responsibility under clause 4(1) wherein he is required to be responsible for *any* breach of Building Regulations, etc., and collapse, etc., would indicate the likelihood of such a breach?

4. The Contractor's own insurances (and the special clause 19(2)(a) policies) will normally exclude faults in design and

the risks listed in this clause will be excluded from his Public Liability Policy.

5. Faults in design can prove lengthy and costly matters to decide; what is the Contractor's position, where such matters arise, in respect of his technical, legal, and consequential costs (delay, expense on the Works, etc.) arising from such events?

All of these matters are bound together. The Contractor's own All Risks Policy would cover his costs in proving he was not responsible with the exception of his consequential costs flowing directly from the event. An extension to his policy can be made to cover such risks and in the light of our movement towards more complex and specialized constructions and the Architect's current problems in obtaining adequate indemnity, it certainly bears earnest consideration.

If the Contractor was found to be in some way responsible for such damage his own insurances would normally cover such events, however policies are usually subjected to a separate and lower indemnity level (usually £10,000) for 'collapse' type risks. In the light of the Contractor's clause 4 responsibilities (see 3 above) this limit must be reassessed by Contractors and Employers who may face ruinous responsibilities which they had though to be insured against, up to the limit of indemnity (normally twenty-five times greater) for all the other risks covered under that policy.

It should be made clear that the Contractor's responsibilities are unfortunately not clearly defined under clause 4 of the Contract. The tortuous and unintelligible Building Regulations describe the most fundamental construction requirements in oblique ways, the possibility exists therefore that the Contractor may in some way have to bear some responsibility for breaching statutory requirements. Furthermore there may possibly be a breach under clause 21 which requires the Contractor not to delay the Works, failing which he pays liquidated damages under clause 22. This hazard may warrant cover under the premise that if the chance of such a happening is remote, the premium will be low, if the chance is not so remote one should have insurance, for certain.

The risks listed in this subclause are all continuing ones which may manifest themselves several years after the Final Certificate. This justifies the Employer insuring accordingly.

The Employer as a 'building owner' should always have an Employer's Liability Policy for his activities as such an 'owner'. The Employer's *Public* Liability Policy would cover him in the example quoted earlier of personal injury occurring to a third party due to collapse, etc., of the Works due to clause 19(2)(a) perils.

Clause 20

The Contract requires the full value of the Works to be insured plus any percentage additions required for professional fee costs (Local Authorities must state a sum attributable to the extra staff costs in the event of a total reconstruction occurring).

The 'full value' in practice varies as the work proceeds due to variations and fluctuations in costs. Insurers therefore adjust the initial premium charged by eventual comparison with the final contract sum on practical completion.

The Contract clearly intends the insurances under clause 20 to provide, in the event of a claim arising, the sum attributable to the Works damaged to be assessed from the prices contained in Contract Bills. Thus to quote an extreme example: A contract for £100,000 is completed but one day prior to Practical Completion a peril listed under clause 20 causes total destruction requiring total reconstruction. The Contract clearly anticipates a clear-cut settlement in the sum of £100,000 for the reconstruction plus the percentage for fees. The Contract does not clearly indicate where sums for demolition, removal of debris, and increases in cost are secured, but it does make clear the fact that only monies due from insurances will be available to the Contractor.

Now in practice certain Assessors may decide that their material damage policies normally simply cover the cost of putting right the material damage suffered and by cost we mean net cost excluding profit! Furthermore if they paid Contract Bill rates *in toto*, the Contractor would benefit handsomely from this calamity by making twice as much profit from the same Works. They will say also that 'if we do not pay you profit, you will make a loss, which you should have insured against with either an extension to the policy in hand or a separate policy'.

Clarification of the interpretation by Assessor and Insurers of the word 'cost' appears necessary.

The Contract clause 20 does not require consequential loss to be covered by formal insurance but there is no reason why the Contractor may not have such cover. This may prove invaluable to a Contractor who negligently (fails to tarpaulin an open roof, etc.) causes a catastrophe listed in this clause. The Contractor might hopefully turn to clause 23(c) to obtain an extension of time to complete, thus saving the payment of liquidated damages, but the Architect should rightly indicate that under clause 23 such extensions are only available *if the Contractor used constantly his best endeavours to prevent such delay*. The liquidated damages would thus be payable by the insurer. (The Employer might also consider taking out an Advanced Profits Policy if he was unable to assess such profits when the liquidated damages sum was being established.)

Clause 14(2)

The Contractor is made responsible for insurances under this clause where under clause 30(2A) materials and goods whose value has been included for payment in an Architect's certificate are stored in premises other than the site (or adjacent).

The clause does not stipulate what insurances are required and the risks to be covered. The Architect is not required to see evidence of insurances or the Contractor to show evidence of satisfactory cover. In the event of the Contractor failing to insure or to maintain such insurances there is no procedure therein for the Employer himself to insure and deduct the costs. The in-transit risks are not dealt with and the subcontractors or suppliers concerned are not mentioned.

Clause 30(2A) lays down numerous conditions before payment can be made. One of the conditions being that the Contractor must be the 'Owner' of such materials or goods. In view of this, insurance must be the sole responsibility of the Contractor otherwise many problems can arise in checking any other persons insurances and any failure on the part of a third person left to insure property could leave the Employer in a defenceless position if a default occurred.

Conclusions

Clauses 19 and 20 (optional 30(2A) and 14(2))

1. The construction industry and insurance profession must agree some measure of standardization of basic terms and conditions that would enable the industry to efficiently compare exclusions, endorsements, and policies, together with the relevant premiums. The final decisions on insurances must lie with either the Employer or Contractor and not the insurance broker.

2. Clarification on the joint name insurance under both clause 19(1) and 19(2)(a) is required in view of the *A.M.F. (International) Ltd.* v. *Magnet Bowling Ltd.* It appears that clause 19(1) would benefit from joint name provision and clause 19(2)(a) would be more sensibly expressed in solely the Employer's name.

3. The procedures and responsibilities in clause 14(2) require clarification, together with clause 19(3) provisions in the event of default in insurances by the Contractor in this respect.

4. The procedures and responsibilities of the Architect, Contractor, and Employer under clause 19(2)(a) require clarification together with the clause 11(3) responsibilities for instructions in respect of this clause.

5. The question of consequential loss, demolition costs, and increases in costs requires clarification under clause 20 together with the procedures for payment of sums from insurance companies to the Contractor in the event of a claim.

6. The optional clause 20(B) is questionable in view of the exception from the indemnity given in clause 18(2) by the Contractor resulting from *Archibald & Co. Ltd.* v. *Comservices Ltd.* (1954), 1 W.L.R. 459.

7. The illogical nature of clause 20(C) requires rectification in particular to enable the Contractor to ensure adequate insurance exists.

8. *Consequential losses.* This matter forms a most important aspect of insurance whether required under the Contract or not.

Clause 18(2) indemnifies the Employer against any 'expense, liability, loss, etc.', if the Contractor has been negligent and clause 19(1)(b) states 'maintain such insurances as may be specifically required . . .'. Therefore clearly the Contractor must cover the financial consequences arising from any event in which he has shown negligence.

However, clause 20 does not require cover for consequential loss arising from the perils listed in that clause; thus nevertheless making him responsible if a breach on his part caused a catastrophe from which stemmed consequential loss.

4. *Standard Form of Tender for Nominated Subcontractors*, R.I.B.A. Publications Ltd., 1970.

Normally a Contractor's All Risks Policy does not provide cover for consequential loss unless it is specially extended. The Contractor's Public Liability Policy will normally contain two important exclusions which insurers are reluctant to remove:

1. Property in the Contractor's care or custody.

2. Property on which the insured is or has been working upon.

Now Public Liability Policies do include cover for consequential loss flowing direct from an event, but bearing in mind exclusion 1 above, a Contractor could have a very vital part of a building stolen whilst in his care or custody and if that part was on an extended delivery period heavy consequential loss could flow from this. Also, bearing in mind 1 and 2 above again, if a Contractor was instructed under clause 6(3) of the Contract to test on site materials or goods (precast components) and in going about these tests caused damage, the Contractor's All Risks Policy would cover the material damage to the materials or goods but in the event of consequential loss arising this would be subject under his Public Liability Policy to the exclusion. The Employer's own consequential loss suffered, due to the delay that calamities cause, is the liquidated damages sum. This sum should be one of the factors to influence a Contractor when considering the need for consequential loss cover coupled to his material damage policies.

Damage to the Works due to impact, theft, vandalism, frost, or malicious damage may be a hazard the Contractor can bear but the consequential loss that could arise may well be several times greater than the material loss suffered.

When sectional completion occurs the Employer is required to take sole risk for the perils listed under clause 20(A) (if applicable) from the date of his possession of the relevant part. Any failure to insure at all could result in consequential loss to the Contractor whilst endeavouring to complete the remainder of the Works. It is therefore essential that the Architect makes certain he informs the Employer of his intention to issue either:

1. His certificate of the value of the relevant part under clause 16(a), or

2. His certificate of Practical Completion under clause 15(1). to enable the Employer to have time to arrange such insurances. Failure to do so may result in a claim of negligence on the Architect's part, by the Employer.

In the event of damage to the Works requiring reconstruction to higher (more expensive) standards imposed by building regulations, difficulties may be encountered in this respect unless cover for such eventualities is included.

DIRECT AND NOMINATED SUBCONTRACTORS

Introduction

It is evident from the table opposite that in practice the majority of work by both direct and nominated subcontractors, is carried out upon the basis of a written inquiry, offer, and acceptance. No standard form of subcontract is used in the majority of cases although both parties have traditionally complained bitterly about each other's apparent unreliability. This has paradoxically not generated any widespread move towards the use of available legal documents or for that matter litigation. The Contractor's original inquiry or main contract conditions frequently cannot be compared with the subcontractor's original offer or counter-offer conditions. To add fuel to the potential fire, the Contractor's subsequent acceptance endeavours to effectively cancel all the offered conditions. In the case of nominated persons, some informal inquiry by the author indicated that although they are often requested to

Subcontract Forms N.F.B.T.E. sales quoted in thousands

	1963	*1964*	*1965*	*1966*	*1967*	*1968*	*1969*	*1970*
Direct	8	13	14	15	14	15	23	21
Direct/Nominated	38	24	17	15	20	18	16	27
Nominated	42	60	58	58	75	66	75	83

quote upon the standard conditions and form of tender, for nominated subcontractors, issued by the J.C.T.(4) they quote conditions at variance with this document which in effect invalidates their tender. Furthermore they are not always aware, even after entering into a formal contract, that their responsibility for defective work or materials is not limited to the replacement or re-execution costs, which is contrary to one offer condition the nominated person will not normally agree to remove.

Direct subcontractors

Great care must be taken to eliminate contradictions between inquiries, offers, counter-offers, and acceptances. When an offer is made with certain conditions attached and this offer is accepted but with conditions attached, in a case of dispute the conditions of the *offeror* may have precedence.

The subcontractor's liabilities should never be inconsistent with or greater than the main contractor's liabilities towards the Employer (one exception occurs in respect of insurances (see no. 7 in the checklist on p. 194 and clauses 18, 19, and 20 in this respect). It is administratively impractical to enter into standard subcontract agreements with all of those likely to be engaged by Contractors in the course of a project, but some policy should be adopted to rapidly check whether such agreements should be entered into. In this connection a check-list of salient points to consider is set out on p. 193.

Direct subcontractors are sometimes requested to enter into agreements based upon conditions drawn up by the main contractor. These agreements are frequently based upon iniquitous documents which should not be accepted. The sub-contractor should instead offer to sign the standard form(5) of subcontract approved by:

5. Standard Conditions for Non-Nominated Subcontract Works.

The National Federation of Building Trades Employers.

The Federation of Associations of Specialists and Subcontractors.

The Committee of Association of Specialist Engineering Contractors.

Nominated subcontractors

A Contractor should treat nominated subcontractors as ordinary subcontractors except that the terms, discounts, and conditions are established without his involvement. As far as the discounts are concerned the Contractor can veto the nomination if those agreed and put forward for acceptance do not accord with the conditions detailed in clause 27. The Contractor can waive his veto if he wishes and agree with the Architect other provisions under a provision detailed in clause 27(a). Presumably a better discount than 2½ per cent for cash would be one reason for agreeing other provisions. However, clause 30(5)(C) states that in settlement of such accounts the Contractor will be paid:

(*a*) the amount paid to the subcontractor, and

(*b*) the discounts for cash stated in clause 27, *which is 2½ per cent only*.

This anomaly also exists in clause 28 dealing with nominated suppliers. Furthermore, if a Contractor fails to pay nominated persons on time according to clause 27(a)(viii) and 28(c), also clause 27(b) and 28(a), the Contractor loses his discount from the nominated person and he loses his contractual right to such discounts. Contractors who fail to pay nominated persons on time in practice are nevertheless frequently still allowed the discount for cash. In these cases clause 30(5)(c) contains the words 'the amounts paid or payable' which should be the sum added into the final account plus the correct contractual discount for cash but only if the Contractor has earned it and not breached the terms of the main contract by not making payment within the stipulated period. If Architects insisted upon complying with this contract provision, subcontractors and suppliers cash flow would be considerably improved.

The main contractor can determine the employment of a nominated person but because only the Architect (clause 11(3)) can issue instructions with regard to the expenditure of prime cost sums the Contractor must beforehand seek the Architect's express instructions in the matter. If no instruction is forthcoming the Contractor should give notice under clause 24(1)(a). If the Architect does instruct in the matter the Contractor should ensure that any possible counter-claim by the nominated person about to be dismissed is drawn to the attention of the Architect and incorporated into the costs upon which instructions are required by the Contractor.

If a nominated person fails or withdraws from a subcontract the Employer is contractually bound to ensure the Architect re-nominates and the costs ensuing fall upon the Employer unless the withdrawal is caused by the main Contractor.

If the Architect does not wish to re-nominate because of, for instance, a very small or non-specialist amount of work, then the Contractor should make an agreement with the Employer to carry out the work himself at either an agreed sum or *quantum meruit*.

Any defects in prime cost sum works carried out by nominated persons, with the possible exception of design faults, are the main contractor's responsibility, but he in turn passes on this responsibility to the nominated person. If any defects first appear after the nominated subcontractor has completed his work then the Contractor cannot obtain an extension of time under clause 23(g) for the main contract. If, however, any defects appear within the nominated subcontractor's work period and cause the nominated subcontractor to exceed the original work period then the Contractor is entitled to an increase of time under clause 23(g) for the main contract. It is clear, therefore, that Contractors should exercise strict quality checks at all times upon nominated subcontractors work and not leave such subcontractors to go their own way. Contractors frequently treat nominated persons differently to direct subcontractors as far as quality and progress standards are concerned, and turn to the Architect if these standards are blatantly ignored by the subcontractor. Architects frequently intervene in such matters, feeling they have some responsibility since they nominated the person concerned. The Contractor should be made to realize that once the nomination is accepted, the relationship is clearly defined in the conditions and he must exercise the rights granted in the subcontract agreement in cases of dilatoriness or failure to work to the specified or implied standards. If the Contractor contemplates determining the employment of a nominated subcontractor, the Architect's express instructions in the matter should be secured to ensure his responsibility to re-nominate, and the Employer's liability to accept possible increases in expenditure against the original prime cost sum, are thoroughly understood.

Design and suitability

Generally speaking, any responsibility for design or suitability imposed upon or accepted from direct or nominated subcontractors must be confirmed and a warranty agreement should be entered into. In the case of nominated subcontractors the main Contractor could regard the lack of such an agreement as a suitable ground under clause 27 for objecting to the nomination. (See also comments under clauses 18, 19, and 20.)

Form of indemnity for final payment to the subcontractor

Nominated subcontractors can be called upon under the main contract clause 27(e) to provide a suitable form of indemnity before a release of early final payment, and retention monies, will be agreed to by the main Contractor.

The Committee of Associations of Specialist Engineering Contractors have published (see Appendix) a suitable form for this purpose with guidance notes for users. However, the kind of security offered with such agreements must be to the reasonable satisfaction of the main Contractor and this should always be in the form of a suitable insurance policy with an established concern.

Warranty forms (6)
A Standard Form of Agreement is available for binding Employers and nominated subcontractors together in respect of:

1. Liabilities for design.
2. Liabilities for delay.
3. Provision for payment direct by the Employer if the main Contractor fails.

Such an agreement rectifies the weakness of the main contract, in respect of these matters, wherein it was necessary to draft a clause that would allow the choice and agreement of financial or other terms with a third person without entering into any contractual relationship. This form now provides for an agreement limited to the three matters listed above.

6. R.I.B.A. Form of Agreement between Employer and Nominated Subcontractor.

Retentions from nominated subcontractors
Clause 27(a)(viii) contains some ambiguity for users when sectional completion occurs. In effect the clause states the limit of retention must not exceed x

where x: subcontract price

as Limit of Retention in Appendix: Contract Sum.

To illustrate this point assume a contract was arranged in the way shown in the table below.

Clause 16(f) dealing with retention upon sectional completion states in effect that the release of retention will be equal to $\frac{1}{2}x$

where $\frac{1}{2}x$: Limit of Retention (original)

as value of Section: Contract Sum (original).

If we apply these rules in Section 1, Case A:

Contractor upon completion of Section 1 is entitled under clause 16(f) to a release of half of the retention $= \frac{1}{2}x$: £5,000 (original Limit of Retention)
as £25,000 (original value of section): £100,000 (original Contract Sum) so $\frac{1}{2}x$ = £625.

If we now turn to clause 27(a)(viii) to see what release of retention in these circumstances is granted in turn to nominated subcontractors we find that the Contractor must retain 'up to a total amount not exceeding x, where x : subcontract price'

as the ('unreduced') Limit of Retention in Retention in Appendix : Contract Sum

In Section 1, Case A this would $= x$: £12,500

£5,000 : £100,000

so x = £625

From this it can be seen that the retention now held from the main Contractor could in fact be financed completely by nominated subcontractors. The position, when variations change the values of sections, is more incongruous. Table C

Contract sum £100,000

Limit of Retention £5,000
Retention held 5 per cent

	Section 1		*Section 2*		*Section 3*		*Section 4*	
CASE A	Value	£25,000	Value	£25,000	Value	£25,000	Value	£25,000
	Nominated subcontract value	£12,500	Nominated subcontract value	£12,500	Nominated subcontract value	£12,500	Nominated subcontract value	£12,500
CASE B	Varied value	£30,000	Varied value	£30,000	Varied value	£30,000	Varied value	£20,000
	Nominated subcontract value	£20,000	Nominated subcontract value	£20,000	Nominated subcontract value	£20,000	Nominated subcontract value	£ 5,000

Table C. Indicating retention when sectional completion occurs

Section	*Contract value*		*Contract retention 5 per cent*		*Retention held by Contractor upon nominated subcontract work as stated in clause 27(a)(viii)*		*Retention held by Employer upon Contractor and Contract after sectional completion entitles the Contractor to a release, as stated in clause 16(f)*	
	Case A	*Case B*	*Case A*	*Case B*	*Case A*	*Case B*	*Case A*	*Case B*
1	25,000	30,000	1,250	1,500	625	1,000	625	750
2	50,000	60,000	2,500	3,000	1,250	2,000	1,250	1,500
3	75,000	90,000	3,750	4,500	1,875	2,500[2]	1,875	2,250
4	100,000	110,000	5,000[1]	5,000[2]	2,500	2,500	2,500	2,500[2]

1. Limit of Retention reached.
2. Limit of Retention or reduced Limit reached.

above indicates the possible extent and effects of the inconsistency between clauses 27(a)(viii) and 16(f).

The Architect has to ‘desire’ in clause 27(e) to release full payment to nominated subcontractors otherwise these retention monies remain in the Contractor’s ‘care’. The Architect’s decision whether or not he exercises his power under clause 27(e) cannot be arbitrated upon.

The words contained in clause 27(a)(viii) would benefit from the addition of references to sectional completion which reduces the sum of the limit of retention, so that in Case A:

Section 1

$$x : £50{,}000 \quad \text{as } £5{,}000 : £100{,}000 \qquad x = £2{,}500$$

Section 2

$$x : £50{,}000 \quad \text{as } £3{,}750 : £100{,}000 \qquad x = £1{,}875$$

Section 3

$$x : £50{,}000 \quad \text{as } £2{,}500 : £100{,}000 \qquad x = £1{,}250$$

Section 4

$$x : £50{,}000 \quad \text{as } £1{,}250 : £100{,}000 \qquad x = £625$$

In addition, references to possible early releases of retention to nominated subcontractors under clause 27(e), with the consequent reduction in the limit of retention, should be included. Some regard to a variation in eventual values must also occur to clarify the differences between original and final values.

If a Contractor became insolvent under the circumstances indicated in Case B in the Table C it appears the Contractor’s trustee or liquidator would have no right to any of the sums held by the Employer as retention, and there would be a deficiency in any event unless Section 4 was reached.

A TWENTY-POINT CHECKLIST TO ENSURE GOOD SUBCONTRACT RELATIONSHIPS

1. *The parties names should be given*
   (*a*) Main Contractor.
   (*b*) Employer.
2. *The Works should be clearly identified*
   (*a*) Location.
   (*b*) Brief description.
3. *The subcontract works should be clearly identified*
   (*a*) Description.
4. *The main Contract form details should be declared*
   (*a*) Standard contract title (or if non-standard a brief description should be given and the effect of a non-standard document should be checked out).
   (*b*) Drawings/specifications/bills available.
   (*c*) Details of alternative clauses in any standard forms or deletions or alterations (e.g. Standard Form, clause 23(j)).
   (*d*) Details of insurances required and optional clauses (e.g. Standard Form, clause 20(A)(B) or (C)).

(*e*) Extracts from Preliminaries of documents details any conditions imposed by Employer (e.g. sequence/phasing).

(*f*) Extracts from any Appendix to the main Contract.
(i) Defects Liability Period.
(ii) Dates for Possession of site and Completion of Works.
(iii) Liquidated Damages.
(iv) Period of Delay (*a*) insurances
(*b*) other reasons.
(v) Period for interim certificates.
(vi) Retention details including any Limit.
(vii) Period for Final Measurement.
(viii) Period for issue of Final Certificate (3 to 6 months.
(ix) Fluctuation details.

5. *The subcontract documents*
(*a*) Bills.
(*b*) Drawings/schedules (production period required if subcontractor responsible for drawings).
(*c*) Specifications.
(*d*) Schedules of Rates.
(*e*) Basic Price Lists.
(*f*) Materials and Goods Lists.

6. *Special working conditions imposed by Contractor*
(*a*) Intermittent.
(*b*) Shift.
(*c*) Night only.
(*d*) Weekend.
(*e*) Overtime.
(*f*) Holiday.
(*g*) Tidal.
(*h*) Order/sequence/phasing (details of possession when given in sections must be given).
(*i*) Any other specific obligation or restriction.

7. *The subcontractor's obligations*
(*a*) To whose reasonable satisfaction must the work comply.

(*b*) Building regulation or other statutory requirements to be complied with in particular respects.

(*c*) Programme or network diagrams required (details of starting and sectional starting and completions to be given or complied with).

(*d*) Samples or tests required with specific details or a provisional sum to be stated.

(*e*) Patent rights or royalties responsibilities (the Architect is responsible to see that nominated subcontractors have obtained and paid for such rights).

(*f*) Warranty or bond details.

(*g*) Insurances required (to comply with clause 19(1)(a) and (b)). It should be made clear that the subcontractor is responsible for claims for damages *by* Persons (his own + third party), or *to* Property or the Works when due *entirely* to the subcontractor's negligence, *except* in the case of fire damage or loss (*even* if it is due to the subcontractor's negligence). This also applies to materials unfixed. The subcontractor's own plant damaged or destroyed by fire, however, is always at his own risk if the fire was caused by his own negligence. If the subcontract works involve vibration (e.g. piling) or subsidence (e.g. lowering ground water) or collapse (e.g. underpinning), then clause 19(2)(a) insurances should be in existence. Damages or loss due to vandalism or theft should be clarified with particular reference to:
(i) Work completed by the subcontractor and formally handed over (the main Contractor is fully responsible).
(ii) Work partially completed (e.g. first fixing) but not formally handed over. If the subcontractor upon leaving considers he has expensive or 'long delivery'

materials at risk due to inadequate security arrangements he should confirm this to the Contractor. Under the main Contract security is the sole responsibility of the main Contractor and damage or loss would therefore fall on him. Certain works by their nature present security problems and the main Contractor may consider that in spite of his security arrangements each subcontractor should be held responsible for his own losses from vandalism or theft. Since the subcontractor is made responsible usually for his own storage arrangements then he is responsible for the materials and goods in such storage even if paid for by the Contractor and Employer. Some materials and goods cannot be conveniently stored and available. This important matter should be resolved between the parties upon commencement.

Both Contractor and subcontractor should satisfy themselves as to the adequacy of each others insurances but the practical difficulties of this are discussed under clauses 18, 19, and 20.

(*h*) Scaffold.
(i) Details of scaffold to be available, its suitability for the purpose, length of time available, etc.
(ii) Details of special scaffold and party responsible (any main Contract provision in respect of special scaffold should be detailed under this section or Contractor's Obligations or Special Attendance).

(*i*) Hoists/plant, etc.
(i) Facilities provided.

(*j*) Removal of rubbish.
(i) Detail who will handle to loading point.
(ii) Detail who will load and remove with any charges clearly defined.

(*k*) Casing and protection.
(i) Party responsible (it should be the sole responsibility of the main Contractor).
(ii) Detail any special provisions required in this respect.

(*l*) Setting out.
(i) Define responsibilities (basic setting out should be the main Contractor's responsibility).
(ii) Detail any templates to be used or provided.

8. *The main Contractor's obligations*

(*a*) Facilities.
(i) Water: details of stand points, pressure, etc.
(ii) Lighting: details and overtime lighting arrangements.
(iii) Power: details 110 V a.c., single-phase, etc.
(iv) Telephone: charge arrangements and facilities available.
(v) Sheds (*a*) space.
(*b*) rates.
(*c*) communal w.c./mess-rooms/first aid/drying.
(*d*) compound details.

(*b*) Security arrangements: details (see also 7(g)).

(*c*) Setting out (see also 7(b)).

(*d*) Scaffold (see also 7(h)).

(*e*) General attendance.
(i) Detail main contract provisions (general attendance is defined in *S.M.M.* 5th edition, to include:
allowing *use* of standing scaffold
use of mess-rooms/w.c./welfare facilities
and providing *space* for storage of plant and materials
space for offices
and providing *free* light (for nominated subcontractors only) but not free power
and providing *free* water (for nominated subcontractors only)
and *clearing away* rubbish (presumably from one collection point accessible by lorry).
(The above definitions are intended to apply to nominated subcontractors but there is no reason why they should not be adopted in general.)

(ii) Special attendance.

(*a*) Detail main Contract provisions (special attendance is defined in *S.M.M.* 5th edition, to include:

Carrying out unloading (but details to be given pre-contract).

Carrying out storing (but details to be given pre-contract).

Carrying out hoisting (but details to be given pre-contract).

Carrying out placing in position (but details to be given pre-contract).

Providing free power.

Providing special scaffold (but details to be given pre-contract).

But all of the above items must be the subject of specific items in the main Contract Bills and any item absent indicates an error if that work or facility is in fact required. (The above definitions are intended to apply to nominated subcontractors only but there is no reason why they should not be adopted in general.)

(*b*) Detail any variation or departure from the above.

9. *Fluctuations in costs*

(*a*) Nominated subcontractors' fluctuations are not subject to the rules of clause 31. Therefore procedures and the basis for such fluctuations should be detailed.

(*b*) The main contract provisions, i.e. 31ACD or 31BCD should be stated and in the case of 31ACD:

(i) A list of Basic Prices of materials and goods is required to detail:

materials or goods

rate or current market price (as at 10 days before the main Contract tender date or any previously announced increased or decreased market price: delivered site with any discounts clarified).

(ii) Verification (photostats) of the above rates or prices from makers' lists or quotations.

(iii) A list of wages, emoluments, and expenses fixed by the recognized body current (as at 10 days before the main contract tender date or any previously announced increased or varied rates proposed).

(iv) Employer's Liability and Third Party insurance premium charges. Adjustments are confined to workpeople and not supervisory or administrative staff. Any changes made to inducement rates or incentives do not qualify for recovery. But any change in or newly imposed tax or statutory payment is recoverable or adjustable even if clause 31ACD does not apply (see clause 31BCD here). Sums adjustable should be included in interim certificates by the Architect and therefore providing the sums have been paid or 'repaid' (in the case of reduced taxes) such sums should be recovered without any retention held upon them. Where a subcontractor is nominated under the standard form the increase or decrease due to fluctuation will vary the 'total value' due therefore the Contractual cash discount of 2½ per cent due to the main Contractor is due on whatever 'total value' is established.

(*c*) Procedures for notification of fluctuations should be detailed.

(*d*) Fluctuations on non-productive time are not adjustable but if fluctuations on productive overtime are permitted in the main contract this fact should be stated. Hours worked on daywork must be priced at the current rate (or quoted rate) and the actual hours worked deducted from the fluctuations claim sheets. (Fluctuations during the defects liability period are not adjustable. Fluctuations during an extension to a subcontract period are recoverable and adjustable even if that subcontractor was responsible for the delay providing the main contract contains a liquidated damages clause and sum contained therein; because that sum is deemed to be a pre-assessment of damage suffered *including* such eventualities as costs rising or falling. Any subcontractor who wishes to use a formula to settle fluctuations should obtain the special agreement necessary at the pre-subcontract stage.)

10. *Subletting*

(*a*) Detail the procedures for subletting or state any ban imposed.

11. *Payments*

(*a*) A definite period and arrangement for interim payments should be stated in detail (this is particularly important if the Contractor and Employer have entered into an arrangement for such payment which is not as laid down in the Standard Form clause 30).

(*b*) Provision for a certificate to be issued by the main Contractor to the subcontractor should be made setting out clearly the sums due:
(i) Value of work properly executed.
(ii) Value of materials and goods for incorporation into the Works as valued upon the site 7 working days prior to the agreed certificate date in the main Contract.
(iii) Special arrangements for the inclusion of materials and goods into such valuations when stored off-site as provided for under clause 30(2A) and 14(2) and the stringent provisions in the main contract for such payments must be accepted in this matter. Insurance provisions for such materials and goods whilst in store or in transit from store to site must be checked before any agreement is settled in this respect.
(iv) Value of authorized variations with details of the basis of such variations should be agreed. Subcontractors must be prepared to submit promptly details in connection with claims for reimbursement when it is considered that a fair valuation has not been made or that loss or expense has been involved due to the issue of variations (see also clause 11 on this).
(v) Value of adjustments to prime cost and provisional sums included.
(vi) Value of authorized and agreed dayworks.
(vii) Retentions should be detailed and arrangements for releases of retention, particularly upon sectional completion, must be stated.
(viii) Fluctuations in costs (not subjected to retentions).
(ix) Discounts.
(x) Previous payments.
(xi) Claims for payment under provisions contained in the subcontract.

(*c*) Contra charges and the method of settlement should be detailed to avoid disagreement and possible claims that the interim payment received by a subcontractor from a Contractor is not the 'total value of the work' as stated in clause 30(2).

(*d*) Any nominated subcontractor should be required to submit a receipt of each payment made to him so that the Contractor has reasonable proof readily available, in the case of nominated subcontractors, that payment has been made. This receipt should be in sufficient detail to indicate to a third party (in this case the Architect) that there is no breach by the Contractor of the terms of the main Contract clause 27(b). Provisions for direct payment, in cases of such breaches by the Employer to the subcontractor are available both in the main Contract and in the Form of Agreement issued by the R.I.B.A.

(*e*) The period of honouring the certificate issued to the subcontractor should be stated (e.g. 14 days from the issue date). The period agreed should not be made subject to a proviso that the main Contractor has himself been paid by the Employer for the value in question. This also applies to releases of retentions.

(*f*) Any indemnity to be provided if early final payment is envisaged must be agreed upon pre-contract. This is particularly important in the case of nominated subcontractors who must under clause 27(e) satisfactorily indemnify the Contractor against any latent defect. C.A.S.E.C. (Committee of Associations of Specialist Engineering Contractors) have issued (November

1970) a Form of Indemnity for this express purpose (see Appendix). It is for the Contractor to determine what security he requires, such as a products guarantee insurance, depending upon the circumstances in each case. If the subcontractor cannot provide an indemnity to the 'reasonable satisfaction' of the Contractor this should be declared at the onset. (A Contractor may well consider this a reasonable ground under clause 27(a) in the main Contract for objecting to the nomination of such a subcontractor even though early final payment is not required by that same subcontractor.)

12. *Errors in Bills of Quantities/Specifications/Drawings/ Details*

(*a*) Procedures in the event of a discovery of an error in subcontract documents should be agreed. The subcontractor's own errors in producing his tender will not be corrected unless both parties agree.

The *Standard Method of Measurement,* 5th edition, provides for bills of quantities to be produced in a standard way to obviate error and ambiguity. However, the Standard Form clause 12 allows departure from such methods providing specific details are given in the bills concerned. This can cause problems if (as is customary practice) the subcontractor is only sent photostat copies of the pages from a bill detailing the quantities in the subcontract work without the specified departures notice. Thus there would be no error in the main contract but possibly an error in the subcontract if the tender was produced assuming the quantities provided were based upon the standard method of measurement. 'Lump Sum' quotations are often submitted by subcontractors even when quantities are provided. Clearly since variations are endemic in the building industry, lump sum quotations are impracticable when valuations or variations are required in the agreement. Furthermore the term 'lump sum' in the legal sense may mean an entire contract for which no stage payment can be implied in law. To avoid confusion the intentions of the parties as to adjustment or otherwise of the quotations given, is desirable.

13. *Delay and grounds for extensions of time*

(*a*) The subcontractor's grounds for obtaining an extension of time for his subcontract works should be defined and include:

(i) Force majeure (an uncontrollable reason).

(ii) Exceptionally inclement weather. (The occurrence of any inclement weather can cause delay to a short-term subcontractor, e.g. if a roofing specialist gives a programme period of 2 weeks but rain falls on 5 working days then there is delay, although 5 days of rain may not constitute *exceptional* inclement weather.)

(iii) Damage to the Works due to any risk formally insured against.

(iv) Industrial strike action, etc.

(v) Authorized variations.

(vi) Non-receipt or delayed receipt of instruction, details, drawings.

(vii) Errors in Contract documents.

(viii) Delay caused by the main Contractor or other subcontractors or Artistic Specialists or others engaged by the Employer.

(ix) Delay due to opening up work (or tests to inspect (unless that was due to the subcontractor's own default).

Optional (x) Inability to obtain key men and/or materials due to unanticipated reasons.

(xi) Discovery and delay due to archaeological objects, etc.

(xii) Contractor's instructions to postpone the Works.

(*b*) In the case of delay due to the reasons in (vi), (vii), (viii), (ix), (xi), and (xii) the detailed procedures for reimbursement (including arbitration in the event of disagreement) of loss and/or expense should be stated. (Prompt submission of such details is imperative to ensure adequate and proper cash flow not only for the subcontractor but for the main Contractor.)

14. *Variations*

(*a*) The procedures for the issue of and authority for variations should be detailed. The person having authority should be identified and the position with regard to variations inherent in drawings or details issued after commencement, but not efficiently identified as such and confirmed, should be clarified.

(*b*) The procedures for distribution of drawings and details both to and from the subcontractor should be stated.

(*c*) The valuation of variations in subcontract work should be defined as laid down in clause 11(4) of the main Contract.

(*d*) The right to claim loss or expense arising from variations which are not reimbursed to the subcontractor from the valuations made in (*c*) above should be stated and provisions for the addition of any sum agreed in this respect should be added to the next payment due without retentions being held.

(*e*) Provision for arbitration should be stated detailing when the hearing could commence.

15. *Completion and sectional completion*

(*a*) The responsibilities of the parties must be clearly defined in the event of either causing a delay in completion or sectional completion. Those responsibilities must be realistic and if possible the damages should be predetermined.

(It is not uncommon to find very small subcontract firms contractually bound in very large projects to carry out an important (but financially insignificant) operation, and to be financially responsible for the enormous consequences of their delay caused to the project. This slavish use of 'standard' subcontract documents in these circumstances seems impracticable and a more realistic arrangement is required of both parties. Rights of determination by the Contractor to determine the employment of the subcontractor coupled with realistic pre-stated damages appears to create a more practical relationship in such circumstances, overcoming the problems caused by dilatory small subcontractors who scorn threats by Contractors to withhold their insignificant retention sum.)

(*b*) Procedures and liabilities in the event of delays to the parties when no delay occurs in 'completion' should be agreed. The acceleration of work by the other parties affected by one parties delay can increase working costs but network diagrams of proposed methods and resources would need to be known by all the parties to enable prompt and accurate settlement of such arrangements. The addition or deduction of any such costs at interim and final payments stage (without retention) should be agreed upon.

(*c*) A definition of practical and sectional completion should in the case of all subcontracts be stated and certificates should be issued by the Contractor to the subcontractor in either case.

(*d*) The certificates issued in (*c*) should:

(i) Establish the start of the defects liabilities period.

(ii) Reduce the insurance responsibilities.

(iii) Establish the start of the final (or sectional) settlement period.

(iv) Establish the release of part of the retentions.

(There is no provision in the Standard Form of (main) Contract for sectionalized liquidated damages to run from the established date of delay in a section. This incongruity can cause problems to all parties and subcontract agreements should not fall into line with the main Contract in this respect. There appears no reason why the section completion date should not be regarded as inviolate and damages recovered accordingly.)

16. *Final account settlement*
   (*a*) The procedures and duties of the respective parties should be detailed:
   (i) The subcontractor should be required to submit his account together with all relevant details (measurements, etc.) to the main contractor within a specified period from the Certificate of Practical Completion of the subcontractor's work as detailed in 15(c).
   (ii) A period for settlement should be defined to commence from the date of submission by the subcontractor of all the final account and relevant details as detailed in (i) above.
   (iii) The issue of the final certificate should be provided for within one calendar month of the period stated in (ii) above expiring.
   (*b*) Reference to arbitration after the proposed date of issue of the final certificate should be provided for, alternatively and perhaps more effectively a variable interest rate should apply to outstanding monies shown due from the date in (iii) above after proper notice has been given and no counter-claim for a reduced balance made and substantiated by the main Contractor.

17. *Defects liabilities*
   (*a*) The period should be stated and commence from the issue of a Certificate of Practical Completion of the subcontractors's work. This is important where sectional completion is provided for in the main Contract.

   If the subcontractor's work and defects liability period expires prior to the main Contractor achieving practical completion both parties must consider such matters with care and evaluate the risk concerned. Prior arrangements to extend the subcontractor's time of responsibility to coincide with the main Contractor's may prove more satisfactory since the main Contractor will then not be motivated to delay issuing the Certificate of Practical completion.
   (*b*) The subcontractor's quotation may exclude certain defects (e.g. shrinkage cracks). Frost damage responsibilities arising when damage occurs after the subcontractor's practical completion should be excluded unless the cause was inherent beforehand.
   (*c*) The subcontractor's liabilities for consequential costs arising from defects can be very onerous. Under the main contract the Contractor is responsible for such damages and he will look to any subcontractor who causes such costs for recompense. These costs are not limited to the liquidated damages quoted in the main Contract Appendix. The direct subcontractor's quotation will usually therefore limit these liabilities to a 'replacement' level, but nominated subcontractors are not permitted this protection under the main and subcontract conditions.

18. *Determination by main Contractor*
   (*a*) Grounds for determination should include:
   (i) Subcontractor suspending work without cause.
   (ii) Subcontractor failing to proceed diligently.
   (iii) Subcontractor refusing to remove or rectify defects.
   (iv) Subcontractor subletting (or assigning) without approval.
   (v) Subcontractor being declared insolvent.
   (*b*) Procedures for two notices should be detailed, the first to state the default and call for rectification within a period of days to be stated, the second notice will state that determination has occurred. In the case of (v) provision for reinstatement should be included.
   (*c*) Procedures for the settlement of accounts, liabilities, and retention money funds must be detailed and include:
   (i) Employment of others (or the main Contractor) to complete.
   (ii) Materials unfixed but paid or unpaid for and materials ordered forward or stored off site.
   (iii) Plant and sheds, etc., on site.

(*d*) The costs arising from default identified as arising directly from such default would include:
(i) Additional costs or expense of employing another (or the main Contractor) to complete.
(ii) Costs or expenses caused to the main Contractor and subcontractors in the Contract.
(iii) Rectification of any defects originally the liability of the defaulting subcontractor.

Pending prompt establishment of the above costs, no payment of any monies due prior to the determination should occur.

19. *Determination by subcontractor*

(*a*) Grounds for determination should include
(i) Main Contractor defaulting in making payments in accordance with the provisions detailed under 11 earlier.
(ii) Main Contractor's own employment being determined.
(iii) Main Contractor suspending work for a period in excess of the agreed period for delay caused by:
(*a*) Force majeure (uncontrollable reason).
(*b*) Damage to the Works due to any risk formally insured against.
(*c*) Industrial strike action, etc.
(*d*) Lack of proper details, drawings, etc.
(*e*) Delay of others employed by the main Contractor or Employer direct.
(*f*) Opening up Works to inspect (unless due to the subcontractor's own default).
(iv) Main Contractor becoming declared insolvent.

(*b*) Procedures for serving proper notice of default must be detailed. It could be said that one notice stating determination will occur automatically within a stated number of days would suffice since the recipient of the notice is bound to be aware of his default and cannot in any case directly control the cause of the breach.

(*c*) Procedures for settlement of account, liabilities, and retention money funds must be detailed and include:
(i) Stipulated periods, in the event of adoption by Trustees, etc., for the appointment of a new Contractor and inclusion of special payment arrangements for materials or goods intended for the Works but unpaid for stored on and off site, also plant and sheds on site.
(ii) The guarding of retention monies. The position here of nominated subcontractors to the recovery of retention monies is somewhat better than direct subcontractors since the case of *Tout* v. *Finch* established that those named subcontractors in the last issued main Contract certificate of payment should not be in the position of ordinary creditors but have their retention reserved by the Trustee, etc.

(*d*) The costs arising from default identified as arising directly from such default would include:
(i) The value of completed and uncompleted work at the date of determination.
(ii) The value of materials unfixed but paid for.
(iii) The costs or expense of and removing plant, sheds, etc., from site.

(*e*) Procedures for settlement of accounts, liabilities, and retention money funds must be detailed and include a stipulated period for the employment of another main Contractor or re-appointment of the original Contractor. This provision would put a responsibility upon the Trustee, etc., to apply pressure upon the Employer in the original main Contract to appoint another or re-appoint as soon as possible. The appointment provisions should detail procedures in the event of the subcontractor not being re-appointed or re-nominated in a new Contract. Materials or goods ordered forward, etc., but unpaid for and intended for the Works should be included in the first interim payment due to the new Contractor.

20. *Arbitration*
   (*a*) Provision should be available for dealing with disputes arising on any matter whatsoever cognate to the subcontractor agreement.
   (*b*) Such arbitration proceedings should be restricted to take place after practical completion of the subcontract works except for disputes concerning interim payments.

Summary
Any problem associated with subcontracts is only one stage removed from becoming a main Contract problem or even dispute. All parties should, therefore, be aware of the need for care and accuracy in defining the relationship and duties in respect of all subcontracts. The widespread use of equitable standard forms of main Contract will require equally widespread use of equitable standard forms of subcontract if the Employer (client) is to be granted deserved protection from 'second phase' problems that can affect his investment.

FINAL SETTLEMENT

Clause 30 clearly envisages that all variations, prime cost, and provisional sum adjustments will have been measured, valued, and agreed during the progress of the Works so that interim duties can be effectively carried out. The original draft is untidy and illogical, but the flowchart has sorted matters out into logical order and annotation covers most of the remaining gaps.

It is evident from these charts that providing all measurement and valuations required by the contract are carried out when the contract in effect requires them (so that interim certificates accord with the conditions) then no delay in theory should occur in the issue of a Final Certificate, except through dilatoriness by the Contractor in dealing with defects at the end of the liability period, or before the issue of the Final Certificate, or by not sending all documents required for the final account to the Architect, as required in subclause (6).

Issue of Final Certificate

Fig. 5.1 indicates that in practice the critical factor in the issue of Final Certificates is most likely therefore to be the Defects Liability Period, if the Appendix footnote in the Local Authorities edition, 'The period inserted must not exceed six months' (from the end of the Defects Liability Period) is accepted by authorities. As far as the Private edition is concerned a period of three months is mandatory here.

Architects may have doubts whether or not to issue a Final Certificate if defects manifest themselves after the issue of a Certificate of Completion of Making Good Defects and before the proposed issue of a Final Certificate. The Contract clause 30(6) states that the Architect must issue the Final Certificate '*so soon as is practicable* . . .' and the statement in clause 30(7) ' . . . unless a notice under clause 35 has been given . . .' makes this Certificate conclusive only if no reference to arbitration has been made and subject in any event to the exceptions listed in subclauses (7)(a)(b) and (c). Under these circumstances the Architect should ascertain that the defect in question is in fact one for which the Contractor is liable and confirm this liability. If the Contractor disputes responsibility then notice to arbitrate should be given. Having taken this step and fully informed the Employers of the position, there is then sufficient reason for the Architect to not find it '*practicable*' to issue the Final Certificate.

It is therefore possible under the Contract to withhold the Final Certificate pending satisfactory rectification of a defect revealing itself outside the declared and agreed periods and Certificates for rectification. The Architect should not withhold the Final Certificate lightly since a subsequent hearing may find for the Contractor, in which case the delay in the issue of the Final Certificate will have incurred interest on the balance due, at the very least. On the other hand if the Architect does issue a Final Certificate even though defects are present, the Employer could recover damages in this event from the Architect. There appears therefore to be in effect no limit on time in this matter even though in a subsequent arbitration the so-called defect may be adjudged a design

Fig. 5.1. Final Certificate Issue

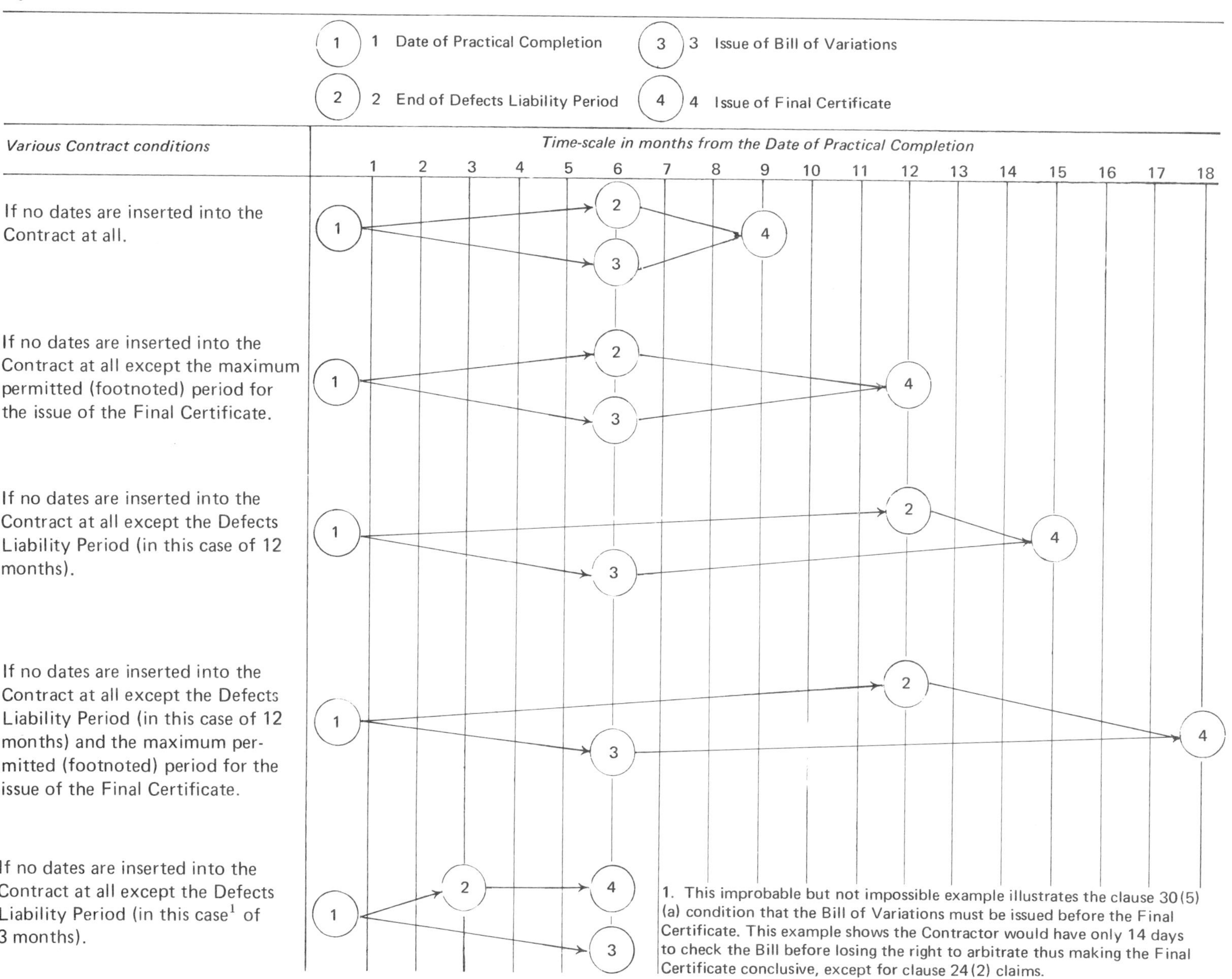
1 Date of Practical Completion
2 End of Defects Liability Period
3 Issue of Bill of Variations
4 Issue of Final Certificate
Various Contract conditions
Time-scale in months from the Date of Practical Completion
1 2 3 4 5 6 7 8 9 10 11 12 13 14 15 16 17 18
If no dates are inserted into the Contract at all.
If no dates are inserted into the Contract at all except the maximum permitted (footnoted) period for the issue of the Final Certificate.
If no dates are inserted into the Contract at all except the Defects Liability Period (in this case of 12 months).
If no dates are inserted into the Contract at all except the Defects Liability Period (in this case of 12 months) and the maximum permitted (footnoted) period for the issue of the Final Certificate.
If no dates are inserted into the Contract at all except the Defects Liability Period (in this case[1] of 3 months).
1. This improbable but not impossible example illustrates the clause 30(5) (a) condition that the Bill of Variations must be issued before the Final Certificate. This example shows the Contractor would have only 14 days to check the Bill before losing the right to arbitrate thus making the Final Certificate conclusive, except for clause 24(2) claims.

fault, or even the fault of a (now insolvent?) nominated sub-contractor. Furthermore the Final Certificate could be awaited by the Employer, for it indicates, of course, that all claims are settled, subject to clause 30(7)(a)(b)(c), and may conceivably show reimbursement due to the Employer (for example, fluctuation net reduction by tax changes not calculated or allowed in the last interim certificate).

Contractors may consider this procedure encourages procrastination so far as the Final Certificate is concerned since it must be remembered that the Contract provides for the withholding of a Certificate of Practical Completion if defects are present at that stage. Later, the Contract provides for the withholding of a Certificate of Completion of Making Good Defects, if defects are present at that particular stage. Then finally the clause 30(7) in effect permits the withholding of a Final Certificate, even though it *must* apparently be issued within an agreed pre-stated period. All of these procedures go by the board if a defect chooses to manifest itself after the Certificate of Making Good Defects but before the due date of issue of a Final Certificate. Clause 6 permits the Architect to issue instructions on defective work, etc., at any time prior to the issue of the Final Certificate.

The so-called finality is not applicable to any defect which the Architect could not have been aware of during the carrying out of the Works. This in effect means, for example, that defective work drawn to the Architect's attention and clearly accepted at the time by him, cannot because of clause 30(7)(b), after the issue of the Final Certificate, be claimed to be defective. If, however, the defect did not reveal itself or could not reasonably be detected at any time during the Works, so that the Architect could not have had an opportunity to condemn it, then that defect can be the subject of an action for damages by the Employer. The period of limitation (6 or 12 years) is the really final and conclusive factor in such matters.

The period of liability for defects stated in the Appendix is therefore only a convenient opportunity for the Contractor to reduce his liability for defects by rectifying them during a specified and convenient period under a provision in the Contract. It does not in any way limit his continuing liability for *any* defects that reveal themselves before the issue of an undisputed Final Certificate, or for *latent* defects outside the contract period until the appropriate limitation date. The building owner must mitigate any loss that defects may cause and usually should give the Contractor an opportunity to remedy his own (latent) defects.

An Architect would be required to investigate any latent defects which manifest themselves outside the contract periods to decide whether they are either designer or contractor responsibilities. Once a defect is identified as a breach of the original Contract, the Architect's responsibility to the Employer is revived for the same or further defects revealing themselves within the limitation period of 6 or 12 years from the date of the cause of the defect. If the date of cause cannot be ascertained then the date of the Certificate of Practical Completion will be taken since the root cause could not possibly have arisen after that date. If increases in costs occur between the date of the cause of the defect and the discovery, the Contractor must stand the additional cost providing the Employer acts, within a reasonable time of the discovery, in accordance with his responsibility to mitigate the loss from any breach of the original contract.

ARCHITECT'S INSTRUCTIONS

Authority to instruct

The Contract is between the Employer and Contractor. The Architect has no authority to waive or vary any Condition contained in the Contract unless the contract gives him that authority or discretion as for example in clause 11(1):

> he may sanction in writing any variation made by the Contractor otherwise than pursuant to an instruction of the Architect . . .

or as the discretionary power granted him in clause 30(2A):

> The amount stated as due in an Interim Certificate may in the discretion of the Architect include the value of any materials or goods before delivery thereof to or adjacent to the Works . . .

Employers do in certain circumstances give to or take from the Architect authority which therefore is at variance with that derived from the Contract. It has been known for a ministry department to issue a directive to local authorities that in effect would certainly influence the Architect or Supervising Officer in making decisions which the Contract expects to be effected by the Architect in a quasi-judicial manner. Local authorities have in the past endeavoured to remove certain authority in connection with final settlement from the Architect and vest those powers in the dreaded District Auditor. This practice is contrary to the framework in which the Joint Contracts Tribunal agreed the Standard Conditions contained in the Contract.

7. *Dutton* v. *Bognor Regis Urban District Council*, (1971), 2 A.E.R. 1003.

The Architect is the agent of the Employer and therefore owes a duty to protect the Employer's interests at all times. However, the Contract (naively it is considered) places a duty upon the Architect in certain matters (for example, clauses 11(6), 24(1), 34(3)) to act in an arbitrary way so that his obligations towards the Employer must not in any way influence or prevent him from preserving the Contractor's rights under the Contract. Contractors in the main, when presenting claims, the cause of which may be dilatoriness or error by the Architect, may find it impossible to accept that the Architect in these circumstances can be both counsel for the defence and judge. The only alternative in these circumstances is to submit to arbitration.

STANDARDS OF MATERIALS, GOODS, AND WORKMANSHIP

Specifications are not included in the contract documents where bills of quantities exist. The work sections in bills instead contain reference to detailed preambles, rather than to a proper specification. Preambles frequently fall short of the standards of comprehensive description required within a specification. This serious failing in documentation can mean that the objective testing of standards to be applied by the Architect (clause 1(1)) is almost impossible to achieve. Some bills of quantities endeavour to blanket the whole problem in one description:

> *Workmanship*
> Except where otherwise stated or contradicted workmanship is to comply with British Standard Codes of Practise where applicable.

Such a description should be set against the fact that there are about 150 relevant, and sometimes voluminous British Standard Codes, some of which contain reference to alternative methods and standards. Responsibilities and liabilities as between the designer and constructor are becoming increasingly difficult to identify. Designer, contractors, subcontractors, and suppliers will in the future increasingly be bound by particular performance parameters rather than the present 'type specification'. These objective methods of the future should suit the algorithmic routine and binary questioning method by enabling the user to respond rapidly and objectively to produce correct conclusions.

In the meantime, however, standards must comply with Regulations and there are really three parties, excluding the Employer, who have responsibilities in this respect, namely the Architect, Contractor, and local authority.

The demarcation of responsibility between the Architect's design function, the Contractor's construction and possible design responsibility, and the local authorities enforcement task, will inevitably create problems, but demarcation must occur if correct solutions are to be obtained to any dispute of this kind. The local authority have been held(7) to owe a duty to a member of the *public* if negligence in inspection occurs causing non-compliance with the statutory requirements of the Regulations.

CONTRACTOR'S INSOLVENCY

If and when a Contractor is declared, or becomes, insolvent to accord with any of the precise Conditions described in clause 25(2) then the Contract provides for automatic determination of the Contractor's employment, but continuation of the Contract. This continuation seems illogical, nevertheless this is what the Contract provides for, and Fig. 5.2 indicates the procedures to adopt in this event.

Fig. 5.2. Procedure in Contractor's insolvency

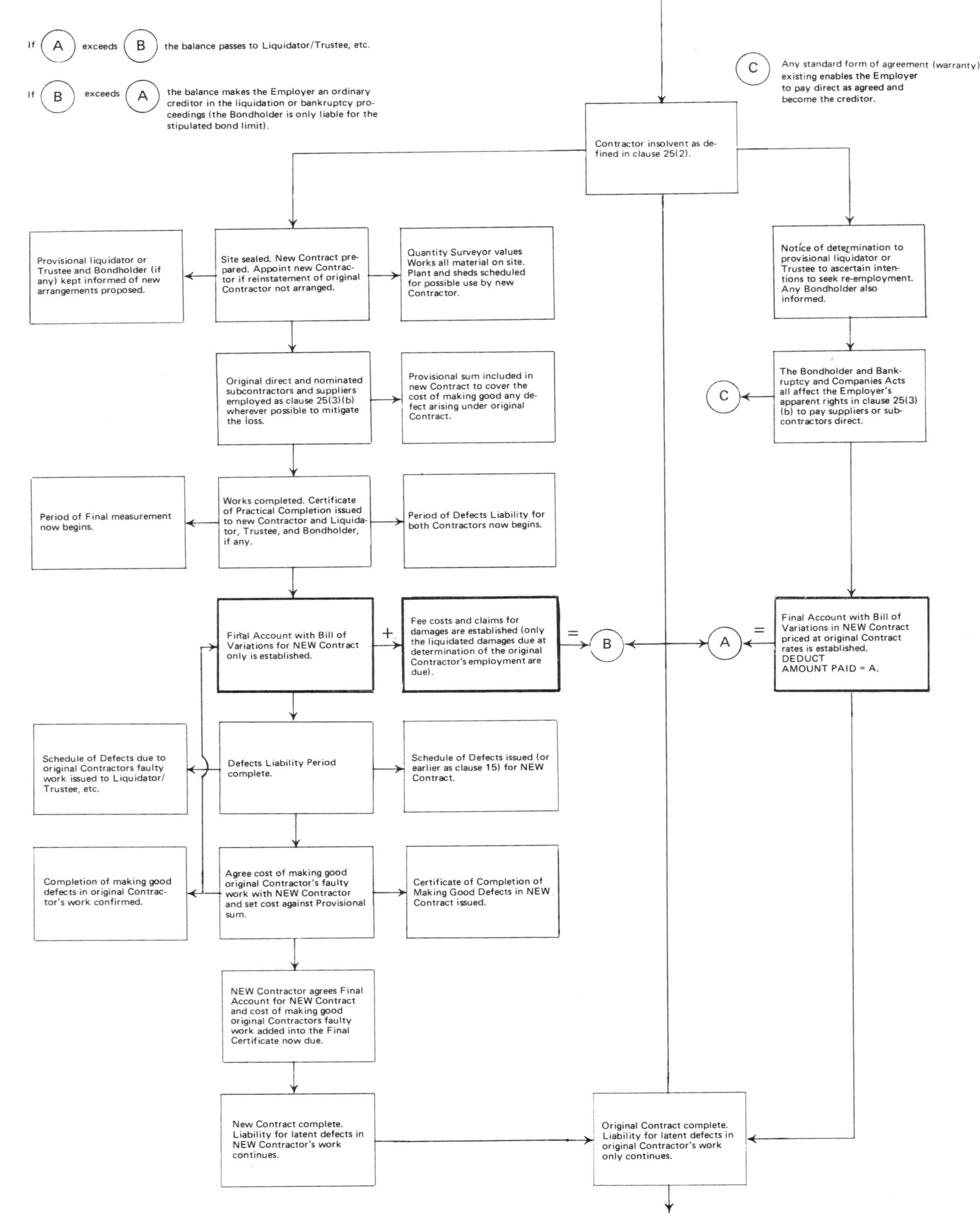

If A exceeds B the balance passes to Liquidator/Trustee, etc.
If B exceeds A the balance makes the Employer an ordinary creditor in the liquidation or bankruptcy proceedings (the Bondholder is only liable for the stipulated bond limit).
C Any standard form of agreement (warranty) existing enables the Employer to pay direct as agreed and become the creditor.
Contractor insolvent as defined in clause 25(2).
Provisional liquidator or Trustee and Bondholder (if any) kept informed of new arrangements proposed.
Site sealed. New Contract prepared. Appoint new Contractor if reinstatement of original Contractor not arranged.
Quantity Surveyor values Works all material on site. Plant and sheds scheduled for possible use by new Contractor.
Notice of determination to provisional liquidator or Trustee to ascertain intentions to seek re-employment. Any Bondholder also informed.
Original direct and nominated subcontractors and suppliers employed as clause 25(3)(b) wherever possible to mitigate the loss.
Provisional sum included in new Contract to cover the cost of making good any defect arising under original Contract.
The Bondholder and Bankruptcy and Companies Acts all affect the Employer's apparent rights in clause 25(3)(b) to pay suppliers or subcontractors direct.
C
Period of Final measurement now begins.
Works completed. Certificate of Practical Completion issued to new Contractor and Liquidator, Trustee, and Bondholder, if any.
Period of Defects Liability for both Contractors now begins.
Final Account with Bill of Variations for NEW Contract only is established.
+
Fee costs and claims for damages are established (only the liquidated damages due at determination of the original Contractor's employment are due).
= B
A =
Final Account with Bill of Variations in NEW Contract priced at original Contract rates is established. DEDUCT AMOUNT PAID = A.
Schedule of Defects due to original Contractors faulty work issued to Liquidator/Trustee, etc.
Defects Liability Period complete.
Schedule of Defects issued (or earlier as clause 15) for NEW Contract.
Completion of making good defects in original Contractor's work confirmed.
Agree cost of making good original Contractor's faulty work with NEW Contractor and set cost against Provisional sum.
Certificate of Completion of Making Good Defects in NEW Contract issued.
NEW Contractor agrees Final Account for NEW Contract and cost of making good original Contractors faulty work added into the Final Certificate now due.
New Contract complete. Liability for latent defects in NEW Contractor's work continues.
Original Contract complete. Liability for latent defects in original Contractor's work only continues.

These procedures are not dealt with in clause 25 charts but nevertheless need to be followed to ensure the Contract provisions are complied with.

SUMMARY AND CONCLUSIONS

This chapter has endeavoured to deal only with certain aspects of Contract practice and some of the associated problems. The object has been to aid the identification, prevention, or solution, of problems which have roots outside the flowchart system. Flowcharts can only solve the kind of problem they have been designed to solve and it is important to realize that untidy problems may have to be cleaned up so that one is left with a purely Contract problem as input to the system.

The chapter concludes with further examples of problems which can arise in practise and are indirectly associated with the Contract.

Consultants

The standard forms are in three sections:

1. *Articles* of Agreement.
2. *Conditions* of Contract.
3. *Appendix* detailing variable *Conditions.*

The Articles of Agreement sets out the names of the parties to the Contract, it also identifies the Works and briefly describes it. In addition to the named parties there is provision for a named Architect or Supervising Officer, and for a Quantity Surveyor. Consultants are not provided for, and their engagement by the Architect or Employer can prove confusing to a Contractor if any form of contractual authority is inadvertently granted or accepted by such persons. The Architect is master under these standard forms, he can delegate his duties but in principle as far as the Contractor is concerned the Architect remains in every way responsible. Direct instructions and even variation orders issued by consultants, un-named in the Contract, are not unfamiliar to Contractors. Bills of Quantities on occasions contain, in the 'Conditions of Contract' section, a reference to the proposed engagement of consultants and confusingly indicate duties which will be delegated to such consultants. Valuations for interim payment of certain specialist works are frequently made subject to the assessment of a consultant. All such arrangements must observe the contractual authority, liability, and responsibility placed upon the Architect in these matters and confirmation of such observance would prevent assumptions of authority in the Contract.

Signing Contracts

Most Contracts are 'under hand' but local authorities in particular do enter into Contracts 'under seal'. This has important effects upon the Contractor's responsibilities for defects which may arise. The Employer is not debarred from a right of action until 12 years after its occurrence, when a Contract is 'under seal'. In simple contracts a right of action elapses after six years. An intention to enter into Contracts 'under seal' is not always made clear in the precontract stage, some Bills may even contain a statement:

The Contract will be signed under hand or seal.

It is clearly desirable to increase the Contractor's responsibility period, particularly for long-term projects, but it is illogical to expect this without some reflection in the tendered sum. The Contractor must always be clearly informed whether the Contract will be under hand or seal.

Contract documents

Basically the work to be carried out is defined and shown on Contract drawings. The quality and quantity of the work is set out in Bills, which must have been prepared strictly according to the *S.M.M.* 5th edition (Metric). (In the editions of Contract without quantities the specifications replaces the Bill.) The Bills also give details of any restriction of method, conditions of site, insurance details, provisional and prime cost sums, temporary work requirements, general and special attendance required upon nominated subcontractors, and protection of the works from inclement weather.

Methods contrary to those set out in the *S.M.M.* can be used providing the precise deviation in method is stated in the

Bills. Deviations in methods of measurement are not uncommon, particularly if computer processes are used to produce the Bills. In addition there is sometimes reluctance on the part of Quantity Surveyors to concern themselves with the Contractor's production problems or methods and this prevents them from thoroughly considering the possibility of any restriction of method that the site, Employer, or Architect may require.

The Contract documents referred to in the standard form Articles of Agreement are:

1. Form of Contract (any Form of Tender used would be included).

2. Contract Drawings (as listed in Bills and Articles of Agreement).

3. Contract Bills (detailed in the Articles of Agreement).

4. Basic Price Schedules (where clause 31ACD applied), Materials, and Goods Schedules.

In addition to the above, the conditions provide that the Architect issues further drawings and details 'necessary either to amplify the Contract Drawings or to carry out and complete the Works . . .' (clause 3(4)). This provision is not always observed by Architects who permit consultants and nominated persons to distribute drawings and details direct to the Contractor without firstly submitting them to the Architect for his approval and issue in the correct way.

Contractors are not always provided with the Contract documents as required by clause 3(2). There is no reason for such delays and Architects or Supervising Officers should ensure they comply with clause 3(2) by putting pressure to bear on the appropriate person or persons preventing their compliance.

Site meetings, instructions, and notices

Verbal instructions are frequently given by the Architect at site meetings and the parties should expressly agree that such instructions are deemed to be in writing (as required by clause 2) once the Architect has issued the minutes of the meeting concerned. The minutes are usually distributed to subcontractors by the Contractor and the Contractor in turn must ensure similar arrangements exist with each subcontractor. Any formal notice required by the Contract must always be made regardless of any references to the subject that may be contained in site meeting minutes.

APPENDICES

APPENDIX 1

Principal condition differences between (1) the Local Authorities edition with quantities and Private Forms with quantities also (2) between the Local Authorities edition with quantities and without quantities.

1. Private Form with quantities

Clause 3. All certificates are issued direct to the *Contractor,* instead of to the Employer.

Clause 17. The *Employer* is prohibited from assigning the Contract without the Contractor's consent. This provision does not appear in the Local Authorities Form with quantities.

Clause 17A. This clause does not appear in the Private Form with quantities.

Clause 19. The *Architect* approves clause 19(2) insurers, instead of the Employer.

Clause 20A. The *Architect* approves clause 20(A) insurers, instead of the Employer.

Clause 20B. The *Contractor* is granted the right to know that proper insurance policies are arranged. In the absence of proper policies the Contractor can himself insure and recover the costs involved. This provision does not appear in the Local Authorities Form with quantities.

Clause 20C. Ditto.

Clause 25. The subclause dealing with corrupt practices and the reference to fair wages (clause 17A) do not appear in the Private Form with quantities.

Clause 26. The *Contractor* can determine his own employment if the Employer is declared insolvent. This provision does not appear in the Local Authority Form.

Clause 30. The Contractor is entitled to payment of certificates within 14 days of *presenting* certificates, instead of within 14 days of issue under the Local Authorities Form.

The period for issue of the Final Certificate is stipulated to be before the expiration of *3 months from:*

(*a*) The end of the Defects Liability Period, or
(*b*) Completion of making good defects, or
(*c*) Receipt of required documents by the Architect instead of a variable period to be stated in the Appendix under the Local Authorities Form.

2. Local Authorities Form without quantities

Clause 3. The Specification and *Schedule of Rates* act jointly as 'substitutes' for the Bills required and used in the Form with quantities.

Clause 11. The Schedule of Rates acts as a 'substitute' for the Bills prices used in the Form with quantities.

Clause 12. The Contract drawings and *the specification* act jointly as 'substitutes' for the Bills referred to in the Form with quantities.

Clause 30. The Schedule of Rates acts as a substitute for the Bills prices used in the Form with quantities.

Clause 31. Ditto.

APPENDIX 2

50p
Stamp to be impressed here if contract is under seal

Standard Form of Building Contract
Local Authorities Edition **WITH** Quantities
1963 Edition (July 1971 Revision)

Articles of Agreement

made the .... day of .... 19........

BETWEEN ....

....

(hereinafter called 'the Employer') of the one part and ....

....

....

of (or whose registered office is situate at) ....

....

....

(hereinafter called 'the Contractor') of the other part. WHEREAS the Employer is desirous of* ....

....

....

(hereinafter called 'the Works') at ....

....

and has caused Drawings and Bills of Quantities showing and describing the work to be done to be prepared by or under the direction of ....

of ....

....

AND WHEREAS the Contractor has supplied the Employer with a fully priced copy of the said Bills of Quantities (which copy is hereinafter referred to as 'the Contract Bills') AND WHEREAS the said Drawings numbered .... to .... inclusive (hereinafter referred to as 'the Contract Drawings') and the Contract Bills have been signed by or on behalf of the parties hereto:

* *State nature of intended Works.*

NOW IT IS HEREBY AGREED AS FOLLOWS:

1 For the consideration hereinafter mentioned the Contractor will upon and subject to the Conditions annexed hereto carry out and complete the Works shown upon the Contract Drawings and described by or referred to in the Contract Bills and in the said Conditions.

2 The Employer will pay to the Contractor the sum of..

....

(£ : :) (hereinafter referred to as 'the Contract Sum') or such other sum as shall become payable hereunder at the times and in the manner specified in the said Conditions.

†*3 [A] The term 'the Architect' in the said Conditions shall mean the said..............................

....of..

....

in the event of his death or ceasing to be the Architect for the purpose of this Contract, such other person as the Employer shall nominate for that purpose, *not being a person to whom the Contractor shall object for reasons considered to be sufficient by an arbitrator appointed in accordance with clause* 35 *of the said Conditions.* ††Provided always that no person subsequently appointed to be the Architect under this Contract shall be entitled to disregard or overrule any certificate or opinion or decision or approval or instruction given or expressed by the Architect for the time being.

†*3 [B] The term 'the Supervising Officer' in the said Conditions shall mean the said..............

....of.. or,

in the event of his death or ceasing to be the Supervising Officer for the purpose of this Contract, such other person as the Employer shall nominate for that purpose, *not being a person to whom the Contractor shall object for reasons considered to be sufficient by an arbitrator appointed in accordance with clause* 35 *of the said Conditions.* ††Provided always that no person consequently appointed to be the Supervising Officer under this Contract shall be entitled to disregard or overrule any certificate or opinion or decision or approval or instruction given or expressed by the Supervising Officer for the time being.

*4 The term 'the Quantity Surveyor' in the said Conditions shall mean..............................

....of..

....

or, in the event of his death or ceasing to be the Quantity Surveyor for the purpose of this Contract, such other person as the Employer shall nominate for that purpose, *not being a person to whom the Contractor shall object for reasons considered to be sufficient by an arbitrator appointed in accordance with clause* 35 *of the said Conditions.*††

†Footnote.—*Article* 3 [A] *is applicable where the person concerned is entitled to the use of the name 'Architect' under and in accordance with the Architects (Registration) Acts,* 1931 *to* 1938. *Article* 3 [B] *is applicable in all other cases. Therefore complete whichever is appropriate and delete the alternative. Where Article* 3 [A] *is completed the expression 'Supervising Officer' shall be deemed to have been deleted throughout the Conditions annexed hereto. Where Article* 3 [B] *is completed the expression 'Architect' shall be deemed to have been deleted throughout the said conditions.*

***Footnote.**—*In cases where the Works are to be carried out under the direction of officials of the Local Authority, insert the names of such officials as are to perform the respective functions of the 'Architect/Supervising Officer' and the 'Quantity Surveyor' under this Contract.*

††Footnote.—*Strike out words in italics in cases where 'the Architect' 'the Supervising Officer' or 'the Quantity Surveyor' is an official of the Local Authority.*

★

***Footnote.**—*This page should be completed with the appropriate Attestation Clause*

The Conditions hereinbefore referred to

Contractor's Obligations.

1 (1) The Contractor shall upon and subject to these Conditions carry out and complete the Works shown upon the Contract Drawings and described by or referred to in the Contract Bills and in these Conditions in every respect to the reasonable satisfaction of the Architect/Supervising Officer.

(2) If the Contractor shall find any discrepancy in or divergence between the Contract Drawings and/or the Contract Bills he shall immediately give to the Architect/Supervising Officer a written notice specifying the discrepancy or divergence, and the Architect/Supervising Officer shall issue instructions in regard thereto.

Architect's/Supervising Officer's instruction

2 (1) The Contractor shall (subject to sub-clauses (2) and (3) of this Condition) forthwith comply with all instructions issued to him by the Architect/Supervising Officer in regard to any matter in respect of which the Architect/Supervising Officer is expressly empowered by these Conditions to issue instructions. If within seven days after receipt of a written notice from the Architect/Supervising Officer requiring compliance with an instruction the Contractor does not comply therewith, then the Employer may employ and pay other persons to execute any work whatsoever which may be necessary to give effect to such instruction and all costs incurred in connection with such employment shall be recoverable from the Contractor by the Employer as a debt or may be deducted by him from any monies due or to become due to the Contractor under this Contract.

(2) Upon receipt of what purports to be an instruction issued to him by the Architect/Supervising Officer the Contractor may request the Architect/Supervising Officer to specify in writing the provision of these Conditions which empowers the issue of the said instruction. The Architect/Supervising Officer shall forthwith comply with any such request, and if the Contractor shall thereafter comply with the said instruction (neither party before such compliance having given to the other a written request to concur in the appointment of an arbitrator under clause 35 of these Conditions in order that it may be decided whether the provision specified by the Architect/Supervising Officer empowers the issue of the said instruction), then the issue of the same shall be deemed for all the purposes of this Contract to have been empowered by the provision of these Conditions specified by the Architect/Supervising Officer in answer to the Contractor's request.

(3) All instructions issued by the Architect/Supervising Officer shall be issued in writing. Any instruction issued orally shall be of no immediate effect, but shall be confirmed in writing by the Contractor to the Architect/Supervising Officer within seven days, and if not dissented from in writing by the Architect/Supervising Officer to the Contractor within seven days from receipt of the Contractor's confirmation shall take effect as from the expiration of the latter said seven days.

Provided always:

(a) That if the Architect/Supervising Officer within seven days of giving such an oral instruction shall himself confirm the same in writing, then the Contractor shall not be obliged to confirm as aforesaid, and the said instruction shall take effect as from the date of the Architect's/Supervising Officer's confirmation, and

(b) That if neither the Contractor nor the Architect/Supervising Officer shall confirm such an oral instruction in the manner and at the time aforesaid but the Contractor shall nevertheless comply with the same, then the Architect/Supervising Officer may confirm the same in writing at any time prior to the issue of the Final Certificate, and the said instruction shall thereupon be deemed to have taken effect on the date on which it was issued.

Contract documents.

3 (1) The Contract Drawings and the Contract Bills shall remain in the custody of the Architect/Supervising Officer or of the Quantity Surveyor so as to be available at all reasonable times for the inspection of the Employer or of the Contractor.

(2) Immediately after the execution of this Contract the Architect/Supervising Officer without charge to the Contractor shall furnish him (unless he shall have been previously furnished) with—

(a) One copy certified on behalf of the Employer of the Articles of Agreement and of these Conditions,

(b) two copies of the Contract Drawings, and

(c) two copies of the unpriced Bills of Quantities, and (if requested by the Contractor) one copy of the Contract Bills.

(3) So soon as is possible after the execution of this Contract the Architect/Supervising Officer without charge to the Contractor shall furnish him (unless he shall have been previously furnished) with two copies of the specification, descriptive schedules or other like document necessary for use in carrying out the Works.

Provided that nothing contained in the said specification, descriptive schedules or other documents shall impose any obligation beyond those imposed by the Contract documents, namely, by the Contract Drawings, the Contract Bills, the Articles of Agreement and these Conditions.

(4) As and when from time to time may be necessary the Architect/Supervising Officer without charge to the Contractor shall furnish him with two copies of such drawings or details as are reasonably necessary either to explain and amplify the Contract Drawings or to enable the Contractor to carry out and complete the Works in accordance with these Conditions.

(5) The Contractor shall keep one copy of the Contract Drawings, one copy of the unpriced Bills of Quantities, one copy of the specification, descriptive schedule or other like documents referred to in sub-clause (3) of this Condition, and one copy of the drawings and details referred to in sub-clause (4) of this Condition upon the Works so as to be available to the Architect/Supervising Officer or his representative at all reasonable times.

(6) Upon final payment under clause 30 (6) of these Conditions the Contractor shall if so requested by the Architect/Supervising Officer forthwith return to the Architect/Supervising Officer all drawings, details, specifications, descriptive schedules and other documents of a like nature which bear his name.

(7) None of the documents hereinbefore mentioned shall be used by the Contractor for any purpose other than this Contract, and neither the Employer, the Architect/Supervising Officer nor the Quantity Surveyor shall divulge or use except for the purposes of this Contract any of the prices in the Contract Bills.

(8) Any certificate to be issued by the Architect/Supervising Officer under these Conditions shall subject to clause 27 (d) hereof, be issued to the Employer, and immediately upon the issue of any certificate the Architect/Supervising Officer shall send a duplicate copy thereof to the Contractor.

Statutory obligations, notices, fees and charges.

4 (1) The Contractor shall comply with and give all notices required by any Act of Parliament, any instrument rule or order made under any Act of Parliament, or any regulation or byelaw of any local authority or of any statutory undertaker which has any jurisdiction with regard to the Works or with whose systems the same are or will be connected. The Contractor before making any variation from the Contract Drawings or the Contract Bills necessitated by such compliance shall give to the Architect/Supervising Officer a written notice specifying and giving the reason for such variation and the Architect/Supervising Officer may issue instructions in regard thereto. If within seven days of having given the said written notice the Contractor does not receive any instructions in regard to the matters therein specified, he shall proceed with the work conforming to the Act of Parliament, instrument, rule, order, regulation or byelaw in question and any variation thereby necessitated shall be deemed to be a variation required by the Architect/Supervising Officer.

(2) The Contractor shall pay and indemnify the Employer against liability in respect of any fees or charges (including any rates or taxes) legally demandable under any Act of Parliament, any instrument, rule or order made under any Act of Parliament, or any regulation or byelaw of any local authority or of any statutory undertaker in respect of the Works. Provided that the amount of any such fees or charges (including any rates or taxes) shall be added to the Contract Sum unless they

(a) arise in respect of work executed or materials or goods supplied by a local authority or statutory undertaker for which a prime cost sum is included in the Contract Bills or for which a prime cost sum has arisen as a result of Architect's/Supervising Officer's instructions given under clause 11 (3) of these Conditions, or

(b) are priced or stated by way of a provisional sum in the Contract Bill.

Levels and setting out of the Works.

5 The Architect/Supervising Officer shall determine any levels which may be required for the execution of the Works, and shall furnish to the Contractor by way of accurately dimensioned drawings such information as shall enable the Contractor to set out the Works at ground level. Unless the Architect/Supervising Officer shall otherwise instruct, in which case the Contract Sum shall be adjusted accordingly, the Contractor shall be responsible for and shall entirely at his own cost amend any errors arising from his own inaccurate setting out.

Materials, goods and workmanship to conform to description, testing and inspection.

6 (1) All materials, goods and workmanship shall so far as procurable be of the respective kinds and standards described in the Contract Bills.

(2) The Contractor shall upon the request of the Architect/Supervising Officer furnish him with vouchers to prove that the materials and goods comply with sub-clause (1) of this Condition.

(3) The Architect/Supervising Officer may issue instructions requiring the Contractor to open up for inspection any work covered up or to arrange for or carry out any test of any materials or goods (whether or not already incorporated in the Works) or of any executed work, and the cost of such opening up or testing (together with the cost of making good in consequence thereof) shall be added to the Contract Sum unless provided for in the Contract Bills or unless the inspection or test shows that the work, materials or goods are not in accordance with this Contract.

(4) The Architect/Supervising Officer may issue instructions in regard to the removal from the site of any work, materials or goods which are not in accordance with this Contract.

(5) The Architect/Supervising Officer may (but not unreasonably or vexatiously) issue instructions requiring the dismissal from the Works of any person employed thereon.

Royalties and patent rights.

7 All royalties or other sums payable in respect of the supply and use in carrying out the Works as described by or referred to in the Contract Bills of any patented articles, processes or inventions shall be deemed to have been included in the Contract Sum, and the Contractor shall indemnify the Employer from and against all claims, proceedings, damages, costs and expenses which may be brought or made against the Employer or to which he may be put by reason of the Contractor infringing or being held to have infringed any patent rights in relation to any such articles, processes and inventions.

Provided that where in compliance with Architect's/Supervising Officer's instructions the Contractor shall supply and use in carrying out the Works any patented articles, processes or inventions, the Contractor shall not be liable in respect of any infringement or alleged infringement of any patent rights in relation to any such articles, processes and inventions and all royalties damages or other monies which the Contractor may be liable to pay to the persons entitled to such patent rights shall be added to the Contract Sum.

Foreman-in-charge.

8 The Contractor shall constantly keep upon the Works a competent foreman-in-charge and any instructions given to him by the Architect/Supervising Officer shall be deemed to have been issued to the Contractor.

Access for Architect/Supervising Officer to the Works.

9 The Architect/Supervising Officer and his representatives shall at all reasonable times have access to the Works and to the workshops or other places of the Contractor where work is being prepared for the Contract, and when work is to be so prepared in workshops or other places of a sub-contractor (whether or not a nominated sub-contractor as defined in clause 27 of these Conditions) the Contractor shall by a term in the sub-contract so far as possible secure a similar right of access to those workshops or places for the Architect/Supervising Officer and his representatives and shall do all things reasonably necessary to make such right effective.

Clerk of Works.

10 The Employer shall be entitled to appoint a clerk of works whose duty shall be to act solely as inspector on behalf of the Employer under the directions of the Architect/Supervising Officer and the Contractor shall afford every reasonable facility for the performance of that duty. If any directions are given to the Contractor or to his foreman upon the Works by the clerk of works the same shall be of no effect unless given in regard to a matter in respect of which the Architect/Supervising Officer is expressly empowered by these Conditions to issue instructions and unless confirmed in writing by the Architect/Supervising Officer within two working days of their being given. If any such directions are so given and confirmed then as from the date of confirmation they shall be deemed to be Architect's/Supervising Officer's instructions.

Variations, provisional and prime cost sums.

11 (1) The Architect/Supervising Officer may issue instructions requiring a variation and he may sanction in writing any variation made by the Contractor otherwise than pursuant to an instruction of the Architect/Supervising Officer. No variation required by the Architect/Supervising Officer or subsequently sanctioned by him shall vitiate this Contract.

(2) The term 'variation' as used in these Conditions means the alteration or modification of the design, quality or quantity of the Works as shown upon the Contract Drawings and described by or referred to in the Contract Bills, and includes the addition, omission or substitution of any work, the alteration of the kind or standard of any of the materials or goods to be used in the Works, and the removal from the site of any work materials or goods executed or brought thereon by the Contractor for the purposes of the Works other than work materials or goods which are not in accordance with this Contract.

(3) The Architect/Supervising Officer shall issue instructions in regard to the expenditure of prime cost* and provisional sums included in the Contract Bills and of prime cost sums which arise as a result of instructions issued in regard to the expenditure of provisional sums.

***Footnote.**—*The term 'prime cost' may be indicated by the abbreviation 'P.C.' in any document relating to this Contract (including the Contract Bills), and wherever the abbreviation is used it shall be deemed to mean 'prime cost'.*

(4) All variations required by the Architect/Supervising Officer or subsequently sanctioned by him in writing and all work executed by the Contractor for which provisional sums are included in the Contract Bills (other than work for which a tender made under clause 27 (g) of these Conditions has been accepted) shall be measured and valued by the Quantity Surveyor who shall give to the Contractor an opportunity of being present at the time of such measurement and of taking such notes and measurements as the Contractor may require. The valuation of variations and of work executed by the Contractor for which a provisional sum is included in the Contract Bills (other than work for which a tender has been accepted as aforesaid) unless otherwise agreed shall be made in accordance with the following rules:—

(a) The prices in the Contract Bills shall determine the valuation of work of similar character executed under similar conditions as work priced therein;

(b) The said prices, where work is not of similar character or executed under similar conditions as aforesaid, shall be the basis of prices for the same so far as may be reasonable, failing which a fair valuation thereof shall be made;

(c) Where work cannot properly be measured and valued the Contractor shall be allowed:

(i) daywork rates at the prices inserted by the Contractor in the Contract Bills; or

(ii) where no such prices have been inserted, the prime cost of such work calculated in accordance with the 'Definition of Prime Cost of Daywork carried out under a Building Contract' last before issued by the Royal Institution of Chartered Surveyors and the National Federation of Building Trades Employers together with percentage additions to each section of the prime cost at the rates set out by the Contractor in the Contract Bills and recorded in the appendix to these Conditions; or

(iii) where the work is within the province of any specialist trade and the said Institution and the appropriate body representing the employers in that trade have agreed and issued a definition of prime cost of daywork, the prime cost of such work calculated in accordance with that definition as last before issued together with percentage additions on the prime cost at the rates set out by the Contractor in the Contract Bills and recorded in the appendix to these Conditions.

Provided that in any case vouchers specifying the time daily spent upon the work (and if required by the Architect/Supervising Officer the workmen's names) and the materials employed shall be delivered for verification to the Architect/Supervising Officer or his authorised representative not later than the end of the week following that in which the work has been executed;

(d) The prices in the Contract Bills shall determine the valuation of items omitted; provided that if omissions substantially vary the conditions under which any remaining items of work are carried out the prices for such remaining items shall be valued under rule (b) of this sub-clause.

(5) Effect shall be given to the measurement and valuation of variations under sub-clause (4) of this Condition in Interim Certificates and by adjustment of the Contract Sum; and effect shall be given to the measurement and valuation of work for which a provisional sum is included in the Contract Bills under the said sub-clause in Interim Certificates and by adjustment of the Contract Sum in accordance with clause 30 (5) (c) of these Conditions.

(6) If upon written application being made to him by the Contractor, the Architect/Supervising Officer is of the opinion that a variation or the execution by the Contractor of work for which a provisional sum is included in the Contract Bills (other than work for which a tender made under clause 27 (g) of these Conditions has been accepted) has involved the Contractor in direct loss and/or expense for which he would not be reimbursed by payment in respect of a valuation made in accordance with the rules contained in sub-clause (4) of this Condition and if the said application is made within a reasonable time of the loss or expense having been incurred, then the Architect/Supervising Officer shall either himself ascertain or shall instruct the Quantity Surveyor to ascertain the amount of such loss or expense. Any amount from time to time so ascertained shall be added to the Contract Sum, and if an Interim Certificate is issued after the date of ascertainment any such amount shall be added to the amount which would otherwise be stated as due in such Certificate.

Contract Bills.

12 (1) The quality and quantity of the work included in the Contract Sum shall be deemed to be that which is set out in the Contract Bills which Bills unless otherwise expressly stated in respect of any specified item or items shall be deemed to have been prepared in accordance with the principles of the Standard Method of Measurement of Building Works 5th edition Imperial, revised March 1964/5th edition Metric* by the Royal Institution of Chartered Surveyors and the National Federation of Building Trades Employers, but save as aforesaid nothing contained in the Contract Bills shall overide, modify, or affect in any way whatsoever the application or interpretation of that which is contained in these Conditions.

***Footnote.**—*Delete whichever edition is inapplicable*

(2) Any error in description or in quantity in or omission of items from the Contract Bills shall not vitiate this Contract but shall be corrected and deemed to be a variation required by the Architect/Supervising Officer.

Contract Sum.

13 The Contract Sum shall not be adjusted or altered in any way whatsoever otherwise than in accordance with the express provisions of these Conditions, and subject to clause 12 (2) of these Conditions any error whether of arithmetic or not in the computation of the Contract Sum shall be deemed to have been accepted by the parties hereto.

Materials and Goods unfixed or off-site.

14 (1) Unfixed materials and goods delivered to, placed on or adjacent to the Works and intended therefor shall not be removed except for use upon the Works unless the Architect/Supervising Officer has consented in writing to such removal which consent shall not be unreasonably withheld. Where the value of any such materials or goods has in accordance with clause 30 (2) of these Conditions been included in any Interim Certificate under which the Contractor has received payment, such materials and goods shall become the property of the Employer, but subject to clause 20 [B] or clause 20 [C] of these Conditions (if applicable), the Contractor shall remain responsible for loss or damage to the same.

(2) Where the value of any materials or goods has in accordance with clause 30 (2A) of these Conditions been included in any Interim Certificate under which the Contractor has received payment, such materials and goods shall become the property of the Employer, and thereafter the Contractor shall not, except for use upon the Works, remove or cause or permit the same to be moved or removed from the premises where they are, but the Contractor shall nevertheless be responsible for any loss thereof or damage thereto and for the cost of storage, handling and insurance of the same until such time as they are delivered to and placed on or adjacent to the Works whereupon the provisions of sub-clause (1) of this clause (except the words 'where the value' to the word 'the Employer but') shall apply thereto.

Practical completion and defects liability.

15 (1) When in the opinion of the Architect/Supervising Officer the Works are practically completed, he shall forthwith issue a certificate to that effect and Practical Completion of the Works shall be deemed for all the purposes of this Contract to have taken place on the day named in such certificate.

(2) Any defects, shrinkages or other faults which shall appear within the Defects Liability Period stated in the appendix to these Conditions and which are due to materials or workmanship not in accordance with this Contract or to frost occurring before Practical Completion of the Works, shall be specified by the Architect/Supervising Officer in a Schedule of Defects which he shall deliver to the Contractor not later than 14 days after the expiration of the said Defects Liability Period, and within a reasonable time after receipt of such Schedule the defects, shrinkages, and other faults therein specified shall be made good by the Contractor and (unless the Architect/Supervising Officer shall otherwise instruct, in which case the Contract Sum shall be adjusted accordingly) entirely at his own cost.

(3) Notwithstanding sub-clause (2) of this Condition the Architect/Supervising Officer may whenever he considers it necessary so to do, issue instructions requiring any defect, shrinkage or other fault which shall appear within the Defects Liability Period named in the appendix to these Conditions and which is due to materials or workmanship not in accordance with this Contract or to frost occurring before Practical Completion of the Works, to be made good, and the Contractor shall within a reasonable time after receipt of such instructions comply with the same and (unless the Architect/Supervising Officer shall otherwise instruct, in which case the Contract Sum shall be adjusted accordingly) entirely at his own cost. Provided that no such instructions shall be issued after delivery of a Schedule of Defects or after 14 days from the expiration of the said Defects Liability Period.

(4) When in the opinion of the Architect/Supervising Officer any defects, shrinkages or other faults which he may have required to be made good under sub-clauses (2) and (3) of this Condition shall have been made good he shall issue a certificate to that effect, and completion of making good defects shall be deemed for all the purposes of this Contract to have taken place on the day named in such certificate.

(5) In no case shall the Contractor be required to make good at his own cost any damage by frost which may appear after Practical Completion of the Works, unless the Architect/Supervising Officer shall certify that such damage is due to injury which took place before Practical Completion of the Works.

Sectional completion.

16 If at any time or times before Practical Completion of the Works the Employer with the consent of the Contractor shall take possession of any part or parts of the same (any such part being hereinafter in this clause referred to as 'the relevant part') then notwithstanding anything expressed or implied elsewhere in this Contract:—

(a) Within seven days from the date on which the Employer shall have taken possession of the relevant part the Architect/Supervising Officer shall issue a certificate stating his estimate of the approximate total value of the said part, and for all the purposes of this Condition (but for no other) the value so stated shall be deemed to be the total value of the said part.

(b) For the purposes of sub-paragraph (ii) of paragraph (f) of this Condition and of sub-clauses (2) (3) and (5) of clause 15 of these Conditions, Practical Completion of the relevant part shall be deemed to have occurred and the Defects Liability Period in respect of the relevant part shall be deemed to have commenced on the date on which the Employer shall have taken possession thereof.

(c) When in the opinion of the Architect/Supervising Officer any defects, shrinkages or other faults in the relevant part which he may have required to be made good under sub-clause (2) or sub-clause (3) of clause 15 of these Conditions shall have been made good he shall issue a certificate to that effect.

(d) The Contractor shall reduce the value insured under clause 20 [A] of these Conditions (if applicable) by the full value of the relevant part, and the said relevant part shall as from the date on which the Employer shall have taken possession thereof be at the sole risk of the Employer as regards any of the contingencies referred to in the said clause.

(e) In lieu of any sum to be paid or allowed by the Contractor under clause 22 of these Conditions in respect of any period during which the Works may remain incomplete occurring after the date on which the Employer shall have taken possession of the relevant part there shall be paid or allowed such sum as bears the same ratio to the sum which would be paid or allowed apart from the provisions of this Condition as does the Contract Sum less the total value of the said relevant part to the Contract Sum.

(f) (i) Within fourteen days of the date on which the Employer shall have taken possession of the relevant part there shall be paid to the Contractor from the sums then retained under clause 30 (3) of these Conditions (if any) one moiety of such amount as bears the same ratio to the unreduced amount named in the appendix to these Conditions as Limit of Retention Fund as does the total value of the said relevant part to the Contract Sum, and the amount named in the appendix to these Conditions as Limit of Retention Fund shall be reduced by the amount of such moiety.

(ii) On the expiration of the Defects Liability Period named in the appendix to these Conditions in respect of the relevant part or on the issue of the Certificate of Completion of Making Good Defects in respect of the relevant part, whichever is the later, there shall be paid to the Contractor from the sums then retained under clause 30 (3) of these Conditions (if any) the other moiety of the amount referred to in the immediately preceding sub-paragraph, and the amount named in the appendix to these Conditions as Limit of Retention Fund shall be reduced by the amount of such moiety.

Assignment or sub-letting.

17 The Contractor shall not without the written consent of the Employer assign this Contract, and shall not without the written consent of the Architect/Supervising Officer (which consent shall not be unreasonably withheld to the prejudice of the Contractor) sub-let any portion of the Works.

Provided that it shall be a condition in any sub-letting which may occur that the employment of the sub-contractor under the sub-contract shall determine immediately upon the determination (for any reason) of the Contractor's employment under this Contract.

Fair Wages.

17A (1) (a) The Contractor shall pay rates of wages and observe hours and conditions of labour not less favourable than those established for the trade or industry in the district where the work is carried out by machinery of negotiation or arbitration to which the parties are organisations of employers and trade unions representative respectively of substantial proportions of the employers and workers engaged in the trade or industry in the district.

(b) In the absence of any rates of wages, hours or conditions of labour so established the Contractor shall pay rates of wages and observe hours and conditions of labour which are not less favourable tha. the general level of wages, hours and conditions observed by other employers whose general circumstances in the trade or industry in which the Contractor is engaged are similar.

(2) The Contractor shall in respect of all persons employed by him (whether in carrying out this Contract or otherwise) in every factory, workshop or other place occupied or used by him for the carrying out of this Contract (including the Works) comply with the general conditions required by this Condition. The Contractor hereby warrants that to the best of his knowledge and belief he has complied with the general conditions required by this Condition for at least three months prior to the date of his tender for this Contract.

(3) In the event of any question arising as to whether the requirements of this Condition are being observed, the question shall, if not otherwise disposed of, and notwithstanding anything in clause 35 of these Conditions (the provisions of which shall not apply to this Condition), be referred through the Minister of Labour to an independent Tribunal for decision.

(4) The Contractor shall recognise the freedom of his workpeople to be members of Trade Unions.

(5) The Contractor shall at all times during the continuance of this Contract display, for the information of his workpeople, in every factory, workshop or place occupied or used by him for the carrying out of this Contract (including the Works) a copy of this Condition. Where rates of wages, hours or conditions of work have been established either by negotiation or arbitration as described in paragraph (a) of sub-clause (1) of this Condition or by any agreement commonly recognised by employers and workers in the district a copy of the award agreement or other document specifying or recording such rates hours or conditions shall also be exhibited by the Contractor or made available by him for inspection in any such place as aforesaid.

(6) The Contractor shall be responsible for the observance of this Condition by sub-contractors employed in the carrying out of this Contract, and shall if required notify the Employer of the names and addresses of all such sub-contractors.

(7) The Contractor shall keep proper wages books and time sheets showing the wages paid to and the time worked by the workpeople in his employ in and about the carrying out of this Contract, and such wages books and time sheets shall be produced whenever required for the inspection of any officer authorised by the Employer.

(8) If the Employer shall have reasonable ground for believing that the requirements of any of the preceding sub-clauses of this Condition are not being observed, he or the Architect/Supervising Officer on his behalf shall be entitled to require proof of the rates of wages paid and hours and conditions observed by the Contractor and sub-contractors in carrying out the Works.

Injury to persons and property and Employer's indemnity.

18 (1) The Contractor shall be liable for, and shall indemnify the Employer against, any liability, loss, claim or proceedings whatsoever arising under any statute or at common law in respect of personal injury to or the death of any person whomsoever arising out of or in the course of or caused by the carrying out of the Works, unless due to any act or neglect of the Employer or of any person for whom the Employer is responsible.

(2) Except for such loss or damage as is at the risk of the Employer under clause 20 [B] or clause 20 [C] of these Conditions (if applicable) the Contractor shall be liable for, and shall indemnify the Employer against, any expense, liability, loss, claim or proceedings in respect of any injury or damage whatsoever to any property real or personal in so far as such injury or damage arises out of or in the course of or by reason of the carrying out of the Works, and provided always that the same is due to any negligence, omission or default of the Contractor, his servants or agents or of any sub-contractor his servants or agents.

Insurance against injury to persons and property.

19 (1) (a) Without prejudice to his liability to indemnify the Employer under clause 18 of these Conditions, the Contractor shall maintain and shall cause any sub-contractor to maintain:

(i) Such insurances as are necessary to cover the liability of the Contractor or, as the case may be, of such sub-contractor, in respect of personal injuries or deaths arising out of or in the course of or caused by the carrying out of the Works; and

(ii) Such insurances as may be specifically required by the Contract Bills in respect of injury or damage to property real or personal arising out of or in the course of or by reason of the carrying out of the Works and caused by any negligence, omission or default of the Contractor, his servants or agents or, as the case may be, of such sub-contractor his servants or agents.

(b) As and when he is reasonably required so to do by the Employer the Contractor shall produce and shall cause any sub-contractor to produce for inspection by the Employer documentary evidence that the insurances required by this sub-clause are properly maintained, but on any occasion the Employer may (but not unreasonably or vexatiously) require to have produced for his inspection the policy or policies and receipts in question.

(c) Should the Contractor or any sub-contractor make default in insuring or in continuing or in causing to insure as provided in this sub-clause the Employer may himself insure against any risk with respect to which the default shall have occurred and may deduct a sum or sums equivalent to the amount paid or payable in respect of premiums from any monies due or to become due to the Contractor.

(2) (a) The Contractor shall maintain in the joint names of the Employer and the Contractor insurances for such amounts of indemnity as may be specified by way of provisional sum items in the Contract Bills in respect of any expense, liability, loss, claim, or proceedings which the Employer may incur or sustain by reason of damage to any property other than the Works caused by collapse, subsidence, vibration, weakening or removal of support or lowering of ground water arising out of or in the course of or by reason of the carrying out of the Works excepting damage

(i) caused by the negligence, omission or default of the Contractor, his servants or agents or of any sub-contractor his servants or agents;

(ii) attributable to errors or omissions in the designing of the Works;

(iii) which can reasonably be foreseen to be inevitable having regard to the nature of the work to be executed or the manner of its execution;

(iv) which is at the risk of the Employer under clause 20 [B] or clause 20 [C] of these Conditions (if applicable);

(v) arising from a nuclear risk or a war risk;

(b) Any such insurance as is referred to in the immediately preceding paragraph shall be placed with insurers to be approved by the Employer, and the Contractor shall deposit with him the policy or policies and the receipts in respect of premiums paid.

(c) Should the Contractor make default in insuring or in continuing to insure as provided in this sub-clause the Employer may himself insure against any risk with respect to which the default shall have occurred and the amounts paid or payable by the Employer in respect of premiums shall not be set against the relevant provisional sum in the settlement of accounts under clause 30 (5) (c) of these Conditions.

Insurance of the Works against Fire, etc.

20 *[A] (1) The Contractor shall in the joint names of the Employer and Contractor insure against loss and damage by fire, lightning, explosion, storm, tempest, flood, bursting or overflowing of water tanks, apparatus or pipes, earthquake, aircraft and other aerial devices or articles dropped therefrom, riot and civil commotion for the full value thereof (plus the percentage (if any) named in the appendix to these Conditions to cover professional fees) all work executed and all unfixed materials and goods, delivered to, placed on or adjacent to the Works and intended therefor but excluding temporary buildings, plant, tools and equipment owned or hired by the Contractor or any sub-contractor, and shall keep such work, materials and goods so insured until Practical Completion of the Works. Such insurance shall be with insurers approved by the Employer and the Contractor shall deposit with him the policy or policies and the receipts in respect of premiums paid; and should the Contractor make default in insuring or continuing to insure as aforesaid the Employer may himself insure against any risk in respect of which the default shall have occurred and deduct a sum equivalent to the amount paid by him in respect of premiums from any monies due or to become due to the Contractor. Provided always that if the Contractor shall independently of his obligations under this Contract maintain a policy of insurance which covers (*inter alia*) the said work, materials and goods against the aforesaid contingencies to the full value thereof (plus the aforesaid percentage (if any)), then the maintenance by the Contractor of such policy shall, if the Employer's interest is endorsed thereon, be a discharge of the Contractor's obligation to insure in the joint names of the Employer and Contractor; if and so long as the Contractor is able to produce for inspection as and when he is reasonably required so to do by the Employer documentary evidence that the said policy is properly endorsed and maintained then the Contractor shall be discharged from his obligation to deposit a policy or policies and receipts with the Employer but on any occasion the Employer may (but not unreasonably or vexatiously) require to have produced for his inspection the policy and receipts in question.

(2) Upon settlement of any claim under the insurances aforesaid the Contractor with due diligence shall restore work damaged replace or repair any unfixed materials or goods which have been destroyed or injured remove and dispose of any debris and proceed with the carrying out and completion of the Works. All monies received from such insurances (less only the aforesaid percentage (if any)) shall be paid to the Contractor by instalments under certificates of the Architect/Supervising Officer issued at the Period of Interim Certificates named in the appendix to these conditions. The Contractor shall not be entitled to any payment in respect of the restoration of work damaged, the replacement and repair of any unfixed materials or goods, and the removal and disposal of debris other than the monies received under the said insurances.

*(B). All work executed and all unfixed materials and goods, delivered to, placed on or adjacent to the Works and intended therefor (except temporary buildings, plant, tools and equipment owned or hired by the Contractor or any sub-contractor) shall be at the sole risk of the Employer as regards loss or damage by fire, lightning, explosion, storm, tempest, flood, bursting or overflowing of water tanks, apparatus or pipes, earthquake, aircraft and other aerial devices or articles dropped therefrom, riot and civil commotion. If any loss or damage affecting the Works or any part thereof or any such unfixed materials or goods is occasioned by any one or more of the said contingencies, then

(a) The occurrence of such loss or damage shall be disregarded in computing any amounts payable to the Contractor under or by virtue of this Contract.

***Footnote.**—*Clause* 20 [*A*] *is applicable to the erection of a new building if the Contractor is required to insure against loss or damage by fire, etc.; clause* 20 [*B*] *is applicable to the erection of a new building if the Employer is to bear the risk in respect of loss or damage by fire, etc.; and clause* 20 [*C*] *is applicable to alterations of or extensions to an existing building; therefore strike out clauses* [*B*] *and* [*C*] *or clauses* [*A*] *and* [*C*] *or clauses* [*A*] *and* [*B*] *as the case may require.*

(b) The Contractor with due diligence shall restore work damaged, replace or repair any unfixed materials or goods which have been destroyed or injured, remove, and dispose of any debris and proceed with the carrying out and completion of the Works. The restoration of work damaged, the replacement and repair of unfixed materials and goods and the removal and disposal of debris shall be deemed to be a variation required by the Architect/Supervising Officer.

*[C]. The existing structures together with the contents thereof owned by him or for which he is responsible and the Works and all unfixed materials and goods, delivered to, placed on or adjacent to the Works and intended therefor (except temporary buildings, plant, tools and equipment owned or hired by the Contractor or any sub-contractor) shall be at the sole risk of the Employer as regards loss or damage by fire, lightning, explosion, storm, tempest, flood, bursting or overflowing of water tanks, apparatus, or pipes, earthquake, aircraft and other aerial devices or articles dropped therefrom, riot and civil commotion and the Employer shall maintain adequate insurance against those risks.** If any loss or damage affecting the Works or any part thereof or any such unfixed materials or goods is occasioned by any one or more of the said contingencies, then

(a) The occurrence of such loss or damage shall be disregarded in computing any amounts payable to the Contractor under or by virtue of this Contract.

(b) (i) If it is just and equitable so to do the employment of the Contractor under this Contract may within 28 days of the occurrence of such loss or damage be determined at the option of either party by notice by registered post or recorded delivery from either party to the other. Within 7 days of receiving such a notice (but not thereafter) either party may give to the other a written request to concur in the appointment of an arbitrator under clause 35 of these Conditions in order that it may be determined whether such determination will be just and equitable.

(ii) Upon the giving or receiving by the Employer of such a notice of determination or, where a reference to arbitration is made as aforesaid, upon the arbitrator upholding the notice of determination, the provisions of sub-clause (2) (except sub-paragraph (vi) of paragraph (b)) of clause 26 of these Conditions shall apply.

(c) If no notice of determination is served as aforesaid, or, where a reference to arbitration is made as aforesaid, if the arbitrator decided against the notice of determination, then

(i) the Contractor with due diligence shall reinstate or make good such loss or damage, and proceed with the carrying out and completion of the Works;

(ii) the Architect/Supervising Officer may issue instructions requiring the Contractor to remove and dispose of any debris; and

(iii) the reinstatement and making good of such loss or damage and (when required) the removal and disposal of debris shall be deemed to be a variation required by the Architect/Supervising Officer.

Possession completion and postponement.

21 (1) On the Date for Possession stated in the appendix to these Conditions possession of the site shall be given to the Contractor who shall thereupon begin the Works and regularly and diligently proceed with the same, and who shall complete the same on or before the Date for Completion stated in the said appendix subject nevertheless to the provisions for extension of time contained in clauses 23 and 33 (1) (c) of these Conditions.

(2) The Architect/Supervising Officer may issue instructions in regard to the postponement of any work to be executed under the provisions of this Contract.

Damages for non-completion.

22 If the Contractor fails to complete the Works by the Date for Completion stated in the appendix to these Conditions or within any extended time fixed under clause 23 or clause 33 (1) (c) of these Conditions and the Architect/Supervising Officer certifies in writing that in his opinion the same ought reasonably so to have been completed, then the Contractor shall pay or allow to the Employer a sum calculated at the rate stated in the said appendix as Liquidated and Ascertained Damages for the period during which the Works shall so remain or have remained incomplete, and the Employer may deduct such sum from any monies due or to become due to the Contractor under this Contract.

***Footnote.**—*See note at foot of page* 11.

****Footnote.**—*In some cases it may not be possible for the Employer to take out insurance against certain of the risks mentioned in this clause. This matter should be arranged between the parties at the tender stage and the clause amended accordingly.*

Extension of time.

23 Upon it becoming reasonably apparent that the progress of the Works is delayed, the Contractor shall forthwith give written notice of the cause of the delay to the Architect/Supervising Officer, and if in the opinion of the Architect/Supervising Officer the completion of the Works is likely to be or has been delayed beyond the Date for Completion stated in the appendix to these Conditions or beyond any extended time previously fixed under either this clause or clause 33 (1) (c) of these Conditions.

(a) by *force majeure*, or

(b) by reason of any exceptionally inclement weather, or

(c) by reason of loss or damage occasioned by any one or more of the contingencies referred to in clause 20 [A], [B] or [C] of these Conditions, or

(d) by reason of civil commotion, local combination of workmen, strike or lockout affecting any of the trades employed upon the Works or any of the trades engaged in the preparation manufacture or transportation of any of the goods or materials required for the Works, or

(e) by reason of Architect's/Supervising Officer's instructions issued under clauses 1 (2), 11 (1) or 21 (2) of these Conditions, or

(f) by reason of the Contractor not having received in due time necessary instructions, drawings, details or levels from the Architect/Supervising Officer for which he specifically applied in writing on a date which having regard to the Date for Completion stated in the appendix to these Conditions or to any extension of time then fixed under this clause or clause 33 (1) (c) of these Conditions was neither unreasonably distant from nor unreasonably close to the date on which it was necessary for him to receive the same, or

(g) by delay on the part of nominated sub-contractors or nominated suppliers which the Contractor has taken all practicable steps to avoid or reduce, or

(h) by delay on the part of artists tradesmen or others engaged by the Employer in executing work not forming part of this Contract, or

(i) by reason of the opening up for inspection of any work covered up or of the testing of any of the work materials or goods in accordance with clause 6 (3) of these Conditions (including making good in consequence of such opening up or testing), unless the inspection or test showed that the work materials or goods were not in accordance with this Contract, or

*(j) (i) by the Contractor's inability for reasons beyond his control and which he could not reasonably have foreseen at the date of this Contract to secure such labour as is essential to the proper carrying out of the Works, or

(ii) by the Contractor's inability for reasons beyond his control and which he could not reasonably have foreseen at the date of this Contract to secure such goods and/or materials as are essential to the proper carrying out of the Works, or

(k) by reason of compliance with the provisions of clause 34 of these Conditions or with Architect's/Supervising Officer's instructions issued thereunder.

then the Architect/Supervising Officer shall so soon as he is able to estimate the length of the delay beyond the date or time aforesaid make in writing a fair and reasonable extension of time for completion of the Works. Provided always that the Contractor shall use constantly his best endeavours to prevent delay and shall do all that may reasonably be required to the satisfaction of the Architect/Supervising Officer to proceed with the Works.

Loss and expense caused by disturbance of regular progress of the Works.

24 (1) If upon written application being made to him by the Contractor the Architect/Supervising Officer is of the opinion that the Contractor has been involved in direct loss and/or expense for which he would not be reimbursed by a payment made under any other provision in this Contract by reason of the regular progress of the Works or of any part thereof having been materially affected by:

(a) The Contractor not having received in due time necessary instructions, drawings, details or levels from the Architect/Supervising Officer for which he specifically applied in writing on a date which having regard to the Date for Completion stated in the appendix to these Conditions or to any extension of time then fixed under clause 23 or clause 33 (1) (c) of these Conditions was neither unreasonably distant from nor unreasonably close to the date on which it was necessary for him to receive the same; or

(b) The opening up for inspection of any work covered up or the testing of any of the work materials or goods in accordance with clause 6 (3) of these Conditions (including making good in consequence of such opening up or testing), unless the inspection or test showed that the work, materials or goods were not in accordance with this Contract; or

(c) Any discrepancy in or divergence between the Contract Drawings and/or the Contract Bills; or

(d) Delay on the part of artists tradesmen or others engaged by the Employer in executing work not forming part of this Contract; or

***Footnote.**—*Strike out either or both of the sub-clauses (j) (i) or (j) (ii) if not to apply.*

(e) Architect's/Supervising Officer's instructions issued in regard to the postponement of any work to be executed under the provisions of this Contract;

and if the written application is made within a reasonable time of it becoming apparent that the progress of the Works or of any part thereof has been affected as aforesaid, then the Architect/Supervising Officer shall either himself ascertain or shall instruct the Quantity Surveyor to ascertain the amount of such loss and/or expense. Any amount from time to time so ascertained shall be added to the Contract Sum, and if an Interim Certificate is issued after the date of ascertainment any such amount shall be added to the amount which would otherwise be stated as due in such Certificate.

(2) The provisions of this Condition are without prejudice to any other rights and remedies which the Contractor may possess.

Determination by Employer.

25 (1) If the Contractor shall make default in any one or more of the following respects, that is to say:—

(a) If he without reasonable cause wholly suspends the carrying out of the Works before completion thereof, or

(b) If he fails to proceed regularly and diligently with the Works, or

(c) If he refuses or persistently neglects to comply with a written notice from the Architect/Supervising Officer requiring him to remove defective work or improper materials or goods and by such refusal or neglect the Works are materially affected, or

(d) If he fails to comply with the provisions of either clause 17 or clause 17A of these Conditions, then the Architect/Supervising Officer may give to him a notice by registered post or recorded delivery specifying the default, and if the Contractor either shall continue such default for fourteen days after receipt of such notice or shall at any time thereafter repeat such default (whether previously repeated or not), then the Employer without prejudice to any other rights or remedies, may within ten days after such continuance or repetition by notice by registered post or recorded delivery forthwith determine the employment of the Contractor under this Contract, provided that such notice shall not be given unreasonably or vexatiously.

(2) In the event of the Contractor becoming bankrupt or making a composition or arrangement with his creditors or having a winding up order made or (except for purposes of reconstruction) a resolution for voluntary winding up passed or a provisional liquidator receiver or manager of his business or undertaking duly appointed, or possession taken, by or on behalf of the holders of any debentures secured by a floating charge, of any property comprised in or subject to the floating charge, the employment of the Contractor under this Contract shall be forthwith automatically determined but the said employment may be reinstated and continued if the Employer and the Contractor his trustee in bankruptcy liquidator provisional liquidator receiver or manager as the case may be shall so agree.

(3) The Employer shall be entitled to determine the employment of the Contractor under this or any other contract, if the Contractor shall have offered or given or agreed to give to any person any gift or consideration of any kind as an inducement or reward for doing or forbearing to do or for having done or forborne to do any action in relation to the obtaining or execution of this or any other contract with the Employer, or for showing or forbearing to show favour or disfavour to any person in relation to this or any other contract with the Employer, or if the like acts shall have been done by any person employed by the Contractor or acting on his behalf (whether with or without the knowledge of the Contractor), or if in relation to this or any other contract with the Employer the Contractor or any person employed by him or acting on his behalf shall have committed any offence under the Prevention of Corruption Acts, 1889 to 1916, or shall have given any fee or reward the receipt of which is an offence under sub-section (2) of section 123 of the Local Government Act, 1933.

(4) In the event of the employment of the Contractor under this Contract being determined as aforesaid and so long as it has not been reinstated and continued, the following shall be the respective rights and duties of the Employer and Contractor:—

(a) The Employer may employ and pay other persons to carry on and complete the Works and he or they may enter upon the Works and use all temporary buildings, plant, tools, equipment, goods and materials intended for, delivered to and placed on or adjacent to the Works, and may purchase all materials and goods necessary for the carrying out and completion of the Works.

(b) The Contractor shall (except where the determination occurs by reason of the bankruptcy of the Contractor or of him having a winding up order made or (except for the purposes of reconstruction) a resolution for voluntary winding up passed), if so required by the Employer or Architect/Supervising Officer within fourteen days of the date of determination, assign to the Employer without payment the benefit of any agreement for the supply of materials or goods and/or for the execution of any work for the purposes of this Contract but on the terms that a supplier or sub-contractor shall be entitled to make any reasonable objection to any further assignment thereof by the Employer. In any case the Employer may pay any supplier or sub-contractor for any materials or goods delivered or works executed for the purposes of this Contract (whether before or after the date of determination) in so far as the price thereof has not already been paid by the Contractor. The Employer's rights under this paragraph are in addition to his rights to pay nominated sub-contractors as provided in clause 27 (c) of these Conditions and payments made under this paragraph may be deducted from any sum due or to become due to the Contractor.

(c) The Contractor shall as and when required in writing by the Architect/Supervising Officer so to do (but not before) remove from the Works any temporary buildings, plant, tools, equipment, goods and materials belonging to or hired by him. If within a reasonable time after any such requirement has been made the Contractor has not complied therewith, then the Employer may (but without being responsible for any loss or damage) remove and sell any such property of the Contractor, holding the proceeds less all costs incurred to the credit of the Contractor.

(d) The Contractor shall allow or pay to the Employer in the manner hereinafter appearing the amount of any direct loss and/or damage caused to the Employer by the determination. Until after completion of the Works under paragraph (a) of this sub-clause the Employer shall not be bound by any provision of this Contract to make any further payment to the Contractor, but upon such completion and the verification within a reasonable time of the accounts therefor the Architect/Supervising Officer shall certify the amount of expenses properly incurred by the Employer and the amount of any direct loss and/or damage caused to the Employer by the determination and, if such amounts when added to the monies paid to the Contractor before the date of determination exceed the total amount which would have been payable on due completion in accordance with this Contract, the difference shall be a debt payable to the Employer by the Contractor; and if the said amounts when added to the said monies be less than the said total amount, the difference shall be a debt payable by the Employer to the Contractor.

Determination by Contractor.

26 (1) Without prejudice to any other rights and remedies which the Contractor may possess, if

(a) The Employer does not pay to the Contractor the amount due on any certificate within 14 days from the issue of that certificate and continues such default for seven days after receipt by registered post or recorded delivery of a notice from the Contractor stating that notice of determination under this Condition will be served if payment is not made within seven days from receipt thereof; or

(b) The Employer interferes with or obstructs the issue of any certificate due under this Contract; or

(c) The carrying out of the whole or substantially the whole of the uncompleted Works (other than the execution of work required under clause 15 of these Conditions) is suspended for a continuous period of the length named in the appendix to these Conditions by reason of:

(i) *force majeure*, or

(ii) loss or damage occasioned by any one or more of the contingencies referred to in clause 20 [A] or clause 20 [B] of these conditions (if applicable), or

(iii) civil commotion, or

(iv) Architect's/Supervising Officer's instructions issued under clauses 1 (2), 11 (1) or 21 (2) of these Conditions, or

(v) the Contractor not having received in due time necessary instructions, drawings, details or levels from the Architect/Supervising Officer for which he specifically applied in writing on a date which having regard to the Date of Completion stated in the appendix to these Conditions or to any extension of time then fixed under clause 23 or clause 33 (1) (c) of these Conditions was neither unreasonably distant from nor unreasonably close to the date on which it was necessary for him to receive the same, or

(vi) delay on the part of artists tradesmen or others engaged by the Employer in executing work not forming part of this Contract, or

(vii) the opening up for inspection of any work covered up or of the testing of any of the work materials or goods in accordance with clause 6 (3) of these Conditions (including making good in consequence of such opening up or testing), unless the inspection or test showed that the work materials or goods were not in accordance with this Contract,

then the Contractor may thereupon by notice by registered post or recorded delivery to the Employer or Architect/Supervising Officer forthwith determine the employment of the Contractor under this Contract; provided that such notice shall not be given unreasonably or vexatiously.

(2) Upon such determination, then without prejudice to the accrued rights or remedies of either party or to any liability of the classes mentioned in clause 18 of these Conditions which may accrue either before the Contractor or any sub-contractors shall have removed his temporary buildings, plant, tools, equipment, goods or materials or by reason of his or their so removing the same, the respective rights and liabilities of the Contractor and the Employer shall be as follows, that is to say:—

(a) The Contractor shall with all reasonable dispatch and in such manner and with such precautions as will prevent injury, death or damage of the classes in respect of which before the date of determination he was liable to indemnify the Employer under clause 18 of these Conditions remove from the site all his temporary buildings, plant, tools, equipment, goods and materials and shall give facilities for his sub-contractors to do the same, but subject always to the provision of sub-paragraph (iv) of paragraph (b) of this sub-clause.

(b) After taking into account amounts previously paid under this Contract the Contractors shall be paid by the Employer:—

(i) The total value of work completed at the date of determination.

(ii) The total value of work begun and executed but not completed at the date of determination, the value being ascertained in accordance with clause 11 (4) of these Conditions as if such work were a variation required by the Architect/Supervising Officer.

(iii) Any sum ascertained in respect of direct loss and/or expense under clauses 11 (6), 24 and 34 (3) of these Conditions (whether ascertained before or after the date of determination).

(iv) The cost of materials or goods properly ordered for the Works for which the Contractor shall have paid or for which the Contractor is legally bound to pay, and on such payment by the Employer any materials or goods so paid for shall become the property of the Employer.

(v) The reasonable cost of removal under paragraph (a) of this sub-clause.

(vi) Any direct loss and/or damage caused to the Contractor by the determination.

Provided that in addition to all other remedies the Contractor upon such determination may take possession of and shall have a lien upon all unfixed goods and materials which may have become the property of the Employer under clause 14 of these Conditions until payment of all monies due to the Contractor from the Employer.

Nominated sub-contractors.

27 The following provisions of this Condition shall apply where prime cost sums are included in the Contract Bills, or arise as a result of Architect's/Supervising Officer's instructions given in regard to the expenditure of provisional sums, in respect of persons to be nominated by the Architect/Supervising Officer to supply and fix materials or goods or to execute work.

(a) Such sums shall be deemed to include 2½ per cent. cash discount and shall be expended in favour of such persons as the Architect/Supervising Officer shall instruct, and all specialists or others who are nominated by the Architect/Supervising Officer are hereby declared to be sub-contractors employed by the Contractor and are referred to in these Conditions as 'nominated sub-contractors'. Provided that the Architect/Supervising Officer shall not nominate any person as a sub-contractor against whom the Contractor shall make reasonable objection, or (save where the Architect/Supervising Officer and Contractor shall otherwise agree) who will not enter into a sub-contract which provides (*inter alia*):—

(i) That the nominated sub-contractor shall carry out and complete the sub-contract Works in every respect to the reasonable satisfaction of the Contractor and of the Architect/Supervising Officer and in conformity with all the reasonable directions and requirements of the Contractor.

(ii) That the nominated sub-contractor shall observe, perform and comply with all the provisions of this Contract on the part of the Contractor to be observed, performed and complied with (other than clause 20 [A] of these Conditions, if applicable) so far as they relate and apply to the sub-contract Works or to any portion of the same.

(iii) That the nominated sub-contractor shall indemnify the Contractor against the same liabilities in respect of the sub-contract Works as those for which the Contractor is liable to indemnify the Employer under this Contract.

(iv) That the nominated sub-contractor shall indemnify the Contractor against claims in respect of any negligence, omission or default of such sub-contractor, his servants or agents or any misuse by him or them of any scaffolding or other plant, and shall insure himself against any such claims and produce the policy or policies and receipts in respect of premiums paid as and when required by either the Employer or the Contractor.

(v) That the sub-contract Works shall be completed within the period or (where they are to be completed in sections) periods therein specified, that the Contractor shall not without the written consent of the Architect/Supervising Officer grant any extension of time for the completion of the sub-contract Works or any section thereof, and that the Contractor shall inform the Architect/Supervising Officer of any representations made by the nominated sub-contractor as to the cause of any delay in the progress or completion of the sub-contract Works or of any section thereof.

(vi) That if the nominated sub-contractor shall fail to complete the sub-contract Works or (where the sub-contract Works are to be completed in sections) any section thereof within the period therein specified or within any extended time granted by the Contractor with the written consent of the Architect/Supervising Officer and the Architect/Supervising Officer certifies in writing to the Contractor that the same ought reasonably so to have been completed, the nominated sub-contractor shall pay or allow to the Contractor either a sum calculated at the rate therein agreed as liquidated and ascertained damages for the period during which the said Works or any section thereof, as the case may be, shall so remain or have remained incomplete or (where no such rate is therein agreed) a sum equivalent to any loss or damage suffered or incurred by the Contractor and caused by the failure of the nominated sub-contractor as aforesaid.

(vii) That payment in respect of any work, materials or goods comprised in the sub-contract shall be made within 14 days after receipt by the Contractor of the duplicate copy of the Architect's/Supervising Officer's certificate under clause 30 of these Conditions which states as due an amount calculated by including the total value of such work, materials or goods, and shall when due be subject to the retention by the Contractor of the sums mentioned in sub-paragraph (viii) of paragraph (a) of this Condition, and to a discount for cash of 2½ per cent. if made within the said period of 14 days.

(viii) That the Contractor shall retain from the sum directed by the Architect/Supervising Officer as having been included in the calculation of the amount stated as due in any certificate issued under clause 30 of these Conditions in respect of the total value of work, materials or goods executed or supplied by the nominated sub-contractor the percentage of such value named in the appendix to these Conditions as Percentage of Certified Value Retained up to a total amount not exceeding a sum which bears the same ratio to the sub-contract price as the unreduced sum named in the appendix to these Conditions as Limit of Retention Fund bears to the Contract Sum; and that the Contractor's interest in any sums so retained (by whomsoever held) shall be fiduciary as trustee for the nominated sub-contractor (but without obligation to invest); and that the nominated sub-contractor's beneficial interest in such sums shall be subject only to the right of the Contractor to have recourse thereto from time to time for payment of any amount which he is entitled under the sub-contract to deduct from any sum due or to become due to the nominated sub-contractor; and that if and when such sums or any part thereof are released to the nominated sub-contractor they shall be paid in full less only a discount for cash of 2½ per cent. if paid within 14 days of the date fixed for their release in the sub-contract.

(ix) That the Architect/Supervising Officer and his representatives shall have a right of access to the workshops and other places of the nominated sub-contractor as mentioned in clause 9 of these Conditions.

(x) That the employment of the nominated sub-contractor under the sub-contract shall determine immediately upon the determination (for any reason) of the Contractor's employment under this Contract.

(b) The Architect/Supervising Officer shall direct the Contractor as to the total value of the work, materials or goods executed or supplied by a nominated sub-contractor included in the calculation of the amount stated as due in any certificate issued under clause 30 of these Conditions and shall forthwith inform the nominated sub-contractor in writing of the amount of the said total value. The sum representing such total value shall be paid by the Contractor to the nominated sub-contractor within 14 days of receiving from the Architect/Supervising Officer the duplicate copy of the certificate less only (i) any retention money which the Contractor may be entitled to deduct under the terms of the sub-contract (ii) any sum to which the Contractor may be entitled in respect of delay in the completion of the sub-contract Works or any section thereof, and (iii) a discount for cash of 2½ per cent.

(c) Before issuing any certificate under clause 30 of these Conditions the Architect/Supervising Officer may request the Contractor to furnish to him reasonable proof that all amounts included in the calculation of the amount stated as due on previous certificates in respect of the total value of work, materials or goods executed or supplied by any nominated sub-contractor have been duly discharged, and if the Contractor fails to comply with any such request the Architect/Supervising Officer shall issue a certificate to that effect and thereupon the Employer may himself pay such amounts to any nominated sub-contractor concerned and deduct the same from any sums due or to become due to the Contractor.

(d) (i) The Contractor shall not grant to any nominated sub-contractor any extension of the period within which the sub-contract Works or (where the sub-contract Works are to be completed in sections) any section thereof is to be completed without the written consent of the Architect/Supervising Officer. Provided always that the Contractor shall inform the Architect/Supervising Officer of any representation made by the nominated sub-contractor as to the cause of any delay in the progress or completion of the sub-contract Works or of any section thereof, and that the consent of the Architect/Supervising Officer shall not be unreasonably withheld.

(ii) If any nominated sub-contractor fails to complete the sub-contract Works or (where the sub-contract Works are to be completed in sections) any section thereof within the period specified in the sub-contract or within any extended time granted by the Contractor with the written consent of the Architect/Supervising Officer, then if the same ought reasonably so to have been completed the Architect/Supervising Officer shall certify in writing accordingly; any such certificate shall be issued to the Contractor and immediately upon issue the Architect/Supervising Officer shall send a duplicate copy thereof to the nominated sub-contractor.

(e) If the Architect/Supervising Officer desires to secure final payment to any nominated sub-contractor before final payment is due to the Contractor, and if such sub-contractor has satisfactorily indemnified the Contractor against any latent defects, then the Architect/Supervising Officer may in an Interim Certificate include an amount to cover the said final payment, and thereupon the Contractor shall pay to such nominated sub-contractor the amount so certified less only a discount for cash of 2½ per cent. Upon such final payment the amount named in the appendix to these Conditions as Limit of Retention Fund shall be reduced by the sum which bears the same ratio to the said amount as does such sub-contractor's sub-contract price to the Contract Sum, and save for latent defects the Contractor shall be discharged from all liability for the work materials or goods executed or supplied by such sub-contractor under the sub-contract to which the payment relates.

(f) Neither the existence nor the exercise of the foregoing powers nor anything else contained in these Conditions shall render the Employer in any way liable to any nominated sub-contractor.

(g) (i) Where the Contractor in the ordinary course of his business directly carries out works for which prime cost sums are included in the Contract Bills and where items of such works are set out in the appendix to these Conditions and the Architect/Supervising Officer is prepared to receive tenders from the Contractor for such items, then the Contractor shall be permitted to tender for the same or any of them but without prejudice to the Employer's right to reject the lowest or any tender. If the Contractor's tender is accepted, he shall not sub-let the work without the consent of the Architect/Supervising Officer.

Provided that where a prime cost sum arises under Architect's/Supervising Officer's instructions issued under clause 11 (3) of these Conditions it shall be deemed for the purposes of this paragraph to have been included in the Contract Bills and the item of work to which it relates shall likewise be deemed to have been set out in the appendix to these Conditions.

(ii) It shall be a condition of any tender accepted under this paragraph that clause 11 of these Conditions shall apply in respect of the items of work included in the tender as if for the reference therein to the Contract Drawings and the Contract Bills there were references to the equivalent documents included in or referred to in the tender.

Nominated suppliers.

28 The following provisions of this Condition shall apply where prime cost sums are included in the Contract Bills, or arise as a result of Architect's/Supervising Officer's instructions given in regard to the expenditure of provisional sums, in respect of any materials or goods to be fixed by the Contractor.

(a) Such sums shall be deemed to include 5 per cent. cash discount and the term prime cost when included or arising as aforesaid shall be understood to mean the net cost to be defrayed as a prime cost after deducting any trade or other discount (except the said discount of 5 per cent.), and shall include purchase tax (where applicable), and the cost of packing carriage and delivery. Provided that, where in the opinion of the Architect/Supervising Officer the Contractor has incurred expense for special packing or special carriage, such special expense shall be allowed as part of the sums actually paid by the Contractor.

(b) Such sums shall be expended in favour of such persons as the Architect/Supervising Officer shall instruct, and all specialists, merchants, tradesmen or others who are nominated by the Architect/Supervising Officer to supply materials or goods are hereby declared to be suppliers to the Contractor and are referred to in these Conditions as 'nominated suppliers'. Provided that the Architect/Supervising Officer shall not (save where the Architect/Supervising Officer and Contractor shall otherwise agree) nominate as a supplier a person who will not enter into a contract of sale which provides (*inter alia*):—

(i) That the materials or goods to be supplied shall be to the reasonable satisfaction of the Architect/Supervising Officer.

(ii) That the nominated supplier shall make good by replacement or otherwise any defects in the materials or goods supplied which appear within such period as is therein mentioned and shall bear any expenses reasonably incurred by the Contractor as a direct consequence of such defects, provided that:—

(1) where the materials or goods have been used or fixed such defects are not such that examination by the Contractor ought to have revealed them before using or fixing;

(2) such defects are due solely to defective workmanship or material in the goods supplied and shall not have been caused by improper storage by the Contractor or by misuse or by any act of neglect of either the Contractor the Architect/Supervising Officer or the Employer or by any person or persons for whom they may be responsible.

(iii) That delivery of the materials or goods supplied shall be commenced and completed at such times as the Contractor may reasonably direct.

(iv) That the nominated supplier shall allow the Contractor a discount for cash of 5 per cent. if the Contractor makes payment in full within 30 days of the end of the month during which delivery is made.

(v) That the nominated supplier shall not be obliged to make any delivery of materials or goods (except any which may have been paid for in full less only the discount for cash) after the determination (for any reason) of the Contractor's employment under this Contract.

(c) All payments by the Contractor for materials or goods supplied by a nominated supplier shall be in full, and shall be paid within 30 days of the end of the month during which delivery is made less only a discount for cash of 5 per cent. if so paid.

29 The Contractor shall permit the execution of work not forming part of this Contract by artists, tradesmen or others engaged by the Employer. Every such person shall for the purposes of clause 18 of these Conditions be deemed to be a person for whom the Employer is responsible and not to be a sub-contractor. **Artists and tradesmen.**

30 (1) At the Period of Interim Certificates named in the appendix to these Conditions the Architect/Supervising Officer shall issue a certificate stating the amount due to the Contractor from the Employer, and the Contractor shall be entitled to payment therefor within 14 days from the issue of that Certificate. Interim valuations shall be made whenever the Architect/Supervising Officer considers them to be necessary for the purpose of ascertaining the amount to be stated as due in an Interim Certificate. **Certificates and payments.**

(2) The amount stated as due in an Interim Certificate shall, subject to any agreement between the parties as to stage payments, be the total value of the work properly executed and of the materials and goods delivered to or adjacent to the Works for use thereon up to and including a date not more than seven days before the date of the said certificate less any amount which may be retained by the Employer (as provided in sub-clause (3) of this Condition) and less any instalments previously paid under this Condition. Provided that such certificate shall only include the value of the said materials and goods as and from such times as they are reasonable, properly and not prematurely brought to or placed adjacent to the Works and then only if adequately protected against weather or other casualties.

(2A) The amount stated as due in an Interim Certificate may in the discretion of the Architect/Supervising Officer include the value of any materials or goods before delivery thereof to or adjacent to the Works provided that:

(a) Such materials or goods are intended for inclusion in the Works;

(b) Nothing remains to be done to such materials or goods to complete the same up to the point of their incorporation in the Works;

(c) Such materials or goods have been and are set apart at the premises where they have been manufactured or assembled or are stored, and have been clearly and visibly marked, individually or in sets, either by letters or figures or by reference to a pre-determined code, so as to identify:

(i) Where they are stored on premises of the Contractor, the Employer, and in any other case, the person to whose order they are held; and

(ii) Their destination as being the Works:

(d) Where such materials or goods were ordered from a supplier by the Contractor or a sub-contractor, the contract for their supply is in writing and expressly provides that the property therein shall pass unconditionally to the Contractor or the sub-contractor (as the case may be) not later than the happening of the events set out in paragraphs (b) and (c) of this sub-clause.

(e) Where such materials or goods were ordered from a supplier by a sub-contractor, the relevant sub-contract is in writing and expressly provides that on the property in such materials or goods passing to the sub-contractor the same shall immediately thereon pass to the Contractor;

(f) Where such materials or goods were manufactured or assembled by a sub-contractor, the sub-contract is in writing and expressly provides that the property in such materials or goods shall pass unconditionally to the Contractor not later than the happening of the events set out in paragraphs (b) and (c) of this sub-clause;

(g) The materials or goods are in accordance with this Contract;

(h) The Contractor furnishes to the Architect/Supervising Officer reasonable proof that the property in such materials or goods is in him and that the appropriate conditions set out in paragraphs (a) to (g) of this sub-clause have been complied with.

(3) The Employer may retain the percentage of the total value of the work, materials and goods referred to in sub-clauses (2) and (2A) of this Condition which is named in the appendix to these Conditions as Percentage of Certified Value Retained. Provided always that when the sum of the amounts so retained equals the amount named in the said appendix as Limit of Retention Fund or that amount as reduced in pursuance of clause 16 (f) and/or clause 27 (e) of these Conditions, as the case may be, no further amounts shall be retained by virtue of this sub-clause.

(4) The amounts retained by virtue of sub-clause (3) of this Condition shall be subject to the following rules:—

(a) The Employer's interest in any amounts so retained shall be fiduciary as trustee for the Contractor (but without obligation to invest), and the Contractor's beneficial interest therein shall be subject only to the right of the Employer to have recourse thereto from time to time for payment of any amount which he is entitled under the provisions of this Contract to deduct from any sum due or to become due to the Contractor.

(b) On the issue of the Certificate of Practical Completion the Architect/Supervising Officer shall issue a certificate for one moiety of the total amounts then so retained and the Contractor shall be entitled to payment of the said moiety within 14 days from the issue of that certificate.

(c) On the expiration of the Defects Liability Period named in the appendix to these Conditions, or on the issue of the Certificate of Completion of Making Good Defects, whichever is the later, the Architect/Supervising Officer shall issue a Certificate for the residue of the amounts then so retained and the Contractor shall be entitled to payment of the said residue within 14 days from the issue of that certificate.

(5) (a) The measurement and valuation of the Works shall be completed within the Period of Final Measurement and Valuation stated in the appendix to these Conditions, and the Contractor shall be supplied with a copy of the priced Bills of Variation not later than the end of the said Period and before the issue of the Final Certificate under sub-clause (6) of this Condition.

(b) Either before or within a reasonable time after Practical Completion of the Works the Contractor shall send to the Architect/Supervising Officer all documents necessary for the purposes of the computations required by these Conditions including all documents relating to the accounts of nominated sub-contractors and nominated suppliers.

(c) In the settlement of accounts the amounts paid or payable under the appropriate contracts by the Contractor to nominated sub-contractors or nominated suppliers (including the discounts for cash mentioned in clauses 27 and 28 of these Conditions), the amounts paid or payable by virtue of clause 4 (2) of these Conditions in respect of fees or charges for which a provisional sum is included in the Contract Bills, the amounts paid or payable in respect of any insurances maintained in compliance with clause 19 (2) of these Conditions, the tender sum (or such other sum as is appropriate in accordance with the terms of the tender) for any work for which a tender made under clause 27 (g) of these Conditions is accepted and the value of any work executed by the Contractor for which a provisional sum is included in the Contract Bills shall be set against the relevant prime cost or provisional sum mentioned in the Contract Bills or arising under Architect's/Supervising Officer's instructions issued under clause 11 (3) of these Conditions as the case may be, and the balance, after allowing in all cases *pro rata* for the Contractor's profit at the rates shown in the Contract Bills, shall be added to or deducted from the Contract Sum. Provided that no deduction shall be made in respect of any damages paid or allowed to the Contractor by any sub-contractor or supplier.

(6) So soon as is practicable but before the expiration of the period the length of which is stated in the appendix to these conditions from the end of the Defects Liability Period also stated in the said appendix or from completion of making good defects under clause 15 of these Conditions or from receipt by the Architect/Supervising Officer of the documents referred to in paragraph (b) of sub-clause (5) of this Condition, whichever is the latest, the Architect/Supervising Officer shall issue the Final Certificate. The Final Certificate shall state:—

(a) The sum of the amount paid to the Contractor under Interim Certificates and the amount named in the said appendix as Limit of Retention Fund, and

(b) The Contract Sum adjusted as necessary in accordance with the terms of these Conditions, and the difference (if any) between the two sums shall be expressed in the said certificate as a balance due to the Contractor from the Employer or to the Employer from the Contractor as the case may be, and subject to any deductions authorised by these Conditions, the said balance shall as from the fourteenth day after the issue of the said certificate be a debt payable as the case may be by the Employer to the Contractor or by the Contractor to the Employer.

(7) Unless a written request to concur in the appointment of an arbitrator shall have been given under clause 35 of these Conditions by either party before the Final Certificate has been issued or by the Contractor within 14 days after such issue, the said certificate shall be conclusive evidence in any proceedings arising out of this Contract (whether by arbitration under clause 35 of these Conditions or otherwise) that the Works have been properly carried out and completed in accordance with the terms of this Contract and that any necessary effect has been given to all the terms of this Contract which require an adjustment to be made to the Contract Sum, except and in so far as any sum mentioned in the said certificate is erroneous by reason of:—

(a) Fraud, dishonesty or fraudulent concealment relating to the Works, or any part thereof, or to any matter dealt with in the said certificate; or

(b) Any defect (including any omission) in the Works, or any part thereof which reasonable inspection or examination at any reasonable time during the carrying out of the Works or before the issue of the said certificate would not have disclosed; or

(c) Any accidental inclusion or exclusion of any work, materials, goods or figure in any computation or any arithmetical error in any computation.

(8) Save as aforesaid no certificate of the Architect/Supervising Officer shall of itself be conclusive evidence that any works materials or goods to which it relates are in accordance with this Contract.

***31A** The Contract Sum shall be deemed to have been calculated in the manner set out below and shall be subject to adjustment on the events specified hereunder:— Fluctuations.

(a) (i) The prices (including the cost of employers' liability insurance and of third party insurance) contained in the Contract Bills are based upon the rates of wages and the other emoluments and expenses (including holiday credits) which will be payable by the Contractor to or in respect of workpeople engaged upon or in connection with the Works in accordance with the rules or decisions of the National Joint Council for the Building Industry and the terms of the Building and Civil Engineering Annual and Public Holidays Agreements which will be applicable to the Works and which have been promulgated at the date of tender, or in the case of workpeople so engaged whose rates of wages and other emoluments and expenses (including holiday credits) are governed by the rules or decisions or agreements of some body other than the National Joint Council for the Building Industry, in accordance with the rules or decisions or agreements of such other body which will be applicable and which have been promulgated as aforesaid.

(ii) If any of the said rates of wages or other emoluments and expenses (including holiday credits) are increased or decreased by reason of any alteration in the said rules, decisions or agreements promulgated after the date of tender, then the net amount of the increase or decrease in wages and other emoluments and expenses (including holiday credits) together with the net amount of any consequential increase or decrease in the cost of employers' liability insurance, of third party insurance, and of any contribution, levy or tax payable by a person in his capacity as an employer shall, as the case may be, be paid to or allowed by the Contractor.

(b) (i) The prices contained in the Contract Bills are based upon the types and rates of contribution, levy and tax payable by a person in his capacity as an employer and which at the date of tender are payable by the Contractor. A type and a rate so payable are in the next sub-paragraph referred to as a 'tender type' and a 'tender rate'.

***Footnote.**—*Parts A, C and D should be used where the parties have agreed to allow full fluctuations. Parts B, C and D should be used whenever Part A is not applicable.*

(ii) If any of the tender rates other than a rate of levy payable by virtue of the Industrial Training Act 1964, is increased or decreased, or if a tender type ceases to be payab,ly or if a new type of contribution, levy or tax which is payable by a person in his capacite as an employer becomes payable after the date of tender, then in any such case the net amount of the difference between what the Contractor actually pays or will pay in respect of workpeople whilst they are engaged upon or in connection with the Works or because of his employment of such workpeople upon or in connection with the Works, and what he would have paid had the alteration, cessation or new type of contribution levy or tax not become effective, shall, as the case may be, be paid to or allowed by the Contractor.

(iii) The prices contained in the Contract Bills are based upon the types and rates of refund of contributions, levies and taxes payable by a person in his capacity as an employer and upon the types and rates of premium receivable by a person in his capacity as an employer being in each case types and rates which at the date of tender are receivable by the Contractor. Such a type and such a rate are, in the next sub-paragraph, referred to as a 'tender type' and a 'tender rate'.

(iv) If any of the tender rates is increased or decreased or if a tender type ceases to be payable or if a new type of refund of any contribution levy or tax payable by a person in his capacity as an employer becomes receivable or if a new type of premium receivable by a person in his capacity as an employer becomes receivable after the date of tender, then in any such case the net amount of the difference between what the Contractor actually receives or will receive in respect of workpeople whilst they are engaged upon or in connection with the Works or because of his employment of such workpeople upon or in connection with the Works, and what he would have received had the alteration, cessation or new type of refund or premium not become effective, shall, as the case may be, be allowed by or paid to the Contractor.

(v) The references in the two preceding sub-paragraphs to premiums shall be construed as meaning all payments howsoever they are described which are made under or by virtue of an Act of Parliament to a person in his capacity as an employer and which affect the cost to an employer of having persons in his employment.

(vi) The references in sub-paragraphs (i) to (iv) of this paragraph to contributions, levies and taxes shall be construed as meaning all impositions payable by a person in his capacity as an employer howsoever they are described and whoever the recipient which are imposed under or by virtue of an Act of Parliament and which affect the cost to an employer of having persons in his employment.

(c) (i) The prices contained in the Contract Bills are based upon the market prices of the materials and goods specified in the list attached thereto which were current at the date of tender. Such prices are hereinafter referred to as 'basic prices', and the prices stated by the Contractor on the said list shall be deemed to be the basic prices of the specified materials and goods.

(ii) If after the date of tender the market price of any of the materials or goods specified as aforesaid increases or decreases, then the net amount of the difference between the basic price thereof and the market price payable by the Contractor and current when the materials or goods are bought shall, as the case may be, be paid to or allowed by the Contractor.

(iii) The references in the two preceding sub-paragraphs to 'market prices' shall be construed as including any duty or tax by whomsoever payable which is payable under or by virtue of any Act of Parliament on the import, purchase, sale, appropriation, processing or use of the materials or goods specified as aforesaid.

***31B** The Contract Sum shall be deemed to have been calculated in the manner set out below and shall be subject to adjustment in the events specified hereunder:—

(a) (i) The prices contained in the Contracts Bills are based upon the types and rates of contribution, levy and tax payable by a person in his capacity as an employer and which at the date of tender are payable by the Contractor. A type and a rate so payable are in the next sub-paragraph referred to as a 'tender type' and a 'tender rate'.

(ii) If any of the tender rates other than a rate of levy payable by virtue of the Industrial Training Act 1964, is increased or decreased, or if a tender type ceases to be payable, or if a new type of contribution, levy or tax which is payable by a person in his capacity as an employer becomes payable after the date of tender, then in any such case the net amount of the difference between what the Contractor actually pays or will pay in respect of workpeople whilst they are engaged upon or in connection with the Works or because of his employment of such workpeople upon or in connection with the Works, and what he would have paid had the alteration, cessation or new type of contribution, levy or tax not become effective, shall, as the case may be, be paid to or allowed by the Contractor.

(iii) The prices contained in the Contract Bills are based upon the types and rates of refund of contributions, levies and taxes payable by a person in his capacity as an employer and upon the types and rates of premium receivable by a person in his capacity as an employer being in each case types and rates which at the date of tender are receivable by the Contractor. Such a type and such a rate are in the next sub-paragraph referred to as a 'tender type' and a 'tender rate'.

(iv) If any of the tender rates is increased or decreased or if a tender type ceases to be payable or if a new type of refund of any contribution levy or tax payable by a person in his capacity as an employer becomes receivable or if a new type of premium receivable by a person in his capacity as an employer becomes receivable, then in any such case the net amount of the difference between what the Contractor actually receives or will receive in respect of workpeople whilst they are engaged upon or in connection with the Works or because of his employment of such workpeople upon or in connection with the Works, and what he would have received had the alteration, cessation or new type of refund or premium not become effective, shall, as the case may be, be allowed by or paid to the Contractor.

(v) The references in the two preceding sub-paragraphs to premiums shall be construed as meaning all payments howsoever they are described which are made under or by virtue of an Act of Parliament to a person in his capacity as an employer and which affect the cost to an employer of having persons in his employment.

(vi) The references in sub-paragraphs (i) to (iv) of this paragraph to contributions, levies and taxes shall be construed as meaning all impositions payable by a person in his capacity as an employer howsoever they are described and whoever the recipient which are imposed under or by virtue of an Act of Parliament and which affect the cost to an employer of having persons in his employment.

(b) (i) The prices contained in the Contract Bills are based upon the types and rates of duty if any and tax if any by whomsoever payable which at the date of tender are payable on the import, purchase, sale, appropriation, processing or use of the materials and goods specified in the list attached thereto under or by virtue of any Act of Parliament. A type and a rate so payable are in the next sub-paragraph referred to as a 'tender type' and a 'tender rate'.

(ii) If in relation to any materials or goods specified as aforesaid a tender rate is increased or decreased, or a tender type ceases to be payable or a new type of duty or tax becomes payable on the import, purchase, sale, appropriation, processing or use of those materials or goods, then in any such case the net amount of the difference between what the Contractor actually pays in respect of those materials or goods, and what he would have paid in respect of them had the alteration, cessation or imposition not occurred, shall, as the case may be, be paid to or allowed by the Contractor. In this sub-paragraph the expression 'a new type of duty or tax' includes an additional duty or tax and a duty or tax imposed in regard to specified materials or goods in respect of which no duty or tax whatever was previously payable.

31C (1) If the Contractor shall decide subject to Clause 17 of these Conditions to sublet any portion of the Works he shall incorporate in the sub-contract provisions to the like effect as the provisions of Clauses 31 A and 31 B which are applicable for the purposes of this Contract.

(2) If the price payable under such a sub-contract as aforesaid is decreased below or increased above the price in such sub-contract by reason of the operation of the said incorporated provisions, then the net amount of such decrease or increase shall, as the case may be, be allowed by or paid to the Contractor under this Contract.

***Footnote.**—*Parts A, C and D should be used where the parties have agreed to allow full fluctuations. Parts B, C and D should be used whenever Part A is not applicable.*

31D (1) The Contractor shall give a written notice to the Architect/Supervising Officer of the occurrence of any of the events referred to in such of the following provisions as are applicable for the purposes of this Contract:

(a) Clause 31 A(a)(ii);
(b) Clause 31 A(b)(ii);
(c) Clause 31 A(b)(iv);
(d) Clause 31 A(c)(ii);
(e) Clause 31 B(a)(ii);
(f) Clause 31 B(a)(iv);
(g) Clause 31 B(b)(ii);
(h) Clause 31 C(2).

(2) Any notice required to be given by the preceding sub-clause shall be given within a reasonable time after the occurrence of that to which the notice relates, and the giving of a written notice in that time shall be a condition precedent to any payment being made to the Contractor in respect of the event in question.

(3) The Quantity Surveyor and the Contractor may agree what shall be deemed for all the purposes of this Contract to be the net amount payable to or allowable by the Contractor in respect of the occurrence of any event such as is referred to in any of the provisions listed in sub-clause (1) of this Condition.

(4) Any amount which from time to time becomes payable to or allowable by the Contractor by virtue of Clause 31 A or Clause 31 B or Clause 31 C of these Conditions shall, as the case may be, be added to or subtracted from:

(a) The Contract Sum; and

(b) Any amounts payable to the Contractor and which are calculated in accordance with either sub-paragraph (i) or sub-paragraph (ii) of paragraph (b) of sub-clause 2 of Clause 26 of these Conditions; and

(c) The amount which would otherwise be stated as due in the next Interim Certificate.

Provided:

(i) No addition to or subtraction from the amount which would otherwise be stated as due in an Interim Certificate shall be made by virtue of this sub-clause unless on or before the date as at which the total value of work, materials and goods is ascertained for the purposes of that Certificate the Contractor shall have actually paid or received the sum which is payable by or to him in consequence of the event in respect of which the payment or allowance arises.

(ii) No addition to or subtraction from the Contract Sum made by virtue of this sub-clause shall alter in any way the amount of profit of the Contractor included in that Sum.

(5) Clause 31 A, Clause 31 B and Clause 31 C shall not apply in respect of:

(a) Work for which the Contractor is allowed daywork rates under Clause 11(4)(c)(ii) of these Conditions.

(b) Work executed or materials or goods supplied by any nominated sub-contractor or nominated supplier (fluctuations in relation to nominated sub-contractors and nominated suppliers shall be dealt with under any provision in relation thereto which may be included in the appropriate sub-contract or contract of sale), or

(c) Work executed by the Contractor for which a tender made under Clause 27(g) of these Conditions has been accepted.

(6) In Clause 31 A and Clause 31 B of these Conditions:

(a) The expression 'the date of tender' means the date 10 days before the date fixed for the receipt of tenders by the Employer; and

(b) The expression 'materials' and 'goods' include timber used in formwork but do not include other consumable stores, plant and machinery.

(c) The expression 'workpeople' means persons whose rates of wages and other emoluments (including holiday credits) are governed by the rules or decisions or agreements of the National Joint Council for the Building Industry or some other like body for trades associated with the building industry.

Outbreak of hostilities.

32* (1) If during the currency of this Contract there shall be an outbreak of hostilities (whether war is declared or not) in which the United Kingdom shall be involved on a scale involving the general mobilisation of the armed forces of the Crown, then either the Employer or the Contractor may at any time by notice by registered post or recorded delivery to the other, forthwith determine the employment of the Contractor under this Contract:

Provided that such a notice shall not be given

(a) Before the expiration of 28 days from the date on which the order is given for general mobilisation as aforesaid, or

(b) After Practical Completion of the Works unless the Works or any part thereof shall have sustained war damage as defined in clause 33 (4) of these Conditions.

(2) The Architect/Supervising Officer may within 14 days after a notice under this Condition shall have been given or received by the Employer issue instructions to the Contractor requiring the execution of such protective work as shall be specified therein and/or the continuation of the Works up to points of stoppage to be specified therein, and the Contractor shall comply with such instructions as if the notice of determination had not been given.

Provided that if the Contractor shall for reasons beyond his control be prevented from completing the work to which the said instructions relate within three months from the date on which the instructions were issued, he may abandon such work.

(3) Upon the expiration of 14 days from the date on which a notice of determination shall have been given or received by the Employer under this Condition or where works are required by the Architect/Supervising Officer under the preceding sub-clause upon completion or abandonment as the case may be of any such works, the provisions of sub-clause (2) (except sub-paragraph (vi) of paragraph (b)) of clause 26 of these Conditions shall apply, and the Contractor shall also be paid by the Employer the value of any work executed pursuant to instructions given under sub-clause (2) of this clause, the value being ascertained in accordance with clause 11 (4) of these Conditions as if such work were a variation required by the Architect/Supervising Officer.

***Footnote.**—*The parties hereto in the event of the outbreak of hostilities may at any time by agreement between them make such further or other arrangements as they may think fit to meet the circumstances.*

33 (1) In the event of the Works or any part thereof or any unfixed materials or goods intended for, delivered to and placed on or adjacent to the Works sustaining war damage then notwithstanding anything expressed or implied elsewhere in this Contract: War Damage.

(a) The occurrence of such war damage shall be disregarded in computing any amounts payable to the Contractor under or by virtue of this Contract.

(b) The Architect/Supervising Officer may issue instructions requiring the Contractor to remove and/or dispose of any debris and/or damaged work and/or to execute such protective work as shall be specified.

(c) The Contractor shall reinstate or make good such war damage and shall proceed with the carrying out and completion of the Works, and the Architect/Supervising Officer shall grant the Contractor a fair and reasonable extension of time for completion of the Works.

(d) The removal and disposal of debris or damaged work, the execution of protective works and the reinstatement and making good of such war damage shall be deemed to be a variation required by the Architect/Supervising Officer.

(2) If at any time after the occurrence of war damage as aforesaid either party serves notice of determination under clause 32 of these Conditions, the expression 'protective work' as used in the said clause shall in such case be deemed to include any matters in respect of which the Architect/Supervising Officer can issue instructions under paragraph (b) of sub-clause (1) of this Condition and any instructions issued under the said paragraph prior to the date on which notice of determination is given or received by the Employer and which shall not then have been completely complied with shall be deemed to have been given under clause 32 (2) of these Conditions.

(3) The Employer shall be entitled to any compensation which may at any time become payable out of monies provided by Parliament in respect of war damage sustained by the Works or any part thereof or any unfixed materials or goods intended for the Works which shall at any time have become the property of the Employer.

(4) The expression 'war damage' as used in this Condition means war damage as defined by section 2 of the War Damage Act, 1943, or any amendment thereof.

34 (1) All fossils, antiquities and other objects of interest or value which may be found on the site or in excavating the same during the progress of the Works shall become the property of the Employer, and upon discovery of such an object the Contractor shall forthwith; Antiquities.

(a) Use his best endeavours not to disturb the object and shall cease work if and insofar as the continuance of work would endanger the object or prevent or impede its excavation or its removal;

(b) Take all steps which may be necessary to preserve the object in the exact position and condition in which it was found; and

(c) Inform the Architect/Supervising Officer or the Clerk of Works of the discovery and precise location of the object.

(2) The Architect/Supervising Officer shall issue instructions in regard to what is to be done concerning an object reported by the Contractor under the preceding sub-clause, and (without prejudice to the generality of this power) such instructions may require the Contractor to permit the examination, excavation or removal of the object by a third party. Any such third party shall for the purposes of clause 18 of these Conditions be deemed to be a person for whom the Employer is responsible and not to be a sub-contractor.

(3) If in the opinion of the Architect/Supervising Officer compliance with the provisions of sub-clause (1) of this Condition or with an instruction issued under sub-clause (2) of this Condition has involved the contractor in direct loss and/or expense for which he would not be reimbursed by a payment made under any other provision in this Contract then the Architect/Supervising Officer shall either himself ascertain or shall instruct the Quantity Surveyor to ascertain the amount of such loss and/or expense. Any amount from time to time so ascertained shall be added to the Contract Sum, and if an Interim Certificate is issued after the date of ascertainment any such amount shall be added to the amount which would otherwise be stated as due in such a Certificate.

Arbitration

35 (1) Provided always that in case any dispute or difference shall arise between the Employer or the Architect/Supervising Officer on his behalf and the Contractor, either during the progress or after the completion or abandonment of the Works, as to the construction of this Contract or as to any matter or thing of whatsoever nature arising thereunder or in connection therewith (including any matter or thing left by this Contract to the discretion of the Architect/Supervising Officer or the withholding by the Architect/Supervising Officer of any certificate to which the Contractor may claim to be entitled or the measurement and valuation mentioned in clause 30 (5) (a) of these Conditions or the rights and liabilities of the parties under clauses 25, 26, 32 or 33 of these Conditions), then such dispute or difference shall be and is hereby referred to the arbitration and final decision of a person to be agreed between the parties, or, failing agreement within 14 days after either party has given to the other a written request to concur in the appointment of an Arbitrator, a person to be appointed on the request of either party by the President or a Vice-President for the time being of the Royal Institute of British Architects.

(2) Such reference, except on article 3 or article 4 of the Articles of Agreement, or on the questions whether or not the issue of an instruction is empowered by these Conditions, whether or not a certificate has been improperly withheld or is not in accordance with these Conditions, or on any dispute or difference under clauses 32 and 33 of these Conditions, shall not be opened until after Practical Completion or alleged Practical Completion of the Works or termination or alleged termination of the Contractor's employment under this Contract or abandonment of the Works, unless with the written consent of the Employer or the Architect/Supervising Officer on his behalf and the Contractor.

(3) Subject to the provisions of clauses 2 (2) 30 (7) and 31 D (3) of these Conditions the Arbitrator shall, without prejudice to the generality of his powers, have power to direct such measurements and/or valuations as may in his opinion be desirable in order to determine the rights of the parties and to ascertain and award any sum which ought to have been the subject of or included in any certificate and to open up, review and revise any certificate, opinion, decision, requirement or notice and to determine all matters in dispute which shall be submitted to him in the same manner as if no such certificate, opinion, decision, requirement or notice had been given.

(4) The award of such Arbitrator shall be final and binding on the parties.

*(5) Whatever the nationality, residence or domicile of the Employer, the Contractor, any sub-contractor or supplier or the Arbitrator, and wherever the Works, or any part thereof, are situated, the law of England shall be the proper law of this Contract and in particular (but not so as to derogate from the generality of the foregoing) the provisions of the Arbitration Act, 1950 (notwithstanding anything in section 34 thereof) shall apply to any arbitration under this Contract wherever the same, or any part of it, shall be conducted.

***Footnote.**—*Where the parties do not wish the proper law of the contract to be the law of England and/or do not wish the provisions of the Arbitration Act, 1950 to apply to any arbitration under the contract held under Scottish procedural law appropriate amendments to this sub-clause should be made.*

Appendix

	Clause
Percentage Additions on Prime Cost	11(4)(c)(ii)

(i) Labour .... % (ii) Materials .... % (iii) Plant .... %

Percentage Additions on Prime Cost	11(4)(c)(iii)

........*	........*	........*
(i) Labour .... %	(i) Labour .... %	(i) Labour .... %
(ii) Materials .... %	(ii) Materials .... %	(ii) Materials .... %
(iii) Plant .... %	(iii) Plant .... %	(iii) Plant .... %

Defects Liability Period [if none other stated is 6 months from the day named in the Certificate of Practical Completion of the Works].	Clause 15, 16 and 30 ....
Percentage to cover Professional fees.**	Clause 20 [A] ....
Date for Possession.	Clause 21 ....
Date for Completion.	Clause 21 ....
Liquidated and Ascertained Damages.	Clause 22 at the rate of £ : : per ....
Period of delay: (i) by reason of loss or damage caused by any one of the contingencies referred to in clause 20[A] or clause 20[B] (if applicable) [if none stated is 3 months]. (ii) for any other reason [if none stated is one month].	Clause 26 ....

***Footnote.**—*State specialist trade to which the percentage additions are applicable.*

****Footnote.**—*Where the professional persons concerned with the Works are all employees of a Local Authority no percentage should be inserted, but care should be taken to include in the sum assured the cost to the Employer of their services.*

APPENDIX continued

Prime cost sums for which the Contractor desires to tender.	Clause 27 (g)	....
Period of Interim Certificates [if none stated is one month].	Clause 30 (1)	....
Percentage of Certified Value Retained.†	Clause 30 (3)	....
Limit of Retention Fund.‡	Clause 30 (3)	£............
Period of Final Measurement and Valuation [if none stated is 6 months from the day named in the Certificate of Practical Completion of the Works].	Clause 30 (5)	....
Period for issue of Final Certificate [if none stated is 3 months]§	Clause 30 (6)	....

†**Footnote.**—*The percentage inserted should be the same percentage as the Limit of Retention Fund is of the Contract Sum, i.e. not normally more than 5 per cent. of the Contract Sum.*

‡**Footnote.**—*The amount inserted should not normally exceed 5 per cent. of the Contract Sum.*

§**Footnote.**—*The period inserted must not exceed 6 months.*

NOTES

(These notes do not form part of the Contract)

A. *The reprint dated April 1966, incorporated the following amendments to the 1963 Edition:—*

- (*i*) *Clauses 14(2) and 30(2A)—Offsite goods and materials.* *(Practice Note 10 and amendment slip published December 1965.)*
- (*ii*) *Clause 31—Redundancy Fund Contributions.* *(Practice Note 11 and amendment slip published April 1966.)*
- (*iii*) *Clause 25(3)—London Government Act, 1963—Local Authority Editions (Practice Note 12).*

B. *The reprint dated December 1967, incorporated the following amendments to the April 1966 edition:—*

- (*i*) *Clause 11(4)(c)—Valuation—Daywork.* *(Amendment slip dated January 1967.)*
- (*ii*) *Clause 31—Fluctuations—revised clause.* *(Amendment slip dated October 1967.)*
- (*iii*) *Building Control Act, 1966—Supplemental Agreement issued March 1967 (Private Editions only).*

C. *The reprint dated July 1968 incorporated the following amendments:—*

- (*i*) *Clauses 19 and 20—Insurances—revised clauses.* *(Amendment slip No. 1 (July 1968), now incorporated.)*
- (*ii*) *Clause 14(1)—Materials and Goods unfixed or offsite—revised clause. Consequential amendment arising out of revised clauses 19 and 20.* *(Amendment slip No. 1 (July 1968), now incorporated.)*
- (*iii*) *Local Authority editions only—existing second footnote deleted and revised footnote substituted page 26 (appendix). Consequential amendment arising out of revised clauses 19 and 20.* *(Amendment slip No. 1 (July 1968), now incorporated in Local Authority editions only.)*
- (*iv*) *Clause 25(3)(b) Private editions only and clause 25(4)(b) Local Authority Editions only—Determination by Employer—additional wording.* *(Amendment slip No. 2 (July 1968) now incorporated.)*
- (*v*) *Clause 17—Assignment or Sub-letting—additional wording.* *(Amendment slip No. 2 (July 1968) now incorporated.)*
- (*vi*) *Clause 27(a)—Nominated Sub-Contractors—additional sub-clause.* *(Amendment slip No. 2 (July 1968) now incorporated.)*
- (*vii*) *Clause 28(b)—Nominated Suppliers—additional sub-clause.* *(Amendment slip No. 2 (July 1968) now incorporated.)*
- (*viii*) *Clause 12(1)—Contract Bills—inclusion of 5th edition, Metric, Standard Method of Measurement—with Quantities edition only.*

D. *The reprint dated July 1969 incorporated the following amendments which appeared on Amendment Sheet 3 (July 1969):—*

- (*i*) *Clause 34—Antiquities—revised clause.*
- (*ii*) *Clause 23—Extension of time—new sub-clause (k).*
- (*iii*) *Appendix—reference to 'Period for Honouring Certificates' deleted.*
- (*iv*) *Clause 26(1)(a)—Determination by Contractor—consequential amendment arising out of item (iii).*
- (*v*) *Clause 30(i) 30(4)(b) and 30(4)(c)—Certificates and payments—consequential amendment arising out of item (iii).*
- (*vi*) *Clause 11(4)(c)(ii) and 11(4)(c)(iii)—Variations, provisional and prime cost sums—amendment.*
- (*vii*) *Appendix: Footnote † Local Authority Editions Page 28 and Footnote ** Private Edition Page 26—revised.*
- (*viii*) *Clause 31—Fluctuations—revised footnotes.*
- (*ix*) *Clause 31D(6)—Fluctuations—revised Sub-Clause.*

(All the above amendments appear on Amendment Sheet No. 3, (July 1969.)

E. *The changes from the previous reprint dated July 1969 are indicated below:—*

- (*i*) *Private Editions only—Clause 17—new sub-clause on assignment.*
- (*ii*) *Clause 19—insurance against injury to persons or property—rearrangement of sub-clauses—revised provisions if default in payment for insurance by Contractor.*
- (*iii*) *Clause 23(j)—sub-clause divided into paragraphs (i) and (ii)—footnote* revised.*
- (*iv*) *Clause 25(2)—determination by Employer—insertion of appointment of provisional liquidator.*
- (*v*) *Local Authority Editions only—Clause 25(3) and (4)—amendments on determination for corruption, etc., by Contractor.*
- (*vi*) *Clause 31A—fluctuations—increase in labour costs—recovery of consequential increase in employer's compulsory contributions.*
- (*vii*) *Clause 31B(b)(i) and (ii)—Tax Fluctuation clause—materials—new duties or taxes.*
- (*viii*) *Clause 31A and 31B—tax, etc., fluctuations—revised basis for inclusion in tenders of increases in existing taxes, etc., or of new taxes, etc.*
- (*ix*) *Clause 35—new sub-clause (5)—proper law of contract—application of Arbitration Act, 1950.*

(All the above amendments E appear on Amendment Sheet No. 4 July 1971.)

- (*x*) *Private editions only—Building Control Act, 1966—supplemental agreement deleted.*

The Joint Contracts Tribunal has published Practice Notes on the use of the Standard Form of Building Contract. Copies are available from RIBA Publications Ltd., NFBTE and the RICS price 15p per set.

The notes listing amendments to the Contract now appear on the preceding page.

Dated..19.........

Standard Form of Building Contract
Local Authorities Edition **WITH** Quantities
1963 Edition (July 1971 Revision)

Agreement

and Schedule of Conditions of Building Contract

between

....

and

....

This Form is issued by the
Joint Contracts Tribunal
Under the sanction of

Royal Institute of British Architects.
National Federation of Building Trades Employers.
Royal Institution of Chartered Surveyors.
County Councils Association.
Association of Municipal Corporations.
Urban District Councils Association.
Rural District Councils Association.
Committee of Associations of Specialist Engineering Contractors.
Federation of Associations of Specialists and Sub-Contractors.

Price 80p

Published for the Joint Contracts Tribunal by RIBA Publications Limited.

Printed by: Charles Knight & Co. Ltd.
11-12 Bury Street, St. Mary Axe, E.C.3.—1199—1969

APPENDIX 3

FOR USE FOR EARLY FINAL PAYMENT (INCLUDING RELEASE OF RETENTION MONEY) TO THE NOMINATED SUB-CONTRACTOR

Form of Indemnity for Final Payment to the Sub-Contractor

THIS AGREEMENT is made the .... day of .... 19....

BETWEEN ....

of (or whose registered office is situate at) ....

....

(hereinafter called the "Contractor") of the one part and ....

....

of (or whose registered office is situate at) ....

....

(hereinafter called the "Sub-Contractor") of the other part

WHEREAS the Contractor and Sub-Contractor have entered into a sub-contract (on the terms printed in the Sub-Contract dated 1963 revised .... issued under the sanction of and approved by the NFBTE and FASS and approved by CASEC) expressed to be supplemental to an agreement between the Contractor and .... on the terms set out in the
(name of Building Owner)
Standard Form of Building Contract issued by the Joint Contracts Tribunal 1963 edition (19.................... revision) (hereinafter called the "Main Contract").

AND WHEREAS the Architect named in the main contract and the Contractor wish to operate the terms of Clause 27(e) of the Main Contract and the Contractor is willing to operate the terms of Clause 11(g) of the sub-contract.

NOW IT IS HEREBY AGREED

The Sub-Contractor in consideration of the Contractor permitting the operation of Clause 27(e) and Clause 11(g) hereinbefore mentioned *indemnifies* the Contractor against any loss or expense the Contractor may suffer or incur due to any latent defects which shall appear in the sub-contract works for such period as the Contractor, whether under the main contract or at common law, remains liable in respect of such defects to the Employer and/or to third parties; †and *secures* the aforementioned indemnity by ....

....

....

....

....

(†Delete if not applicable; see Notes for Guidance 3 and 5 attached hereto)

*(A) IN WITNESS WHEREOF the parties hereto have hereunto set their hands the day and year first above written.

Signed by the above-named Contractor in the presence of

....

....

Signed by the above-named Sub-Contractor in the presence of

....

....

*(B) IN WITNESS WHEREOF *the Common Seals of the parties hereto have hereunto been affixed the day and year first above written.*

The Common Seal *of the above-named Contractor was hereunto affixed in the presence of*

....

....

SEAL

The Common Seal *of the above-named Sub-Contractor was hereunto affixed in the presence of*

....

....

SEAL

***Footnote.**—*Where the Form of Indemnity is executed under hand, alternative* (B) *above should be struck out and the parties should sign in the spaces provided in alternative* (A).

Where the Form of Indemnity is executed under seal, alternative (A) *above should be struck out and the Common Seals of the parties should be affixed in the spaces provided in alternative* (B). *A ten shilling stamp must be impressed within thirty days of the date of the Form of Indemnity.*

Where the Contract to which the Form of Indemity relates is under hand, the Form should be executed under hand; where it is under seal, the Form should be executed under seal.

Form of Indemnity: Notes for Guidance

1. The Standard (RIBA) Form of Building Contract 1963 Edition issued by the Joint Contracts Tribunal provides in Clause 27(e):—

   "If the Architect desires to secure final payment to any nominated sub-contractor before final payment is due to the Contractor, and if such sub-contractor has satisfactorily indemnified the Contractor against any latent defects then the Architect may in an Interim Certificate include an amount to cover the said final payment . . . . .".

   The Form of Sub-Contract issued under the sanction of and approved by the NFBTE and FASS and approved by CASEC and endorsed "For use where the Sub-Contractor is nominated under the 1963 edition of the RIBA Form of Main Contract" provides in Clause 11(g) that if the Architect is desirous of acting under Clause 27(e) quoted above the Contractor shall pay any sums certified as a result of the exercise of the powers under Clause 27(e) but "such payment shall only be made if the Sub-Contractor indemnifies and secures the Contractor to the reasonable satisfaction of the Contractor against all latent defects in the Sub-Contract Works and if by such final payment the Contractor will be discharged under the Main Contract from all liabilities in respect of the Sub-Contract Works except for any latent defects".

2. The Architect cannot exercise his powers under Clause 27(e) unless the Contractor tells him that he has been satisfactorily indemnified by the Sub-Contractor; and the Contractor is not obliged to pay over any final payment certified as a result of the exercise of the power in Clause 27(e) unless he has been satisfactorily indemnified and secured as stated in Clause 11(g). The Form of Indemnity seeks to provide the necessary indemnity and security to enable Clause 27(e) and Clause 11(g) to be operated.

3. The Form leaves blank for the parties to insert the security to which the Contractor is entitled under Clause 11(g) over and above the already existing obligations of the Sub-Contractor under his sub-contract. It is for the Contractor to determine what security is to be requested and for the Sub-Contractor to weigh up whether the benefit of early final payment is worth the cost of the security that the Contractor requests. It must be noted however that the Contractor must always act reasonably in what security he requires since his entitlement is only to indemnity and security to his "reasonable satisfaction".

   If the Contractor is satisfied with the indemnity alone, together with the still subsisting obligations of the Sub-Contractor under the sub-contract, then that part of the Form referring to security should be deleted and the deletion initialled by the parties.

4. The phrase in the Form "any loss or expense" is intended to cover any injury or damage to third parties or to property and the Sub-Contractor should therefore make sure that he is adequately insured for public liability with no exclusion in regard to goods sold or supplied.

5. In regard to the kind of security that might be required it is pointed out that this should be related to the degree of loss or expense which a latent defect in the sub-contract works would be likely to cause. If the amount is likely to be small then it may not be necessary to require any specific security; if the amount is larger, the Contractor might wish the Sub-Contractor to offer reasonable security (for example, products guarantee insurance if available). In any case, however, the Sub-Contractor should be asked for adequate public insurance cover and required to provide any reasonable proof from time to time that that insurance is being maintained.

SELECT BIBLIOGRAPHY

Bindslev, Bjorn, 'Contract Procedures and Techniques in Europe and Scandinavia', *Chartered Surveyor* (September 1971).

British Standards Institute, *Specification for Data Processing Problem, Definition and Analysis, Part 1, Flow Chart Symbols*, BSS 4058 (Part 1): 1966 (London: British Standards Institute, 1966).

Chomsky, Noam, *Aspects of the Theory of Syntax* (Massachusetts: M.I.T. Press, 1965).

Conservative Trade Unionist Annual Conference (London: 1970).

Consumer Council Study, *Justice out of Reach* (July 1970).

Contractor's Guide to the Joint Contract Tribunal's Standard Forms of Building Contract (Building & Contract Journals Ltd., 1970).

Duncan Wallace, I. N., *Bickerton* v. *N.W.R.H.B.* (1967), 1 A.E.R. 977, *Hudson's Building and Engineering Contracts,* 9th and 10th editions, (London: Sweet and Maxwell, 1965, 1970).

——, *Building and Civil Engineering Standard Forms* (London: Sweet & Maxwell, 1969).

Eaglestone, F. N., *The RIBA Contract and the Insurance Market* (P.H. Press Ltd., 1964).

Gill, W. H., *Emden and Gill's Building Contract and Practise* (London: Butterworths, 1969).

Gowers, Sir Ernest, *The Complete Plain Words* (London: H.M.S.O., 1960).

Gunning, R., A Formula to Establish a Measure of Readability.

Joint Contracts Tribunal, *Practise Notes on Standard Forms issued by the Joint Contracts Tribunal* (London: R.I.B.A. Publications Ltd., 1971).

Jones, Harry W. (ed.), *Law and the Social Role of Science* (New York: Rockefeller University Press, 1966).

Keating, D., *Law and Practise of Building Contract*, 2nd edition (London: Sweet & Maxwell, 1963).

Lewis, B. N., *Decision Logic Tables for Algorithms and Logical Trees* (London: H.M.S.O., 1970).

——, Horabin, I. S., and Gane, C. P., *Flow Charts, Logical Trees and Algorithms for Rules and Regulations,* CAS Occasional Paper 2 (London: H.M.S.O., 1967).

Lyons, John, *Chomsky* (W. M. Collins & Co. Ltd., 1965).

McLuhan, Marshall, *Understanding Media: The Extension of Man,* (London: Routledge & Kegan Paul Ltd., 1964).

Piesse, E. L. and Gilchrist-Smith, J., *The Elements of Drafting* (Stevens & Sons, 1965).

Sawer, G., *Law in Society* (Oxford: Clarendon Press, 1965).

Skoyles, E. R., *Architects Journal* (28 January 1970).

Standard Form of Tender for Nominated Subcontractors (R.I.B.A. Publications Ltd., 1970).

Walker-Smith, Sir Derek, *et al., The Standard Form of Building Contract* (Charles Knight & Co. Ltd., 1965).

Wilson, J. F., *Evolution or Revolution?–Prospects for Contract Law Reform* (University of Southampton, 1969).

Zander, M., *et al., What's Wrong with the Law* (London: British Broadcasting Corporation, 1970).